An Instructional Guide to the Woodcock-Johnson Psycho-Educational Battery—Revised

Nancy Mather
University of Arizona
Division of Special Education
and Rehabilitation

John Wiley & Sons, Inc.

New York • Chichester • Brisbane • Toronto
Singapore • Weinheim

This text is printed on acid-free paper.

Copyright © 1991 by John Wiley & Sons, Inc.

All rights reserved. Published simultaneously in Canada.

ISBN 0-471-16189-6

Printed in the United States of America

10 9 8 7 6 5 4

Acknowledgments

Several individuals have provided support and assistance during this project. Dr. Samuel A. Kirk encouraged and guided me in a literature review of instructional methods during a year of postdoctoral study. Dr. R. W. Woodcock and two reviewers provided helpful comments and ideas on an earlier draft of the manuscript. Dr. Lynne Jaffe contributed to the case studies in the Appendix. Ms. Mary Kord helped in preparing several figures. Ms. Jeanne King-Friedrichs assisted with the literature review. Mr. David A. McPhail created record forms for the Appendix. Ms. Jane Todorski, my copy editor, contributed to the project with her careful editing and sense of humor. I would like to write another book just to have the opportunity to work with her again. Finally, I would like to thank George, Benjamin, and my parents for their love and support during the preparation of this book.

Library of Congress Catalog Card Number: 90-82412
ISBN: 0-88422-108-3

4 Conant Square
Brandon, Vermont 05733

Printed in the United States of America.

Permission to reprint all material from the *Woodcock-Johnson Psycho-Educational Battery — Revised* by R. W. Woodcock and M. B. Johnson has been generously granted by DLM. © 1977, 1989 DLM.

To Dr. Richard W. Woodcock who taught me about testing . . .

To Dr. Samuel A. Kirk who taught me about teaching . . .

TABLE OF CONTENTS

LIST OF FIGURES AND TABLES

Figures

Tables

INTRODUCTION

In training seminars on the Woodcock-Johnson Psycho-Educational Battery (WJ) (Woodcock & Johnson, 1977) and the Woodcock-Johnson Psycho-Educational Battery—Revised (WJ-R) (Woodcock & Johnson, 1989), participants frequently ask questions regarding the relationship between assessment results and instructional planning. Examples of these questions include:

- Now that I have all of these test results, what am I supposed to do?
- What other skills should I assess?
- How may I use this information to assist in designing an instructional program?
- What recommendations should I make to a classroom teacher?
- What types of methods and strategies may I recommend to improve performance?

The intent of this guide is to help examiners who use the WJ-R translate a student's test results into meaningful information for program development. Although the WJ-R is appropriate for use with ages 2 through 90+, this book emphasizes assessment and instruction for elementary, secondary, and college students who require special services for learning.

The guide is organized into seven chapters. The first chapter presents a brief overview of the diagnostic/pre-

scriptive process. Chapter 2 describes the tests and clusters of the WJ-R and the interpretive information that is available. The next four chapters directly address performance in the curricular areas assessed by the WJ-R Tests of Achievement (WJ-R ACH): Reading, Written Language, Knowledge, and Mathematics. The Reading chapter is divided into two sections of basic reading skills and reading comprehension. The Written Language chapter is divided into sections on handwriting, basic writing skills, and written expression. The Knowledge chapter presents information that is pertinent to content area instruction. The Mathematics chapter is separated into sections on computation and problem solving. Each chapter presents information on test content, procedures for error analysis, informal assessments, modifications and compensatory strategies, and instructional methods. The last chapter addresses instructional implications that may be obtained from WJ-R Tests of Cognitive Ability (WJ-R COG). Relevant research is presented, and specific modifications are suggested for students with low performance in one or more of the cognitive areas.

With careful analysis of a student's WJ-R performance, an examiner may gain important insights regarding both cognitive and academic strengths and weaknesses. When WJ-R results are supplemented with informal assessments and classroom observations, appropriate individualized instructional programs may be designed for each student.

1

THE DIAGNOSTIC/PRESCRIPTIVE PROCESS

Clinicians, educators, and research scientists should strive to become the best possible describers of children. In other words, when studying a child or a group of children, we should attempt to depict essential elements of developmental function and performance that need to be accounted for; the best description leads to the best prescription. The description is an account not only of problems and weaknesses but also (perhaps more important) of talents and advantages, the exploitation of which may go a long way toward alleviating the burdens imposed by the dysfunction.

(Levine, 1987, p. 7)

Simple test administration is rarely an end goal. Most testing is conducted to help answer specific referral questions, such as Why is a student having reading problems? and How can reading skills be improved? Once testing is recommended, the goal is to answer the referral question and, subsequently, to make recommendations for solving the prevailing concern.

In school settings, assessments are often performed to determine whether a student qualifies for a special program. If, after testing and a multidisciplinary meeting, the decision is made that a student does not qualify for services, the initial question is answered but the referring problem is not solved: Some type of intervention plan is still needed. Conversely, if a student does qualify for a program, the same problem must be addressed: Some type of instructional program must be designed. Presently, the majority of public school referrals are for students experiencing academic problems. For example, Ownby, Wallbrown, D'Atri, and Armstrong (1985) recorded the referrals made for assessment services in a small school population. They found that from first grade through high school, referrals for academic problems exceeded referrals for behavior problems by almost 5 to 1. These findings illustrate the need for assessments that will produce information relevant to instructional planning. Diagnosis must be followed by prescription.

A diagnostic/prescriptive process follows these seven steps: (a) define and clarify the referral problem, (b) assess and diagnose the problem, (c) brainstorm interventions, (d) evaluate and choose among alternatives, (e) specify responsibilities, (f) implement the selected strategies, and (g) monitor program effectiveness (Reynolds, Gutkin, Elliott, & Witt, 1984). A simplified model of this spiral or cyclic process is presented in Figure 1-1. The diagnostic/prescriptive process requires use of assessment procedures that provide educationally relevant information for helping students overcome academic difficulties.

Depending upon the nature of the referral question and the severity of the problem, assessment measures are differentially applied. In other words, what is assessed and how it is assessed depend upon the purposes of the evaluation. For example, the tests administered for screening students will differ from the tests administered for a detailed psychoeducational evaluation. Similarly, the tests selected to be used in placement decisions may differ from the ones used in planning individual educational programs. As a rule, developing instructional programs requires in-depth assessment. In designing instructional programs, two major goals exist: (a) to determine appropriate modifications, compensatory strategies, and materials and (b) to select appropriate teaching methods.

Modifications and Compensations

Many times a multidisciplinary team recommends specific compensations for an individual. Compensations are adaptations in a student's regular education program that enable the individual to perform successfully. These modifications are needed for students who are faced with instructional demands that they cannot meet because of insufficient skill. Various strategies exist to enhance stu-

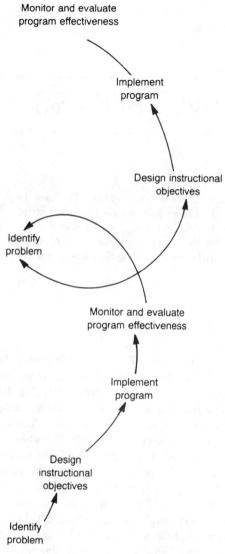

Figure 1–1. The Diagnostic/Prescriptive Process.

In some cases, the use of supplementary or teacher-designed materials may be recommended. For example, a student reading several years above grade level may benefit more from a reading program based on trade books than a reading program based on higher level books from a basal reading series. In another case, a student with severe spelling difficulty may be best served with individualized spelling lists, rather than a basal spelling book. After test administration, an examiner will recognize the types of compensations and modifications that are most appropriate for a student based upon considerations of age, ability level, and severity of disability. As a resource, Riegel, Mayle, and McCarthy-Henkel (1988) have compiled an extensive manual of suggestions and guidelines for adapting materials for students with special needs in the regular classroom.

Specific Teaching Methods

A multidisciplinary team may also suggest specific strategies and methods to use with an individual. These special techniques may be implemented in a regular or special education classroom or, in some instances, in the home by a tutor or parent. After considering a student's learning characteristics, educational history, and present performance level, a team will brainstorm alternatives and recommend a technique. For example, if an elementary student has failed to learn to read using the classroom approach, the team will consider what other reading methods may be more effective with the student. Or, if a secondary student is having trouble mastering content area vocabulary, a specific study strategy may be recommended. Unfortunately, linking assessment to remediation is an inexact science. In many instances, an instructor must trial-teach a selected method and monitor student progress carefully to ascertain the effectiveness of the technique. If the technique is not effective, another method is selected and implemented.

Effective program design requires the coordination of all facets of the instructional plan. After modifications and recommendations are made, examiners, classroom and special education teachers, and, in some instances, family members, must work together to coordinate and implement program objectives. The student must also be a willing participant and understand and agree to any program modifications. In many instances, the student will participate in the instructional planning process and assume responsibility for monitoring progress. Before recommending specific modifications and teaching methods, an examiner should also consider a student's academic and nonacademic strengths, as well as any affective and environmental factors that influence performance.

dent performance. For example, one appropriate recommendation that applies to all academic areas and ages is to coordinate the use of cross-age or peer tutors or classroom volunteers to provide extra assistance. Another effective technique, referred to as "cooperative learning," is to have low- and high-ability students work in pairs or small groups on a shared project or activity. A third, and perhaps the most important, is to alter the level of difficulty of the instructional material.

If a student is performing significantly below or above grade level, it may be necessary to modify or extend educational materials. Whenever possible the examiner and instructor should work together to identify the specific materials to be used for instruction and review. All assigned seatwork and homework should be at a student's instructional or independent level.

Academic Strengths

A thorough psychoeducational assessment involves the identification of strengths, as well as weaknesses. A student may perform at grade level in mathematics but be several years below grade level in reading. In some instances, performance in one area may be used to facilitate performance in another area. For example, a student may have above-average performance in science but below-average performance in basic reading skills. A reading program may be developed around the student's specific science interests.

Specific Nonacademic Strengths

In designing an instructional program, an examiner will also consider a student's nonacademic strengths. Some students with generalized low academic performance have special talents, interests, or knowledge in areas that are not traditionally included in an assessment or an academic curriculum. For example, one student may excel in a particular artistic, athletic, musical, or mechanical skill but be experiencing extreme difficulty with some type of academic skill. Another student may be a talented dancer but have trouble with reading. Still another student may be mechanically gifted but have trouble with spelling. In planning an educational program, an examiner should consider each student's unique strengths and interests. In addition to promoting self-esteem, integration of a student's interests into the curriculum provides motivation for building academic skills. Furthermore, students should be encouraged to develop special talents, as these abilities may provide the basis for an occupation or avocation.

Affective and Environmental Factors

In addition to a student's abilities, an examiner must consider a variety of affective and environmental factors that may influence performance. Problems in either motivational or social development may contribute to academic difficulties. Affective factors are the emotional characteristics of the learner. Examples of factors that may influence performance include: motivation, interest, values and attitudes, expectations, and self-concept. Environmental factors are the conditions within the school and home. Examples of school-related factors that may affect student performance include: teacher characteristics, instructional methods, response requirements of the tasks, social adjustment, and popularity in the classroom. Examples of home variables that may affect performance include: socioeconomic status, family support system, relationships with siblings, and behavioral management techniques. In analyzing student performance, an examiner should attempt to determine the influence that external environmental factors have upon student performance. School and home factors may contribute to or alleviate a problem. By considering both a learner's characteristics and the relevant environmental and situational variables, an examiner will be more equipped to answer a specific referral question, develop an instructional plan, and monitor and evaluate program effectiveness.

2

OVERVIEW OF THE WOODCOCK-JOHNSON PSYCHO-EDUCATIONAL BATTERY—REVISED

The purpose of this chapter is to provide an overview of the Woodcock-Johnson Psycho-Educational Battery—Revised (WJ-R) (Woodcock & Johnson, 1989). The chapter may assist an examiner in explaining various tests, clusters, scores, and profiles to others. The first section of the chapter provides a brief description of the WJ-R tests and clusters. The next section provides an explanation of the various scores, profiles, and types of discrepancies that facilitate test interpretation. More detailed descriptions of tests and interpretive features are provided in the WJ-R Examiner's Manuals (Woodcock & Mather, 1989a, 1989b), the Technical Manual (McGrew, Werder, & Woodcock, 1990), and Hessler (in press).

Test and Cluster Descriptions

The WJ-R is divided into two main parts: the Tests of Cognitive Ability (WJ-R COG) and the Tests of Achievement (WJ-R ACH). Each of these parts is divided into a Standard and Supplemental Battery. First, the theoretical model, tests, and clusters of the WJ-R COG are described, followed by a description of the WJ-R ACH tests and clusters. Examiners who do not use the WJ-R COG may wish to turn directly to the description of the WJ-R ACH tests and clusters.

WJ-R COG Theoretical Model

The WJ-R COG is based upon the *Gf-Gc* theory of intellectual processing (Cattell, 1963; Horn, 1985, 1986; Horn & Cattell, 1966). This theory provides a data-based theoretical foundation for psychoeducational diagnosis.

The WJ-R factors derived from this theory include eight broad intellectual abilities. A brief description of the factors and the WJ-R COG abbreviations used for these abilities follows.

Long-term retrieval (Glr) measures the effectiveness in storing and fluently retrieving information over extended time periods. The period of time may range from several minutes to several days.

Short-term memory (Gsm) measures the ability to apprehend information and repeat it within a short period of time.

Processing speed (Gs) measures the ability to perform relatively trivial tasks quickly.

Auditory processing (Ga) measures the ability to analyze and synthesize auditory patterns.

Visual processing (Gv) measures capability in perceiving and thinking with visual patterns.

Comprehension-knowledge (Gc) measures breadth and depth of knowledge and its application.

Fluid reasoning (Gf) measures capacity for abstraction or ability to reason in novel situations.

Quantitative ability (Gq), an eighth cognitive factor, may be obtained from the WJ-R ACH Broad Mathematics cluster. This factor measures comprehension of quantitative concepts and skill in using numerical symbols.

Cognitive Tests

The Cognitive battery contains 21 tests. The Standard Battery includes tests 1 to 7, and the Supplemental Battery contains Tests 8 through 21.

Standard Battery

The Standard Battery is designed to provide a full-scale cognitive score. The tests may be administered in any order. The Standard Battery provides one measure of each of the seven cognitive factors and takes approximately 40 minutes to administer. Five of the measures are Early Development tests (EDev) that may be used to assess preschool or low-functioning individuals of any age. A description of each test follows.

Test 1: Memory for Names measures the ability to form and retrieve auditory-visual associations. On the introduction page, the student is shown a picture of a space creature and told its name. The student is then shown a response page that contains nine space creatures and is asked to identify the creature. Additional space creatures are introduced on subsequent pages. The student is asked to point to the space creature just introduced and to other previously introduced characters. During the test, the student is informed whether responses are correct or incorrect, and all errors are corrected. Memory for Names requires the student to retain the names and identify up to 12 space creatures. This test primarily measures long-term retrieval. Figure 2-1 illustrates the subject and examiner pages from Item 1.

Test 2: Memory for Sentences measures the ability to repeat words, phrases, and sentences that are presented by a tape player. This test primarily measures short-term memory.

Test 3: Visual Matching measures the ability to identify and circle quickly the two identical numbers in a row of six numbers. The test is timed for 3 minutes, and the level of difficulty increases from single-digit to triple-digit numbers. Figure 2-2 illustrates several rows from the Visual Matching test.

Test 4: Incomplete Words measures auditory closure, or the ability to identify a word with missing sounds. This test is presented with a tape player and progresses in difficulty from words missing single phonemes to words missing multiple phonemes. This test primarily measures auditory processing.

Test 5: Visual Closure measures the ability to identify a drawing or picture that has been altered in one of several ways. The picture may be distorted, may be missing lines, or may have a pattern superimposed. This test primarily measures visual processing. Figure 2-3 illustrates several different types of items from this test.

Test 6: Picture Vocabulary measures the ability to identify and name pictured objects. On several of the beginning items the student is required to point to the correct response. Thereafter, the student is required to name the pictured object or action. This test primarily measures comprehension-knowledge.

Test 7: Analysis-Synthesis measures the ability to de-termine the missing components of an incomplete logic puzzle. In this controlled learning test, the student is given feedback and instruction. The test involves a miniature system of mathematics and primarily measures fluid reasoning. Figure 2-4 illustrates the key and several sample puzzles from this test. Using the key to solve the puzzles, the student identifies the color(s) of the blank square(s).

Supplemental Battery

The Supplemental Battery consists of 14 tests that provide further information about seven cognitive factors. A description of each test follows.

Test 8: Visual-Auditory Learning measures the ability to retain visual-auditory associations. This test requires the student to retain and identify up to 28 rebuses (symbols) that are read within the context of a meaningful phrase or sentence. This test primarily measures long-term retrieval. Figure 2-5 illustrates examiner and subject pages from the first story in this test.

Test 9: Memory for Words measures the ability to repeat lists of unrelated words in the correct order. This taped test proceeds in difficulty from single words to lists containing eight words.

Test 10: Cross Out measures the ability to scan and compare visual information rapidly. The student is asked to mark the 5 drawings in a row of 20 geometric drawings that are identical to the first drawing. The test is timed for 3 minutes and primarily measures processing speed. Figure 2-6 illustrates several rows from the Cross Out test.

Test 11: Sound Blending measures the ability to synthesize a series of sounds into whole words. On this taped test, word parts are presented first in syllables and then in phonemes. This test primarily measures auditory processing.

Test 12: Picture Recognition measures the ability to recognize a subset of previously presented pictures within a field of distracting pictures. The student is exposed to a set of pictures, such as several different dolls, for five seconds, and then asked to recognize the pictures on the following page. The item difficulty increases as the number of pictures that the student must identify increases and varies from one to four. This test primarily measures visual processing. Figure 2-7 illustrates a stimulus, response, and examiner page from this test.

Test 13: Oral Vocabulary measures knowledge of word meanings. The student is asked to provide synonyms and antonyms for words that are orally presented by the examiner. This test primarily measures comprehension-knowledge.

Test 14: Concept Formation measures categorical reasoning ability. The student is asked to derive and identify rules for concepts when shown illustrations of both the

Examiner Page

I am going to show you a space creature and tell you its name. Then I will show you a page with more space creatures and ask you to point to the one I name.

Point to the picture on the subject's side and say:

Look at Jawf (jawf). Point to Jawf.

Proceed immediately to the next page after the subject points to Jawf.

Subject Page

Examiner Page

1.   **Now point to Jawf.**

▶**Correct:** points to Jawf

1: Error or No Response

Point to the correct drawing and say

This is Jawf. Point to Jawf

Proceed immediately to the next page after the subject points to Jawf.

Figure 2–1. Test Item 1 from the Memory for Names Test.

8 (9) 5 2 (9) 7
(8) 3 7 0 4 (8)
2 7 4 (1) (1) 6
5 (3) 9 (3) 1 4
(7) 2 6 5 (7) 8
0 7 (4) 2 9 (4)
(5) (5) 8 1 6 3
2 (6) 7 (6) 3 0
8 (2) 4 7 (2) 9
3 6 (0) 8 9 (0)
(8) 7 1 (8) 2 4
5 0 7 (3) (3) 6
2 (9) 6 4 1 (9)

84 48 (94) 49 47 (94)
36 55 66 (56) (56) 65
(41) 61 16 14 64 (41)
32 (23) (23) 83 38 28
89 98 97 87 (78) (78)
(13) 12 23 (13) 31 21
56 (68) 65 86 (68) 26
(32) 20 40 (32) 23 34
49 94 (59) 95 45 (59)
74 24 (27) 24 (72) 77
(968) 689 869 (968) 986 896
524 (542) 245 425 452 (542)
679 976 (967) (976) 697 796

Figure 2–2. Several Rows from the Visual Matching Test.

7.

▶**Correct:** duck, ducky, bird, chicken, goose

Incorrect: horse

Query: stripes, lines, picture, square—*What picture do you see?* **animal**—*What kind of animal?*

No Response in 30 Seconds

Say: *Let's try another one.* Turn to the next page.

17.

▶**Correct:** fan, air

Incorrect: air conditioner, heater, lamp, light

Query: cooler—*Tell me another word.*

No Response in 30 Seconds

Say: *Let's try another one.* Turn to the next page.

23.

▶**Correct:** doll, Raggedy Ann, Annie

Incorrect: boy, man

Query: baby, clown, girl, kid, toy—*What else do we call it?*

No Response in 30 Seconds

Say: *Let's try another one.* Turn to the next page.

Figure 2–3. Test Items 7, 17, and 23 from the Visual Closure Test.

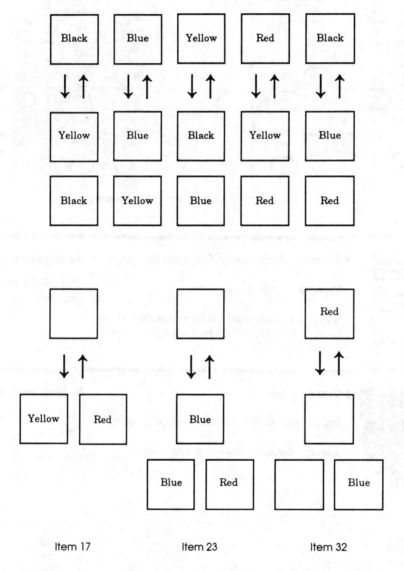

Figure 2–4. Key and Items 17, 23, and 32 from the Analysis-Synthesis Test.

Examiner Page

Introduction 1

Each of these drawings is a word. As soon as I tell you what a drawing says, I want you to say it back to me.

Do not discuss any symbol, say its name more than once, or allow the subject to review or practice the words.

 Point to the first symbol on the subject's side and say:
cowboy. Pause for the subject to repeat the word once. (It may be necessary to remind the subject to say the word.) Move immediately to the next symbol.

 Point to the second symbol and say:
dog. Pause for the subject to repeat the word.

Point to the next symbol and say:
horse. Pause for the subject to repeat the word.

 Point to the last symbol and say:
and. Pause for the subject to repeat the word.

Proceed immediately to the next page, Test Story 1.

Subject Page

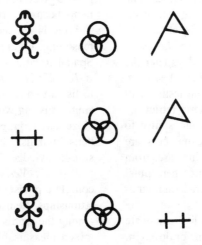

Figure 2-5. Test Story 1 from the Visual-Auditory Learning Test.

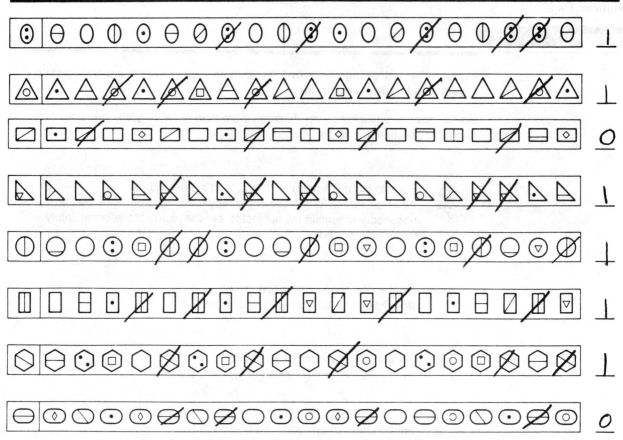

Figure 2–6. Several Rows from the Cross Out Test.

concept and non-instances of the concept. The student is given feedback regarding the correctness of each response. This test primarily measures fluid reasoning. Figure 2-8 illustrates several items from this test.

Test 15: Delayed Recall—Memory for Names measures the ability to recall from 1 to 8 days later the space creatures presented in Test 1: Memory for Names. The student is not informed that subsequent testing will occur. This test primarily measures long-term retrieval.

Test 16: Delayed Recall—Visual-Auditory Learning measures the ability to recall from 1 to 8 days later the rebuses presented in Test 8: Visual-Auditory Learning. The student is not informed that subsequent testing will occur. This test primarily measures long-term retrieval.

Test 17: Numbers Reversed measures the ability to repeat a series of digits backwards. The numbers are presented with the test tape. Item difficulty increases from two digits to eight digits. This test requires perceptual reorganization and primarily measures short-term memory and fluid reasoning.

Test 18: Sound Patterns measures the ability to indicate whether pairs of sound patterns are the same or different. The pairs may differ in pitch, rhythm, or duration. All items are presented with the test tape. This test primarily measures auditory processing, but is more a measure of fluid reasoning with young children.

Test 19: Spatial Relations measures the ability to match shapes visually with the component parts. The student must select the correct pieces from a series of shapes to make a given whole shape. Difficulty level increases as the items become progressively more abstract and complex. This test is a mixed measure of visual processing and fluid reasoning. Figure 2-9 illustrates several items from the Spatial Relations test.

Test 20: Listening Comprehension measures the ability to listen to a short tape-recorded passage and supply the single missing word at the end of the passage. This oral cloze task requires a variety of vocabulary and comprehension skills. This test primarily measures comprehension-knowledge.

Test 21: Verbal Analogies measures the ability to complete phrases with words to indicate appropriate relationships. Item difficulty increases as the relationship among the words becomes more complex. This test is a mixed measure of fluid reasoning and comprehension-knowledge.

Stimulus Page

Response Page

A   **B**   **F**

Examiner Page

A*   **B**   **F***

▶ **Correct:** A and F

Figure 2–7. Test Item 6 from the Picture Recognition Test.

1.

Point to the first puzzle on the subject's side and say: **What is the rule for this puzzle?**

▶**Correct:** red

Query: color—*What color?*
red square—*Both drawings are squares.
What is different about the drawing inside the box?*

1: Error or No Response

Point to the drawing inside the box and say: *The answer is "red." The drawing inside the box is red, but the drawing outside the box is yellow.*

13.

▶**Correct:** one

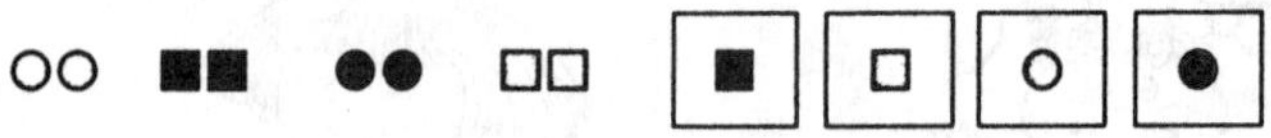

13: Error or No Response

Point to the drawings inside the boxes and say: *The answer is "one."* Do not explain further.

Go ahead.

22.

▶**Correct:** big *or* yellow *or* square

22: Error or Over One Minute

Say: *The answer is "big or yellow or square." For a drawing to be inside a box, it has to be either big or yellow or square.* Do not explain further.

Figure 2–8. Test Items 1, 13, and 22 from the Concept Formation Test.

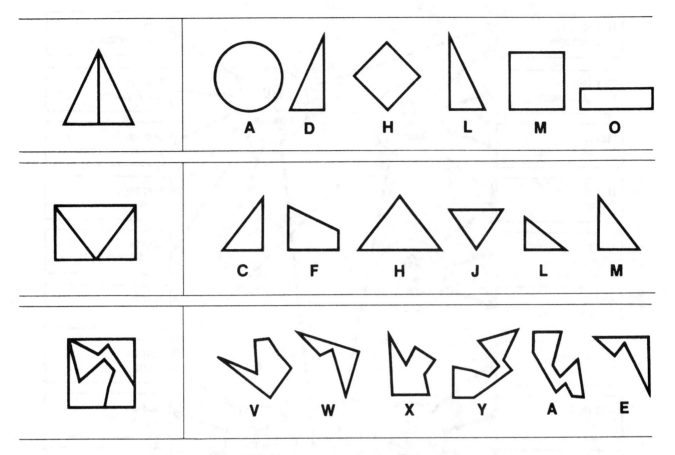

Figure 2–9. Test Items 2, 16, and 28 from the Spatial Relations Test.

Cognitive Clusters

In addition to the individual test scores, an examiner may determine several cluster scores.

Broad Cognitive Ability

The Cognitive battery provides three broad-based measures of intellectual ability.

Broad Cognitive Ability—Early Development is appropriate for children at the preschool level or for low-functioning individuals of any age. This cluster consists of five tests: Test 1: Memory for Names, Test 2: Memory for Sentences, Test 4: Incomplete Words, Test 5: Visual Closure, and Test 6: Picture Vocabulary.

Broad Cognitive Ability—Standard Scale is composed of all seven tests in the Standard Battery and provides a broad-based measure of intellectual ability. This cluster is usually administered to students at kindergarten level and older.

Broad Cognitive Ability—Extended Scale is based on a combination of the first 14 cognitive tests. If all 14 tests have been administered, this score is used as the broad-based measure of intellectual ability.

Cognitive Factors

The eight cognitive factors are briefly described in the section discussing the theoretical model underlying the WJ-R COG. The hypothesized model of the factorial structure is presented in Figure 2-10. Each of the seven WJ-R COG factors contains two tests. The 14 tests connected with solid arrows in the illustration are the primary measures of the seven cognitive factors. The tests connected with dotted arrow lines are secondary measures of the seven factors.

As noted, quantitative ability, the eighth factor, is obtained from the WJ-R ACH Broad Mathematics cluster score. In addition, several other achievement tests may be used to provide further information regarding performance in a cognitive area. The Knowledge tests may be used as additional measures of comprehension-knowledge; the Word Attack test is an additional measure of auditory processing; and the Writing Fluency test provides supplemental information about processing speed.

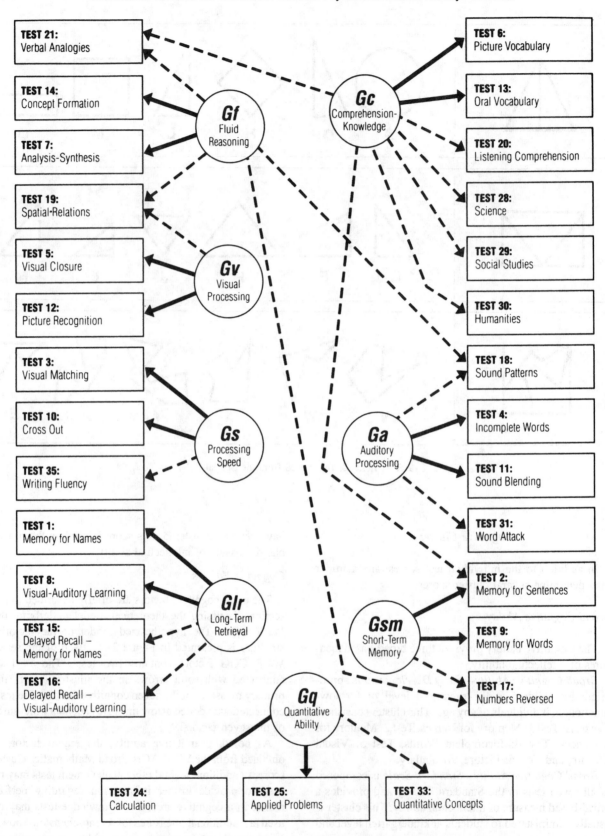

Figure 2–10. Hypothesized Model of the Factorial Structure Underlying the WJ-R. *Note.* From *WJ-R Technical Manual* by K. S. McGrew, J. K. Werder, and R. W. Woodcock (1990), Allen, TX: DLM. Reprinted by permission.

Aptitude Clusters

Five aptitude clusters provide information regarding a student's expected or predicted level of achievement. Figure 2-11 illustrates the content of each of the aptitude clusters. These ability clusters are used to determine the existence and severity of an aptitude-achievement discrepancy.

Reading
    2. Memory for Sentences
    3. Visual Matching
    11. Sound Blending
    13. Oral Vocabulary

Mathematics
    3. Visual Matching
    7. Analysis-Synthesis
    13. Oral Vocabulary
    14. Concept Formation

Written Language
    3. Visual Matching
    8. Visual-Auditory Learning
    11. Sound Blending
    13. Oral Vocabulary

Knowledge
    2. Memory for Sentences
    5. Visual Closure
    11. Sound Blending
    14. Concept Formation

Oral Language
    12. Picture Recognition
    14. Concept Formation
    17. Numbers Reversed
    18. Sound Patterns

Figure 2–11. Content of the WJ-R COG Aptitude Clusters.

Oral Language

The Oral Language cluster provides a broad-based measure of a student's oral language performance. This cluster is composed of Test 2: Memory for Sentences, Test 6: Picture Vocabulary, Test 13: Oral Vocabulary, Test 20: Listening Comprehension, and Test 21: Verbal Analogies.

Achievement Tests

The Achievement battery contains 14 tests and four auxiliary written language measures. The Standard Battery contains Tests 22 through 30. The Supplemental Battery contains Tests 31 through 35, and measures of Punctuation & Capitalization, Spelling, Usage, and Handwriting.

Standard Battery

The Standard Battery is designed to provide an overview of academic performance in four broad curricular areas: Reading, Mathematics, Written Language, and Knowledge. The tests may be administered in any order and the battery takes approximately 50 to 60 minutes to administer with about 15 minutes of that time required by the Writing Samples test. The Standard Battery tests provide two measures of reading, mathematics, and written language, and three measures of knowledge. Six of these measures are Early Development tests (EDev) that may be used to assess preschool or low-functioning individuals of any age.

Test 22: Letter-Word Identification measures the ability to identify letters and words. The items progress from rebuses, to individual letters, to high-frequency words, to words that appear less frequently in written English. Successful word identification does not require comprehension: A subject may or may not know the meaning of a word.

Test 23: Passage Comprehension, a modified cloze procedure, measures an individual's ability to use syntactic clues and semantic clues. Syntactic clues refer to the grammatical aspects of language or inferences about word meaning based upon the roles, or part of speech, a word assumes in a sentence. The reader tends to select words that sound correct in the passage. Semantic clues refer to the meaningful aspects of language or inferences about word meanings based upon passage content. The reader tends to select words that make sense. To produce a correct response, a student must integrate syntactic and semantic clues. Figure 2-12 illustrates several items from the Passage Comprehension test.

Test 24: Calculation measures an individual's ability to perform a variety of mathematical calculations, including the four operations of addition, subtraction, multiplication, and division. Operations involving whole numbers, negative numbers, decimals, fractions, and percents are also included. The problems progress from simple addition to more advanced geometric, trigonometric, logarithmic, and calculus operations.

Test 25: Applied Problems measures an individual's skill in solving practical problems. Emphasis is placed on ability to apply knowledge to determine the correct solutions. To solve these verbal problems successfully, the individual must: (a) determine the steps to be followed, (b) identify the relevant data and eliminate extraneous information, and (c) perform the relatively simple calculations required.

Test 26: Dictation, administered like a traditional spelling test, measures knowledge of prewriting skills, punctuation and capitalization, spelling, and usage. The student responds in writing to a variety of oral prompts.

7.   Something is on the chair. It is a ___ .

▶**Correct:** book

   Incorrect: ball, box, chair

7: No Response

If the subject does not respond in about 30 seconds *after* completely reading the passage, encourage a response. If the subject still does not respond, point to the next item and say: *Try this one.*

15.   "I didn't do it," said Tom. "Yes, you ___ ," they said.

▶**Correct:** did

   Incorrect: do

15: No Response

If the subject does not respond in about 30 seconds *after* completely reading the passage, encourage a response. If the subject still does not respond, point to the next item and say: *Try this one.*

33.   It is one thing to demonstrate that modern war is harmful to the species. It is another thing to do something about ___ it.

▶**Correct:** stopping, preventing

   Incorrect: demonstrating

33: No Response

If the subject does not respond in about 30 seconds *after* completely reading the passage, encourage a response. If the subject still does not respond, point to the next item and say: *Try this one.*

Figure 2–12. Test Items 7, 15, and 33 from the Passage Comprehension Test.

Test 27: Writing Samples measures ability to produce meaningful sentences to satisfy a variety of task demands. The emphasis is on the quality of writing or the expression of ideas, rather than on basic skills. Task demands progress from writing single words and simple sentences to producing complex sentences that require imitation of a writing style. Figure 2-13 illustrates several items from the Writing Samples test.

Test 28: Science measures knowledge of both biological and physical sciences. The student is asked a variety of questions concerning body parts and functions, nature, astronomy, weather, geology, chemistry, and physics.

Test 29: Social Studies measures knowledge of a variety of aspects of social studies. The student is asked questions involving history, geography, government, and economics.

Test 30: Humanities measures knowledge of several branches of cultural studies. The student is asked a variety of questions that sample knowledge of art, music, and literature.

Supplemental Battery

The Supplemental Battery includes five tests that may be used to provide additional information about a student's achievement in reading, mathematics, and written language. In addition, the examiner may obtain measures of punctuation/capitalization, spelling, usage, and handwriting.

Test 31: Word Attack measures a subject's ability to apply phonic and structural analysis skills in pronouncing phonically regular nonsense words. All of the nonsense words follow the patterns of regular English pronunciation and spelling. To decode the nonsense words, a student must remember the phoneme associated with each sound and then blend or synthesize the phonemes into a word. The successful identification of the multisyllabic nonsense words requires increased knowledge of word structure.

Test 32: Reading Vocabulary measures knowledge of word meanings. The Reading Vocabulary Test has two parts: Synonyms and Antonyms. For Synonyms, the

2.

This is a _____

12.

_____

_____

_____

18.

(1) When my father agrees to build a house, he follows several steps. (2) _____

_____

_____

(3) Next, he determines the exact plan his customer has in mind.

27.

(1) Robert was an eccentric, perversely perky little man, hesitantly alert. (2) _____

_____

_____ (3) Simultaneously, but independently,

they devised a scheme that would astound the entire community.

Figure 2–13. Test Items 2, 12, 18, and 27 from the Writing Samples Test.

student reads words and is asked to supply words similar in meaning. For Antonyms, the student reads words and is asked to supply words that are opposite in meaning. Together these tests provide a measure of comprehension of reading vocabulary.

Test 33: Quantitative Concepts measures an individual's knowledge of basic mathematical concepts and vocabulary. A variety of problems are presented that measure: (a) numeration skills, including sequencing, number recognition, and counting, and (b) recognition and identification of mathematical signs, abbreviations, formulas, and vocabulary. Some mental arithmetic is required.

Test 34: Proofing measures an individual's ability to detect and correct errors in punctuation and capitalization, spelling, and usage in written passages.

Test 35: Writing Fluency measures automaticity, or the ability to produce writing rapidly with ease. Minimal analytic attention or problem solving is involved. The task requires the production of legible, simple sentences with acceptable English syntax. This timed test assesses the number of sentences that an individual is able to write within 7 minutes. Figure 2-14 illustrates several items from the Writing Fluency test.

Punctuation & Capitalization, Spelling, and Usage measure the abilities to produce correct forms and to detect and correct errors in written passages. When both

Dictation and Proofing have been administered, separate scores may be obtained for Punctuation & Capitalization (P), Spelling (S), and Usage (U).

Handwriting (H) measures both overall legibility and several aspects of handwriting skill. Handwriting is evaluated by matching samples of a student's writing from the Writing Samples test to a ranked scale of handwriting samples provided in Appendix D of the Examiner's Manual. Additionally, the Test Record contains an informal checklist that includes six aspects of handwriting skill. This form may be completed to provide further information regarding the legibility and appearance of a student's handwriting.

Achievement Clusters

In addition to the scores from the individual tests, an examiner may determine scores for 11 clusters. The Standard Battery contains five cluster scores—the four Broad clusters and the Skills cluster. An additional six achievement clusters are derived from combinations of tests in the Standard and Supplemental batteries. A brief description of the clusters follows.

Broad Reading provides a broad measure of reading achievement. The cluster is a combination of the Letter-Word Identification and Passage Comprehension tests.

Figure 2–14. Test Items 1, 19, and 31 from the Writing Fluency Test.

Basic Reading Skills measures ability to identify sight vocabulary and apply phonic and structural analysis skills. This cluster is composed of the Letter-Word Identification and Word Attack tests.

Reading Comprehension measures understanding of single words and context-embedded stimuli. This cluster is composed of the Passage Comprehension and Reading Vocabulary tests.

Broad Mathematics provides a broad measure of math achievement. This cluster is a combination of the Calculation and Applied Problems tests.

Basic Mathematics Skills measures knowledge of basic mathematical skills, including computation, concepts, and vocabulary. This cluster is a combination of the Calculation and Quantitative Concepts tests.

Mathematics Reasoning measures ability to analyze and solve practical mathematical problems. Although not an actual cluster, the Applied Problems test is used to plot the Mathematics Reasoning cluster on a profile.

Broad Written Language provides a broad measure of written language achievement. This cluster is composed of the Dictation and Writing Samples tests.

Basic Writing Skills measures ability to produce correct spellings and to identify and correct errors in spelling, punctuation, capitalization, and word usage. This cluster is composed of the Dictation and Proofing tests.

Written Expression measures the ability to produce simple sentences with ease and to write increasingly complex sentences in response to a variety of prompts. This cluster is composed of the Writing Samples and Writing Fluency tests.

Broad Knowledge measures knowledge in three content areas. This cluster is composed of the Science, Social Studies, and Humanities tests and may be used as an Early Development measure.

Skills provides a broad measure of basic school skills. This cluster is composed of the Letter-Word Identification, Applied Problems, and Dictation tests and may be used as an Early Development cluster.

Understanding and explaining a student's performance on any standardized test require knowledge of the types of information and scores that may be derived. The next section provides the user with an overview of the variety of scores available to facilitate test interpretation.

Interpretive Information

All too often the only data derived from testing are scores that are recorded and filed into a cumulative folder. The examiner does not consider or report the variety of interpretive information available from observations, error analysis, and test scores. The WJ-R provides four broad levels of interpretive information (Woodcock & Mather,

1989a, 1989b). Figure 2-15 illustrates the four levels of performance and provides examples of the types of information obtained at each level.

Level 1 information is obtained through error analysis and behavioral observations. These qualitative observations are critical to understanding an individual's performance and planning an instructional program. Observations may include a description of a student's responses, attention to task, level of motivation and interest, emotional status, or task persistence. Level 2 information describes an individual's stage of development and includes scores such as age and grade equivalents. Level 3 information indicates the quality of an individual's performance on reference tasks. This type of information is helpful for identifying an appropriate level of instructional materials by determining the range of tasks that a student would perceive as quite easy to a level that would be perceived as quite difficult. Level 4 information describes an individual's relative position when compared to his or her peers and includes scores such as standard scores and percentile ranks. Although Level 4 information is helpful for determining program eligibility, the first three levels are the most meaningful for instructional planning and the diagnostic/prescriptive process. To assist an examiner in using the full range of interpretive information available, further explanation is provided regarding: (a) error analysis, (b) behavioral observations, (c) test scores, (d) profile interpretation, and (e) discrepancy interpretation.

Error Analysis

Error analysis, Level 1 information, involves a systematic examination of a student's correct and incorrect responses to individual items in an attempt to discern whether a particular response pattern exists. For example, specific error patterns may be noted when a student is reading a passage orally or performing math computations. Once an error pattern is identified, instructional objectives are determined.

In analyzing errors, an examiner should consider the quality of the response. Every error exists somewhere on a continuum from a reasonable response that demonstrates tangential knowledge to an unreasonable response that demonstrates limited experience or understanding of a concept. For example, when presented with a picture of a toga, Chris, a second-grade boy, responded that he could not remember what to call it, but that it was what the Romans wore. Although Chris would not receive credit for this item, an examiner would note his understanding. Similarly, a student may not be able to name an object but may explain its function. When shown a picture of door hinges, Janet, a third-grade girl, remarked that she did not know what to call them but they were the things that let

Level	Type of Information	Basis	Information and Scores
1	Qualitative	Observations during testing and error analysis	Description of subject's reaction to the test situation and performance on finely defined skills
2	Level of development	Sum of item scores	Raw Score *Rasch Ability Score (Example: Test or cluster W score) Age Equivalent Grade Equivalent
3	Degree of mastery	Quality of performance on reference tasks	*Rasch Difference Score (Example: Test or cluster difference score) Relative Mastery Index (RMI) Developmental Level Band Instructional Range
4	Comparison with peers	Deviation from a reference point in a group	Rank Order *Standard Score Percentile Rank

*Equal interval units preferred for statistical calculations

Figure 2–15. Hierarchy of Test Information Available in the WJ-R. *Note.* From *WJ-R Tests of Cognitive Ability—Standard and Supplemental Batteries: Examiner's Manual* (p. 62) by R. W. Woodcock and N. Mather, 1989, Allen, TX: DLM. Copyright 1989 by DLM. Reprinted by permission.

the door swing back and forth. Janet illustrates her knowledge of function but cannot retrieve the specific word. In contrast, when presented with a picture of a globe, Jessica, a sixth-grade girl, responded that it was the United States of Earth. Clearly, Jessica's response demonstrates her confusion or limited experience regarding this vocabulary item. Evaluating the quality of a learner's response will help an examiner to determine the nature and severity of an instructional problem.

Error analysis will also help an examiner determine what areas to explore in more depth. The WJ-R provides a sampling of a wide span of skills. By evaluating a student's responses, an examiner will be able to form hypotheses regarding areas of concern. When an examiner notes specific errors, a more in-depth assessment, if needed, may be performed after testing is completed. For example, on the Calculation test, an examiner observed that Jeff, a seventh-grade student, had difficulty adding and subtracting fractions. At a later date, the examiner asked Jeff to complete additional problems and to explain the process involved in adding and subtracting fractions. At this time, the examiner was able to check Jeff's procedural and conceptual understanding and, subsequently, design an appropriate teaching strategy based upon the results.

Behavioral Observations

During an assessment, an examiner should be a careful observer of behavior. Behavioral observations provide additional Level 1 information. As a rule, any relevant observations are recorded on the Test Record for further consideration. Many times, the comments made by a student during an evaluation reveal important information regarding abilities and performance. For example, when asked whether he liked to read, Marty, a second-grade boy, responded that he did not know how to read. After hearing this statement, the examiner was surprised to discover that Marty possessed average reading skills. In this instance, Marty's school difficulties were more a result of low self-esteem than limited academic skill, and a plan was designed to enhance his self-concept and his image of himself as a capable reader.

The checklist in Figure 2-16 provides examples of several types of behaviors an examiner may observe. For the first ten items, a rating of "1" is the highest or best performance and a rating of "5" is the lowest performance. The ratings on Items 11 through 15 are not ordered from high to low. Instead, they reflect student characteristics and learning styles that vary from individual to individual. Additional comments may be added after any area of concern.

Student: _____ Examiner: _____ Date: _____

1.   Attitude toward testing
         1   2   3   4   5
         positive   negative
     Comments:

2.   Attitude toward examiner
         1   2   3   4   5
         friendly   hostile
     Comments:

3.   Student remarks
         1   2   3   4   5
         relevant   irrelevant
     Comments:

4.   Task perseverance
         1   2   3   4   5
         high   low
     Comments:

5.   Attention to specific tasks
         1   2   3   4   5
         high   low
     Comments:

6.   Consistency of attention
         1   2   3   4   5
         high   low
     Comments:

7.   Ability to follow directions
         1   2   3   4   5
         high   low
     Comments:

Figure 2–16. WJ-R Behavioral Observation Checklist. Permission is granted to reproduce this form. (*Continued on next page.*)

8. <u>Tolerance for frustration</u>

      1   2   3   4   5

    high   low

Comments:

9. **<u>Interest in tests</u>**

      1   2   3   4   **5**

    high   low

Comments:

10. <u>General attitude toward school</u>

      1   2   3   4   5

    positive   negative

Comments:

11. <u>Activity level of student</u>

      1   2   3   4   5

    high   low

Comments:

12. <u>Communicativeness</u>

      1   2   3   4   5

    talkative   quiet

Comments:

13. <u>Response - style</u>

(length of response time between question and answer)

      1   2   3   4   5

    fast   slow

Comments:

14. <u>General body language</u>

      1   2   3   4   5

    tense   relaxed

Comments:

15. <u>Need for reassurance</u>

      1   2   3   4   5

    high   low

Comments:

In describing and reporting a student's behaviors, the examiner should provide specific behavioral descriptions. A child who appears anxious about testing may grip the table top, tap his or her foot on the floor, or frequently change responses. A student who appears disinterested in testing may fall out of the chair during the testing session or remark about how boring the experience is. In some instances, these types of behaviors may simply be signs of frustration as the test items increase in difficulty. The examiner should report observable behaviors that are pertinent to a student's learning problem. Before recommending some type of intervention, the examiner should verify with the classroom teacher that the presenting behavior is a concern and, if so, perform a systematic classroom observation.

Test Scores

The WJ-R contains a full array of test scores. The variety of scores available will assist the user in test interpretation. Based upon the type of information required, an examiner will select which scores to determine and report. For example, in a special education placement conference, an examiner may wish to report standard scores or percentile ranks. When considering instructional planning, an examiner will be most interested in grade equivalents, Relative Mastery Indexes (RMIs), and instructional ranges. A brief discussion of WJ-R test scores follows.

Raw Score

A raw score is the summation of the total number of correct responses. On the majority of tests, each correct response receives 1 point. On the Memory for Sentences and Writing Samples tests, items may receive 2 or 1 raw score points. Raw scores are converted into W scores.

W Score

W scores, Level 2 information, are not usually reported by the user; however, the mathematical properties of this scale make it well suited for use as an intermediate step in test interpretation. The W scale provides a common scale of equal-interval measurement that represents both a person's ability and the task difficulty. The distance between points on the scale has the same meaning. When a student is presented a test item that has a difficulty level on the W scale equal to the person's ability, the probability of success is 50%.

Standard Error of Measurement

The standard error of measurement (SEM) is an estimate of the standard deviation that would be obtained by an individual if he or she were tested again and again on the same test. The SEM is directly related to the reliability of a test and estimates the amount of error that is attached to an individual's obtained score.

The SEM is used to communicate the degree of confidence in a score using confidence intervals. First, the examiner must determine the desired level of confidence. Two common levels of confidence are the 68% and the 95% level. To determine the lower and upper limits of the interval for the 68% confidence level, the examiner subtracts and then adds one SEM to the obtained score. For example, if a student obtained a standard score of 100 on a test and the SEM is 4, the confidence interval would range from 96 to 104. This interval indicates that the chances are about 68 out of 100 that the student's true score falls within this range. To estimate the 95% level, an examiner may multiply the SEM by 2 (or 1.96), and then subtract this figure from and add this figure to the obtained score. Confidence intervals may be constructed around grade equivalents, age equivalents, standard scores, and percentile ranks. For age and grade equivalents, the SEM for the W score is used. For standard scores and percentile ranks, the SEM for the standard score (SS) is used.

Grade and Age Equivalents

Grade and age equivalent scores are determined by comparing a student's performance to the average score obtained by students at different grades or ages in the norm sample. These scores provide Level 2 information. The WJ-R provides *extended* grade and age score scales. These scales use superscripts to indicate the percentile rank of students who are above or below the average score of students at both ends of the scale. For example, the grade scale ranges from beginning kindergarten (K.0) to seniors completing college (16.9). If a student scores below the average for students entering kindergarten, the grade equivalent is accompanied by a percentile rank superscript, such as K.0[13]. This score indicates that the student's score was equal to the 13th percentile of entering kindergarten students.

The extended age score scale is used with students who score below the average for 2-year-olds on the early development tests, below the average for 4-year-olds on the other tests, or above the average for mature adults on any of the tests. The highest age on the age scale indicates median peak performance for adults. Beyond this age, performance declined in the norm sample. For example, if the scale plateaus at 33 years of age, the superscript percentile rank is used to describe people who scored at a higher level. An age score of 33[87] indicates that the individual scored at the 87th percentile for subjects at the peak median level of performance.

Relative Mastery Index

The Relative Mastery Index (RMI), Level 3 information, describes the student's expected quality of performance on tasks of a given difficulty level. The RMI is represented as an index: the constant term (90) is in the denominator, while the numerator predicts the percentage of success for an individual on similar tasks. For example, an RMI of 30/90 indicates that a student would perform tasks with 30% mastery, while average people at the student's age or grade will perform at 90% mastery.

RMIs are of particular value in determining instructional implications. Unlike standard scores and percentile ranks that represent group standing, the RMI depicts the expected performance of an individual on similar tasks. Depending on the grade or age of an individual and the type of task, the significance of deficits in relative performance may vary. For example, a student beginning second grade who is at the 5th percentile on the Word Attack test would have an RMI of 11/90. This means that she would have 11% success on word attack tasks that average classmates would complete with 90 percent success. In contrast, a college senior who is at the 5th percentile would have an RMI of 68/90, meaning that she would have 68% success on word attack tasks that average seniors perform with 90% success. The second-grade student has a much greater performance deficit and a greater instructional need than the college student, even though both students stand at the 5th percentile for their grade.

Percentile Rank

A percentile rank, Level 4 information, describes a score in terms of its position within a group of 100 scores. This score indicates the point equal to or below which a percentage of individuals in the norm sample fall. For example, a percentile rank score of 45 would indicate that a person has scored as well as or better than 45% of the people in the norm sample.

The traditional percentile rank scale extends from 1 to 99. The WJ-R provides an extended percentile rank scale that ranges from .1 to 99.9. A percentile rank score of .1 indicates that one person out of 1,000 in the reference group would obtain a score that low or lower. A score of 99.9 would indicate that the person's performance was equal to or better than 999 persons out of 1,000.

Standard Score

A standard score, Level 4 information, is a statistical transformation of the percentile rank. This score is useful in determining a student's group standing. The WJ-R standard scores are based on a mean of 100 and a standard deviation of 15. Table E in the WJ-R Norm Tables may be used to convert standard scores into percentile ranks and three other types of standard scores: *T* scores, stanines, and normal curve equivalents.

Profile Interpretation

In addition to analyzing scores, an examiner may want to interpret a student's results on the two major profiles: the Age/Grade Profile and the Standard Score/Percentile Rank Profile.

Interpreting the Age/Grade Profile

The Age/Grade Profile is located on the front and back covers of the Test Record. This profile provides Level 2 and 3 information and depicts the level of development, the quality of a student's performance, and the instructional range from an easy to difficult level. These bands represent the developmental levels on the WJ-R COG and the instructional ranges on the WJ-R ACH. Figures 2-17 and 2-18 provide illustrations of the Age/Grade Profile from several tests of the WJ-R COG and the WJ-R ACH.

The profile bands are plotted using the W score and are based on 20 W units in length: 10 W points above and 10 W points below where a person scored on the scale. To assist in interpretation, a student's grade or age placement is plotted with a vertical line.

An examiner may note on this profile that some bands are wider than other bands. For example, the band for the Memory for Names test in Figure 2-17 is much wider than the band for Letter-Word Identification in Figure 2-18. The length of the band directly reflects the rate of growth. In an area of rapid development with much change over age, such as Letter-Word Identification, the band is quite short. In an area where less change occurs over the course of development, such as Memory for Names, the band is quite wide.

The purpose of the band is to assist the examiner in understanding the educational significance of a student's performance and determining appropriate instructional levels for an individual on various tasks. To estimate a student's developmental level or instructional range, note the grade or age equivalent scales at the top and bottom of the profile. The shaded bands, along an age or grade developmental scale, range from those tasks that a student would perceive as easy to those that would be perceived as difficult.

The WJ-R ACH Instructional Range Band is similar to the *independent* and *frustration* reading levels of an informal reading inventory as described by Betts (1957). Figure 2-19 illustrates the relationship between informal reading inventory criteria and the Instructional Range Band on the Age/Grade Profile.

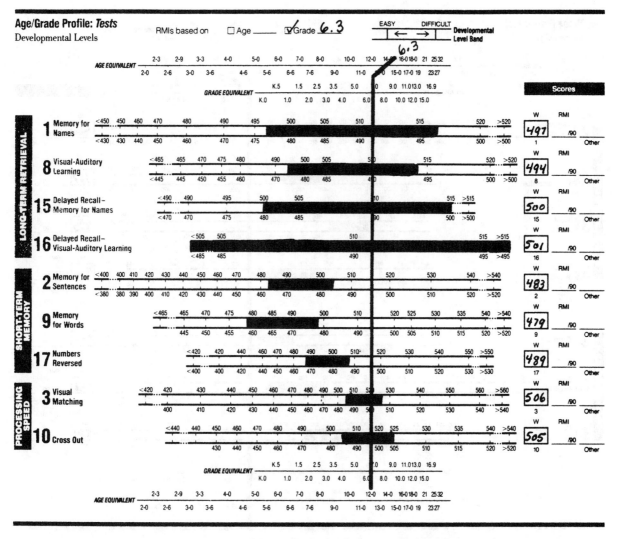

Figure 2–17. WJ-R COG Age/Grade Profile for a Sixth-Grade Student.

In analyzing the Age/Grade Profile, an examiner may observe: (a) generalized low, average, or high performance or (b) specific strengths and weaknesses among the cluster or test results. For example, the student in Figure 2-18 has below grade-level performance on all four reading tests and would be at the frustration level when presented with reading tasks at grade level. Based upon a student's performance within an area, the examiner may recommend a lower or higher level of instructional material than currently in use or suggest compensations that will enable a student to cope with the curricular demands.

In some cases, students will not be performing consistently below or above grade level in all academic areas. For example, a student may score below grade level on the Reading and Writing clusters of the WJ-R ACH, but score above grade level on the Mathematics and Knowledge clusters. Conversely, a student may score significantly below grade level on the Mathematics cluster but perform within the average range on the Reading cluster. In these cases, an examiner will recommend different instructional levels for different areas of performance.

Interpreting the Standard Score/Percentile Rank Profile

The Standard Score/Percentile Rank Profile provides Level 4 test information and describes an individual's strengths and weaknesses in comparison to peers. Three interpretation guidelines exist for interpreting performance on the Standard Score/Percentile Rank Profile (Woodcock & Johnson, 1977; Woodcock & Mather, 1989a, 1989b): (a) if the confidence bands overlap, no difference exists; (b) if the separation is less than the width of the wider band, a possible difference exists (84%

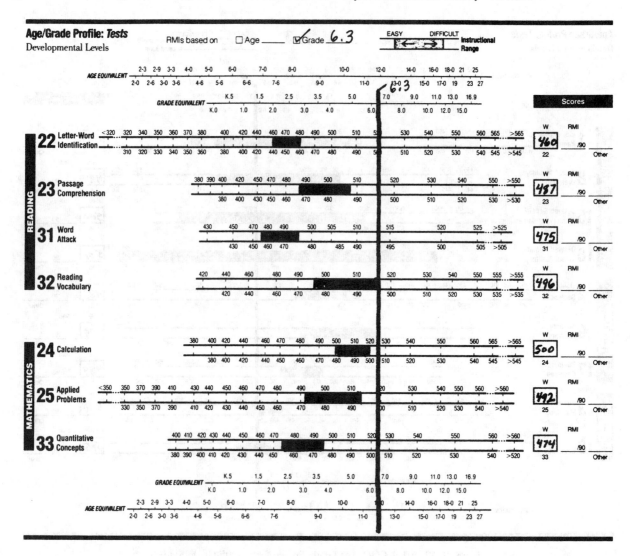

Figure 2–18. WJ-R ACH Age/Grade Profile for a Sixth-Grade Student.

confidence); and (c) if the separation is greater than the width of the wider band, a real difference exists (95% confidence).

Figure 2-20 depicts the conditions of no difference, possible difference, and real difference between tests and then clusters. On the test profile, a real difference exists between Picture Vocabulary and the other tests. On the cluster profile, a real difference exists between performance on Broad Mathematics and Broad Reading and Basic Reading Skills. These guidelines are applied to estimate statistically significant differences. The examiner must determine further whether or not a difference is educationally or practically significant.

Discrepancy Interpretation

The WJ-R provides procedures for documenting three types of psychoeducational discrepancies: Type 1, aptitude-achievement discrepancies; Type 2, intracognitive discrepancies; and Type 3, intra-achievement discrepancies. These discrepancies provide additional Level 4 information. Figure 2-21 illustrates the relationship among these three types of intra-ability discrepancies.

Type 1, an aptitude-achievement discrepancy, reflects the amount of disparity between an individual's intellec-

IRI	Independent*	Instructional*	Frustration
Accuracy	99+%	95+%	<95%
Comprehension	90+%	75+%	<75%
Frustration signs	No	No	Yes
WJ-R Instructional Range band	Easy level	Grade equivalent	Difficult level

*Both oral reading accuracy and comprehension criteria must be met.

Figure 2–19. Relationship Between Informal Reading Criteria and the WJ-R ACH Instructional Range Band.

tual abilities and actual academic achievement. In the WJ-R, the most relevant set of cognitive skills are compared to performance in a specific achievement area.

Although controversial, this type of discrepancy is frequently used as part of the selection criteria for learning disability programs. Mather and Healey (1990) address several issues surrounding the use of aptitude-achievement discrepancies for identifying students with learning disabilities.

Type 2, an intracognitive discrepancy, is present within individuals who have specific cognitive dysfunctions, such as a deficit in short-term memory. The deficit may be circumscribed, such as difficulty with one type of short-term memory task, or more generalized, such as difficulty with several different types of memory tasks.

Type 3, an intra-achievement discrepancy, is present within individuals who have specific academic deficits. Discrepancies may exist between academic areas, such as a discrepancy between overall reading and mathematics performance, or within academic areas, such as a discrepancy between basic reading skills and reading comprehension.

In the WJ-R, the presence of intracognitive and intra-achievement discrepancies is most apparent when a student has difficulty in a specific area, rather than in several areas. For example, in considering intra-achievement discrepancies, one area is compared to average performance in the other three areas. If mathematics performance is considerably lower than the other three broad achievement clusters, a significant difference will be detected. With some students, however, performance may be low in several areas. For example, a student may have low performance on both Broad Reading and Broad Written Language, but average performance on Broad Mathematics and Broad Knowledge. The expected score for Broad Reading is influenced by the low score for Broad Written Language, and, consequently, the size of the intra-achievement discrepancy is reduced.

Two scores may be used for interpreting the significance of a discrepancy. The discrepancy percentile rank, the most meaningful interpretive score, indicates the percentage of the students with the same expected or predicted score whose achievement is as low or lower. A discrepancy percentile rank over 50 indicates achievement that is higher than predicted achievement. This discrepancy percentile rank may also be transformed into a standard deviation statistic. The SD DIFF score refers to the difference, in units of the standard error of estimate, between the student's actual and predicted scores. A negative value indicates that the student's actual achievement is lower than predicted, whereas a positive value indicates that the student's achievement is higher than predicted. This statement of significance may be used instead of the discrepancy percentile rank in programs that have a selection criterion similar to "a difference equal to or greater than, one and one-half times the standard deviation" (Woodcock & Mather, 1989a). For this type of application, the standard error of the estimate is the correct standard deviation statistic.

Figure 2-22 presents the Compuscore printout for Christopher, a fifth-grade boy, who has significant intracognitive, aptitude-achievement, and intra-achievement discrepancies. In examining intracognitive discrepancies, based on his average performance on the other six cognitive factors, only 1 out of a 1,000 students with the same predicted score would obtain a score as low or lower than Christopher in Long-Term Retrieval. In contrast, only 3 out of 1,000 students with the same predicted score would obtain a score as high or higher than Christopher on Fluid Reasoning. Christopher also has an aptitude-achievement discrepancy between his Reading Aptitude score and his Broad Reading score. Only 2% of the student's peer group with the same predicted scores would have achievement as low or lower. In examining intra-achievement discrepancies, Christopher's performance in Broad Reading is significantly lower than predicted when compared to his average performance in the other three achievement areas. Only 1 out of 1,000 students with the same predicted score would have achievement as low or lower.

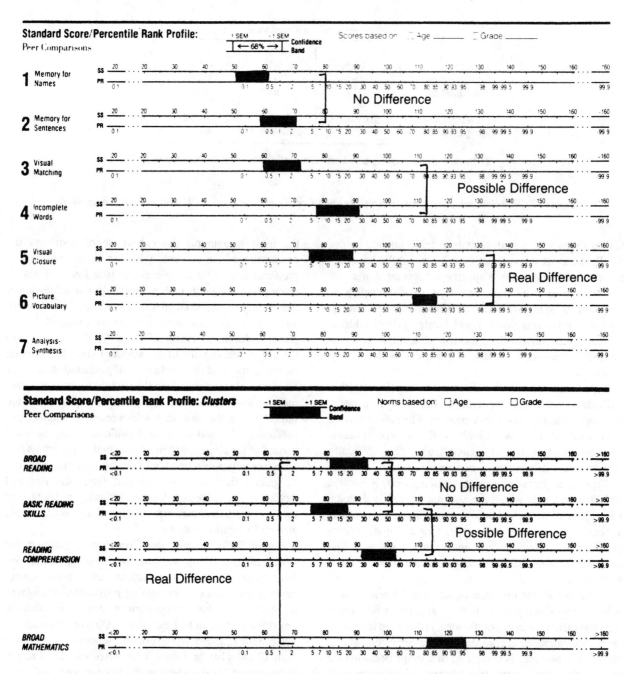

Figure 2–20. Interpretation Guidelines for the Standard Score/Percentile Rank Profile.

Understanding the full range or levels of interpretive material available on the WJ-R allows an examiner to maximize the information obtained from a testing session. Depending upon the nature of the assessment, an examiner may consider all of the information or only some of the information. In some instances, grade equivalents and RMIs will be the only scores necessary. In other instances, an examiner will want to obtain selected derived scores and plot profiles. An examiner should not waste time with unnecessary testing or scoring. The goal of every assessment is to provide the most useful description of a student's behavior and performance for the given purpose.

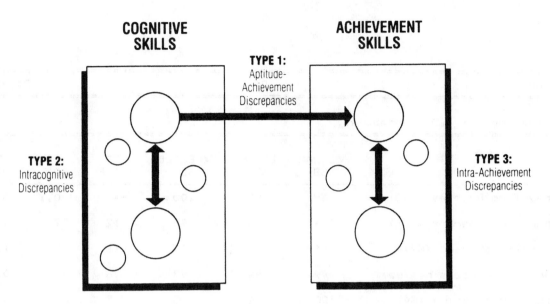

Figure 2–21. A Model of Psychoeducational Discrepancies. *Note.* From *WJ-R Tests of Cognitive Ability—Standard and Supplemental Batteries: Examiner's Manual* (p. 7) by R.W. Woodcock and N. Mather, 1989, Allen, TX: DLM. Copyright 1989 by DLM. Reprinted by permission.

```
==========================================================================
Name:                          ID:                          Page: 6
==========================================================================

Intra-Cognitive Discrepancies
==========================================================================
```

	ACTUAL SS	OTHER SS	EXPECTED SS	SS DIFF	PR	SD DIFF
Long-Term Retrieval (Glr)	59	100	100	-41	0.1	-3.33
Short-Term Memory (Gsm)	104	93	92	12	82	0.92
Processing Speed (Gs)	81	97	97	-16	12	-1.18
Auditory Processing (Ga)	99	94	93	6	69	0.49
Visual Processing (Gv)	100	94	95	5	64	0.37
Comprehension-Knowledge (Gc)	99	94	91	8	76	0.71
Fluid Reasoning (Gf)	120	90	87	33	99.7	2.80

```
Aptitude/Achievement Discrepancies
==========================================================================
```

	ACTUAL ACH SS	APTITUDE SS	EXPECTED SS	SS DIFF	PR	SD DIFF
Oral Language	107	108	105	2	57	0.18
Broad Reading	75	96	97	-22	2	-2.16
Broad Mathematics	113	106	104	9	80	0.84
Broad Written Language	88	86	91	-3	39	-0.27
Broad Knowledge	109	115	110	-1	46	-0.09

```
Intra-Achievement Discrepancies
==========================================================================
```

	ACTUAL SS	OTHER SS	EXPECTED SS	SS DIFF	PR	SD DIFF
Broad Reading (R)	75	103	103	-28	0.1	-3.04
Broad Mathematics (M)	113	91	92	21	98	2.06
Broad Written Language (W)	88	99	99	-11	13	-1.13
Broad Knowledge (K)	109	92	93	16	94	1.57

Figure 2–22. A Fifth-Grade Student on the Three Types of Psychoeducational Discrepancies.

3

READING

The student's definition of reading that 'Reading is thinking and feeling about ideas suggested by printed matter,' is an ideal toward which we all should strive and which gives reading the place it should have as a mental process of the highest level and of the greatest possible educative value.

(Dolch, 1941, p. 8)

Several aspects of reading skill are measured on the WJ-R ACH. Two tests, Letter-Word Identification in the Standard Battery and Word Attack in the Supplemental Battery, measure basic reading skills. Two additional tests, Passage Comprehension in the Standard Battery and Reading Vocabulary in the Supplementary Battery, measure reading comprehension. Each of the four reading tests measures a different aspect of reading performance.

Content of the Reading Tests

The measured abilities include skills in identifying letters and words (Letter-Word Identification), applying phonic and structural analysis (Word Attack), producing word associations (Reading Vocabulary), and using syntactic and semantic cues (Passage Comprehension). Figure 3-1 illustrates the relationships among the WJ-R ACH reading tests.

The WJ-R ACH tests measure several stages of reading development. Chall (1983) outlined a five-stage model to illustrate the way reading proficiency changes throughout development. During the first stage, accurate decoding, students learn to use grapheme-phoneme relationships to decode the printed word. In the second stage, fluency, students learn to read words rapidly and accurately. In the third stage, knowledge acquisition, attention is directed toward reading to learn. In the fourth stage, the student is able to evaluate and compare information from a variety of sources. In the fifth stage, the student is able to acquire highly specialized knowledge at an advanced level. In this five-stage model, the WJ-R ACH reading tests measure the first three stages of reading development. Although important, proficiency in the last two stages is based more upon critical thinking, reasoning abilities, language skills, and specialized knowledge and vocabulary, rather than reading comprehension per se.

Determining Instructional Level

One major goal of any reading assessment is to determine a student's instructional reading level. Helpful information may be obtained by plotting performance on the Instructional Level Profile on the front and back covers of the WJ-R Test Record. By viewing the grade scale above or below the instructional band, an examiner may estimate a student's present performance ranging from an easy to difficult level. In determining an instructional level, an examiner should consider both a student's strengths and weaknesses and expected reading achievement.

Strengths and Weaknesses

Analysis of a student's strengths and weaknesses among the four reading tests will help an examiner develop an appropriate instructional program. Some students have good basic reading skills but difficulty with reading comprehension. Other students have good reading comprehension but low performance in basic reading skills. After analyzing performance, an examiner may determine that a student has: (a) low basic reading skills,

MORE COMPLEX

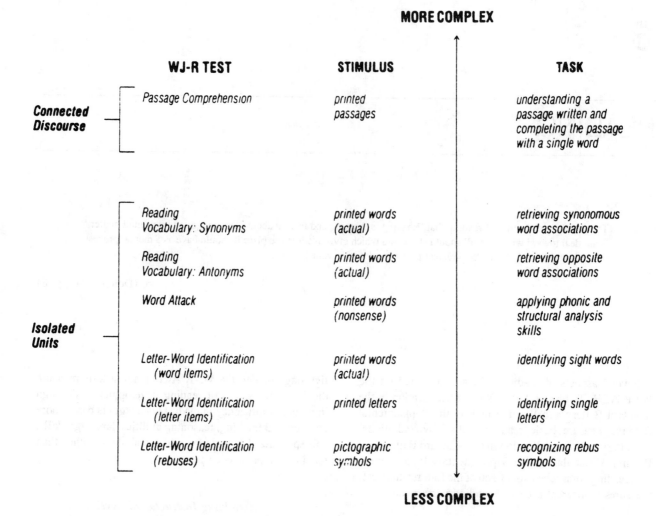

	WJ-R TEST	STIMULUS	TASK
Connected Discourse	Passage Comprehension	printed passages	understanding a passage written and completing the passage with a single word
Isolated Units	Reading Vocabulary: Synonyms	printed words (actual)	retrieving synonomous word associations
	Reading Vocabulary: Antonyms	printed words (actual)	retrieving opposite word associations
	Word Attack	printed words (nonsense)	applying phonic and structural analysis skills
	Letter-Word Identification (word items)	printed words (actual)	identifying sight words
	Letter-Word Identification (letter items)	printed letters	identifying single letters
	Letter-Word Identification (rebuses)	pictographic symbols	recognizing rebus symbols

LESS COMPLEX

Figure 3–1. Various Skills Measured by the WJ-R ACH Reading Tests. *Note*. From *WJ-R Tests of Achievement: Examiner's Manual* (p. 18) by R.W. Woodcock and N. Mather, 1989, Allen, TX: DLM. Copyright 1989 by DLM. Reprinted by permission.

but average or above-average reading comprehension; (b) high or average basic reading skills but low reading comprehension; or (c) generalized low, average, or high reading performance. Figure 3-2 depicts the performance of three different sixth-grade students on the Age/Grade Profile. Instructional objectives and reading programs will differ for these three students.

When a significant discrepancy occurs between performance in basic reading skills and reading comprehension, an examiner should base a general instructional level for independent reading upon the lower area of skill. For example, for the first student in Figure 3-2, an estimate of the instructional level would be based upon performance in basic reading skills, whereas for the second student, an estimate would be based upon reading comprehension performance. For teacher-directed or remedial instruction, an examiner may wish to base the instructional level on the higher level of performance. For example, for the first

student, selected reading materials would be at the comprehension level, and the teacher would provide intensive remediation of basic skills in the context of the written material. In identifying individual needs and planning instructional programs, an examiner may also wish to consider a student's predicted achievement levels.

Predicting Reading Achievement

The purpose of comparing a student's predicted achievement to actual achievement is to determine whether or not a student is functioning within this estimate of performance. In many instances, a student's aptitude is similar to his or her level of performance.

A student with high performance on the WJ-R COG Reading Aptitude cluster is likely to exhibit high performance on the Basic Skills and Reading Comprehension clusters. Even when no discrepancies are noted, a student

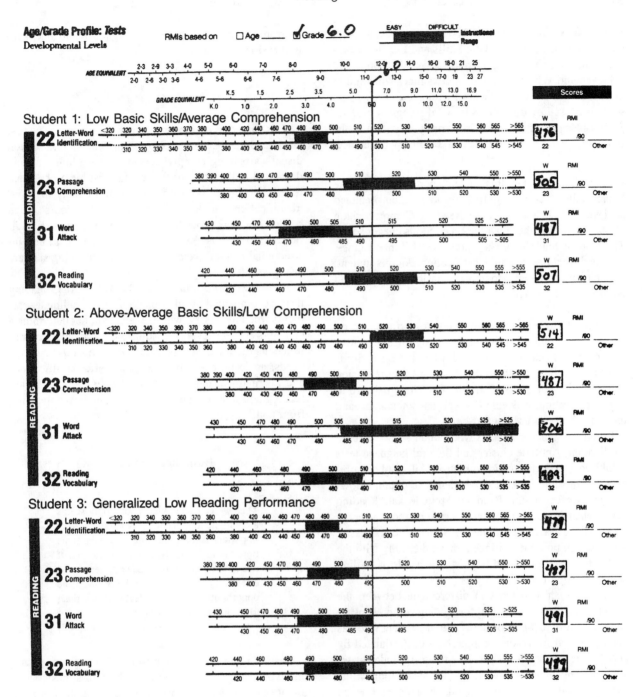

Figure 3–2. Three Sixth-Grade Students on the Age/Grade Profile.

who is significantly above or below grade level in performance will need some type of classroom modifications.

Performance Patterns

When differences in performance occur, several types of patterns emerge. For example, a student may have high or average reading potential, but low basic reading skills and comprehension. Three different performance patterns are described for students who have high or average predicted achievement based on the WJ-R COG Reading Aptitude cluster or the oral language tests: (a) low basic skills and comprehension, (b) low basic skills, and (c) low comprehension.

Low basic skills and comprehension. For this student, performance on both the Basic Skills and Reading Comprehension clusters is significantly lower than predicted achievement. With this pattern, an examiner will want to determine whether or not the low Reading Comprehension score is caused by difficulties in word recognition. If so, emphasis is placed on improving word recognition skills. If not, the goal is to improve general reading performance.

Low basic skills. For this student, performance on the Basic Skills cluster is significantly lower than predicted achievement. In addition, the Reading Comprehension cluster score is higher than the Basic Skills cluster score. The student tends to make good use of context clues, despite difficulties in word identification. For this student, the first remedial goal is to improve basic word attack and word recognition skills.

Low comprehension. For this student, performance on the Reading Comprehension cluster is significantly lower than predicted achievement. In addition, the Basic Skills cluster score is higher than the Reading Comprehension cluster score. For this student, the remedial goals are to improve vocabulary, develop background knowledge, and increase ability to use context clues.

In most instances, students who obtain a low score on the Reading Aptitude cluster and the oral language tests exhibit low performance in both basic skills and comprehension. In some instances, a student will obtain below-average scores on the Reading Aptitude and Reading Comprehension clusters but an average or above-average score on the Basic Skills cluster. Some students master word recognition but continue to have difficulty with the higher level cognitive and linguistic demands of reading comprehension tasks.

An examiner will want to differentiate between the student who has low potential for reading comprehension and good word recognition skills and the student who has good potential for reading comprehension (estimated by performance on the WJ-R COG Reading Aptitude cluster and oral language tests) but low word recognition skills. Although both of these students will obtain low scores on the Reading Comprehension cluster, the first student has a word recognition problem that is interfering with comprehension ability and has good prognosis for reading development; the second student has low aptitude and oral language and will likely benefit from enrichment activities to enhance oral language development and background knowledge.

The purpose of all reading instruction is to enhance a student's ability to derive meaning from text. To achieve this aim, some students will need direct instruction in basic reading skills, whereas other students will benefit primar-

ily from instructional strategies designed to enhance comprehension.

Chapter Organization

This chapter is divided into two main sections. The first section addresses basic reading skills. The second section discusses reading comprehension. The reading tests are discussed in the order of the reading test hierarchy illustrated in Figure 3-1, progressing from skill in word identification to understanding connected discourse. Each section contains procedures for error analysis and additional informal assessments. Several modifications, instructional methods, and strategies for improving skill are also presented.

Analysis of performance on the WJ-R ACH reading tests, accompanied by additional informal reading assessments when necessary, will help an examiner determine a student's present level of reading skill and select appropriate instructional strategies. Based upon an individual's needs, an examiner may suggest specific modifications and instructional methods that will help a student enjoy reading and improve his or her ability to derive meaning from text.

Basic Reading Skills

> Thus we can state what at first only seems a contradiction: decoding is at once a least important aspect of reading, and at the same time the most crucial aspect of reading. If one does not learn to decode efficiently and effectively, one will never be allowed the opportunity to read, i.e., deal with and react to meaning via the printed word.
>
> (Glass, 1973, pp. 4-5)

Basic reading skills include both sight word recognition and word analysis skills. As noted by Glass, basic skills are at once the least important aspect of reading and the most crucial aspect. Students with poor word identification skills have difficulty deciphering the code and, consequently, obtaining meaning from text.

The two WJ-R ACH basic reading skills tests are Letter-Word Identification in the Standard Battery and Word Attack in the Supplemental Battery. When administering these tests, an examiner should record the student's incorrect responses verbatim for later error analysis. If more detailed information is desired for error analysis, the examiner may administer both Forms A and B of these tests.

Error Analysis of Letter-Word Identification

The initial items of the Letter-Word Identification test measure reading readiness skills. The first several items involve symbolic learning, or the ability to match a pictorial representation (rebus) with an actual picture of the object. Success in this early development task is dependent on the knowledge that drawings or pictograph representations may be used to symbolize objects. The next set of items requires the identification of the letter names of several capital and small letters.

Most of the items on the Letter-Word Identification test require the identification of words. In performing an error analysis on these items, an examiner should consider a student's: (a) error types, (b) response style, and (c) error patterns.

Error Types

One purpose of examining a student's performance on the Letter-Word Identification test is to determine whether or not the student has developed efficient strategies for word identification. In analyzing responses, several different types of errors may emerge. As with all tests, possible responses range on a continuum from minor errors to more serious errors. A hierarchy of error types, ranging from least to most serious follows.

Type 1: Minor mispronunciation. The student may mispronounce a word, such as putting the accent on the wrong syllable, and not self-correct. This error may indicate that the student has good word recognition skills but is not familiar with the meaning or correct pronunciation of the word.

Type 2: Meaningful word/close visual resemblance. The student's response is a real word that is very similar in appearance to the correct response. For example, Jeff, a high school student, pronounced "significance" as "significant." He also identified the word "shoulder" as "shudder" and the word "process" as "progress." Jeff's responses are real words that closely resemble the stimulus words and demonstrate some word identification skill.

Type 3: Meaningless word/close auditory resemblance. The student's response is a nonsense word that is somewhat similar in pronunciation to the stimulus word. For example, Shiela, a sixth-grade student, pronounced "bounties" as "bourties," and "doubtful" as "dubful."

Type 4: Meaningful word/little resemblance. The student's response is a real word that only minimally re-

sembles the stimulus word. As examples, Clinton, a second-grade student, pronounced the word "dog" as "pig." John, a high school student, pronounced the word "significance" as "sealant." With these types of mistake, the student may just look at the general configuration of the word, or at the initial consonant, and then take a guess.

Type 5: Meaningless word/little resemblance. The student produces a nonsense word that has little phonological resemblance to the real word.

Type 6: No response. The student does not attempt to pronounce the word. He or she may not attempt a word when it is not immediately recognized. In observing the student, the examiner may note that the student quickly glances at the word, and then states: "I don't know." Or, the student may look quickly at the lists of words on the page and remark: "I don't know any of these words." When encouraged to try, the student refuses. In some cases, a student may have developed some word identification skill, but is unwilling to try, extremely frustrated, or afraid to risk making an error. In most cases, students who are unwilling to attempt words have not developed an effective strategy for word identification or lack confidence in their skill.

Response Style

In listening to a student read the words on the Letter-Word Identification test, the examiner should note how easily and rapidly the student responds. A student with good sight word recognition skills recognizes many words rapidly with little effort. A student with nonautomatic word identification skills may identify several words accurately but may require increased time and greater attention to phonological analysis to determine the correct response. This type of reader may attempt to sound out each word and then self-correct initial responses. In many instances, a close approximation of a word provides the student with enough information to identify the word. For example, Mary, a high school student, initially mispronounced the word "island" as two separate words, "is" and "land," and then immediately self-corrected. Mary used her oral vocabulary skills to aid in word identification but she has not developed automatic word identification skills.

Error Patterns

In analyzing a student's errors, the examiner may gain insight into the student's knowledge of sound-symbol relationships. The items on Forms A and B of the Letter-Word Identification tests contain words with both regular and irregular sound/symbol correspondence. In analyzing errors, an examiner may note that the student has more difficulty with nonphonic or irregular words, than words that have predictable sound/symbol correspondence. Table 3-1 delineates regular, infrequent, and irregular words from Forms A and B. Words are considered regular if the orthographic pattern is predictable in English and sounding out the word produces the correct response. Correct pronunciation requires knowledge of sound/symbol correspondence. For example, the word "knew" is considered to be regular, but the student must know that the letters *k* and *n* together produce one sound. Words are considered infrequent if a phonic rule exists to guide pronunciation, but the pattern occurs infrequently. Irregular words cannot be pronounced correctly using phonic rules.

Specific error patterns may also be observed. For example, an examiner may note that a student has difficulty with particular phonic elements, such as vowel sounds or final consonants. Figure 3-3 illustrates the performance of Gina, a fourth-grade student, referred for reading difficulty. Gina's responses suggest that she identifies initial and final consonant sounds but has difficulty with medial vowel sounds.

Error Analysis of Word Attack

Evaluation of performance on the Word Attack test will provide the examiner with additional information regarding a student's phonological word analysis abilities. Because no context is provided and nonsense words are used, a student must rely solely on ability to pronounce phonically regular word patterns.

Error Patterns

By analyzing the errors a student makes, an examiner may formulate some initial hypotheses regarding an individual's word attack skills. Figure 3-4 illustrates the responses of Josh, a high school sophomore, who was having extreme difficulty with word identification, spelling, and learning Spanish. His limited word attack skill was a contributing factor to his scholastic difficulties. These types of observations will assist the examiner in making appropriate recommendations for educational programming.

A more in-depth analysis of word identification skill may be performed by combining a student's errors from both the Letter-Word Identification and Word Attack tests and then underlining the part of the word that contained an error. By looking at the missed word parts, the examiner may determine whether a student tends to make errors or lacks mastery of a certain phonic element. For example, the examiner may note that the student has not mastered beginning or ending consonant sounds. Or, the examiner may observe that single consonant sounds are mastered,

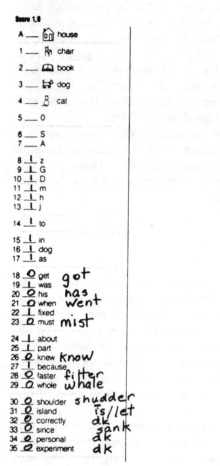

Figure 3–3. A Fourth-Grade Student on the Letter-Word Identification Test.

but the student is having difficulty with another phonic element, such as short vowel sounds or consonant blends. Table 3-2 groups several items from the Letter-Word Identification and Word Attack tests by different phonic elements, including: (a) short vowel sounds; (b) long vowel sounds; (c) consonant blends, two sounds that are partially merged but each letter maintains its sound; (d) consonant digraphs, two successive consonants that produce a single sound that differs from the sounds each letter would make in isolation; (e) vowel digraphs, two successive vowel letters that produce one sound; and (f) vowel diphthongs, two successive vowels that represent a single blended sound.

Strategies

On the longer nonsense words containing two or more syllables, an examiner may observe whether or not the

Table 3–1. List of Words with Regular, Infrequent, and Irregular Sound/Symbol Correspondence.

	Form A			Form B		
	Regular	Infrequent	Irregular	Regular	Infrequent	Irregular
14.			to	is		
15.	in			go		
16.	dog			not		
17.	as			but		
18.			get			from
19.			was	had		
20.	his			keep		
21.	when					said
22.	fixed			got		
23.	must				their	
24.	about			light		
25.	part					once
26.	knew			use		
27.	because				young	
28.	faster			point		
29.	whole			piece		
30.		shoulder			built	
31.			island	however		
32.	correctly			bachelor		
33.	since			social		
34.	personal					knowledge
35.	experiment			bought		
36.	distance			investigate		
37.	bounties			thermostsat		
38.	process			fierce		
39.	doubtful			curious		
40.			moustache	authority		
41.			cologne		courageous	
42.	hesitating			megaphone		
43.	masculine			illiteracy		
44.	sufficient			acrylic		
45.	domesticated				irregularities	
46.	preyed				silhouette	
47.		therapeutic		precipitate		
48.	significance			reminiscent		
49.			bouquet	chorused		
50.		apparatus				debris
51.	diacritical			municipality		
52.			debutante	subsidiary		
53.	trivialities			melodious		
54.	expostulate			semiarid		
55.	stochastic			facetious		
56.	ubiquitous			satiate		
57.			enceinte			puisne

student sounds out the words letter by letter or proceeds syllable by syllable. Some students may place a finger under the word and then produce a sound for each letter. Although the response may be correct when the sounds are blended together, recognizing a word by its parts, clusters, or syllables is a more efficient strategy for longer words than pronouncing single letters.

Occasionally, an examiner may observe that a student bypasses direct phonological analysis and identifies the nonsense words on the Word Attack test by relating a word's visual configuration and pattern to a known sight word. For example, Kevin, a high school student, used the following strategy. He looked at the stimulus word, thought of and pronounced a real word, and then pronounced the stimulus word. For example, for "zoop," Kevin said "loop," then "zoop." For "loast," he said "toast," then "loast." Although this strategy worked effectively for pronouncing many of the items, it was inefficient for pronouncing the multisyllabic words and impractical in terms of the time demands. Kevin had not developed

TEST 31

Word Attack   **Basal:** Item 1
                         Ceiling: 6 highest-numbered items failed

Figure 3–4. A High School Sophomore on the Word Attack Test.

automatic decoding skills and had difficulty applying phonological analysis to real words that were not recognized immediately.

Additional Assessment of Basic Reading Skills

In some cases, an examiner may want to perform a more in-depth analysis of basic reading skills. This assessment may be conducted to provide more information about: (a) letter knowledge, (b) word recognition skill in context, or (c) reading fluency.

Letter Knowledge

If a student misses one or more of the letter names on the Letter-Word Identification test, an examiner may wish to determine exactly which capital and small letters the student recognizes and/or determine which letter sounds are known. For this procedure, all 26 letters (52 with capitals) are written on index cards and presented in a random order. Or, the student may be presented with a list of letters to read. Figure 3-5 presents a list of lowercase and capital letters that may be used for this purpose. The student may be asked to give both the letter name and the letter sound. To check consistency, the letters may be presented again. The student may also be asked to match lowercase with uppercase letters.

Word Recognition in Context

A comprehensive evaluation of word recognition involves both listening to a student read aloud both words in lists and passages from text. By listening to a student read aloud, an examiner will obtain further information regarding a student's word recognition skills in context. For this assessment, an examiner may wish to use graded passages from the school's basal reading series, an informal reading inventory, or the student's textbooks. As an alternative, the examiner may wish to create word lists and stories using a similar set of words to determine if some words are identified correctly in context but not in isolation.

For most students, word identification skills improve in context. The provision of text provides the student with additional syntactic and semantic clues that make it easier to identify words. In some instances, however, students make fewer mistakes when reading words in isolation than in context (Allington, 1978; Reisberg, 1982). Allington hypothesized that some students with extreme reading difficulty are able to read words more easily in isolation because of past remedial training that focused on word analysis in isolation. Another possibility is that for students with language impairments, the demands of processing whole sentences reduce attention to word identification.

In examining individual differences among 20 students with learning disabilities who were poor readers, Reisberg (1982) found that the majority of students made fewer word identification errors in context than on words presented in isolation. Three of the subjects, however, made fewer errors with words in isolation than with words in connected text. For these students, contextual cues did not improve word identification. In listening to a student's oral reading performance, the examiner will want to determine whether or not word identification skill improves with the addition of context. If not, instructional programming should include strategies for enhancing attention to syntactic and semantic information.

Reading Fluency

An important aspect of reading skill that is not assessed by the WJ-R ACH reading tests is fluency. Reading fluency is the ability to read easily and rapidly with proper

Table 3–2. Different Phonic Elements for the Letter-Word Identification and Word Attack Tests.

	Letter-Word Identification			Word Attack	
	Form A	Form B		Form A	Form B
Short Vowel	14.	is	A.	nat	nat
	15. in		B.	ib	ib
	16. dog	not	1.	tiff	hap
	17. as	but	2.	nan	mell
	18. get		3.	rox	fim
	19.	had	4.		ven
	20. his		5.	lish	jop
	21. when		6.		floxy
	22. fixed	got	7.	jox	leck
	23. must		9.	gusp	distrum
	28. faster		11.	yosh	
			13.		gradly
			16.	thrept	
			18.	mibgus	shomble
			21.		quog
			22.		centizen
			25.		hudned
			27.		cimp
			29.		depnonlel
Long Vowel	15.	go	6.	dright	
	20.	keep	12.	tayed	
	24.	light	14.		blighten
	26.	use	15.	sluke	wreet
	29. whole	piece	20.		gnobe
			22.	saist	
Consonant Blends	18.	from	6.	dright	floxy
	23. mu<u>st</u>		9.	gu<u>sp</u>	di<u>str</u>um
	25.	on<u>ce</u>	10.	<u>sn</u>irk	
	28. fa<u>st</u>er	poi<u>nt</u>	13.	<u>gr</u>awl	<u>gr</u>adly
	30.	bui<u>lt</u>	14.	loa<u>st</u>	<u>bl</u>ighten
	33. si<u>nce</u>		15.	<u>sl</u>uke	
	36. dista<u>nce</u>		16.	<u>thr</u>ept	
	37.	thermo<u>st</u>at	19.	<u>spl</u>aunch	
	40. mou<u>st</u>ache		20.	quan<u>tr</u>ic	
	50.	de<u>br</u>is	21.	li<u>nd</u>ify	
	53. <u>tr</u>ivialities		22.	sai<u>st</u>	
	55. <u>st</u>ochastic		27.		ci<u>mp</u>
			30.		querpo<u>st</u>onious
Consonant Digraphs	23.	<u>th</u>eir	5.	li<u>sh</u>	
	30. <u>sh</u>oulder		11.	yo<u>sh</u>	<u>ch</u>ur
	32.	ba<u>ch</u>elor	17.	<u>wh</u>eeg	
	37.	<u>th</u>ermostat	18.		<u>sh</u>omble
	40. au<u>th</u>ority		19.	<u>spl</u>aunch	
	42.	mega<u>ph</u>one	21.		quog
	47. <u>th</u>erapeutic		23.		wrou<u>tch</u>
	49. bou<u>qu</u>et		24.	<u>wh</u>umb	<u>ph</u>intober
			26.	<u>ph</u>igh	cy<u>the</u>
			28.	para<u>ph</u>onity	
			30.		<u>qu</u>erpostonious

Table 3–2. (*Continued on next page.*)

Table 3–2 (*continued*)

| | | Letter-Word Identification | | Word Attack | |
		Form A	Form B	Form A	Form B
Vowel	20.		keep		
Digraphs	26.	knew			
	27.	because	young	4. zoop	
	29.		piece	8. feap	pawk
	30.	shoulder	built	12. tayed	
				13. grawl	
	38.		fierce	14. loast	
	40.	moustache	authority	15.	wreet
	46.	preyed		17. wheeg	koodoo
	47.	therapeutic		19. splaunch	baunted
	49.	bouquet		22. saist	
				25. mafreatsun	
Vowel	24.	about		10.	foy
Diphthongs	28.		point	23. knoink	wroutch
	31.		however	28.	doitibility
	37.	bounties			
	39.	doubtful			

phrasing. Reading dysfluency is characterized by: (a) slow rate, (b) word-by-word reading, (c) hesitations, (d) repetitions, and (e) lack of expression. A student may point to each word as it is being read. When using graded passages to assess fluency, an examiner may note that a student is fluent at a certain level of reading skill, but not with grade-level text. In another case, an examiner may note that the student tends to read word-by-word regardless of the difficulty level.

Samuels (1987) described several simple techniques for determining whether or not a student is automatic in decoding. The examiner gives the student a text that he or she has not read before. The student reads the text orally and then recalls it in as much detail as possible. Because automatic decoders are usually able to recognize and comprehend words simultaneously, a satisfactory retelling of the story suggests that the student is automatic in decoding. The examiner should also listen to the vocal expression as the student reads the passage orally. Students who are not automatic in decoding tend to read with little expression. In some cases, a student may read a passage fluently but be unable to restate the content. This type of student will benefit from language and reading comprehension strategies, rather than fluency techniques.

Students who have not yet developed automatic decoding skills will likely benefit from instructional techniques designed to improve fluency. Several techniques for increasing fluency are described in the section on Instructional Strategies for Reading Fluency.

Instructional Compensations and Modifications

Reading compensations are used to alter tasks in the learning environment so students with reading disabilities may obtain information in ways that either limit the amount of required reading or do not require reading. An examiner may recommend several different compensatory strategies or program modifications for students with difficulty in word recognition.

Instructional Level

One modification is to match the readability level of all materials to the student's reading level. Additionally, it may be necessary to lower the readability level of classroom worksheets and exams. Riegel, Mayle, and McCarthy-Henkel (1988) describe an easy way to determine if the reading material is too difficult for a student based upon the standard of 95% accuracy for word recognition. The student opens the book at random and counts out 100 words. He or she places four fingers under the cover of the book and the thumb on the top of the page. The student reads out loud and presses a finger down for each word that cannot be identified easily. If the student gets to his or her thumb, the reading material is probably too difficult to read independently.

Interest Level

During assessment, an examiner may determine a student's interests. An instructor may provide supplemental

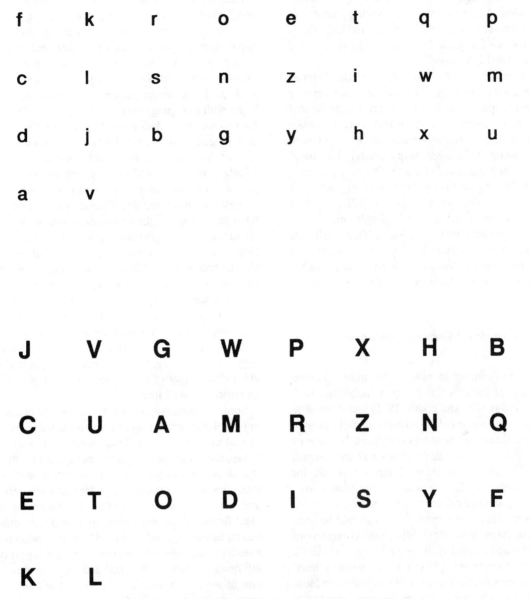

Figure 3–5. Small and Capital Letters for Informal Evaluation.

reading materials that address specific interests. High-interest, low vocabulary readers are also available.

Other Media

Important information may be presented using other media, such as filmstrips, television, and audiotapes. A peer or volunteer may read material to a student or the student may listen to a tape-recorded book.

Oral Reading

An examiner may recommend that time spent in oral reading activities be reduced. This may decrease any frustration associated with low word recognition skill.

Shorten Assignments

The number of assigned pages may be based upon a student's reading rate and skill. For some students, abridged versions of classroom readings may be appropriate.

Skip and Drill

One technique that may be used to reduce the amount of material that a student is expected to cover and increase student motivation is a skip-and-drill procedure (Lovitt, 1984; Lovitt & Hansen, 1976). Lovitt and Hansen found that this procedure was effective for improving oral reading rates, reducing error rates, and developing reading comprehension. As an alternative to placing students in lower level materials, students may be permitted to skip certain portions of a grade-level text when the desired performance level is reached.

To begin, the instructor establishes the student's baseline performance in the target skill, such as reading rate or comprehension questions. A criterion level is set so that once the student reaches or exceeds that score, he or she is allowed to skip a selected amount of text. Although Lovitt and Hansen had students skip a quarter of the basal reading text, they suggested that a teacher may just have the student skip the next story. If the student goes for 7 days without reaching the criterion, a drill procedure appropriate to the targeted area is implemented. For example, the student may practice reading orally or rework comprehension questions with the teacher or a peer. Drill procedures continue until the student reaches the established criterion level for skipping a section.

Instructional Strategies: Overview

Difficulty in learning to read is the most common problem found in students with learning disabilities (Kirk & Chalfant, 1984). Kirk and Elkins (1975) found that 60% to 70% of the students in federal projects for children with learning disabilities had reading disabilities. Because of the high prevalence of reading problems, an examiner will need to be familiar with many different methods for enhancing word identification skill and comprehension.

In designing an instructional program to improve word identification skill, three important facts should be considered. First, the purpose of providing instruction in word identification and decoding is to facilitate a student's ability to construct meaning from text or translate printed symbols into meaningful thoughts. When low word identification skill interferes with comprehension, a method is selected that will help the student to develop efficient, automatic decoding strategies. In addition to a method to improve word identification skill, the instructor should provide separate or simultaneous attention to the comprehension process. It is important to strike a careful balance between the direct instruction of word identification skills and the direct instruction and monitoring of comprehension skills (Palincsar & Englert, 1988).

Second, no single reading approach is effective with all students. With many students a language experience approach is most effective, but some students require a more structured, intensive approach. An instructor needs to be flexible with methods as each reading approach has advantages and disadvantages for students with learning disabilities. D'Zamko and Hedges (1985) summarized several common reading approaches and their advantages and disadvantages for students with learning disabilities.

Finally, as students develop in reading skill, different approaches are often necessary at different times in development. Methods change as the student progresses. For example, when initially assessing Charlie, a second-grade student, the examiner recommended that the instructor begin with a language experience approach. The rationale for this recommendation was based upon Charlie's good oral language skills, his interest in drawing, and his present lack of motivation and disinterest in reading. Charlie had not learned to read with the classroom approach and was resistant to books and reading. Once interest was increased and Charlie was willing to try to learn to read again, the examiner recommended that the instructor shift to a phonics approach for a few months to help Charlie improve his word attack skill. As soon as Charlie had developed fairly accurate decoding skills, the examiner recommended that a fluency method be used to help Charlie develop his reading rate and expression. Throughout the use of all of these different reading methods, the instructor supplemented lessons with interesting books that she and Charlie read and discussed together. In this way, Charlie learned to enjoy reading and did not lose sight of the purpose of reading as his word identification skill increased.

Some controversy exists regarding whether instruction in word identification should be embedded in the context of reading or decontextualized, using word cards and lists. No approach has been identified as superior for the reason that different students learn by different methods and strategies. In one instance, a student may overrely on the use of context and picture clues. Improvement in word identification skills may be accomplished more efficiently and rapidly using word cards and lists. In another instance, a student may need assistance with integrating all types of information when reading text and supplemental instruction in word identification is provided within the classroom reading materials. The important consideration to remember is when word identification skills are taught in isolation, they must generalize to reading text; that is, a student must demonstrate improved word identification skill in context and, consequently, increased ability to obtain meaning from text.

In selecting an approach for teaching word identification, an examiner should consider a student's: (a) motivation, (b) interests, (c) strengths and weaknesses in word recognition, (d) strengths and weaknesses in cognitive areas, and (e) past instructional experiences. Other relevant environmental factors include the instructional setting and availability of materials. After analyzing test performance and considering relevant student and environmental variables, an examiner may wish to suggest a specific instructional strategy for building basic reading skill in: (a) whole-word recognition, (b) phonological word analysis, or (c) reading fluency. The intent of these strategies is to eliminate any factors that are inhibiting a student's ability to understand text.

Instructional Strategies for Whole-Word Recognition

Several different methods may be used that emphasize learning words as wholes or sight words. Sight words are words that the student recognizes instantly. During an evaluation, an examiner may observe that a student has developed a limited sight vocabulary. Consequently, the examiner may recommend a technique designed to help the student develop or expand sight word vocabulary.

Paul, a third-grade student, was referred for an evaluation based on his difficulty learning to read. In reviewing his educational history, the examiner found that Paul had been exposed to both a basal reading approach and a structured phonics method. When listening to Paul read, the examiner noted that Paul attempted to sound out words but was unable to use this strategy effectively. After pronouncing the initial consonant sound, Paul would often take a wild guess at the word. Although he correctly identified many initial and final consonant sounds, Paul did not pronounce any of the items on the Word Attack test correctly. In contrast, Paul rapidly identified several of the initial words on the Letter-Word Identification test.

The examiner recommended that Paul receive reading instruction using the Language Experience Approach. In addition to reading and writing stories, Paul would keep word cards filed alphabetically for additional practice and review. For words that were difficult to learn, the examiner recommended that Paul trace and pronounce each word and then attempt to write the word from memory. After 6 months of instruction, Paul was able to engage in independent reading in his classroom. He continued to use word cards and tracing for any words that he found difficult to master.

Sight Word List

In teaching students to master sight words, an instructor should use a comprehensive list of words to record student progress. Fry, Polk, and Fountoukidis (1984) presented a list of the most commonly used words in the English language that students should recognize instantly. The 1,000 instant words on this well-researched list, provided in Figure 3-6, are ranked in order of frequency of occurrence. These words make up about 90% of all written material. The first 100 words constitute about 50% of all written material. These words should be recognized instantaneously by students. Once appropriate words are selected, several methods may be used for instruction.

Sight Word Association Procedure

Bos and Vaughn (1988) described a sight word association procedure (SWAP) for use as a supplemental activity in teaching sight word vocabulary to the automatic level. To begin, five to ten words are written on word cards. The teacher and student discuss the meaning of the words. Each word is presented for 5 seconds, and the teacher says the word twice. The cards are shuffled and the student is asked to identify the words. Corrective feedback is provided by telling the student when a word is correct or by supplying the correct response if an error is made or if the student does not respond in 5 seconds. All words are then presented again for 5 seconds and the instructor pronounces each word twice. The student then attempts to identify each word, and the instructor provides corrective feedback. This procedure continues until the student easily identifies all of the words. A record sheet may be used to record the words, the number of exposures required to master each word, and the results of retention checks. If the student does not retain the words using this type of systematic teaching, a more intensive multisensory technique, such as the Fernald method, may be necessary.

Rebus Method

If a student is having difficulty with beginning reading, but scores above average on the WJ-R COG Visual-Auditory Learning test, the examiner may wish to consider the *Peabody Rebus Reading Program* (Woodcock, Clark, & Davies, 1968). Rebuses are pictures or symbols used to represent words, such as on the Visual-Auditory Learning test. The rebuses are presented in three forms: (a) pictorial, such as for the word "cat"; (b) relational, such as a square with a dot inside to represent "in"; and (c) abstract, such as a dash to represent the word "is". The program, which is divided into three parts, simplifies initial reading. In Part One, 35 rebuses are introduced. In Part Two, rebuses and traditional orthography are combined to form words and sentences. In Part Three, the transitional level, students are taught punctuation, traditional orthography, and some phonic skills.

In using the rebus method in a school in England, Oosterom and Devereux (1982) noted that students learned many of the subskills of reading without the added burden of decoding. The program provides: (a) reading for meaning, (b) decision making, (c) immediate knowledge of results, and (d) overlearning of material. An important facet of the program is that learning to read rebuses is much easier than learning to read traditional orthography (Woodcock, 1968). For this reason, this type of approach may be effective in initial reading instruction for students with mental retardation or students with severe learning disabilities. Additionally, some evidence suggests that

1. the	52. up	103. sound	154. does	205. food	256. car	307. fish	358. hold
2. of	53. other	104. take	155. another	206. between	257. miles	308. area	359. himself
3. and	54. about	105. only	156. well	207. own	258. night	309. mark	360. toward
4. a	55. out	106. little	157. large	208. below	259. walked	310. dog	361. five
5. to	56. many	107. work	158. must	209. country	260. white	311. horse	362. step
6. in	57. then	108. know	159. big	210. plants	261. sea	312. birds	363. morning
7. is	58. them	109. place	160. even	211. last	262. began	313. problem	364. passed
8. you	59. these	110. years	161. such	212. school	263. grow	314. complete	365. vowel
9. that	60. so	111. live	162. because	213. father	264. took	315. room	366. true
10. it	61. some	112. me	163. turned	214. keep	265. river	316. knew	367. hundred
11. he	62. her	113. back	164. here	215. trees	266. four	317. since	368. against
12. was	63. would	114. give	165. why	216. never	267. carry	318. ever	369. pattern
13. for	64. make	115. most	166. asked	217. started	268. state	319. piece	370. numeral
14. on	65. like	116. very	167. went	218. city	269. once	320. told	371. table
15. are	66. him	117. after	168. men	219. earth	270. book	321. usually	372. north
16. as	67. into	118. things	169. read	220. eyes	271. hear	322. didn't	373. slowly
17. with	68. time	119. our	170. need	221. light	272. stop	323. friends	374. money
18. his	69. has	120. just	171. land	222. thought	273. without	324. easy	375. map
19. they	70. look	121. name	172. different	223. head	274. second	325. heard	376. farm
20. I	71. two	122. good	173. home	224. under	275. later	326. order	377. pulled
21. at	72. more	123. sentence	174. us	225. story	276. miss	327. red	378. draw
22. be	73. write	124. man	175. move	226. saw	277. idea	328. door	379. voice
23. this	74. go	125. think	176. try	227. left	278. enough	329. sure	380. seen
24. have	75. see	126. say	177. kind	228. don't	279. eat	330. become	381. cold
25. from	76. number	127. great	178. hand	229. few	280. face	331. top	382. cried
26. or	77. no	128. where	179. picture	230. while	281. watch	332. ship	383. plan
27. one	78. way	129. help	180. again	231. along	282. far	333. across	384. notice
28. had	79. could	130. through	181. change	232. might	283. Indians	334. today	385. south
29. by	80. people	131. much	182. off	233. close	284. really	335. during	386. sing
30. words	81. my	132. before	183. play	234. something	285. almost	336. short	387. war
31. but	82. than	133. line	184. spell	235. seemed	286. let	337. better	388. ground
32. not	83. first	134. right	185. air	236. next	287. above	338. best	389. fall
33. what	84. water	135. too	186. away	237. hard	288. girl	339. however	390. kind
34. all	85. been	136. means	187. animals	238. open	289. sometimes	340. low	391. town
35. were	86. called	137. old	188. house	239. example	290. mountains	341. hours	392. I'll
36. we	87. who	138. any	189. point	240. beginning	291. cut	342. black	393. unit
37. when	88. oil	139. same	190. page	241. life	292. young	343. products	394. figure
38. your	89. its	140. tell	191. letters	242. always	293. talk	344. happened	395. certain
39. can	90. now	141. boy	192. mother	243. those	294. soon	345. whole	396. field
40. said	91. find	142. following	193. answer	244. both	295. list	346. measure	397. travel
41. there	92. long	143. came	194. found	245. paper	296. song	347. remember	398. wood
42. use	93. down	144. want	195. study	246. together	297. being	348. early	399. fire
43. an	94. day	145. show	196. still	247. got	298. leave	349. waves	400. upon
44. each	95. did	146. also	197. learn	248. group	299. family	350. reached	401. done
45. which	96. get	147. around	198. should	249. often	300. it's	351. listen	402. English
46. she	97. come	148. form	199. American	250. run	301. body	352. wind	403. road
47. do	98. made	149. three	200. world	251. important	302. music	353. rock	404. half
48. how	99. may	150. small	201. high	252. until	303. color	354. space	405. ten
49. their	100. part	151. set	202. every	253. children	304. stand	355. covered	406. fly
50. if	101. over	152. put	203. near	254. side	305. sun	356. fast	407. gave
51. will	102. new	153. end	204. add	255. feet	306. questions	357. several	408. box

Figure 3–6. 1,000 Instant Words. *Note* From *The Reading Teacher's Book of Lists* (pp. 22-28) by E. Fry, J. Polk, and D. Fountoukidis, 1984, Englewood Cliffs, NJ: Prentice-Hall. Copyright 1984 by Edward Fry. Reprinted by permission.

Figure 3–6 (*continued*).

409. finally	462. common	515. divided	568. edge	621. buy	674. someone	727. brown
410. wait	463. bring	516. general	569. past	622. century	675. sail	728. trouble
411. correct	464. explain	517. energy	570. sign	623. outside	676. rolled	729. cool
412. oh	465. dry	518. subject	571. record	624. everything	677. bear	730. cloud
413. quickly	466. though	519. Europe	572. finished	625. tall	678. wonder	731. lost
414. person	467. language	520. moon	573. discovered	626. already	679. smiled	732. sent
415. became	468. shape	521. region	574. wild	627. instead	680. angle	733. symbols
416. shown	469. deep	522. return	575. happy	628. phrase	681. fraction	734. wear
417. minutes	470. thousands	523. believe	576. beside	629. soil	682. Africa	735. bad
418. strong	471. yes	524. dance	577. gone	630. bed	683. killed	736. save
419. verb	472. clear	525. members	578. sky	631. copy	684. melody	737. experiment
420. stars	473. equation	526. picked	579. glass	632. free	685. bottom	738. engine
421. front	474. yet	527. simple	580. million	633. hope	686. trip	739. alone
422. feel	475. government	528. cells	581. west	634. spring	687. hole	740. drawing
423. fact	476. filled	529. paint	582. lay	635. case	688. poor	741. east
424. inches	477. heat	530. mind	583. weather	636. laughed	689. let's	742. pay
425. street	478. full	531. love	584. root	637. nation	690. fight	743. single
426. decided	479. hot	532. cause	585. instruments	638. quite	691. surprise	744. touch
427. contain	480. check	533. rain	586. meet	639. type	692. French	745. information
428. course	481. object	534. exercise	587. third	640. themselves	693. died	746. express
429. surface	482. am	535. eggs	588. months	641. temperature	694. beat	747. mouth
430. produce	483. rule	536. train	589. paragraph	642. bright	695. exactly	748. yard
431. building	484. among	537. blue	590. raise	643. lead	696. remain	749. equal
432. ocean	485. noun	538. wish	591. represent	644. everyone	697. dress	750. decimal
433. class	486. power	539. drop	592. soft	645. method	698. iron	751. yourself
434. note	487. cannot	540. developed	593. whether	646. section	699. couldn't	752. control
435. nothing	488. able	541. window	594. clothes	647. lake	700. fingers	753. practice
436. rest	489. six	542. difference	595. flowers	648. consonant	701. row	754. report
437. carefully	490. size	543. distance	596. shall	649. within	702. least	755. straight
438. scientists	491. dark	544. heart	597. teacher	650. dictionary	703. catch	756. rise
439. inside	492. ball	545. sit	598. held	651. hair	704. climbed	757. statement
440. wheels	493. material	546. sum	599. describe	652. age	705. wrote	758. stick
441. stay	494. special	547. summer	600. drive	653. amount	706. shouted	759. party
442. green	495. heavy	548. wall	601. cross	654. scale	707. continued	760. seeds
443. known	496. fine	549. forest	602. speak	655. pounds	708. itself	761. suppose
444. island	497. pair	550. probably	603. solve	656. although	709. else	762. woman
445. week	498. circle	551. legs	604. appear	657. per	710. plains	763. coast
446. less	499. include	552. sat	605. metal	658. broken	711. gas	764. bank
447. machine	500. built	553. main	606. son	659. moment	712. England	765. period
448. base	501. can't	554. winter	607. either	660. tiny	713. burning	766. wire
449. ago	502. matter	555. wide	608. ice	661. possible	714. design	767. choose
450. stood	503. square	556. written	609. sleep	662. gold	715. joined	768. clean
451. plane	504. syllables	557. length	610. village	663. mild	716. foot	769. visit
452. system	505. perhaps	558. reason	611. factors	664. quiet	717. law	770. bit
453. behind	506. bill	559. kept	612. result	665. natural	718. ears	771. whose
454. ran	507. felt	560. interest	613. jumped	666. lot	719. grass	772. received
455. round	508. suddenly	561. arms	614. snow	667. stone	720. you're	773. garden
456. boat	509. test	562. brother	615. ride	668. act	721. grew	774. please
457. game	510. direction	563. race	616. care	669. build	722. skin	775. strange
458. force	511. center	564. present	617. floor	670. middle	723. valley	776. caught
459. brought	512. farmers	565. beautiful	618. hill	671. speed	724. cents	777. fell
460. understand	513. ready	566. store	619. pushed	672. count	725. key	778. team
461. warm	514. anything	567. job	620. baby	673. cat	726. president	779. God

Figure 3–6 (*continued*).

780. captain	833. enjoy	886. property	938. shop	990. conditions
781. direct	834. elements	887. particular	939. suffix	991. cows
782. ring	835. indicate	888. swim	940. especially	992. track
783. serve	836. except	889. terms	941. shoes	993. arrived
784. child	837. expect	890. current	942. actually	994. located
785. desert	838. flat	891. park	943. nose	995. sir
786. increase	839. seven	892. sell	944. afraid	996. seat
787. history	840. interesting	893. shoulder	945. dead	997. division
788. cost	841. sense	894. industry	946. sugar	998. effect
789. maybe	842. string	895. wash	947. adjective	999. underline
790. business	843. blow	896. block	948. fig	1000. view
791. separate	844. famous	897. spread	949. office	
792. break	845. value	898. cattle	950. huge	
793. uncle	846. wings	899. wife	951. gun	
794. hunting	847. movement	900. sharp	952. similar	
795. flow	848. pole	901. company	953. death	
796. lady	849. exciting	902. radio	954. score	
797. students	850. branches	903. we'll	955. forward	
798. human	851. thick	904. action	956. stretched	
799. art	852. blood	905. capital	957. experience	
800. feeling	853. lie	906. factories	958. rose	
801. supply	854. spot	907. settled	959. allow	
802. corner	855. bell	908. yellow	960. fear	
803. electric	856. fun	909. isn't	961. workers	
804. insects	857. loud	910. southern	962. Washington	
805. crops	858. consider	911. truck	963. Greek	
806. tone	859. suggested	912. fair	964. women	
807. hit	860. thin	913. printed	965. bought	
808. sand	861. position	914. wouldn't	966. led	
809. doctor	862. entered	915. ahead	967. march	
810. provide	863. fruit	916. chance	968. northern	
811. thus	864. tied	917. born	969. create	
812. won't	865. rich	918. level	970. British	
813. cook	866. dollars	919. triangle	971. difficult	
814. bones	867. send	920. molecules	972. match	
815. tail	868. sight	921. France	973. win	
816. board	869. chief	922. repeated	974. doesn't	
817. modern	870. Japanese	923. column	975. steel	
818. compound	871. stream	924. western	976. total	
819. mine	872. planets	925. church	977. deal	
820. wasn't	873. rhythm	926. sister	978. determine	
821. fit	874. eight	927. oxygen	979. evening	
822. addition	875. science	928. plural	980. nor	
823. belong	876. major	929. various	981. rope	
824. safe	877. observe	930. agreed	982. cotton	
825. soldiers	878. tube	931. opposite	983. apple	
826. guess	879. necessary	932. wrong	984. details	
827. silent	880. weight	933. chart	985. entire	
828. trade	881. meat	934. prepared	986. corn	
829. rather	882. lifted	935. pretty	987. substances	
830. compare	883. process	936. solution	988. smell	
831. crowd	884. army	937. fresh	989. tools	
832. poem	885. hat			

kindergarten students who participate in a rebus reading readiness program are more capable of segmenting oral language or identifying the number of words in orally presented sentences (Begy & Cahill, 1978).

Language Experience Approach

Another meaning-centered approach is the language experience approach (LEA). This method of reading and writing instruction capitalizes upon a student's oral language and background knowledge. The LEA is adaptable to individual, group, and class instruction and may be used with young children as well as adolescents and adults. The approach involves writing down a story that is dictated by a student. The student retells an experience in his or her own words and the teacher (or student) records the experience. The following steps may be used:

1. Discuss an experience shared by the group.
2. Have students summarize the main ideas from the discussion.
3. Write down the story as the class or student dictates it.
4. Reread the story together. Edit and revise, if desired.
5. Type the story and have the class or student reread the story the next day.
6. Place all stories in a book for frequent rereadings on subsequent days.

For increased skill learning, this method may be adapted to provide more review and repetition of words. A student may make word cards for any vocabulary or sight words that he or she is having trouble retaining. These words are then filed alphabetically in a box. When sight words are recognized immediately, these words may be used as a word bank. To increase the number of known words, the instructor may introduce similar words with common linguistic patterns. Words are practiced and reviewed as needed. The goal of this type of strategy is to promote generalization to new words.

The LEA integrates listening, reading, and writing skills and is most suitable for students who learn easily with a visually oriented whole-word approach to reading. Students may also illustrate their stories. Additionally, the approach helps an instructor accommodate students from divergent experiential and language backgrounds (Van Allen, 1976). The type of students who may benefit from the method include: (a) a student who learns to read easily, (b) an unmotivated student who has failed in reading, (c) a student who acquires and retains sight vocabulary easily, (d) a student who is learning English as a second language, and (e) a student with good artistic skills. Students who enjoy drawing are often highly motivated by the opportunity to illustrate their stories.

Although instruction in specific skills may be integrated into an LEA approach, some students need a more sequential, systematic approach to word identification than that provided by the LEA. For these students, the method does not provide enough overlearning, repetition, and review or enough instruction in phonological analysis. Additionally, the method may not provide enough language and vocabulary enrichment for students with low language skills or enough stimulation for students who are accelerated in reading and writing skill.

Fernald Method

Throughout history, multisensory methods for teaching word recognition have been recommended for instructing students with learning difficulty. Early Greek and Roman educators noted that tracing words on wax or ivory tablets improved retention. The most well-known and researched method for instructing students with learning disabilities is the Fernald method (Fernald, 1943). This approach provides instruction in a systematic, multisensory way, in which visual, auditory, kinesthetic, and tactile channels are used simultaneously by the learner.

Steps. To begin, the instructor informs the student that they will use a new way of learning words. The student selects the words and the words are taught. After several words are mastered, story writing begins. When the student does not know how to write a word, the word is written and learned before it is included in the story. The following description provides a summary of Fernald's four stages of teaching students with extreme reading disability.

Stage 1: Child learns by tracing the word: To begin, the student selects a word that is then written by the teacher with crayon, in manuscript or cursive, on an index card. The student then traces the word, saying the word while moving a finger over the written copy, matching sound with letter. This process is repeated as many times as needed until the word can be written from memory without looking at the copy. Initially, some students with severe reading disabilities may require more than 50 tracings to master a word. Once the word has been written correctly from memory, it is written in the story. After the story has been completed, typed, and read, the new words are filed alphabetically by the student in a word box.

The following points are noted regarding the first stage: (a) finger contact is important; (b) a word should always be written without looking at the copy as looking back and forth breaks up the word into small, meaningless units; (c) words are crossed out or covered up if an error occurs; and (d) words should always be meaningful and used in context.

Although the length of the tracing period varies with individuals, the majority of students discontinue tracing after several months. Before long the individual begins to acquire new words without needing to trace.

Stage 2: Tracing is no longer needed: In the second stage, the student is able to learn words directly from the word cards. The student looks at the word, says the word, and then writes the word from memory while pronouncing the word. This vocalization should be exactly as the word sounds; that is, the word should be pronounced as a whole, not in separate units.

The following important points are noted regarding the second stage: (a) a word must be pronounced either silently or aloud as it is traced and written; (b) a story must be typed and read within a 24-hour period; and (c) the content of what is written should not be simplified. Material should be at the level of listening comprehension. Longer, more difficult words are often easier for a student to remember than easier, shorter ones.

Stage 3: Student learns directly from printed word: In the third stage, the student does not need to have words written on cards. The student is able to glance over a word of four to five syllables, say the word once or twice, and write it from memory. Book reading also begins at this stage, and the student is told words that are not immediately recognized. These words may be written on word cards for later reinforcement. In this stage, small words may still cause some confusion.

A teacher can verify that a student is able to learn words without writing them by giving a student two lists of words. For the first list, the student looks at and pronounces the words. For the second list, the student writes and pronounces the words. The following day, retention is checked by asking the student to read the two word lists. Performance should be equal if writing is no longer necessary for word learning.

Stage 4: Ability to generalize to new words: In the fourth stage, the student begins to notice resemblances between words and is able to recognize new words from their similarity to already learned words. Word meanings are provided by the teacher. In this stage, retention of words the student pronounces and writes one time is between 88% to 95%. Remedial work is continued until a student is able to return to classroom reading instruction.

The following important points are noted regarding the third and fourth stages: (a) Students must do all of their own reading and not rely on others for obtaining information and (b) words are not sounded out by the student or teacher.

Research. Mather (1985) conducted a thorough literature review on the Fernald method to answer three questions: (a) Why does the method work? (b) With what type of student does it work? and (c) What modifications have been successful?

Why the method works: Many experimenters have attempted to determine why the Fernald method is successful with disabled readers. Research and clinical observations suggest that tracing words: (a) provides a kinesthetic memory trace that improves the retention of letters and words, (b) improves visual discrimination and visual recognition skills, (c) directs a student's attention to word learning, (d) increases visual memory capacity for words, (e) assists in developing an association between the spoken and written word, and (f) improves visual-auditory matching of letters (graphemes) or word parts and sounds (phonemes).

Type of student: The Fernald method has been used effectively with students of all ages across intelligence ranges. Additionally, the method is useful as an adjunct procedure in first-grade classrooms to reduce reading failure. Results from research investigating student characteristics suggest that students who seem to benefit most from the method are those with severe deficits in visual perception, attention, and/or visual-verbal memory. The method is also effective for the student with a language impairment whose memory is enhanced by the tactile/kinesthetic component.

Successful modifications: Several modifications of the Fernald method have been successful with disabled readers. These modifications include: (a) the AKT (auditory, kinesthetic, tactile) or blind writing method, (b) use of the non-dominant hand for tracing, (c) group applications, (d) combination of Fernald and the language experience approach, and (e) use with high-utility sight words. Different types of media may be used for tracing activities, such as the chalkboard, wet sand, or screen writing. Additionally, tracing procedures may be used to assist in eliminating inversions or reversals. The student traces repeatedly over the letter or word form, while pronouncing the letter name or word.

Although the majority of students do not need an approach as intensive as the Fernald method, the method is appropriate for students with severe reading disabilities who have not responded to other methods of reading instruction. Before recommending this procedure, an examiner should consider the severity of the student's reading problem and past history of reading instruction. This approach may be easily combined with the language experience approach for use in a regular classroom setting.

Computers

Some evidence suggests that microcomputers may be used effectively to improve the word recognition skills of students with learning disabilities (Torgesen, 1986). Torgesen described several software programs that were effective in increasing sight word acquisition and decoding fluency. Jones, Torgesen, and Sexton (1987) found that the decoding skills of reading disabled children improved when they were provided with mastery-oriented practice on the microcomputer. These initial results suggest that the use of computers may enhance the decoding skills of students with learning and reading disabilities.

Instructional Strategies for Phonological Word Analysis

When an examiner notices that a student has extreme difficulty pronouncing unknown words or phonically regular nonsense words such as on the Word Attack test, a phonics method may be appropriate. Most students do not need phonics instruction as they intuitively learn these skills through reading; the rules of written language are discovered without formal instruction. Essentially, three types of students exist: students who need phonics to become good readers, students who can learn phonics but do not need phonics, and students who are unable to master phonics (Carbo, 1987). Intensive phonics instruction is only recommended for students who need a more structured approach for learning to decode and do not learn to read naturally.

Beth, a third-grade student, had not learned to read using the whole-language approach taught in her classroom. Although she enjoyed looking at books and had maintained a positive attitude toward reading, her limited word identification skills prevented her from reading even primer-level texts with fluency. Beth seemed unable to learn sight words. In fact, her mother reported that Beth had ripped up all of her sight word cards one evening in frustration. Based on knowledge of her above-average auditory processing skills (WJ-R COG) and her average oral language abilities, the examiner recommended direct instruction in phonics to teach Beth how to identify words. After 4 months of instruction, Beth had developed adequate word identification skills and she was able to comprehend and enjoy the books used in her classroom. Additionally, she started reading books independently.

The goal of phonological word analysis methods is to teach the student a strategy for identifying and pronouncing unknown words by increasing knowledge of sound-symbol correspondence. Ability to apply phonic generalizations lessens the demands on memory. Consequently, students who have difficulty memorizing sight words often benefit from a systematic phonics approach. Even students who memorize words easily need some knowledge of sound-symbol correspondence to identify and pronounce unfamiliar words. In most instances, students gain this knowledge through reading.

Many different methods exist for teaching phonics or structural analysis. The three basic approaches that are used for phonics instruction include: (a) analytic, which begins with the whole word and has the student learn to determine the parts, either letter sounds or letter names; (b) synthetic, which begins with attention to individual letter names or sounds, and has the student learn to blend the sounds to form a word; and (c) linguistic, which begins with word families and phonograms, and encourages the student to make generalizations regarding new words. For each of these three approaches, sound blending skill is a prerequisite.

Sound Blending

Decoding phonically regular nonsense words, as presented on the WJ-R ACH Word Attack test, requires ability in sound blending. Before instruction in a program for phonological word analysis is recommended, an examiner should determine the student's level of skill in this area. In some cases, a student's low performance on the Word Attack test is the result of low sound blending skill. This may be substantiated by administering the Incomplete Words and Sound Blending tests from the WJ-R COG. If difficulty is noted, blending skill should be developed prior to addressing the word recognition problem. In other cases, the student has developed adequate skill in sound blending but does not know how to apply the skill to decode words.

The two tasks that are most highly related to the early stages of reading development are sound blending and oral segmentation (Lewkowicz, 1980). Sound blending requires the ability to synthesize a sequence of sounds into the word that they represent. Oral segmentation requires the ability to analyze and separate all of the sounds in a word in correct order. When blending skill is low, direct instruction in phonological awareness improves reading skill (Bradley & Bryant, 1985). Various methods may be used to increase phonemic awareness.

Selecting a phonemic training method depends upon the characteristics of the student (Williams, 1984). Some students perform better when visual representations of phonemes, either letters, tokens, or tiles, are associated with the sounds. Initially, objects such as poker chips may be used to represent the sounds and then, as skill develops, the chips are replaced with letters. Other students respond better to a purely auditory approach of just listening to and counting the number of syllables, then phonemes or sounds, in words. Several approaches are described below.

ABDs of Reading. Williams (1980) described a program for improving decoding, called The ABDs of Reading, that provides explicit training in phoneme analysis and sound blending. The program was highly successful for teaching general decoding strategies to children with learning disabilities. To begin, the child was taught to identify the first, middle, and final syllables in a three-syllable word. The syllables were represented with wooden squares. Next, the squares were used to represent phonemes, progressing from combinations of two to three phonemes. Seven consonants and two vowels were used. Students then learned to blend consonant-vowel-consonant (CVC) units and learned the letter names for the nine phonemes. Letters were written on the wooden blocks and students practiced constructing all the possible CVC patterns. In the next section, additional phonemes were introduced and practiced. In the final section more complex patterns were practiced: CCVC, followed by CVCC, then CCVCC, and then two-syllable words. Students who participated in this instructional program performed significantly better than first- and second-grade controls and developed general decoding strategies. Williams indicated that the use of this type of program shows promise for teaching decoding to students with severe learning disabilities.

Phonic Remedial Reading Lessons. In the introduction to the *Phonic Remedial Reading Lessons*, Kirk, Kirk, and Minskoff (1985) advised that if a student is deficient in sound blending and has difficulty or is unable to synthesize words with three or four sounds, auditory sound blending training is needed prior to phonics instruction. In conducting this training, the teacher should attend to two factors: (a) the duration of time between the sounds and (b) the number of sounds in the sequence. The longer the interval between the sounds, the more difficult it is to blend the sounds. Consequently, in the early stages of training, the instructor begins with short intervals between sounds and gradually progresses until 1-second intervals are reached. Similarly, the greater the number of sounds that are presented, the more difficult it is to remember and synthesize the sounds. Kirk et al. recommended that the instructor begin sound blending training with words with two sounds, then three sounds, and finally progress to words with four sounds. The following steps are used to train sound blending:

1. The teacher has the student say the word.
2. The teacher then presents the word with prolonged sounds, but no break between the sounds, and asks the student to say the word.
3. The teacher presents the sounds with a short break. The student says the word.

4. The teacher presents the word with a quarter-second, then a half-second, and finally a 1-second break between the sounds. The student says the word after each presentation.

Low-functioning students. Hoogeveen and Smeets (1988) evaluated a program for teaching sound blending and word skills to trainable mentally retarded students. The procedure was effective for all steps, and the training resulted in significant increases in blending and word attack skills. The program consisted of the following eight steps.

Step 1: Blending words: The students were taught to produce compound words by blending sets of two meaningful words into compound words, such as "rain" and "drop" into "raindrop." Four pictures were presented, one of a raindrop, and the students were asked to imitate the response and then point to the corresponding picture. Practice trials continued with the experimenter eliminating the pictures, gradually extending the pause between the two words, and then asking the subject to say the word. The pause increased from 0 seconds, to 0.8 seconds, to 1.1 seconds, to 1.5 seconds.

Step 2: Blending syllables of meaningful words: The same procedures were followed using two-syllable meaningful words, such as "ti . . . ger" and "mo . . . vie," with pictures.

Step 3: Blending syllables and phonemes of meaningful words: Training proceeded with pictures and phonemes and syllables of meaningful words.

Step 4: Blending syllables and phonemes of meaningless words: Training proceeded with phonemes and syllables of meaningless words with no pictures.

Step 5: Blending phonemes of meaningful consonant-vowel (CV) and vowel-consonant (VC) words: Words like "toe" and "ear" were used for training.

Step 6: Blending phonemes of meaningless CV and VC words: Students were presented with phonemes that they could match with the corresponding graphemes.

Step 7: Reading CV and VC words: Both meaningful and meaningless words were used. Students were asked to read each word on a card.

Step 8: Reading CVC words: Students were asked to read meaningful words presented on cards.

This program, that uses picture prompts to introduce blending skills, was effective for improving the blending skill and decoding of mentally retarded students. Hoogeveen and Smeets suggested that a shortened version may be effective with higher functioning students who need sound blending training. Conceivably, for some students with learning disabilities, several steps may be eliminated, such as the use of pictures and/or the meaningless words.

Phonemic Segmentation

Segmentation involves the ability to perceive the separate sounds in words. Two separate conclusions have emerged regarding teaching segmentation: (a) Word pronunciation should be slowed and the sounds elongated so that a student may perceive the separate sounds, and (b) the student must perform the slow pronouncing because articulatory clues are important (Lewkowicz, 1980). Additionally, students should be familiar with the speech sounds in isolation before they attempt to detect them in words and should be told the number of sound elements that exist in the word.

Lewkowicz identified several stages in teaching segmentation. To begin, the student is taught to isolate the initial phoneme. This may be accomplished by prolonging the initial sound when pronouncing the word or by using the more effective technique of repeating the initial sound several times before pronouncing the word. Next, the student is taught two-chunk segmentation, consonant/vowel-consonant (C/VC) and consonant-vowel/consonant (CV/C), before learning to identify the three sounds in CVC words. In training, the instructor provides pauses between the sounds. Gradually, more complex patterns are introduced.

Once a student has developed phonemic analysis skill, a phonics approach, if deemed appropriate, may be used to build word recognition skill. Direct instruction in phonics should also contribute to improvement in sound blending skill. Many different methods exist for teaching phonics. Several widely used programs are presented.

Orton-Gillingham Approach

The Orton-Gillingham or Gillingham-Stillman approach (Gillingham & Stillman, 1973) uses a multisensory teaching approach that emphasizes tactile and kinesthetic input coupled with the visual and auditory modalities. This synthetic approach teaches the 48 English phonemes and presents rules governing their use in a systematic, structured way. Initial instruction begins with single letters of the alphabet and progresses to one syllable, short vowel words.

The procedures are principally designed to: (a) reduce the tendency to reverse letters and transpose letters within syllables and words; (b) strengthen visual and auditory associations through a kinesthetic linkage; (c) establish the left-right sequential process for reading, spelling, and writing; (d) strengthen mnemonic processes; and (e) provide a phonetic and syllabic basis for building an extensive reading vocabulary (Ansara, 1982). Through repetitious practice and usage, students learn to decode automatically. Results of research conducted to evaluate program effectiveness over a 3-year period indicated that students in the lower quartile of reading performance in the elementary grades made significant academic gains when the Orton-Gillingham approach was used (Enfield & Greene, 1981). Additionally, many students with mild to moderate learning disabilities did not require special services when this structured approach was used.

Thorpe, Nash, and Chiang (1981) found that secondary students with learning disabilities improved their ability to read words and retain words using a simultaneous multisensory approach that was similar to Orton-Gillingham. The following instructional procedure was used:

1. Mark and pronounce the vowel or vowel combinations.
2. Underline and pronounce the phonemes from left to right.
3. Look at and pronounce the phonemes.
4. Underline and say the word fast.
5. Trace the word on the desk five times using the index finger and saying the letter sounds simultaneously.
6. Underline and say the word fast.

This study offers support for using a procedure like this to improve the word recognition skill of secondary students with learning disabilities. This procedure may also be effective for enhancing sight vocabulary.

Guyer and Sabatino (1989) found that college students who had been diagnosed as learning disabled made significant reading improvement in a summer program when taught by an adaptation of the Orton-Gillingham approach. The Orton-Gillingham group made greater gains in decoding skill than did two other groups of students: one using a nonphonetic approach and the other receiving no educational activity.

The main advantages of the Orton-Gillingham approach are that: (a) it may be used with groups of students; (b) it provides a comprehensive, organized, carefully sequenced approach; and (c) it promotes proficiency in sound blending. The major disadvantages are that: (a) it is time-consuming and (b) it requires intensive teacher training to implement.

One adaptation of the Orton-Gillingham approach is the Slingerland method (Slingerland, 1971). This multisensory approach may be used with groups of children but requires specific teacher training to implement. After comparing the Slingerland approach to a linguistic reading program, Lovitt and DeMier (1984) reported that although effective with students with learning disabilities, other structured, remedial reading programs were equally as effective.

Spalding Method

The Spalding method is a language arts program that integrates handwriting, spelling, reading, speaking, and writing (Spalding & Spalding, 1986). Students are taught to recognize and write 70 common phonograms, which include single letters or two, three, or four letters that make one sound. The text includes a complete list of the rules to be taught and the individual phonograms. Phonogram cards are used to present the sounds.

Although research supporting the effectiveness of this approach is limited, positive testimonials from principals and elementary teachers are reported throughout the book. Additionally, the method has been used with students from age 6 through college to promote automatic decoding skills. Advantages of this approach are that it is easy to use, systematic, and inexpensive. Some students, however, may be confused by the presented rules or may benefit more from an approach that does not directly teach rules.

Phonic Remedial Reading Lessons

The Phonic Remedial Reading Lessons (Kirk, Kirk, & Minskoff, 1985) are based on the Remedial Reading Drills, originally published in 1936. This systematic, programmed method provides a step-by-step procedure for teaching phonics and is based upon principles of successful learning. No phonics rules are taught. Instead, sounds are introduced one at a time in a variety of words so that the student develops an automatic response to each symbol. As a supplement to the program, the student is asked to write words, while carefully pronouncing each sound.

Type of student. These drills have been used successfully with students of low, average, and superior intelligence. Kirk et al. described the type of student for whom these lessons are most appropriate. The following characteristics are included: (a) The student is 7 1/2 or more years of age and has been in school for at least 1 year, (b) has adequate mental ability to learn to read, (c) understands at least second- or third-grade material when it is read to him or her, (d) has an educationally significant reading problem, (e) has no efficient method of decoding new words, and (f) is motivated for learning to read. Additionally, the procedure is particularly useful for students who show marked reversal tendencies in reading and writing.

Advantages of this program are that students learn to apply phonic skills, not to memorize phonic rules, and

teacher training and expense are minimal. Although stories are included, the reading material is minimal and the instructor may wish to supplement the program with a linguistic reading series.

Linguistic Approach

Many different linguistic reading series exist. For some students, this type of approach is more effective than a basal reading approach. In a linguistic approach, the student learns various word families, such as *cat, fat, rat,* and *mat* or *ran, fan,* and *man*. Word families are word elements that contain both vowels and consonants to which an initial consonant may be synthetically blended (Aukerman, 1984). Sight words are introduced gradually.

Cunningham, Moore, Cunningham, and Moore (1983) described a four-step exercise to promote independence in the use of word families in beginning reading instruction. Five cards are created for each student using words known to the students. For example, the word cards may include: *tell, hop, ran, car,* and *cow*. The teacher writes a word such as *star* on the board, and the students are asked to locate the card that most closely resembles the word. The teacher then demonstrates the similarities and differences between the words. Word cards are added until the student has mastered 15 cards and their matches. In the next steps, students are asked to provide matches with words written on the board without looking at their word cards. Then, the words from the word cards are written on the board and the students are asked to produce new words. Students then attempt to apply word families in their reading. If they encounter an unknown word, they are asked to think of a similar word family. Conceivably, this type of procedure may be used with older students using prefixes, root words, and suffixes.

Glass-Analysis for Decoding Only

The Glass-Analysis method is a supplemental reading approach developed out of a stimulus-response reinforcement model (Glass, 1973). The method is based on a perceptual conditioning process. This process requires the reader to examine words and identify the visual and auditory clusters or the word parts and their associated sounds. The goal of the approach is to help the student develop the habits of successful readers at all developmental levels. Fluent readers recognize clusters automatically, whereas poor readers must devote considerable attention to these letter combinations (Samuels, 1987).

Glass differentiated between reading and decoding. Decoding is a simplistic, prerequisite skill to the act of reading. In reading, students derive meaning from the printed word and then use the meaning for academic and personal growth. The method does not teach students how to identify specific words, but instead develops ability to identify, generalize, and produce an automatic response to common letter clusters and sounds. Letter clusters are a combination of letters that frequently occur in the English spelling system. When used judiciously, students with reading disabilities may be taught to perceive specific letter cluster patterns and distinctive features in words (Miccinati, 1981).

Steps. To begin, a word is written on an index card and shown to the student. Five general steps are followed:

1. Identify the whole word and ask the student to repeat the word. For example, while showing the word, say: "This is the word 'carpenter.' What is the word?"
2. Give the sound(s) and ask for the letter or letters. For example, say: "What letters make the 'car' sound?" "What letters make the 'pen' sound?" etc.
3. Give the letter or letter names and ask for the sound(s). For example, say: "What sound does 'ar' make?" "What sound does 'ter' make?"
4. Take away the letters auditorially, not visually, and ask for the remaining sound. For example, say: "If I took off the 'car' sound, what would be left?" "If I took off the 'ter' sound, what would be left?" etc.
5. Finish by asking: "What is the whole word?"

Figure 3-7 illustrates several sample dialogues from the Teacher Guide.

Glass recommended two 15-minute sessions daily for initial decoding practice. In practicing word analysis, parts of the word are never covered up, nor are the structural units displayed separately. The correct letter clusters are always presented in the context of a whole word. For instructional purposes, Glass devised the list shown in Figure 3-8 of the most common letter clusters in whole words. These clusters are presented in the four program kits.

Materials. Although special program materials are available, this method may be adapted to teacher-selected words. A teacher may carefully select words containing common visual and auditory letter clusters and print them on flash cards. An instructor may also select words and letter clusters from a linguistic basal reading series, as an alternative to the Glass-Analysis program (Miccinati, 1981). The order of presentation of clusters does not seem to make a difference as long as transfer is made to new words in context. Transfer is accomplished by providing practice with this method during oral reading. When a student has difficulty with a word, he or she is encouraged to look for the common clusters and then attempt to pronounce the word.

Type of student. The Glass-Analysis method is designed for students with low decoding skill. If a student scores poorly on Letter-Word Identification and Word Attack, this type of technique may help the student increase decoding skills. Glass also indicated that the method is particularly effective for teaching decoding to non-English speaking children. Conceivably, this type of approach provides students with considerable practice in English sound/symbol correspondence and may reduce the frustration inherent in the mastery of the sounds of a new language. Improved decoding ability may then assist students with language acquisition, English phonological awareness, and, subsequently, reading comprehension.

Word Identification Strategy

Secondary students may also benefit from specific strategies to improve word recognition skill. One word identification strategy, DISSECT, has been used effectively by students in middle and secondary school (Lenz & Hughes, 1990; Lenz, Schumaker, Deshler, & Beals, 1984). Research has indicated that nearly all low-achieving students and students with learning disabilities are able to master the learning strategy and improve their ability to decode words if the eight-step instructional procedure, summarized in the manual, is carefully followed.

The DISSECT strategy is used to help students identify unfamiliar, multisyllabic words in text. Students are advised to apply the strategy whenever they come to a word that they do not know how to pronounce. The steps of this strategy, presented on a cue card, are as follows:

Step 1: *D*iscover the context. The student skips over the word and reads the rest of the sentence to see if the word can be determined from the meaning of the surrounding words. If not, the student progresses to Step 2.

Step 2: *I*solate the prefix. First the student is taught common prefixes. When analyzing a word, the student is instructed to examine the initial letters and, if there is a prefix, to place a mark, like this: dis cover.

Step 3: *S*eparate the suffix. The student is taught common suffixes. When analyzing a word, the student is instructed to look at the last letters and match them to any known suffixes. If the word contains a suffix, a mark is added like this: dis cov er.

Step 4: *S*ay the stem. Once the prefix and/or suffix have been isolated, the student attempts to pronounce the stem. If the student cannot pronounce the stem, he or she moves to the next step.

Step 5: *E*xamine the stem. Examining the stem involves dissecting it into easy-to-pronounce parts. Several rules are applied. The first is the Rule of Twos and Threes: If a stem begins with a vowel, separate and pronounce the first two letters. If the stem begins with a consonant,

STEP-BY-STEP

Expose one word page from the Cluster Word Booklet to the individual or group. Keep decoders as close to you as practical. Make sure all can see the word and are always looking toward the booklet. If you keep the booklet away from your own line of vision, it will be easier to maintain the attentiveness of the individual or group.

Always begin a target cluster by reading aloud from the first page of the Cluster Word Booklet. This will orient the learner(s) to the sound of and the letters in the up-coming target cluster. The giving of examples of the cluster in whole words will aid in gaining a correct perspective as to clusters and whole words.

Remember, never separate, either auditorily or visually, letters that form a blend (bl, st, pr), a consonant digraph (wh, th, sh), or a vowel cluster (ate, ing, ea). Don't be a Cluster-Buster! Always show the whole word; do not cover up any part of the word. In GLASS-ANALYSIS the training for decoding is only with whole words, as is decoding in all independent word attack.

The following script demonstrates how cluster words are to be utilized to form audile/visile perceptual conditioning to the "ong", "et", and "ire" clusters. (The questions asked are summarized on the inside back cover of the Cluster Word Booklet.)

"ong" cluster

song

[From sound to letters]

This word is "song". What is the word?
- In the word, "song", what letter make the "sss" sound?
What letters make the "ong" sound?

[From letters to sound]

- In the word, "song, what sound does the "ong" sound?
- In the word, "song, what sound does the letter /s/ make? What sound does o/n/g make?
- If I took off the /s/ what sound would be left?
- What is the whole word?

longest

[For each word, say the whole word and ask that the word be repeated.]
- In the word, "longest", what letter makes the "lll" sound? What letters make the "ong" sound? What letters make the "long" sound? What letters make the "est" sound? What letters make the "ongest" sound?

[From sound to letters]

- In the word, "longest", what sound does the /l/ make?
What sound does the o/n/g make?
What sound does the l/o/n/g make?
- In the word "longest", what sound does e/s/t make?

[From letters to sound]

What sound does o/n/g/e/s/t make?
- If I took off the l/o/n/g, what sound would I have left?
If I took off the "est" sound, what sound would be left?

[Take off letters or sound]

- What is the whole word?

stronger

[Remember, always tell the word and ask for its repetition]
- In the word, "stronger", what letters make the "st" sound?

[Ask for letters first]

What letters make the "ong" sound?
What letters make the "rong" sound?
What letters make the "strong" sound?
What letters make the "er" sound?
- In the word, "stronger", what sound does s/t make?

[Then ask for sounds]

What sound does the o/n/g make?
What sound does the r/o/n/g make?
What sound does the s/t/r/o/n/g make?
- In the word, "stronger", what sound does the e/r make?
The o/n/g/e/r?
- If I took off the s/t, what sound would be left?
If I took off the e/r what sound would be left?
- What is the whole word?

Figure 3–7. Sample Dialogue from Glass-Analysis for Decoding Only. *Note.* From *Glass-Analysis for Decoding Only Teacher Guide* (pp. 4–9) by G.G. Glass, 1976, Garden City, NY: Easier to Learn. Copyright 1976 by G.G. Glass. Reprinted by permission.

"et" cluster

set

[Again, note how we go from giving sound to asking for letter(s)—to giving letter(s) and asking for sound]

- *In the word, "set"*, what letter makes the "sss" sound?
What letters make the "et" sound?
- *In the word, "set"*, what sound does the /s/ make?
What sound does e/t make?
- If I took off the "sss" what sound would be left?
If I took off the e/t, what sound would I have left?
- What is the whole word?

better

[Form contiguous clusters into one]

- *In the word, "better"*, what letter makes the "bbb" sound?
What letters make the "et" sound?
What letters make the "bet" sound?
What letters make the "er" sound?
The "eter" sound?
- *In the word, "better"*, what sound does the /b/ make?
What sound does the e/t make?
What sound does b/e/t make?
What sound does t/e/r make?
The e/t/t/e/r?
- *In the word, "better"* if I took off the b/e/t, what sound would be left?
If I took off the e/r, what sound would be left?

[Begin and end with the whole word]
- What is the whole word?

forgetfulness

- *In the word "forgetfulness"*, what letters make the "for" sound?
The "or" sound?
What letters make the "et" sound?
The "get" sound?
What letters make the "forget" sound?
In the word, "forgetfulness", what letters make the "ful" sound?
The "forgetful" sound?

What letters make the "ess" sound?
The "ness" sound?
What letters make the "fulness" sound?
What letters make the "getfulness" sound?
- *In the word "forgetfulness"*, what sound does f/o/r make?
What sound does o/r make?
What sound does e/t make?
The g/e/t?
The f/o/r/g/e/t?
What sound does f/u/l make?
What sound does g/e/t/f/u/l make?
What sound does e/s/s make?
n/e/s/s?
In the word, "forgetfulness", what sound does f/u/l/n/e/s/s make?
g/e/t/f/u/l/n/e/s/s?
- If I took off the f/o/r, what sound would be left?
If I took off the "ness" sound, what sound would be left?
- What is the whole word?

[Notice how many audile/visile structures can be learned in just one word. All transferable to other words]

"ire" cluster

fire

- *In the word, "fire"*, what letter makes the "fff" sound?
In the word, "fire", what letters make the "ire" sound?
- What sound does the /f/ make?
In the word, "fire", what sound does i/r/e make?
- If I took off the "fff", what sound would be left?
- What is the whole word?

umpires

- *In the word, "umpires"*, what letters make the "um" sound?
What letters make the "ump" sound?
What letters make the "ire" sound?
The "ires" sound?

The following is an example of the letter clustering that can be done for the cluster words in the "at" cluster.

sat	bat	mat	fat	cats
s	b	m	f	c
at	at	at	at	at
				ats

patting	batter	fatten	chatter	flatten
p	b	f	ch	fl
at	at	at	at	at
pat	bat	fat	chat	flat
ting	ter	ten	ter	ten
ing	er	en	er	en
atting	atter	atten	atter	

that	clatter	catch	matching	battery
th	cl	c	m	b
at	at	at	at	at
	clat	cat	mat	bat
	ter	ch	ch	ter
	er	atch	ing	er
	atter		ching	ery
			atching	attery

smattering	attack	rattles	scratching	platform
sm	at	rat	sc	pl
at	tack	at	ratch	at
smat	ack	tles	at	plat
ter		attles	ch	form
er			atch	orm
smatter			scratch	atform
ing			ing	
ering			ching	
attering			atching	
			ratching	

attic	scatter	satellite
at	sc	sat
tic	at	at
ic	scat	ell
	ter	satell
	er	lite
	atter	ite
		ellite
		atellite

In the word, "umpires", what letters make the "pire" sound?
The "pires" sound?
• *In the word "umpires", what sound does u/m make?*
u/m/p?
What sound does i/r/e make?
i/r/e/s?
What sound does p/i/r/e make?
p/i/r/e/s?
In the word "umpires", if I took off the u/m, what sound would be left?
If I took away the "ires" sound, what sound would be left?
• What is the whole word?

entirely

• *In the word, "entirely", what letters make the "en" sound?*
What letters make the "ent" sound?
The "ire" sound?
The "tire" sound?
What letters make the "entire" sound?
What letters make the "ly" sound?
What letters make the "irely" sound?
• *In the word, "entirely", what letters make the "tirely" sound?*
• What sound does the e/n make?
The e/n/t?
In the word, "entirely", what sound does i/r/e make?
t/i/r/e?
What sound does e/n/t/i/r/e make?
What sound does l/y make?
What sound does i/r/e/l/y make?
What sound does t/i/r/e/l/y make?
• *In the word, "entirely", if I took off the e/n, what sound would be left?*
If I took off the l/y, what sound would be left?
• What is the whole word?

[Quicken the pace by shortening the verbiage in the questioning]

[After a good beginning repeat the whole word only randomly.]

Figure 3–7. (*continued.*)

STARTERS KIT

(Non-Reader, 1st grade decoding level,
weak 2nd grade decoding level)

1. at	11. am	21. ash
2. ing	12. un	22. ish
3. et	13. in	23. ed
4. it	14. ap	24. ig
5. ot	15. and	25. ip
6. im	16. ack	26. ud
7. op	17. um	27. id
8. an	18. ab	28. en
9. ay	19. ag	29. ug
10. ad	20. old	30. ut

MEDIUMS KIT

(2nd grade decoding level and/or
weak 3rd grade decoding level)

31. ar	41. ame	51. ice
32. em	42. ape	52. ick
33. up	43. ace	53. if(f)
34. ate	44. ang	54. ink
35. ent	45. ank	55. ob
36. est	46. ong	56. od
37. ake	47. all	57. og
38. ide	48. aw	58. ub
39. ock	49. el(l)	59. uf(f)
40. ade	50. eck	60. ush

HARDERS KIT

(3rd grade decoding level and above)

61. able	71. us	81. eat
62. ight	72. il(l)	82. as(s)
63. is(s)	73. ite	83. ev
64. on	74. es(s)	84. ind
65. or	75. om	85. oss
66. ul(l)	76. oke	86. eam
67. ac	77. ore	87. ost
68. af(f)	78. tow	88. rol(l)
69. ook	79. ast	89. one
70. fowl	80. ane	90. ale

COMPLETERS KIT

(Use after Harders)

91. ave	101. eal	111. ure
92. ove	102. tea	112. ur
93. folly	103. ee	113. ir
94. age	104. care	114. ai
95. er	105. deaf	115. au
96. air	106. oat	116. oi
97. ied	107. ue	117. tion
98. ew	108. soon	118. ture
99. ire	109. ou	119. al
100. ear	110. ound	

Figure 3–8. Glass-Analysis Clusters for Decoding. *Note.* From *Glass-Analysis for Decoding Only* by G.G. Glass, 1982, Garden City, NY: Easier to Learn. Copyright 1982 by Easier to Learn. Reprinted by permission.

separate the first three. The second rule is that if the first rule does not work, divide off the first letter of the stem and apply the Rule of Twos and Threes again. The third rule applies to vowels: When two vowels are together, try pronouncing both of the vowels together and, if that doesn't work, then try making just one of the vowel sounds. If the student still cannot determine the word, he or she moves to Step 6.

Step 6: *C*heck with someone. The student is instructed to ask a peer, teacher, or parent for assistance.

Step 7: *T*ry the dictionary. If no one is available to help the student, the student is instructed to look up the word in the dictionary and consult the pronunciation guide.

An important aspect of introducing and implementing this strategy is to obtain a verbal commitment from students that they wish to improve decoding skills.

Lenz and Hughes (1990) found that use of this instructional strategy improved the word identification of 12 adolescents with learning disabilities. Improvement in word identification, however, differentially affected reading comprehension performance. Performance in reading comprehension increased for the majority of the 12 students, but not all. In considering this finding, Lenz and Hughes suggested that some students need to reach a certain level of automatization with the word identification strategy and then be taught additional comprehension strategies, whereas other students would benefit from simultaneous instruction using appropriate comprehension strategies.

Instructional Strategies for Reading Fluency

> In the Orient, children bawl in concert over a book, imitating their fellows or their teacher until they come to know what the page says and to read it for themselves.
>
> (Huey, 1968, p. 274)

When an examiner notes that a student reads slowly in a word-by-word fashion, the student may benefit from a listening/reading or fluency technique. Many reading techniques have been developed to help a reader progress from word-by-word reading to more rapid, automatic word recognition and fluent reading. The purpose of fluency techniques is to make decoding automatic, so that the reader is able to concentrate more fully on comprehension. Most listening/reading techniques attempt to improve reading ability through a global approach, rather than an individual skill development approach. The majority of these techniques share three common elements: (a) presence of a reading model, either a person or a tape; (b) tracking the line of print with a finger or a marker; and (c) reading while listening to the same material (Janiak, 1983). With most of these methods, the student listens to the passage while reading. The teacher may assist the student by modeling the reading, reading along simultaneously, or by providing taped recordings (Hagedorn & McLaughlin, 1982). Table 3-3 provides an overview of various listening/reading techniques. This table includes descriptions of the materials, the advantages and disadvantages of the technique, and the type of student who may benefit from the technique. These methods may be most effective with students whose reading skills are below their listening ability (Carver & Hoffman, 1981); in other words, their progress in reading comprehension is being hindered by a slow reading rate.

Ivan, a secondary student, was referred for an evaluation because of limited reading skill and poor grades in his courses. His content area teachers reported that Ivan was unable to read the textbooks and, consequently, that he failed all examinations. In contrast, they noted that Ivan appeared interested in class and participated in all class discussions. In the evaluation, the examiner observed that Ivan had fairly accurate word identification skills but was a slow word-by-word reader. His slow reading rate and lack of fluency interfered with his understanding of the text.

Based on these observations, the examiner recommended that Ivan read together with a special education teacher for 10 minutes daily and that weekly measures of fluency be taken and the results charted on a graph. Additionally, taped books of all his content area textbooks were obtained and Ivan listened to these tapes while he followed along with the text. By using choral reading and taped books, Ivan was able to increase his reading fluency, understand and learn the material presented in his content area textbooks, and, subsequently, obtain passing grades in his classes.

Beginning Techniques

Several methods may be used to introduce young or severely disabled readers to the reading process. These methods are success oriented and are appropriate for culturally diverse or low language children because they build familiarity and competence with the English language without subjecting a student to failure. Additionally, these methods may be effective with emotionally disturbed or unmotivated students who require positive, nonthreatening reading experiences.

Presenting method. The Presenting method was designed to help beginning readers, children at the lowest levels of reading achievement, or children with oral language or bilingual difficulties or deviant speech patterns (Heckelman, 1974, 1986). Heckelman (1986) suggested that the Presenting technique is also effective with students who have difficulty with tasks involving auditory processing or short-term memory.

The Presenting method contains three main phases: (a) the auditory phase, (b) the paraphrasing or comprehension phase, and (c) the echo phase (Gibbs & Proctor, 1982).

The auditory phase: A simple but interesting story with a definite story line is selected. The teacher sits opposite the student and reads the story while the student watches the instructor's face. The story is read several times.

The paraphrasing phase: The teacher paraphrases the story using vocabulary that is within the child's listening level. Ideas, feelings, and actions are explained to the student, and then the story is read again. If desired, the teacher may ask the child to retell the story, providing ample cueing as needed. The purpose of this introduction process is to increase the listener's comprehension and familiarity with the story by building background knowledge and understanding of details prior to introducing written symbols. Heckelman (1986) indicated that in extremely severe cases, the initial steps may be repeated

Table 3–3. Overview of Listening/Reading Techniques.

	Materials Teacher/Student Ratio	Advantages	Disadvantages	Type of Students
Neurological Impress	High-interest, student selected books. 1:1 instruction. Gradually move to reading materials at frustration level. Sessions 10-15 minutes daily. Not effective if student hasn't responded in four hours of instruction time.	Provides good reading model. Use of age-appropriate materials. Encourages correct eye movement. Low cost of materials. Builds rapport. Multisensory. May cover lots of material.	Physical discomfort and voice fatigue. Time-consuming. Student may not watch words. May not make gains in comprehension.	Word-by-word reader. Problems with phrasing. Student should have at least progressed to mid-2nd grade reading development. Auditory processing impairment. Oral language problems. Speech problems. Emotional problems.
Presenting Method Echoing Assisted Reading Predictable Books	High-interest books with simple, clear story line. Books with repetitive rhythmical pattern. May be used with group.	Builds oral language skills. Enhances auditory memory. Emphasis on meaning and understanding. Builds vocabulary. Uses phonological, syntactic, and semantic systems.	Student may not master basic reading skills. Student may need more control of material. Early phases may interrupt the rhythm of natural reading.	Beginning readers, oral language problems. Limited English proficiency. Low auditory memory. Auditory-visual impairment. Students who fail to learn by phonics instruction. May help older students integrate and see the relationship between auditory and visual information. Emotionally disturbed or unmotivated children.
Taped Books	Book, tape, tape recorder. Listening center. May use high-interest, class textbooks. Rate of tape should be matched to individual fluency rates. May develop classroom tape library. Once technique is mastered, students may work without teacher assistance.	Puts student in control of own learning. Can listen to materials at frustration level. Emphasizes relationship between spoken and written language. Reduces amount of attention devoted to word recognition. May improve listening skills.	Students may not track print with eyes. Students may lose place in reading. Students may not receive enough repetition to acquire new sight vocabulary words. Commercial materials may not meet student needs. Materials may be expensive.	Word-by-word reader, Auditory processing impairments. Attention and memory impairments. Speech impaired. Secondary students and adults. All students may benefit when it is used as a supplemental program.
Repeated Readings	Graph, stopwatch. Passages with a length of 50-200 words. Students may practice independently between timed readings.	Graph and timings may serve as a motivator. Word accuracy and rate improve. May provide sufficient repetition to learn words.	Small amount of material is covered. Comprehension is not emphasized. Student may become bored with passage.	May be most beneficial for students who have listening ability higher than reading ability. Most effective with students with adequate word recognition skills. Unmotivated students.

to strengthen receptive language, expressive language, and memory.

The echo phase: The teacher breaks the story into short phrases and has the student repeat back the story word-for-word. In rare instances, the teacher may have to begin with single words. This process is repeated as often as the teacher feels is necessary.

After the echo phase is completed, the student is introduced to the neurological impress method (Heckelman, 1974), described more fully in the next section. The teacher may begin by reading phrases or sentences repeatedly in unison and may gradually progress to reading the entire story without interruption. Correction of errors and further questioning are not recommended.

Gibbs and Proctor (1982) used the Presenting method for 15 minutes daily for 6 weeks with 21 first- and second-grade students enrolled in a remedial reading program. Students at the second-grade level made the most progress. In considering the results, Gibbs and Proctor suggested that the Presenting method of listen-model-read is most effective with more mature beginners assessed as nonreaders.

Echo reading. In echo or imitative reading, the teacher reads a phrase or sentence while pointing to the words, and the student repeats the words. The procedure is repeated until the student is able to read the passage fluently. This technique may be useful for second language students. The primary goals of echo reading are to improve word recognition skills, intonation, phrasing, and confidence. The method begins with small segments of easy text and gradually progresses in length and difficulty (Henk, Helfeldt, & Platt, 1986).

Assisted reading. In this type of reading, the teacher assists the child by supplying any words not recognized (Hoskisson, 1975, 1979). For the method to be effective, the child must have adequate language so that story comprehension is not a problem. To begin, a parent or teacher reads a short segment of an interesting story. Then the child reads the phrase or sentence as the adult moves a finger along the line of print. When some words are recognized without assistance, the adult pauses and lets the child say the word. Gradually, the student gains increasing independence and the teacher only supplies words the child does not know. This method has been used successfully by elementary and remedial reading teachers with slow readers and students who failed to learn to read by phonics methods (Hoskisson, 1975, 1979).

Predictable books. Predictable books have a repetitive, rhythmical pattern that makes it easy for children to guess what comes next. McClure (1985) described three types of predictable books. In the repetitive book, the author repeats certain words, phrases, or themes; in the cumulative book, the author incorporates previous ideas into subsequent ones; in the familiar sequence book, the author repeats sequences, such as numbers and days of the week. Use of predictable books encourages the use of syntactic, semantic, and graphic cues to aid in comprehension (McClure, 1985). Stories are read again and again with the students joining in when they are ready.

Another type of predictable reader uses the verses of well-known children's songs. These song-picture books may be helpful in teaching a student with language disabilities (Bromley & Jalongo, 1984). Bromley and Jalongo suggested that children with language delays may benefit from creating and adding verses to familiar songs. Because song lyrics have a strong motivational appeal for children, they may be used effectively to develop language competence and to expand reading and writing skills.

Bridge, Winograd, and Haley (1983) found that a patterned language approach with first-grade students who were low readers was more effective than the basal reading approach. In this approach, the teacher read aloud to the students and then reread the story asking students to join in when ready. Students then read the story together. The text was then put on a large chart without pictures. Students read the story from the chart together.

Sentence and word matching procedures were used to encourage students to attend to graphophonic clues. Sentences were cut into strips, and students matched the sentences to the chart and then read the sentences. Students were then given word cards from the story and asked to place each card under the matching word in the chart. Students read the story. Word cards were placed in random order at the bottom of the chart, and the students matched the words in the story. This approach combines the use of predictable reading materials with individual word analysis and was effective in helping first-grade students learn sight words.

Neurological Impress Method

Another unison reading procedure is the neurological impress method (NIM), an adapted choral reading approach, developed by Heckelman (1965, 1966, 1969, 1986). The NIM should be used 15 minutes daily for a total instructional period of 8 to 12 hours. The method seems most effective when used daily for short periods rather than twice a week for more extended periods (Cook, Nolan, & Zanotti, 1980). The student sits slightly in front of the instructor and the material is read in unison. The teacher's voice is directed into the student's ear. The instructor attempts to find a comfortable speed for the student with the goal of establishing a normal, fluid reading pattern.

Finger as a guide. While reading, the instructor slides a finger under the words in a smooth, continuous motion. Voices are synchronized so that the finger is pointing to the word as it is spoken. Eventually, as the method becomes familiar, the student may use his or her finger as a guide. Use of a finger for tracking provides a visual cue and helps train the eyes to move smoothly across the line.

Pacing. In the beginning sessions, the instructor reads in a louder voice and at a slightly faster pace than the student. The student is encouraged to forget about mistakes. Periodically in the session, the material is speeded up for a few minutes. After 2 hours of instruction time, reading can be done at the fastest speed at which a teacher can read without discomfort.

Materials. The instructor should begin with books that are at a slightly lower level than the student can handle. By the end of 2 hours of total instruction time, the student is exposed to more difficult materials. A goal of the method is to cover as much material as possible.

Evaluation. If a student has not responded after 4 hours of total instruction time, it is most likely that the NIM is not an effective procedure to use. After 8 hours of total instruction time, the instructor should observe a sharp rise in achievement.

Type of student. This method may be particularly beneficial for students who are "phonics-bound," or who have received intensive instruction in phonics and still cannot read (Heckelman, 1965, 1969; Memory, 1981; Otto & Smith, 1980). Cook, Nolan, and Zanotti (1980) found that the approach was effective for students with auditory processing impairments. In their experience with the approach, Otto and Smith observed that NIM was most effective with students who lacked a proper concept of reading, had serious phrasing problems, or attempted to sound out every word. Brown (1982) indicated that NIM is most effective with extremely disabled readers who have developed at least a small basic sight vocabulary and have progressed to mid to upper second-grade reading development.

NIM modification. Henk (1983) described a NIM modification that could be used to enhance reading comprehension by incorporating the procedure into the Directed Reading Activity model (DRA). The modification contains the four basic steps of a DRA lesson (Harris & Sipay, 1985; Henk, 1983): (a) pre-reading, (b) guided silent reading, (c) skills and abilities, and (d) extension and enrichment activities.

For the pre-reading step, students are asked to discuss material from their previous NIM session. They may retell what happened in the story or be asked to speculate what may happen next. In the second step, the student and teacher read orally for 10 minutes. The teacher interrupts the reading process at appropriate places, discusses the topic, and asks the student questions. The teacher may ask the student to predict what will happen next. When used with severely disabled or beginning readers, the teacher may question the student after each paragraph; more advanced readers may read the entire 10 minutes without interruptions. For the last two steps, the teacher presents and reviews specific skills related to the lesson and extends the activity to related instructional tasks. In addition to improving fluency, this type of strategy provides a balance of skill development and reinforces the idea that the primary purpose for reading is understanding the material (Henk, 1983).

Paired Reading

Paired Reading is a method that involves a parent or peer reading aloud in a synchronized voice with the student. Although similar to NIM, this method also places emphasis on accurate reading. This technique has been widely implemented in the United Kingdom as a procedure for use by parents to assist with reading progress at home (Topping, 1987a). More recently, use has been expanded to include peer tutoring (Topping, 1987b).

Steps. To begin, the student and tutor read aloud together at a rate comfortable for the student. Finger pointing may be used. The student attempts to read slightly faster than the tutor. If the student makes an error, the tutor supplies the correct word, and the student reads the word correctly. When the student wants to proceed independently, he or she signals to the tutor with a nudge or a tap to discontinue reading. The student then reads aloud independently until an error is made. At this point the tutor provides the correct word, the student says the correct word, and then the pair resumes reading together. Throughout the process, the tutor praises the student for accurate reading. The pair may stop the reading process to discuss the story content or any new vocabulary words. Initially, the procedure should take place five times a week for a minimum of 5 minutes daily over a period of 6 to 8 weeks (Topping, 1987a).

Topping (1987a) stated that initial research on the Paired Reading procedure has shown that average children who participate in Paired Reading make three times the normal progress in reading accuracy and five times the normal progress in reading comprehension. He also noted that the technique has been effective with students from ages six to thirteen, across intelligence ranges and socioeconomic status. In a review of 10 peer tutoring projects,

Topping (1987b) found that overall gain in reading skills for both the remedial students and the tutors was four times the normal rate. Topping acknowledged, however, that these studies, conducted in real-life educational settings, had substantial methodological problems. Pumfrey (1986) cautioned regarding the unjustified overoptimism of Paired Reading researchers and noted that studies of parents listening to their children read at home have also produced significant gains. Despite reservations, Pumfrey concluded that this method is a positive and useful technique for improving reading performance.

Both Paired Reading and NIM are appropriate techniques for an examiner to recommend for home use. The procedures are simple and the materials are inexpensive. The major difference between Paired Reading and NIM that may influence an examiner's recommendation is the attention to errors. In some cases, this correction procedure may influence a parent-child interaction in a negative way. In other situations, the correction procedure may produce greater gains. Further research is needed to substantiate the effectiveness of this approach.

Repeated Readings

Another technique for improving reading fluency is repeated readings (Samuels, 1979). The major difference between NIM and repeated readings is that in NIM, a student continues to read new passages, whereas in repeated readings, the passages are reread until fluency is obtained (Kann, 1983). The rationale for this method emerged from the theory of automatic information processing in reading (LaBerge & Samuels, 1974). The nonfluent reader must focus attention on each individual word, leaving little attention free for semantic level processing. In contrast, the fluent reader is able to decode automatically so that attention is directed to comprehension.

Although intended as a supplement to a developmental reading program, the method has been effective for students with special learning problems (Moyer, 1982; Samuels, 1979) and appears to produce gains in fluency and reading achievement (Carver & Hoffman, 1981; Gonzales & Elijah, 1975).

The method involves rereading a short, meaningful passage several times until fluency is reached. Fluency is separated into reading speed and word recognition accuracy. Although speed is emphasized, both words per minute and errors in word recognition may be charted on a graph for each reading. Figure 3-9 illustrates a sample graph for recording student performance.

A student's rate may be recorded by the number of seconds required to read a passage or by the number of words read per minute. Each reading may be timed or a student may reread the passage independently until it is

time to try again. As speed increases, errors decrease. The number of rereadings may be set by the student or teacher. As speed improves, fewer readings are needed to reach criterion.

Depending upon the age and ability of the student, a length of between 50 to 200 words is selected. In early experimental work with mentally retarded students, the subjects began with passages of 50 words and progressed to 200 words, while students with average intelligence began with a 200-word passage (Samuels, 1979).

The number of rereadings may also vary. Samuels (1979) recommended that students read passages until they reach a criterion of 85 words per minute. O'Shea, Sindelar, and O'Shea (1987) recommended that the number of readings of any passage be limited to three. In using repeated readings with elementary students with learning disabilities, they found that additional readings did not improve comprehension and that, by the third reading, students had reached a fluency level of 100 wpm. Selection of an appropriate criterion level and the number of rereadings may be determined by the teacher and student on an individualized basis.

Group adaptation. O'Shea and O'Shea (1988) described an adaptation of the repeated readings method that may be used by large groups of students in regular classrooms. To begin, the teacher reads a passage with expression while the students follow along, pointing to each word as it is read. The teacher reads the first sentence aloud, and the students then read the sentence in unison. The teacher and students alternate until the passage is finished. Students may then choral-read the entire passage, practice the passage with a peer, or use language masters or tape recorders. To complete the procedure, the same passage is read with a comprehension task, such as a cloze or maze procedure.

Secondary students. Repeated readings may be an effective method for increasing interest, comprehension, and speed in secondary students with learning disabilities and students with behavior problems who resist or have a negative attitude toward reading (Neill, 1979). Neill recommended the following procedure:

1. With the teacher's help, the student selects a 100- to 200-word passage of average difficulty.
2. The student reads the passage while the teacher times and counts the number of errors.
3. The timing and number of words are recorded on the individual's chart.
4. The student reviews, rereads, or asks for the pronunciation of any words in the passage. A list of problem words may be created for study.
5. With the teacher's help, a goal in time and percentage of words correct is set.

Number of Words in Passage: _____   Date: _____

Estimated Grade Level: _____   Student's Name: _____

Book: _____

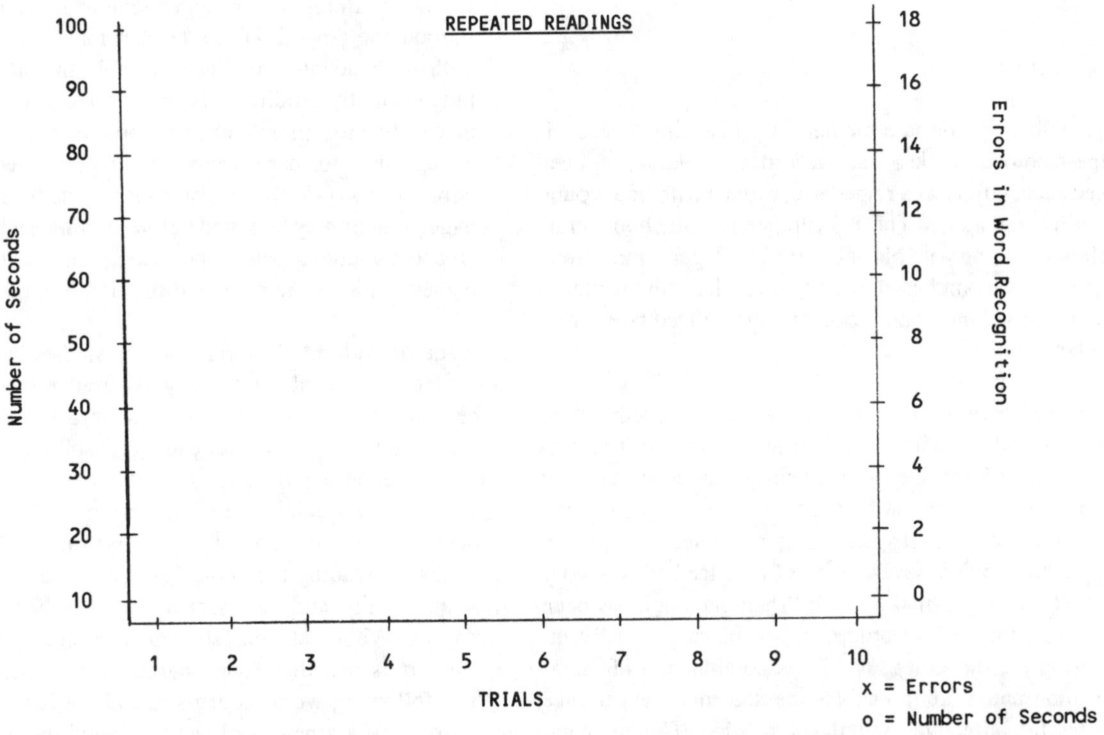

Figure 3–9. Repeated Readings Graph. Permission is granted to reproduce this form.

6. The student rereads and practices the passage.
7. When the goal is reached, a new passage is selected.

Students of all ages find repeated readings to be highly motivating, and the chart provides additional reinforcement (Henk, Helfeldt, & Platt, 1986; Moyer, 1982). One advantage of repeated readings over NIM is that it promotes development of syntactic competency—a student hears and practices appropriate phrasing (Kann, 1983). The main disadvantage is the repetitious nature of the task.

Choral Repeated Reading

Bos and Vaughn (1988) described a modification of the repeated readings method, entitled choral repeated reading. This method combines the teaching of word identification and comprehension with a fluency technique, and is designed for students who have a higher level of listening comprehension than word identification skill and have developed a sight vocabulary of at least 25 words.

To begin, the teacher explains the procedure and the student selects a book of interest that is one or two instructional levels above present performance. Word

recognition should range from 75% to 85% accuracy. The teacher and student briefly review the book and make predictions about what will happen. The following three-step procedure is used:

Teacher reads. The teacher reads several sentences or a short paragraph of the text aloud to the student at a normal reading rate while running his or her finger underneath the words as the student watches.

Teacher and student read. While pointing to the words, the teacher and the student read the passage together. The passage may be read as many times as necessary until the student feels ready to read the passage independently.

Student reads. The student reads the passage aloud. The teacher pronounces and records any unknown words.

After reading each section, the teacher and student may discuss what was learned, review predictions, and make new predictions. The three-step process is then repeated for a new section. To measure progress, a teacher may record the number of words read in a minute. Students may then record the results on a graph or chart.

To build word identification skill, the teacher may write any of the unknown words on word cards. These words are then practiced using a variety of instructional activities for building word identification skill. One advantage of this type of procedure is that it integrates instruction in word identification and comprehension with a fluency technique.

Taped Books

Another appropriate method for enhancing fluency is tape-recorded books. Tape-recorded books have been used successfully as a remedial approach with both young children and adults. The student listens to the book while following along with his or her eyes or finger. Prerecorded tapes may be purchased, rented, or created. An instructor, parent, or volunteer may make individualized tapes for a student.

Repeated listenings. In this procedure, a student listens and reads along with a book or story as many times as necessary to read the story fluently. Sessions may last from 5 minutes to half an hour, depending upon the student's age and motivation. Using repeated listenings, it may take a student several days of practice before a story is read fluently (Janiak, 1983). When one book has been mastered, the student proceeds to another, gradually increasing the difficulty level. This combination of memorization and reading enables the student to experience successful, effective, and fluent reading (Cunningham, 1979).

Selecting or preparing materials. Several factors should be considered in selecting taped books for a student. One consideration is the reading rate of the taped book. On some commercial tapes, the rate is too fast. Research conducted by Neville and Pugh (1975) suggested that poor readers benefit more when the rate of the tape is slowed to match their reading skills. On other beginning reading books, the pause between words is too long. Students appear to make the most progress when the tapes are paced to their approximate reading rates (Hoskisson & Krohm, 1974). In developing tapes for elementary students, Carbo (1978) adapted the rate and phrase length for each student. The greatest gains were made when individualized tapes, based upon a student's reading ability, were used.

Another consideration in using taped books is the instructional level of the material. Mikkelsen (1981) found that in using taped books with students in first through eighth grade that the students who used tape-recorded materials at their frustration level performed significantly better than students who used taped books at their independent reading level. Meyer (1981) suggested that

instead of considering the difficulty level of the material, a teacher should record material based upon the student's interests.

One limitation of taped books is that students, particularly of elementary age, may just listen to the recording and not follow along with the print. Listening to a tape and following along with a finger require some practice. In introducing taped books, a teacher may want to practice with the students until they are able to follow the text independently. Additionally, some students may lose their place while reading. Some prerecorded books do not allow enough time for page turning. In preparing recordings of books, Carbo (1978) suggested that to cue the listener, the page number may be stated before starting each page with an accompanying pause that is long enough to allow the reader to locate the page and the first line of print.

Type of student. Several research studies have demonstrated that taped books may be used effectively with certain types of remedial readers. In a research project with children with severe reading disability, van der Leij (1981) found that the use of taped books was as effective as intensive special help from the remedial teacher. Students listened to a tape three or four times while simultaneously reading the book. Sessions were conducted 10 minutes daily, and students read aloud to the teacher once a week. While listening, students recorded in a notebook any words that they found particularly difficult to read. The following week students reread the lists of difficult words, chose a new book, and repeated the procedure.

Carbo (1978) found that teaching reading with talking books was effective for students with auditory processing, attention, or memory problems. Additionally, talking books were used successfully with learning disabled, emotionally disturbed, educable mentally retarded, and speech impaired students. All students made gains in comprehension, word recognition, and vocabulary, and gained an intuitive knowledge of phonics. Taped books were also effective with students who had difficulty learning phonics and for older students who were frustrated by reading.

Secondary and adult readers. Taped books may also be used in secondary reading instruction. Tape libraries may be developed that include cassette recordings of all required textbooks, or a teacher may create a tape library for a particular classroom. Smith and Smith (1985) described a program in which students could check out tapes and listen to the chapters as they read along visually. Taping may be done by volunteers, including retired citizens, drama students, honor students, other teachers, or parents.

Wearing headphones and following along with books also improves the sight vocabulary of adult readers. Using this technique, adults who identified themselves as "nonreaders" were able to read short articles independently after as little as 1 to 2 hours of instruction (Meyer, 1981).

A major advantage of using taped books is that they do not require individualized instruction. Additionally, secondary and college students may listen to required textbooks that they would be unable to read independently.

Word lists. Shapiro and McCurdy (1989) used a taped-words intervention to increase the reading proficiency of five ninth- and tenth-grade students with behavior disorders. Three of the students had also been diagnosed as learning disabled, and one of the students was diagnosed as educable mentally retarded. All subjects were reading at or below a sixth-grade reading level. Eighty vocabulary words were selected from passages that ranged from seventh- to ninth-grade level. Six lists were developed that contained the 80 words in random order. Students were instructed to read along with an audiotape that presented the list of 80 words within 1 minute. For the second reading, the oral reading rate was timed. The intervention increased the reading rate of word lists, but little improvement was noted on the measure of generalization or reading passages that contained the words. These findings suggest that this type of procedure may not be effective for improving overall reading fluency but may increase sight word recognition and encourage students to attempt to read faster.

Previewing Techniques

Previewing techniques involve any method that has a learner read or listen to a passage prior to instruction or testing (Rose & Sherry, 1984). Three types of previewing techniques may be used: (a) oral previewing, reading a passage aloud before a lesson; (b) silent previewing, reading a passage silently before instruction; and (c) listening previewing, following along with the passage as the teacher reads aloud (Hansen & Eaton, 1978).

Rose and Sherry (1984) conducted an experiment to explore the effects of oral reading preview procedures with five learning disabled adolescents. With the exception of one student, silent and listening previewing were more effective than no previewing, and listening previewing was superior to silent previewing. They concluded that listening previewing appears to be a viable instructional technique for increasing the oral reading performance of secondary students with learning disabilities. This method may be used with groups or individuals, or the teacher may prerecord selected passages for students. In another study, comparing the effects of listening and silent previewing with learning disabled students, listening previewing was superior to silent previewing (Rose, 1984). These findings suggest that allowing a student to preview material improves performance.

A final consideration in building reading rate is that time spent reading may be the single most important factor in improving fluency (Palincsar & Englert, 1988). Palincsar and Englert suggested that stressing oral fluency without regard for comprehension seems counterproductive. With many students, a fluency method should be combined with strategies for comprehension monitoring; with some students, particularly those whose listening comprehension is higher than their present level of reading performance, direct instruction using a fluency method will improve rate and, as a result, comprehension. The goal is to select for each student the method that will be most effective for enhancing ability to derive meaning from text.

Conclusion

Based upon a student's WJ-R performance, other informal assessments, and teacher reports, an examiner will be able to prescribe an effective instructional program for increasing word identification skill. The selection of an instructional approach for word identification is dependent upon a student's characteristics. For example, the Fernald approach places emphasis on the meaningfulness of symbols and the development of visualization skill, whereas the Phonic Remedial Reading Lessons emphasize the sounds of the language and the development of sound blending skill. The neurological impress method emphasizes rapid, fluent reading and promotes automaticity in decoding. Different students will profit from different instructional methods. One general principle applies, however: When providing supplemental instruction in word identification, students should not lose sight of the purpose of reading. The sole purpose of increasing word identification skill is to facilitate a student's ability to obtain meaning from text. For some students, improvement in word identification skill and fluency allows them to devote more attention to comprehension of text.

Although an important facet of overall reading competency, improved word identification skill and fluency do not guarantee improvement in reading comprehension or vocabulary. For some students, an examiner will also recommend additional strategies to be used separately or simultaneously for enhancing reading comprehension.

Reading Comprehension

Again, reading began to be regarded as a
form of experience, like hearing or seeing,
as well as a form of learning. It became

apparent that the efficient reader not only recognizes words and grasps the ideas presented, but also reflects on their significance, relates them, and sees their implications. If he is to benefit from these ideas, moreover, he must react thoughtfully to what he reads, weighing its value and the soundness of the judgments or conclusions. It is equally important for him to apprehend the value and the significance of the content. Finally, if reading is to help him solve problems or direct his own activities, he must learn to apply the ideas acquired.

(W. S. Gray, 1956, p. 62)

The two measures of reading comprehension on the WJ-R ACH are Reading Vocabulary in the Supplemental Battery and Passage Comprehension in the Standard Battery. These tests measure the abilities to understand word meanings and to use syntactic and semantic clues. When administering these tests, an examiner should record all incorrect responses for later error analysis.

Successful performance on both of these tests requires basic reading skill. Ability to identify words is a prerequisite for comprehending written text. Consequently, in analyzing performance, an examiner must determine whether a student's errors result primarily from comprehension difficulties, limited basic reading skills, or a combination of both.

Error Analysis of Reading Vocabulary

The Reading Vocabulary test requires the student to read words aloud and then state an appropriate synonym (Part A) or antonym (Part B). Although a student is not penalized for oral reading errors on Reading Vocabulary, an examiner will want to listen to the individual's oral pronunciation of each of the stimulus items and record the response. Noting the pronunciation will provide an examiner with further information regarding an individual's word identification performance.

Error Types

Several types of diagnostically significant error patterns may occur. A description of these error types follows.

Mispronunciation/correct response. A student may mispronounce or even not say the stimulus word but still produce a correct response. For example, Sandra, an eighth-grade student, mispronounced the word "residence" and then said, "It's a place to live, like a house." When she came to the word "genuine," she said, "I don't know how to pronounce that word, but it means 'real.' "

Correct pronunciation/incorrect response. A student may pronounce a word correctly but then not produce a correct response. For example, Mary, a fifth-grade student, pronounced the word "cogitate" correctly and then replied, "I've never heard of that word." Despite lack of familiarity with the word, the student's response revealed her good word identification or decoding skill.

Misidentification/appropriate response. A student may misread a word and then supply a response that would be correct for the misidentified word. For example, Megan, a fourth-grade student, read Item 12 "moist" as "most" and then supplied the synonym of "best." She pronounced Item 21 "restrain" as "restrict" and then provided the synonym of "limit." In Megan's case, difficulty with these reading vocabulary items appears to be attributed to low decoding skill, rather than low vocabulary knowledge.

Homophones. On some items, a student may pronounce a word correctly but then confuse the word with a homophone. For example, Kevin, a seventh-grade student, pronounced the word "haul" correctly and then responded "corridor." On the Antonyms test he pronounced the word "hire" correctly, and then supplied the antonym of "lower" and for the word "cellar," responded "buyer." Even though these responses are incorrect, Kevin demonstrated good oral vocabulary. Kevin's errors may primarily reflect low word recognition and spelling skill.

Incorrect pronunciation/incorrect response. A student may mispronounce a word, and then produce an incorrect response. The mispronunciation may be a real word or the student may produce a nonsense word and then fail to provide an antonym or synonym.

By listening to a student's pronunciation and analyzing the responses, an examiner will acquire a broader understanding of a student's present level of reading skill and instructional needs. Harris and Sipay (1985) discussed three types of explanations for why a student does not recognize a vocabulary word when reading. In Type 1, the student would know the meaning if he or she could pronounce the word (mispronunciation/correct response). In many instances, this type of error has to be validated through observations of a student's oral vocabulary performance, such as on the WJ-R COG Oral Vocabulary test. In Type 2, the student pronounces the printed form, but the meaning is unknown (correct pronunciation/incorrect response). In Type 3, both the pronunciation and meaning are unknown (incorrect pronunciation/incorrect response). For instructional planning in the first situation, emphasis is placed on building word recognition skills. In the second situation, emphasis is placed on expanding the student's vocabulary. For the third situation, attention is directed to both areas.

Performance on Synonyms and Antonyms

An examiner may also wish to compare a student's performance on the two parts of the Reading Vocabulary test: Synonyms and Antonyms. Developmentally, Antonyms is an easier task than Synonyms, and so in most instances students will score higher on Antonyms than Synonyms. Opposite meanings are more automatic and easier to retrieve than words that have the same or nearly the same meanings. An examiner may also note that a student provides antonyms as responses for one or more of the synonym items. As items increase in difficulty for the student, he or she may resort to the easier, more automatic response. In some instances, a student will obtain similar scores on the two parts. Similar scores may result when the student has: (a) difficulty in word identification that interferes with vocabulary or (b) limited (low scores) or extensive (high scores) linguistic experience. An examiner may differentiate between these two factors by analyzing a student's performance on the WJ-R COG Oral Vocabulary test and comparing these results to performance on the Reading Vocabulary test.

Comparing Reading Vocabulary to Oral Vocabulary

An examiner may obtain further insights into reading skill by comparing a student's performance on the WJ-R ACH Reading Vocabulary test to performance on the WJ-R COG Oral Vocabulary test. On the Oral Vocabulary test, words are presented orally and no reading is required. If performance is significantly higher on Oral Vocabulary than on Reading Vocabulary, difficulty with reading vocabulary is most likely attributed to low word identification skill rather than lack of vocabulary knowledge.

Error Analysis of Passage Comprehension

Item analysis of students' responses to cloze tasks may reveal difficulty with various parts of speech, grammatical structures, or sentence patterns (Henk & Selders, 1984). Although the Passage Comprehension test does not provide extensive information for error analysis, examination of a student's responses may provide meaningful diagnostic information. If further analysis is needed, the assessment may be supplemented by preparing a cloze or maze passage from the student's instructional material. Procedures for this type of informal assessment are described in the section on Additional Assessment of Reading Comprehension Skills.

Error Categories

To delineate specific weaknesses, Rye (1982) proposed a system of cloze error categories. Although these cate-gories were developed for verbatim scoring of the cloze passages, the different types and hierarchy of errors are relevant to the interpretation of Passage Comprehension and to assessments in which the Passage Comprehension test is supplemented with informal cloze passages. The examiner begins by making a list of a student's incorrect responses and then identifies each error as Type 1, 2, 3, or 4.

Type 1. Type 1, the least serious of errors, are responses that are semantically and syntactically correct but do not match the exact wording of the author. In informal cloze analysis a Type 1 response is an appropriate, but not verbatim response. On many of the Passage Comprehension items, several responses are accepted as correct. Consequently, on this test, a Type 1 error is a response that is almost acceptable. In other words, the response, although scored as incorrect, demonstrates correct syntactical use and some passage understanding.

Type 2. Type 2 errors are responses that are syntactically appropriate, but semantically inappropriate. The response is appropriate in terms of word class, tense, person, case, and number but does not maintain the intended passage meaning. For example, Item 21 states:

> "Is this my hat?" asked Wendy. "No, it is not *yours*," said Brian.

For this item, the response: "hers" or "mine" is a Type 2 error. The student has selected a response that is syntactically appropriate but semantically inappropriate.

A Type 2 error may result from one of the following factors: (a) too little attention to passage meaning; (b) careless reading; or (c) word calling, decoding words without understanding the meaning. Figure 3-10 illustrates the performance of Josh, a fifth-grade student, on the Passage Comprehension test. Error analysis indicates that all of his errors are Type 2; the responses are syntactically appropriate, but semantically inappropriate. A high proportion of this type of error indicates that a student has developed a sense of language structure and the relationships among words, but needs to learn more about inferring meaning from text and attending to contextual cues.

Type 3. Type 3 errors are responses that are semantically acceptable, but syntactically unacceptable. The word may share the same stem with the correct response but be unacceptable in terms of word class, tense, person, case, or number. Two types of errors are found in this category: (a) words of the correct class but not the precise form, such as a wrong verb tense; or, of a more serious nature, (b) complete failure to understand the syntactic pattern. On Item 21 above, previously described, the response "you"

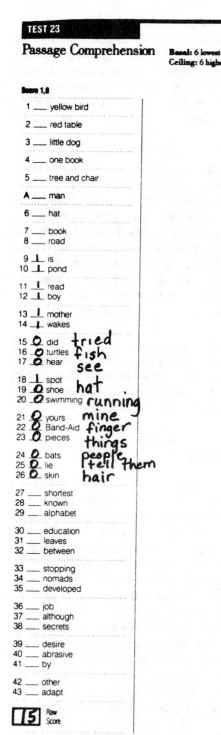

Figure 3–10. Type 2 Errors on the Passage Comprehension Test.

would be a Type 3 error. The student has selected a response that shares the same word stem, but is syntactically inappropriate.

In assessing a student with limited English proficiency, an examiner should attempt to determine whether Type 3 errors are caused by a lack of familiarity with English language structure, rather than a failure to comprehend a passage.

One general principle employed in the WJ-R is not to penalize a subject for mispronunciations resulting from speech defects, dialects, or regional speech patterns. For this reason, on Passage Comprehension and Reading Vocabulary, responses are accepted as correct when they differ from the correct response only in verb tense or number (singular/plural). Responses are scored as incorrect when a different part of speech, such as a noun for a verb or an adjective for an adverb, is given.

Type 4. Type 4 errors, the most serious of errors, are syntactically and semantically unacceptable. This type of response indicates failure to use either of the two main sources of information available on the Passage Comprehension test. For example on Item 21, the responses "Sam" or "is" are Type 4 errors. The student has selected a response that is both syntactically and semantically inappropriate. A marked difference in skill exists between a student who provides responses that are syntactically and semantically correct and a student who provides meaningless responses.

When a high proportion of Type 4 errors exists, the examiner should attempt to determine the reason for the difficulty. In some instances, a Type 4 response results from failure to comprehend the passage. In other instances, a student produces Type 4 errors when the word identification demands have become too difficult and, consequently, the student is unable to decode the passage and ventures a wild guess. In this situation, the examiner may observe that the student reads the word before the blank or makes no attempt to decode the passage.

In some instances, an in-depth error analysis is not necessary. Even when responses are not analyzed in detail, an examiner should still ask, when considering the quality of a student's answers: To what extent do the individual's responses demonstrate syntactic and semantic knowledge?

Comparing the Oral Language to Reading Tests

To gain further understanding of a student's oral language and reading development, an examiner may compare a student's performance on several of the WJ-R COG oral language tests to his or her performance on the WJ-R ACH reading tests. These comparisons allow the examiner to determine whether a significant difference exists between a student's performance on orally administered tests and his or her performance on reading tests. For example, an examiner may wish to compare a student's performance on the Oral Language cluster to his or her performance on the Broad Reading cluster. Or, an examiner may compare the Listening Comprehension test to the Passage

Comprehension test to gain insights into the effect of word recognition on reading comprehension performance. The Passage Comprehension test presents modified reading cloze tasks whereas the Listening Comprehension test presents modified oral cloze tasks. Significantly higher performance on the Listening Comprehension test suggests that word recognition skill is interfering with reading comprehension performance. These types of comparisons, presented in Figure 3-11, will provide the examiner with increased information regarding a student's expected reading achievement and present performance level.

Additional Assessment of Reading Comprehension Skills

When difficulty with reading comprehension is cited as a referral concern, an examiner may wish to assess other aspects of reading comprehension. After noting that the student has difficulty on the WJ-R ACH reading comprehension tests, an examiner may perform a more in-depth evaluation of reading comprehension skill. More extensive testing will help an examiner to determine exactly which factors are affecting a student's performance.

Even when a student attains an average or above-average score on the WJ-R ACH reading comprehension tests, he or she may still have difficulty with certain classroom comprehension tasks. Factors that contribute to a discrepancy between test and classroom performance include: (a) the length of the passage, (b) the complexity of the text(s), (c) the nature of the instructional assignments, (d) the instructional methods, and (e) the teacher-student interaction.

In one case, a student may have difficulty sustaining concentration on longer passages. In another case, a student may be using a classroom text that is too difficult, either in the word identification or comprehension requirements. In conducting an assessment, an examiner should consider the relationships between the reader, criterial task, material, and strategies (Englert & Palincsar, 1988). Several methods for informal assessment are described below.

Passage Reading

To assist in estimating an appropriate instructional level, an examiner may ask a student to read a set of graded passages from his or her basal reading series or content area textbooks. The examiner records all reading errors on a second copy of the test and then asks a series of comprehension questions. After the student has completed a selected passage, the examiner may either ask the student to retell what he or she read or ask the student text-dependent questions. The material is appropriate if

WJ-R ORAL LANGUAGE AND READING COMPARISONS

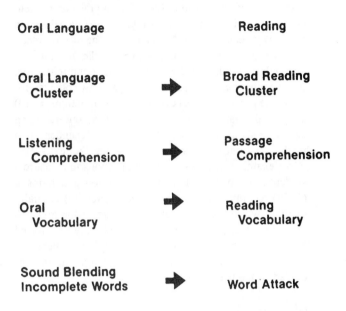

Oral Language		Reading
Oral Language Cluster	➡	Broad Reading Cluster
Listening Comprehension	➡	Passage Comprehension
Oral Vocabulary	➡	Reading Vocabulary
Sound Blending Incomplete Words	➡	Word Attack

Figure 3–11. Comparison of Oral Language and Reading Tests.

the student misses fewer than 10% of the words, reads at an appropriate rate, and answers 75% or more of the comprehension questions (Englert & Palincsar, 1988).

Retelling. An examiner may ask a student to paraphrase the important points in a story or a factual passage. To begin, the examiner may say, "Tell me what the story was about" or "Tell me the important points from the material that you just read." The examiner may tape record the retelling for further analysis or for comparison with performance at a later date. When analyzing retellings, an examiner may note different patterns. Some students may recall the gist of the passage but omit specific details. Other students may cite specific details but fail to comprehend the central ideas. An examiner may count and record the number of story elements or important ideas that are recalled.

Questions. Several different questions may be developed to guide the retelling. After a student has read a story or factual passage, an examiner may ask the student to answer questions based upon who, what, where, when, how, and why. Or, an examiner may ask questions about the story structure, such as the setting, problem, outcome, and conclusion.

The examiner may also develop specific questions to assess different types of comprehension: literal reading comprehension (understanding the passage) or inferential comprehension (using information beyond what is presented in the passage). McLoughlin and Lewis (1990) suggest the following types of questions for informally assessing comprehension. To assess literal comprehension, an examiner may ask the student to: (a) state the main idea, (b) propose a title, (c) recall passage details, (d) recall a sequence of events, or (e) explain the meaning of vocabulary words. To assess inferential comprehension, the examiner may ask the student to: (a) draw conclusions, (b) make predictions, (c) evaluate ideas or actions, or (d) suggest alternate endings. In preparing the questions, an examiner should ensure that they are text-dependent: that is, they can only be answered by reading the text.

An examiner may also classify questions to measure a student's use of prior knowledge. Pearson and Johnson (1978) recommended three question types: (a) textually explicit, where the information is found in the text; (b) textually implicit, where the information may be inferred from the text; and (c) scriptually implicit, where the information is based upon prior knowledge and not included in the text.

Cloze Procedure

When an examiner notes difficulty on the Passage Comprehension test, a more in-depth informal evaluation may be accomplished using the cloze procedure. Informal assessment using this procedure may be used to determine a student's level of reading comprehension in the school reading series or in content area textbooks.

Passage development. Bormuth (1975) outlined the following procedure for developing passages:

1. Select a passage of 250 words. If the evaluation is being done for instructional placement purposes, select passages from the school reading series.
2. Begin with 1 of the words in the second sentence, and delete every 5th word until 50 words are deleted.
3. Type the passage, double spaced, and replace the deleted words with an underlined blank, 15 spaces long.
4. Give students a sample cloze test before administering the actual test. Instruct the students to write the word they think was omitted in each blank.

Number of deletions. Because the number of deletions increases the level of task difficulty, Miller (1986) suggested varying the number of deletions according to the grade level of the student: primary grades every 10th word, intermediate grades every 8th word, and upper-intermediate and secondary levels, every 5th word. The number of deletions may also be based on an estimate of the reader's competency. Rankin and Overholser

(1969) suggested beginning with deletions of every 10th word to provide maximum content, then gradually progressing to every 7th word, and then finally to every 5th word.

As an alternative to deleting every nth word, selective deletions may be a better tool for assessing bilingual or multilingual students than strict cloze testing (Ashby-Davis, 1984). Students with limited English proficiency may demonstrate a lack of familiarity with English language structure, rather than a lack of reading comprehension.

Guidelines for instructional placement. When the cloze procedure is used as a test to determine appropriate instructional placement, typically only exact or verbatim responses are scored as correct. A student's performance may be interpreted using the following guidelines (Bormuth, 1968; Jones & Pikulski, 1974; Rye, 1982):

> Independent level: About 60% accuracy
> Instructional level: About 40% to 60% accuracy
> Frustration level: Below 40% accuracy

Several authors indicate that 50% accuracy should represent the Independent level when students are required to match the exact words of the author (Ashby-Davis, 1984). Even though only verbatim responses are accepted for the total score, an examiner should analyze the responses and types of errors in a manner similar to the procedure described for the Passage Comprehension test. If the majority of errors are Type 1, the student is demonstrating understanding.

Maze Procedure

As an alternative to an informal cloze procedure, an examiner may use the maze procedure. The maze procedure may be used for determining instructional level, identifying students with comprehension difficulties, and monitoring reading growth (Guthrie, Seifert, Burnham, & Caplan, 1974). Guthrie et al. (1974) outlined the following procedure for developing a passage:

1. Extract a passage from a story or book.
2. Replace every 5th or 10th word with three alternate choices.
3. Instruct the students to read the material silently and to circle the correct alternative.

The percentage of correct choices indicates the level of passage comprehension. For example, if a student was given a 100-word passage with 20 maze items and made 15 errors, his or her comprehension proficiency would be 25%. Because optimal teaching levels are 60% to 70%

accuracy when three alternate choices are supplied, the material is too difficult.

The maze technique may also be used to assess growth in comprehension. Different stories from the basal reading series are transcribed into maze form and then administered periodically to the student. Guthrie et al. (1974) suggested the following procedure: (a) select new passages that do not exceed 120 words, (b) delete every 5th word or less, and (c) vary the word positions of the deletions. When constructing the alternative choices, include the word originally contained in the text, an incorrect replacement that is the same part of speech, and an incorrect replacement that is a different part of speech. Again, 60% to 70% is the optimal instructional level. If a student performs consistently at or above a 90% accuracy level for three to four maze administrations, introduce more difficult materials, such as a book from the next highest reading level.

Although the maze procedure may be used effectively with elementary students, in most instances an examiner would want to use the cloze procedure when assessing secondary and college students.

Oral and Silent Reading

An examiner may wish to compare a student's reading comprehension performance under two conditions: oral and silent reading. For some students, performance in silent reading is significantly higher than performance in oral reading. Harris and Sipay (1985) noted several reasons why this might be true. As examples, a student may: (a) make minor errors that cause him or her to fail the word-recognition criterion but do not significantly affect comprehension, (b) reread as needed in silent reading, (c) have good language skills and be expert in using context despite weaknesses in word recognition, or (d) become anxious when reading orally and so concerned about word recognition that comprehension suffers.

For other students, oral reading performance may be better than silent reading performance. Differences may occur when a student has had more practice reading orally or when a student is aided by hearing the words. The most likely reason for higher oral reading performance in older students is that oral reading requires sustained attention to the task (Harris & Sipay, 1985).

To compare oral and silent reading, an examiner may use an informal reading inventory that has two comparable passages at each reading level. The student reads one set of passages orally and answers comprehension questions and reads one set silently and answers questions. A difference of at least two reader levels is needed to conclude that the oral and silent reading levels differ significantly (Harris & Sipay, 1985).

Vocabulary

The Reading Vocabulary test measures a student's ability to retrieve the specific meanings of individual words. In some cases, an examiner may wish to explore a student's word knowledge in more depth. Word understanding is not an all or none phenomenon; accuracy in defining a word does not guarantee that the student has acquired full understanding of the word (Glaser, Lesgold, & Lajoie, 1987). Informal inventories may be created to test a student's vocabulary knowledge in one context or to measure an individual's flexibility of usage in different contexts. To assess qualitative differences in levels of word knowledge, the examiner may present items that require specific and precise discriminations, such as discriminating whether a word is used appropriately in a variety of contexts or selecting a variety of synonyms that relate to a word (Curtis & Glaser, 1983).

Listening Comprehension

In some instances, an examiner may wish to analyze reading potential informally. Two factors are highly predictive of reading success: In the primary grades, word recognition speed is the best predictor of reading performance (Lesgold, Resnick, & Hammond, 1985); after the primary grades, listening comprehension tasks are the best predictors of reading comprehension (Curtis, 1980). Reading comprehension reflects listening comprehension which reflects thinking and knowledge (Juel & Leavall, 1988).

Betts (1946, 1957) defined the capacity level as the highest level of readability of material that the learner is able to comprehend when the material is read to him or her. Because successful reading performance ultimately depends upon language facility and understanding of what is read, the capacity level provides an estimate of reading potential. To confirm results from a standardized assessment or to obtain an estimate with the basal series or text used in a classroom, the capacity level may be assessed informally. This is accomplished by reading graded passages from a basal reading series or an informal reading inventory and then asking comprehension questions or asking the student to paraphrase the passage. The capacity or listening level is the highest level at which a student understands the material. This type of procedure is most useful for determining a student's expected achievement in a specific set of instructional materials.

Additional Factors

Many factors affect a student's performance on reading comprehension tasks. Reading comprehension is an interactive, complex process that is influenced by a student's attitude, motivation, interest, background knowledge, and application of strategies. Based upon prior knowledge, experiences, or interest, a student may have good comprehension for one type of material, but low comprehension for another type. Text characteristics, such as the length, structure, and writing style of the author, influence performance. Task requirements, such as the type of questions asked and the type of responses required, may also alter performance. In interpreting student performance and making instructional decisions, an examiner must consider the effects of a variety of factors and the interactive nature of the reading process.

Instructional Modifications

> No one can justify ordering thirty similar third-grade workbooks for the thirty dissimilar third-grade pupils found in any classroom in the country.
>
> (Betts, 1946, p. 525)

An examiner may recommend several different modifications or compensatory strategies for students with difficulty in reading comprehension. The purpose of these modifications is to allow students to work on comprehension tasks independently. Additional modifications that may be appropriate for students with difficulty in reading comprehension are presented in Chapter 5.

Adjust Instructional Level

One critical modification is to adjust the level of the reading material. For teaching comprehension skills, an instructor should present material that is one to two reading levels below the student's instructional reading level for word identification (Choate & Rakes, 1987). This allows the student to concentrate on the comprehension task and not struggle with word identification. If the word identification demands are too difficult, the student encounters too many disruptions in reading.

Identify Interests

During assessment, an examiner may identify a student's interests. Initially, comprehension exercises may be constructed using materials that are related to a student's specific interests and prior knowledge. The student should also be encouraged to engage in independent reading regarding topics of interest.

Alter Assignments

An examiner may recommend that an instructor reduce the number of pages of required reading. As an alternative to reducing the number of pages, an instructor may extend the amount of time allotted for reading assignments and reduce the number of assignments. Or, a procedure such as Skip and Drill, described earlier in the Instructional Modifications for Basic Reading Skills section, may be implemented. In using this procedure for reading comprehension, the mastery criterion is successful completion of the comprehension questions provided with the story.

Identify Important Information

Important information may be identified for a student prior to reading. An instructor may color-code, such as with a yellow highlighter, the sections in the text that a student should read. Advance organizers and study guides may also be used to help students identify and remember the most important information in an assignment. Students may also highlight important facts in a text by writing notes in the margin. In some instances, students will need to purchase books so they may record notes directly in their textbooks.

Use Other Media

Comprehension may be enhanced by providing experiences through other media, such as filmstrips and television. Students may also read along silently while listening to a taped presentation of the text.

Instructional Strategies for Reading Vocabulary

When an examiner notes that a student is low in vocabulary development on the WJ-R ACH Reading Vocabulary, the WJ-R COG Picture Vocabulary, and/or the Oral Vocabulary tests, specific instructional techniques may be recommended. Results from several studies have suggested that reading comprehension improves as a direct result of vocabulary training (Beck, Perfetti, & McKeown, 1982; Stahl, 1983). The common factor in methods for teaching vocabulary is to help students relate new words to words they already know. The goal is for students to develop the ability to learn words independently. Several principles and techniques for teaching vocabulary are described. Additional strategies for vocabulary instruction are discussed in Chapter 5 in the section on Content Area Vocabulary.

Instructional Principles

Englert and Palincsar (1988) suggested three valuable principles for teaching vocabulary. First, the instruction should stimulate interest in learning and using new vocabulary. Second, procedures should be used that emphasize inferring word meanings from word parts by calling attention to the processes used in word formation. For example, the relationships among word families, such as *restrict, restricted,* and *restriction,* would be discussed. Finally, students should be encouraged to derive word meanings from the surrounding context as they read.

Teacher Interaction Method

Eeds and Cockrum (1985) compared three methods of teaching vocabulary: expanding schemata (Teacher Interaction Method), dictionary work, and reading in context. They found that the Teacher Interaction Method was significantly more effective than the other two approaches. The intent of this method was to link new vocabulary to previously learned concepts or schemas. A sequence of four steps was suggested.

1. Activating common experiences. The teacher asks questions that will help the students relate a word to their own personal knowledge. For example, in explaining the word *peculiar,* the teacher may ask the students to recall and discuss strange experiences.
2. Recording an individual experience. The students write down a personal experience that they found to be *peculiar.*
3. Recording a nonexample. The students write down something that is not *peculiar.*
4. Translating into their own words. The students write down in their own words what they think the word *peculiar* means.

Eeds and Cockrum reported that this method is easily adapted for classroom use and appropriate for students of all ages. The method was especially effective for students who had been identified as "less able."

Semantic Feature Analysis

Semantic feature analysis is a vocabulary-building technique that helps students see the relationships among familiar and unfamiliar words. For this exercise, students complete a matrix that identifies both common and unique traits of words classified into the same category. Johnson and Pearson (1984) described the following procedure for developing the matrix:

1. Organize a list of words that share some common features, such as a list of different vehicles, dwellings, or animals. Write these words down the side of the paper or chalkboard.
2. With student assistance, list some features in a row across the top of the paper that are commonly associated with at least one of the words.
3. Have students complete the chart by supplying pluses (+) if the word shares the feature and minuses (−) beside each word that does not share the feature. Students may use a 0 to signify no relationship and a ? when more information is needed (Bos & Vaughn, 1988).
4. If desired, expand the matrix by adding additional words or features.
5. Discuss the completed matrix with students. Examine the patterns of pluses and minuses as they appear on the chart. Help the students to understand that no two words have exactly the same pattern of pluses and minuses and that this fact results in slightly different word meanings.

Figure 3-12 illustrates a matrix that was completed by a group of first-grade students who were studying animals. This type of activity may be used prior to reading to enhance background knowledge or after reading to consolidate information.

Semantic Maps

Semantic maps may also be used in vocabulary instruction to help students see the relationships among words (Johnson & Pearson, 1984). Johnson and Pearson described the following steps for developing semantic vocabulary maps:

1. Choose a key word from a story that the class will be asked to read, or from any other source related to classroom work.
2. Write the word on a large chart tablet or on the chalkboard.
3. Encourage the class to brainstorm as many words as they can that are related to the selected key word and to list them by categories on the paper.
4. Have students share the prepared lists orally and place all words on the map in categories.
5. Have students label the categories on the map. Once the map is complete, a discussion is conducted that encourages students to become aware of new words, gather new meanings from old words, and see the relationships among words.

Animals

	Furry	Wings	Four legs	Pet	Shell
Dog	+	-	+	+	-
Cat	+	-	+	+	-
Bird	-	+	-	+	-
Elephant	-	-	+		-
Turtle	-	-	+	+	+

Figure 3–12. Semantic Feature Analysis Vocabulary Matrix.

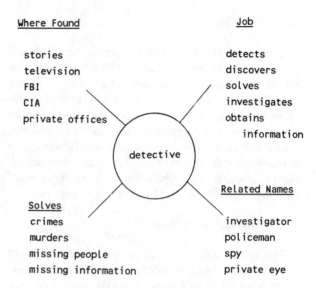

Figure 3–13. Semantic Vocabulary Map.

Figure 3-13 illustrates a sample semantic vocabulary map that was developed by a group of seventh-grade students prior to reading a story about a detective.

Conceivably, both semantic maps and semantic feature analysis would be especially appropriate activities for students with learning disabilities or English as a Second Language (ESL) students who have strengths in visual processing or reasoning, but weaknesses in auditory processing or short-term memory. Both of these techniques may also be adapted to stimulate vocabulary development for writing activities.

Instructional Strategies for Reading Comprehension

> To be effective, remedial instruction in reading must be preceded by careful diagnosis.
>
> (Monroe & Backus, 1937, p. 12)

After assessment, an examiner may wish to recommend specific techniques for improving reading comprehension. The majority of instructional strategies for reading comprehension have two common elements. The first element is an attempt to build background knowledge prior to reading passages. Students are encouraged to identify and clarify the central ideas prior to reading and to become familiar with new vocabulary. The second element is active participation. Students are encouraged to engage actively in the reading process by monitoring their comprehension while they read.

In developing comprehension activities, an instructor should consider the amount of background knowledge that a student possesses regarding the story prior to assigning reading. Pace (1978) investigated the influence of prior knowledge on reading comprehension for students in kindergarten, second, fourth, and sixth grades. The results suggested that even young students are able to perform seemingly sophisticated cognitive operations, such as reconstructing implicit relationships, provided they are familiar with the story situation. In contrast, the more unfamiliar the topic, the more difficulty students had in understanding it. Pace suggested that semantics, not syntax or sentence length, should be the primary consideration in the construction and selection of reading materials. For this reason, a reading method like the Language Experience Approach, described in the Basic Skills section, reduces comprehension demands and may be highly motivating to some students.

In summarizing the research on the use of reading strategies, Wong (1982) reported that efficient readers clarify the purposes for reading, identify and attend to important aspects in the passage, monitor their reading when comprehension falters, and evaluate their comprehension of materials read. Students with poor comprehension require additional instruction and assistance to become more efficient, active readers.

Ernie, a freshman in high school, was referred for an evaluation because of poor reading comprehension in his English class. The English teacher reported that although Ernie pronounced most words correctly and could read passages orally in class, he did not appear to understand what he was reading. In analyzing performance on the WJ-R ACH, the examiner noted that Ernie had above-average performance on the Letter-Word Identification and Word Attack tests. On the Passage Comprehension test, the examiner noted that Ernie had difficulty using both syntactic and semantic information. When asked by the examiner to paraphrase a short story, Ernie cited several minor details about the story, but was unable to explain the plot. When asked what strategies he used to aid his understanding, Ernie commented that he just read all of the words and tried to remember what they meant. When asked to ask the examiner questions about the story, Ernie replied that he couldn't think of anything to ask. The results of the assessment suggested that Ernie did not engage in comprehension-monitoring strategies. As a result, the examiner recommended that Ernie receive instruction using an intervention called reciprocal teaching. This technique involves summarizing, generating questions, clarifying, and predicting text. After using this method for 1 month, Ernie was able to identify and discuss the significant information in a story and employ this strategy independently as an aid for increasing his comprehension.

When an examiner determines that a student has difficulty in reading comprehension, several different remedial techniques may be appropriate. Since the WJ-R ACH Passage Comprehension test is based upon a modified cloze procedure, a student who has difficulty on this type of task may benefit from an instructional strategy such as the cloze technique that is designed to increase ability to use syntactic and semantic clues when reading. A detailed description of this method and several adaptations follow.

Cloze Procedure

Use of the cloze procedure helps a student focus on the conceptual aspect of reading, rather than the perceptual aspect (Kennedy, 1974). One major advantage of the cloze procedure is that language skills are not taught in isolation, but in the context in which they naturally occur (Bortnick & Lopardo, 1973). By providing an experience similar to that which occurs in the actual reading process, the cloze procedure promotes independent reading (Bortnick & Lopardo, 1976). Students involved in cloze exercises are more able to develop, understand, and use the basic resources they bring to the reading act (Valmont, 1983c).

When carefully constructed, cloze passages require the reader to engage in reasoning while reading (Thomas, 1978). This type of instruction not only forces the student to interpret the passage meaning, but also increases awareness of other contextual clues, such as syntactic and semantic information (Bortnick & Lopardo, 1973; Thomas, 1978; Valmont, 1983c). This holistic process promotes reading comprehension and development in students of all ages and abilities. With careful planning and selection of materials, the cloze method and various adaptations help students develop language/reading comprehension abilities when used in both group and individualized instruction.

Materials. Materials are easily adapted to individual needs using the cloze procedure. Passages may be developed from a student's instructional materials. Additionally, materials may be developed for content area instruction.

Guidelines for passage construction. Care must be taken in constructing cloze exercises. If too difficult, the exercises may create frustration for students because the chance of error is much greater than in typical reading exercises (Dwyer, 1980). Several guidelines apply to developing cloze exercises. To begin, an instructor selects materials at the student's independent reading level (Schoenfeld, 1980; Thomas, 1978). Reading difficulty increases when words are deleted (Rye, 1979). An important aspect of the effectiveness of the cloze procedure is the instructor's ability to adjust passages systematically to a student's reading level (Jongsma, 1980).

An estimate of the independent reading level may be obtained by analyzing a student's performance on WJ-R ACH reading tests on the Age/Grade Profile. This profile depicts the level of reading tasks that will be easy (independent) and difficult (frustration) for a student. In estimating this level, an examiner should consider performance in both basic reading skills and reading comprehension.

Initially, an instructor may begin with single sentences and then expand to passages that are no more than 150 words. Further guidelines for passage construction specify that: (a) words should not be deleted from the first and last sentence, (b) the number of spaces between deleted words should vary, (c) deleted words should appear frequently, and (d) the meaning of the deleted words should be understood (Schoenfeld, 1980; Valmont, 1983a). An additional consideration is the position of the deleted words. Words in the middle of the sentence are easiest to predict, followed by words at the end of the sentence, and then words at the beginning (Rye, 1982).

The level of the reading material, the number of omitted words, and the type of omitted words determine the difficulty and appropriateness of the task (Kennedy, 1974). Another factor is the level of required reasoning. To help students develop a foundation in using context clues, an instructor should develop cloze activities that progress from the use of highly predictable content to more abstract text (Choate & Rakes, 1987). As a general principle, cloze tasks should be demanding, but not too difficult or frustrating for the student (Rye, 1982). Adherence to this principle is particularly important when instructing students with special learning needs.

Active student participation. Teacher-directed learning activities are essential for ensuring the success of the cloze procedure (Bortnick & Lopardo, 1973). When using cloze as a teaching tool, a teacher will want to credit acceptable synonyms. This practice provides greater learning opportunity and makes the procedure a more interactive and dynamic teaching method. Thomas (1978) recommended three general steps to follow when implementing cloze:

1. Presentation and preparation: Using short practice sessions, the teacher models how to select responses.
2. Preview and completion: Students read the passages three times. In the first step, preview, the blanks are filled in mentally. In the second step, the student rereads the passage and responses are written. In the final step, completion, the student rereads the passage to ensure that the written responses make sense.
3. Follow-up: The final, most critical step, is the follow-up conference. For this activity, the teacher and students share choices, discuss other acceptable responses, and explain and defend word choices. Discussion of alternative responses and provision of a follow-up conference result in the most effective use of the cloze procedure as a teaching technique (Rye, 1979; Valmont, 1983a). To maximize benefit, students must be involved in the learning activity. One advantage of the cloze procedure is that unlike some remedial methods, this technique provides an opportunity for group oral work in which students are instructed to discuss and determine the deleted word and then provide justifications for their choices (Rye, 1979).

Cloze applications. Cloze exercises may be designed to meet specific instructional objectives (Schoenfeld, 1980; Thomas, 1978). These exercises may emphasize graphophonic (word shape and/or letter sounds), syntactic (grammatical word functions), or semantic (meaning) cueing systems (Lutes, 1982). Several different types of deletions are described below (Schoenfeld, 1980; Thomas, 1978, 1979a).

Context/content: Content words that complete key ideas in the selection are deleted. In relative order of predictive difficulty, content words include nouns, main verbs, adjectives, and adverbs (Rye, 1982). By removing only content words, greater emphasis is placed on comprehension, and the potential for discussion is increased (Rye, 1979, 1982).

Specific word class: A particular part of speech may be deleted from the passage. For example, an instructor may delete all of the nouns to improve understanding of noun functions in a sentence. Or, an instructor may delete all of the adjectives to improve understanding of the role of descriptive words.

Specific phonic elements: Specific phonic elements, such as consonant digraphs or short vowel sounds, may be

deleted from the passage. As an alternative, specific phonic elements may be highlighted throughout an entire passage with the rest of the word deleted to aid in transfer of skills. For example, the student would have to complete all words beginning with "th."

Specific morphemic elements: Specific morphemes, such as prefixes, suffixes, or root words, may be deleted. Practice with this type of deletion may be particularly effective for secondary or college students who tend to omit word endings in their writing.

Function or structure words: Specific function words such as prepositions, articles, auxiliary verbs, or conjunctions may be eliminated from the text. Perceiving relationships among ideas is basic to reading comprehension. Because function words often cue these relationships, practice with these words will assist readers in attending to these language features.

Pronouns and pronoun referents: Pronouns, pronoun referents, or a combination of the two may be deleted. Because misuse of pronouns and pronoun referents may produce ambiguity and confusion when reading, cloze exercises may be designed to highlight and improve an individual's understanding of these relationships.

Organizational patterns: In the various types of organizational patterns used by authors, specific key words that signal organizational type are used. By deleting these key words in a cloze pattern, the reader discovers paragraph patterns. The following organizational types with example key words may be presented: (a) simple listing—*first, second, next, then,* and *finally*; (b) time order—*on* (date), *not long after, now, before, after,* and *when*; (c) comparison/contrast—*however, but, as well as, different, on the other hand,* and *similarly*; and (d) cause/effect—*because, therefore, consequently, as a result, so that, nevertheless,* and *since.* Figure 3-14 provides sample illustrations of several types of cloze deletions.

Different objectives may be accomplished using a variety of cloze exercises. In some instances, specific cloze deletions may be used to supplement instruction, such as a lesson on prefixes, conjunctions, or a certain phonic skill; in other instances, an examiner may recommend a specific type of deletion to address a problem area for an individual student, such as a difficulty in forming plurals or using conjunctions.

Cloze adaptations for the primary grades. Several adaptations of the cloze procedure are appropriate for elementary students. These adaptations simplify the procedure.

1. Context/content clues

    The largest country in the world is _____,

    located to the _____ of the United States.

2. Specific word class

    As the young _____ walked into _____,

    he saw his good _____, the _____.

3. Specific phonic elements

    The d___g r___n away from the b___g c___t.

4. Specific morphemic elements

    After the third strike, the catch___ threw the

    ball to the pitcher___.

5. Function or structure words

    It was twelve o'clock _____ night when Martha

    went _____ bed.

6. Pronouns

    The man ran around the track as fast as ____ could.

7. Pronoun referents

    Sara was happy to receive a letter from her son.

    It was the first time _____ had written _____.

8. Organizational patterns

    First, sand the wood, _____ paint it red,

    _____ assemble the pieces.

Figure 3–14. Sample Deletion Patterns for Cloze Exercises.

Visual clues: One method for simplifying the cloze procedure is to provide additional visual clues, such as several of the missing letters of a word. The missing letters are then combined with the blanks that approximate the length of the deleted word (Valmont, 1983c). For example, if the deleted word is *school*, the blank may appear: sc___l. A more difficult variation is to just present the corresponding number of word blanks (Dwyer, 1980; Quillin & Dwyer, 1978). The word *school* is represented by six blanks. Boxes that display word configuration and shape may also be used (Rye, 1982). For example, the box for the word *night* would be presented as follows:

Although these visual clues help ensure success in the early stages of learning the cloze procedure, they limit the demands on the student. For this reason, reliance on supplementary clues, such as visual patterns, should be reduced as soon as possible (Rye, 1982).

Maze: The most familiar adaptation of the cloze procedure is the maze technique. The major difference between the two techniques is that in the cloze procedure, graphic information is removed; in the maze procedure, graphic information is added (Valmont, 1983b, 1983c; Wiseman & McKenna, 1978). In this approach, the student selects the best response from choices of responses.

The maze procedure may be used to introduce early elementary students to the cloze procedure. Initially, a few choices are provided for the deleted word and the number of choices is increased gradually as the student gains experience with the procedure. Blachowicz (1977) suggested that the first exercises should contain two unambiguous distractors. Later, more difficult exercises may be constructed and attention may be drawn to specific word classes or features, such as graphophonic clues. The following example emphasizes the use of graphophonic clues:

horse.

The girl rides her favorite house.

harsh.

Pearson and Spiro (1980) recommended the use of a maze procedure for directing attention to specific word meanings. Students are given maze activities that provide three semantically correct choices: however, only one has a precise semantic fit. The following example emphasizes the use of precise semantic clues:

walked

Sallie was so happy, she   ran   to the park.

skipped

Even though the maze procedure provides a simple format for introducing primary students to prediction procedures (Blachowicz, 1977), a teacher will want to move a child from the maze procedure to the cloze

procedure as rapidly as possible. Cloze is a recall task, whereas maze is a recognition task (Wiseman & McKenna, 1978). When alternative responses are provided, a student's attention is focused on the alternatives, rather than on the context. The most effective procedure requires the reader to generate the language (Rye, 1982).

An instructor may use a continuum to progress from the maze to the cloze procedure. First, provide two choices; then provide three choices; then place all the deleted words at the end of a passage with a few distractor words; finally, introduce a standard cloze format (Silky, 1979).

Maze exercises may continue to be appropriate for activities such as vocabulary development or introduction of the cloze method in content areas. Because of its success-oriented nature, the maze procedure may initially be more appropriate for students with a history of learning failure. In addition to the maze procedure, three other variations may be used to introduce students to the cloze procedure: Zip, Oral Cloze, and Synonym Cloze (Blachowicz, 1977).

Zip: Zip is a group adaptation of the cloze procedure that provides instantaneous feedback. To begin, a story or short passage is copied onto an overhead transparency. The words that are selected for deletion are covered with masking tape. The story is then placed on an overhead projector, and students are asked to read the story. In the next reading, words are predicted and the choices are discussed one at a time. After the children have suggested possible responses, the tape is pulled off to reveal the actual word. The class then discusses the choices. The transparency may be used again with different words masked or students may prepare their own transparencies for class. An instructor may increase awareness of word classes by asking the children to tape over all the nouns or verbs. In addition to being a highly motivating technique, this procedure is particularly appropriate for introducing young students to the cloze procedure.

Oral cloze: Oral cloze tasks involve listening to a passage and then supplying a missing word. The WJ-R COG Listening Comprehension test is a modified oral cloze task. In addition to an assessment procedure, this exercise may also be used as an instructional technique. The following procedure may be used: (a) instructor deletes content words from a high-interest selection and then reads the altered passage aloud, (b) instructor reads the passage aloud again to the class and pauses for the deleted words, and (c) students suggest words that would make sense. After each response is given, the instructor and students discuss the choice. As a final step, students may tape-record different versions of the story using varied responses.

Hasson (1983) found that oral cloze instruction was an effective instructional technique for improving kindergarten children's ability to supply words. Stories were selected from kindergarten story books. Words in the book were covered as the teacher showed the story to the students while reading it. When the teacher came to a deletion, she stopped reading and the children guessed the word. Each response was discussed as to whether it was appropriate for the story context.

In addition to preparing children for written cloze exercises, a teacher may find that oral variations of the cloze procedure are useful for children with low reading or listening comprehension skills, reasoning difficulties, or language problems or differences. A student who performs poorly on the WJ-R COG Listening Comprehension test may benefit from oral cloze activities.

Synonym cloze: In synonym cloze selected words are deleted and replaced with lines and then synonyms or synonym phrases are placed below the lines. In addition to helping young children, this procedure may also help older students who need additional clues to complete cloze exercises.

Cloze adaptations for upper elementary, secondary, and college students. Several adaptations of the cloze procedure may be used with upper elementary, secondary, and college students. A description of these techniques follows.

Synonym cloze: Synonym cloze may be used as a more advanced procedure to help students expand their vocabulary. One adaptation is to prepare a worksheet in which the student is asked to replace simple vocabulary with words that are more precise. An instructor may also use a student's written work. Words that are to be replaced with more precise vocabulary are underlined or erased and written underneath the blank.

Restoration: Another adaptation is to take a story or report that a student has written and delete certain words with correction fluid (Giordano, 1983b). The student then attempts to restore the deleted words. More advanced students may use a passage written by someone else and attempt to restore words that are grammatical and maintain sentence meaning. Another variation is to have a student delete words from a story and then exchange papers with another student who attempts to restore the words.

Cloze passages may also be developed using language experience stories (Lopardo, 1975). Students may exchange papers or attempt to reconstruct their own story. Once the deletions have been restored to a story, the student compares the restored story to the original typed version.

Reading fluency: In order for a student to become a fluent reader, decoding must become automatic. A component

skill of fluent automatic decoding is the ability to combine prior context with sound-symbol relationships quickly so that an unknown word does not have to be completely processed before it is identified (Cunningham, 1979). (Several methods of building fluency are discussed in the section on Instructional Strategies for Reading Fluency). Cunningham outlined a procedure that combines a fluency technique and a modified cloze procedure to build reading comprehension. A summary of this procedure follows:

1. Select a passage at the student's independent reading level.
2. Delete part of every 20th word that starts with a consonant or consonant cluster, exposing only the initial consonant or consonant cluster. No more than 5% of the words are deleted.
3. Have the student read the passage silently and then answer at least one comprehension question.
4. When students request help, such as the pronunciation or meaning of unknown words, direct them to guess and continue reading.
5. After students have read the passage silently, guessing at the deleted words, have one student read the passage orally.
6. Finally, instruct students to reread the passage and fill in the blanks.

In initially considering the use of this procedure, an instructor may feel that cloze is incompatible with promoting reading fluency and speed. The difference between this adaptation and a standard cloze format is that the teacher encourages the students to make rapid responses rather than to ponder over an answer. The purpose is to increase a student's capacity to decode words rapidly by sampling graphophonic information, in this instance, initial consonants. This added graphic information may help create an automatic response to the deleted word and help a student develop the habit of anticipating and predicting words using a combination of graphophonic, syntactic, and semantic clues.

If an examiner observes that a student is having trouble with other aspects of comprehension, such as using background knowledge, maintaining interest, or understanding vocabulary, other strategies for increasing reading performance would be more appropriate. The following techniques encourage the student to become an active participant in the reading process.

Semantic Maps

Semantic maps may be used as a prereading, during reading, or postreading activity. (The procedure for this technique is described more fully in Chapter 4). Semantic maps provide a graphic outline of a story or passage. The concepts or story parts are linked together to illustrate the interrelationships. Sinatra, Berg, and Dunn (1985) used this approach to improve the reading comprehension of three upper elementary students with learning disabilities. Following map development on the chalkboard, students were asked to read passages silently and then answer multiple-choice comprehension questions. In most instances, comprehension scores improved when semantic maps were constructed prior to reading. Sinatra et al. hypothesized that the visualization of this schema helps students to organize and predict content while it is being read. Furthermore, they suggested that this technique should appeal to students with nonverbal strengths.

Story Grammar

Story grammar (also discussed in Chapter 4) may be used to increase reading comprehension. Results from recent research have indicated that students with learning disabilities differ from normally achieving peers in the amount as well as the type of information they include in both oral retellings and written stories (Montague, Maddux, & Dereshiwsky, 1990). In summarizing the findings of story grammar research, Whaley (1981) presented two important implications for classroom practice: (a) Knowledge of story components facilitates comprehension and memory of stories and (b) knowledge of story components increases developmentally. Additionally, story grammar instruction appears to improve comprehension of students with low achievement and students with learning disabilities. Newby, Caldwell, and Recht (1989) found that when a story grammar strategy was taught and applied by students with learning disabilities, their reading comprehension improved. The students using this strategy were able to recall an increased number of story elements.

Similarly, Carnine and Kinder (1985) demonstrated that schema-based strategies improved the reading comprehension of low-performing elementary students. This story grammar strategy may be introduced to the students by saying: "We are going to read an action story. In an action story we ask four questions." The teacher then states the four questions:

1. Who is the story about?
2. What is he or she trying to do?
3. What happens when he or she tries to do it?
4. What happens in the end?

Three stages are used for instruction. In the first stage, the teacher reads a story aloud and asks story grammar questions at relevant points. In the second stage, the students read the story aloud and the teacher asks story grammar questions at appropriate times throughout the story. In these two stages, the teacher responds to any errors on questions by modeling a correct answer. In the third stage, the students read a story silently and ask themselves the four questions while they are reading. Students may be encouraged to write responses to the questions.

Griffey, Zigmond, and Leinhardt (1988) found that combining the identification of story structure elements with a self-questioning strategy was effective for improving reading comprehension of students with learning disabilities in third through fifth grade. Strategy training was accomplished in four 30-minute training sessions. The script presented in Table 3-4 was used to teach self-questioning and the story structure strategy CAPS (Character, Aim, Problem, Solution).

This type of technique also appears to be effective with upper-level secondary students. Singer and Donlan (1982) taught nonhandicapped eleventh-grade students how to generate story-specific questions for better comprehension of complex short stories. Students generated and answered questions regarding text structure elements such as the main characters, the setting, the goal, the obstacles, the outcomes, and the general theme. Students in a control group were presented with teacher-generated questions prior to reading and were then asked to write essays about the stories based upon the questions. In postsession evaluations, students instructed in the story grammar strategy answered significantly more comprehension questions than did students in the control group who read and studied the story.

Similarly, Gurney, Gersten, Dimino, and Carnine (1990) found that a story grammar procedure was an effective instructional strategy for high school students with learning disabilities. The structure of the story grammar strategy provided a framework that helped the students analyze short stories and answer questions based on the stories they read. In teaching the strategy, the instructor modeled the process and the students recorded the components on a notesheet. Through direct instruction, followed by guided practice, the students were able to learn to use the strategy independently. The story grammar strategy included four major components:

1. Identifying the main problem or conflict. Students were asked to identify the main character and the conflict that he or she faced. Both major and minor problems were identified.
2. Character clues. Students were asked to draw inferences from the text about the personalities and motivations of the main characters. The character clues included a description of the action, dialogue, thoughts, physical attributes, or reactions to other characters.

Session One

Self-Questioning Plus CAPS Strategy

"The method you are going to learn today is called *CAPS*, and can be used to help you find answers to *your own* questions about what is important in a story."

1—WRITE CAPS ON BOARD

"Most stories, although not all of them, have the same story parts. These stories have at least one main character and sometimes more. These characters are usually people or, even sometimes, they can be animals. Second, the main character or characters have a goal or an aim. I'm going to tell you a very short story that will help you understand. Bobby and Sally, the characters in this story, want to earn money so they can go to the circus. Going to the circus is the aim of the characters. Third, in most stories something will happen that will make it harder for the characters to do what they want to do. For instance, Bobby and Sally may decide to mow lawns in order to get enough money to go to the circus, but find out that they have no gas for the lawn mower. The next part of the story will be about how they solve this problem. They may go to a gas station and ask if they could "borrow" some gas until they make enough money cutting lawns to pay for it. The gas station attendant agrees to "loan" them some gas and the problem is solved. Finally, they spend the rest of the day cutting lawns and raise enough money not only for the gas but also to go to the circus."

"Let's see if we can name the different parts of the story we just heard—OK? First, we met the main *characters*, Bobby and Sally, then we learned that they wanted to go to the circus, which was their *aim*. Next we found out that they had a *problem*, they wanted to mow lawns to raise money for the circus but they had no gas for their lawn mower. They *solved* this problem by "borrowing" some gas, and were able to raise enough money to go to the circus."

"So, we have the *characters*, the *aim* of the story, a *problem*, and a *solution*."

2—INSTRUCTOR WRITES THE STORY STRUCTURE ELEMENTS ON CHALKBOARD

CAPS Means   C = CHARACTERS
              A = AIM
              P = PROBLEM
              S = SOLUTION

3—MAKE SURE STUDENTS ARE PAYING ATTENTION

Session Two

Model Self-Questioning Plus CAPS Strategy

"The next thing you are going to do is to learn a way which will help you remember these story parts so that you can locate them in the stories that you read."

"A good way to do this is to ask yourself questions as you are reading. These questions should be about the story parts we talked about yesterday. Here is a story that we will use to help you learn the CAPS method."

1—GIVE EACH STUDENT A COPY OF GOING TO THE ZOO

"Let's take a few minutes and read the story called *Going to the Zoo*. I'll read slowly so everyone can keep up—OK? Also I will be asking myself the CAPS questions as I am reading—so please listen to the story and to my questions."

2—AS INSTRUCTOR READS THE STORY AT A SLOW PACE, MONITOR STUDENT'S ATTENTION

3—THE FIRST QUESTIONS SHOULD RELATE TO ALL STORY STRUCTURE ELEMENTS

"What do I want to know? I want to know who the main *characters* are, what the *aim* of the story is, if a *problem* happens, and how the problem is *solved*. As I read the story I want to keep the idea of CAPS in mind to help me answer the questions."

4—AS THE STORY IS READ THE INSTRUCTOR SHOULD ASK STORY STRUCTURE QUESTIONS AT THE APPROPRIATE STORY STRUCTURE LOCATIONS

"Who are the characters?—Sue, Sam and Mary."
"What is the aim of the story?—To go to the zoo."
"Is there a problem?—Yes, it started to rain."
"How did the characters solve the problem?—They played inside and dressed up like zoo animals."

5—AFTER READING THE STORY AND ASKING THE QUESTIONS THE INSTRUCTOR SHOULD SUMMARIZE THE PASSAGE BY STATING THE ANSWERS TO THE STORY AND WRITE THEM ON THE BOARD; FOR EXAMPLE:

"*Sue, Sam, and Mary* wanted *to go to the zoo*, but it *started to rain*, so they *stayed home and dressed up like zoo animals.*"

6—THE INSTRUCTOR SHOULD REVIEW THE CAPS STRATEGY BY ASKING THE STUDENTS THE FOLLOWING QUESTIONS (GROUP RESPONSE)

"Who were the main characters in this story?—Sue, Sam and Mary."
"What was the aim of the story?—To go to the zoo."
"What problem happened?—It started to rain."
"How did they solve the problem?—They stayed home and dressed up like zoo animals."

7—THEN ASK: (GROUP RESPONSE)

"What do the letters in *CAPS* mean?"

8—THE INSTRUCTOR SHOULD TELL THE STUDENTS THAT TOMORROW THEY WILL REVIEW THE CAPS METHOD AGAIN AND HAVE A CHANCE TO PRACTICE USING IT WHILE READING A STORY

Session Three

Practice and Feedback

1—INSTRUCTOR SHOULD REVIEW THE CAPS STRATEGY

A. WRITE CAPS ON CHALKBOARD
B. REMIND STUDENTS TO USE CAPS WHEN READING A STORY BY ASKING QUESTIONS
C. REVIEW THE QUESTIONS
    1. WHO ARE THE CHARACTERS?
    2. WHAT IS THE AIM OF THE STORY?
    3. WHAT PROBLEM HAPPENS?
    4. HOW IS THE PROBLEM SOLVED?
D. GO OVER THE EXAMPLE FROM SESSION TWO—GOING TO THE ZOO

Table 3–4. Script for the Story Structure Strategy CAPS. *Note.* From "The Effects of Self-Questioning and Story Structure Training on the Reading Comprehension of Poor Readers" by Q.L. Griffey, N. Zigmond, and G. Leinhardt, 1988, *Learning Disabilities Research*, *4*, pp. 48–49. Copyright 1988 by the Division of Learning Disabilities. Reprinted by permission.

3. Resolution. Students were asked to identify how the main character solves or fails to solve the problems.
4. Theme. Students were asked to identify what the author was trying to say to the reader. In determining the theme, students were asked to consider the main characters, the major conflict, the character clues related to the conflict, and the resolution or solution to the problem. The stated theme needed to be appropriately related to the other story grammar components.

In teaching the strategy, Gurney et al. noted that the theme was the most difficult story grammar component to teach and required more extensive modeling and explanation than the other components. Once students had mastered the strategy, they were able to use it to help them identify and articulate the most important ideas in a story.

Whaley (1981) described several additional instructional techniques that may be applied to story grammar instruction, including: (a) prediction task, (b) macrocloze task, (c) scrambled stories, (d) sorting task, and (e) retelling stories. In a prediction task, the students read incomplete stories and then tell aloud or write what they think will come next. For example, after reading about the setting, students may predict that the beginning will come next. In the macrocloze task, a whole story category is deleted, and the students read the text and attempt to fill in the missing material either orally or in writing. The instructor may omit the setting, problem, outcome, or conclusion. In the scrambled stories activity, a story is separated into story element parts and then scrambled. The reader is asked to reorder the parts to make a good story. In the sorting task, students read a brief story and then the teacher gives them sentence strips of all the sentences in the story. The students are asked to sort the sentences into piles that go together. For retelling stories, students are asked to retell simple stories following the sequence of story components.

Initial research findings suggest that the combination of questioning strategies with story grammar techniques is an effective procedure for improving reading comprehension in students of all ages with and without learning problems. These types of techniques help students understand the structure of stories and monitor their comprehension while reading.

Story Frames and Maps

Both story frames and story maps may be used to provide additional practice with story grammar and assist students in attending to the important information in the story. These types of techniques may be most effective with students who have developed basic reading skills but who need assistance in reading comprehension.

Story maps. The purpose of story maps is to help students develop strategies for understanding a story. A story map is a unified representation of a story that is based upon a logical organization and the interrelationships of the central ideas and events (Beck & McKeown, 1981). Beck, Omanson, and McKeown (1982) found that students who were asked questions related to a story map recalled more of the important information than students who were given questions from the teacher's manual of the basal reader. Beck and McKeown described the following steps for constructing and applying maps:

1. The teacher identifies the starting point of the story.
2. The teacher and students summarize the important events and ideas that form the plot or theme of the story and draw these events in a map. The transitions are discussed and attention is directed to both explicit and implicit ideas.
3. This outline or map then serves as the basis for questions. Questions that follow the form of the map are presented to the class for discussion.

In contrast to the questions in basal reading series, questions based upon a story map provide increased emphasis to the sequential and relational aspects of the story. By identifying the primary ideas and the relationships among them, students' comprehension and retention of stories are enhanced. As an alternate activity, an instructor may separate a story into its components and then have a student reassemble the story pieces in the correct sequence, as in the scrambled stories activity.

This technique has been used to improve the comprehension of groups of high-achieving students as well as students with learning disabilities. One advantage of story maps is that they may be used for large group instruction. Idol (1987) used a story mapping technique that improved the reading comprehension of low achieving students and students with learning disabilities and allowed these students to work together with classmates on comprehension exercises. The higher achieving students' progress was not impeded by this technique.

Four phases were used in this method. In the first phase, the teacher modeled the desired responses. In the second phase, the teacher assisted students with responses. In the third phase, the test phase, students wrote in responses independently. In the last phase, comprehension responses were monitored without the use of the story map. This phase was implemented when students had 80% correct responses to the questions for two consecutive days. This design promoted generalization by teaching students to apply the strategy independently. Figures 3-15 and 3-16 illustrate the story map and the questions.

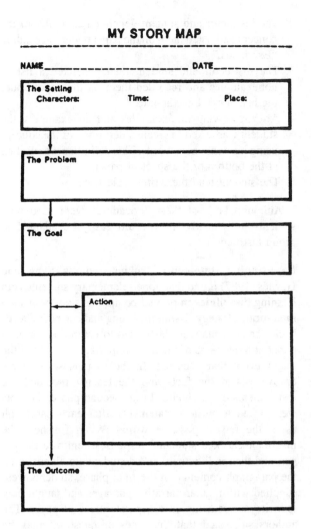

MY STORY MAP

NAME_____ DATE_____

The Setting
Characters: Time: Place:

The Problem

The Goal

Action

The Outcome

Figure 3–15. Story Map Form. *Note.* From "Group Story Mapping: A Comprehension Strategy for Both Skilled and Unskilled Readers" by L. Idol, 1987, *Journal of Learning Disabilities, 20*, p. 199. Copyright 1987 by Pro-Ed. Reprinted by permission.

Story frames. Story frames may also be used to provide students with an outline to link information together. Students complete the frame while reading, and then the frames may be used to guide discussions. An example of a story frame used by Fowler and Davis (1985) is presented in Chapter 4. Once students have learned to apply story frames in groups, they can use them individually. Fowler (1982) described the following steps for constructing story frames:

1. Read a passage or story and identify the problem on which you want the students to focus.
2. Select the paragraph that addresses the problem.
3. Delete all words, phrases, and sentences except those needed to sustain the purpose of the paragraph.

Name: _____

Date: _____

1. Where did this story take place?
2. When did this story take place?
3. Who were the main characters in the story?
4. Were there any other important characters in the story? Who?
5. What was the problem in the story?
6. How did _____ try to solve the problem?
7. Was it hard to solve the problem? Explain.
8. Was the problem solved? Explain.
9. What did you learn from reading this story? Explain.
10. Can you think of a different ending?

Figure 3–16. Story Map Questions. *Note.* From "Group Story Mapping: A Comprehension Strategy for Both Skilled and Unskilled Readers" by L. Idol, 1987, *Journal of Learning Disabilities, 20*, p. 197. Copyright 1987 by Pro-Ed. Reprinted by permission.

4. Try the frame with other passages or stories that are similar in theme. Modify the frame so that it may be used in several situations.

Teachers may develop frames that are based upon a specific story, using such phrases as: *To begin, . . .* ; *The problem starts when . . .* ; *The main character decides to . . .* ; *The problem is solved when . . .* ; and, *At the end . . .* , etc. To complete the frames, students write in the specific details as they read the stories.

When presenting reading assignments using story frames and story maps, the instructor should provide stories that are at a student's independent reading level in basic reading skills. As noted, an estimate of the student's independent reading level may be obtained by analyzing performance on the WJ-R ACH reading tests on the Age/Grade Profile. Presenting material at the independent reading level allows students to focus their attention on answering the questions and understanding the stories.

Direct Strategy Instruction

The purpose of direct instruction in strategies is to teach a student how to comprehend. For some students with special learning needs, this may be accomplished by exposing them to what goes on in the mind. The teacher models in a step-by-step manner the unobservable process or steps that a reader uses to comprehend text (Samuels, 1986). Darch and Kameenui (1987) found that direct instruction was superior to discussion/workbook activities for teaching critical reading skills to elementary students with learning disabilities. Similarly, Sachs (1983) found that using intervention strategies prior to reading was more effective than worksheet activities for improving the comprehension of elementary students with learning disabilities. Several strategies may be used either prior to reading, during reading, or after reading to help students improve their comprehension. These types of activities may be especially beneficial to students with low oral language.

Directed Reading Activity and Concept Analysis Activity. Sachs (1983) described two prereading procedures, Directed Reading Activity (DRA) and Concept Analysis Activity (CAA), that were effective for improving the evaluative reading comprehension of students with learning disabilities.

In the modified DRA, the following steps were used:

1. To promote interest in the story, the instructor asked the student to preview the text and find the illustration that was most interesting.
2. After discussing the illustration, the instructor displayed pictures that were related to the story, such as zoo animals for a story about an animal in the jungle. The student was then encouraged to discuss past experiences related to the narrative.
3. The instructor presented five vocabulary words from the story. The instructor and student read the sentence with each vocabulary word and then the student made up a sentence that contained the word.
4. A 5-minute information question-answer session was conducted to discuss the central story theme.
5. To set the purpose for reading, the last step required the student to predict what the story was about based upon the title.

The intent of the modified CAA was to help students understand the story's central concept by drawing upon their background experience and prior knowledge. For the CAA, the following steps were used:

1. Using magic marker, the instructor wrote the central concept of the written selection on a sheet of unlined paper.

2. The instructor and student generated examples of the concept and listed them on the paper under the heading "Examples."
3. The instructor and student then generated a list of nonexamples and recorded them on the paper under the heading "Nonexamples."
4. After reviewing the examples and nonexamples, the student was asked to create a definition of the concept using his or her own words. This definition was written at the bottom of the sheet of paper.
5. The student read the written selection.

Although both of these procedures were used with students individually, they could easily be adapted to group instruction.

Paragraph restatements. Jenkins, Heliotis, Stein, and Haynes (1987) found that upper-elementary students with learning disabilities improved comprehension by using a monitoring strategy. Using modeling and corrective feedback, the students were instructed to determine for each paragraph the name of the most important person and the major event that occurred. In the first phase, students orally restated the facts and the teacher recorded the restatements on the board. In the second phase, students were asked to write restatements after each paragraph using the fewest possible words. When finished, the instructor checked students' responses, removed the paper, and then individually asked students to elaborate on the paragraph contents. In the final phase, students were supplied with regular narrative passages and taught how to write restatements on a separate piece of paper. The authors suggested that the types of questions may be modified according to the type of material. This technique may also be effective for non-fiction and content area reading.

TELLS Fact or Fiction. Idol-Maestas (1985) found that four learning disabled elementary and two secondary students were able to improve their performance on comprehension questions when an advance organizer, named TELLS Fact or Fiction, was used. This organizer helped familiarize students with stories prior to reading them. The strategy steps included:

T: Study story titles.
E: Examine and skim pages to discover what the story is about.
L: Look for important words.
L: Look for hard words.
S: Think about the setting.

As a last step, students were asked to decide whether the story was fact or fiction. When the teacher-guided assistance was discontinued, the secondary students maintained their improved performance in inferential comprehension, but the elementary students did not. Idol-Maestas hypothesized that the older students were more cognitively aware of when to apply strategies.

An important aspect of strategy instruction is to ensure that the techniques generalize to new situations. Elementary students may require substantially more practice with application of strategies than secondary students. Additionally, students with learning disabilities are most successful when instruction provides a detailed strategy and ample practice opportunities for applying the technique to written materials (Darch & Kameenui, 1987).

Self-questioning strategies. Asking students to form questions prior to reading is another procedure used to increase recall. Wong and Jones (1982) found that the comprehension of junior high students with learning disabilities improved with instruction in a self-questioning strategy. To begin, students were instructed in how to turn the main idea statement into a paraphrased question. Prompt cards were provided to help students remember the strategy. The strategy consisted of the following steps:

1. Identify the purpose for studying the passage.
2. Find the main idea and underline it.
3. Develop a question about the main idea.
4. Learn the answer to your question.
5. Review questions and answers to see how each successive question provides you with further information.

After the exercises, students were provided with individual corrective feedback. Using this self-questioning training, students' awareness of important textual elements improved substantially, as did their ability to formulate questions about the main ideas. Additionally, Wong (1979) found that simply supplying questions prior to reading improved the comprehension of fifth-grade students with learning disabilities. Forming questions prior to reading enabled the students to become active participants in the reading process.

Billingsley and Wildman (1988) found that secondary students with learning disabilities could improve their ability to monitor their comprehension during reading using a brief prereading activity that combined a structured overview and self-questioning activity. In this procedure the students were first presented with a visual framework of the main ideas in the passage. Following presentation of the structured overview, the students were asked to formulate questions related to the passage. The instructor recorded all of the questions that were generated by the students. Providing a structured overview and encouraging students to form questions prior to reading promote active involvement with text.

Reciprocal teaching. Another procedure for teaching self-questioning and comprehension monitoring that promotes active involvement is reciprocal teaching (Palincsar, 1986b; Palincsar & Brown, 1984, 1986). The focus of this method is on critical thinking skills rather than on isolated reading skills: A student is taught to monitor comprehension and to read for meaning. All instruction is embedded in the context of reading for a purpose. This interactive procedure has been used successfully for improving the comprehension of seventh-grade students who were poor readers (Palincsar & Brown, 1984). Additionally, Palincsar and Brown (1986) reported that reciprocal teaching has been used effectively in larger, heterogeneous groups of students in middle school remedial reading classes. The method is designed primarily for students who are able to decode grade-level material, but whose comprehension of test is below grade level (Palincsar & Brown, 1986).

In the procedure, the following four skills are taught: questioning, summarizing, clarifying, and predicting. Questioning and summarizing help students identify and paraphrase the important information in the text. Clarifying alerts the teacher to any comprehension difficulties. Predicting helps students link their background knowledge with the information they will acquire.

The procedure is based on five principles: (a) teacher models the desired comprehension activities; (b) strategies are always modeled in context not as isolated activities; (c) discussion emphasizes both text content and the student's understanding of why the strategies are being used; (d) teacher provides feedback based on student progress; and (e) teacher gives control of activities to the student as soon as possible (Palincsar, 1986b).

To begin, the instructor and student read a paragraph or segment of a passage. After the passage is completed, the instructor and student generate questions about the segment, summarize the content in a sentence, discuss and clarify any hard parts, and then predict what will happen in the next paragraph or segment. These activities are conducted in a natural dialogue with the teacher and student giving feedback to each other and alternating roles as dialogue leader. The teacher or leader takes responsibility for generating the summary, asking questions, leading the discussion about difficult parts, and predicting the next topic. Sessions last for about 30 minutes and may be conducted individually or in small groups of from four to seven students (Palincsar & Brown, 1984). At the end of the 30-minute teaching period, students receive a new passage to read independently and then generate a summary or answer questions.

Reciprocal teaching may also be used effectively with first-grade students as a listening activity: The teacher reads the text aloud and then the teacher and students discuss it (Palincsar, 1986a).

Other specific learning strategies have been developed for junior high and secondary students. To use any of these strategies, a student must possess at least fourth-grade-level reading skill.

RIDER. Clark, Deshler, Schumaker, Alley, and Warner (1984) taught a visual imagery and a self-questioning strategy with the acronym RIDER to secondary students with learning disabilities, to facilitate reading comprehension and increase their interaction with text. Practice was first provided on materials at the student's ability level and then on materials from grade level. The results supported the conclusion that students with learning disabilities may be taught to use strategies to improve their reading comprehension and that they are able to apply these strategies to grade-level materials.

In the RIDER visual imagery strategy, students were instructed to:

1. *Read.* Read the first sentence.
2. *Image.* Try to make a picture in your mind.
3. *Describe.* Describe your image. Continue reading if you can't make one. Modify and add to the image as you read on.
4. *Evaluate.* Evaluate the image for completeness. If the image is comprehensive, continue.
5. *Repeat.* Read the next sentence and repeat the first four steps.

The self-questioning strategy encourages students to form questions to maintain interest and enhance recall. While reading, a student asks and answers five common types of "WH" questions: who, what, where, when, and why. This type of strategy may be applied to both fiction and nonfiction.

Paraphrasing strategy. The paraphrasing strategy was developed at the University of Kansas Institute of Research in Learning Disabilities (Schumaker, Denton, & Deshler, 1984). The students are taught the following steps that are represented with the acronym RAP: (a) *R*ead a paragraph and think of what the words mean; (b) *A*sk yourself what the main ideas and details in this paragraph were?; and (c) *P*ut the main ideas and details into your own words.

When paraphrasing the student makes one general statement about each paragraph. The statements are tape-recorded or written. Each statement must be accurate, have new and useful information, make sense, and be in the student's own words. Students with learning disabilities who used this paraphrasing strategy were able to increase their ability to answer comprehension questions about grade-level material.

Multipass. Schumaker, Deshler, Alley, Warner, and Denton (1982) described Multipass, a learning strategy that has been used successfully with secondary students with learning disabilities. This strategy and others that are particularly appropriate for content area textbooks are described in Chapter 5 in the section on Content Area Reading.

Conclusion

After analyzing a student's performance on the WJ-R ACH reading comprehension tests and administering other informal assessments, as needed, an examiner will be able to recommend an effective program for enhancing an individual's vocabulary and ability to derive meaning from text. For vocabulary development, activities that help students relate new words to known words and increase their ability to learn words independently are the most effective. For reading comprehension, methods and strategies that encourage active involvement and comprehension monitoring are the most productive. A variety of instructional approaches may be used to enhance students' abilities to identify, predict, and construct meaning. Instruction in the application of these strategies will help students become independent learners and use reading to expand their world knowledge.

4

WRITTEN LANGUAGE

Written language is the quintessence of verbal language. It allows for the ultimate integration of all linguistic processes. To neglect it is to ignore a buried treasure.

(Dagenais & Beadle, 1984, p. 83)

The WJ-R ACH written language tests provide information regarding several facets of writing. Although these tests do not measure all aspects of writing skill, analysis of a student's results on the writing tests will provide an examiner with considerable diagnostic information for instructional planning. Two tests, Dictation in the Standard Battery and Proofing in the Supplemental Battery, measure basic writing skills. Two other tests, Writing Samples in the Standard Battery and Writing Fluency in the Supplemental Battery, measure written expression.

Content of the Writing Tests

The aspects of writing measured on the WJ-R ACH include: handwriting, knowledge of punctuation, capitalization, spelling, and usage (Dictation and Proofing); syntactical competence and automaticity (Writing Fluency); and ability to generate meaningful writing to specific task demands (Writing Samples). Figure 4-1 illustrates the hierarchical relationship of the WJ-R ACH writing tests.

Determining Instructional Level

One major goal of a writing assessment is to determine an appropriate instructional level for a student. Helpful information is obtained by plotting performance on the Age/Grade Profile. By viewing the grade scale above or

below the instructional band, an examiner may estimate a student's present level of functioning ranging from an easy to difficult level.

Strengths and Weaknesses

Analysis of a student's strengths and weaknesses within the various writing tests will help an examiner develop an appropriate instructional program. For example, some students have trouble with basic writing skills, such as spelling and proofreading; other students have developed adequate basic skills but have difficulty expressing and organizing their ideas. After analyzing a student's performance, an examiner may determine that a student has: (a) low basic skills, but average or above-average written expression; (b) high basic skills, but average or below-average written expression; or (c) generalized low, average, or high writing performance. Figure 4-2 depicts the performance of three different third-grade students on the Age/Grade Profile. Instructional planning and objectives will differ for these students.

Minimal Writing Skill

In some cases, an examiner may note that a student has developed minimal writing skill. For example, a student may have adequate visual-motor skills but not respond to the simplest writing assignments. The student may write a few letters and simple words on the Dictation test, but only a few simple words or sentences on the Writing Samples and Writing Fluency tests. Some students are

87

MORE COMPLEX

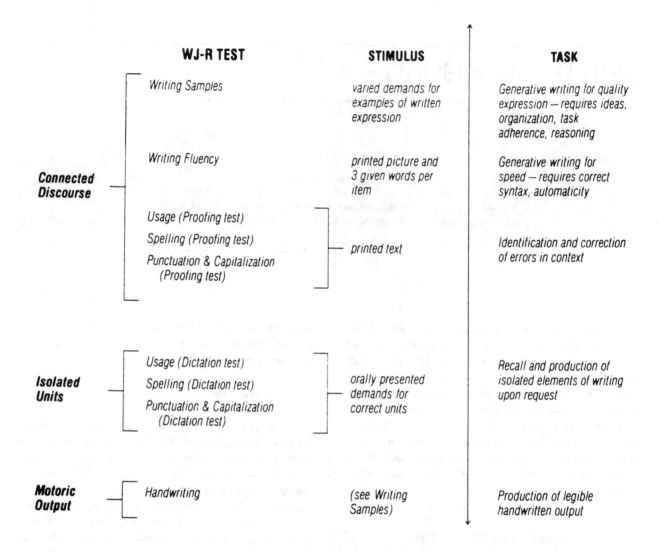

Figure 4–1. Various Skills Measured by the WJ-R ACH Writing Tests. *Note.* From *WJ-R Tests of Achievement: Examiner's Manual* (p. 20) by R.W. Woodcock and N. Mather, 1989, Allen, TX: DLM. Copyright 1989 by DLM. Reprinted by permission.

willing to write but do not know how to proceed; other students, because of past writing failures, are unwilling to write. A carefully planned instructional program is essential for both severely disabled and extremely reluctant writers.

Chapter Organization

This chapter is divided into three major sections: (a) Handwriting; (b) Basic Writing Skills, including Spelling and Proofreading; and (c) Written Expression, including Writing Fluency and Writing Samples. Discussions of the writing tests and instructional modifications and methods are presented in the order of the writing test hierarchy illustrated in Figure 4-1. These writing skills range from the production of legible handwriting to the production of complex sentences. The purpose of analyzing performance in handwriting and basic skills and, subsequently, providing supplemental instruction in these areas is to

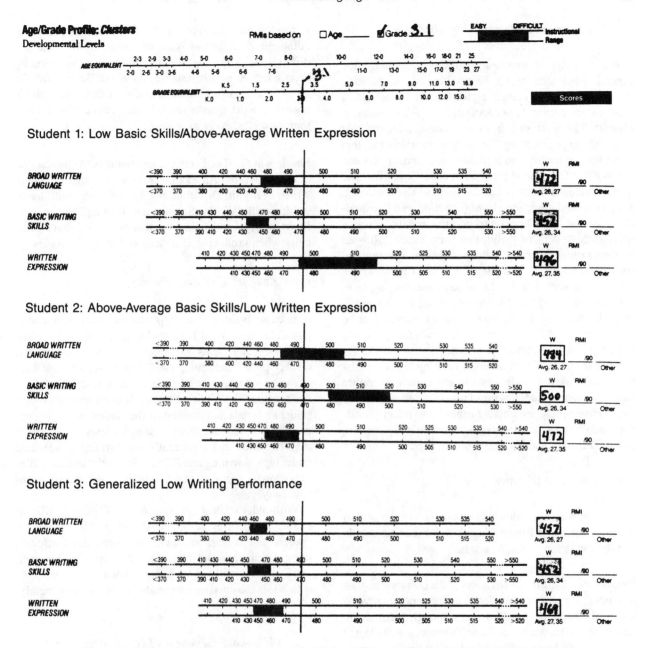

Figure 4–2. Three Third-Grade Students on the Written Language Clusters of the Age/Grade Profile.

remove any barriers that inhibit a student's writing performance. For many individuals, improvement in basic writing skills enhances both independence in writing and ability to express thoughts and ideas on paper.

Analysis of performance on the WJ-R ACH writing tests, accompanied by additional informal writing assessments when necessary, will help an examiner determine a student's present level of skill and select appropriate instructional interventions. Based upon an individual's needs, an examiner may suggest specific modifications, strategies, and/or methods that will help students enjoy writing and increase their ability to communicate effectively.

Handwriting

Handwriting is for writing.
(Graves, 1978, p. 393)

The WJ-R ACH Handwriting test provides an examiner with both a standardized method of scoring handwriting and an informal method for evaluating handwriting. If an examiner assigns a low rating to a student's handwriting, the results may be verified by analyzing the quality of samples of a student's typical classroom writing. If unsatisfactory handwriting is also apparent in the instructional setting, specific handwriting instruction may be necessary.

Error Analysis of Handwriting

The first step in assessing legibility is to judge the general appearance of the handwriting. A handwriting rating is obtained by comparing the student's handwriting to ranked samples in Appendix D of the WJ-R Examiner's Manual. The next step is to evaluate the factors that contribute to poor writing. To analyze several factors that affect writing quality and legibility, an examiner may use the WJ-R ACH Handwriting Elements: Checklist. The factors evaluated in this checklist include: slant, spacing, size, horizontal alignment, letter formation, and line quality. Figure 4-3 illustrates the performance of Terry, a sixth-grade student, on the Writing Samples test, followed by the examiner's general rating of the handwriting and completion of the Handwriting Elements: Checklist.

Although Terry has developed some handwriting skill, the examiner noted several elements to target for improvement. In watching Terry, the examiner observed that he wrote very slowly. In general, poor handwriting is often characterized by illegibility, slowness, tension, and fatigue (Larsen, 1987). In addition to using this checklist with the Writing Samples test, an examiner may gather classroom writing samples for a more in-depth evaluation. An examiner may also obtain further information regarding handwriting skill by analyzing a student's handwriting on the Dictation and Writing Fluency tests.

Error Analysis of Dictation

The Dictation test allows an examiner to analyze two different aspects of handwriting skill: (a) readiness skills and (b) formation of single words.

Readiness. Using the initial items of the Dictation test, an examiner may observe a student's performance on several handwriting readiness skills. Items 1 through 6 require the student to: (a) draw a vertical line, (b) make a scribble, (c) draw a straight horizontal line (or vertical line in Form B) within boundaries, (d) draw a line within the boundaries of a circle (or square), (e) trace the letter *Z* (or *B*), and (f) produce an *E* (or *S*) from a model. A student may not have developed the muscular control or visual-motor skill needed in beginning handwriting. For example, Figure 4-4 illustrates the performance of Ruby, a first-grade girl, on the initial Dictation items. Analysis of performance suggests that Ruby has not yet developed the visual-motor skill necessary for forming letters. If a student is unable to complete several of these items, an examiner may recommend that the student focus on readiness skills, before beginning specific handwriting instruction.

Some primary students also have difficulty with visual-motor skill. Figure 4-5 illustrates the performance of Zach, a third-grade student, on the Writing Samples test. Although Zach knows what he wants to write, he has difficulty with spacing, staying on the lines, and forming certain letters. In this instance, Zach's difficulty with the motor requirements of handwriting affects his attitude regarding writing tasks and influences his ability to communicate effectively in writing.

Single words. The Dictation test requires the production of single words. An examiner may note that a student writes neatly on Dictation, but has difficulty with handwriting on the Writing Samples and Writing Fluency tests. Some students write single words neatly, but have difficulty when producing sentences and longer passages.

Error Analysis of Writing Fluency

Because Writing Fluency is a timed test, a student may pay little attention to handwriting in an attempt to complete as many items as possible. Some students will display poor handwriting on Writing Fluency, but adequate handwriting on Writing Samples and Dictation. Performance on Writing Fluency is most indicative of a student's fastest handwriting. If the student writes legibly on the Dictation and Writing Samples tests, an examiner may conclude that a student's handwriting is adequate under typical writing conditions. Unless the student writes very slowly, supplemental handwriting instruction is unnecessary.

With older students, writing rate is a more significant factor. In analyses of the handwriting skills of eighth graders and college students, rate more often affected writing skill than did poor quality (Phelps & Stempel, 1987). Additionally, a tendency existed for the students who wrote the most rapidly to also write the most legibly.

Additional Assessment of Handwriting Skills

The WJ-R ACH Handwriting test and the informal Handwriting Elements: Checklist provide measures of the quality of handwriting. Information regarding a student's rate of writing may be obtained from analysis of performance on the Writing Fluency test. Although Writing Fluency is not purely a measure of speed, the examiner may observe whether or not the student writes slowly or rapidly under timed conditions. An examiner may use informal procedures to assess further a student's: (a) writing rate, (b) performance under varied conditions, and (c) specific illegibilities. Additionally, an examiner may use a more detailed handwriting evaluation checklist for secondary students.

TEST 27

Writing Samples (cont.)

21.

who found the   *The boy who found the lost dog was nice.*

22.

mosquitoes   butterflies   *Most of these bugs bite.*

bees   lady bugs

black flies   beetles

23.

(1) When doing the laundry, always separate the light clothes from the dark clothes.

(2) *I put in my blue jeans. Guess what!!*

(3) **My white tennis shorts were covered with blue spots!**

(continued)

Figure 4–3. Writing Samples and Handwriting Elements: Checklist for a Sixth-Grade Student.

Rate

For students who have difficulty with writing speed, an examiner may wish to measure writing rate. Determination of a student's handwriting rate allows an examiner to: (a) evaluate if performance is significantly below grade level and (b) measure growth in writing speed. To determine writing rate, an examiner asks the student to write a sentence over and over as many times as possible within a 2-minute period. The selected sentence should be memorized or well-known to the student in order to measure speed of writing and not the speed of thinking (West & Freeman, 1950). The handwriting rate, or the average number of letters written per minute (lpm), is obtained by dividing the total number of letters written by the number of minutes.

Table 4-1 presents average writing rates for first through seventh grades from Zaner-Bloser (1979) and an estimate of writing rate for college students (Phelps & Stempel, 1987).

Estimated writing speeds vary among different handwriting programs and research studies. Groff (1969) reported the average writing speeds for elementary students who wrote the first three sentences of the *Gettysburg Address*. Before writing, the students practiced reading the sentences until they could identify all words. Students printed the passage on the chalkboard. The following mean norms were obtained for over 1,500 students in each grade: Grade 4: 35 lpm; Grade 5: 41 lpm; and Grade 6: 50 lpm.

Although estimates of writing rate vary, the average attainment of students at each grade level increases. Based on the large sample size and careful control of factors affecting writing speed, the speeds reported by Groff may be most accurate in determining grade-level expectancies for elementary students.

TEST H

Handwriting
(From Test 27: Writing Samples)

HANDWRITING ELEMENTS: CHECKLIST
Check boxes that are appropriate.

	Needs Improvement	Satisfactory	Excellent
Slant	☑	☐	☐

☐ inconsistent
☐ too extreme

Comments: *Most letters vertical*

Spacing	☑	☐	☐

☐ too wide
☐ crowded
☐ poor between letters
☑ poor between parts of letter
☑ poor between words

Comments: *inconsistent spacing between words*

Size	☑	☐	☐

☑ not uniform
☐ too big
☐ too small

Comments: *e's too small*

Horizontal Alignment	☐	☑	☐

☐ uneven height
☐ above the line
☐ below the line

Comments: *Ending e's go above the line.*

Letter Formation	☑	☐	☐

☐ poor general form
☑ poor loop letters
☐ letters too thin
☑ letters too round

List specific letter formation errors: *t's too round, connecting cursive b's, o and u, w and h*

Line Quality	☐	☑	☐

☐ too heavy
☐ too light
☐ broken
☐ shaky

Comments:

OVERALL LEGIBILITY:
(Based on specimens in Appendix D)

First rater   _40_

Optional second rater   _____

☐ Rating (Average, if more than one rater)

Test H — Handwriting
Form A
SCORING TABLE
Encircle entire row for the Raw Score

Rating	AE	GE
0	4-0^2	K.0^2
5	4-0^8	K.0^6
10	4-0^{23}	K.0^{12}
15	4-0^{44}	K.0^{26}
20	4-10	K.0^{44}
25	5-10	K.8
30	7-0	2.0
35	8-3	3.2
40	9-8	4.4
45	11-3	5.8
50	13-1	7.7
55	17-6	10.2
60	24	13.8
65	32^{56}	16.9^{58}
70	32^{68}	16.9^{70}
75	32^{78}	16.9^{81}
80	32^{86}	16.9^{88}
85	32^{92}	16.9^{94}
90	32^{96}	16.9^{97}
95	32^{97}	16.9^{99}
100	32^{98}	16.9^{99}

Figure 4–3. (*continued*)

Varied Conditions

A student's typical writing is evaluated on the WJ-R ACH Handwriting test. An examiner may also wish to collect samples under three different conditions to com-pare writing performance. The student may be asked to copy several sentences using his or her: (a) normal writing, (b) fastest writing, and (c) best writing. Analysis of a student's best writing will help an examiner determine what an individual is capable of producing. Some students

TEST 26

Dictation

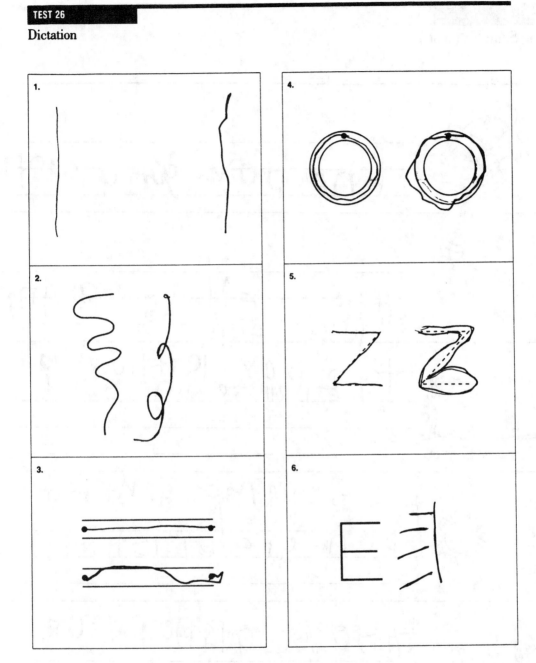

Figure 4–4. A First-Grade Girl on the First Items of the Dictation Test.

only write neatly and legibly when asked to do so. This may be particularly true for older students.

In a classic study, Newland (1932) analyzed the writing of individuals from first graders to adults for specific illegibilities. Groups were divided into elementary, high school, and adult levels. The results indicated that the adults wrote three times more (350%) illegibly than elementary children, whereas high school students wrote 136% more illegibly than elementary children. These findings are most likely not attributed to differences in ability, but rather to the fact that writing quality in adults varies from task to task and reflects the demands placed upon an individual for legibility (West & Freeman, 1950).

Specific Illegibilities

> No letter should vary from its conventional form in such a way that it is likely to be confused with another letter or to lose its characteristic form.
>
> (Freeman, 1914, p. 132)

TEST 27

Writing Samples (cont.)

11. the boy got a airplane

12. with the sell is flying the ball

13. the boy is thowing the ball to the girl

and

14. the lamp andthe sun are brief

15. the boy cannot run because he has qeqst

because

Figure 4–5. A Third-Grade Student on the Writing Samples Test.

For students with poor handwriting skill, an examiner will want to determine exactly which letters are causing difficulty. Further assessment of specific illegibilities may be conducted by asking the student to write the sentence "The quick brown fox jumps over the lazy dog" six times at his or her usual writing rate. This sample, which contains all the letters of the alphabet, may be analyzed to determine any specific malformed letters (Graham & Madan, 1981). An alternate sentence is "Big oxen, quick zebras, fighting monkeys, and wild pigs have jungle

Table 4–1. Average Handwriting Rates by Grade.

Grade	Rate
1	25
2	30
3	38
4	45
5	60
6	67
7	74
College	83

homes" (Tagatz, Otto, Klausmeier, Goodwin, & Cook, 1968). Although specific errors in joining letters may not be observed, these sentences allow an examiner to check for errors in the formation of individual letters.

Several letter formation errors occur frequently. In examining the different types of illegibilities, Newland found that failure to close letters was the most consistent error. One-half of all the illegibilities were caused by four types of difficulties in letter formation: (a) failure to close letters; (b) closing looped strokes, such as writing *i* like *e*; (c) looping nonlooped strokes, such as a *t* like an *l*; and (d) using straight up strokes instead of rounded strokes, such as making an *n* like a *u*, a *c* like an *i*, an *h* like an *li*. Across all age groups, writing an *e* like an *i* accounted for 15% of all illegibilities. Nearly one-half of the illegibilities involved the letters *a*, *e*, *r*, and *t*.

The implications of these findings, particularly for secondary students and adults, is that corrective work may be directed toward resolving an individual's specific illegibilities. In analyzing the handwriting performance of college students, Phelps and Stempel (1987) found that one-third of the errors resulted from poor spacing and letter formation errors.

Secondary Students

Some high school and college students continue to have difficulty with legibility. Ruedy (1983) developed two handwriting evaluation checklists, presented in Figures 4-6 and 4-7, for use with secondary students. The Student Handwriting Evaluation Sheet in Figure 4-6 is completed by an examiner or instructor. The Handwriting Checklist and Writing Sample Pretest in Figure 4-7 is completed by the student.

Once the instructor has completed the evaluation, the recommendations are shared with the student, and a remedial program is planned, if necessary. When assessing the handwriting ability of students at the secondary or college level, the goal is to determine how an individual may improve legibility. By the time students reach the secondary level, emphasis must switch from the extrinsic

direction of the teacher to the intrinsic motivation of an individual who desires to improve handwriting appearance (Davis & Miller, 1983). Upper-elementary level students may also become extrinsically motivated to improve writing as they participate in meaningful writing activities.

Instructional Modifications

In extreme cases, a student's handwriting may be totally illegible, and, consequently, an examiner or teacher is unable to evaluate the content of the written message. For students who are unable to develop a legible writing style, instructional modifications are necessary. For some assignments, the student may use a transcriber, such as a peer, parent, or volunteer. An examiner may also wish to recommend that the student receive typing or word processing instruction.

Several additional modifications may improve handwriting performance. A student may: (a) use a clipboard, (b) tape the paper to the desk prior to writing, and (c) keep a chart with all letter forms or difficult letters affixed to the top of the desk for easy reference. An instructor may: (a) increase the allotted time for writing assignments, (b) permit the student to use either manuscript or cursive, (c) teach a new writing style, or (d) teach cursive writing early, when appropriate.

For some secondary and college students, writing habits are firmly established and limited progress is made in improving legibility. Figure 4-8 illustrates the handwriting performance of Betsy, a high school junior, on several items of the Writing Samples test.

Despite good motor control and consistent slant and spacing, her writing is nearly illegible. Betsy commented to the examiner that her teachers had always complained about having difficulty reading her exams and papers. She also stated that she had tried to write more legibly, but could not alter her style. The examiner recommended that Betsy be given opportunities to type, dictate, or write and then read to her instructors all written work, including exams, prior to grading.

For young students with poor motor control, typing or word processing, if a computer is available, should be introduced in elementary school. While learning to use the typewriter or computer, the student should still be encouraged to practice and improve handwriting skill.

Instructional Sequence

Some educators believe that letters are most easily learned when presented in a developmental sequence that is based on the similarity of the motor patterns used to form the letter. Although no definitive research exists to

Student Handwriting Evaluation Sheet

	O.K.	Needs Review
1. Performance observation.		
a. pen or pencil is held properly	☐	☐
b. paper is positioned at a "normal" slant	☐	☐
c. writing posture is acceptable	☐	☐
d. writing speed is acceptable	☐	☐
2. Correct letter formation.		
a. closed letters are closed	☐	☐
b. looped letters are looped	☐	☐
c. stick letters are not loops	☐	☐
d. i's and j's are dotted directly above	☐	☐
e. x's and t's are crossed accurately	☐	☐
f. m's and n's have the correct number of humps	☐	☐
g. all lower case letters begin on the line (unless they follow b, o, v, or w)	☐	☐
h. b, o, v, and w end above the line	☐	☐
i. all lower case letters end on the line	☐	☐
j. v's and u's are clearly differentiated	☐	☐
k. connecting strokes of v and y are clearly not ry and ry	☐	☐
l. upper case letters are correctly or acceptably formed	☐	☐
m. numbers are correctly formed	☐	☐
3. Fluency.		
a. writing is smooth, not choppy	☐	☐
b. pencil pressure appears even	☐	☐
c. words appear to be written as complete units	☐	☐
d. letter connection is smooth	☐	☐
4. Letter size, slant, and spacing.		
a. lower case letter: are uniform size	☐	☐
b. upper case letters are clearly larger than lower case letters	☐	☐
c. upper case letters are uniform in size	☐	☐
d. tail lengths are consistent and do not interfere with letters on the line below	☐	☐
e. tall letters are a consistent height and are clearly taller than other letters	☐	☐
f. writing is not too small or too large	☐	☐
g. slant of letters is acceptable	☐	☐
h. slant of letters is consistent	☐	☐
i. spacing of letters and words is consistent	☐	☐
5. Student attitude toward writing		
a. student's opinion of his writing skills	☐	☐
b. "writing is hard"	☐	☐
c. writes too slowly	☐	☐
d. feels good about writing	☐	☐
6. Overall teacher evaluation.	☐	☐

Teacher Recommendation:

☐ You appear to write smoothly and easily. Your letters are formed correctly. Letter size, slant, and spacing are good. Your writing is neat and legible. It is not necessary for you to complete the handwriting exercises.

☐ You appear to write smoothly and easily. You have developed your own writing style which is acceptable, neat and legible. It is not necessary for you to complete the handwriting exercises.

☐ You appear to write smoothly and easily. However, your letter formation, neatness, and legibility need some work. Please complete the handwriting exercises.

☐ **Writing seems to be difficult for you. You need practice in handwriting skills. Please complete the handwriting exercises.**

Figure 4–6. Student Handwriting Evaluation Sheet. *Note.* From "Handwriting Instruction: It Can Be Part of the High School Curriculum" by L.R. Ruedy, 1983, *Academic Therapy, 18*, pp. 427–428. Copyright 1983 by Academic Therapy. Reprinted by permission.

Handwriting Checklist and Writing Sample Pre-test

1. Into which handwriting category do you fit? (Circle one.)
   a. I am not comfortable with my writing skills so I print or use a combination of printing and writing.
   b. I have the basic writing skills and use them, but I would like my written work to look better, and I do not want to have to use so much energy when I write.
   c. Writing is easy for me, but my teachers often complain that they can't read my writing or that my written work is too sloppy.
   d. My writing is easy to read and neat. It flows easily. I do not have to "think" about writing, and it does not take much effort for me to write.

Check "yes" or "no" in answering the following questions.

	YES	NO
2. I know and use an acceptable form of all the written lower case letters.	☐	☐
3. I know and use an acceptable form of all the written upper case letters.	☐	☐
4. I hold my pen or pencil lightly, and my hand does not get too tired when I write.	☐	☐
5. I "choke" the end of my pen or pencil.	☐	☐
6. I hold my pen or pencil so tightly that my hand gets tired or cramped when I write.	☐	☐
7. I place my paper at a comfortable slant when I write.	☐	☐
8. I sit up straight when I write.	☐	☐
9. All my written letters slant the same amount.	☐	☐
10. The shapes and sizes of my letters are even.	☐	☐
11. The pressure I put on the paper is even.	☐	☐
12. I completely close all letters that have circles (a, d, g, o, p, q).	☐	☐
13. The "loops" on my "loop letters" are all clearly open (b, e, f, g, h, j, k, l, p, y, z).	☐	☐
14. My "stick letters" do not have loops (d, i, t).	☐	☐
15. I cross or dot letters carefully (i, j, t, x).	☐	☐
16. I write on a firm surface.	☐	☐
17. My upper case letters are clearly larger than my lower case letters	☐	☐
18. I write each word as a unit, going back to add crosses or dots only after I have written the whole word.	☐	☐
19. I do not add extra loops or squiggles which may make my writing hard to read.	☐	☐
20. I connect my letters carefully so my connecting lines are not confused with letters or parts of letters.	☐	☐
21. Writing is hard for me and I avoid it whenever possible.	☐	☐
22. I am a good speller.	☐	☐
23. I am usually happy with the way my papers look.	☐	☐
24. Taking notes is hard for me.	☐	☐
25. I think I would write more if I felt better about my writing.	☐	☐
26. It is hard for me to write on unlined paper.	☐	☐
27. I sometimes make mistakes in math because my numbers are not lined up properly.	☐	☐
28. I sometimes lose my "train of thought" because I write so slowly.	☐	☐
29. I seldom re-copy my papers.	☐	☐
30. I use pens and pencils that feel comfortable.	☐	☐

31. Write this sentence: The quick brown fox jumped over the lazy dogs.
32. Write the lower case alphabet as if it were a single word (with each letter connected to the next).
33. Write the upper case alphabet.
34. Write your full name.
35. Write the numbers from zero through nine.

Figure 4–7. Handwriting Checklist and Writing Sample Pretest. *Note.* From "Handwriting Instruction: It Can Be Part of the High School Curriculum" by L.R. Ruedy, 1983, *Academic Therapy, 18*, pp. 425–426. Copyright 1983 by Academic Therapy. Reprinted by permission.

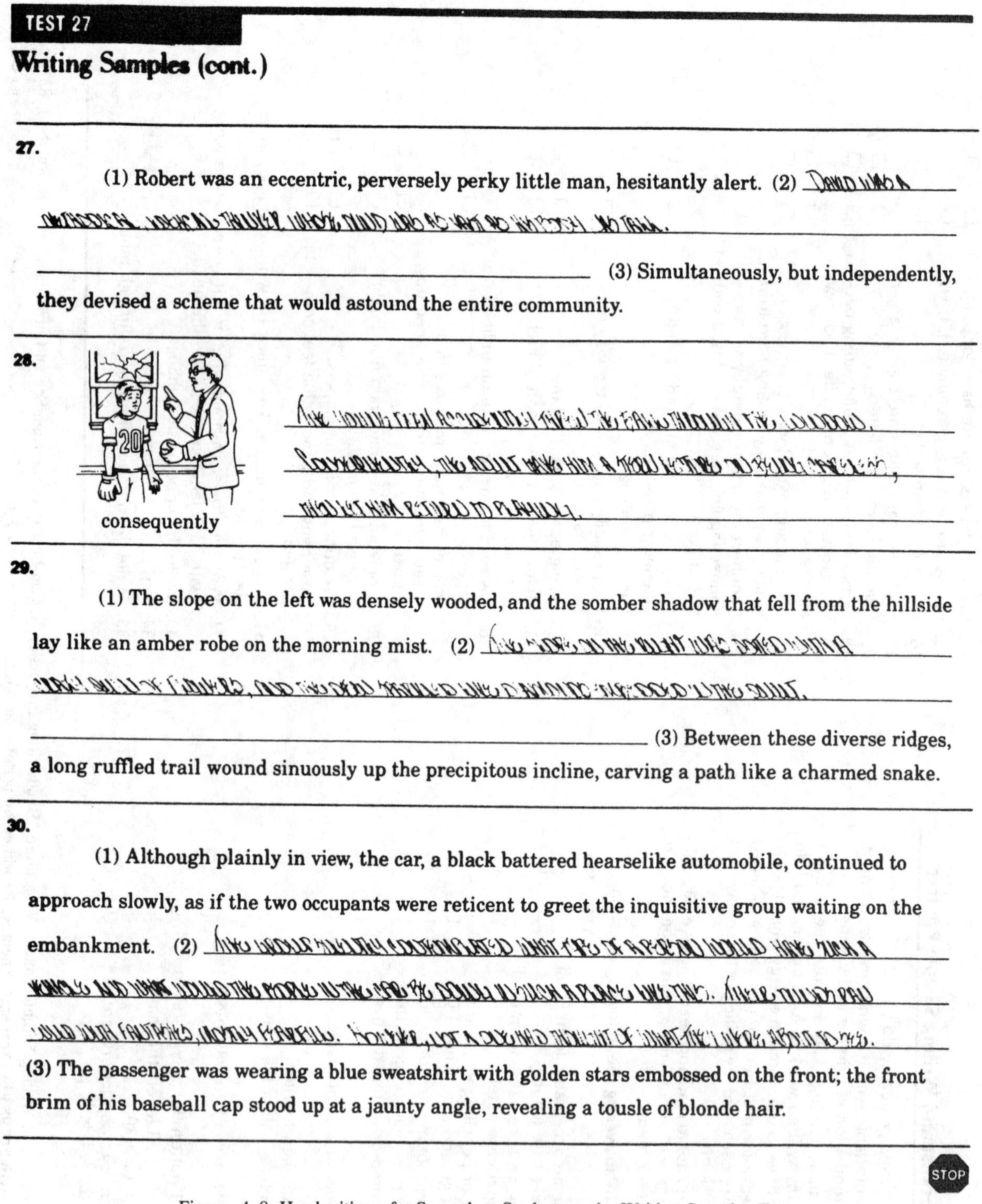

TEST 27

Writing Samples (cont.)

27.

(1) Robert was an eccentric, perversely perky little man, hesitantly alert. (2) ______ (3) Simultaneously, but independently, they devised a scheme that would astound the entire community.

28.

consequently

29.

(1) The slope on the left was densely wooded, and the somber shadow that fell from the hillside lay like an amber robe on the morning mist. (2) ______ (3) Between these diverse ridges, a long ruffled trail wound sinuously up the precipitous incline, carving a path like a charmed snake.

30.

(1) Although plainly in view, the car, a black battered hearselike automobile, continued to approach slowly, as if the two occupants were reticent to greet the inquisitive group waiting on the embankment. (2) ______

(3) The passenger was wearing a blue sweatshirt with golden stars embossed on the front; the front brim of his baseball cap stood up at a jaunty angle, revealing a tousle of blonde hair.

STOP

Figure 4–8. Handwriting of a Secondary Student on the Writing Samples Test.

support the teaching of letter formation in groups, this type of instructional strategy may benefit students who have trouble remembering letter forms or producing consistent motor patterns. For a student with poor handwriting or unusual letter formation, an examiner may recommend that the student review letter formation by practicing letters in groups.

Manuscript

Cohen and Plaskon (1980) presented a sequence for teaching manuscript letters that organizes lowercase and capital letters according to the basic strokes of straight line, circle, and parts of circle:

1) L, E, F, T, I, H (straight lines)
2) O, C, G, Q (circles and straight lines)
3) t, i, l (vertical and horizontal lines)
4) v, w, x, y, z, k (straight and slant lines)
5) V, N, M, W, K, A, Z, X, Y (straight and slant lines)
6) o, c, e, d, a, g, q (counterclockwise circles and lines)
7) b, p, r, n, m, h (lines, clockwise circles, part circles)
8) D, P, B, R, J (straight lines and half circles)
9) s, u, j, f (straight lines and half circles)
10) S, U (half circles)

Cursive

Groupings of letters may also be used to teach cursive writing. Getman (1985) presented the following developmental grouping for teaching lowercase cursive letters.

Group 1: o, a, c, d, g, q, y, and z
Group 2: e, l, f, k, b, and h
Group 3: i, t, j, and p
Group 4: n, m, u, y, w, and v
Group 5: r, x, and s

When skill has become apparent with the letters of Group 1, Group 2 letters are introduced. Group 1 letters are then reviewed before progressing to Group 3 and Group 4. The three letters in Group 5 do not follow any of the patterns set by other letters and, consequently, are introduced last. Getman stated that clinical evidence from vision therapy programs suggests that progress is greater when this developmental sequence is followed.

Hanover (1983) described a similar method for learning families of cursive letters based on groupings. Letters are presented and practiced in the following sequence:

1) the *e* family: e, l, h, f, b, and k
2) the *c* family: c, a, d, o, q, and g
3) the hump family: n, m, v, y, and x
4) letters with tails tied in the back: f, q
5) letters with tails tied in the front: g, p, y, and z
6) r and s
7) letters with a handle: b, o, v, and w

Several letters are in more than one group to emphasize the similar characteristics. Depending upon the student's ability, more than one letter family may be introduced in a lesson. After the lowercase letters are learned, the capital letters are introduced in groups. This type of strategy may ease demands on memory by helping students associate and group common letter formation patterns.

Instructional Styles

In designing a handwriting program, an examiner may wish to recommend that the student be encouraged to use or to learn a specific writing style. Handwriting instruction may be provided in manuscript, cursive, or manu-cursive. Depending upon a student's age, ability, and interest, instructional training in a particular writing style may be recommended.

Manuscript and Cursive

Many commercial handwriting programs exist that teach varying styles of manuscript and cursive. After analyzing a student's capabilities in both manuscript and cursive writing, an examiner may wish to recommend that the student concentrate on developing or improving one writing style. The style of writing should match the student's level of motor control (Hagin, 1983). For example, in one instance, an examiner recommended that Frank, a third-grade student with legible manuscript, should continue to develop this writing form, rather than switch to cursive writing. The reasons for this recommendation were that Frank was having extreme difficulty with the rhythmic movements required for cursive writing and with the memorization of the new letter forms.

In another instance, an examiner recommended that Marisa, a second-grade student with good visual-motor skill, begin cursive writing instruction. The reasons for this recommendation were to help Marisa perceive words as units and to reduce the frequency of letter reversals. One conclusion from a decade of research in handwriting is that there is no need to change from manuscript to cursive writing (Askov, Otto, & Askov, 1970). Many adults prefer manuscript writing, and neither method is superior to the other in terms of increased legibility or writing rate. Additionally, many students with learning disabilities have trouble transferring from manuscript to cursive writing (Thurber, 1983).

Manu-cursive

Manu-cursive writing styles emphasize the use of shared motor patterns between manuscript and cursive. The most well-known example of a manu-cursive writing style is D'Nealian (Thurber, 1983, 1984). In this continuous stroke method, the movements required to make letters are minimized. Additionally, 90% of the letters are skill-progressed from manuscript to cursive, allowing for a natural transition to cursive writing, if or when a student desires.

A major advantage of D'Nealian is that the method offers visual, auditory, and tactile-kinesthetic clues to aid the memory process. Several steps may be followed in teaching letter formation. To begin, the teacher tells the student the letter name. The instructor forms the letter in the air while saying the audio directions. Next, the teacher and student repeat the directions while writing the letter in the air, coordinating the audio directions with the air-writing. The student then practices writing the letters in short words. Because students are expected to make mistakes when learning new letter forms, erasing is discouraged.

For students who have difficulty remembering letter formation patterns, two additional steps may be added. The teacher traces the letter on the student's hand, back, or arm, saying the audio directions in exact synchronization with the movements. Instructions are repeated several times so that the student associates the oral directions with the kinesthetic-tactile formation of the letter. As a final step, the student traces the letter on the teacher's hand, while saying the audio directions.

Figure 4-9 illustrates D'Nealian numbers and lower and uppercase letters, with the suggested audio phraseology. A teacher may modify these descriptions as needed (Thurber, 1984).

Several factors make D'Nealian an effective tool for students with learning disabilities. This method: (a) provides audio descriptions of letter formation, (b) reduces the number of strokes needed to form letters, (c) eliminates component parts needed to form letters, (d) increases the discrimination among letters, (e) provides a natural transition from manuscript to cursive writing, and (f) encourages acceptance of individuality (Thurber, 1983, 1984). Additionally, research results suggest that students make fewer reversal and substitution errors using D'Nealian as opposed to a traditional ball-stick method for both near and far point copying (Thurber, 1984).

Hagin (1983) presented a simplified manu-cursive method for students who have difficulty learning cursive writing. This method, based upon a vertical downstroke rather than a diagonal slant, builds on the motor patterns taught in manuscript. Several motifs are used to teach joining strokes and pivoting movements. An example of a motif, or an activity that forms the foundation for letter practice, includes making a string of waves shaped like the letter *c* across the page.

Five steps are used to practice letters: (a) tracing the letter on a transparency placed over a printed model, (b) writing a letter on the transparency over blank printed lines, (c) placing the letter over the printed model to judge the writing, (d) recording the letters and motifs that were practiced, and (e) engaging in copying and spontaneous writing. This method may be useful with students who have difficulty with slant and prefer a vertical alignment of letters in cursive writing.

Instructional Strategies for Handwriting

As with other skill areas, individualized instruction is a critical factor in improving handwriting skill. In examining the effects of three different instructional approaches on handwriting performance, Tagatz, Otto, Klausmeier, Goodwin, and Cook (1968) found that for third-grade students, an individualized diagnostic approach was superior to a formal group method using commercial materials. Such training should be provided before handwriting habits are firmly established. Additionally, copying letter forms for practice is more effective than repeated tracings of letter forms (Cohen & Plaskon, 1980). Tracing, however, may be more effective for students who have fine-motor problems or difficulty remembering the movements for letter formation.

In reviewing the research on handwriting, Hofmeister (1973) summarized several common instructional errors: (a) massed practice without supervision, (b) no immediate feedback, (c) emphasis on rote practice rather than discrimination, (d) failure to provide close-range models of correct letter formation, (e) lack of emphasis on student evaluation of errors, and (f) failure to reward good work. Additionally, in some instances, handwriting instruction may begin before the student has developed prerequisite skills.

Readiness

Before beginning handwriting instruction, some students will benefit from additional development in readiness skills. Activities should be selected that develop increased muscular control and visual-motor skill. Mercer and Mercer (1985) suggested that a student should be able to perform the following activities prior to handwriting instruction: (a) perform directional hand movements; (b) trace geometric shapes and lines; (c) connect dots on paper; (d) draw horizontal and vertical lines; (e) draw a backward circle, a curved line, and a forward circle; (f) draw slanted lines; (g) copy simple shapes; and (h) name letters and see likenesses and differences in letter forms.

In addition, hand preference should be determined, and the student should be taught the proper position of the paper and pencil. In some cases, an examiner may wish to recommend that a student spend instructional time on readiness skills until he or she can successfully perform the activities that are outlined above.

Improving Factors That Influence Handwriting

The WJ-R ACH Handwriting Elements Checklist includes several factors that affect writing quality and legibility. These factors include: (a) slant, (b) spacing, (c)

Number Descriptions

1 — Start at the top; slant down to the bottom.
[Top start; slant down.]

2 — Start a little below the top; curve up right to the top; curve down right to the middle; slant down left to the bottom; make a bar to the right.
[Start below the top; curve up, around; slant down left; and over right.]

3 — Start a little below the top; curve up right to the top; curve down right to the middle; curve down right again to the bottom; curve up left, and stop.
[Start below the top; curve up, around halfway; around again, up, and stop.]

4 — Start at the top; slant down to the middle; make a bar to the right. Start again at the top, to the right of the first start; slant down through the bar to the bottom.
[Top start; down halfway; over right. Another top start, to the right; slant down, and through.]

5 — Start at the top; make a bar to the left; slant down to the middle; curve down right to the bottom; curve up left, and stop.
[Top start; over left; slant down halfway; curve around, down, up, and stop.]

6 — Start at the top; slant down left to the middle; curve down left to the bottom; curve up right to the middle; curve left, and close.
[Top start; slant down, and curve around; up; and close.]

7 — Start at the top; make a bar to the right; slant down left to the bottom.
[Top start; over right; slant down left.]

8 — Start a little below the top; curve up left to the top and down left to the middle; curve down right to the bottom; curve up left; slant up right, through the middle, to the beginning, and touch.
[Start below the top; curve up, around, down; a snake tail; slant up right; through; and touch.]

9 — Start at the top; curve down left to the middle; curve up right to the beginning, and close; slant down to the bottom.
[Top start; curve down, around, close; slant down.]

10 — Start at the top; slant down to the bottom. Start again at the top, to the right of the first start; curve down left to the bottom; curve up right to the top, and close.
[Top start; slant down. Another top start, to the right; curve down, around, and close.]

Figure 4–9. D'Nealian Numbers and Letters. *Note.* From D'Nealian® Handwriting by Donald Neal Thurber. Copyright © 1987 by Scott, Foresman and Company. Reprinted by permission.

Figure 4–9 (*Continued on next page.*)

size, (d) horizontal alignment, (e) letter formation, and (f) line quality. In addition, a student's grip may affect handwriting. When one or more of these factors is affecting legibility, specific instructional strategies may be used.

Slant. Students who demonstrate inconsistent slant may be given paper that is marked with slant indicators (Larsen, 1987). These diagonal slashes are made in the same direction as the student's natural slant: left slant, right slant, or no slant. For example, if a left-handed student writes with a backhand slant, the slashes would be angled from left to right. These slash marks will help the student produce consistent slant.

Some students tend to write specific letters with an atypical slant. The examiner should identify letters by drawing lines through letters to determine which letters have an inconsistent slant.

In some instances, slant may be improved by demonstrating the proper position of the arm, hand, and paper and pencil. For manuscript writing, the paper is placed directly in front of the student. For cursive writing, the paper is slanted so that the lower corner points toward the center of the body. A right-handed student points toward the lower left corner and a left-handed student points toward the lower right corner. The hand and arm stay aligned with the position of the paper.

Lowercase Manuscript Letter Descriptions

ā — Start in the middle; curve down left to the bottom; curve up right to the beginning, and close; retrace down, and swing up.
[Middle start; around down, close up, down, and a monkey tail.]

b — Start at the top; slant down to the bottom; curve up right to the middle; curve left, and close.
[Top start; slant down, around, up, and a tummy.]

c — Start a little below the middle; curve up left to the middle; curve down left to the bottom; curve up right, and stop.
[Start below the middle; curve up, around, down, up, and stop.]

d — Start in the middle; curve down left to the bottom; curve up right to the beginning; touch, and keep going up to the top; retrace down, and swing up.
[Middle start; around down, touch, up high, down, and a monkey tail.]

e — Start between the middle and the bottom; curve up right to the middle; curve down left; touch, and keep going down to the bottom; curve up right, and stop.
[Start between the middle and bottom; curve up, around, touch, down, up, and stop.]

f — Start a little below the top; curve up left to the top; slant down to the bottom. Make a crossbar in the middle.
[Start below the top; curve up, around, and slant down. Cross.]

g — Start in the middle; curve down left to the bottom; curve up right to the beginning, and close; retrace down to halfway below the bottom, and hook left.
[Middle start; around down, close up, down under water, and a fishhook.]

h — Start at the top; slant down to the bottom; retrace up halfway; make a hill to the right, and swing up.
[Top start; slant down, up over the hill, and a monkey tail.]

i — Start in the middle; slant down to the bottom, and swing up. Make a dot above the letter.
[Middle start; slant down, and a monkey tail. Add a dot.]

j — Start in the middle; slant down to halfway below the bottom, and hook left. Make a dot above the letter.
[Middle start; slant down under water, and a fishhook. Add a dot.]

k — Start at the top; slant down to the bottom; retrace up halfway; curve right; make a small loop left, and close; slant down right to the bottom, and swing up.
[Top start; slant down, up into a little tummy, and a monkey tail.]

l — Start at the top; slant down to the bottom, and swing up.
[Top start; slant down, and a monkey tail.]

m — Start in the middle; slant down to the bottom; retrace up, and make a hill to the right; retrace up; make another hill to the right, and swing up.
[Middle start; slant down, up over the hill, up over the hill again, and a monkey tail.]

n — Start in the middle; slant down to the bottom; retrace up; make a hill to the right, and swing up.
[Middle start; slant down, up over the hill, and a monkey tail.]

ō — Start in the middle; curve down left to the bottom; curve up right to the beginning, and close.
[Middle start; around down, and close up.]

p — Start in the middle; slant down to halfway below the bottom; retrace up; curve down right to the bottom; curve left, and close.
[Middle start; slant down under water, up, around, and a tummy.]

q — Start in the middle; curve down left to the bottom; curve up right to the beginning, and close; retrace down to halfway below the bottom, and hook right.
[Middle start; around down, close up, down under water, and a backwards fishhook.]

r — Start in the middle; slant down to the bottom; retrace up; curve right, and stop.
[Middle start; slant down, up, and a roof.]

s — Start a little below the middle; curve up left to the middle and down left halfway; curve down right to the bottom; curve up left, and stop.
[Start below the middle; curve up, around, down, and a snake tail.]

t — Start at the top; slant down to the bottom, and swing up. Make a crossbar in the middle.
[Top start; slant down, and a monkey tail. Cross.]

u — Start in the middle; slant down to the bottom, and curve right; slant up to the middle; retrace down, and swing up.
[Middle start; down, around, up, down, and a monkey tail.]

v — Start in the middle; slant down right to the bottom; slant up right to the middle.
[Middle start; slant down right, and slant up right.]

w — Start in the middle; slant down to the bottom, and curve right; slant up to the middle; retrace down, and curve right; slant up to the middle.
[Middle start; down, around, up, and down, around, up again.]

x — Start in the middle; slant down right to the bottom, and swing up. Cross through the letter with a slant down left.
[Middle start; slant down right, and a monkey tail. Cross down left.]

y — Start in the middle; slant down to the bottom, and curve right; slant up to the middle; retrace down to halfway below the bottom, and hook left.
[Middle start; down, around, up, down under water, and a fishhook.]

z — Start in the middle; make a bar to the right; slant down left to the bottom; make a bar to the right.
[Middle start; over right, slant down left, and over right.]

Figure 4–9. (*continued*)

Capital Manuscript Letter Descriptions

  Start at the top; slant down left to the bottom. Start again at the same point; slant down right to the bottom. Make a crossbar in the middle.
[Top start; slant down left. Same start; slant down right. Middle bar across.]

B Start at the top; slant down to the bottom; retrace up; curve down right to the middle; curve left, and close; curve down right to the bottom; curve left, and close.
[Top start; slant down, up, around halfway, close, around again, and close.]

C Start a little below the top; curve up left to the top; curve down left to the bottom; curve up right, and stop.
[Start below the top; curve up, around, down, up, and stop.]

 D Start at the top; slant down to the bottom; retrace up; curve down right to the bottom; curve left, and close.
[Top start; slant down, up, around, and close.]

 E Start at the top; make a bar to the left; slant down to the bottom; make a bar to the right. Make a bar to the right in the middle.
[Top start; over left, slant down, and over right. Middle bar across.]

 F Start at the top; make a bar to the left; slant down to the bottom. Make a bar to the right in the middle.
[Top start; over left, and slant down. Middle bar across.]

G Start a little below the top; curve up left to the top; curve down left to the bottom; curve up right to the middle; make a bar to the left.
[Start below the top; curve up, around, down, up, and over left.]

 H Start at the top; slant down to the bottom. Start again at the top, to the right of the first start; slant down to the bottom. Make a crossbar in the middle.
[Top start; slant down. Another top start, to the right; slant down. Middle bar across.]

 I Start at the top; slant down to the bottom. Make a small crossbar at the top, and another at the bottom.
[Top start; slant down. Cross the top and the bottom.]

J Start at the top; slant down to the bottom; curve up left, and stop.
[Top start; slant down, and curve up left.]

 K Start at the top; slant down to the bottom. Start again at the top, to the right of the first start; slant down left to the middle, and touch; slant down right to the bottom, and swing up.
[Top start; slant down. Another top start, to the right; slant down left, touch, slant down right, and a monkey tail.]

 L Start at the top; slant down to the bottom; make a bar to the right.
[Top start; slant down, and over right.]

 M Start at the top; slant down to the bottom. Start again at the same point; slant down right to the middle; slant up right to the top; slant down to the bottom.
[Top start; slant down. Same start; slant down right halfway, slant up right, and slant down.]

 N Start at the top; slant down to the bottom. Start again at the same point; slant down right to the bottom; slant up to the top.
[Top start; slant down. Same start; slant down right, and slant up.]

 O Start at the top; curve down left to the bottom; curve up right to the beginning, and close.
[Top start; around down, and close up.]

 P Start at the top; slant down to the bottom; retrace up; curve down right to the middle; curve left, and close.
[Top start; slant down, up, around halfway, and close.]

 Q Start at the top; curve down left to the bottom; curve up right to the beginning, and close. Cross through the bottom of the letter with a curve down right.
[Top start; around down, and close up. Cross with a curve down right.]

 R Start at the top; slant down to the bottom; retrace up; curve down right to the middle; curve left, and close; slant down right to the bottom, and swing up.
[Top start; slant down, up, around halfway, close, slant down right, and a monkey tail.]

S Start a little below the top; curve up left to the top and down left to the middle; curve down right to the bottom; curve up left, and stop.
[Start below the top; curve up, around, down, and a snake tail.]

 T Start at the top; slant down to the bottom. Make a crossbar at the top.
[Top start; slant down. Cross the top.]

 U Start at the top; slant down to the bottom, and curve right; slant up to the top; retrace down, and swing up.
[Top start; down, around, up, down, and a monkey tail.]

 V Start at the top; slant down right to the bottom; slant up right to the top.
[Top start; slant down right, and slant up right.]

 W Start at the top; slant down right to the bottom; slant up right to the top; slant down right to the bottom; slant up right to the top.
[Top start; slant down right, slant up right, slant down right, and slant up right again.]

 X Start at the top; slant down right to the bottom, and swing up. Cross through the letter with a slant down left.
[Top start; slant down right, and a monkey tail. Cross down left.]

 Y Start at the top; slant down right to the middle. Start again at the top, to the right of the first start; slant down left to the middle; touch, and keep going down to the bottom.
[Top start; slant down right halfway. Another top start, to the right; slant down left, and touch on the way.]

 Z Start at the top; make a bar to the right; slant down left to the bottom; make a bar to the right.
[Top start; over right, slant down left, and over right.]

Figure 4–9. (*continued*)

Lowercase Cursive Letter Descriptions

a — Go overhill; retrace halfway; curve down to the bottom; curve up right to the middle, and close; retrace down, and swing up.
[Overhill; back, around down, close up, down, and up.]

b — Go uphill to the top; loop left down to the bottom; curve up right to the middle; curve left; and sidestroke right.
[Uphill high; loop down, around, up, and sidestroke.]

c — Go overhill; retrace halfway; curve down to the bottom, and swing up.
[Overhill; back, around, down, and up.]

d — Go overhill; retrace halfway; curve down to the bottom; curve up right to the middle; touch, and keep going up to the top; retrace down, and swing up.
[Overhill; back, around down, touch, up high, down, and up.]

e — Go uphill to the middle; loop left down to the bottom, and swing up.
[Uphill; loop down, through, and up.]

 f — Go uphill to the top; loop left down to halfway below the bottom; loop right up to the bottom line; close; and swing up.
[Uphill high; loop down under water, loop up right, touch, and up.]

 g — Go overhill; retrace halfway; curve down to the bottom; curve up right to the middle, and close; retrace down to halfway below the bottom; and loop left up through the bottom line.
[Overhill; back, around down, close up, down under water, loop up left, and through.]

h — Go uphill to the top; loop left down to the bottom; retrace up halfway; make a hill to the right, and swing up.
[Uphill high; loop down, up over the hill, and up.]

 i — Go uphill to the middle; retrace down, and swing up. Make a dot above the letter.
[Uphill; down, and up. Add a dot.]

 j — Go uphill to the middle; retrace down to halfway below the bottom; and loop left up through the bottom line. Make a dot above the letter.
[Uphill; down under water, loop up left, and through. Add a dot.]

k — Go uphill to the top; loop left down to the bottom; retrace up halfway; curve right; make a small loop left, and close; slant down right to the bottom, and swing up.
[Uphill high; loop down, up into a little tummy, slant down right, and up.]

l — Go uphill to the top; loop left down to the bottom, and swing up.
[Uphill high; loop down, and up.]

m — Go overhill; slant down to the bottom; retrace up, and make a hill to the right; retrace up; make another hill to the right, and swing up.
[Overhill; down, up over the hill, up over the hill again, and up.]

n — Go overhill; slant down to the bottom; retrace up; make a hill to the right, and swing up.
[Overhill; down, up over the hill, and up.]

o — Go overhill; retrace halfway; curve down to the bottom; curve up right to the middle; close; and sidestroke right.
[Overhill; back, around down, close up, and sidestroke.]

p — Go uphill to the middle; retrace down to halfway below the bottom; retrace up; curve down right to the bottom; curve left; close; and swing up.
[Uphill; down under water, up, around into a tummy, and up.]

 q — Go overhill; retrace halfway; curve down to the bottom; curve up right to the middle, and close; retrace down to halfway below the bottom; loop right up to the bottom line; close; and swing up.
[Overhill; back, around down, close up, down under water, loop up right, touch, and up.]

r — Go uphill to the middle; sidestroke right; slant down to the bottom, and swing up.
[Uphill; sidestroke, down, and up.]

s — Go uphill to the middle; slant down to the bottom; curve left, and close; retrace to the bottom, and swing up.
[Uphill; down, around, close, and up.]

 t — Go uphill to the top; retrace down, and swing up. Make a crossbar in the middle.
[Uphill high; down, and up. Cross.]

u — Go uphill to the middle; retrace down, and curve right; slant up to the middle; retrace down, and swing up.
[Uphill; down, around, up, down, and up.]

v — Go overhill; slant down to the bottom, and curve right; slant up to the middle; and sidestroke right.
[Overhill; down, around, up, and sidestroke.]

w — Go uphill to the middle; retrace down, and curve right; slant up to the middle; retrace down, and curve right; slant up to the middle; and sidestroke right.
[Uphill; down, around, up, down, around, up again, and sidestroke.]

x — Go overhill; slant down right to the bottom, and swing up. Cross through the letter with a slant down left.
[Overhill; slant down right, and up. Cross down left.]

y — Go overhill; slant down to the bottom, and curve right; slant up to the middle; retrace down to halfway below the bottom; and loop left up through the bottom line.
[Overhill; down, around, up, down under water, loop up left, and through.]

z — Go overhill; curve down right to the bottom; curve down right again to halfway below the bottom; and loop left up through the bottom line.
[Overhill; around down, around again, and down under water, loop up left, and through.]

Figure 4–9. (*continued*)

Capital Cursive Letter Descriptions

 Start at the top; curve down left to the bottom; curve up right to the beginning, and close; retrace down, and swing up.
[Top start; around down, close up, down, and up.]

 Start at the top; slant down to the bottom; retrace up; curve down right to the middle; curve down right again to the bottom; curve up left; touch; sidestroke right, and stop.
[Top start; down, up, around halfway, around again, touch, sidestroke, and stop.]

C Start a little below the top; curve up left to the top; curve down left to the bottom; and curve up right.
[Start below the top; curve up, around, down, and up.]

D Start at the top; slant down to the bottom; curve left, and loop right; curve up right to the beginning; close; loop right, swing up, and stop.
[Top start; down, loop right, curve up, around, close, loop right, through, and stop.]

E Start a little below the top; curve up left to the top; curve down left to the middle; curve down left again to the bottom; and curve up right.
[Start below the top; curve up, around to the middle, around again to the bottom, and up.]

 Start a little below the top; slant down to the bottom, and curve up left; sidestroke right. Make an overhill-underhill crossbar at the top; and a straight crossbar in the middle.
[Start below the top; down, around, up, and sidestroke. Wavy cross and a straight cross.]

 Start at the bottom; go uphill to the top; loop left down to the middle, and swing up; slant down to the bottom; curve up left, across the uphill; sidestroke right, and stop.
[Bottom start; uphill high, loop through the middle, up, curve down, around, through the uphill, sidestroke, and stop.]

H Start a little below the top; curve up right to the top; slant down to the bottom. Start again at the top, to the right of the first start; slant down to the bottom; retrace up halfway; curve left, touch, loop right, swing up, and stop.
[Start below the top; make a cane. Top start, to the right; down, up, left, touch, loop right, through, and stop.]

 Start a little below the middle; sidestroke left; curve down right to the bottom; go uphill to the top; loop left down to the bottom, and swing up.
[Start below the middle; sidestroke left, curve down, around, uphill high, loop down, and up.]

 Start at the bottom; curve up left to the top; loop right down to halfway below the bottom line; loop up left, and through.
[Bottom start; curve up, around, touch on the way down under water, loop up left, and through.]

 Start a little below the top; curve up right to the top; slant down to the bottom. Start again at the top, to the right of the first start; slant down left to the middle, and touch; slant down right to the bottom, and swing up.
[Start below the top; make a cane. Top start, to the right; slant down left, touch, slant down right, and up.]

 Start a little below the top; curve up right to the top; loop left, and keep going down to the bottom; curve left; loop right, and swing up.
[Start below the top; uphill; loop down, loop right, and up.]

m Start a little below the top; curve up right to the top; slant down to the bottom; retrace up, and make a hill to the right; retrace up; make another hill to the right, and swing up.
[Start below the top; make a cane, up over the hill, up over the hill again, and up.]

n Start a little below the top; curve up right to the top; slant down to the bottom; retrace up; make a hill to the right, and swing up.
[Start below the top; make a cane, up over the hill, and up.]

O Start at the top; curve down left to the bottom; curve up right to the beginning, and close; loop right, swing up, and stop.
[Top start; around down, close up, loop right, through, and stop.]

P Start at the top; slant down to the bottom; retrace up; curve down right to the middle; curve left, and close.
[Top start; down, up, around halfway, and close.]

 Start a little below the top; curve up right to the top; curve down right to the bottom; loop right, and swing up.
[Start below the top; curve up, around, down, loop right, and up.]

R Start at the top; slant down to the bottom; retrace up; curve down right to the middle; curve left, and close; slant down right to the bottom, and swing up.
[Top start; down, up, around halfway, close, slant down right, and up.]

 Start at the bottom; go uphill to the top; loop left down to the middle; curve down right to the bottom; curve up left, across the uphill; sidestroke right, and stop.
[Bottom start; uphill high, loop through the middle, curve down, around, through the uphill, sidestroke, and stop.]

 Start a little below the top; slant down to the bottom, and curve up left; sidestroke right. Make an overhill-underhill crossbar at the top.
[Start below the top; down, around, up, and sidestroke. Wavy cross.]

 Start a little below the top; curve up right to the top; slant down to the bottom, and curve right; slant up to the top; retrace down, and swing up.
[Start below the top; make a cane, around, up, down, and up.]

V Start a little below the top; curve up right to the top; slant down to the bottom, and curve right; slant up right to the top; sidestroke right, and stop.
[Start below the top; make a cane, around, slant up right, sidestroke, and stop.]

W Start a little below the top; curve up right to the top; slant down to the bottom, and curve right; slant up to the top; retrace down, and curve right; slant up to the top; sidestroke right, and stop.
[Start below the top; make a cane, around, up, down, around, up again, sidestroke, and stop.]

X Start a little below the top; curve up right to the top; slant down right to the bottom, and swing up. Cross through the letter with a slant down left.
[Start below the top; curve up, slant down right, and up. Cross down left.]

y Start a little below the top; curve up right to the top; slant down to the bottom, and curve right; slant up to the top; retrace down to halfway below the bottom line; loop up left, and through.
[Start below the top; make a cane, around, up, down under water, loop up left, and through.]

 Start a little below the top; curve up right to the top; curve down right to the bottom; curve down right again to halfway below the bottom line; loop up left, and through.
[Start below the top; curve up, around, down, around again, and down under water, loop up left, and through.]

Figure 4–9. *(continued)*

Spacing. Students who have difficulty with spacing between letters in words and between words need additional practice with uniform spacing. One technique is to have students use graph paper for writing, putting one letter or a space between words in each square.

A difficulty some young children have with spacing between words is that they were taught to use their thumb or a finger as a spacer to separate words, which results in too much spacing. A better rule is to tell students to make the space between words the size of their letter *o* (Cohen & Plaskon, 1980; Sassoon, 1983).

Size. Difficulties with the size of letters are often caused by improper arm or finger movement, poor understanding of the writing lines, or an improper mental image of the letter (Mercer & Mercer, 1985). To improve letter size, the student may need to increase or reduce arm movement. Additionally, the instructor may need to review the concept of letter size and the various sizes of letters.

The student may practice problem letters on worksheets, the chalkboard, or using transparencies. Development of proper and consistent size may be aided by using paper that provides clear bottom, middle, and top lines. Although the one-half space middle line may be dotted, it should be clear. Figure 4-10 illustrates sample lined paper that may be used with upper elementary and secondary students who need to monitor letter size.

Horizontal alignment. Proper alignment requires that the base of each letter is touching the line on the writing paper. The student should be encouraged to bring each letter down to the baseline. In addition to the use of lined paper, younger students may benefit from the use of colored lines. Lines may also be emphasized with the use of string, yarn, or Elmer's glue, or by folding the paper (Cohen & Plaskon, 1980). For older students, repetitive exercises, such as writing several rows of difficult letter combinations, may be used to assist in the development of rhythmic, accurate writing movements.

Letter formation. Once an examiner has identified the illegibilities in a student's writing, specific techniques may be used to promote mastery of letter formation. Having the student practice the problematic letters may increase the overall legibility of the student's writing (Larsen, 1987).

Graham and Madan (1981) described a technique for correcting errors in manuscript or cursive letter formation. Letters are taught one at a time and then practiced first in isolation, then in context. For the initial step, the instructor analyzes a writing sample and identifies the specific letters that cause the student difficulty. In the second step, a single letter is targeted for instruction. The teacher models correct letter formation while verbalizing the process. This

procedure is continued until the student can first verbalize the steps for forming the letter in unison with the teacher and then trace the letter and self-verbalize the steps. For the third step, the target letter is traced or copied and the student verbally directs the writing task, correcting errors as they occur. This step is repeated until the student can copy the letter successfully five times. For the fourth step, the teacher verbally describes how to form the letter, while the student attempts to visualize and then write the letter. If the letter is formed incorrectly, the teacher provides corrective feedback. This step is repeated until the student can write the letter successfully five times from memory. In the final step, the letter is practiced in meaningful contexts, first within single words, and then within phrases and sentences. These steps could also be applied to correcting difficulties in connecting two letters, such as a cursive *b*, *v*, *o*, or *w,* with another letter. This intensive remedial method could be used effectively with both elementary and secondary students who are able to work independently and are motivated to improve their handwriting.

Line quality. The line quality of a student's handwriting is determined by the evenness and intensity of pressure placed upon the writing tool. In some cases, simply altering the writing instrument improves line quality. A variety of different writing implements exist, including pens, pencils, felt- and nylon-tipped markers, and erasable ballpoint pens. Students should experiment with different writing implements and then select an instrument with which they are comfortable (Davis & Miller, 1983).

Grip. A student should hold a pencil or pen in a comfortable manner. If a student tends to grip the writing implement too hard, placing a wadded paper tissue in the palm of the writing hand will relax the grip (Mercer & Mercer, 1985). In some instances, an alternative grip may be recommended. Thurber (1988) described a grip that does not require much fingertip pressure to hold the writing instrument. The pencil is held between the index and middle fingers with about a 25-degree slant. Figure 4-11 illustrates this grip.

Direct Instruction

Direct instruction in handwriting often includes the following components: modeling, copying, feedback, correction of errors, and positive reinforcement. Results from many intervention studies have indicated that students improve both manuscript and cursive handwriting when provided with feedback, modeling, prompting, and rewards contingent upon improved performance (Shapiro, 1989). When drill and practice activities are used, rein-

Figure 4–10. Sample Lined Paper for Upper-Elementary and Secondary Students. Permission is granted to reproduce this page.

Figure 4–11. D'Nealian Pencil Grip. Photograph provided by D.N. Thurber.

forcement systems such as points or contracts enhance student motivation.

Progressive approximation procedure. Hofmeister (1973) described a method called the Progressive Approximation Procedure that was designed to eliminate common instructional errors in handwriting instruction. For this technique, a worksheet is created with a writing model at the top and several blank practice lines below. The model may consist of individual manuscript or cursive letters or short sentences. Four steps are followed:

1. Using a pencil, the student completes the first line and informs the teacher.
2. The teacher corrects the paper by overmarking with a highlighter the letters that need improvement. Letters that represent significant improvements are not corrected.
3. The student erases the incorrect portion of letters and traces over the entire letter that the teacher has highlighted.
4. On the next line, the student repeats the parts that needed improvement on the preceding line.

The steps are repeated until a student demonstrates mastery. Using this type of procedure provides students with a good model for writing, immediate feedback, and specific practice on letters and letter combinations that need improvement.

Self-instruction and self-correction. Students who are encouraged to recognize their own errors and work on

their personal difficulties make the most progress (Tagatz, Otto, Klausmeier, Goodwin, & Cook, 1968). Kosiewicz, Hallahan, Lloyd, and Graves (1982) found that self-instructions, self-correction, and a combination of the two treatments were all highly effective in improving the handwriting performance of an elementary student with learning disabilities. Prior to that, in spite of previous skill training, the boy had consistently produced illegible handwriting.

The steps of the self-instruction strategy were applied to both list and paragraph copying and consisted of the following sequence: (a) saying aloud the word that was to be written, (b) saying the first syllable of the word, (c) naming each of the three letters in that syllable three times, (d) repeating each letter as it was written down, and (e) repeating the steps for each syllable. For the self-correction strategy, the student circled errors made on the previous day before beginning that day's copying assignment. Progress was measured on the percentage of correctly produced letters and punctuation marks. Both methods and a combined approach resulted in considerable improvement in handwriting skill. Kosiewicz et al. hypothesized that these types of self-instruction/correction procedures may only be effective once a skill, such as letter formation, has been learned. Conceivably, this type of technique would also be useful for students with difficulties in spelling and writing fluency.

Another approach for emphasizing self-correction is to provide the student with transparencies that have a row of model letters or numbers across the top. Once a student has completed practicing the letter forms on the transparencies, letter forms may be checked and corrected by laying the transparency over a master copy of correctly formed letters. This procedure frees the teacher from constantly checking each student's work and frees students from practicing and copying letters that they already form competently (Stowitschek & Stowitschek, 1979). As an alternative, a comparison may be made by placing a prepared transparency over a student's letters to determine accuracy.

Conclusion

The WJ-R ACH provides procedures for rating handwriting and evaluating several factors that may influence handwriting performance. Although handwriting is a motoric rather than a cognitive process, a student's legibility may affect both academic and vocational success. Poor handwriting contributes to lower grades, whereas legible handwriting contributes to higher grades on written assignments (Briggs, 1970; Bull & Stevens, 1979; Markham, 1976). Additionally, legible handwriting influences an employer's impression of job applicants (Davis & Miller, 1983). The development of legible handwriting is an important goal for all students. When students are able to write legibly and easily, their full attention may be directed to communication. In providing modifications and instruction in handwriting to students of all ages, the purpose of instruction, improving ability to communicate effectively, must be clear. As students engage in meaningful writing activities and develop ability to express their ideas, they see a need for developing a legible handwriting style.

Basic Writing Skills

The two basic writing skills tests on the WJ-R ACH are Dictation and Proofing. Additionally, separate test scores may be obtained for Spelling, Punctuation/Capitalization, and Usage. Basic skills, such as spelling, punctuation, capitalization, and usage are important facets of a writer's competence and are among the factors that most influence the judgment of writing quality (Brown, 1981). For some students, difficulty with basic skills is the major barrier to writing competence as their difficulties interfere with the communication of meaning. Research results have indicated that students with learning disabilities have greater deficits in basic writing skills, reflecting the conventional aspects of grammar and spelling, than in areas reflecting the expression of ideas (Poplin, Gray, Larsen, Banikowski, and Mehring, 1980). Additionally, these deficits persist into postsecondary environments. For example, in analyzing the performance of 36 college freshmen with learning disabilities on all of the WJ clusters (Woodcock & Johnson, 1977), Dalke (1988) found that their lowest mean standard score was on the Written Language cluster, a measure of basic writing skills. Students with learning disabilities often have significant spelling problems that persist into secondary school and college (Cone, Wilson, Bradley, & Reese, 1985; Gregg, 1983; Leuenberger & Morris, 1990; Vogel, 1989; Vogel & Moran, 1982). Vogel and Moran found that college students with learning disabilities made significantly more spelling, punctuation, and usage errors than their nondisabled peers.

In this section the two curricular areas of spelling and proofreading are discussed. Specific punctuation, capitalization, and usage skills, such as measured on the WJ-R ACH, are presented within the section on proofreading instruction. When a student demonstrates difficulty on the basic writing skill tests, an examiner should analyze a student's errors, decide whether or not additional assessment is necessary, and then make specific instructional recommendations for improving skill.

Spelling

Children's spelling, perhaps even more than their reading, can provide a window onto the

way in which they conceptualize the sounds of speech.

(Treiman, 1985, p. 12)

The WJ-R ACH Spelling score is obtained by totalling the responses to spelling items across the Dictation and Proofing tests. After examining the scores obtained from this test, an examiner may wish to perform a more in-depth analysis of spelling skill. Further information regarding a student's spelling performance may be obtained by analyzing a student's specific spelling errors. This type of analysis is necessary to plan appropriate remedial strategies.

Error Analysis of Spelling

In reviewing spelling errors, an examiner will want to consider a student's performance on the Proofing, Dictation, and Writing Samples tests. Although a spelling score is not derived from the Writing Samples test, informal analysis of a student's responses on this test will provide additional diagnostic information regarding spelling skill.

Error Analysis of Proofing

Analysis of an individual's responses on the Proofing test may provide the examiner with further insights into spelling skill. In some instances, a subject may identify a correct spelling as being incorrect. For example, on Item 10 of the Proofing test, Anita, a third-grade student, stated that "girl" should be changed to "gril." On two items measuring punctuation and capitalization, Anita also identified a correctly spelled word as being misspelled. Notations of these types of responses, when coupled with further information from Dictation and Writing Samples, assist in determining an individual's present level of spelling skill.

In another instance, a student will identify the spelling error on a Proofing item, but fail to produce the correct spelling. For example, on Item 21, Dick, a sixth-grade student, identified the word "column" as being misspelled but then stated that the correct spelling was "colum." Although his response is scored as incorrect, the student has demonstrated "spelling awareness" or the recognition that a word is spelled incorrectly. The ability to detect misspellings is an essential component of proofreading skill as it enables an individual to locate the correct spelling from an external source, such as a teacher, parent, or dictionary. If several responses of this nature occur, an examiner may hypothesize that a student has developed good spelling awareness, but has not yet mastered correct spelling.

Error Analysis of Dictation and Writing Samples

Although the Spelling score is obtained from the Dictation and Proofing tests, analysis of spelling errors is enhanced by examining a student's errors on both Dictation and Writing Samples, two tests that require written responses. On the Dictation test the subject is required to write words of increasing difficulty that are dictated orally. Figure 4-12 illustrates the performance of Luke, a fifth-grade boy, on the Dictation test.

On the Writing Samples test the examiner analyzes spelling performance in the context of a student's writing vocabulary. Although misspellings are not penalized, analysis of a student's spelling errors provides additional diagnostic information. Figure 4-13 illustrates Luke's performance on several items of the Writing Samples test.

Although Luke has adequate written expression, his difficulty with spelling is apparent. On Item 14, after writing the word *bouth*, Luke looked at his spelling, commented that it didn't look right, and then added in the letter *g*. Although the spelling for the word *both* was still incorrect, Luke demonstrated that he is applying the knowledge he possesses and trying to detect mistakes in spelling.

An examiner may also compare the student's performance on the Dictation and Writing Samples test. For example, the examiner may note that a student misspells several words on the Dictation test, but has few misspellings on the Writing Samples test. A critical difference between a dictated spelling list and a writing sample is that on the dictated test the student does not select the words to write. In contrast, when a student is creating sentences, he or she may only select words in which the spelling is known. Use of this strategy results in correct spelling, but an impoverished writing vocabulary. For example, a student may wish to write the word *excellent*, but be unsure of the correct spelling. After pondering the spelling for a moment, the student opts to write a less precise but easier to spell synonym, such as *good*. Although this student has adequate oral expression, his or her written expression is diminished as a result of spelling difficulty.

In another case, a student may demonstrate good spelling ability on the Dictation test, but have many misspellings on the Writing Samples test. The student is able to spell isolated words but when writing sentences, his or her spelling falters. For this student, the task of expressing ideas in writing may be such a complex mental activity that little energy is available for monitoring spelling. The student's attention is monopolized by trying to capture and record an idea. Although this type of student may have adequate written expression, assistance in the postwriting activity of proofreading is needed. Another important distinction between Dictation and Writing Samples is that on a dictated list the student hears the examiner pronounce the word to be spelled, whereas on Writing Samples, the student does not hear a word pronounced. The student must produce a word and may or may not subvocalize the pronunciation. For most students, spelling performance improves when they listen carefully to word pronunciation.

Developmental Spelling Stages

An important aspect of error analysis is to identify an individual's developmental level in spelling. In acquiring spelling skill, students progress through a consistent succession of qualitatively different approaches to spelling words. Several stages that characterize misspellings have been identified (Ehri, 1986, 1989; Gentry, 1982a, 1982b, 1984; Reid, 1988).

Stage 1: Precommunicative or prephonemic. In the initial stage of learning to spell, spellers randomly string together letters of the alphabet without regard to sound-symbol correspondence. In this early stage of development, an individual may know only a few letters and the letters may be combined with numbers or scribbles. Ernie, a first-grade student, wrote a string of unrelated letters and numbers and then asked his teacher to read the communication. At this stage, the learner has developed the understanding that letters and words convey messages to others. Figure 4-14 illustrates the prephonemic spelling of Ernie on the Writing Samples test.

Stage 2: Semi-phonetic. In this stage, letters are used to represent sounds, but only a few sounds are represented. Memory for correct spellings is unstable during this stage, and very few correct spellings are known (Ehri, 1989). A student is likely to know consonant sounds, long vowel sounds, and an occasional sight word. The individual applies the knowledge that he or she possesses regarding the spelling system to construct words.

Stage 3: Phonetic. At this stage, individuals produce spellings that demonstrate sound-symbol correspondence. Letters are used to represent the sounds that the person hears in a word without regard for conventional aspects of English spelling. Initially, an individual may represent all of the sounds in a word on the basis of letter names, thus becoming *letter name* spellers (Rhodes & Dudley-Marling, 1988). Even secondary and college students who have extreme spelling difficulty continue to rely on letter names for spelling. As proficiency increases, the learner captures all of the sounds within a word and presents them in the correct sound sequence. Figure 4-15 illustrates the spelling of Andrea, a fourth-grade student, on the Dictation test. At this point in development, Andrea is making

TEST 26

Dictation (cont.)

7. _____

8. _____

9. H R _____

10. S F _____

11. e h _*l*_ _____

12. The dog is big,

13. _*Ø*_ _____

14. _*le*_ _____

15. _*six*_ _____

16. _*green*_ _____

17. _*hose*_   _*horse*_ _____

18. _*?*_ _____

19. One man, two _*men*_ _____

20. _*Tabee*_ _____

21. tall, taller, _*taller*_ ___

22. One tooth, two _*teeht*_ ____

23. _*dont*_ _____

24. One dress, two _*dresses*_ __

25. _*wost*_ _____

26. _*Dull*_ _____

27. One child, two _*chden*_ ____

28. _*come*_ _____

29. _*parsks*_ _____

30. _*grog*_ _____

31. elegant, more elegant, _____

32. _____

33. One knife, two _____

34. _____

35. _____

36. Dear Mr. Smith

37. _____

38. One ox, two _____

39. _____

40. _____

41. _____

42. The foxes den.

43. _____

44. _____

45. _____

46. _____

47. One crisis, two _____

48. _____

49. _____

50. _____

51. _____

52. _____

53. _____

54. _____

55. _____

56. _____

STOP

Figure 4–12. A Fifth-Grade Boy on the Dictation Test.

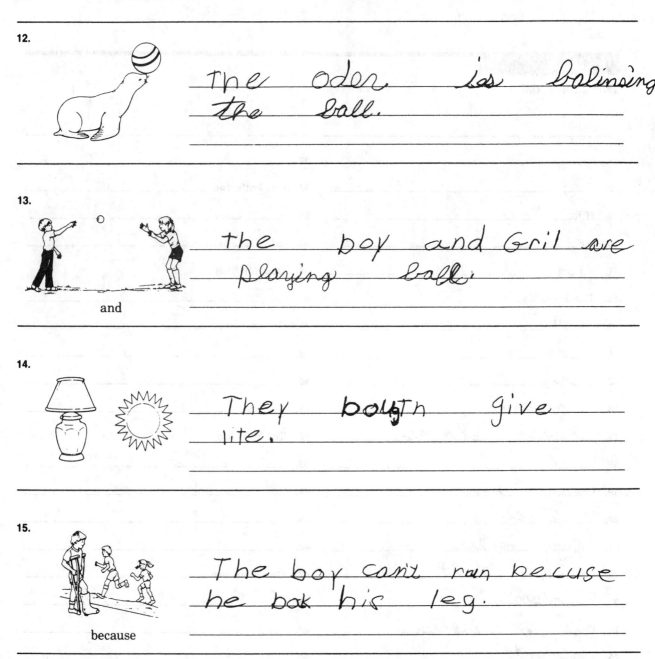

12. The oder is balinsing the ball.

13. and the boy and Gril are playing ball.

14. They bolgTn give lite.

15. because The boy can't ran becuse he bak his leg.

Figure 4–13. A Fifth-Grade Boy on the Writing Samples Test.

the transition from semi-phonetic to phonetic spelling. It is interesting to note that for both the words *children* and *dresses*, Andrea spells the *dr* sound with a *gr*.

Stage 4: Transitional. In this stage, visual memory of spelling patterns becomes apparent. The individual de-

velops awareness of the conventions of English orthography. For example, the individual produces frequent spelling patterns, such as *ight* and *tion*. As spelling knowledge develops, the individual may overgeneralize these features. For example, a student may spell the word *bite* as *bight*.

TEST 27

Writing Samples

1.

My name is _Er h lP_

2.

This is a _YN\e3_

3.

This is an _lPFNVIYEIE_

4.

This is a little dog.

This is a _lPYE5E?_

5.

This is a new hat.

This is an _V?3I+_

Figure 4–14. Prephonemic Spelling of a First-Grade Student on the Writing Samples Test.

TEST 26

Dictation (cont.)

7. _____

8. _____

9. H R   D Y _____

10. S F   Y _____

11. e h   i _____

12. The dog is big.

13.   I _____

14.   he _____

15.   SIX _____

16.   hoas _____

17.   grha _____

18.   ! _____

19. One man, two   one _____

20.   taebl _____

21. tall, taller,   tlit _____

22. One tooth, two   teth _____

23.   dont _____

24. One dress, two   grasls _____

25.   wakte _____

26. _____

27. One child, two   cllgran _____

28.   kome _____

29.   preis _____

30.   grag _____

31. elegant, more elegant,   algtly

32.   Dae tin awhel _____

33. One knife, two   lnifes _____

34.   cafe _____

35.   fran strt _____

36. Dear Mr. Smith

37.   I _____

38. One ox, two _____

39. _____

40. _____

41. _____

42. The foxes den.

43. _____

44. _____

45. _____

46. _____

47. One crisis, two _____

48. _____

49. _____

50. _____

51. _____

52. _____

53. _____

54. _____

55. _____

56. _____

STOP

Figure 4–15. A Fourth-Grade Student on the Dictation Test.

Stage 5: Correct or standard spelling. In this stage, the individual possesses multiple strategies for deriving correct spelling and has mastered words that involve roots, prefixes, suffixes and rules for combining them. Although not all words are spelled correctly, the individual regularly employs the visual features of standard English spelling (Rhodes & Dudley-Marling, 1988).

Individuals of all ages with varying abilities and disabilities progress through comparable developmental stages in learning to spell. For many students, the transition to standard spelling is generally completed by the third grade (Gentry, 1978). For children with learning disabilities, who are often noted for their aberrant spellings, the progression is slower. In examining the acquisition of spelling knowledge, research findings indicate that intermediate-grade students with learning disabilities use error patterns that are similar to their younger, non-disabled counterparts (Carpenter, 1983; Carpenter & Miller, 1982; Poplin, 1983). Even college students with learning disabilities progress in a similar developmental sequence (Bookman, 1984). When considering a speller's knowledge level, the errors are systematic and logical products of problem solving (Bookman, 1984; Gentry, 1984; Gerber & Hall, 1987).

Carla, a community college student, was receiving a failing grade in her English composition course. Prior to testing, Carla informed the examiner that the reason for her low grade was that her instructor penalized for spelling mistakes on in-class essays and exams. In fact, the instructor had informed Carla that she wouldn't be able to pass English composition class with "spelling like that." After analyzing Carla's spelling patterns, the examiner recognized that Carla's spellings were primarily phonetic. Although Carla was able to use a word processor with a spelling checker successfully for homework assignments, she was not able to produce correct spellings independently. In Carla's case, the examiner recommended that the instructor either permit Carla to revise written work or not penalize for misspellings on in-class assignments. Once the requirement of correct spelling had been removed, Carla was able to receive a passing grade in her composition class.

When evaluating the developmental level of spelling skill, an examiner may analyze and classify a student's spelling errors on the Dictation test. Table 4-2 illustrates sample semi-phonetic, phonetic, and transitional responses.

In addition to indicating the present level of spelling performance and suggesting ways to facilitate development, this type of error analysis also aids in the evaluation of spelling progress. All spelling errors fall somewhere on a continuum from being totally unrecognizable to being perfectly reasonable spellings. Considerable diagnostic information is lost by relying solely on the score for the

Dictation test which requires correct spelling as the sole criterion for evaluation.

Sometimes a student's obtained grade scores from one year to the next do not reflect the developmental progress a student has made in spelling. For example, on the first assessment, Mary, a third-grade student, wrote one or two consonants to represent words. One year later, she produced spellings that contained all of the sounds: Her spellings had evolved from semi-phonetic to phonetic. This type of qualitative error analysis helps an examiner and teacher document spelling growth and continue to plan an appropriate instructional program.

To perform a more in-depth analysis, the examiner may compile a list of all of a student's misspelled words from both the Dictation and Writing Samples tests. Table 4-3 illustrates a list of misspellings from Tom, a 15-year-old student, on Dictation and Writing Samples. Analysis suggests that Tom has a mixture of both phonetic and transitional spellings. Additionally, analysis reveals that he does not understand when and how to use apostrophes to form contractions or to show possession.

Specific Error Patterns

In addition to estimating developmental level, an examiner should determine whether or not a specific error pattern exists. Edgington (1967) presented the following list of error patterns that are found in students' misspellings: (a) addition of unneeded letters; (b) omissions of needed letters; (c) mispronunciations or dialectal speech patterns; (d) reversals of whole words, vowels, consonant order, or syllables; (e) consonant or vowel directionality (e.g., *brithday*); (f) phonetic spellings of nonphonetic words; (g) wrong association of sounds with letters; and (h) no relationship to the dictated word.

In analyzing the spelling error patterns of able and disabled readers, Carpenter (1983) found that the majority of errors were omissions, unrecognizable words, and medial position errors. Additionally, use of phonetic strategies by able readers in fourth through sixth grade distinguished them from students with learning disabilities. This finding suggests that elementary students with learning disabilities may benefit from specific instruction in listening to and writing the correct sequence of sounds.

An examiner should also differentiate between phonetically accurate and phonetically inaccurate spellers. This distinction, even at fairly young ages, is important. Phonetically inaccurate spellers are in need of more intensive remedial aid in a much wider range of areas than phonetically accurate spellers (Rourke, 1983).

Analysis of a student's performance on Dictation and Writing Samples will enable the examiner to determine whether the individual produces accurate or inaccurate

Table 4–2. Example Spellings from the Dictation Test Representing Three Developmental Stages.

Words	Semi-phonetic	Phonetic	Transitional
house	hs	hows	hous
table	tapl	tabul	tabel
don't	dt	dont	do'nt
walked	wkt	wokt	waked
comb	km	com	combe
garage	gj	garaj	gerage
cough	kf	cauf	caugh
annually	anly	anuale	annully
per se	pr	persay	per sa
inflammation	ifmasn	influmashum	inflamation

phonic alternatives. If a student writes many unrecognizable words on the Dictation and Writing Samples tests, the first spelling goal may be to help the student produce reasonable phonic alternatives, or "good" misspellings. For example, Sandra, a secondary student with a severe spelling disability, primarily produced semi-phonetic spellings. In writing words, she included the major consonant sounds in the correct sound sequence. The instructional goal for Sandra was to help her master phonetic spelling, so she would be able to use a word processor with a spelling checker for her writing assignments.

Additionally, in analyzing a student's responses, the examiner will want to note whether or not a difference exists in the student's ability to spell words that have regular grapheme-phoneme correspondence and those that require the memorization of visual features. Figure 4-16 illustrates the performance of Rosa, a sixth-grade student, on the Dictation test. Although Rosa attempts to represent some of the sounds in words, she appears to overrely on the visual appearance of words, and, consequently, many of the sound sequences are unreasonable.

In contrast, Figure 4-17 illustrates the performance of Kevin, a secondary student who maintains grapheme-phoneme correspondence but has trouble recalling the visual appearance of words. Kevin attempts to spell all words exactly as they sound.

Initially, instructional goals and remedial methods would differ for these two students. For Rosa, a spelling strategy would be selected that will help her attend to the sequence of sounds within a word so that she can produce phonetic spellings. For Kevin, a spelling strategy would be selected with a visual emphasis that will help him move from phonetic spellings into transitional/correct spellings. Effective spelling instruction is planned, monitored, and based on assessment information (Graham, 1983).

Additional Assessment of Spelling Skills

To assess spelling skill further, an examiner may analyze a student's classroom spelling tests and his or her spontaneous writing samples. An estimate of spelling competency should not be based on an individual's spelling test scores. Sometimes an individual has perfect scores on weekly spelling tests but then misspells the same words when writing a story. An individual may even misspell the studied word when asked to write a sentence using it. Unfortunately, the studied words are not retained for use in writing.

Retention of Spelling Words

A method for verifying difficulty with retention is to give the student a list of unknown words to study and then administer a spelling test several days later. A week later, the examiner may re-administer the same list unannounced. Retention is checked by comparing the percentage of words correct on the first and second administrations. As an alternative, if a weekly spelling test is administered, these results may be used. This procedure will help the examiner identify students who are able to memorize a list of words for a weekly test but who do not retain the spellings of the words for future application.

Spelling Paragraphs

An examiner may also wish to dictate an age-appropriate paragraph for a student to write that contains 100 words and then record the percentage of words spelled correctly. A 100-word passage may be selected from a basal reading series or classroom text at the student's independent reading level.

As an alternative, Peters (1979) presented three levels of paragraphs that may be used for analyzing spelling performance. The same paragraph may be dictated some time in the future for analysis of spelling growth. Figure 4-18 presents these three paragraphs and the recommended ages for use. For older students with limited spelling skill, an examiner should select a lower-level paragraph.

Table 4–3. Spelling Errors from the Dictation and Writing Samples Tests.

Word	Student's Spelling
table	tabale
I'll	I'wll
don't	do'nt
clothes	cloghths
against	agenst
purchase	pearches
cough	coffe
annually	anuly
whistling	whisoling
chick	cheack
catching	keching
both	bouth
fell	feel
off	of
mountain	mounten
gets	get's
don't	dount
legs	leg's
tongue	tonge
mad	made
hammer	hamer
tools	tooles

Peters (1979) delineated four broad categories for classifying the observed spelling errors: reasonable phonic alternatives; unreasonable phonic alternatives, including transpositions; handwriting errors, including perseveration (e.g., *openened* for *opened*); and unclassified words. She indicated that if the majority of errors are reasonable phonic alternatives, spelling prognosis is good. Unclassified errors are the most serious as they indicate that the student lacks awareness of the English spelling system. If many errors fall in the unclassified category, a remedial spelling program is essential. In presenting spelling instruction, the examiner and teacher should be familiar with: (a) modifications, (b) research results and learning principles, (c) word study methods with a visual emphasis, (d) word study methods with an auditory emphasis, and (e) word study strategies.

Instructional Modifications

Great harm may be done both to the child's development in spelling and to his personality by holding him to standards of performance which, because of his disabilities, he cannot meet.

(Horn, 1954, p. 28)

Although poor spelling skill is a concern, teachers should ensure that it is not the central focus of written language instruction or become a barrier to a student's performance in other academic areas. Mastery of lower-level functions, such as spelling, should not interfere with instruction in higher-order abilities, such as expository writing (Reid & Hresko, 1981). Students with spelling difficulties at both elementary and secondary levels need to receive both sympathetic understanding and realistic instructional goals from their teachers. Students also must see a purpose for correct spelling as they write on topics of interest. Additionally, students of all ages should be involved in setting personal goals and assuming responsibility for learning to spell.

Before recommending compensations and modifications to the spelling program, the examiner should ascertain the classroom demands by analyzing the student's performance in the present spelling program. Unfortunately, many classroom teachers use the same grade-level spelling books for all students regardless of their level in spelling skill. When analyzing the classroom spelling program, an examiner should determine whether a student is able to read all of the words that he or she is expected to learn to spell. If not, the words are too difficult. For example, Matthew, a fifth-grade student, received a list of 20 words to learn each week. His past success rate on spelling tests was 25% accuracy. When Matthew was asked to read the list of words to the examiner, he pronounced 5 of the 20 words correctly. After practicing the list of words four times, Matthew was able to identify the words accurately. Clearly, the words were too difficult for him.

Next, an examiner should determine whether a student understands the word meanings and is able to use these words in writing. In Matthew's case, he understood the meaning of the words once he was able to pronounce them. In other cases, poor spellers are unable to use the words from grade-level spelling lists their own writing.

Finally, the examiner should determine appropriate modifications to the spelling program. Although reducing the number of words on the weekly spelling test may be necessary for some low spellers, it is more important to modify the selection of words. Grade-level spelling lists are developed for the average speller, not the below-average speller. In designing an instructional spelling program for the classroom, an examiner may suggest one or more of the following modifications.

Simplify the List

Several procedures may be used to simplify a spelling list. One method is to select spelling lists from lower-grade spelling books. Another method is to shorten the list of

Dictation (cont.)

7. _____

8. _____

9. H R _____

10. S F _____

11. e h _____

12. The dog is big

13. _____ *l* _____

14. _____ *he* _____

15. _____ *six* _____

16. _____ *green* _____

17. _____ *house* _____

18. _____ *!* _____

19. One man, two _____ *men* _____

20. _____ *tald* _____

21. tall, taller, _____ *taltest* _____

22. One tooth, two _____ *teeht* _____

23. _____ *dont* _____

24. One dress, two _____ *brees* _____

25. _____ *wackf* _____

26. _____ *I will* _____

27. One child, two _____ *chisl* _____

28. _____ *cole* _____

29. _____

30. _____

31. elegant, more elegant, _____

32. _____

33. One knife, two _____

34. _____

35. _____

36. Dear Mr. Smith

37. _____

38. One ox, two _____

39. _____

40. _____

41. _____

42. The foxes den.

43. _____

44. _____

45. _____

46. _____

47. One crisis, two _____

48. _____

49. _____

50. _____

51. _____

52. _____

53. _____

54. _____

55. _____

56. _____

STOP

Figure 4–16. A Sixth-Grade Student Who Overrelies on Visual Features.

TEST 26

Dictation (cont.)

7. _____

8. _____

9. H R _____

10. S F _____

11. e h _____

12. The dog is big

13. _____

14. *he*

15. *six*

16. *green*

17. *house*

18. *!*

19. One man, two *men*

20. *taybal*

21. tall, taller, *tallist*

22. One tooth, two *teethe*

23. *don·t*

24. One dress, two *dreses*

25. *woldt*

26. *I'll*

27. One child, two *children*

28. _____

29. *perchis*

30. *geroje*

31. elegant, more elegant, *most elegnt*

32. *Dayton, OH*

33. One knife, two *knives*

34. *coff*

35. *Front St.*

36. Dear Mr. Smith **;**

37. *french*

38. One ox, two *ox*

39. *anuale*

40. *fifty one*

41. *ed.*

42. The foxes den.

43. _____

44. _____

45. _____

46. _____

47. One crisis, two _____

48. _____

49. _____

50. _____

51. _____

52. _____

53. _____

54. _____

55. _____

56. _____

STOP

Figure 4–17. A Secondary Student with Phonetic Spelling.

Diagnostic dictation (8-9 years)
One day, as I was walking down Bridge Street, I heard the
sound of trotting. I turned and saw behind me the shaggy
dark hair of a frightened little horse. I searched in my
pockets for an apple from my dinner to give him. 'I know
where you should be,' I said. So I removed the belt of my
raincoat and tied it around his neck and led him back. I
opened the gate, and with satisfaction he galloped into his
own field. I was certainly very happy that now he was safe,
away from the noisy and dangerous traffic.

Diagnostic dictation (9-10 years)
Late one night my friend woke me, saying, 'Would you
enjoy a trial-run in my new helicopter?'
I had scarcely scrambled into my track-suit before we were
away. The lights of the city glowed beneath: the stars above.
I was beginning to wonder about our destination when I
caught sight of the spinning knife edge and the surface of
what must have been a type of flying saucer whistling round
us. We dodged skilfully to avoid an accident. To our relief,
the space-craft regained height and we sank down to earth
and the comfortable bed I had never actually left.

Diagnostic dictation (10-11 years)
A peculiar shape was approaching from the southern valley.
Gradually they distinguished a recently designed airplane
circling above.

The machine touched down with precision in the rough
mountainous region, without even scraping its surface. The
children surrounded the pilot, who explained that his
altimeter and temperature gauge were damaged and he was
anxious about increasing altitude in these freezing conditions.
From the alpine school he telephoned his base, requesting
spare instruments to be delivered and fitted immediately.

The children viewed the repairs with enthusiasm, especially
when they were taken in groups for an unforgettable flight
before the pilot's final departure.

Figure 4–18. Diagnostic Spelling Paragraphs. *Note.* From
Diagnostic and Remedial Spelling Manual (pp. 20–22) by M.L.
Peters, 1979, London: Macmillan Education. Copyright 1979 by
Macmillan Education. Reprinted by permission.

words by reducing the number that a student has to learn.
The list may also be shortened by selecting the easiest
words, high-frequency words, or the words with regular
grapheme-phoneme correspondence.

Classify Types of Words

In presenting spelling words for study, words can be
divided into three main groups: sound words that are
spelled the way they sound, think words that contain an
unpredictable element, and see words that require memorization of the irregular element (Childs, 1960). A similar

classification for spelling patterns is: green-flag words,
purely phonetic; yellow-flag words, spelled in more than
one way; and red-flag words, irregular words to be learned
as wholes (Venezky, 1970). Color may be used to highlight words that have regular (green), irregular but predictable (yellow), and irregular grapheme-phoneme correspondence (red). These types of classifications help
students know which words to study and how to study
certain words.

Spelling Notebook

Students can develop their own spelling notebooks to
record words difficult to spell that they use frequently in
their own writing. These words may be entered alphabetically for quick reference when writing (Harp, 1988).

Individualized Word Lists

As early as first grade, students can keep individualized
lists of words that have not been learned yet. For first-
through fourth-grade students, James (1986) found that
having students select their own words to study was more
motivating and more effective for retention than having
students learn teacher-selected words from the basal spelling list.

An effective solution for developing word lists is to
select misspelled words from students' compositions to
serve as the basis of the instructional program (Personke
& Yee, 1971). Peers may administer the individualized
weekly spelling test to each other. For secondary students
enrolled in a vocational program, or college students, the
examiner and student may select words relevant to the area
of study or identify high-frequency words for the student
to master.

High-Frequency Words

High-frequency words are words that a student encounters on a regular basis. For individuals with mild
mental retardation or severe spelling difficulties, a functional spelling vocabulary that is relevant to the student's
current and future life success should be determined
(Graham, 1983; Luftig, 1987). Figure 4-19 illustrates a list
of functional words provided by Petty, Petty, and Salzer
(1989) that are used frequently in writing.

Fitzgerald (1951) compiled a list of frequent errors and
spelling demons. These 222 high-frequency words accounted for more than 61% of the total words used in
writing. In second through sixth grade, these errors accounted for approximately 55% of the misspellings in
spontaneous writing. Figure 4-20 presents the 50 persis-

a	cold	girls	line	part	the	work
about	come	give	little	people	their	would
after	coming	glad	live	place	them	write
again	could	go	long	play	then	
ago	country	going	look	played	there	year
all	cut	good	looked	please	these	years
along		got	lost	pretty	they	yes
also		grade	lot	put	thing	yet
always	daddy	great	lots		things	you
am	day	grow	love	rain	think	your
an	days			ran	this	yours
and	dear	had	made	read	thought	
another	did	hand	make	red	three	
any	didn't	happy	man	rest	through	
are	do	hard	many	ride	time	
around	does	has	may	right	to	
as	dog	hat	me	room	today	
asked	doing	have	men	run	told	
at	doll	he	milk		too	
away	don't	hear	more	said	took	
	door	heard	morning	same	top	
baby	down	help	most	sat	town	
back		her	mother	saw	tree	
bad	each	here	much	say	two	
ball	eat	him	must	school		
be	end	his	my	see	until	
because	even	hold		seen	up	
bed	every	home	name	send	use	
been		hope	never	she		
before	fall	hot	new	should	very	
best	far	house	next	show		
better	fast	how	nice	side	walk	
big	fat		night	sister	want	
black	father	I	no	sleep	wanted	
book	feet	if	not	snow	was	
boy	few	I'm	now	so	water	
boys	find	in		some	way	
bring	fire	into	of	something	we	
brother	first	is	off	soon	week	
but	five	it	old	started	well	
buy	for	its	on	stay	went	
by	found		once	stop	were	
	four	just	one	such	what	
call	friend		only	summer	when	
called	from	know	open	sun	where	
came	fun		or	sure	which	
can		land	order		while	
car	game	large	other	take	white	
cat	gave	last	our	teacher	who	
children	get	let	out	tell	will	
close	getting	letter	over	than	wish	
coat	girl	like		that	with	

Figure 4–19. A Functional Spelling Word List. *Note.* From *Experience in Language: Tools and Techniques for Language Arts Methods* (5th ed.) (pp. 295–296) by W.T. Petty, D.C. Petty, and R.T. Salzer (M.F. Becking contributed to previous editions), 1989, Boston: Allyn and Bacon. Copyright© 1989 by Allyn and Bacon. Reprinted with permission.

am	our
and	received
because	Saturday
coming	some
cousin	sometimes
don't	Sunday
everybody	teacher
February	teacher's
for	Thanksgiving
friend	that's
from	their
getting	there
going	time
good-by	to
guess	today
Halloween	tomorrow
have	too
hello	two
here	very
I'm	we
January	write
know	writing
Mrs.	you
name	your
now	you're

Figure 4–20. Frequent Spelling Errors and Demons.

tent demons that were found in four or five of the grades. Based upon the high utility and difficulty of these words, an instructor should present these words systematically and students should study them until mastery is achieved (Fitzgerald, 1951).

A comprehensive word list, appropriate for use with upper-elementary, secondary, and college students with spelling difficulty, is presented in Figure 3-6 in Chapter 3 (Fry, Polk, & Fountoukidis, 1984). Mastery of these 1,000 words will provide a student with a solid foundation in spelling skill.

Flow List

Another modification that may be applied with students is a flow list, or a list that changes daily, rather than a fixed spelling list (McCoy & Prehm, 1987). For the flow list, a chart is made where correct words are marked with a *C* and incorrect words are marked with a check. The teacher decides how many days a word should be spelled correctly before it is crossed off the list. As words are mastered, new words are added to the bottom of the list. The crossed out words are reviewed periodically. Figure 4-21 illustrates a sample flow list in which the words were selected from the student's writing.

A similar procedure, called "Add-a-Word," was described by Pratt-Struthers, Struthers, and Williams (1983). Students copied a list of 10 words and then covered each word and attempted to write it from memory. If a word was spelled correctly on 2 consecutive days, the word was dropped from the list and replaced with a new word. Using this procedure, fifth- and sixth-grade students with learning disabilities increased their percentage of correct spelling.

This type of flexible spelling list allows a teacher to individualize the spelling program and lets each student progress at his or her own rate with as much review and repetition as needed. A flow list could also be recommended for students who are accelerated in spelling skill: Students select relevant words to study and then cross them off as they are mastered.

Peer Tutors

Classwide peer tutoring or peer tutoring for selected individuals is also an effective instructional procedure for improving spelling performance (Delquadri, Greenwood, Whorton, Carta, & Hall, 1986; Maheady & Harper, 1987; Mandoli, Mandoli, & McLaughlin, 1982). Delquadri, Greenwood, Stretton, and Hall (1983) developed a peer tutoring game that increased spelling accuracy of average peers and students with learning disabilities on the weekly Friday test. With all students, high-interest activities are an important aspect of a spelling program.

Spelling Checkers

Most word processing programs include built-in spelling checkers. These programs identify misspelled words and also provide correct spellings. Spelling checkers similar in appearance to a calculator are also available. To profit from spelling checkers, a student must be able to spell words as they sound. This enables the system to recognize the word and then provide the correct spelling. For students with severe spelling disabilities, particularly at the secondary level, an examiner may wish to recommend that the individual be allowed to use a spelling checker for all written assignments.

Research Results and Learning Principles

There is no question that the behavior of the teacher determines, more than any other factor, whether a child learns or does not learn to spell.

(Peters, 1974, p. 40)

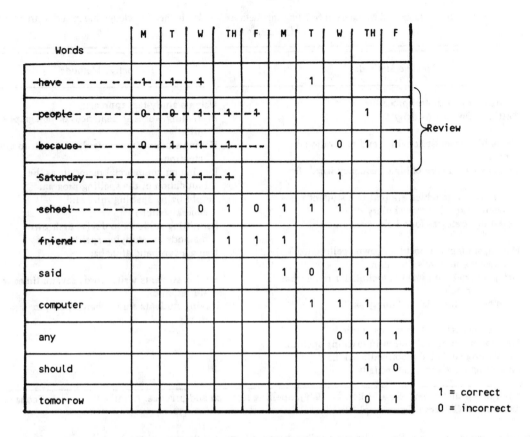

Figure 4–21. Sample Spelling Flow List.

Many teachers are not aware of empirically supported methods of spelling instruction. In fact, teachers routinely employ as many nonsupported spelling methods as they do supported methods (Vallecorsa, Zigmond, & Henderson, 1985). Examinations of current school practices show that many of the employed spelling procedures are based on tradition or habit rather than sound instructional principles (Gettinger, 1984; Graham, 1983; Graham & Miller, 1979). For mainstreamed handicapped students, spelling instruction should be direct, comprehensive, student-oriented, individualized, varied, and based upon a foundation of research evidence (Graham, 1985). Vallecorsa, Zigmond, and Henderson (1985) presented a table adopted from Graham and Miller (1979) that summarized effective and ineffective methods of spelling instruction. (See Table 4-4.)

Self-Correction

The single most effective method for helping students learn to spell is to have them correct their own errors after taking a spelling test (Christine & Hollingsworth, 1966; Graham & Miller, 1979; Personke & Yee, 1971). Self-correction encourages the student to identify the part of the word that was missed and then correct the error. Words are

learned in the process of correction. As soon as a test is complete, a teacher should spell words aloud and the student should study any missed words as soon as possible.

Copying Words

Perhaps the most commonly used ineffective spelling study strategy is to have students copy words a specific number of times. Writing a word does not guarantee retention (Graham, 1983). When practicing spelling words, students should look at the word and then attempt to write the word from memory.

Spelling Books

In many classrooms, the spelling book is the only material used for instruction. Students should not be required to complete all spelling activities in the workbook. Instead, the teacher should select the activities that will promote spelling competence. In addition to a spelling workbook, other methods, techniques, and instructional games should be used to promote spelling growth.

Table 4-4. Supported and Nonsupported Methods of Spelling Instruction Included in the Knowledge Index and Instructional Practices Questionnaire[*]

Effective Methods	Ineffective Methods
Using a test-study-test procedure	Using a study-test approach
Testing a few words daily	Presenting words in sentences or paragraphs initially
Using high interest activities and motivational games	Having students write words in the air to aid retention
Emphasizing a core of high frequency words first	Relying on commercial materials as the foundation of the spelling program
Teaching words which are part of a student's listening/speaking vocabulary	Emphasizing spelling rules and generalizations
Teaching strategies for whole-word study	Permitting students to devise their own methods for studying spelling words
Having students correct their own spelling work under the teacher's direction	Using a synthetic alphabet
Using a variety of remedial techniques rather than one approach	Having students write words several times to aid retention
Developing students' dictionary skills	Having students study "hard spots" in words
Frequently reevaluating words studied	
Limiting phonics instruction in teaching spelling	
Developing students' proofreading skills	
Presenting words in a list initially	

[*]Adapted from Graham, S., & Miller, L. (1979). Spelling research and practice: A unified approach. *Focus on Exceptional Children*, October, p. 10.

Note. From "Spelling Instruction in Special Education Classrooms: A Survey of Practices" by A.L. Vallecorsa, N. Zigmond, and L.M. Henderson, 1985, *Exceptional Children, 52*, p. 21. Copyright 1985 by The Council for Exceptional Children. Reprinted by permission.

Distributed Practice

Spelling performance also increases when a few words are presented daily, rather than presenting all words at the beginning of the week. Poor spellers perform better if three phonemically irregular or four regular words are introduced daily (Gettinger, 1984). After reviewing the results of their study comparing the two systems of word presentation, Rieth, Axelrod, Anderson, Hathaway, Wook, and Fitzgerald (1974) suggested that presenting students with a few words daily should replace the customary practice of presenting a list of words at the beginning of the week. The procedure was more effective for retention even without daily testing. Distributed practice was most helpful for poor spellers. For good spellers, the two procedures were equally effective.

Spelling Rules

Providing students with direct instruction in spelling rules is not effective in improving spelling achievement (Graham & Miller, 1979). Graham and Miller suggested teaching only the following six spelling rules:

1. Proper nouns and most adjectives formed from proper nouns begin with capital letters.
2. Rules for adding suffixes (e.g., changing *y* to *i*, dropping the final *e*, and doubling the final consonant).
3. Periods are used for writing abbreviations.
4. Apostrophes are used to show possession.
5. The letter *q* is followed by a *u*.
6. English words do not end in the letter *v*.

Gettinger, Bryant, and Fayne (1982) found that elementary students with learning disabilities could improve their spelling performance when remedial procedures based upon learning principles were employed. The following strategies were employed to teach both regular and irregular words: oral spelling, presentation of practice words one at a time with three to four words per day, daily mastery practice with three consecutive correct trials, corrective feedback after each dictation, focus on difficult word parts, distributing practice across three weeks of instruction, and sentence writing practice. The sentence writing practice began with fill-ins, followed by sentence dictation, and then sentence generation. In providing spelling instruction to individuals with learning disabilities, the results from this study supported several practices: (a) reduced number of words, (b) distributed practice, and (c) specific training for transfer to novel words and sentence writing.

Although knowledge of validated methods makes spelling instruction more effective for all students, methods not supported by group research should not be discarded. A method that is ineffective for a group of students, such as tracing in the air or writing a word several times, may be quite effective when used by a specific individual.

Once an examiner has determined that a student needs spelling assistance, a systematic instructional program is planned. An important point to keep in mind is that the purpose of spelling instruction is to improve a student's ability to communicate in writing, not to improve his or her performance on weekly spelling tests. Improved spelling performance requires active involvement, interest, and commitment of the learner. This purpose can only be accomplished by providing an atmosphere in which students engage in meaningful writing activities and their initial written products are valued, regardless of spelling errors. Students must see a need for correct spelling.

Matching Instruction to the Developmental Level

In planning instruction, an examiner should consider the student's present developmental level in spelling skill. After identifying where a student's performance falls on the developmental continuum, an examiner may make appropriate recommendations and set appropriate instructional goals. For example, it is unreasonable to expect a student who spells semi-phonetically to become a correct speller without first progressing through other developmental stages.

Gentry (1982a) discussed instruction that would be appropriate for the various developmental levels. The precommunicative speller should increase knowledge of the alphabet and book awareness but not receive formal spelling instruction. Semi-phonetic spellers should enhance their print awareness through continued immersion in print. Word families, alphabet and beginning reading instruction, and the language experience approach are appropriate for semi-phonetic spellers. At this stage, correct spelling is not emphasized. Peters (1979) discussed how children who write freely and confidently at an early age will deviate from conventional spelling. In these early stages, the teacher must welcome what a child writes, irrespective of how it is written.

As students are making the transition to phonetic spelling, they should be introduced to word families, spelling patterns, phonics, and word structure. These skills should be taught in the context of written language. Transitional spellers are ready for formal spelling instruction in a spelling textbook. Students should engage in creative writing activities to enhance their understanding of English spelling. Correct spellers should also receive formal spelling instruction as well as extensive writing opportunities to increase their written vocabulary.

In many instances, an examiner will wish to recommend a specific strategy for studying spelling words. As with reading, one best way to teach spelling does not exist (Gerber & Lydiatt, 1984; Stanback, 1979-1980). Different techniques are effective for different students at different times in their educational careers. Depending upon a student's characteristics, an examiner may wish to recommend the use of: (a) a visual method of word study, (b) an auditory method of word study, or (c) a specific strategy to promote generalization.

Word Study Methods with a Visual Emphasis

Some students have difficulty remembering how words look and, consequently, spell words exactly as they sound. When learning to spell irregular words, it is necessary to store specific visual information about orthographic forms (Ehri, 1980).

Phonetically accurate spellers may have difficulty remembering letter orientation and the spelling of basic sight words or high-frequency words. In elementary-age students, an examiner may note frequent omissions, insertions, reversals, and transpositions in a student's spelling. These types of errors suggest that a student will benefit from a look and write method to teaching spelling (Peters, 1979). Phonetically accurate spellers tend to direct too much attention to the analysis of sounds, and as a consequence, remedial efforts should focus on appreciation of orthographic relationships (Rourke, 1983).

The goal is to move students from phonetic to transitional/correct spellings by teaching students to look at words with the intent of remembering their spelling patterns. When learning a difficult word, an individual with a severe spelling disability should look at the word, cover it, and attempt to write it from memory while saying the word (Cotterell, 1974). As a further aid to retention, several of these methods add a tracing component.

Figure 4-22 illustrates the spelling of Carolyn, a college sophomore, on the Dictation test. When analyzing Carolyn's spellings the examiner observed that she overrelies on phonetic information. Carolyn was highly motivated to improve her spelling skills and decided that she wanted to master the 1,000 high-frequency words presented in Figure 3-6 in Chapter 3. She decided to try to master 3 words daily and then recheck her accuracy on all words at the end of the week. Carolyn also decided to keep a spelling notebook and record alphabetically any words that she had difficulty spelling when she was writing. The examiner suggested a study strategy of looking carefully at the word and its parts, saying the word, covering it up, and writing the word correctly from memory three times. Carolyn used this approach and was able to improve her spelling proficiency. The next section presents several examples of specific remedial spelling methods that will increase attention to the visual features of words.

Fernald Method

The intent of the Fernald remedial spelling method (Fernald, 1943) is to help a student develop a distinct perception and image of a word so that the individual can reproduce a word after the stimulus has been removed. Fernald believed that the major characteristic of poor spellers was vague, indistinct, or nonexistent visual imagery. She also believed that the most satisfactory spelling vocabulary is one that is determined by the student; consequently, an essential element of this method is that the student selects the words to study.

The steps of the method include:

1. The teacher writes the selected word on the blackboard or paper.
2. The teacher pronounces the word clearly and distinctly. The student looks at the word while pronouncing the word correctly.
3. The student studies the word in order to develop a visual image before attempting to write the word. A visual student tries to picture the word; an auditory student vocalizes the word; and a kinesthetic student traces the word.
4. When the student indicates that the word is known, the word is erased and the student writes the word from memory.
5. Once the word has been written correctly, the paper is turned over and the word is written a second time from memory.
6. Finally, the teacher creates situations in which the student will use the word in writing.

For some students, tracing a word several times while simultaneously pronouncing it, and then attempting to write the word from memory, is an effective study technique. This technique: (a) ensures that a student is looking at a word, (b) provides an association between what is heard and what is seen, and (c) determines the direction of word inspection, thus supplanting and correcting faulty eye-movements (Anderson, 1938).

Cover-Write Methods

Kirk and Chalfant (1984) described another useful procedure for students with severe spelling difficulties who have difficulty retrieving word images. The following steps are used:

1. Select a word to be learned, write it on a card, and pronounce it.
2. Have the student look at and pronounce the word.
3. While looking at the word and saying the letter names or sounds, the student traces each letter in the air.
4. Remove the word and ask the student to trace the word in the air while pronouncing it.
5. Repeat step 3 if needed.
6. Repeat the tracing in the air with pronouncing until the student feels that he or she knows how to spell the word.
7. Have the student write the word from memory and pronounce it. Repeat tracing, if incorrect.
8. Teach a new word following the same steps.
9. Ask the student to trace the first word in the air and write it from memory.
10. Write the word in a notebook that can be used for review.
11. Encourage the student to use the words in sentences and homework whenever possible.

When using this method, a teacher may wish to modify it by having the student trace over the word instead of tracing the word in the air. The main problem with air-tracing is that it does not produce a distinct visual image. It does, however, provide the individual with kinesthetic feedback, provided by large muscle movement, that may aid in recall.

A similar approach was described by Edgington (1967). Three to five words are presented on individual cards using the following steps:

1. Look at and say the word.
2. Write the word, pronouncing the sounds while writing the letters.
3. Compare the written word to the model letter by letter.
4. If the word is correct, repeat the second and third steps four more times.
5. Cover the word, write and sound out the word.
6. Repeat all five steps.

Depending upon the severity of the spelling problem, the teacher may modify the number of repetitions in this approach.

Five-Step Study Strategy

A simple procedure developed by Graham and Freeman (1985) was used effectively with elementary students with learning disabilities. In addition to aiding recall, students demonstrated ability to apply this procedure without teacher assistance. The students memorized the steps and practiced them with a teacher and then independently. The steps included:

TEST 26

Dictation (cont.)

7. _____

8. _____

9. H R _____

10. S F _____

11. e h _____

12. The dog is big

13. _____

14. _____

15. _____

16. _____

17. _____

18. _____

19. One man, two _____

20. _____

21. tall, taller, *tallest*

22. One tooth, two *teeth*

23. *don't*

24. One dress, two *dresses*

25. *walked*

26. *I'll*

27. One child, two *children*

28. *comb*

29. *perchise*

30. *giraje*

31. elegant, more elegant, *most elegant*

32. *Dates, OH*

33. One knife, two *knives*

34. *cauf*

35. *front street*

36. Dear Mr. Smith :

37. *french*

38. One ox, two *oxin*

39. *anualy*

40. *fifty one*

41. *ect.*

42. The foxes den.

43. *exsapt*

44. *embaresed*

45. *sirogence*

46. _____

47. One crisis, two _____

48. _____

49. _____

50. _____

51. _____

52. _____

53. _____

54. _____

55. _____

56. _____

STOP

Figure 4–22. A College Sophomore on the Dictation Test.

1. Say the word.
2. Write and say the word.
3. Check the word.
4. Trace and say the word.
5. Write the word from memory and check it.
6. Repeat the steps.

As a further component of strategy training, each student was asked to predict the number of words that he or she would spell correctly.

In a later study, Harris, Graham, and Freeman (1988) found that training in this strategy and asking students to predict the number of words that would be spelled correctly improved the metamemory performance (self-monitoring of spelling accuracy) of students with learning disabilities. Subjects in the teacher-monitored group were more accurate in their predictions than subjects in the free-study group. The results suggested that prediction accuracy was related to improved spelling performance.

Because of its simplicity, some secondary students could also apply this strategy when studying unknown words. Tracing would be eliminated when it was no longer necessary for retention. Additionally, asking students to predict the accuracy of their spellings may help increase awareness of correct spelling patterns.

Whole-Word Approach

An approach outlined by Smith (1975) for whole-word learning was found to be effective with groups of students. The approach consisted of these steps.

1. Look at the word.
2. Close your eyes and try to visualize the word.
3. Check the word.
4. Copy or look at the letters of the word.
5. Recheck the spelling.
6. Attempt to write the word from memory.
7. Check to see if the spelling is correct.
8. Repeat steps 6 and 7 until the word is spelled correctly two times in succession.

Chalkboard Spelling

Chalkboards are useful for presenting and practicing spelling words. A teacher may write the word, pronounce it, have the student study the word, erase the word, and have the student write the word from memory (Hildreth, 1955). A similar procedure is to write a word with a wet sponge and have students copy the word before it evaporates from the board (Sisneros & Bullock, 1983). A modification of this procedure is to have children watch the word until it evaporates and then to attempt to write

the word from memory. In this way, the student must produce the spelling independently.

TV Spelling

Peters (1979) described a simple procedure that parents may use at home to improve spelling. The method includes the following steps:

1. Have a pad and pencil ready when watching TV.
2. Watch the beginning of an advertisement.
3. Try to write the name of what is being advertised without looking up in the middle.
4. Check the word and rewrite the name. Say the name as you write it.

Parents may provide help by checking the student's spelling when the advertisement disappears from the screen.

Microcomputer Spelling

Effective study may also be accomplished with the help of a microcomputer in preschool through high school in both regular and special education classrooms (Rieth, Polsgrove, & Eckert, 1984). Several companies have developed software programs that use a "look and write from memory" approach. The word is flashed on the screen for a pre-selected length of time, and then the student types the word from memory. If an error is made, the computer flashes the word again until mastery is achieved.

Typing

Touch typing is another remedial strategy for children who do not retain the visual forms of words easily (Edgington, 1967). Typing instruction may also be provided using a microcomputer.

Misspellings

Another spelling strategy that has been recommended is to imitate a student's errors (Kauffman, Hallahan, Haas, Brame, & Boren, 1978; Nulman & Gerber, 1984). The teacher writes the student's misspelling, followed by the correct spelling. The student is asked to compare the two spellings and determine the mistake. In other approaches, students are exposed to misspellings of words, such as eliminating nonphonetic letters in standard spellings. Increased exposure to incorrect spellings may not be effective for slow-learning students, ESL students, or students with learning disabilities who may be as likely to remember the visual appearance of the incorrect spelling as the correct spelling.

Word Study Methods with an Auditory Emphasis

In some remedial spelling methods, increased emphasis is placed on word pronunciation. When analyzing a subject's performance on the Dictation and Writing Samples tests, an examiner may observe that a student is overrelying on visual cues. Figure 4-16 (see page 118) illustrates the performance of Rosa, a sixth-grade girl, on the Dictation test. Analysis of Rosa's spellings suggests that she overrelies on the visual features of words. Her misspellings contain many of the right letters, but the sequence of the letters demonstrates lack of attention to the order of sounds. Noting this pattern, the examiner recommended that Rosa would benefit from a spelling method that emphasized word pronunciation.

Many techniques may be used to help students listen to and sequence the sounds within words. The following remedial spelling methods may be helpful to students who have difficulty attending to sound sequences.

Horn Method

Horn (1954) described the following method:

1. Pronounce each word carefully.
2. Look at each word part while pronouncing the word.
3. Say the letters in sequence.
4. Attempt to recall how the word looks, then spell the word.
5. Check the attempt.
6. Write the word.
7. Check.
8. Repeat all steps if necessary.

This method emphasizes both the careful pronunciation of spelling words and attention to visual appearance.

Bannatyne's System

Although Bannatyne's (1971) spelling approach is similar to the Fernald method, the primary emphasis of this technique is placed on word pronunciation. Study begins with nonvisual training and careful articulation of the word. The following steps are used for word study:

1. Pronounce the word carefully.
2. Repeat the word separating the phonemes.
3. Study the visual word, breaking down the graphemes to match the phonemes.

4. As the teacher points to the graphemes in sequence, articulate each phoneme.
5. Write the graphemes as lightly spaced units while articulating the phonemes in rhythmic sequence.
6. Continue using this technique with copying and tracing until the word is easily recalled.

This type of approach helps a student develop grapheme-phoneme awareness, or the relationship between written symbols and their corresponding sounds.

Adaptation of the Glass-Analysis Method

Although the Glass-Analysis method was developed primarily for teaching decoding skills (see the Basic Skills section in Chapter 3 for a complete description of this method), it may also be adapted to improve spelling skills. Once the visual and auditory clusters are identified in a word, the teacher may ask a student to write the various clusters that make the different sounds. For example, in learning to spell the word "adaptation," a teacher may say:

1. Write the letters that make the "a" sound.
2. Write the letters that make the "dap" sound.
3. Write the letters that make the "ta" sound.
4. Write the letters that make the "tion" sound.
5. Write the word "adaptation" as you say each part: a-dap-ta-tion.
6. Turn over your paper and write the word "adaptation" from memory. Be sure to say the word while you write it.

In using Glass-Analysis for spelling, the visual and auditory clusters should be presented in the order that they appear within words to emphasize correct sound sequencing.

Finger Spelling

Finger spelling is a procedure for reinforcing auditory discrimination, auditory sequencing, and phonetic spelling for remedial spellers that is taught in conjunction with sound blending (Stein, 1983). The approach is used to teach young children or remedial spellers short words that include consonants, short vowels, digraphs, and beginning and ending blends. The teacher presents a short word on a card, pronounces the word, and then spells the word raising one finger for each sound. The process is repeated as the children say the word and raise a finger with each sound they hear. Two fingers are raised together for digraphs and beginning blends. Next, the teacher dictates the word, the children repeat it, raise fingers for each sound, and then write the word on paper, saying each sound as they write the letter. Stein suggested that the kinesthetic feedback from raising a finger helps to eliminate confusion in the sequencing of sounds. Similarly, a teacher may have students clap out or push forward chips or tokens to represent the number of syllables or phonemes within a word. Developmentally, students are able to indicate the number of syllables in a word before they can indicate the number of phonemes (Treiman, 1985).

Spelling requires careful listening to the sequence of sounds in words. Moving from speech to sequencing of letters is a necessary substructure for developing spelling ability (Stanback, 1979-1980). Use of these types of activities may help a student progress from the precommunicative level to the semi-phonetic level, or from the semi-phonetic level to the phonetic level of spelling development.

Adaptation of Simultaneous Oral Spelling

An adaptation of the Simultaneous Oral Spelling (SOS) procedure (Gillingham & Stillman, 1973) was more effective than other methods in helping poor spellers improve their skill (Bradley, 1981, 1983). The steps were as follows:

1. The student selects a word to learn.
2. The word is written or formed with plastic script letters.
3. The student pronounces the word.
4. The student writes the word, while saying the alphabetic name of each letter as it is being written.
5. The student pronounces the word again and checks to see that it is written correctly. Steps 2 through 5 are then repeated twice.
6. The student practices the word in this way for six consecutive days.

Bradley (1983) suggested the reason that the multisensory SOS procedure was more effective than other techniques was because it establishes one-to-one correspondence between the spoken and written symbol and teaches the student to label, discriminate, recall, and organize. For some poor spellers, saying letter names, as in the SOS procedure, instead of sounds may be more effective. Saying letter names did not, however, improve the spelling performance of average spellers.

Syllable Approach

Cicci (1980) described a syllable approach to teaching spelling that was useful for students with problems in auditory processing. To begin, syllables are presented on flash cards. The student looks at the syllable card, the teacher pronounces the syllable, and the student says the syllable. Several syllables are then presented to form words. Once the student has practiced the separate syllables, the syllables are moved together to form a whole word. The student then sees the word, hears the word, and pronounces the word. Gradually, words are introduced on paper typed in parts. For spelling, the student hears the word, says the word in syllables, and then writes the word in syllables. If in the beginning the student is unable to divide the word into syllables, the instructor pronounces the word in separate syllables as the student writes each syllable. This type of method will help a student isolate word parts. This technique is most applicable to words with regular phoneme-grapheme correspondence.

Word Study Strategies

Specific strategies may be used to increase students' knowledge of the linguistic structure of words. Careful analysis of word patterns may help students generalize knowledge to new words.

Analogy Strategy

An analogy strategy, described by Englert, Hiebert, and Stewart (1985), may help students use spelling patterns from known words to spell new or unfamiliar words. With this approach, students look for orthographic similarities among words and then use these spelling patterns to spell new words. Each instructional lesson takes approximately 10 minutes and can be done with a small group or entire class.

To begin, the instructor identifies words that a student has missed on pretests. A spelling bank of 15 words is then developed by matching the missed words to words that the student already knows how to spell. For example, if the student missed the word *neat* then the word *eat* may be selected for the spelling bank.

In the first step, the teacher demonstrates that when words rhyme, the last parts are often spelled the same way. The teacher presents a set of words and then says a new word that rhymes with one of the words. The students are asked to select the word that rhymes with the auditorily presented word. Students then identify which letters of the printed and dictated word would be spelled the same based upon the rhyming rule.

In the second step, the students practice the words by spelling them aloud from memory and then writing the words from memory two times and once in a test of delayed recall.

Using this analogy strategy, students are given a practice list of transfer words. Words are presented auditorily and the student finds the spelling bank word that rhymes with the presented word. After identifying the part of both words that rhymes and is spelled the same way, the student attempts to spell the word using the rhyming word from the spelling bank. Transfer words are then practiced in a cloze passage. Students are asked to fill in the missing words from sentences without looking at the spelling bank. If the word is not written correctly, the student is reminded to think of the rhyming word in the spelling bank that rhymes with the transfer word. A transfer list may also be constructed using words that share the same phonetic features but do not rhyme (Gerber, 1984). A teacher may identify the phonetic features that are troublesome to a student and then provide further practice with these features.

Looking for orthographic similarities between known and unknown words may help students of all ages generalize spelling patterns. If a remedial method is to be effective, the teacher must continue to help students generalize from known spelling words to new words with similar phonemic elements (Bradley, 1981).

Self-Questioning Strategy

Wong (1986) described an exploratory study in which students were taught structural word analysis and a self-questioning strategy. To begin, words were read aloud by the teacher. Students were taught how to break words into syllables and to identify root words and suffixes. Students were shown how parts of the root word changes when a suffix is added. A prompt card containing several steps for self-questioning was provided. Sample questions included: Do I know this word? Do I have the right number of syllables? Is there a part of the word I am not sure how to spell? If so, the student underlines the difficult part of the word and then attempts to spell the word again and see if the word looks correct. This type of self-questioning strategy may help students improve their ability to monitor their spellings.

Conclusion

Analysis of student performance on the WJ-R ACH Dictation, Proofing, and Writing Samples tests, and the results of informal assessments as needed, will help an examiner determine a student's present developmental level in spelling. After analyzing student performance, an appropriate instructional method or study strategy may be selected. Remedial spelling approaches share several common features that promote active participation. These methods involve the student in: (a) choosing words to learn, (b) writing words from memory, (c) pronouncing words with careful attention to the sequence of sounds, and (d) applying learning to new words. Knowledge and use of a variety of spelling methods and strategies will help all students increase their spelling competency.

The intent of spelling instruction is not to improve grades on weekly spelling tests, but rather to improve competence in written expression so that students are able to communicate more effectively. The learning environment should provide a risk-free atmosphere that is rich with print and provides many opportunities for experimentation with language, including learning words misspelled in daily writing, generalizing spelling knowledge, and mastering objectives in progressive developmental stages (Grinnell, 1988). For spelling instruction to be meaningful, students must engage in purposeful writing activities and have a need for increasing their spelling competence.

Proofreading

Analysis of an individual's proofreading skill is a critical component of a comprehensive written language evaluation. Many students have difficulty detecting and correcting errors in their written work. The WJ-R ACH Proofing test measures a student's ability to identify and correct errors in punctuation, capitalization, spelling, and usage in short written passages.

Error Analysis of Proofing

The Proofing test contains punctuation and capitalization (P) items, spelling (S) items, and usage (U) items. Error analysis, instructional modifications, and strategies for Spelling are discussed in the previous section. The Punctuation and Capitalization test samples a student's knowledge of standard rules, such as beginning sentences with capital letters, capitalizing proper names, using commas in dates, using apostrophes to form contractions, and using quotation marks. The Usage test samples an individual's knowledge and detection of several types of usage errors. As examples, the subject is asked to identify and correct errors in: subject-verb agreement, verb tense, formation of irregular plurals, word endings, standard usage (e.g., *anywheres*), and pronoun case (e.g., *whom* for *who*).

Type of Item

In analyzing a student's performance on the Proofing test, an examiner may observe that the student is more successful on one type of item than another. For example, a student with low oral language skills may have difficulty on the usage items, but demonstrate above average mastery on the punctuation and capitalization items. Another student with above average oral language skills may detect usage and spelling errors more readily than errors in punctuation and capitalization. When desired, an examiner may determine separate scores for the punctuation and capitalization, spelling, and usage measures from the Dictation and Proofing tests.

Knowledge or Error Monitoring

A goal of error analysis is to determine whether a student's proofreading mistakes result from a lack of knowledge or a lack of error-monitoring skill. Two situations exist: A student may have not been taught how to apply a specific convention, such as quotation marks, or a student may understand the use of quotation marks but not notice that they are missing. The first student is likely to benefit from direct instruction in the specific skill, whereas the second student will benefit from error-monitoring strategies. In some cases, additional informal assessment is necessary to determine the reasons for errors.

Reading Performance

Proofreading ability requires reading skill; consequently, low word recognition ability may affect performance on the Proofing test. Although the examiner is allowed to pronounce any words that a student requests, a student may not ask for an unknown word or may misread one or more words in the passage. For example, on Item 10: "The girl has *to* mittens," a fourth-grade student, Shiela, responded that the word *minutes* was misspelled and then provided an incorrect spelling for *minutes*. An examiner should note these types of errors to assist in determining whether the student's limited proofreading skill may be primarily attributed to low word recognition.

On some occasions, a student may read a Proofing item aloud and correct the mistake orally while reading. This type of automatic correction occurs primarily with the Usage items. In this instance, the student is demonstrating good oral language skills, but poor proofreading skill, and, consequently, the item is scored as incorrect. Accurate proofreading requires both detection and correction of errors.

Additional Assessment of Proofreading Skills

When a student obtains a low score on the Proofing test, an examiner may further assess proofreading skill by having the student proofread the first draft of one of his or her written assignments. The examiner may then observe the types of errors that the student fails to detect or is able to detect but unable to correct. A student may not notice misspelled words, missing punctuation marks, improper capitalization, or deleted word endings. Precise identifica-

tion of skills not mastered will assist the examiner in developing an instructional program.

In some cases, an examiner may wish to construct a passage or use a preprinted worksheet to assess knowledge of specific proofreading skills. For example, if the student seems to have difficulty with items that involve subject-verb agreement, an examiner may prepare a worksheet to substantiate the difficulty further. Similarly, if a student tends to miss items involving capitalization, an examiner may conduct a more extensive review of a student's knowledge and application of specific capitalization rules. To control for the effects of word recognition difficulties, the material for this proofreading assessment should be text written by the student or material at the student's independent reading level.

Error Types

After analyzing hundreds of writing samples from students with learning disabilities, Goodman (1987) indicated that the errors occurred in relatively few categories as compared to the numerous possibilities presented in preprinted informal proofreading inventories. Consequently, an examiner may wish to develop an error analysis worksheet when assessing a specific individual. Using this worksheet, the examiner records relevant error types across the top of the page and down the side of the page on each numbered line of the written text. The error types that are listed are developed as the error analysis progresses. For example, when analyzing the written work of Mark, an eighth-grade student, an examiner noted errors in the following categories: spelling, capitalization, plurals, word endings, verb tense, and punctuation. These errors were listed across the top of the page, and a check was placed for each line in which an error occurred. When the examiner had finished the analysis, he noted that the majority of Mark's errors were in spelling and capitalization. Using this strategy, the examiner was able to summarize quickly the frequency of the types of errors and pinpoint appropriate instructional objectives for Mark.

Types of errors vary based upon the age and writing skill of the student. Additionally, students with learning disabilities may exhibit error patterns that differ from their peers. Gregg (1983) reported that when compared to normal writers, college students with learning disabilities had a greater percentage of comma errors, spelling errors, omission of articles, and dropped endings. Identification of the specific errors that an individual makes is necessary for instructional planning.

Revision

Another aspect of proofreading involves the more complex conceptual skills needed for revision. Revision refers to the reexamination of the whole product in light of content modifications (Hillocks, 1987). A skilled writer makes spelling and punctuation corrections, as well as content revisions (Isaacson, 1987). This aspect of proofreading is not measured on the WJ-R ACH. Assessing skills in revision requires direct observation of a student engaged in revising an original piece. After the student has completed the first draft, the examiner and student may discuss what types of content modifications may be appropriate. After suggestions are made, the student revises the piece, and the examiner then analyzes the revision. This type of analysis may be done with several different writing assignments.

Measuring Growth

Informal analysis may also be used to measure growth in proofreading skill. Cooper (1975) described a procedure to measure growth in standard usage. Errors are counted within 300 word samples from two early papers and two later papers. The early papers are collected to provide a baseline for performance and additional diagnostic information. Students are informed of which papers will be rated. Growth is measured by the difference in the number of errors between the first papers and the subsequent samples. This type of procedure may help an examiner or instructor monitor growth in the proofreading skill of upper-elementary and secondary students.

Instructional Modifications

If a student has limited proofreading skill, several modifications may be appropriate. A student should not be penalized with poor grades or red pencil markings for failure to correct errors during editing. Instead, an effort should be made to enhance proofreading skill. Initially, the student may require direct assistance from an instructor, parent, or peer in editing written work. As proofreading skill develops, the instructor will be able to select appropriate instructional strategies to increase independence.

Microcomputers with word processing programs may also be used to improve proofreading skill. Upper-elementary and secondary students will benefit from the use of a word processing program that contains a spelling checker. Punctuation, capitalization, and usage checkers are also available for some systems. After the student has written the first draft, edits are made on a printed copy, and the student enters the text revisions. Use of a word processor eliminates much of the tedious recopying that is involved when a paper is revised several times. Students may also be provided with pocket-size spell checkers to use when proofreading.

Instructional Strategies for Proofreading

Proofreading is one of the last stages of the writing process. Editing and making corrections occur after a draft of a composition has been written so as not to detract from the goal of writing: communicating a message. In working with students with learning disabilities, mechanics, handwriting, and spelling are ignored until the student has received reinforcement for expression of ideas (Silverman, Zigmond, Zimmerman, & Vallecorsa, 1981; Walmsly, 1984). In this way, students do not lose sight of the purpose of writing. Additionally, students must eventually assume responsibility for error monitoring and develop independence in proofreading skill. The best way to teach proofreading skills is within the context of a student's own writing, not as individual and independent prerequisite skills (Cohen & Plaskon, 1980; Walmsly, 1984).

Direct Instruction

Punctuation and capitalization are matters of courtesy to the reader to help make meanings clear (Van Allen, 1976). In most instances, the best way to teach a student punctuation, capitalization, and usage rules is to introduce these elements within natural writing situations. Students are directly taught specific writing conventions when they are ready to apply them or when errors are observed in their writing.

Punctuation. For students with mild handicaps, direct and systematic teaching of punctuation is essential. In mastering punctuation, a student should be able to identify the punctuation element, recognize when it should be used, and apply it to new situations (Cohen & Plaskon, 1980). Cohen and Plaskon presented a list of punctuation elements that should be included in the instructional program for students across grade levels. These elements, presented in Figure 4-23, are sequenced according to the order of presentation in a writing program.

Capitalization. An instructional sequence should also be followed in teaching capitalization. Cohen and Plaskon presented a list of the standard uses of capital letters. These applications, presented in Figure 4-24, follow the order of introduction in a writing program.

Thomas, Englert, and Morsink (1984) presented a similar instructional sequence for capital letters:

1. first and last names
2. first word in a sentence
3. the word *I*
4. days, months, and holidays
5. proper names (people, schools, parks, rivers)
6. addresses (streets, roads, cities, states, countries)
7. personal titles (Mr., Mrs., Miss, Dr.)
8. commercial product names

1. **Period**
   a. At the end of a sentence
   b. Following a command
   c. After an abbreviation
   d. After numbers in a list
   e. Following an initial
   f. After numerals and letters in an outline
2. **Comma**
   a. In dates (between the day of the month and the year)
   b. In addresses (between the name of the city and state)
   c. After the greeting of a friendly letter
   d. After the closing of a friendly letter
   e. Between words given in a series
   f. To set off appositives
   g. After "yes" and "no" when they are used as parenthetical expressions
   h. After the name of a person being addressed
   i. To separate a quotation from the explanatory part of a sentence
   j. After a person's last name when it is written before the first name
3. **Question Mark**
   a. At the close of a question
4. **Quotation Marks**
   a. Before and after the direct words of a speaker
   b. Around the title of a story, poem, or an article
5. **Apostrophe**
   a. To establish a possessive noun
   b. In a contraction
6. **Exclamation Point**
   a. At the end of an exclamatory sentence
   b. After a word or group of words showing surprise or strong feeling
7. **Hyphen**
   a. In compound words
   b. In compound numbers (e.g. telephone numbers)
   c. Separating syllables of a word that is divided at the end of the line
8. **Colon**
   a. Between the hour and minutes in the time of day (e.g. 3:25)
   b. After the salutation in a business letter

Figure 4–23. Punctuation for an Instructional Program. *Note.* From *Language Arts for the Mildly Handicapped* (pp. 291–92) by S.B. Cohen and S.P. Plaskon, 1980, Columbus: Charles E. Merrill. Copyright 1980 by S.B. Cohen and S.P. Plaskon. Reprinted by permission.

1. A person's first name
2. A person's last name
3. The first word of a sentence
4. The word *I*
5. The date
6. Proper names: holidays, months, places, days of the week
7. Names of streets and cities
8. Titles of compositions and books
9. Title names: *Mrs., Ms., Mr., Miss, Dr., President* Washington
10. Mother and Father, when used as proper names
11. First word in the salutation of a letter
12. First word in the closing of a letter
13. Names of organizations and clubs
14. Geographical names
15. Names of states
16. Commercial product names
17. First word of a quotation
18. Race and nationality

Figure 4–24. Capitalization for an Instructional Program. *Note.* From *Language Arts for the Mildly Handicapped* (p. 291) by S.B. Cohen and S.P. Plaskon, 1980, Columbus: Charles E. Merrill. Copyright 1980 by S.B. Cohen and S.P. Plaskon. Reprinted by permission.

Usage. When analyzing a student's writing, the examiner should note all usage errors, such as: verb tense, subject-verb agreement, possessive pronoun forms, and pronoun agreement. If a student is having difficulty with a particular aspect of usage, such as the formation of plurals or subject-verb agreement, supplemental instruction may be provided. English grammar books provide specific practice in usage. The instructor should insure that the practiced skills generalize to natural writing situations.

Providing Feedback

> Where teachers wield the red pencil, children will inevitably be wary of writing adventurously.
>
> (Peters, 1979, p. 1)

An important aspect of proofreading instruction is the provision of appropriate feedback. Immediate, reasonable, and knowledgeable feedback is the most effective method for improving knowledge of basic writing skills without interfering with the meaning that a student intends to communicate (Poplin, Gray, Larsen, Banikowski, & Mehring, 1980). Providing appropriate feedback is particularly critical for poor writers; inappropriate feedback decreases motivation and increases frustration with writing tasks.

Simms (1983) outlined several techniques that teachers should avoid when responding to written assignments. These techniques include: (a) applying the "red pencil treatment" based solely on mechanics, (b) marking excessive corrections, (c) correcting skills that have not been taught, and (d) presenting isolated pattern practice or formal instruction in grammar. Another important point is that feedback is not necessary for every assignment. When daily writing is required, papers may be returned without grades or corrections. At the end of the week, students may decide which paper should be evaluated.

Although untaught skills should not be corrected, if an examiner or instructor notes that a student is attempting to use a skill that has not yet been introduced, such as quotation marks, the teacher should introduce the skill, regardless of where it lies in a curricular skill sequence (Poteet, 1987). Conversely, a teacher should not introduce skills that a student is not ready to incorporate into writing. Further guidelines recommended by Simms for applying appropriate feedback include:

1. Maintain a positive attitude in evaluation. Note the paper's strengths as well as providing constructive corrections.
2. Offer feedback at the prewriting stage.
3. Identify and mark only a small number of mechanical errors.
4. Provide feedback on an individualized basis.

With students of all ages, feedback should be as specific as possible. Van De Weghe (1978) found that providing text-specific comments had a greater positive effect on the writing performance of secondary students than more generalized comments, such as "Excellent" or "Try to do better."

Proofreading for Mechanical Errors

Different strategies may be used to help students improve their proofreading ability. As with the teaching of any skill, some students will require more assistance and structure than others in finding their errors in text. For example, Deshler, Ferrell, and Kass (1978) reported that secondary students with learning disabilities detected only one-third of the mechanical errors made in their writing. In many cases, simply identifying the errors does not provide a student with enough assistance. Research results suggest that even when errors are marked, students with learning disabilities are unable to correct the errors; the proportion of errors does not change from the initial to the revised drafts (Espin & Sindelar, 1988; MacArthur, Graham, & Skarvoed, 1986). These findings indicate that in many cases simply marking errors is insufficient for improving student performance.

One effective strategy for improving proofreading skill is to have the students begin the editing process simply, focusing on only one or two aspects of the proofreading task. For example, an elementary student may check the capital letters in a writing assignment; a secondary student may check a paper for consistent verb tense and subject-verb agreement. As skill develops, additional aspects are added (Polloway, Patton, & Cohen, 1981).

Checklist. Specific guidelines may be provided to help students with proofreading. The guidelines should gradually become more general with the aim of encouraging increased student independence (Moulton & Bader, 1986). Checklists should be individualized. A student with less proofreading skill may initially need line-by-line guidance, whereas another student may only require general reminders. For one student a checklist may include a reminder to check words in a personal spelling dictionary, or to refer to a list of words that the student uses frequently but has not mastered. Another student may be asked to make sure that each sentence begins with a capital letter.

A third student, with more advanced spelling skill, may be reminded to use a dictionary to check the spelling of difficult words. Figure 4-25 illustrates a sample proofreading checklist developed by Weiss and Weiss (1982) for use with secondary students with learning disabilities. The checklist is filled out, checked, and signed for each written assignment. This type of list is adapted to meet individual needs.

Proofreading symbols. To aid students in revision, a schoolwide set of proofreading symbols may be developed. When students are familiar with symbols, they can readily understand the type of error. Figure 4-26 illustrates a sample set of symbols that may be posted in elementary classrooms. In early elementary programs, an instructor may begin with only a few symbols, such as spelling, capital letters, and a period. Additional symbols are added to a chart as they are learned.

Standard editing and proofreading symbols, such as presented in writing manuals and English textbooks, may be used with secondary students; or, a more extensive coding system may be developed. Hayward and LeBuffe (1985) developed a self-correction coding system that was used successfully with secondary students with hearing impairments. No marks were put on the writing, but the students' compositions were returned with codes written in the margins near where the errors were made. Each student then identified, reviewed, and corrected mistakes. Table 4-5 contains a list of the most commonly used codes.

Although the codes are sequenced in order of presentation, the order may be varied to meet individual needs. For example, a high school senior may simply review the codes. This type of approach has two main advantages: (a) no marks are put directly on the paper and (b) students are involved in the self-identification and correction of their mistakes.

Oral proofreading. One effective strategy for helping students note errors is to have them read stories aloud while they listen for inconsistencies in the text (Polloway, Patton, & Cohen, 1981). For elementary students, oral proofreading appears to be more effective than silent proofreading (Van De Weghe, 1978). This procedure is also effective with upper-elementary and secondary students and students with learning disabilities.

Espin and Sindelar (1988) compared sixth- through eighth-grade students with learning disabilities to two groups: one matched on reading level and the other on chronological age. Although the students with learning disabilities identified fewer errors in word usage, word order, word endings, and punctuation than nondisabled students of the same chronological age, students from all three groups who listened to passages located significantly

Sample Checklist

1. I have written on every other line on the paper so that I can leave space for corrections. _____ (Student checks here.)
2. I have begun all sentences with a capital letter. _____
3. I have begun all names of persons and places with a capital letter. _____
4. I have put a period at the end of each sentence. _____
5. I have put a question mark at the end of questions. _____
6. I have checked the words for misspelling. _____ I have changed any word that I could to its correct spelling and placed a check under any other word that looked wrong wrong even though I could not correct the spelling. _____
7. I have reread my sentences aloud (or subvocally) to be sure that they made sense and are sentences containing a subject and action word (verb). _____
8. I have made sure that I wrote an introduction to tell about the main idea of my paper (essay) _____ and a summary that sums up the things I tried to say. _____
9. I can read my own handwriting on this paper. _____
10. I think that my writing is readable to someone else. _____

Figure 4–25. Sample Proofreading Checklist. *Note.* From "Training Kids to Be Winners in the Handling of Writing Skills" by H.G. Weiss and M.S. Weiss, 1982, *Academic Therapy, 18,* p. 81. Copyright 1982 by Academic Therapy Publications. Reprinted by permission.

more errors than students who read the material. The auditory feedback helped students identify errors in punctuation, grammar, and syntax. Although the passages were not written by the students in this study, auditory feedback may also help students revise their own papers.

This type of procedure may be incorporated into a classroom by having a student read a story or paper to another student, a small group, or an entire class. Other students may then assist the writer with corrections. As an alternative, students may exchange papers and have the writer listen to his or her story being read by another student. Written work may also be tape-recorded and an individual may listen to written passages while editing.

Guided proofreading. Another effective procedure for proofreading instruction is to gradually decrease instructor assistance with the editing process. Mehlmann and Waters (1985) described a proofreading program that was effective for teaching proofreading skills to slow learners and students with learning disabilities who had marked skill deficiencies. In this method, students are guided through a gradual progression of editing steps using anonymous student writing samples. The following steps were used.

1. A sentence is presented and all errors are underlined. Clues are provided in the order of mistakes. For example, the teacher may write under a sentence with three errors *capital letter,* *spelling,* and *plural.*

2. The error clues are presented in random order.
3. All errors are underlined but no clues are given.
4. Only a clue regarding the number of errors is provided.
5. The student must locate errors independently.

Once this method is mastered with sentences, students may focus on correcting errors in paragraphs. Gradually reducing the amount of assistance will promote student success and build independence in proofreading skill.

For some students, a simple count of errors provides enough guidance for making corrections. A teacher may total the number of mechanical errors and circle the number on top of the paper. When needed, clues or additional assistance may be provided. For other students, a check mark placed in the margin by each line that has an error is sufficient. With any of these strategies, an instructor should ensure that students apply the technique to their own written product.

SCOPE. Bos and Vaughn (1988) described a strategy called SCOPE used to assist students in developing proofreading skills. This strategy, appropriate for use in the upper-elementary through secondary level, is a series of questions that a student applies to a piece of writing.

S: Is the *spelling* correct?
C: Are the first words and proper names and nouns *capitalized?*
O: Is the syntax or word *order* correct?
P: Are there *punctuation* marks where needed?
E: Does the sentence *express* a complete thought? Does the sentence contain a noun and verb?

COPS. Another error-monitoring strategy, COPS, was designed to help secondary students with learning disabilities identify four types of errors (Schumaker, Deshler, Nolan, Clark, Alley, & Warner, 1981). After writing a rough draft, a student asks the COPS questions while editing the paper. The following questions are asked:

C: Have I *capitalized* the first word of each sentence and proper names?
O: How is the *overall* appearance? The student reviews the paper for errors involving neatness, legibility, indentation of paragraphs, margins, and complete sentences.
P: Have I included commas and end *punctuation*?
S: Are words *spelled* correctly?

Students are encouraged to apply this approach independently before submitting written work. In implementing this strategy, adolescents with learning disabilities were able to detect and correct 90% of the errors in teacher-prepared material and 95% of errors in their own work, after a maximum of six practice sessions (Schu-

PROOFREADING SYMBOLS

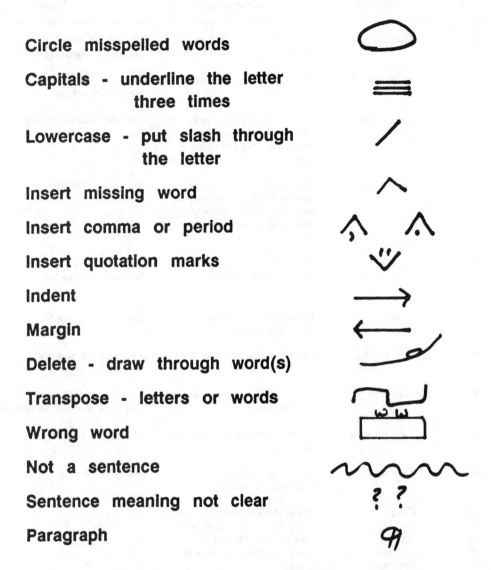

Circle misspelled words

Capitals - underline the letter
three times

Lowercase - put slash through
the letter

Insert missing word

Insert comma or period

Insert quotation marks

Indent

Margin

Delete - draw through word(s)

Transpose - letters or words

Wrong word

Not a sentence

Sentence meaning not clear

Paragraph

Figure 4–26. Sample Proofreading Symbols for an Elementary Classroom.

maker, Deshler, Alley, Warner, Clark, & Nolan, 1982). Reynolds, Hill, Swassing, and Ward (1988) found that instruction in the COPS strategy significantly improved the performance of sixth- through eighth-grade students with learning disabilities in revision of mechanics.

Revision

Revision is an important part of the writing process. Very young writers often do not revise their writing at all. Once something has been written, they believe it cannot be altered because that is the way it was written. Teachers may use many strategies to help students improve their ability to revise. When several steps are provided in the revision process, drafts may be edited both for mechanical errors and organizational problems.

Revision conference. A revision conference may be used to help students with language disabilities revise the content of their writing (Moulton & Bader, 1986). To help students modify content, a teacher prepares a list of questions and comments about the draft. For example, major questions might include:

1. How well does the draft correspond to the topic?
2. How well does the draft compare to the prewriting plan?
3. Is the information clearly organized?
4. Is the "word choice" appropriate?

Once a student has reviewed and considered each question, a conference is held. The student reads the draft aloud and responds to the teacher's questions and com-

Table 4–5. Self-Correction Codes.

	Code	Meaning	Interpretation	Example
1.	sp	Spelling	A word in this line is spelled wrong.	The gril sat down. He though about the problem.
2.	C	Capitalization	A capital letter is needed in this line.	She and i are friends. we went to school.
3.	lc	Lower case	A word in this line has an incorrect capital letter that should be changed to lower case.	The Man chased the Dog.
4.	p	Punctuation	There is an error in punctuation in this line. To clarify in early use, it is possible to specify the punctuation needed, e.g., ᵽ ᵽ̇.	John said, Stop that!
5.	#	Number—singular or plural	A word in this line is singular when it should be plural, or vice versa.	These car were stolen. We saw only one birds.
6.	ill	Illegible	Something on this line is illegible. I can't read it.	Do you like ppo⧫le?
7.	vt	Verb tense	A verb in this line is in the wrong tense.	Tom was lost and cries.
8.	V	Verb error	A verb in this line is in the wrong form.	Sue is go to college. Mary has laugh at the jokes before.
9.	pro	Pronoun error	There is a wrong pronoun on this line.	The boy ate him supper.
10.	prep	Preposition	An incorrect preposition has been used in this line.	The girl walked at school.
11.	w N adj adv det conj	Word Noun Adjective Adverb Determiner Conjunction	These abbreviations are used, along with 8, 9, and 10, with codes 12, 13, 14, and 15, or alone, to signify an error in usage.	
12.	∧	Insert	Something has been left out. (Often used with a word code.)	The boy saw cat. (det) ∧
13.	ℓ	Delete	Something in this line must be taken out.	Alex lost the his ball.
14.	w	Wrong	Used with the codes for the parts of speech. Indicates wrong choice of words.	The girl see at the TV.
15.	?	Not clear	I don't understand what you are trying to say. This may stand alone to show the whole sentence is unclear, or be linked with a word code.	

16.	SV	Subject-verb agreement	The subject and verb in this line do not agree.	The boys is happy.
17.	cont	Contraction	There is a mistake in a contraction on this line.	They cant come.
18.	syl	Error in syllabication	The word at the end of this line is divided wrong.	They lived happ-ily ever after.
19.	poss	Possessive	Mistake in a possessive form. This could be lack of a needed possessive or misplaced apostrophe.	Ann father left early today.
20.	ab	Abbreviation	Spell out the abbreviation.	Will he come w/ you?
21.	adj→adv	Change adjective to adverb	An adjective in this line needs to be changed to an adverb. This is usually a matter of form only.	The chorus sings good.
22.	adv→adj	Change adverb to adjective	An adverb needs to be changed to an adjective.	The bitterly old woman laughed.
23.	¶	Paragraph	A new paragraph is needed, starting with a sentence that starts on this line.	
24.	no ¶	No paragraph	Combine this paragraph with the one above.	
25.	rep	Repetitious	The words or sentences on this line are repetitious. Cut something out or reword it.	
26.	frag	Sentence fragment	This sentence is not complete. This code is used with students who are comfortable with the term. Prior to this, a code is used for the specific part of the sentence that is missing.	
27.	RO	Run-on sentence	There is a run-on sentence. Before students know this term, this error is coded with p,C.	The children laughed and played outside they had fun.
28.	awk	Awkward	The phrasing is awkward. Rewrite.	
29.	wordy	Wordy	The sentence is too wordy. Find a more precise way to say this.	

Table 4–5 (continued).

30.	trans	Transition error	The transition from one idea to the next is rough or unclear.	Sam is a good player. He is not dependable.
31.	MM	Misplaced modifier	An adjective or adverb or phrase is in the wrong place making the sentence grammatically wrong or just unclear.	The girl tall is afraid. He studied a disease that is caused by a virus at the University of Michigan.
32.	F	Faulty parallelism	There is a lack of parallel form in a conjoined construction. This code is also useful in correcting outlines.	I like to eat and skiing.
33.	DM	Dangling modifier	There is a phrase misplaced so that its referent is unclear.	Taking our seats, the game started.
34.	shift	Shift in perspective	There has been a change in point of view; for example, from first to third person in a narrative.	Most teenagers have fights with their parents. I will try to understand my parents. Then people will have fewer fights.

Source: Marie H. Katzenbach School for the Deaf, West Trenton, New Jersey.
Compiled by Ann Fajgier, Linda Hayward, Marion Weisbrot, and Elsie Winters.

Note. From "Self-Correction: A Positive Method for Improving Writing Skills" by L.R. Hayward and J.R. LeBuffe, 1985, *Teaching Exceptional Children, 18,* pp. 69–71. Copyright 1985 by the Council for Exceptional Children. Reprinted by permission.

ments. The student uses a colored pen to revise the draft at the conference. It is not necessary to revise all aspects of the paper. The teacher provides guidance, but the student is encouraged to suggest any changes. The goals are to have a student identify and propose solutions to problems in a paper and develop independence in the revision process.

Step-by-step revising. Cohen (1985) outlined the following approach to the revision process that was used successfully with high school seniors with learning disabilities:

1. The student completes and turns in a free writing assignment.
2. The teacher writes down reactions to the first draft without corrections.
3. Papers are returned and read aloud to other students. During oral reading, errors in structure and word usage become obvious.
4. After receiving feedback from other students, students are asked to revise, reorganize, and correct their work.
5. Papers are turned in and the teacher places a check by each line containing an error. If more than one error exists, a check is placed next to the number of errors

written in parentheses.
6. Students correct teacher-indicated errors and turn in the third draft. At this point, the teacher may use a red pencil to mark any additional corrections.
7. Students prepare a final paper that incorporates a teacher's corrections.

This type of approach is used with many writing assignments and the student may choose one piece for the final paper. Students with language and learning disabilities will benefit from the ample teacher feedback and the several opportunities to correct and revise work provided in this structured approach.

Conclusion

Analysis of performance on the WJ-R ACH Proofreading test will help an examiner determine a student's present level of proofreading skill. Ability to monitor and correct errors in written work is an important aspect of writing competence as it allows students to prepare and share their written work with an audience. Providing corrective feedback, a variety of strategies, modeling, practice, and reinforcement will help students enhance their proofreading skill and develop independence in writing. As with studying spelling, students must see a need for improving their proofreading skill. When proofreading instruction is provided in the context of meaningful assignments, students understand the importance of this skill and, consequently, improve their ability to communicate more effectively in writing.

Written Expression

The two WJ-R ACH tests of written expression are Writing Fluency and Writing Samples. These tests measure two different aspects of written production. Some students do not write easily. Other students write easily, but have difficulty expressing their ideas. Both of these problems influence a student's ability to communicate effectively in writing. If a student demonstrates difficulty on either or both of these writing tests, an examiner should analyze a student's errors, decide whether or not additional assessment is necessary, and then make specific instructional recommendations for improving written language skill.

Writing Fluency

Hence the well-known fact that young children cannot express their thoughts fluently by writing. The mechanics of the writing process stand in the forefront of attention and interrupt the flow of thought. As practice proceeds, these steps follow one another more rapidly and more closely so that they interrupt the thought process less. The writing process becomes more nearly automatic—that is, it becomes capable of being carried on without the direction of attention. The attention can then be occupied more fully with the meaning which is to be expressed.

(Freeman, 1914, p. 23)

The Writing Fluency test measures the ability to write rapidly with ease. Litowitz (1981) described the spiral development of written language. When first learning to write, conscious attention is needed to acquire the linguistic system. Gradually, the mechanics of writing become unconscious and automatic, and attention is used to pursue another consciously attended problem. In the final stage, conscious attention is redirected to language and its uses.

When writing is not automatic, a student's attention is focused primarily on the linguistic system or the mechanics of writing, rather than on the formulation or expression of ideas. With practice, students become increasingly automatic in their writing. Automaticity is obtained when a student is able to write with a pencil as easily as he or she can dictate the ideas to another person (Samuels, 1986). Ability to write fluently affords the writer the opportunity to focus on the communication of ideas.

Error Analysis of Writing Fluency

When a student has difficulty on the Writing Fluency test, an examiner may wish to determine the reason for the low performance. Successful performance on the Writing Fluency test requires: motor speed, production of simple sentences, ability to follow and remember directions, ability to sustain concentration, and attention to detail. Poor muscular or motor control may also affect an individual's performance on this test. In performing an error analysis, an examiner will want to consider the student's: (a) response style; (b) level of automaticity; (c) types of errors, including incomplete sentences and omission or alteration of words; (d) sustained concentration; and (e) reading and spelling skill.

Response Style

Writing Fluency requires ability to write rapidly. This test may also be used as a supplemental measure of processing speed in the WJ-R COG. Processing speed measures the ability to respond rapidly under timed conditions to tasks of trivial difficulty. In observing student performance, several different response styles may be observed. For some students, low performance on this test results from their approach to timed tasks. For example, the examiner noted that Rich, a secondary student, approached and completed all tasks at a slow, consistent pace, regardless of imposed time constraints. Although Rich obtained a low score on the timed tests, his responses were always accurate. Additionally, he did quite well on untimed tests. For Rich, the examiner recommended that he be provided with sufficient time to complete all written assignments. In contrast, Steven, a seventh-grade student, approached tasks in a very different manner. When tasks were timed, Steven worked very rapidly, but tended to make a lot of careless errors.

In analyzing a student's performance, attempt to determine whether the student works: (a) slowly but inaccurately, (b) slowly and accurately, (c) rapidly but inaccurately, or (d) rapidly and accurately. Identification of a student's response style may have important implications for instructional planning. An examiner should ask: How will this student's response style affect instructional performance?

Automaticity

Most students who score low on Writing Fluency have not yet developed automatic writing skills. They struggle with the complex demands of writing. Figure 4-27 illustrates the performance of Dick, a fourth-grade student, on Writing Fluency. After 7 minutes, Dick had completed the first six items. Although he was able to write several simple, complete sentences, Dick's production was slow and labored. Although errors in punctuation and capitalization are not penalized, the examiner also noted that Dick did not use capital letters to begin sentences, with the exception of the word "I," or use periods at the end of sentences. The examiner also observed that Dick had difficulty staying on the writing line. The examiner recommended that Dick should spend at least one half-hour daily engaged in meaningful writing assignments. Through increased involvement and interest in writing, Dick's skill improved.

Types of Errors

A student may also miss several items and, subsequently, obtain a low score on the Writing Fluency test. Examples of error types include writing incomplete sentences, omitting important words, or altering the stimulus words.

Incomplete sentences. A student may respond to many items but not produce complete sentences on several of the items. When analyzing the performance of Helen, a third-grade student, on the Writing Fluency test, the examiner observed that she had difficulty formulating simple sentences. Despite good motor control and ability to write easily and rapidly, Helen lacked understanding of how to combine words to form complete simple sentence patterns. For some students, the convention of syntax makes an enormous demand on attention. The examiner recognized that an immediate instructional goal for Helen was to provide direct teaching in how to compose simple sentence patterns.

Omission or alteration of words. Some students may omit critical words from sentences on the Writing Fluency test. This lack of attention to detail affects effective communication in writing. When words critical to sentence meaning are omitted on several items, an examiner may wish to assess proofreading skill and recommend specific strategies for error monitoring.

The examiner may also observe that the student tends to omit less important words, such as the articles *the* and *a,* from sentences. Although these omissions are not penalized, an examiner should note the frequency of omissions as this information may have implications for instructional planning. In general, students with writing difficulty are likely to have a higher occurrence of omissions. For example, Gregg (1983) found that college students with learning disabilities tended to omit more articles and word endings than college students with average writing skill.

Occasionally, a student may write many sentences within the 7-minute time limit but alter the stimulus words in some way. When the stimulus words are altered, the sentence is scored as incorrect. This stringent criterion is required because the difficulty level for each item is based upon the exact words presented. When a word is changed, the difficulty level is altered.

If a student does produce an appropriate quantity of sentences, based upon ability and grade-level expectations, poor performance may be attributed to factors other than a lack of writing fluency. Possible factors could include: attention to detail, difficulty remembering or following the specific directions, lack of familiarity with English syntax, or poor copying skill. An examiner should use caution when interpreting the test performance of ESL students. Low performance may result from a lack of familiarity with the English language structure rather than low writing fluency. Figure 4-28 illustrates the performance of George, an ESL secondary student, who altered and omitted words. George will benefit from further instruction and practice in writing in English.

Sustained Concentration

The Writing Fluency test has a 7-minute time limit. Some students will have difficulty sustaining concentration on a writing task for a 7-minute period. For example, when testing Andy, a third-grade student, the examiner needed to keep refocusing him to the task. Andy would write a few words and then look up around the room. When redirected to the task, Andy would check the words he had written and then complete the sentence. On four occasions, Andy asked the examiner how much time had elapsed. Andy's low performance may be more attributed to difficulty sustaining attention than to low writing fluency. His difficulty sustaining attention could, however, be caused by frustration with writing tasks.

Reading or Spelling Skill

Although the stimulus words on the Writing Fluency test are controlled in terms of reading difficulty, word recognition and spelling skill may affect performance of younger students or older students with limited skill. Although the examiner may read any requested word, some students may not bother to ask for the pronunciation of an unrecognized word or may misread a word.

TEST 35

Writing Fluency (cont.)

1. this
   bat
   is

   this bat is long

2. boy
   happy
   is

   is that boy happy

3. hot
   soup
   my

   my hot soup is ready

4. the
   foot
   little

   the foot is little

5. a
   jumping
   boy

   a boy is jumping

6. milk
   like
   cold

   I like cold milk

Go on to the next page →

Figure 4–27. A Fourth-Grade Student on the Writing Fluency Test.

TEST 35

Writing Fluency (cont.)

31. mail
    puts
    for

    He put mail for me. O

32. packed
    shirt
    in

    Shirt packs in case. O

33. jumped
    pass
    first

    They jump to pass. O

34. into
    bite
    when

    The girl bite into then eats. O

35. land
    tractor
    drives

    Tractor is driving the land. O

36. money
    rich
    ground

    He rich money on ground. O

Figure 4–28. An ESL Secondary Student on the Writing Fluency Test.

An examiner may also note that a student glances at each stimulus word several times to copy it correctly. In observing Matthew, a fifth-grade student with extreme spelling difficulty, the examiner observed that he placed a finger underneath each word as he copied it. After writing one letter, he would glance back at the word. This slow copying process decreased Matthew's writing speed. His difficulty with spelling affects his ability to write with ease. For students like Matthew with limited reading and spelling skill, writing fluency may be influenced by several factors.

Additional Assessment of Writing Fluency

The Writing Fluency test measures a student's ability to write short, simple sentences. An examiner also may wish to know how many words a student typically writes within sentences or stories. For informal assessment, writing fluency is often measured by counting the number of sentences and/or words that a student writes. A writing sample may be collected under timed or untimed conditions. A student's performance may vary based upon the conditions of assessment and the nature of the writing assignment. Two procedures for informally assessing writing fluency follow.

Sentence Length

To measure the student's average sentence length, the examiner should collect a writing sample, count the number of words, the number of sentences, and then divide the word total by the sentence total (Cohen & Plaskon, 1980). This procedure may be done with several samples, and then an average index may be determined. A student's writing growth may be analyzed over a period of time by evaluating increased sentence length. As writing skill progresses, students write more words in gradually longer messages (Isaacson, 1988).

Word Count

An examiner may also count the number of written words. To establish a student's baseline performance, three written stories may be used (Deno, Mirkin, & Wesson, 1984). Deno, Marston, and Mirkin (1982) found support for counting and recording the total number of words written as a method of evaluating the performance of regular classroom students and students with learning disabilities in third through sixth grade. They suggested that for beginning writers, counting the correct letter sequences may be an appropriate alternative. When fluency is a concern, an examiner may recommend that a teacher keep an ongoing record of the number of words or sentences that a student produces within a time period.

Instructional Modifications

A student who performs poorly on Writing Fluency may not be able to write rapidly under timed constraints. The student may require additional or extended time to complete written assignments or an adjusted amount of written work. A student who lacks fluency may also have difficulty expressing his or her ideas in writing. Whenever appropriate, provisions should be made for oral reports and assistance with writing. Initially, the type of writing assignments may need to be simplified so that a student may focus on writing production with minimal cognitive demands.

A student with low performance on the Writing Fluency test may also have difficulty copying words from the blackboard or from books. To help a student compensate for this difficulty, an examiner may recommend: (a) preferential seating or (b) limited or no required copying from the board.

After reviewing several of Matthew's classroom work samples, the examiner noted that when Matthew was copying problems from his math textbook, he often miscopied the problem. On several of the miscopied problems, he had obtained the correct solution, but the problems were marked as incorrect. In making instructional recommendations, the examiner suggested that Matthew not be required to copy math problems or long sentences from workbooks.

Instructional Strategies for Writing Fluency

In assisting in the development of writing competence, the first goal is to help a student develop fluency, or the ability to write simple declarative sentences with ease (Isaacson, 1987). An important consideration is that writing becomes increasingly automatic with practice. Research results have indicated that in composing stories, nondisabled students write twice as many words as their learning disabled peers (Nodine, Barenbaum, & Newcomer, 1985). To help students develop automaticity, writing must be done regularly beginning at an early age (Samuels, 1986). Several instructional strategies are particularly appropriate for helping students develop beginning writing skill and build their writing fluency.

Developing Beginning Writing Skill

Most young students enjoy learning to write. Writing develops naturally as students are provided with opportunities to explore and record their experiences for others to share. On occasion, an examiner will encounter an older student who has developed minimal writing skill and is highly resistant to writing. This student is likely to obtain a low score on both the WJ-R ACH Writing Fluency and Writing Samples tests.

In working with reluctant writers, the first goal is to get the student to write. Skills must be carefully sequenced from simple to complex, emphasizing the gradual development of communicative competencies. Additionally, a supportive, accepting environment is essential for promoting writing growth. Several techniques that are appropriate for reluctant writers are presented in the previous section on Writing Fluency.

Giordano (1983a, 1983b, 1984) presented several prewriting and remedial exercises that may be used with reluctant writers or students with limited writing skill. Sample activities include:

1. Scribbling: Scribbling is used to prepare students for the motor movements required in handwriting. Practice may begin with fingerpaints and progress to pencils and crayons. The instructor may model either manuscript or cursive writing.
2. Imitation: Students are encouraged to copy words or parts of words in manuscript writing. The instructor may write down what students say and then encourage them to copy parts of the dialogue.
3. Tracing: Students dictate several sentences that the instructor writes. Students choose one or two words from the sample and trace them with a yellow marker.
4. Completion: While saying the words, the instructor writes a sentence and then pauses before the final word. The students choose the appropriate response from one of two word cards.
5. Automatic writing: To begin this activity, the instructor selects a word that the students are able to write without analytic attention, such as their first names. Students then sign their names next to selected items in a list or catalog. As another example, the instructor may write three sentences and have students sign their names by the sentences that they like best.
6. Ordered writing: To develop passage comprehension, the instructor has the students record observations in a sequence, such as describing the beginning, middle, and end of an experience.
7. Incomplete sentence exercises: The instructor provides students with various incomplete sentences. At first a selection of responses may be included, and then students can create responses.
8. Paraphrasing: Students can summarize lower-grade books for students having reading difficulty and then attach their summaries to the inside cover. As another activity, students may rewrite sentences for different audiences.
9. Dialogue: For this activity, students write dialogue for cartoon or fictional characters. Dialogue may be deleted from newspaper cartoon balloons and the cartoons enlarged on a copier. Several microcomputer programs are also available for developing cartoons and designing posters.
10. Correspondence: Students write in personal notebooks and the teacher responds. The teacher may model writing strategies appropriate for each student.

Another activity for reluctant writers suggested by Giordano (1982) is the CATS (copy, alter, transform, supply) exercises. To begin, a teacher writes three sentences leaving spaces beneath them. The student is asked to copy his or her favorite sentence. If the student is unable to copy a sentence, the sentence may be traced with a yellow marker pen. After the sentence is written, the student alters one word in the copied sentence. Next, the student is asked to transform the sentence into a different form, such as turning the sentence into a question. Finally, the student is asked to supply a response in writing to the transformed question.

The goal of these types of activities is to involve the student in writing and motivate the student to want to write. Once a student has developed some interest in writing and some beginning skill, activities that involve increased participation, such as those provided in the next section, should be used. These methods are designed to improve writing rate, automaticity, ability to control written syntax, and production of simple to complex sentence patterns. The reason for increasing fluency is to enable students to write easily so that their full attention may be directed to expression of ideas. Several of the methods that emphasize the communicative aspect of writing are also appropriate for use with reluctant or unmotivated writers.

Timed Writings

One method for improving writing rate and fluency is to have students engage in daily timed writing. Houten, Morrison, Jarvis, and McDonald (1974) found that the quantity and quality of second- and fifth-grade elementary students' writing increased significantly when timing and feedback were provided. In this procedure, a topic was written on the board. Students were told that they were being timed for 10 minutes and that they should try to beat their previous day's number of words written. Words from repetitious sentences or incomplete sentences were not counted. At the end of the 10-minute period, students counted the number of words and wrote the number on top of their paper. Scores were verified and the ones that exceeded the word count from previous days were recorded on a chart. Impartial judges and other elementary teachers rated the compositions on mechanical aspects, vocabulary, number of ideas, development of ideas, and internal consistency. The judges also rated the compositions from the timing and feedback conditions higher than the compositions written prior to use of the procedure. Teachers reported that students showed an improved attitude toward writing and decreased socialization during the timed period.

The components in this technique, timing, self-scoring, public display of scores, and instructions to beat their previous high scores, may be adapted for classroom use. Instead of a public display of scores, each individual may keep a personal chart of scores, recording a daily score. As alternatives to focusing on the number of words written, on some days emphasis may be placed on the number of ideas a student could record or the number of specific vocabulary words a student could integrate into writing. Although this approach was effective with an entire class, these types of procedures will be most effective for students who need to increase their writing fluency.

Alvarez (1983) described a similar activity for increasing the writing output of secondary students enrolled in a remedial reading class. The objective was to write as many words as possible within 6 minutes. Students were told to write on a self-selected topic or to write whatever thoughts came into their minds. During writing, the teacher spelled any words requested. After the 6 minutes elapsed, all words in sentences were counted, written at the top of the paper, and recorded on an individual graph. As a variation, the teacher may select topics of interest for the writing activity. In addition to increasing written output, the procedure helped students develop positive attitudes toward writing.

Similarly, Douglass (1984) described a 5-minute writing procedure that was effective with secondary students with learning disabilities. The students and teacher wrote daily for 5 minutes on a topic of their choice. After the 5 minutes, students who wished to share their writing were encouraged to do so. Douglass observed that students' confidence increased as they realized they could put their thoughts on paper and that they had something significant to say.

As with other skills areas, principles of behavior modification have been used successfully to increase the fluency and written productivity of elementary and secondary students with learning disabilities and behavior problems (Brigham, Graubard, & Stans, 1972; Rumsey & Ballard, 1985; Seabaugh & Schumaker, 1981). Students may count and record the number of letters, words, or sentences written daily. Contingent reinforcements, such as points for each word written, may be earned and traded for various privileges.

When the examiner first assessed Charlie, a third-grade student referred for writing difficulty, Charlie refused to write. Charlie informed the examiner that he could write his name, but that he did not know how to write any words. His classroom teacher also reported that Charlie refused to engage in any writing activities in the classroom. Initially, the examiner and Charlie worked out a plan in which Charlie would keep count of all the words that he could write in a 15-minute session. For each word, Charlie received one point. Points were then traded in for stickers which Charlie collected in a small book. To monitor his progress, Charlie placed his daily results on a graph. Once Charlie began to experience some success in a writing task, he began to experiment more with written language. In several weeks, he began producing simple sentences using a beginning sentence combining technique. After several months, Charlie engaged in all classroom writing activities. He took pride in his writing and enjoyed sharing his thoughts with classmates.

Sentence Combining

One reason that a student may perform poorly on the Writing Fluency test is difficulty manipulating English syntax. Sentence combining is an effective method for increasing a student's syntactic maturity and control of written syntax (Isaacson, 1985; Nutter & Safran, 1984). This procedure teaches students how to build more complex sentences from simple ones and helps students to develop control of English syntax and, consequently, to write more complex, mature sentences.

Research results indicate that this procedure is twice as effective as free writing for enhancing writing quality (Hillocks, 1987). Instruction in sentence combining may replace any teaching of formal grammar, as it fulfills the same goals as grammar study: development of standard usage and control of written syntax (Cooper, 1973). This technique has been effective for improving student writing at every academic level (Lawlor, 1983). Additionally, research indicates that students with learning disabilities may be taught to improve their syntactic complexity using sentence combining activities (Isaacson, 1985).

Basic procedure. Sentence combining exercises, presented as a language game, may be used with individuals, pairs of students, or as an entire class activity (Cooper, 1973). To begin, simple sentences are written on paper, an overhead projector, or on the chalkboard. Students are then asked to combine the short sentences in different ways to form one longer, more elaborate sentence. The teacher and class discuss all suggestions and write out the new sentences. Two simple combined sentences are presented in Figure 4-29 to illustrate the basic procedure.

Beginning sentence combining activities. Some students who perform poorly on the Writing Fluency test have difficulty producing simple sentences. In some cases, a student may not understand how to write a simple sentence pattern. Simple sentence combining exercises

```
Martha lives in an apartment.

The apartment is large.

The apartment is near Chicago.
```

Combined sentence:

```
Martha lives in a large apartment near Chicago.
```


```
It was Saturday.

We went to see a movie.

It was science fiction.
```

Combined sentence:

```
On Saturday we went to see a science fiction movie.
```

Figure 4–29. Sample Sentence-Combining Exercises.

may help beginning or reluctant writers learn how to compose sentences. To begin, simple words are written on index cards and the student moves the words around to form a sentence, adding any words that are needed on blank cards. Next, the student copies the sentence. As a challenge, the student may be asked to create as many different sentences as possible using the set of index cards.

Constructing exercises. To develop exercises, simple sentences may be written using spelling lists, vocabulary lists, or a student's own written work. Another approach is to break apart complex sentences from a basal reader, trade book, or a content area textbook. Exercises may focus on a specific aspect of syntax, such as combining sentences with a variety of connectives. For example, a teacher may ask the students to join sentences selecting one of these words: *but, because, and, or.* Cooper (1973) presented an outline for constructing sentence combining problems that illustrates all of the different types of embeddings and substitutions that students need to master to become mature writers. Even capable writers at the secondary level benefit from practice with multiple embeddings.

Principles. Nutter and Safran (1984) presented several general principles to follow in implementing sentence combining exercises. These principles include:

1. Teach unfamiliar words before they are used in exercises.
2. Allow students to be creative, not just correct. Discuss the addition of words and any alterations in meaning.
3. Accept any grammatically correct response. If the response is ungrammatical, help students solve the problem.
4. Provide any spellings of words, as needed.
5. Emphasize oral practice of combining and reading sentences. Oral practice helps students remember and process longer discourse.
6. Present exercises several times a week for 5 to 15 minutes.

One important benefit of sentence combining practice is that it reduces the mental demands of composing by making sentence construction more automatic (Lawlor, 1983). Sentence combining exercises help students practice the composing processes of manipulating language, considering alternate meanings, and revising syntax (Nutter & Safran, 1984). As students move from simple to more complex sentence patterns, they develop the ability to use a variety of sentence structures.

Sentence Guides

Students who have difficulty formulating simple sentences may also benefit from a method like the Phelps Sentence Guide Program (Phelps-Teraski & Phelps, 1980). This program, developed for levels first grade through adulthood, teaches three skills: generation, elaboration, and ordering of sentences. The student learns sentence elements by answering questions. The program progresses from simple sentences, based on concrete picture images, to editing skills and paragraph writing. The sentence guide consists of nine columns placed across the top of the sheet, each containing a question. By answering the questions, the student produces then writes sentences.

This type of guide may be adapted for use and easily applied in a regular classroom. For example, an instructor may develop different sentence guides for students by listing on the top of a sheet questions that will elicit basic sentence patterns, such as: (a) *Who? What doing? To whom?* or (b) *Who? What doing? When? Where?* or *Why?* These questions may refer to a story or a picture. After answering each question, the student attempts to write a sentence. As skill develops, the order of the questions may be modified. For example, the first question may ask *When?* instead of beginning with *Who?* Once sentence writing becomes more proficient, attention is directed toward paragraph writing. Initially, pictures that tell a story in sequence may be used to facilitate writing longer passages. Additional methods for developing paragraph organization are discussed in the section on Writing Samples.

Shared Writing

An additional method that may be used to motivate reluctant writers and reduce the "burden" of independent writing is shared writing (Mather & Lachowicz, in press). Williams and Wason (1977) indicated that this type of collaborative writing can help students overcome their fear of writing and that secondary students in English classes enjoy using the technique. In this gamelike procedure, a student and teacher or peer, or small group of students, share the composition of a paper. After selecting a topic, the paper is passed back and forth between the partners with each individual making a contribution. Depending upon the established parameters, the required contribution may be a sentence, a single word, or a paragraph. The rules of the writing game may be modified depending upon the age and writing skill of the students.

For example, the activity may be conducted with or without talking between partners. When the story is completed, the pair may edit and revise the piece as needed or desired. The goal is to create a unified story that sounds as if it were written by one person.

For reluctant writers, this type of activity may focus on a conversation, rather than creation of a story. The first writer asks his or her partner a question based upon past experience, such as "What is your favorite TV show?" or "What was something fun that you did this weekend?" After responding, the second writer may then ask the first writer a question, or pass the paper back for another question. This type of method emphasizes communication and may increase a student's interest in writing and willingness to participate in writing activities.

Conclusion

The WJ-R ACH Writing Fluency test measures a student's ability to write easily and rapidly. Automaticity in writing allows a student to concentrate on the expression of ideas and provides a foundation that facilitates further advancement in writing skill. When an examiner notes that an individual is reluctant to write or dysfluent in writing, he or she should recommend appropriate activities for improving writing skill. Perhaps, the most important recommendation is increased time devoted to writing activities. When combined with opportunities for practice and meaningful writing activities, the use of suitable methods will help students increase their easiness with writing.

Writing Samples

A perfect healthy sentence, it is true, is extremely rare.
(Henry David Thoreau, from "A Week on the Concord and Merrimack Rivers," 1983, p. 103)

The WJ-R ACH Writing Samples test measures a student's ability to respond in writing to a variety of tasks and provides an examiner with information regarding an individual's present developmental level in writing skill. Most students who obtain a low score on Writing Samples have difficulty conveying their ideas in writing. Additional information may be obtained by performing an in-depth analysis of a student's written responses.

Error Analysis of Writing Samples

Analysis of a student's responses will help an examiner interpret performance and, in some cases, determine the reason for a student's low test performance. An examiner may evaluate a student's: (a) attitude toward writing, (b) basic writing skills, (c) oral language performance, (d) vocabulary, and (e) organizational ability. Also, an examiner may determine whether or not additional writing assessment and a remedial plan are necessary.

Attitude

On occasion, an examiner may encounter a student who is highly resistant to writing. An examiner may note that the student produces short, simple sentences or, in rare cases, refuses to write. For example, when asked to write responses for the Writing Samples test, Tony, a seventh-grade student, responded: "Do I have to? I hate writing." Most likely, Tony has experienced considerable past failure in attempting to write and will benefit from techniques and strategies that facilitate a positive attitude by emphasizing meaningful applications of writing.

Basic Writing Skills

Although students are not penalized for basic skill errors on Writing Samples, an examiner may analyze errors in punctuation, capitalization, usage, and spelling. For example, an examiner may want to compare a student's spelling ability on a dictated list (Dictation) to his or her ability when producing sentences (Writing Samples). Additionally, the examiner may note whether a student uses standard usage, capitalization, and punctuation in writing. Figure 4-30 illustrates a checklist for evaluating basic skills on the Writing Samples test.

Oral Language

An important aspect of analyzing writing performance is to compare the student's written expression to his or her oral expression. Dialects and cultural influences may affect the way students pronounce words and how they write. Listening to how a student pronounces words will help an examiner determine if usage errors in written expression should receive high or low instructional priority. For example, if a student spells the word *went* as *wint*, the misspelling may reflect his or her pronunciation. Figure 4-31 illustrates several items written by Diana, a fourth-grade student who speaks with a dialect. The examiner noted that her spelling mirrored her oral pronunciation patterns. Diana substituted a "d" sound in words beginning with "th." With some students, simply pointing out the differences between oral pronunciation and spelling is sufficient to reduce writing errors.

An examiner may also note that a student makes a particular type of error, such as using improper verb tenses or omitting word endings. If these errors are also present in the student's speech, the writing difficulty may reflect the student's oral language performance. For instructional planning, attention would be directed to development of both oral and written language.

Vocabulary

Vocabulary is an important aspect of both oral and written language. Many students have similar abilities in oral and written vocabulary. Some students, however, have significant discrepancies between their oral vocabulary and their written vocabulary. By comparing a student's performance on the Writing Samples test to his or her performance on the oral language tests of the WJ-R COG, an examiner may observe discrepancies between these skills. In one case, the examiner may note that a student possesses a good oral vocabulary, but has an impoverished written vocabulary. Difficulty with some aspect of written expression prevents the student from fully employing his or her vocabulary in writing. For example, because of difficulty with spelling, a student may write simple nouns and verbs and select the same words over and over again.

Several of the more difficult items require the student to model a writing style. Figure 4-32 illustrates the performance of Ben, a high school senior, on Items 26 through 30. Although he understood the meaning of the passages, his written responses are simplistic. Ben will likely benefit from techniques designed to increase sentence maturity and expand written vocabulary.

An examiner may also note that a student has developed a rich writing vocabulary, despite difficulties in other area of writing skill. Figure 4-33 illustrates the responses of Katie, a fifth-grade student with good use of vocabulary but relatively low spelling skill.

The sample responses, provided in the WJ-R Examiner's Manual, are based upon both the task requirements and the level of item difficulty. Many of the initial items require short, simple sentences that explain what is happening in a picture for full credit. In some instances, a student may produce sentences that are better than the sample illustrations provided for a two-point or superior response. Figure 4-34 illustrates the performance of Sandy, a second-grade student accelerated in writing skill, on Items 6 through 10.

Organizational Ability

One item type on the Writing Samples test requires a student to fill in the missing middle sentence in a paragraph. Successful completion of this task requires both

	Good	Needs Review
1. Begins sentences with capital letters	☐	☐
2. Ends sentences with periods	☐	☐
3. Writes complete sentences	☐	☐
4. Writes: simple sentences	☐	☐
compound sentences	☐	☐
compound/complex	☐	☐
5. Letter formation	☐	☐

List reversed or misformed letters:

6. Word Endings	☐	☐

List omitted word endings:

7. Spelling	☐	☐

List any misspelled words:

Figure 4–30. Error Analysis Checklist for the Writing Samples Test. Permission is granted to reproduce this form.

TEST 27

Writing Samples (cont.)

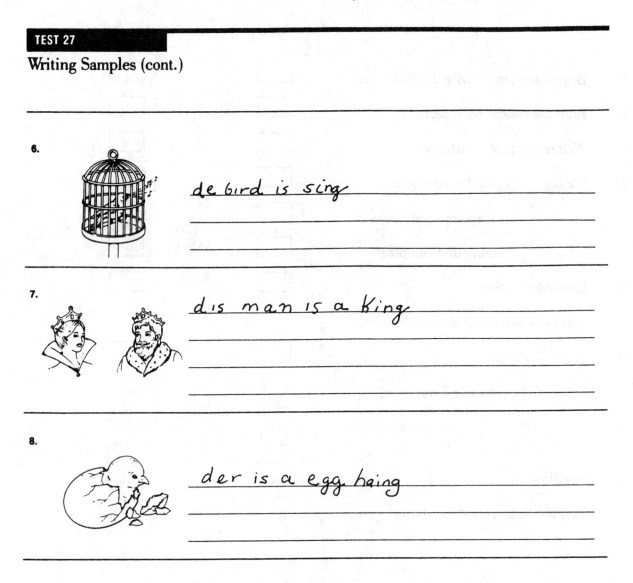

6. de bird is sing

7. dis man is a king

8. der is a egg haing

Figure 4–31. A Fourth-Grade Student with a Dialect.

sequencing and organization skill, or the ability to arrange thoughts logically in writing. The student must create a sentence that will unify the first and last sentences of a paragraph. In analyzing a student's responses, an examiner may note that the student has difficulty determining an appropriate sentence to write based upon the supplied context. Figure 4-35 illustrates responses from two different third-grade students on Item 18. In the first example, the step is out of sequence. In the second example, the student's response does not unify the first and last sentence. He wrote: *You gave me a motor home directions.* Students that make these types of errors will benefit from

writing techniques that are designed to assist with text structure and organization of ideas.

Additional Assessment of Written Expression Skills

One important feature of the Writing Samples test is that a student responds to several different types of writing tasks. This allows the examiner to sample performance on a variety of miniature writing tasks. All standardized writing tests, however, measure a student's performance at one point in time. Within an instructional setting, depend-

TEST 27

Writing Samples (cont.)

26.

Few people understood the extent of his disappointment, the loss of his desire, or _____

his reasons

27.

(1) Robert was an eccentric, perversely perky little man, hesitantly alert. (2) _____

Sally lived next door

_____ (3) Simultaneously, but independently,

they devised a scheme that would astound the entire community.

28.

Consequently you can't play ball

consequently

29.

(1) The slope on the left was densely wooded, and the somber shadow that fell from the hillside

lay like an amber robe on the morning mist. (2) ___ *The other ridge*

was sunny

_____ (3) Between these diverse ridges,

a long ruffled trail wound sinuously up the precipitous incline, carving a path like a charmed snake.

30.

(1) Although plainly in view, the car, a black battered hearselike automobile, continued to

approach slowly, as if the two occupants were reticent to greet the inquisitive group waiting on the

embankment. (2) ___ *The driver was old and wearing*

old clothes

(3) The passenger was wearing a blue sweatshirt with golden stars embossed on the front; the front

brim of his baseball cap stood up at a jaunty angle, revealing a tousle of blonde hair.

Figure 4–32. A High School Senior on the Writing Samples Test.

STOP

TEST 27

Writing Samples (cont.)

11. Tom is
unwraping a prasent that had a
green and red ariplane.

12. The seal is playing with a white Ball
with black strips at the zoo.

13. Bill and Mary are throughing a white
beach ball on Saterday.

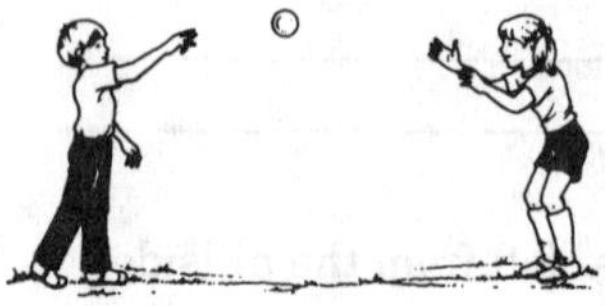

    and

14. The sun and lamp are both light
sorsus

15. Marty cannot play with Anne and
John because he broke his leg riding
his bike.

    because

Figure 4–33. A Fifth-Grade Student on the Writing Samples Test.

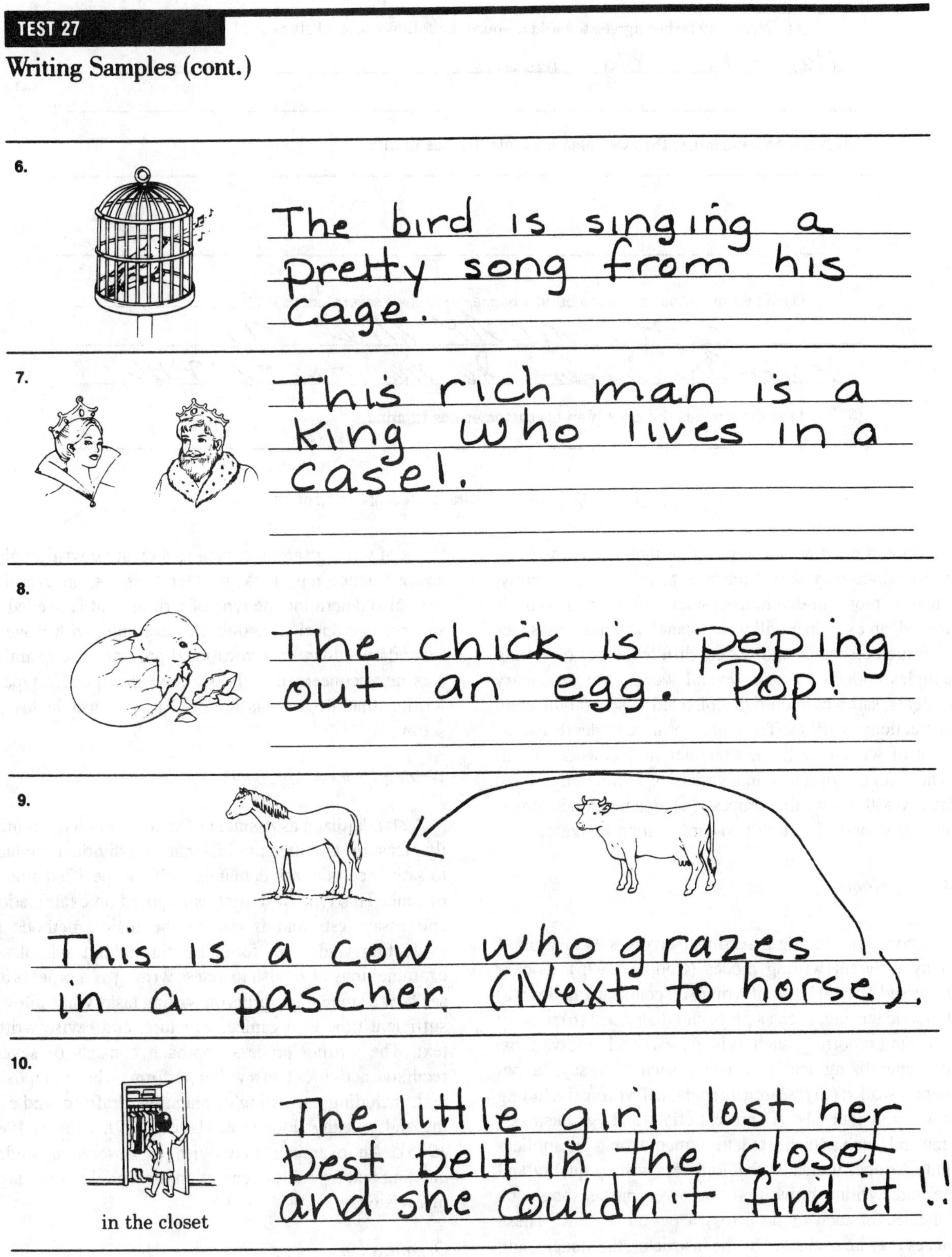

TEST 27

Writing Samples (cont.)

6.

The bird is singing a pretty song from his cage.

7.

This rich man is a king who lives in a casel.

8.

The chick is peping out an egg. Pop!

9.

This is a cow who grazes in a pascher. (Next to horse).

10.

in the closet

The little girl lost her best belt in the closet and she couldn't find it!!

Figure 4–34. A Second-Grade Student on the Writing Samples Test.

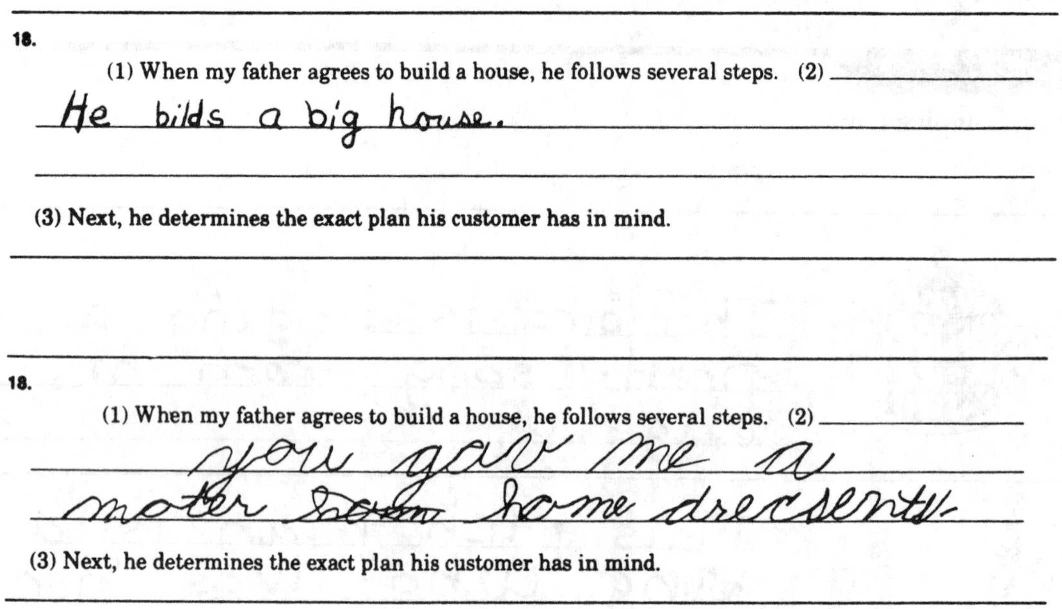

18.

(1) When my father agrees to build a house, he follows several steps.   (2) _____

He bilds a big house.

_____

(3) Next, he determines the exact plan his customer has in mind.

_____

18.

(1) When my father agrees to build a house, he follows several steps.   (2) _____

you gav me a moter home dresents.

(3) Next, he determines the exact plan his customer has in mind.

Figure 4–35. Two Third-Grade Students on Item 18.

ing upon the nature and types of assignments, a writer's performance may vary from task to task. Consequently, when a more in-depth assessment of writing skill is needed, an examiner will want to analyze longer passages of written discourse and several different types of writing samples collected across several weeks. For secondary students, samples should be collected in several different instructional settings. To conduct a more in-depth assessment of writing skill, an examiner may consider a student's: (a) performance in a variety of writing modes, (b) facility with the writing process, (c) organization in longer discourse, and (d) attitude toward writing assignments.

Writing Modes

A complete writing assessment involves evaluation of many different writing modes (Cooper, 1975). Cooper discussed several kinds of written discourse, including: (a) dramatic writing, such as plays and dialogues; (b) sensory recording reporting, such as interviews and observations; (c) generalizing and theorizing, such as essays about literary works; (d) research; (e) personal writing, including letters and journals; (f) prose fiction, and (g) business-practical, such as business letters, memos, and job applications. Cooper indicated that to assess writing quality and measure writing growth, six or seven pieces should be collected in each mode across a period of time. These pieces may be evaluated by the instructor, the student, and peers.

For an informal assessment, based upon the student's age and ability, an examiner may wish to collect different types of writing samples, such as a creative writing piece and a science report. With older students, an examiner may also determine the type of writing that is needed for success in a specific setting. For example, with Roger, a secondary student in a vocational program, the examiner was most concerned with assessing the specific type of writing that Roger was required to perform in his job setting.

Writing Process Approach

A standardized assessment of written language primarily measures a written product that an individual produces to satisfy certain task demands within a specified amount of time. This type of writing is required on examinations and essay tests and is one of the major methods for evaluating student performance throughout school. An examiner may also wish to assess writing as a process and see how a student performs on writing tasks when allowed sufficient time to organize, structure, and revise written text. The writing process approach consists of several recursive activities that a writer performs when composing text, including prewriting or planning, drafting, and editing and revising (Flower & Hayes, 1980; Graves, 1983, 1985). An examiner may wish to observe a student creating text from idea generation through the final stages of revision.

Organization

In some cases, an examiner will want to analyze a student's ability to organize and sequence text in longer written passages, such as in a story, report, or essay. Hall (1981) included the following evaluation components for analyzing a story. The examiner may ask whether the student includes: (a) a title; (b) a clear introduction; (c) relevant supportive information, such as facts, details, and examples; (d) more than one paragraph; (e) indentation at the start of each paragraph; and (f) appropriate sequencing of information. Additionally, the examiner may ask whether the student includes only relevant information and avoids gaps in the story line. When critiquing a writing sample, an examiner should record the student's strengths and weaknesses in organizational skill.

Attitude

Before planning and recommending an instructional program, the examiner will want to consider the student's attitude toward writing. When an examiner observes that a student has a poor attitude, remedial efforts are directed toward increasing motivation and confidence by providing reasons for writing and successful writing experiences. Further assessment may be performed with evaluative inquiries or writing attitude checklists. These questions will help an examiner or instructor plan for appropriate types of experiences. An examiner should attempt to determine: (a) valued purposes for writing, (b) student interests, and, with secondary students, (c) career goals (Polloway, Patton, & Cohen, 1981). Instruction then focuses on the communicative aspects of writing using meaningful activities.

Instructional Modifications

Some students have such extreme writing difficulty that an examiner will have to identify and recommend appropriate curricular modifications. Although a remedial program will be designed, a student may need alternate means for completing assignments as writing skill develops. The purpose of modifications is to alter tasks in the learning environment so that students with writing disabilities are able to discuss information and express themselves in ways that reduce or eliminate required writing.

Dagenais and Beadle (1984) listed several modifications that may be employed with students with language and learning disabilities in the regular classroom. These modifications include: (a) providing oral examinations; (b) allowing students to dictate writing to a transcriber such as a parent, peer, or tutor; (c) allowing the student and transcriber to proofread the assignment together; (d) reducing the length or number of writing assignments; (e) providing extended time for assignments; (f) giving separate grades for content, grammar, punctuation, and

spelling; (g) encouraging students to take responsibility for requesting certain modifications for assignments; (h) allowing students to ask other students to take notes for them; and (i) providing students with one more chance to improve their final draft of a paper before a grade is assigned.

The major accommodations for secondary students with moderate and severe writing difficulties include: (a) tape-recording lectures, (b) tape-recording responses to written assignments, (c) using dictated transcripts for assignments, and (d) using word processors with spelling checkers to complete classroom assignments (Masters & Mori, 1986). Efforts must be made to accommodate students with writing disabilities, while encouraging them to develop their writing skill.

When assessing Bryan, an eighth-grade student, the examiner noted that he had extreme difficulty with writing. Despite above-average oral language proficiency, Bryan had trouble producing even simple sentences. His classroom teachers reported that he received failing grades on all writing assignments, but participated fully in all class discussions and seemed to understand all of the concepts. As a compensation, the examiner recommended that Bryan be allowed to dictate all of his written assignments and examinations into a tape recorder. As time permitted, Bryan would transcribe a portion of his oral dictations using a word processor. This compensation allowed Bryan to succeed in the learning environment, communicate and develop his knowledge, and gradually increase his competency in written language.

Writing Instruction

> While instruction and evaluation may prove helpful, the more valuable opportunity is the actual writing practice, the expression of ideas.
>
> (Lickteig, 1981, p. 47)

Several factors will influence a student's progress in writing. An examiner may wish to determine the amount of time devoted to writing activities and the general approach that is used in the instructional setting. Writing instruction needs to be ongoing, systematic, and meaningful.

Amount of Daily Writing

In planning a writing program, an examiner may wish to determine the amount of time that is allocated to writing in the instructional setting. Some students lack writing skill because they have had limited opportunity to write. In discussing several research studies by the National

Study of Writing in the Secondary School, Applebee (1984) summarized that the majority of student writing time was devoted to recording responses without composing text. Only 3% of student time for class or homework was spent writing text longer than a paragraph.

Even in elementary, self-contained learning disability classrooms, little actual writing may occur. Leinhardt, Zigmond, and Cooley (1980) observed that 25 minutes of each 270-minute day were spent in writing, but that 19 of those minutes were spent on copying activities rather than on generating written language. One general recommendation that an examiner may make to help a student improve writing skill is that the student engage in daily writing for a specified time period.

Instructional Approach

The examiner may also wish to consider the instructional approach used in the classroom. In traditional writing instruction, little time was spent in prewriting activities or revising. Additionally, no feedback was provided until the writing assignment was complete. Research has demonstrated that effective writing instruction places emphasis on the process of writing, rather than the product (Hillocks, 1987). In some instances, an examiner may wish to recommend that a student participate in increased prewriting activities, receive constructive feedback, and have several opportunities to revise a piece before final grading.

Writing Process Approach

One approach to teaching writing that has been effective with students with learning disabilities is the writing process approach (Graves, 1983, 1985). The writing process approach stresses meaning first, and then skills in the context of meaning. In this approach, students write daily for 30 minutes or more at least four times a week. Students select topics for writing based upon their areas of expertise. Writing examples are saved in a folder to share with others. The teacher is a full participant by sharing his or her own writing and moving throughout the class during writing time asking clarifying questions. At the end of each writing period, several students share their pieces with the group.

At the beginning of the school year, Megan, a fifth-grade student, was reluctant to write because of previous failures. In the past, Megan had received negative feedback regarding both poor spelling and handwriting. In exasperation, her fourth-grade teacher had written on her papers: "Please spell words correctly!" Megan had received low grades in writing because of difficulty with spelling, proofreading, and editing and, consequently, had become anxious and discouraged about attempting to express her ideas in writing. In fifth grade, Megan's classroom teacher incorporated the instructional principles of the writing process approach into her classroom. In this risk-free environment, Megan was encouraged to first capture her ideas on paper, and then concentrate on organization in subsequent drafts. For the final draft, Megan received help in editing her paper for spelling and punctuation errors. As her confidence in her writing skill increased, Megan assumed more responsibility for proofreading her final drafts. Additionally, she regained her interest in writing.

Graves (1985) stated that students with learning disabilities learn more than just how to write when they are involved in a writing process approach. They learn to see themselves as thinkers with a message to convey to others. Instructor acceptance of each individual student as a writer with ideas to share is an important facet of effective instruction for students with writing difficulties. The purpose of students' writing is to fulfill personal intentions, not to master the content of instructional lessons (Rhodes & Dudley-Marling, 1988).

Instructional Strategies for Written Expression

As with other academic areas, the choice of an instructional strategy is based upon an individual's specific needs. Several techniques may be used to help students: (a) activate and record their background knowledge and (b) organize their stories, paragraphs, and reports. These interactive techniques are appropriate for individualized instruction or with groups of students and are used to develop and organize ideas in writing.

Activating and Recording Background Knowledge

> What we lack is not ideas but a direct means
> of getting in touch with them.
> (Rico, 1983, p. 28)

Several techniques are appropriate for assisting students to activate and enhance their background knowledge to facilitate the writing process. Research on methods for teaching written expression has demonstrated that the most effective instructional techniques emphasize strategies for collecting and transforming data in various ways (Hillocks, 1987). Sample techniques for activating background knowledge include: (a) the language experience approach, (b) clustering, (c) semantic mapping, and (d) a self-control strategy.

Language experience approach. Most teachers are familiar with the language experience approach to reading: A child dictates a story, the teacher writes down the story, and then the child reads the story. This type of approach may also be used successfully with writing (Simms, 1984). As with reading, the language experience approach and adaptations may be successful with students of all ages who are reluctant to write.

The emphasis of this approach is placed on having the student write down material based on experiences. After informal discussion about a topic, the student dictates the story as the teacher writes the story on the chalkboard or a piece of paper. A teacher may encourage a student to write aspects of the story as it is being recorded. Once the dictated story is written, a teacher encourages a student to copy the story from the teacher's text. During the writing process or after the story has been written, the teacher may explain aspects of capitalization and punctuation as they are needed, such as when to use a capital letter or a period. This type of approach may also be used with groups of students. When guided by teacher questions, the technique improves understanding of the story-writing process (Thomas, Englert, & Morsink, 1984).

In addition, the language experience approach may be used to help students increase vocabulary. After the story is dictated, the teacher and student discuss alternative word choices that would enhance the story. For example, if a student wrote that it was a *good* day, the teacher and student search for a more descriptive word. Poteet (1987) discussed a procedure called "slotting" that may be used in later grades to help students expand sentences and produce more mature writing. The purpose is to add phrases, clauses, and parts of speech that will make the writing more mature. Blanks are inserted where context may be elaborated. The student may be asked to list alternative choices, both words and phrases, below the slot. The student and teacher, or the class if conducted as a group activity, may select the best choice. An example of the slotting technique is presented for a sentence in Figure 4-36. This procedure may be particularly useful for secondary students who write simple, unembellished sentences.

Another adaptation for secondary students who are able to work independently is to have them dictate a story, report, or essay into a tape recorder and then write the story from the tape (Simms, 1984). If necessary, the story may be transcribed by a peer, parent, or teacher and the student may then be encouraged to type the paper. This procedure allows a student to concentrate on the language and organization of the report before engaging in writing.

Clustering. Rico (1983) described a prewriting technique called clustering. The intent of this process is self-organization by generating ideas. Rico recommended clustering and writing daily for approximately 10 minutes. To begin, the writer jots down a nucleus word or idea in the center of the page and circles the word. From the nucleus word, lines are drawn from the center in any direction and other associated words or ideas are added, each in its own circle. The writer is encouraged to free-associate by recording and connecting rapidly any word that comes to mind. When a new idea emerges, the writer begins at the central nucleus word. Arrows are added between connected associations. The clustering process continues until a pattern emerges in the seemingly random spilling of associations around the nucleus (Rico, 1983). At this point, the writer experiences a sudden sense of knowing what to write about.

Clustering helps the writer generate a point of departure for writing as a result of the ideas that emerge during the clustering process. This process helps students release associations and ideas prior to writing. Additionally, some evidence suggests that techniques such as clustering and brainstorming prior to writing help students recall pertinent information to include in their writing (Hillocks, 1987).

Semantic mapping. Another prewriting technique, called mapping, teaches students how to recall, organize, and structure ideas. This visual and verbal technique is most helpful for students who have never developed strategies for thinking through what they will write and how they will write it (Buckley, 1981). The purpose is to help a student organize ideas starting with the central thesis to the subordinate details. The major purposes of mapping are: (a) to add a visual dimension, (b) to aid organization in planning, and (c) to improve ability to see relationships among the component parts (Tompkins & Friend, 1985).

To begin, students brainstorm as many ideas as possible relating to a topic. The teacher writes all ideas on the board. Next, the ideas are organized into categories. The topic and categories are then placed into a map. In beginning instruction, a student may draw a map to look like a spider. For a more detailed map, a student may draw a large geometric shape in the middle of the paper. Several arms are drawn from the shape that may be used as categories. Small lines that represent supporting details are drawn down from the categories. When these types of maps become too restrictive, students may produce maps in any shape and size. Figure 4-37 illustrates several different forms of maps. Once a map is developed, the student is ready to begin writing.

Although similar in purpose to outlining, mapping seems to be a more effective prewriting strategy. Boyle (1981) noted several reasons for teaching mapping rather than traditional outlining. Semantic mapping (a) is easy to share with others, (b) clearly illustrates relationships, (c) presents the whole structure, (d) is personal and idiosyncratic, and (e) is easy to learn. Additionally, semantic mapping moves students from fluency with ideas to a form for organizing ideas.

```
The roadrunner ran across the road.


The _____ roadrunner ran across


        quick


        swift


        smart


        desert


the road   _____


    on Saturday afternoon


    in front of my station wagon


    as we watched the sun setting


    before the dog could catch him
```

Figure 4–36. Slotting Technique for the Language Experience Approach.

Self-control strategy. Harris and Graham (1985) found that a self-control strategy training procedure was effective in improving the compositions of upper-elementary students with learning disabilities. To begin, a particular composition skill is targeted for improvement such as action words, or doing words; action helpers, or words that tell how the action is done; or describing words, words that tell more about the picture. Only one type of word is targeted at a time, and then the procedure is repeated for another type of word. A five-step strategy is introduced on a small chart. The strategy steps include:

1. Look at the picture and write down a list of the type of targeted word, such as good action words.
2. Think of a story that will use the selected words.
3. Write the story. Make sure it makes sense and uses the words.
4. Read the story and ask these questions: Did I write a good story? Did I use the words I selected?
5. Edit the story. Try to use more of the type of words selected.

The student sets a goal for the number of action words to use in the story. The student practices the learning strategy and self-instructions while writing the story. After each practice story, the teacher and student count the number of targeted words used. This number may then be charted on a graph. This procedure may assist in activating background knowledge and developing writing vocabulary.

Organizing Stories

Many students with learning and reading disabilities lack understanding of story schema necessary for writing stories and comprehending stories (Nodine, Barenbaum, & Newcomer, 1985). Research has demonstrated that the quality of writing of students with learning disabilities improves when specific instructions about text structure are provided (Graham & Harris, 1986; Harris & Graham, 1985; Raphael, Englert, & Kirschner, 1986). The following techniques may be used to enhance the ability to use story or text structure organization as a writing strategy. To be effective, these strategies require the use of examples, teacher modeling, and group and individual efforts (Stewart, 1985). The emphasis of these strategies is to provide students with material for writing and a structure for organization prior to composing.

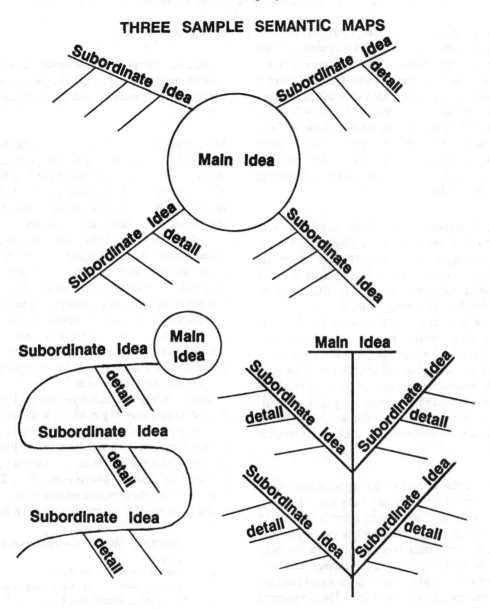

Figure 4–37. Three Sample Semantic Maps.

Story grammar. A story grammar is a set of rules that illustrate how stories are typically organized (Gordon & Braun, 1983). Knowledge of story elements and text regularities enhances both reading comprehension and ability to write a well-organized story. Research results indicate that when students are directly taught how to recognize and apply narrative structures, the quality and organization of their stories improve (Fitzgerald & Teasley, 1986). Results also suggest that upper-elementary students with learning disabilities include fewer story grammar components in written narratives than do their peers (Laughton & Morris, 1989).

The major story elements include: a setting; the char-

acters; a plot, problem, or the action; and a resolution. A simplified story grammar includes these four major story parts: (a) setting, the introduction of the characters, time, and place; (b) problem or initiating event, a predicament that confronts the main characters; (c) response or goal, the characters' reactions and attempts to solve the problem; and (d) outcome, the success or failure of the characters to accomplish the goal or resolve the problem (Nodine, Barenbaum, & Newcomer, 1985; Thomas, Englert, & Morsink, 1984). Thomas et al. recommended using this simplified story grammar with mildly handicapped students.

Initially, a teacher models the process by having students write a group story, using a story grammar guide as a framework or outline for writing. Next, students generate the story components. After the questions are answered, the story is written. If a student has trouble completing a question or fails to answer a question with sufficient detail, a teacher or peers provide assistance. Figure 4-38 illustrates a sample story guide, developed by Thomas, Englert, and Morsink (1984), that students may use to direct their thoughts prior to writing. Story guides may be adapted for use with different age groups and varying levels of student ability.

Macrocloze. A technique that may be used in conjunction with story grammar to help students handle text structure variability is macrocloze (Gordon & Braun, 1983). For this procedure, sentences, paragraphs, or major story elements are deleted from a story. Students then attempt to complete the missing portion.

This type of procedure is used on several of the items of the WJ-R ACH Writing Samples test. The middle sentence is deleted from a paragraph, and the student is asked to write a sentence that will fit or that the writer may have used. Successful completion of macrocloze exercises requires organizational ability, sequencing skill, and ability to model a writing style. Practice with this type of activity may increase a student's awareness of text structure.

Story frame. A similar method for applying knowledge of story grammar to writing is the story frame (Fowler, 1982; Fowler & Davis, 1985). A story frame is the scaffold or foundation of the story that is hooked together by key language, such as transition words that indicate the story sequence (Fowler, 1982). All words, phrases, and sentences that are not needed to sustain the story purpose are deleted. For example, Fowler and Davis (1985) presented the following sample story frame:

> *The problem in this story was . . .*
> *It started when . . .*
> *After that . . .*
> *Then . . .*
> *The problem is solved when . . .*
> *The story ends . . .*

In learning to use a story frame, Fowler suggested that students follow this sequence of steps: (a) listen to the story, (b) discuss the story while the story frame is displayed, (c) fill in missing information, (d) finish the frame individually, and then (e) practice using a story frame while portions are omitted systematically. As with other strategies for improving written expression, this technique is useful for instruction in both writing and reading comprehension.

Organizing Paragraphs

Specific strategies may be employed to teach students how to organize paragraphs. The purpose of these strategies is to assist students with the sequencing of information.

Statement-pie. A strategy that is useful for introducing expository writing, writing for the purpose of providing information, is called statement-pie (Englert & Lichter, 1982; Thomas, Englert, & Morsink, 1984). The statement is the main idea or the topic sentence, and the pie includes the *p*roofs, *i*nformation, and *e*xamples.

Wallace and Bott (1989) found that use of this technique improved the paragraph-writing skills of eighth-grade students with learning disabilities. The teacher modeled detecting and generating the "Pies." The students completed a paragraph-planning guide prior to writing the paragraphs and were given immediate feedback upon the appropriateness of their "Statement" and the "Pies." After learning this strategy in the special education classroom, students were able to generalize their paragraph-writing skills to different classrooms.

In introducing this technique, the teacher explains that any paragraph may begin with a statement, or the main idea or topic. The rest of the paragraph is the "pie" or information pertaining to that statement. Initially, a teacher may provide the statements and have the students write in the related details (Thomas et al., 1984). Later, students may complete the structure without cues.

An example of a statement-pie format follows:

> Statement: Maggie is a champion tennis player.
> pie: practices 5 hours daily
> pie: has won several major tournaments
> pie: ranked second in the state

The pie details may be written as sentence fragments or complete sentences. When writing the paragraph, the pies are then transformed into complete sentences. Once students have successfully mastered the statement-pie outline for paragraphs, they begin to construct compositions. Each statement with its set of related pies forms a separate paragraph. Filler sentences and transitions are added to improve the composition. In addition to a writing technique, this strategy is useful for note taking or outlining for upper-elementary and secondary students in content area courses (Thomas et al., 1984).

Paragraph types. Students may be taught to write several different types of formula paragraphs, including: (a) enumerative, (b) sequential, (c) compare and contrast, and (d) descriptive. A brief description of these paragraph types follows.

1. *Setting.*

   a. Where does the story take place? _____

   _____

   b. Who is the story about? _____

   c. What does the person look like? _____

   _____

2. *Problem.*

   a. What is the problem confronting the main characters? _____

   _____

   _____

   b. What caused the problem? _____

   _____

3. *Response.*

   a. How do the people feel about the problem? _____

   _____

   b. What does the main character do? _____

   _____

   c. Does anyone/anything help the main character? _____

4. *Outcome.*

   a. What happens to solve the problem? _____

   _____

   _____

   b. What happens at the end of the story? _____

   _____

   c. How does everyone feel at the end of the story?_____

   _____

Figure 4–38. Sample Story Guide. *Note.* From "Modifying the Classroom Program in Language" by C.C. Thomas, C.S. Englert, and C.V. Morsink in *Teaching Special Needs Students in Regular Classrooms* (p. 258) by C.V. Morsink, 1984, Boston: Little Brown, and Company. Copyright 1984 by Catherine Voelker Morsink. Reprinted by permission.

Enumerative: An enumerative paragraph involves a series of points that relate to a specific topic. A student writes the main idea, followed by several supporting details. For example, a topic sentence may read: "The causes of the Civil War were political, economic, and social" (Moran, 1983). A student would then write a detail sentence to support each major point.

Sequential: A sequential paragraph involves the serial presentation of a number of steps or ideas. Events may be presented in chronological order. A sequence guide in which the topic and numbered lines for each step (e.g., First, Then, Next, Finally) are laid out may help some students (Stewart, 1985). The student completes the sequence guide and then writes an organized paragraph.

Compare and contrast: A compare and contrast paragraph presents a discussion of the likenesses and differences between two or more items. To aid in this process, a data chart may be compiled in which the topic categories for comparison are listed across the top of the page and the attributes of interest are listed down the side of the page (Hennings, 1982). The student enters information into the chart before writing the paragraph or report.

Descriptive: Students may also write descriptive paragraphs. For this type of paragraph, an attribute guide may help a student identify and organize the information to be included (Stewart, 1985). At the top of the attribute guide, the topic is identified. Headings for different characteristics are then listed down the side. The writer records the details and then uses them as a framework for composing. As students become proficient in using teacher-made guides, they may create their own guides using self-questioning techniques (Stewart, 1985).

Research studies have demonstrated the effectiveness of teaching formula paragraphs. For example, Moran, Schumaker, and Vetter (1981) used a strategy to help adolescents with learning disabilities improve their paragraph organization. Students were told to write a topic sentence, at least three detail sentences, and a clincher statement. This strategy was then applied to three paragraph types: enumerative, sequential, and compare and contrast.

Similarly, Moran (1983) conducted a series of interventions with secondary students with learning disabilities using a paragraph-organization strategy to produce the three paragraph types. The results of these experiments indicated that secondary students with learning disabilities improve their paragraph organization skills with 10 to 20 hours of instruction and practice in writing formula paragraphs. Additionally, as students gained control over the form, they became freer in expression. These findings suggest that secondary students with writing difficulty benefit from direct instruction in structured approaches that use a student's writing as the material and provide students with positive and corrective feedback. When teaching formula paragraphs, instructors should provide students with practice in integrating the different paragraph types into longer themes or essays.

Organizing Reports and Themes

Once a student has learned to write well-organized paragraphs, several techniques may be used to help students compose longer compositions. As early as third grade, students have to prepare reports on a variety of topics.

Report writing. Beach (1983) described activities to include in instructing elementary students on informational report writing. The unit begins with activities that will arouse topic interest. Next, students generate a list of questions that will be answered in the report. The question list is revised and then organized into a logical sequence for content and paragraph organization. After the teacher models the entire process, students write their own first draft. These drafts are then revised with the help of peers; the author reads the report to another student and then together they list suggestions for improvement.

To help students of all ages organize writing, a set of questions may be developed through oral discussion. For example, once a writing assignment has been presented, students and teachers may generate orally a list of questions that should be addressed in the writing assignment. These questions serve as response organizers. For students needing additional assistance with organization, questions are grouped by paragraph or a more structured technique is recommended.

Weiss and Weiss (1982) recommended a graphic procedure for organizing materials, illustrated in Figure 4-39. A student writes a main idea and then develops several subtopics. Envelopes are fastened under each subtopic. As a student researches the topic, notes taken on index cards are filed in the appropriate envelopes. This type of strategy could also be done using "post-its" or sticky paper (Bos & Anders, in press). Students write several subtopics on a paper or poster board and then record and post their notes under the appropriate headings. These types of procedures help students organize information to be included in a report prior to writing.

Kerrigan's method. Kerrigan (1979) described a structured process for theme organization that may be used by students individually or within an English composition class. The strategy is appropriate for upper-elementary through secondary-level students. The following steps are outlined:

Step 1: Write a sentence that you can say much more about. The sentence should be a short, simple declarative sentence that makes one statement.

Step 2: Write three sentences about the sentence in Step 1 that are clearly and directly about that sentence, not just something in it. Do not simply repeat the same idea in different words, but rather provide sentences that are more specific than the initial sentence. These three sentences form the topic sentences for three separate paragraphs.

Step 3: Write four or five sentences about each of the sentences in Step 2. Make the material in these sentences

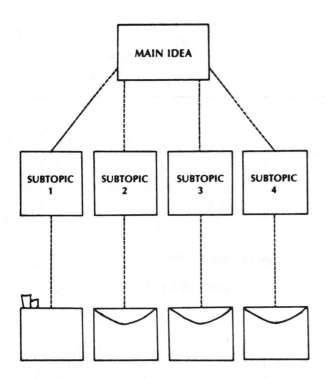

Figure 4–39. A Simple Graphic Outline. *Note.* From "Training Kids to Be Winners in the Handling of Writing Skills" by H.G. Weiss and M.S. Weiss, 1982, *Academic Therapy, 18,* p. 79. Copyright 1982 by Academic Therapy Publications. Reprinted by permission.

as concrete and specific as possible. Go into detail and provide specific examples. The goal is to say more about what has just been said. These sentences form the body for each of the three paragraphs.

Step 4: In the first sentence of the second paragraph and every paragraph following, insert a clear reference to the idea in the preceding paragraph.

Step 5: Make sure every sentence in the theme is connected to and makes a clear reference to the preceding sentence. This is done by using explicit references to the previous sentence, such as: (a) repeating a word; (b) using a synonym or antonym for a word used in the previous

sentence; (c) using a pronoun to refer to an antecedent; (d) repeating a sentence structure; or (e) using connectives, such as *for example, consequently,* and *however.*

Kerrigan also presented examples for writing various types of themes that require specific rules, including: themes of contrast, themes of comparison, and themes of expression. An examiner may recommend the use of this method to an instructor or to an individual who needs assistance in developing and writing organized compositions.

Power Writing. Power Writing is another example of a program for teaching subordination of ideas (Sparks, 1982). The powers refer to the various levels of organization, such as 1st Power for main ideas, 2nd Power for major details or subtopics, and 3rd Power for minor details. The program progresses from practice in subordinating single words and sentences to construction of essays. Additionally, grammar and punctuation rules are reviewed and more than 28 sentence patterns are introduced. A major advantage of both the Kerrigan method and the Power Writing program is that motivated secondary and college students may enhance their expository writing skill by working independently through these programs stage-by-stage.

Conclusion

The WJ-R ACH writing tests sample a variety of skills important to writing development, ranging from the tools of writing, handwriting, spelling, and proofreading, to the abilities to write with ease and express and organize ideas. The central aim of writing assessment and provision of supplemental instruction is to help students increase ability to express and organize their ideas effectively. In composing, students must attend first to meaning, and then later to form. Writing is an expressive, interactive, and communicative process through which students demonstrate their world knowledge and share their ideas with others. With careful diagnosis, followed by sound instructional practices and meaningful writing experiences, students will increase proficiency and ability to communicate effectively in writing.

5

KNOWLEDGE

What learners are able to learn is dependent to a large extent upon what they already know.

(Reid, 1988, p.13)

The WJ-R ACH Knowledge tests sample an individual's knowledge in three content areas: Science, Social Studies, and Humanities. These three tests contain items that range in difficulty from early preschool (age 2) through college and adult levels. Although the initial items require the student to point to the correct response, the majority of items require single word or open-ended responses. All three tests are administered orally. Additionally, the Knowledge tests may be used as a supplemental measure of Comprehension-Knowledge (Gc) when analyzing a student's performance on the WJ-R COG factors.

Content of the Knowledge Tests

Figure 5-1 illustrates the relationship among the three Knowledge tests. In contrast to the other achievement tests, the relationship among these tests is overlapping rather than hierarchical. With each test, as items progress in difficulty, the content questions require an increased amount of specialized content area knowledge.

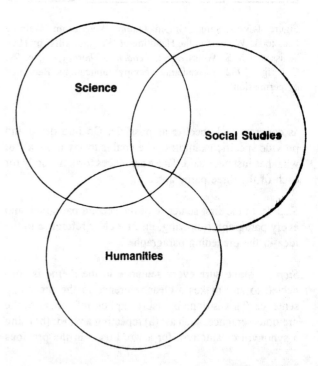

Figure 5–1. Relationship Among the Three Knowledge Tests.

the three tests, (b) types of errors, (c) responses to certain item types, and (d) classroom performance in content area subjects.

Strengths and Weaknesses Among the Tests

An examiner may note strengths and weaknesses in student performance on the three Knowledge tests. For

Error Analysis of the Knowledge Tests

An analysis of performance on these tests will help an examiner estimate a student's content-specific knowledge when no reading is required. When interpreting results, an examiner may consider the following factors regarding student performance: (a) strengths and weaknesses among example, Robert, a fifth-grade student with a reading disability, received average scores on the Science and Social Studies tests but a below-average score on the Humanities test. In this case, the examiner hypothesized that Robert's below-average score resulted from his limited reading skill and, as a result, his reduced exposure to literature. His average scores on the Science and Social Studies tests suggested, however, that Robert is acquiring and retaining orally presented content information. Figure 5-2 depicts Robert's Age/Grade Profile on the three Knowledge tests.

In another situation, a student may excel in one content area, but have average or below-average performance in another. Figure 5-3 illustrates the performance of Carla, a high school student, on the Age/Grade Profile for the Knowledge tests. Her high performance on the Science test suggests that courses involving science content will be easier for her than courses that emphasize either social studies or humanities content.

Types of Errors

When administering the Knowledge tests, the examiner should record a student's responses verbatim for subsequent qualitative error analysis. A student's response to an item may reveal: (a) thorough knowledge, (b) partial knowledge, (c) minimal knowledge, or (d) no knowledge. Considering the quality of a student's responses will help an examiner determine the need for supplemental instruction in a content area.

Thorough knowledge. A response that indicates thorough knowledge demonstrates that the student possesses detailed understanding of the question. In some cases, the student may respond correctly and then provide an additional embellishment. For example, when asked Social Studies Item 15: "What does an astronaut do?" Melissa, a third-grade student, explained the role and then briefly summarized several recent missions accomplished by astronauts.

Partial knowledge. Partial knowledge is indicated when the student demonstrates some experience with the concept but may not be able to produce a specific or exact response. The concept may be in the process of developing but may not be fully formed. For example, when asked Item 30: "What would someone be doing if they were involved in espionage activities?" Todd, a college sophomore, responded: "It would be like James Bond." Although Todd demonstrated some knowledge of the concept, he was not able to express the precise meaning of the word "espionage."

Similarly, when asked Social Studies Item 26: "The people of India live on which continent?" Doris, a sixth-grade student, replied: "South America." Although incorrect, her response indicates that she does know that South America is a continent. When answering Social Studies Item 32: "Why did the Pony Express end?" Doris responded: "It was because the mailman was introduced." Although Doris lacks the necessary historic information, her response indicates she knew that the Pony Express delivered mail and that alternative, more efficient methods for delivering mail were created.

For some items, a student may produce one correct response to a two-part item. For example, when asked Social Studies Item 26: "Which country borders the United States on the north, and which country borders the United States on the south?" Susan, a seventh-grade student, responded: "Canada on the north, but I can't remember the south." On other items, a student may reverse concepts, such as defining fiction as nonfiction or confusing a biography with an autobiography. Although these types of responses are scored as incorrect, they indicate that a student possesses some knowledge of the vocabulary or concept being presented.

On several items, specific queries are listed in the examiner key for responses that demonstrate partial knowledge. After hearing the query, a student may produce a correct or incorrect response.

Minimal knowledge. A minimal knowledge response suggests that the student may have had some exposure to the concept but is missing the necessary information for a correct response or is confused about the concept. When asked Social Studies Item 23: "How does a town get money to pay for its streets and school?" Jamie, a third-grade student, responded: "They have bake sales or skating parties."

No knowledge. A response that indicates no knowledge suggests that a student has not been exposed to, does not recall, or lacks understanding of a concept. These types of responses often reveal a student's confusion regarding a concept. For example, when asked Social Studies Item 28: "Where did Columbus sail from in 1492?" John, a fifth-grade boy, responded: "I have no idea, but it must have been Columbus, Ohio." Although John's response may indicate a sense of humor, it also reveals his lack of knowledge regarding this specific fact. When asked Social Studies Item 16: "What is paper made from?" Tom, a secondary student, responded: "Sodium." Tom's response indicates his misconception or lack of knowledge regarding the raw materials used in making paper.

A failure to respond to an item does not necessarily indicate that the student has no knowledge of the question. In some situations, a student may choose to say "I don't know" rather than risk producing an incorrect response or

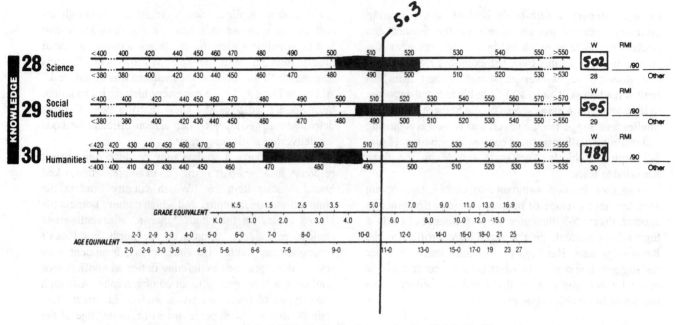

Figure 5–2. A Fifth-Grade Student on the Age/Grade Profile.

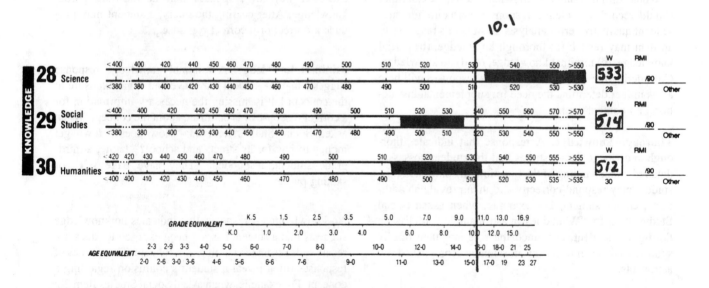

Figure 5–3. A High School Student on the Age/Grade Profile.

revealing a lack of knowledge. When administering test items to Lois, a third-grade student, the examiner noted that Lois often responded that she did not know the answer. When asked to try, she would typically produce a correct response. Lois would only respond without prompting when she was certain that a response was correct. The classroom teacher also reported that Lois would rarely participate in class or volunteer responses to questions. The examiner recommended that Lois be encouraged to venture guesses and express her opinions. A

student like Lois needs a risk-free classroom environment where she learns that making mistakes is not symptomatic of failure, but merely part of the learning process.

Item Types

More specific error analyses may be performed by examining a student's responses to different item types within each of the three tests.

Science. On the Science test, the examiner may note that a student performs well on items involving biology, but seems to have difficulty with questions covering another area of science, such as astronomy. In some instances, an examiner may wish to administer questions from both Forms A and B to obtain a more in-depth analysis of performance. As an example, when assessing a young student, an examiner may wish to obtain additional information regarding a student's knowledge of body parts. Figure 5-4 provides a list of the items that require identification of body parts for Forms A and B.

Social Studies. The Social Studies test samples a student's knowledge of tools, occupations, signs, maps, weather, geography, history, government, and economics. An examiner may note that a student has difficulty on a particular type of item, such as geography. For example, an examiner noted that Roger, a high school junior, had developed limited knowledge regarding geographic concepts. On Item 25: "The people of India live on which continent?," he responded: "Egypt." This response indicates that Roger does not know the location of India and most likely does not understand the concept of "continent." On Item 26: "Which country borders the United States on the north, and which country borders the United States on the south?" he responded: "Hawaii on the north, and England on the south." This response suggests that Roger: (a) is confused about directions (North, South, East, West), (b) may not understand the difference between a state (Hawaii) and a country, and (c) may not understand the meaning of the word "border." This type of analysis will help an examiner to determine specific areas of weakness within a content area. The necessity of additional informal assessment and the type of instructional modifications required may also be determined.

Humanities. The Humanities test is composed of three specific item types: art, music, and literature. When desired, a more detailed error analysis may be performed by examining a student's responses to the three item types. An examiner may observe that a student has developed a substantial knowledge base in one or two of these areas, but not in another. For example, Paul, a sixth-grade student enrolled in the school band, answered music questions at a higher level than art and literature questions. Figures 5-5 and 5-6 categorize the Humanities items in Forms A and B into art (A), music (M), or literature (L). When performing an error analysis, an examiner may enter a "1" for all passed items, and a "0" for all failed items.

The knowledge bases of art and music are shared by most cultures, as is knowledge of the classic works in literature. Knowledge of early development literature, such as nursery rhymes and tales, is more culturally based.

Students with diverse cultural experiences or from different countries may not have been exposed to some of the initial literature items on the Humanities test. In analyzing performance, an examiner should attempt to determine whether the student's responses reflect limited experience with literature in general or a lack of exposure to the literature base of a culture. In some instances, a student may have acquired knowledge of the early development literature of another culture. Through informal analysis and discussion with parents, an examiner may ascertain a student's past exposure to nursery rhymes, stories, and books.

Performance in Content Area Courses

For some evaluations, an examiner will want to compare a student's test performance to his or her classroom performance. Several different performance patterns may occur.

Similar test and classroom performance. In many instances, a student's performance on the Knowledge tests will be similar to performance in the instructional setting. Students who perform at an average or above-average level on the orally administered Knowledge tests have developed background or topical knowledge in content areas. The more extensive experience a student has with the vocabulary and concepts in a content area, the easier it is to comprehend the text. Conversely, students who perform poorly on the Knowledge tests have limited background knowledge in content areas and are likely to have difficulty with content area classes unless specific modifications are made. For these students, the instructional emphasis should be placed on developing relevant background knowledge prior to reading.

High test but low classroom performance. In some instances, a student's performance on the Knowledge tests is above average, but the student receives low grades in content area courses. Lack of classroom success may be attributed to student-related factors, such as low motivation or interest, or environmental factors, such as poor instruction or a mismatch between the learning and teaching styles of the student and instructor.

Limited classroom success may also be attributed to low performance in other areas, such as in reading or writing, rather than limited background knowledge. Students who have below grade-level skill in reading or writing are likely to have trouble completing required course assignments unless the assignments are modified to the student's skill level. For these students, instruction should focus on developing basic reading and writing skills and on learning and applying strategies that will assist with the mastery of difficult content area material.

Form A		Form B	
1. nose	☐	1. ear	☐
2. eye	☐	2. foot	☐
3. knee	☐	3. chin	☐
7. mouth	☐	8. tongue	☐
15. wrist	☐	14. elbow	☐
		16. heel	☐

Figure 5–4. Error Analysis for Science: Body Parts.

Low test but high classroom performance. In other instances, a student's performance on the Knowledge tests is low, but the student receives high grades in content area courses. Again, classroom success may be attributed to student-related factors, such as high motivation and strong family support, or environmental factors, such as adaptation of materials to the student's performance level.

Additional Assessment of Content Area Skills

The WJ-R ACH Knowledge tests provide an examiner with an estimate of background knowledge in three content areas. For some assessments, an examiner may wish to perform a more in-depth analysis of a student's performance within one or more content area subjects. Because the necessary knowledge base and student performance expectations differ for each instructional course, an examiner may analyze a student's reading performance in the content area textbook and determine his or her instructional demands. For example, factors such as types of assignments, examinations, and homework are considered.

To begin, an examiner should determine whether the reading level of the instructional text is too difficult for the student. An estimate of reading skill may be obtained by analyzing a student's performance on the WJ-R ACH reading tests. Performance in both basic reading skills and comprehension should be considered.

Retelling

Informal analysis may also be conducted using a student's textbook. To determine if word identification is interfering with performance, an examiner may compare a student's ability to answer questions or retell information under two conditions: after reading a passage independently and after listening to a passage. An examiner may have the student first read a portion of the text and answer questions and then listen to a portion of the text and answer questions. Questions may be provided prior to reading or presented orally after reading. If performance is significantly higher in the listening condition, difficulty in word identification skill is most likely affecting the student's ability to comprehend the content area text.

Cloze Procedure

The cloze procedure, described more fully in Chapter 3, may also be used for informal assessment of comprehension of a subject area textbook.

Steps. Rakes and McWilliams (1981) described the following procedure for constructing a cloze test using content material:

1. Select a passage of approximately 400 words from the first 50 pages of the book.
2. Retype the selection deleting every 7th word. Do not change the first and last sentence. Delete a minimum of 50 blanks. When finished, record a number under each blank.
3. Prior to administering the informal test, have students complete a sample cloze test containing 6 to 10 blanks.
4. Prepare an answer sheet with the exact word that appeared in the book.

Scores. Only exact responses are scored as correct. Recognizable misspellings are not penalized. Rakes and McWilliams indicated that the percentage of correct scores may be interpreted as follows:

58% and above: book is at the independent level and appropriate for the student.

		Art	Music	Literature
1.	scissors	—		
2.	drum		—	
3.	blue	—		
4.	crayons	—		
5.	piano		—	
6.	newspaper			—
7.	brown	—		
8.	Once upon a ...			—
9.	jewelry	—		
10.	Jack and Jill			—
11.	brushes	—		
12.	Donald Duck			—
13.	black	—		
14.	playing horn		—	
15.	Mary/lamb			—
16.	Humpty Dumpty			—
17.	ballerina		—	
18.	Dennis			—
19.	Goldilocks			—
20.	Wizard of Oz			—
21.	tambourine		—	
22.	blue and yellow	—		
23.	solo		—	
24.	fiction			—
25.	saxophone		—	
26.	Picasso	—		
27.	Mark Twain			—
28.	pick		—	
29.	orchestra		—	
30.	treble clef		—	
31.	anonymous			—
32.	palette	—		
33.	Homer			—
34.	sharp		—	
35.	autobiography			—
36.	acappella		—	
37.	epilogue			—
38.	secondary colors	—		
39.	pottery	—		
40.	dialogue			—
41.	sepia	—		
42.	Yearling			—
43.	limerick			—
44.	festoon	—		
45.	interval		—	

Figure 5–5. Error Analysis of Humanities, Form A. Permission is granted to reproduce this form.

		Art	Music	Literature
1.	crayons	—		
2.	horn		—	
3.	red	—		
4.	Mickey			—
5.	blue	—		
6.	green	—		
7.	playing piano		—	
8.	Humpty Dumpty			—
9.	painting	—		
10.	guitar		—	
11.	three pigs			—
12.	shake them		—	
13.	Red Riding Hood			—
14.	Jack/candlestick			—
15.	violin		—	
16.	Pinocchio			—
17.	dwarfs			—
18.	Jack/beanstalk			—
19.	Cinderella			—
20.	notes		—	
21.	Mary Poppins			—
22.	harmonica		—	
23.	choir		—	
24.	Robin Hood			—
25.	portrait	—		
26.	duet		—	
27.	Zeus			—
28.	accordion		—	
29.	la		—	
30.	setting			—
31.	sculpture	—		
32.	Hamlet			—
33.	fables			—
34.	woodwind		—	
35.	simile			—
36.	c		—	
37.	papier-mache	—		
38.	silhouettes	—		
39.	troupe		—	
40.	chartreuse	—		
41.	Hans Christian Andersen			—
42.	Origami	—		
43.	cornucopia	—		
44.	impressionism	—		
45.	Baroque		—	

Figure 5–6. Error Analysis of Humanities, Form B. Permission is granted to reproduce this form.

37-57%: book is at the instructional level but the reader will require instructional assistance for understanding.

Below 37%: book is at the frustration level and the reader will require extensive assistance to use the book.

Although only verbatim responses are scored as correct, an examiner may wish to analyze a student's responses in more depth by identifying the types of errors that a student makes. This procedure is described in the section on Error Analysis of the Passage Comprehension test. Examination of error types will assist the examiner in interpreting the quality of a student's performance and identifying instructional needs. An examiner may wish to use other informal techniques to assess a student's: (a) vocabulary knowledge, (b) background knowledge, or (c) study skills.

Vocabulary Knowledge

Vocabulary knowledge is critical to success in content areas. Each content area has its own technical or specialized vocabulary and concepts to be learned. After administering the Knowledge tests, an examiner may note that the student is low in content area vocabulary. Rakes (1987) described an informal procedure for assessing a student's knowledge of science or social studies vocabulary. To begin, select textbooks equal to, above, and below the student's expected performance level. From each textbook, choose 20 technical vocabulary words from the glossary and list the words vertically on a page. Ask the student to pronounce each word and then, if desired, ask the student to provide the word meaning. If the student is unable to produce the meaning, ask the student to use the word in a sentence that will demonstrate understanding. Rakes indicated that the student should have 75% to 80% accuracy on word identification and at least 70% accuracy for word definitions in a text at the instructional reading level.

Background Knowledge

Background knowledge and experience are important aspects of successful reading performance and are critical for understanding the concepts and vocabulary presented in content area textbooks. A student's difficulty with content material in the classroom may stem from limited background knowledge.

The Pre Reading Plan (PReP) is a three-step procedure that may be used for assessing relevant background knowledge prior to reading (Langer, 1981). The assessment is intended to determine whether or not students need to develop additional background knowledge prior to reading the text. To begin, the students brainstorm or free-associate with key words, concepts, or pictures from the text, saying anything that comes to mind. Next, students are instructed to reflect on their initial associations and responses by answering the question: "What

made you think of . . . ?" This process allows students to evaluate their knowledge and determine how it relates to the text. Finally, the students are encouraged to formulate new questions that result from the previous discussion. For example, the instructor asks: "Based on our discussion, what new ideas do you have?"

To determine if further concept development is necessary prior to reading, a student's responses are classified into three levels: much, some, or little knowledge. Students with much knowledge produce responses, such as definitions and analogies, that demonstrate integration of the key concepts. These students will not have difficulty with comprehension. Students with some knowledge produce responses such as examples, qualities, or defining characteristics and may benefit from additional instructional activities. Students with little knowledge produce examples such as rhyming words or unrelated firsthand experiences. These students will require concept and vocabulary instruction prior to reading.

In addition to assessment, this procedure may also be used as an instructional technique to activate and enhance prior knowledge. When used for teaching, the instructor selects key words and concepts that are central to the passage that the students will read. The teacher and students then proceed through the three teaching phases: (a) initial associations with the concept, "What comes to mind when you think of . . . ?"; (b) reflections on the initial associations, "What made you think of . . . ?"; and (c) reformulation of knowledge, "Based on discussion, have you any new ideas about . . . " Langer (1984) found that the use of the PReP activity significantly increased students' text comprehension.

Study Skills

Another important aspect of success in content areas is well-established study skills. An examiner may want to interview a student to determine whether he or she has developed efficient studying methods.

Figure 5-7 illustrates a Study-Skills Questionnaire developed by McCabe (1982) for interviewing secondary students with learning disabilities. McCabe recommended that each question be followed by a discussion with the student regarding independent study habits. This type of questionnaire may be easily adapted for use with upper-elementary students.

Instructional Modifications and Strategies for Content Areas

> When students are mainstreamed into regular classes, the textbooks they use must aid their learning, not prevent it.
>
> (Beech, 1983, p. 401)

Study-Skills Questionnaire

1.	I study in the same place each day at a desk or table.	yes no
2.	I keep distractions to a minimum (music, desk top clear).	yes no
3.	I study immediately after I sit down at my desk.	yes no
4.	I know how I learn best (visual, auditory, kinesthetic).	yes no
5.	I intend to learn.	yes no
6.	I am aware when I am not concentrating.	yes no
7.	I take short breaks when I get tired.	yes no
8.	I write down all assignments with the date they are due.	yes no
9.	I plan how long an assignment will take to finish.	yes no
10.	I keep a calendar or time sheet of my work schedule.	yes no
11.	I keep dated assignments and tests for study and review.	yes no
12.	I keep an organized binder (subjects separated).	yes no
13.	I spend enough time studying.	yes no
14.	I study each subject one half hour per night.	yes no
15.	I do something while studying (write notes, recite).	yes no
16.	I make up illustrations (diagrams, maps).	yes no
17.	I pay attention to illustrations, graphs, etc., in books.	yes no
18.	I make a list of new vocabulary words and study them.	yes no
19.	I use the SQR3 method of studying.	yes no
20.	I test myself (flashcards, study questions).	yes no
21.	I review often. (Review is worth 4 months of remembering.)	yes no
22.	I overlearn the material.	yes no
23.	I actively participate in class (discuss, take notes).	yes no
24.	I use group study techniques.	yes no
25.	I use new information in my daily life (vocabulary, etc.)	yes no

Figure 5–7. Study-Skills Questionnaire. *Note.* From "Developing Study Skills: The LD High School Student" by D. McCabe, 1982, *Academic Therapy, 18*, p. 200. Copyright 1982 by Academic Therapy Publications. Reprinted by permission.

Students with learning problems often have difficulty obtaining the content from textbooks. Too often, a student's progress in a content area course is impeded by lack of proficiency in reading and writing. Rudy, who had recently transitioned from an ESL program, was failing his high school biology and American history classes. In discussing his performance with the examiner, Rudy complained that it took him too long to complete the reading assignments. After assessing Rudy's reading skill, the examiner estimated that Rudy had a fourth-grade independent reading level. In contrast, Rudy's performance on the Science and Social Studies tests was slightly above grade level. Through informal assessment, the examiner determined that Rudy was able to understand the content of his textbooks but could not read them independently. To solve this problem, the examiner recom-

mended that Rudy listen to taped copies of his textbooks, allowing Rudy to complete his reading assignments on time.

In preparing recommendations, an examiner will want to determine if content area modifications are needed to circumvent a reading problem, a writing problem, limited background knowledge, or a combination of factors. Once the contributing factors are identified, one or more of the following modifications or strategies may be appropriate.

Modification of Materials

One option for improving student performance is to select an alternate text that is written on the student's independent or instructional reading level. An increasing amount of material is available for use in content areas with students who are reading significantly below grade level. If these types of texts are not available, volunteers may paraphrase and rewrite the material into a simpler format.

Simplifying content. Summarizing guidelines from psycholinguistic research, Beech (1983) presented several strategies for simplifying content, sentences, and vocabulary in context area textbooks for mainstreamed students. The guidelines for content include: (a) present ideas logically, include the main idea first followed by supporting details; (b) present sequences in chronological order; (c) cluster related information together; (d) keep points as simple as possible; and (e) eliminate all extraneous or irrelevant information.

Sentences are simplified by using basic sentence structures that include only a subject, verb, and a modifier. Clauses may be maintained for more advanced readers. Complex sentences may be broken into separate sentences. In some cases, however, clear communication of complex concepts requires longer sentences. A disadvantage of decombining sentences is that when a word signifying the relationships between clauses is omitted, the reader must infer that relationship, which may increase task difficulty.

Vocabulary is controlled by using familiar and frequently used words. The meaning of any specialized vocabulary is presented in context. Additionally, words with high visual imagery are selected whenever possible.

Abrahamsen and Shelton (1989) found that the comprehension of adolescents with learning disabilities was significantly increased when text modifications were made. The text was simplified by making both syntactic and semantic modifications. The syntactic modifications included changing passive voice to active voice, changing past perfect tense to simple past tense, and clarifying pronoun antecedents. The semantic modifications included reducing the number of multimeaning words and eliminating double negatives. Although rewriting a content area text involves a significant time commitment, the investment will help ESL students and students with language and learning disabilities understand and retain more information.

Color-coding. Color-coding is another method for simplifying textbooks. Using a yellow highlighter, an instructor may color-code the main ideas in a textbook so the amount of required reading is reduced or so the most important ideas are immediately apparent. If desired, different colors may be used to highlight other types of information, such as green for vocabulary words and pink for important names and dates.

Content Reduction or Alteration

It may also be necessary to reduce the amount of content presented or assessed at any one time. A student may be assigned a few pages daily. Or, a student may need weekly chapter tests, rather than periodic unit tests that cover several chapters. Additionally, alternate assignments should be made available if the required reading or writing is too difficult for the student. Text supplements, such as trade books, magazines, or journals, may be used, and special projects, such as drawings, maps, debates, or models, may be substituted for exams or written reports.

Advance Organizers

An advance organizer is any method, such as an outline or diagram, that provides an organizational format to material prior to its presentation. The format of organizers may be verbal, written, or incorporate a combination of forms. For example, prior to beginning a lecture, an instructor may enumerate the important points to be covered. These types of organizational cues assist students in recognizing and establishing a mental framework for critical information.

In reviewing studies that assessed the effectiveness of advance organizers, Mayer (1979) found that advance organizers were most effective when presented prior to reading and were most helpful for students with lower ability or limited background knowledge. Lenz, Alley, and Schumaker (1987) found that advance organizers significantly improved the learning performance of secondary students with learning disabilities. Content area teachers were able to implement the strategy after 45 minutes of training. Figure 5-8 illustrates ten steps identified by Lenz (1983) for developing and teaching students how to apply advance organizers.

Study Guides

Study guides may be used as advance organizers or may be applied when the student is reading. Most typically, study guides present open-ended questions that follow the sequence of the written material. The questions direct a student to locate specific information, including facts, concepts, vocabulary, and details. Maring and Furman (1985) described several special adaptations for study guides that may be helpful for mainstreamed students. One recommendation is to categorize the questions into three levels of difficulty: literal, inferential, and applicative. The questions may be coded with asterisks, such as one star for literal questions, two for inferential, and three for applicative. Different students may then be required to answer a specific type of question, or students can work in cooperative learning teams to discuss and answer the most difficult questions.

```
STEPS IN DEVELOPING AN ADVANCE ORGANIZER

Step 1:   Inform students of advance organizers
          a.  Announce advance organizer
          b.  State benefits of advance organizer
          c.  Suggest that students take notes on the advance organizer

Step 2:   Identify topics of tasks
          a.  Identify major topics or activities
          b.  Identify subtopics or component activities

Step 3:   Provide an organizational framework
          a.  Present an outline, list, or narrative of the lesson's
              content

Step 4:   Clarify action to be taken
          a.  State teachers' actions
          b.  State student's actions

Step 5:   Provide background information
          a.  Relate topic to the course or previous lesson
          b.  Relate topic to new information

Step 6:   State the concepts to be learned
          a.  State specific concepts/ideas from the lesson
          b.  State general concepts/ideas broader than the lesson's
              content

Step 7:   Clarify the concepts to be learned
          a.  Clarify by examples or analogies
          b.  Clarify by nonexamples
          c.  Caution students of possible misunderstandings

Step 8:   Motivate student to learn
          a.  Point out relevance to students
          b.  Be specific, short-term, personalized, and believable

Step 9:   Introduce vocabulary
          a.  Identify the new terms and define
          b.  Repeat difficult terms and define

Step 10:  State the general outcome desired
          a.  State objectives of instruction/learning
          b.  Relate outcomes to test performance
```

Figure 5–8. Ten Steps for Teaching Advance Organizers. *Note.* From "Promoting Active Learning Through Effective Instruction: Using Advance Organizers" by B.K. Lenz, 1983, *Pointer*, *27*(2), p. 12. Copyright 1983 by B.K. Lenz. Reprinted by permission.

Another suggestion is to put the page, column, and paragraph number after certain questions to help the student locate the information. For some students, recording only the page number will be sufficient.

Lovitt, Rudsit, Jenkins, Pious, and Benedetti (1985) found that a study guide method and a precision teaching approach were equally effective for adapting instruction in a seventh-grade physical science text. The approaches, described below, improved performance of students of all achievement levels, but were particularly effective for average and low-achieving students.

Study guide method. In the study guide method, students are presented with a framed outline that consists of a sequenced list of the main ideas in the chapter with key words deleted. Students are instructed to write in the missing key words as they listen to the teacher lecture. Supplemental vocabulary instruction is supplied with worksheets containing two types of problems: Some vocabulary words are supplied but the definitions are missing, and some definitions are supplied but the vocabulary words are missing.

Precision teaching method. The precision teaching method involves pairing students for vocabulary drill and see-to-write activities. For the vocabulary drill sheet, the students alternate turns reading isolated words for 1-minute periods. When the goal of 80 words per minute is reached, students receive a phrase drill sheet. At the end of 1 minute, the number of words read is recorded and the students change roles. For the see-to-write activities, students receive a clear acetate sheet that is placed over a worksheet containing sentences from which key words are missing. The correct words are listed at the top of the sheet in a random order. During 1-minute timings the students are instructed to fill in as many blanks as possible. After timing, answers are checked and scores recorded. These two adaptations both emphasize basic vocabulary development and require students to practice ideas and words repeatedly. Although these types of drill procedures promote familiarity and fluency with key vocabulary words, an instructor should ensure that this knowledge generalizes to improved understanding of the concepts presented in the text.

Worksheets

Specific worksheets may also be developed to enhance student performance. Following are two examples of procedures for developing worksheets. These procedures may be adapted to any content area course.

Content guide. Thomas (1979b) described a content guide designed to help readers identify and locate key ideas and information. This type of guide is especially suitable for short selections of textual material. A three-step process is used to develop the guide. First, the instructor identifies the important ideas within the reading. Next, the instructor identifies the specific sentences in which the key ideas appear and then deletes the terms that reflect the key ideas within the sentences.

After the worksheet is prepared, students are asked to read the selections and write in responses for the blanks. At the end of the lesson, the responses are discussed. This type of approach may help some students attend to and recall the important information in the text. It also integrates reading and writing with content area study. Additionally, a content guide may be used for review prior to examinations.

K-W-L procedure. Ogle (1986) described the K-W-L procedure that may be used to help students recall information, increase their knowledge, and participate more actively in the reading process. The procedure assesses students' present topical knowledge and activates their predictions about what they are going to read. Once they have finished reading, students summarize the main ideas. A strategy worksheet is developed with the following three columns across the top of the paper: (K) What we know, (W) What we want to find out, and (L) What we learned and still need to learn. As an adaptation, four columns may be used. The last column may be divided into two columns: (L) What we learned and (S) What we still need to know.

Three steps are involved in completing the worksheet. In the first step, students brainstorm about a key concept that is specific enough to generate information that will be pertinent to the reading. For example, the instructor may ask: "What do you know about sea turtles?" After the students list what they already know about sea turtles, they then brainstorm and list under the first column other categories of information that they may encounter in the material. For example, in a description of sea turtles, students may encounter information regarding characteristics and habitat. In the second step, the students develop reasons for reading by deciding what they want to learn. The instructor helps the students raise questions, and then each student writes down his or her own list of questions in the second column. After the group has read the story together, the students write down in the third column what they have learned from reading. They then check back to the second column to see whether or not their questions were answered.

Graphic Organizers

Many different types of graphic organizers exist, including semantic maps, flow charts, and structured overviews. The common element of these graphic displays is the visuospatial arrangement of information, in which words or statements, are connected to form a meaningful diagram (Horton, Lovitt, & Bergerud, 1990). Supplementing textbook material with graphic organizers appears to enhance retention. Bergerud, Lovitt, and Horton (1988) found that the use of graphics helped secondary students with learning disabilities comprehend passages in a life science textbook. An example of a graphic is a picture of blood circulation with blanks to identify information such as the size, location, and number of chambers in the heart. After students read for 10 minutes, they are given a graphic with missing information and instructed to find as many answers as they can in 15 minutes. After the 15 minutes, the teacher places the graphic on an overhead projector. The missing information is revealed and discussed one blank at a time.

The results of this investigation indicated that the use of graphics was more effective than either study guides or self-study for improving performance on multiple-choice tests. Students recalled a greater number of facts from the life science text when the material was presented graphically. For the majority of students, both graphics or study guides were more effective than self-study. These results suggest that methods that promote student involvement increase the retention of students with learning disabilities.

Horton, Lovitt, and Bergerud (1990) found that graphic organizers were effective in secondary-level content area courses for three classifications of students: students with learning disabilities, remedial students, and regular education students. In this study, an attempt was made to investigate the use of graphic displays with students ranging from low to high achievement who were enrolled in general education classes in social studies, science, and health.

Prior to teaching, graphic organizers were prepared for reading passages using a hierarchical format in which information is arranged by major and minor categories. Each student was given instructions on how to complete the diagram. For example, in this study, the student was told the main idea of a passage: the difficult time Canadian leaders had in uniting Canada because of the many different special-interest groups. Using the organizer, the student was then asked to locate five special-interest groups and write the names in the numbered boxes. The student was then instructed to locate and write in two important facts about each group.

The use of graphic organizers resulted in higher performance than self-study for both the remedial and regular education students. One teacher observed that he was able to cover textual material at a faster pace because the method combined reading, studying, and evaluation within one class period. The use of graphic organizers helps students arrange ideas using meaningful visual patterns. To use the technique effectively, students require both instruction and practice with it. Students could also develop their own graphic organizers as they worked in small cooperative learning groups. The choice of whether to use graphic organizers or study guides as forms of text adaptation may depend upon the type of material being learned and the preference of the learner. Additionally, the type of guide may be varied to maintain interest.

Philip, a secondary student, was referred for difficulty with all content area courses. He had received failing grades in both his American History and Biology courses. Philip's scores on the WJ-R ACH Science and Social Studies tests were several years below grade level. In analyzing his responses, the examiner noted that Philip did not understand some basic concepts. When asked about his classroom performance, Philip explained that he read all material for these two classes, but he did not know what to study when he was preparing for tests. Using informal techniques, the examiner discovered that Philip could not summarize the main ideas from paragraphs in his classroom texts or paraphrase the material after reading. The examiner recognized that Philip would require significant amounts of guided instruction to master the content of these two courses. At a meeting with Philip's instructors, a decision was made to incorporate graphic organizers during both listening and reading activities and study guides as a postreading activity. Using visual organizers and completed study guides for review, Philip was able to understand and retain the presented material and, subsequently, pass his examinations.

Taped Books

One modification that allows students with limited basic reading skills to acquire textbook content is taped books. All content area textbooks are recorded on tape, and students listen to the readings. In preparing the materials, the tapes may be either paraphrased to a simpler level of vocabulary or recorded verbatim. The main advantage of recording books verbatim is that a student may follow along with the text while listening.

Wiseman, Hartwell, and Hannafin (1980) found that listening to textbook content was as effective or more effective than reading textbook content for many mildly handicapped secondary students. The data from this study also illustrated a high degree of variability among students in listening comprehension. Some high and some low readers had difficulty listening to a taped textbook. As with all methods, these findings suggest that listening to taped content-area textbooks will benefit some students, but not others.

Torgesen, Dahlem, and Greenstein (1987) conducted three experiments to examine the effects of taped text recordings on the comprehension performance of secondary students with learning disabilities. In the first experiment, a read and listen condition and a listen-only condition were more effective than a read-only condition on paragraph-length selections. In the second experiment, the use of supplemental auditory tapes did not improve performance on chapter-length material. In the third experiment, a read and listen condition coupled with completion of a worksheet while reading significantly improved performance on chapter-length material.

These findings suggest that combining taped books with study guides or teacher-created worksheets is effective as a supplemental strategy for enhancing student comprehension of content area textbooks. In constructing the worksheets, Torgesen et al. recommended that the questions focus on the most important concepts in the text.

Additionally, the reading level should be relatively easy, and marks should be placed in the student's text to indicate when to stop reading to answer a question.

Torgesen et al. hypothesized that supplemental auditory materials may be most beneficial for learning disabled students with average intelligence but poor word identification skills. Additionally, they cautioned that although taped recordings may improve the performance of students with below-average intelligence, their reading comprehension difficulties will continue without substantial text modifications or extensive supplemental discussion.

Peer Tutoring

Peer tutoring may also be an effective procedure for improving a student's performance in content areas. Maheady, Sacca, and Harper (1988) found that classwide peer tutoring improved the performance of both nondisabled and mildly handicapped students enrolled in tenth-grade social studies classrooms. Each week 30-item study guides, consisting of a series of questions from the social studies text, were developed collaboratively by the regular and special education teachers.

The tutoring procedure lasted for 30 minutes with the tutoring pairs reversing roles after 15 minutes. During the tutoring, the tutor dictated each study guide question and the tutee wrote and said the response. The tutor provided feedback for each response and immediately corrected any error. When an error occurred, the tutee wrote the correct response three times. The students continued to review the list of questions for the 15-minute time period. This tutoring procedure was combined with a game in which the class was divided into teams who competed for the highest number of points. Maheady et al. recommended this type of procedure as an instructional alternative for secondary classroom teachers attempting to meet the needs of a diverse range of students in content area classrooms. Peer tutoring and cooperative learning activities may also be used successfully for content area instruction in elementary classrooms.

Examinations

In some instances, an examiner will want to recommend specific modifications for classroom examinations. When oral language performance is significantly higher than reading or writing performance, content area exams should be administered orally so that the student is not penalized for limited skill in written language. In assessing content area knowledge, an examiner should evaluate knowledge of material rather than reading performance.

Written examinations may also be adapted and simplified. One procedure is to select specific questions for the student to answer and to place an asterisk or check mark next to the questions. Another procedure is to provide alternate formats of exams. In general, recognition questions, such as multiple-choice, matching, or true or false, are easier than recall exams, such as fill-in-the-blank or short answer. Students who require additional structure may be provided with a study guide that highlights the specific information to be covered in an exam.

Valencia and Pearson (1988) presented several techniques for modifying the format of multiple-choice tests. One technique was to have students locate several acceptable answers rather than one single correct answer. Another variation was to ask students to rate the acceptability of the multiple-choice responses by indicating if the choice is very good (2), on the right track (1), or completely wrong (0). For other variations, students may be asked to justify why they selected a particular response, or to select more than one answer for each question. Modifications of test format will help maximize student performance.

Content Area Study Skills

When a student has difficulty in a content area, the examiner may recommend a specific instructional study strategy for improving performance. If general reading comprehension is a concern, one or more of the techniques discussed in the Reading Comprehension section may be appropriate. Additionally, students with low reading comprehension often require specific guidance for understanding and retaining information presented in content area textbooks.

In teaching content area study skills, an instructor should help a student learn not only the steps of a strategy, but how and when to apply it. Three different types of knowledge exist: (a) declarative, or facts and vocabulary; (b) procedural, or information about how to perform activities; and (c) conditional, or information about how, when, and why tasks are performed (Reid, 1988). In planning activities, attention should be directed toward providing instruction in the three different types of knowledge. In this way, students will both acquire knowledge and learn how to apply knowledge. Considering the three types of knowledge, several supplemental procedures may be recommended to build content area vocabulary and reading comprehension.

Content Area Vocabulary

Each content area has a specialized vocabulary that must be learned for a student to understand the text fully. Preteaching key vocabulary may help activate a student's background knowledge (Harris & Sipay, 1985). Fry, Polk, and Fountoukidis (1984) provided an extensive list of subject area vocabulary listed for primary, intermediate, and secondary students. In most instances, however, an instructor will want to select relevant words for study from the student's content area textbook.

Although no single best method exists for teaching vocabulary, effective methods share certain features. These features include: (a) multiple exposures to the word, (b) presentation in a variety of different contexts, and (c) involvement of students in active thinking about word meanings (McKeown & Beck, 1988). Examples of several specific techniques to help students learn content area vocabulary are described.

Mnemonic method. Mnemonic strategies focus on the use of memory cues to improve student performance. This type of method is most useful for assisting students with the memorization of vocabulary terms or declarative knowledge. Mastropieri and Scruggs (1988) found that secondary students with learning disabilities benefited from the use of mnemonic strategies for instruction in U.S. history. The mnemonic instruction facilitated both learning and recall of content. Mastropieri and Scruggs reported that this type of instruction was particularly useful for students who lacked the basic skills necessary for independent studying. Similar results were obtained with mildly handicapped elementary students (Mastropieri & Scruggs, 1989). Additionally, Scruggs, Mastropieri, Levin, McLoone, Gaffney, and Prater (1985) found that mnemonic instruction was more effective than free study or a visual-spatial display for teaching elementary and junior high students with learning disabilities the attributes of North American minerals.

One mnemonic technique that research has shown to be effective for assisting students in learning new vocabulary is the keyword method (Mastropieri, 1988). The purpose of this method is to expedite initial learning and improve the delayed recall of declarative or factual knowledge. The mnemonic keyword method involves the association of an unfamiliar term with familiar, meaningful information using visual and auditory clues. This method has been used successfully with learning disabled, mentally retarded, gifted, and average students and is easily adapted for classroom use in any content area (Mastropieri, 1988). It also may be effective for teaching concrete as well as abstract vocabulary to adolescents with learning disabilities (Mastropieri, Scruggs, & Mushinski Fulk, 1990).

Mastropieri (1988) described three steps in this method: recoding, relating, and retrieving. For recoding, the new vocabulary word is changed into a known word or concept, referred to as the keyword, that sounds similar and is easily pictured. In relating, the keyword is associated with its definition by creating either a mental image or a sentence using the keyword and its definition in interaction. Recall is strongest when good interactive images are created. Retrieving involves recalling the definition when presented with the original vocabulary word. The student is instructed to think of the keyword, remember the picture or sentence, and then retrieve the desired response. After students have learned the new vocabulary, they practice the words in a variety of contexts in both oral and written work.

Mastropieri (1989) provided the following example for learning the definition of the word "apex," which means "the highest point." First, apex is reconstructed into an acoustically similar and easily pictured word: *ape*. Next, ape is related to its definition through a picture: an ape sitting on the highest point. Finally, when asked to retrieve the definition, the student recalls the keyword "ape," retrieves the interactive picture, and then provides the definition of highest point.

Mastropieri reported that students with mental retardation, learning disabilities, and behavior disorders were successful with this method after one or two practice examples were presented. Additionally, McLoone, Scruggs, Mastropieri, and Zucker (1986) found that students with learning disabilities were able to generate keywords and interactive images independently for similar lists of words after working in a one-to-one situation with the keyword method.

Students were most successful with the keyword strategy when they were provided with elaborated instruction regarding when and how to use the strategy (O'Sullivan & Pressley, 1984). For example, students were told that the strategy only works well when you have to remember two things that go together. The students were then provided with examples of how to employ the strategy. These findings illustrate the importance of practicing and applying strategies in a variety of situations and of direct instruction in conditional knowledge, or when and how to apply the strategy. Additional studies in strategy instruction and generalization are needed (Pressley, Scruggs, & Mastropieri, 1989).

This type of strategy is most effective with tasks that require formation and retention of associations, such as facts and word meanings. The technique facilitates memorization by allowing students to relate new material to familiar images. Although this type of strategy will facilitate rote learning, the intent is not just to learn words for an examination. Once students are able to recall word meanings, the vocabulary words are applied in a variety of contexts. Both vocabulary and important concepts are reviewed as needed. Because the selected words often represent concepts presented in the text, an instructor may wish to integrate the vocabulary and concepts with a postreading activity such as semantic mapping (Palincsar & Englert, 1988). With this technique, vocabulary words are integrated in a visual display with relevant content information.

Semantic mapping. Semantic mapping or webbing techniques may be used to increase content area vocabulary by helping students associate known words with new words. A target word is drawn in the center of a circle, and then related words are drawn in connected circles. If desired, the related words are grouped into categories and labeled. The maps may also be used to present a combination of main ideas and concepts with specific content-related vocabulary. In addition to use with elementary students, mapping techniques have also been effective for improving the vocabulary and comprehension of secondary students and adults with minimal reading skill (Gold, 1984; Solon, 1980).

Semantic feature analysis. Semantic feature analysis, discussed in more detail in the Instructional Strategies for Reading Comprehension section, has also been used effectively for vocabulary instruction in science and social studies. Cunningham and Cunningham (1987) discussed the use of a feature matrix for science books. Prior to reading, a class matrix is constructed and each student completes an individual matrix based upon what he or she already knows. The purpose for reading is then to confirm the pluses and minuses that are entered into the matrix and to fill the empty spaces. After reading, the class matrix is completed by having students share their responses. If a fact is in question, students may prove a point by locating and reading the supporting information from the text. In some cases, additional library research is needed to fill all of the boxes.

Similarly, Bos, Anders, Filip, and Jaffe (1989) found that semantic feature analysis was effective for improving the comprehension of secondary students with learning disabilities. Prior to reading, the students completed a chart individually. Then to activate and build background knowledge, the students and teacher discussed the important vocabulary items as they related to selected key concepts from the chapter. Students then read the chapter. After reading, the group reviewed and completed the relationship chart, filling in any missing data. This method immediately improved comprehension, and the students maintained gains 6 months after the initial instruction.

In addition to semantic feature analysis, Readence and Searfoss (1980) described two further categorization methods that incorporate active student participation. The methods are effective for students from primary grades through graduate school and may be used to help students develop prerequisite skills for semantic feature analysis. Readence and Searfoss indicated that the greatest benefits come from learning the methods in the following order: (a) word fluency, (b) list-group-label lesson, and (c) semantic feature analysis.

Word fluency method. For the word fluency method, a teacher and a student or two students work in pairs. One of the students generates as many text-related words as possible in 1 minute, while the other participant tallies the number of words on a sheet of paper. Students then alternate roles. When the instructor has a turn, he or she models producing categories of words. All words receive one point with the exception of number words, words presented in a sentence, and repetitions. Extra points are awarded for word categories that contain at least four words. Words may also be limited to a certain category or a specific area of study, such as a chapter in a Social Studies text. For example, the student may be asked to think of any words that are related to the unit of study. As soon as students have developed the ability to categorize, procedures that associate known and new words are employed.

List-group-label lesson. Another procedure for enhancing vocabulary in social studies and science classes is the list-group-label lesson. For the list-group-label procedure, students are asked to think of words or expressions that are related to one topic word that is written on the top of the chalkboard. The words are recorded on the board, and the teacher rereads the list orally, pointing to each word. The students are then asked to construct smaller lists by grouping words that have something in common. This activity may be performed individually, with partners, or in small groups. Once this activity is completed, the categories are labeled and recorded on another part of the board. When each category is recorded, students must explain their reason for grouping the words together. Initially, a teacher may need to model the thinking process that occurs when attempting to categorize words. Once students have become proficient in this procedure, they may concentrate on the more complex activity of semantic feature analysis.

Content Area Reading

> Strategies such as predicting, questioning, summarizing, and clarifying induce readers to anticipate information they will encounter, to integrate what is presented in the text with prior knowledge, to reconstruct prior knowledge, and to monitor for understanding.
>
> (Palincsar & Brown, 1988, p. 57)

The most effective techniques for content area instruction are ones that encourage students to be active participants in the learning process and to integrate reading, writing, and thinking. As with general instruction in reading comprehension, these strategies involve building background knowledge, associating new knowledge with prior knowledge, predicting and establishing relationships between and among concepts, and monitoring and con-

firming understanding. In synthesizing the research on effective reading instruction in social studies, Wade (1983) found that effective instructional programs provide instruction in both reading and study skills. Additionally, teachers play an active role in instruction and use a variety of materials and activities.

Several effective study strategies may be taught to improve performance in content area reading assignments. The goal of these approaches is to help the student become an active reader who engages in questioning, predicting, and comprehension monitoring. These types of strategy help students develop the ability to ask questions in order to guide their reading and thinking. The goal of instruction in task-appropriate strategies is to provide students with methods to solve problems (Reid, 1988). Examples of several widely used techniques follow.

DRTA. The purpose of a Directed Reading Thinking Activity (DRTA) is to help a student develop critical reading skills (Stauffer, 1975). The steps of the DRTA center around a process in which students predict or set purposes for reading, read to process their ideas, and prove or test their answers. Stauffer indicated that the DRTA develops abilities to ask relevant questions, process information, and validate answers. The teaching sequence follows these steps:

1. Students are asked to read the title of a story silently and then to evaluate how this title may relate to the story. Once a number of predictions are made and discussed, the students begin reading a designated amount of the story.

2. Once the designated amount is read, books are closed for a comprehension check. The instructor asks three primary questions: "Were you correct?" "What do you think now?" "What do you think will happen next?" When students are asked whether their initial prediction was correct, they must read the lines aloud that prove or disprove their prediction.

3. Approximately halfway through the story, students stop reading again and similar questions are asked. Another brief comprehension check is made about five-sixths of the way through the story. Students then continue reading until the end of the story.

This type of approach is easily adapted. For example, the instructor may not wish to interrupt the reading process by asking questions. Otto, Peters, and Peters (1977) described a directed reading activity (DRA) that preteaches vocabulary and sets the purposes for reading. The strategy consists of several steps. To begin, students are taught technical vocabulary. Next, purposes for reading and a list of questions are developed through class discussion. The teacher then models the process for answering questions. Students read the entire passage silently, attempting to answer the questions. After reading, the answers to questions are discussed.

SQ3R. The Survey, Question, Read, Recite, Review (SQ3R) study procedure, developed by Robinson (1946), involves five steps for promoting independence in studying. For the first step, *Survey*, the student skims the chapter noting all headings, pictures, graphs, captions, and summary paragraphs. The purposes are to identify the author's intent and gain understanding of the text structure. In the next step, *Question*, the student goes to each heading and turns it into a question prior to reading. This questioning procedure provides the student with a reason for reading. The 3*R* steps are *Read*, *Recite*, and *Review*. Reading is an active process wherein the student seeks answers to the self-generated questions. Reciting involves review of the information by stating the answers to the questions, underlining important information, or outlining the material. Reviewing includes rehearsing the major points in the material during and immediately after reading. For this step, students may write the major ideas found in the selection. This procedure may be modified and adapted for student use by omitting one or more of the steps. Some students will require extended practice with each step.

In summarizing the results of six research studies on the SQ3R procedure, Johns and McNamara (1980) found that the method was as effective, but not more effective, than other studying procedures. Adams, Carnine, and Gersten (1982) reported that fifth-grade students who used SQ3R scored higher than the control group on short-answer questions involving factual information.

In addition to being useful with science and social studies texts, this procedure or an adaptation may improve ability to comprehend fiction. When reading fiction, students may generate and answer questions as the story progresses. Singer and Donlan (1982) found that high school juniors who were taught how to create questions to a story while reading outperformed the control group on complex short stories. Additionally, supplying students with questions or detailed previews prior to reading improves student ability to comprehend text. Graves, Cooke, and LaBerge (1983) found that providing poor readers in junior high school with detailed previews of difficult short stories significantly increased their comprehension. As with all study techniques, students must receive instruction in how and when to use the technique and have opportunities to apply the strategy with classroom materials.

Reciprocal teaching. In addition to general reading comprehension instruction, reciprocal teaching may also be applied to content area instruction (Palincsar & Brown, 1986). In a research review evaluating the effectiveness of this teaching procedure, Palincsar and Brown described a study in which several classes of middle school students improved their performance on weekly science tests.

Instruction was provided for 20 days, and the following procedure was used:

1. Students were assigned segments of the text to read.
2. Using the heading of each segment, students were instructed to write two statements regarding what they expected to learn from the portion of text.
3. The teacher and students then discussed the different predictions made by students.
4. The students then read one segment (approximately four paragraphs) and wrote two questions and a brief summary of what they read.
5. Students noted in writing any further points that needed clarification.
6. A discussion was held to review the questions, summaries, and clarifications noted by the students.

Reciprocal teaching has been used effectively in small and large group settings and for peer tutoring. In this instructional technique, reading comprehension is conceptualized as a problem-solving activity (Palincsar & Brown, 1988). The procedure may be most effective for students who have grade-level decoding skills but comprehension 2 years below grade level. Additionally, Palincsar and Brown (1986) suggested that this procedure may be used effectively with beginning readers, nonreaders, and poor decoders as a listening comprehension activity by having the teacher or another student read the segments aloud. The goal of this method is to help students enhance comprehension and become independent in the use of strategies. This type of content area instruction is especially effective because it integrates reading, writing, and thinking and helps students assume responsibility and become independent learners.

Multipass. Schumaker, Deshler, Alley, Warner, and Denton (1982) found that Multipass, an adaptation of the SQ3R learning strategy, helped secondary students with learning disabilities improve their ability to comprehend content area textbooks both at their instructional level and at their current grade level. Additionally, students were able to improve their grades in content area courses.

To begin, an instructor explains the steps and rationale of the strategy and then demonstrates the strategy by thinking aloud. Students then verbally rehearse the strategy. Once a student is successful with materials at his or her reading level, the strategy is practiced in grade-level materials. The steps of the procedure involve three substrategies: survey, size-up, and sort-out. Using this strategy, the student never reads the passage in its entirety.

Survey: The purpose of the survey pass is to familiarize the student with the chapter organization and the main ideas. This is accomplished by reading the (a) chapter title,

(b) introductory paragraph, (c) table of contents (to understand the chapter's relationship to adjacent chapters), (d) subtitles, (e) illustrations and captions, and (f) summary paragraphs. The student may then paraphrase all the information gained from the first pass through the chapter.

Size-up: For the size-up pass, the student reads the questions at the end of the chapter and places a check mark by any questions that may be already answered. The student then progresses through the chapter searching for textual cues that highlight headings or important information, such as boldface, italics, or colored print. The student turns each of these cues into a question and skims the text to find the answer. When the answer is located, the student paraphrases the answer. At the end of the chapter, the student paraphrases all remembered facts and ideas.

Sort-out: For the sort-out pass, the student reads each question at the end of the chapter and places a check mark by any that he or she can answer immediately. If a question cannot be answered, the student attempts to locate the answer by skimming through the appropriate section.

Schumaker et al. suggested that this strategy is most

effective for students who are reading at or above a fourth-grade level. Readers functioning below a fourth-grade level may be able to apply the strategy to ability-level materials, but not to grade-level materials.

Conclusion

Careful analysis of a student's performance on the WJ-R ACH Knowledge tests will assist an examiner in making appropriate instructional recommendations. In addition to assessment of knowledge in the content areas, an examiner will also want to consider whether a student's present levels of reading and writing skill affect classroom performance. To accommodate students with learning problems and low achievement, a variety of instructional modifications and strategies are needed. The methods selected should promote active student participation, acquisition of knowledge in the content area, development and integration of reading and writing skill, and independent learning. Using these types of instructional techniques, students will become effective, efficient managers of their learning.

6

MATHEMATICS

> In the Clinic School at the university all the children look forward eagerly to
> the arithmetic period. This attitude is due to the fact that they are never without
> the security of means by which they can succeed in the problems that confront
> them.
>
> (Fernald, 1943, p. 254)

Several aspects of mathematical skill are measured on the WJ-R ACH. Two tests, Calculation in the Standard Battery and Quantitative Concepts in the Supplemental Battery, comprise the Basic Mathematics Skills cluster. One test, Applied Problems in the Standard Battery, is used as the Mathematics Reasoning cluster score.

Content of the Mathematics Tests

Each of the three tests measures a different aspect of mathematical ability. The measured abilities include: knowledge of mathematical vocabulary and symbols (Quantitative Concepts); computational skills, ranging from basic operations to advanced calculations (Calculation); and mathematical reasoning and problem solving (Applied Problems). Figure 6-1 illustrates the hierarchical relationship of the three WJ-R ACH mathematics tests.

Determining Instructional Level

One major goal of a mathematics assessment is to determine an appropriate instructional level for a student. Helpful information is obtained by plotting a student's performance on the Instructional Level Profile on the front and back covers of the WJ-R Test Record. By viewing the grade scale above or below the instructional band, an examiner may estimate a student's present functioning with tasks ranging from an easy to difficult level.

Strengths and Weaknesses

Examination of a student's strengths and weaknesses among the three mathematics tests will help an examiner develop an appropriate instructional program. Some students have good calculation skill but have trouble with mathematical concepts and problem solving, whereas others have good problem-solving ability but limited calculation skill. In some cases, student performance is above or below level in all aspects of math. After analyzing performance, an examiner may determine that a student has: (a) low basic skills, but average or above-average mathematics reasoning; (b) high basic skills, but average or below-average mathematics reasoning; or (c) generalized low, average, or high mathematical performance. Figure 6-2 depicts the performance of three different ninth-grade students on the mathematics tests on the Age/Grade Profile. Instructional objectives and planning will differ for these three students.

Attitude

While administering the WJ-R ACH math tests, an examiner may note a student's attitude toward math tasks. Some students enjoy solving mathematical problems. Other students become anxious or resistant when presented with mathematical problems. A dislike for mathematics may stem from poor instruction, resulting in failure. Students with a history of failure must be placed in a high-interest, success-oriented environment where an attempt will be made to decrease anxiety and improve

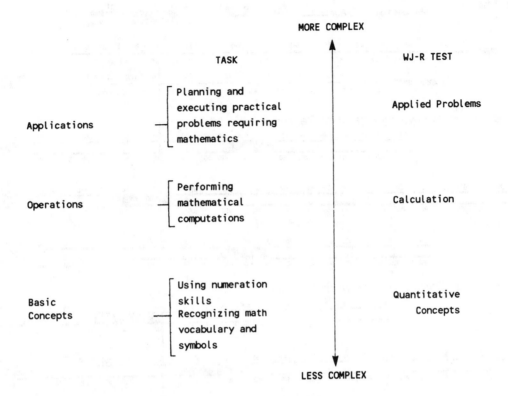

Figure 6–1. Various Skills Measured by the WJ-R ACH Mathematics Tests.

attitude by providing meaningful instruction in the application of mathematics to problem solving.

Chapter Organization

This chapter is divided into two main sections. In the first section, error analysis and interventions for problems in basic skills are discussed. In the second section, information related to mathematical reasoning and problem solving is presented. The tests are discussed in order of the math hierarchy presented in Figure 6-1, ranging from skills in basic operations to problem-solving applications of these skills.

Analysis of performance on the WJ-R ACH math tests, accompanied by additional informal assessments when necessary, will help an examiner design an appropriate instructional program. Based upon an individual's skills, an examiner may suggest specific modifications, strategies, or methods for improving a student's skill and understanding of mathematics.

Basic Math Skills

Arithmetic is where the answer is right and
everything is nice and you can look out of

the window and see blue sky—or the answer
is wrong and you have to start all over and
try again and see how it comes out this time.
(Carl Sandburg, cited in Ashlock, 1982, p.1)

Many children with learning problems experience difficulty with math calculations, both in memorizing the facts and in understanding the basic vocabulary or concepts. In some cases, a student may not understand or remember the algorithm or step-by-step procedure used to solve a problem. In other cases, a student may not have been taught how to perform a certain operation. The two WJ-R ACH tests that measure basic math skill are Quantitative Concepts and Calculation. If further information is needed for error analysis, an examiner may administer both Forms A and B.

Error Analysis of Quantitative Concepts

Analysis of an individual's performance on the Quantitative Concepts test provides further information regarding basic math skills. Several different types of skills are measured on this test, including: (a) counting, forwards and/or backwards; (b) identifying numbers; (c) understanding math vocabulary, (d) determining the missing number (or information) in a sequence; and (e) identifying

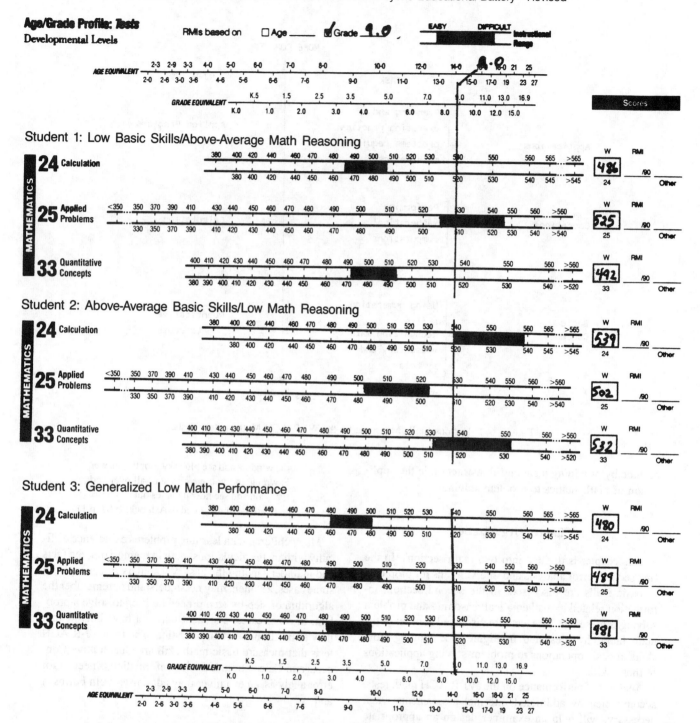

Figure 6–2. Three Ninth-Grade Students on the Age/Grade Profile.

math symbols, geometric shapes, and common math abbreviations. Figure 6-3 illustrates an error analysis sheet for the Quantitative Concepts test for Forms A and B. The items are grouped by several categories. The grade equivalent score after each item number indicates that the item would be answered correctly by approximately 50% of the students at that grade placement.

When analyzing a student's performance, an examiner may note that the student tends to miss a certain type of item. One student may have difficulty with items that require identifying the missing number in a sequence. Another student may not recognize common math abbreviations. In some cases, an examiner may note inconsistent performance within the item types. A student may miss certain item types at an easy level, while getting other item types correct at a more difficult level. Error analysis will help an examiner gather information relevant to instructional planning.

Error Analysis of Calculation

When administering the Calculation test, an examiner will want to observe a student's behaviors and the strategies used to solve problems. As examples, an examiner may note whether a student: (a) makes comments, expressions, or gestures during the test that provide additional information regarding math performance; (b) uses finger counting to obtain answers; (c) knows facts rapidly and automatically; or (d) skips over certain types of problems. Observation and notation of relevant comments, error patterns, strategies, and responses will assist with instructional planning.

Student Comments

A student's remarks often reveal misunderstanding of or confusion regarding basic concepts. For example, when confronted with the problem in Item 20: 13 × 7, Cindy, a fifth-grade student, commented: "I can't do that problem because I haven't memorized the 13s." In performing the computation on Item 12: 17 − 9, Ted, an eighth-grade student, remarked that it was impossible. He explained further by saying, "You borrow from the one, and bring it over and it's still a one." These types of comments reveal a student's present level of conceptual development and will help an examiner develop appropriate supplemental mathematics instruction.

Mini-Error Analysis

The WJ-R ACH Calculation test samples many different computational skills. Computations include application of the four processes of addition, subtraction, multiplication, and division with whole numbers, negative numbers, fractions, decimals, and percents.

Figure 6-4 provides additional information for examining student performance on Forms A and B of the Calculation test. The problems are grouped by: addition, subtraction, multiplication, division, fractions, decimals and percents, and algebra. The median grade equivalent score next to each number indicates that approximately 50% of the students at that grade placement would answer the item correctly.

Even though the Calculation test does not contain enough problems for an in-depth error analysis, an examiner will want to perform a mini-error analysis of a student's performance. This is done by carefully evaluat-

ing a student's responses to individual problems and attempting to determine why an error was made. The general purposes for analyzing a student's answers on the Calculation test are to: (a) note the student's methods for solving various calculations, (b) determine whether an expanded evaluation is necessary, and, if so, (c) identify the problem areas that require further assessment.

In analyzing a student's responses, several questions may be asked. Examples include:

Do the student's answers demonstrate understanding of the concept?
Are the answers sensible?
Do the errors indicate the source of the confusion?
Is there a pattern to the student's mistakes?
Does the student seem to understand the algorithms, but have trouble with the basic facts?

In one instance, after analyzing an individual's responses on the Calculation test, an examiner may note that the student does not understand place value, regrouping, or operations involving fractions. In another instance, an examiner may note that the student seems to understand the basic steps for solving problems, but tends to make errors on the facts. Before analyzing responses, an examiner may wish to review various types of errors and failure strategies that may appear in responses on the Calculation test.

Error Patterns

Several types of error patterns and failure strategies have been observed in students' computations. In fact, Cox (1975) identified over 200 discernible types of systematic errors in the basic operations. Computational errors may be classified in several different ways. An examiner may note any of the following errors on a Calculation test: (a) errors in basic facts, (b) errors in regrouping (carrying or borrowing), (c) errors in problems with zero, (d) errors in basic algorithms, (e) errors caused by poor column alignment, or (f) errors caused by lack of attention to the sign.

Other types of errors may also be observed. For example, Wagner (1981) described several common math perceptual errors, including: (a) directionality problems, where the directionality of the sequence is confused; (b) mirror writing, where numbers or number positions are reversed; (c) visually misperceived signs, where the plus or multiplication sign is rotated; and (d) mixed process, where the student switches operations in the middle of the problem. For example, the student begins a problem with addition, and then shifts in the middle of the operation to subtraction or multiplication. Figure 6-5 illustrates these four error types on items from the Calculation test.

FORM A   FORM B

Counting

Grade   Grade

1.   <K.0 2   1.   <K.0 2

2.   <K.0 3   2.   <K.0 1...5

4.   <K.0 1...10   5.   <K.0 5

20.   1.6 2-4-6-8-10   22.   1.9 10-20-30-40...100

27.   3.2 80-75-70-65-60-55-50-45

Number Identification

3.   <K.0 (1)   3.   <K.0 4

9.   <K.0 (12)   6.   <K.0 10

Symbols

15.   1.1 ¢   13.   K.4 +

16.   1.2 =   18.   1.2 -

24.   2.9 ÷   19.   1.4 $

26.   3.2 %   35.   6.0 $\sqrt{}$

34.   5.8 $\sqrt{36}$ 36.   6.7 3^3

37.   7.4 7^2 40.   11.2 π

47.   >16.9 $\int$ 42.   >16.9 ∞

48.   >16.9 ≡   43.   >16.9 10^{-2}

                                          44.   >16.9 log 1 =

Figure 6–3. Error Analysis for the Quantitative Concepts Test.

Vocabulary

	Grade			Grade	
5.	<K.0	first	7.	<K.0	largest
		last			smallest
		middle			
8.	<K.0	largest	8.	<K.0	highest
		smallest			lowest
10.	<K.0	last	10.	K.2	between
		first			
		middle			
11.	K.2	before	11.	K.3	before
13.	K.6	before	15.	1.1	tallest
					shortest
35.	6.7	parallel	16.	1.1	after
			27.	3.1	dozen
			48.	>16.9	ordinate

Sequencing

7.	<K.0	1 2 3 __ 5	9.	K.2	5 6 7 8 __
11.	K.2	before 3	11.	K.3	before eight
12.	K.3	11 12 __ 14 15	12.	K.3	Days of week
13.	K.6	before 16	14.	K.9	10 9 8 7 __
14.	1.1	40 50 60 70 __	16.	1.1	after 37
18.	1.6	5 10 15 __ 25	17.	1.1	40 50 60 __ 80
19.	1.6	before Tuesday (Monday)	20.	1.5	2 4 6 __ 10
32.	5.4	90 75 60 45 __	21.	1.7	19 18 17 16 __
			24.	2.5	after December
			30.	4.0	125 __ 75 50 25

(continued)

Money

Grade			Grade		
17.	1.3	pennies in nickel	23.	2.1	nickels in dime
23.	2.7	nickels in quarter			

Fractions

25.	3.0	1/2 of four fish	32.	4.6	1/4 of 4 books
33.	5.5	1/3 of 18	33.	5.5	17/5 (mixed number)
36.	6.9	12/5 (mixed number)	34.	5.9	1/3 of 12 apples
40.	12.2	9/20 what percent?	38.	7.7	3/4 of 12
			41.	13.3	lowest common denominator

Geometric Shapes

6.	<K.0	square	4.	<K.0	circle
21.	2.3	triangle	26.	3.1	rectangle

Abbreviations

22.	2.6	yd.	25.	2.9	ft.
28.	3.3	hr.	28.	3.4	min.
29.	3.6	lbs.	29.	3.5	oz.
30.	3.7	in.	31.	4.2	yr.

Figure 6–3. (*continued*)

Using a more general classification system, Englehardt (1982) described four computational error classes that may be found in isolation or in combination: (a) mechanical errors, including misformed and misaligned symbols; (b) careless errors; (c) conceptual errors, resulting from absent or incorrect concepts; and (d) procedural errors, including misordered or inappropriate procedures. Instructional interventions will differ based upon the types of errors a student makes.

Failure Strategies

In examining strategies of third-grade students, Gerhard (1968) found that many computational errors resulted from confusion regarding the basic concepts or procedures to be followed. Gerhard identified four main failure strategies: (a) wrong operation, such as adding instead of multiplying; (b) computational errors, usually based on incorrect recall of facts; (c) defective algorithm, or appli-

	Form A			Form B		
	Grade			Grade		
Addition	1.	K.5	2 + 2	1.	K.4	1 + 1
	2.	K.5	1 + 3	2.	K.4	1 + 2
	3.	K.6	2 + 1	3.	K.8	2 + 3
	4.	K.6	6 + 1	4.	1.0	5 + 1
	5.	1.2	2 + 4	9.	1.7	15 + 6
	10.	2.2	9 + 7	11.	2.4	76 + 9
	15.	3.4	476 + 61 + 2,611	15.	3.0	189 + 274
	19.	4.4	28.6 + 27.08	26.	6.4	1/4 + 1/4
	21.	5.0	.045 + 11.26	30.	7.4	2 3/4 + 4 1/8
	25.	5.5	2/5 + 1/5	35.	9.1	-15 + 6
	30.	7.4	5/8 + 9/8			
	31.	8.2	2 6/7 + 5 1/2			
	34.	9.0	-18 + 12			
Subtraction	6.	1.2	3 - 2	5.	1.5	4 - 1
	9.	1.5	7 - 3	6.	1.2	6 - 2
	11.	2.0	89 - 18	7.	1.5	4 - 3
	12.	2.9	17 - 9	8.	1.6	5 - 1
	23.	5.0	48 - 19	10.	2.3	18 - 9
	27.	6.0	2/3 - 1/3	12.	2.9	69 - 28
				18.	3.7	88 - 29
				22.	5.1	503 - 254
				24.	5.9	3/4 - 1/4
				39.	11.9	1/2 - 1/3 - 1/5
Multiplication	13.	2.9	5 x 3	13.	2.7	4 x 2
	14.	3.2	7 x 4	14.	3.1	3 x 6
	17.	3.8	2 x 7	17.	4.0	3 x 3
	18.	4.3	8 x 5	19.	3.9	8 x 7
	20.	4.3	13 x 7	21.	4.8	75 x 9
	24.	5.2	102 x 12	27.	6.5	58 x 64
	32.	8.3	0.045 x 0.03	32.	8.3	-9 x 7
	35.	9.3	-6 x 7	33.	8.8	2.05 x .3
	36.	8.9	1.05 x .2	37.	10.9	120 x 3/2
	40.	>16.9	12% of 6.0	38.	11.9	5% of 100
Division	16.	3.7	8/2	16.	3.6	10/5
	22.	4.9	12/6	20.	4.8	120/12
	26.	5.4	126/42	23.	5.2	96/3
	28.	6.5	288/48	25.	5.9	$26.50/5
	29.	6.6	5936/112	28.	6.2	3250/25
	38.	12.5	4/7 ÷ 1/2	29.	6.7	5202/102
	42.	>16.9	8 1/2 ÷ 4 1/8	36.	10.7	3/5 ÷ 2/3
				44.	>16.9	6 2/3 ÷ 4 1/9

Figure 6–4. Error Analysis of the Basic Operations for the Calculation Test.

	Form A	Form B

	Grade		Grade	

Fractions	25.	5.5	2/5 + 1/5	24.	5.9	3/4 - 1/4
	27.	6.0	2/3 - 1/3	26.	6.4	1/4 + 1/4
	30.	7.4	5/8 + 9/8	30.	7.4	2 3/4 + 4 1/8
	31.	8.2	2 6/7 + 5 1/2	36.	10.7	3/5 ÷ 2/3
	38.	12.5	4/7 ÷ 1/2	37.	10.9	120 x 3/2
	42.	>16.9	8 1/2 ÷ 4 1/8	39.	11.9	1/2 - 1/3 - 1/5
				44.	>16.9	6 2/3 ÷ 4 1/9

Decimals	19.	4.4	28.6 + 27.08	25.	5.9	$26.50/5
and	21.	5.0	.045 + 11.26	33.	8.8	2.05 x .3
Percents	32.	8.3	0.045 x 0.03	38.	11.9	5% of 100
	36.	8.9	1.05 x .2	42.	>16.9	162% of 90
	40.	>16.9	12% of 6.0			

Algebra	33.	8.6	$2x + 3 = 11$	31.	7.3	$3x + 4 = 16$
	37.	10.4	$4 + 5(7)$	34.	8.8	$3 + 6(8)$
	41.	14.4	$2x + 4y = 16$	40.	11.3	$10 - x = 3x$
			$3x - y = 3$			
	43.	>16.9	$8 - x = 2x$	41.	>16.9	$x^2 + x =$
	44.	>16.9	$x^2 + 2x - 3 = 0$	43.	>16.9	$4x + 2y = 14$ and
						$2x - y = 5$
	45.	>16.9	If $1/5x = 11$, then	45.	>16.9	$aba^2 b^3 a^3 b$
			$3/5x =$			
	46.	>16.9	$\sqrt{\dfrac{4a^2}{16}}$	46.	>16.9	$\sqrt{\dfrac{9b^2}{36}}$
	47.	>16.9	$\left(\dfrac{4b}{3y}\right)\left(\dfrac{-4y}{12b^2}\right)$	47.	>16.9	$\left(\dfrac{5b}{2y}\right)\left(\dfrac{-3y}{10b^2}\right)$
	49.	>16.9	If $x = -3$, then $x^3 - x^2 - x - 1$	48.	>16.9	$\sqrt[3]{1000}$
	50.	>16.9	$\sqrt{0.0025}$	50.	>16.9	2^{-3}
				54.	>16.9	$8a^2 x^2 + 4a^3 x$

Figure 6–4. (*continued*)

cation of an incorrect strategy; and (d) random response, where no discernible relationship existed between the problem and the solution. The majority of students made systematic errors. The largest numbers of mistakes were caused by the following three faulty algorithms:

Inversion of order. These errors include: (a) subtracting in the direction that causes the least difficulty, (b) working from left to right instead of right to left on addition problems, and (c) carrying the units' digit instead of the tens' digit.

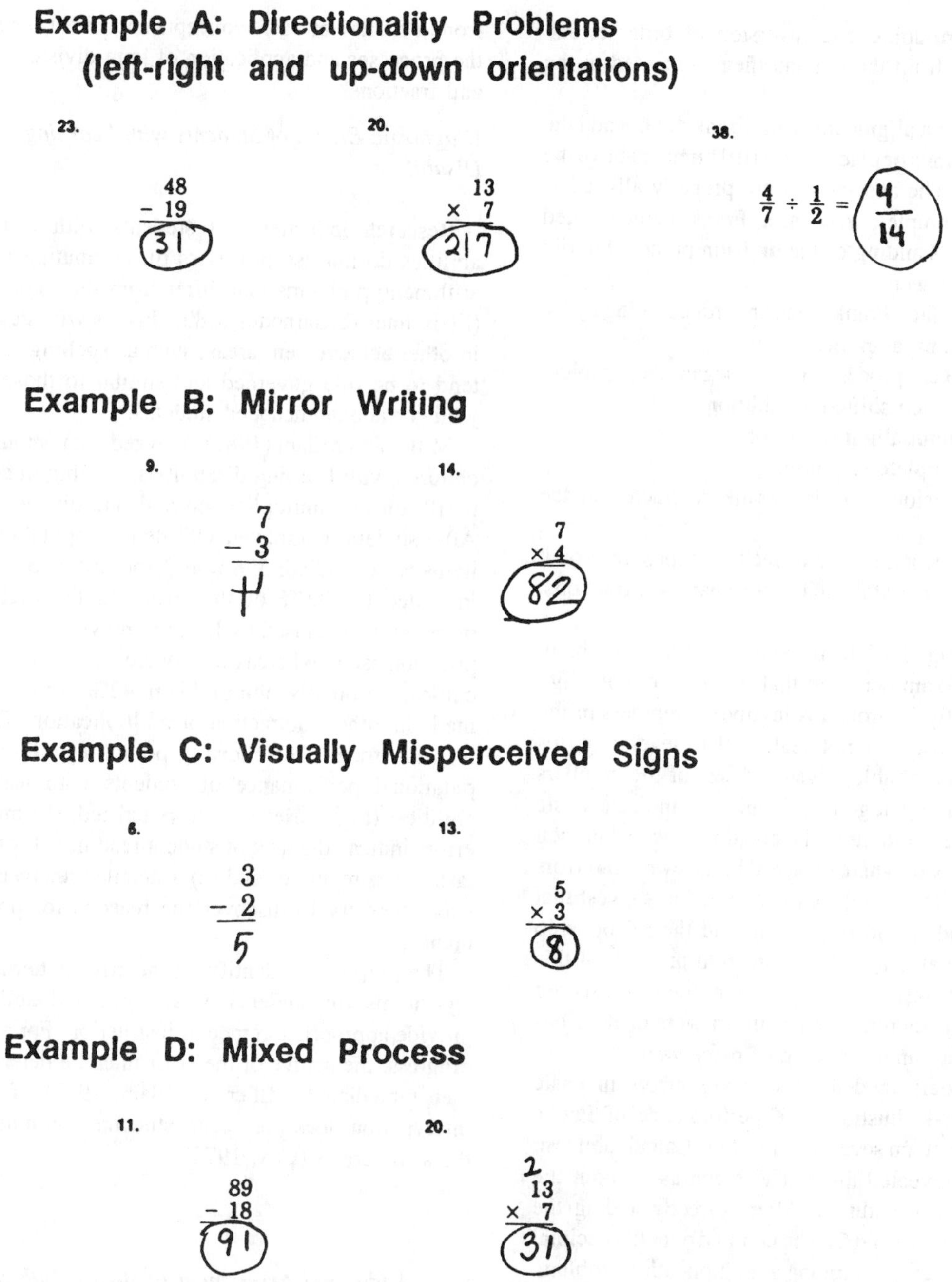

Example A: Directionality Problems
(left-right and up-down orientations)

23.

$$\begin{array}{r} 48 \\ -\ 19 \\ \hline \boxed{31} \end{array}$$

20.

$$\begin{array}{r} 13 \\ \times\ 7 \\ \hline \boxed{2|7} \end{array}$$

38.

$$\frac{4}{7} \div \frac{1}{2} = \boxed{\frac{4}{14}}$$

Example B: Mirror Writing

9.

$$\begin{array}{r} 7 \\ -\ 3 \\ \hline \end{array}$$ ꜩ

14.

$$\begin{array}{r} 7 \\ \times\ 4 \\ \hline \boxed{82} \end{array}$$

Example C: Visually Misperceived Signs

6.

$$\begin{array}{r} 3 \\ -\ 2 \\ \hline 5 \end{array}$$

13.

$$\begin{array}{r} 5 \\ \times\ 3 \\ \hline \boxed{8} \end{array}$$

Example D: Mixed Process

11.

$$\begin{array}{r} 89 \\ -\ 18 \\ \hline \boxed{91} \end{array}$$

20.

$$\begin{array}{r} {}^{2}13 \\ \times\ 7 \\ \hline \boxed{31} \end{array}$$

Figure 6–5. Common Math Perceptual Errors.

Grouping errors. These errors include: (a) adding columns without carrying and (b) failing to align columns. In analyzing a student's responses, the examiner may note that a student does not use regrouping or has difficulty keeping columns in a straight line.

Mixed operations. With this type of error, the student starts the problem with the correct operation and then shifts to the wrong operation.

Analyzing Student Responses

An examiner will often note several different types of errors on a student's test. For example, Figure 6-6 illustrates the performance of Frank, a fourth-grade student, on the Calculation test.

Frank made the following mistakes on individual items:

Item 10: Sign error. Frank did not pay attention to the sign. He subtracted instead of adding.

Item 12: Regrouping and inversion of order errors. Frank borrowed from the ten and then subtracted in the easiest direction.

Item 15: Column alignment error. Frank did not add the appropriate columns or place the carried number above the correct column. The answer was not properly aligned.

Item 16: Incomplete response. Frank demonstrated conceptual understanding of the division process but did not record his answer.

Item 18: Basic fact. Frank made an error counting by 5s.

Item 19: Column alignment error.

Item 20: Mixed process. Frank began the problem multiplying and then shifted to addition.

Item 21: Column alignment error.

Item 22: Incomplete response.

Item 23: Inversion of order. Frank subtracted in the easiest direction.

Item 25: Conceptual error or lack of exposure. Frank added together numerators and denominators of fractions.

After analyzing all of the responses, one basic problem noted by the examiner was that Frank did not align columns correctly in problems involving numbers in the 1,000s. Frank also did not realize that several of his answers were impossible, given the size of the numbers that he was adding together. Frank did indicate basic conceptual understanding of the division process but then did not know how or where to record his answer. His errors involving subtraction in the easiest direction suggest that he does not understand regrouping and the relationship between place value and the subtraction process. In this instance, further informal analysis is needed to discover whether Frank does not monitor his answers or if he has not developed an understanding of place value.

Some secondary students also make errors in basic skills. Figure 6-7 illustrates the performance of Pat, a secondary student, on several items of the Calculation test. Error analysis revealed that Pat was confused about the use of decimals in addition. After correctly adding the numbers on Items 19 and 21, she counted over the decimal points as if she were performing a multiplication problem. When adding fractions, she added the denominators together, as well as the numerators. On Item 30, although the answer is incorrect, she correctly reduced the solution. Pat also missed the two problems, Items 28 and 29, involving long division. When she failed to estimate the correct number, she did not check her answer to make sure that she had removed all of the 48s within 288. When there was one left over, she recorded it as a remainder of one. A similar type of mistake was made on the subsequent problem. The analysis indicates that Pat would benefit from a review of basic concepts and direct instruction in the processes and application of long division, decimals, and fractions.

Diagnostic Errors of Students with Learning Disabilities

Research indicates that students with learning disabilities do not use processes for computing answers to arithmetic problems that differ from their normal peers' (Fleischner & Garnette, 1980). Just as with development in other achievement areas, such as spelling, their errors tend to be rule governed and similar to those made by younger nonhandicapped students.

Miller and Milam (1987) analyzed the responses of 213 children with learning disabilities, ranging in age from 9 to 18, on one multiplication and one division problem. After students completed a 92-item computation test, two items were studied: 396×498 and 4060/46. The results indicated that 40% of the errors on the multiplication problem were caused by lack of knowledge of the multiplication facts, whereas 25% were due to addition difficulties. On the division problem, 42% of the errors were made in either subtraction or multiplication. These findings illustrated the following points regarding the computational performance of students with learning disabilities: (a) a variety of errors existed; (b) many of the errors indicated a lack of student readiness for the type of task being required; and (c) a detailed analysis of errors was necessary to discover the reasons for poor performance.

The purpose of identifying the error patterns or faulty algorithms for students of all ages and abilities is to provide appropriate remedial instruction. For a student to progress, the source of the error must be determined and then remediated (Miller & Milam, 1987). If systematic intervention does not occur, students continue to repeat the same errors (Cox, 1975).

Additional Assessment of Basic Math Skills

As noted, an important aspect of math assessment is to determine the factors contributing to computational errors. Students may have difficulty on the Quantitative Concepts and Calculation tests for several reasons. Some students do not understand numeration, place value, and/or the procedure used to solve the problem. Other students lack prerequisite knowledge and vocabulary. Still others lack knowledge of basic facts or do not monitor their responses.

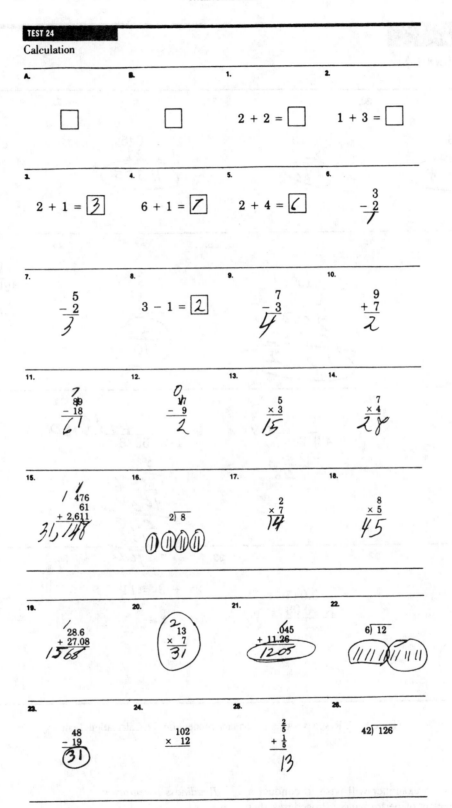

Figure 6–6. Responses of a Fourth-Grade Student on the Calculation Test.

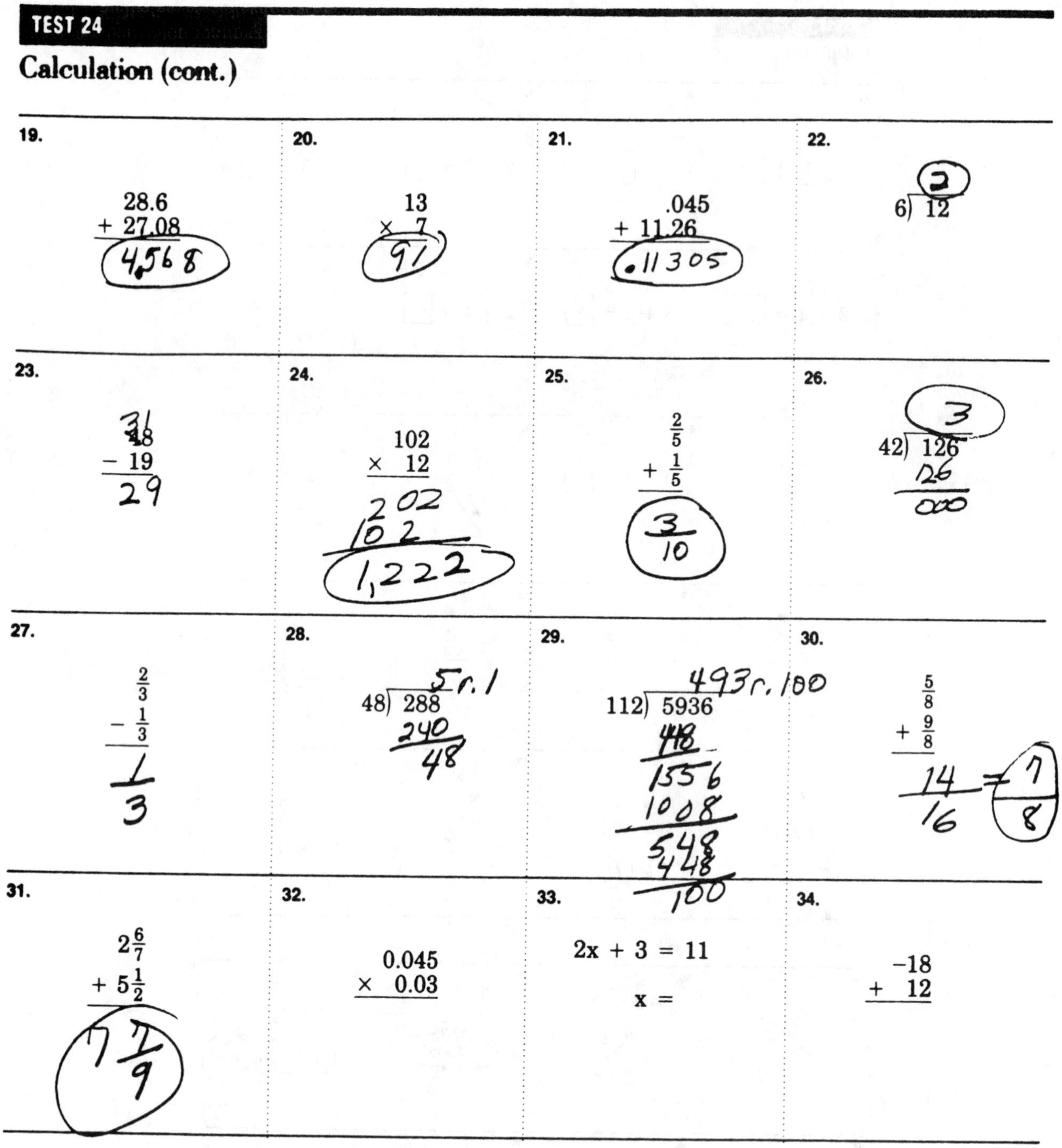

TEST 24

Calculation (cont.)

19.
$$28.6$$
$$+ \ 27.08$$
$$\overline{\;4{,}568\;}$$

20.
$$13$$
$$\times \ 7$$
$$\overline{\;91\;}$$

21.
$$.045$$
$$+ \ 11.26$$
$$\overline{\;.11305\;}$$

22.
$$6\overline{)\ 12} \quad 2$$

23.
$$3\!\!\!/6\ \!\!\!/8$$
$$- \ 19$$
$$\overline{\;29\;}$$

24.
$$102$$
$$\times \ 12$$
$$\overline{\;202\;}$$
$$102$$
$$\overline{\;1{,}222\;}$$

25.
$$\frac{2}{5}$$
$$+ \ \frac{1}{5}$$
$$\overline{\;\frac{3}{10}\;}$$

26.
$$42\overline{)\ 126} \quad 3$$
$$126$$
$$\overline{\;000\;}$$

27.
$$\frac{2}{3}$$
$$- \ \frac{1}{3}$$
$$\overline{\;\frac{1}{3}\;}$$

28.
$$48\overline{)\ 288} \quad 5\,r.\,1$$
$$240$$
$$\overline{\;48\;}$$

29.
$$112\overline{)\ 5936} \quad 493\,r.\,100$$
$$448$$
$$\overline{\;1556\;}$$
$$1008$$
$$\overline{\;548\;}$$
$$448$$
$$\overline{\;100\;}$$

30.
$$\frac{5}{8}$$
$$+ \ \frac{9}{8}$$
$$\overline{\;\frac{14}{16}\;} = \frac{7}{8}$$

31.
$$2\frac{6}{7}$$
$$+ \ 5\frac{1}{2}$$
$$\overline{\;7\frac{7}{9}\;}$$

32.
$$0.045$$
$$\times \ 0.03$$

33.
$$2x + 3 = 11$$
$$x =$$

34.
$$-18$$
$$+ \ 12$$

Figure 6–7. Responses of a Secondary Student on the Calculation Test.

In some situations, an examiner will wish to conduct a more in-depth analysis of performance. Procedures that may be used for further evaluation include: (a) readiness inventories, (b) an oral interview, (c) additional problems, (d) timed tests, (e) cloze procedure, and (f) math vocabulary lists.

Readiness Inventories

In some cases, the examiner may note that the student has developed minimal knowledge of numerals. Some students may fail to make progress in computational skill because they lack understanding of numeration and place value. Engelhardt, Ashlock, and Wiebe (1984) identified 17 numeration readiness concepts that an examiner may wish to assess using paper, pencil, and interview. Bos and Vaughn (1988) presented a succinct summary of these concepts and how they can be assessed. When needed, this in-depth assessment of concepts will help the examiner to determine a student's present knowledge of numeration.

Oral Interview

If an examiner cannot determine how a student has derived certain answers on the Calculation test or on a math worksheet, an oral math interview may be conducted. The purpose of this interview is to identify the steps or procedures a student uses to solve various types of mathematical problems and to determine the inaccurate strategies that are causing problems (Lowenthal, 1987; Pieper, 1983). Sometimes a student will make several mistakes on computations, and an examiner or teacher will not be able to determine any specific error pattern. If an examiner is unsure of why a student is missing problems, the most efficient way to discover the student's thinking processes is to ask the student to explain the computational strategies used to solve selected math problems. This interview may provide the examiner with information concerning the student's: (a) current level of computational skill, (b) use of strategies and procedures, and (c) specific error patterns (Skrtic, Kvam, & Beals, 1983). Additionally, an examiner will be able to determine a student's mastery of the underlying concepts.

Two techniques may be used to conduct the interview. An examiner may ask a student to explain how certain problems were completed on a worksheet, or the examiner may give the student new problems and ask the student to describe the steps while performing the problem. To insure that no information is lost, the interview may be tape recorded (Pieper, 1983). A tape-recorded interview also allows an examiner or instructor to analyze a student's conceptual development over time.

Additional Problems

When a student misses certain problems on the Calculation test, the examiner may wish to create an additional set of problems, similar to the ones missed, for the student to complete. In this way, an examiner may determine exactly what the student does and doesn't know. For example, a student may ignore a computational sign when working a problem, such as using addition on a multiplication problem. At a later date, an examiner may develop a worksheet with a mixture of problems for the student to complete to see whether the student notes each computational sign. Or, an examiner may wish to have a student complete more problems involving fractions, negative numbers, or quadratic equations, based upon the initial assessment. To

measure mastery of a skill, Gregory and Morsink (1984) recommended that a typical probe would have about 20 stimulus items, with some items presented more than once, administered several days in a row. This mini-test would only measure one skill, such as adding fractions with like denominators and no reducing. In some instances, an examiner may wish to have a student use a chart or calculator to control for factual errors when informally assessing a student's error patterns (Enright, 1987).

In other instances, an examiner may wish to provide a student with a mixture of problems using a variety of processes, such as addition, subtraction, multiplication, and division of fractions. The purpose is to determine whether the student applies the correct algorithm. For example, Ernie, a seventh-grade student, missed several of the problems involving fractions on the Calculation test. When the examiner spoke with the math teacher, she commented that Ernie knew how to do all of the algorithms associated with fractions. In analyzing Ernie's classroom work and tests, the examiner realized that Ernie performed problems correctly because they were all the same process, such as adding fractions. On the Calculation test, Ernie found common denominators for both addition and multiplication problems. Although Ernie knew the steps of various algorithms, he did not know when a particular operation was appropriate. Essentially, Ernie had learned how to find solutions when only one type of problem was presented, but he did not know how to apply this knowledge.

Timed Tests

The WJ-R ACH Calculation test is untimed. This allows an examiner to determine whether or not the student is accurate in performance. In some cases, an examiner will also want to determine how rapidly a student solves simple computational problems. Retrieving facts automatically from memory is another important aspect of competence in arithmetic. Failure to automatize number facts leads to future difficulty in math achievement (Ackerman, Anhalt, & Dykman, 1986). Ackerman et al. noted that reliance on a counting strategy rather than a mental-retrieval strategy requires attention, and, consequently, mental operations are not performed efficiently. By third grade, most students with normally developing arithmetic skills rely on known number facts rather than a counting strategy to solve simple problems (Ashcraft, 1982).

Depending upon a student's grade level, an examiner may prepare a worksheet that consists of simple addition, subtraction, multiplication, or division problems, or a mixture of problems. The examiner may then determine how many problems a student is able to complete within a 1- or 2-minute period. Identifying and remedying automatization failure is an important aspect in the assessment and remediation of calculation skill. Figure 6-8 provides an assessment sheet for the multiplication facts (2s through 9s). This type of data sheet may be used in an initial assessment and/or to chart increases in computational rate over a period of time.

Cloze Procedure

Another technique that may be applied to the diagnosis and remediation of a student's comprehension of an algorithm, or the steps in a problem, is the cloze technique (Russell & Dunlap, 1977). To use this technique, certain numbers are omitted from the problem. The student is asked to determine the missing numbers that belong in the squares. Figure 6-9 illustrates several sample applications of the cloze technique for various computations.

In using this assessment technique, the difficulty level of the cloze deletions is determined by the student's ability level, computational skill, and conceptual understanding. The examiner will want to begin with easier problems and gradually increase the difficulty level. If a student has trouble solving cloze problems, an oral math interview may be conducted to determine the specific reasons for difficulty.

Math Vocabulary Lists

Although the Quantitative Concepts test has several items of math vocabulary, an examiner may wish to assess this area in more depth. Some students have not mastered specific vocabulary and, subsequently, are confused by their teacher's instructions. For example, when the examiner asked Sue, an eighth-grade student, to define terminology related to fractions, she incorrectly identified the numerator and denominator. Sue noted that when her teacher used these terms and modeled the procedures for multiplying and dividing fractions, she had trouble following the demonstration. In this instance, the examiner recommended that Sue review and master specific terminology associated with fractions.

To determine vocabulary knowledge, an examiner may ask a student to explain selected words from his or her math textbook. Or, an examiner may develop a list of math vocabulary from the glossary or use a prepared list for informal assessment. When a student has not mastered important math terminology, specific instruction in math vocabulary is necessary.

Instructional Program

In designing an instructional program in mathematics, an examiner will need to be familiar with the curriculum of the instructional setting. Mathematics, more than any other academic area, is introduced and taught in a hierarchical sequence that varies from school to school. For example, in some schools, multiplication is introduced in second grade; in others, it is introduced at the end of third grade. Some programs stress the use of manipulatives for solving computations in early elementary school, whereas other programs emphasize developing automaticity with computations. Knowledge of the instructional program will assist the examiner in error analysis and in designing and selecting appropriate modifications and instructional strategies.

Instructional Modifications

As with reading, each student's math program should be presented at his or her instructional level. If teachers have not targeted the right objectives, students will not profit from instruction and will view math as an endless series of problems (Blankenship, 1984). For example, a fifth-grade student who has not mastered basic addition and subtraction should not be expected to perform long division problems. Research results indicate that retention is increased when meaningful materials are matched to a student's achievement level and learning rate (Suydam & Dessart, 1976). In addition to modifying the level of materials, an examiner may wish to suggest several adaptations and modifications.

Adaptation of Worksheets

A worksheet should contain only the number of problems a student is able to perform successfully. For some students, the pages of commercial workbooks contain too many problems that are crowded too close together. Worksheets may be redesigned for the needs of a specific student by reducing the number of problems, enlarging the problems, or repositioning the problems. Students also may be asked to complete a specified number of problems on a worksheet, such as 5 out of 25.

Distributed Practice

Instead of giving a student an entire sheet of math problems in which error patterns may be reinforced, a teacher may present the student with five to eight problems. A student should demonstrate understanding of a process before extended practice is assigned (Ashlock, 1982). Extended practice may be provided for homework once the instructor is certain that the student understands the procedures.

```
  2        6        7        8        5        2        3
x 7      x 5      x 9      x 8      x 4      x 2      x 6
____     ____     ____     ____     ____     ____     ____


  6        8        5        9        4        7        2
x 6      x 2      x 8      x 8      x 9      x 3      x 3
____     ____     ____     ____     ____     ____     ____


  4        9        4        3        2        7        4
x 6      x 9      x 2      x 3      x 5      x 6      x 4
____     ____     ____     ____     ____     ____     ____


  8        6        8        7        9        5        4
x 7      x 2      x 3      x 4      x 3      x 5      x 8
____     ____     ____     ____     ____     ____     ____


  9        7        9        3        5        7        3
x 10     x 5      x 2      x 4      x 9      x 7      x 5
____     ____     ____     ____     ____     ____     ____
```

Figure 6–8. Assessment Sheet for Multiplication Facts. Permission is granted to reproduce this form.

Progress Charts

Individual charts and graphs may be constructed for monitoring progress. Most students are highly motivated by a chart that illustrates the skills they possess, the skills they are mastering, and the skills they need to acquire.

Color-Coding and Directional Arrows

The purposeful use of color-coding or directional arrows may help a student attend to the task and follow the proper procedures. For example, a green dot may be used to identify a starting point and a red dot to identify the ending point. As another adaptation, addition signs may be colored green and subtraction signs colored red. Negative numbers may be introduced with a red sign. Arrows may be used to illustrate the directional steps of an algorithm.

Graph Paper

Graph paper may be used throughout the math curriculum. The rows and columns help students keep numbers aligned and complete computations more accurately and efficiently. Adult professionals who specialize in math fields continue to use some type of ledger paper. Graph paper may be particularly effective for students who are having difficulty with regrouping and placement of numbers. If an examiner notes this type of difficulty on the Calculation test, the use of graph paper in the classroom and for homework should be recommended.

Supplementary Material

An examiner may want to recommend supplemental materials for students who need extended practice with

$$7 \times 3 = \square 1$$

$$56 + 79 = 1\square5$$

$$50 - 23 = 4\square$$

$$5\overline{)16} \quad 3\ r.\ \square$$

$$9\overline{)107} \quad 11\ r.\ 8$$
$$\underline{9}$$
$$\square7$$
$$\underline{9}$$
$$\square$$

$$\frac{1}{4} \div \frac{1}{7} = \frac{7}{\square}$$

$$\frac{2}{3} \times \frac{5}{6} = \frac{1\square}{\square 8}$$

$$\frac{3}{\square} \times \frac{2}{3} = \frac{\square}{12} = \frac{1}{\square}$$

Figure 6–9. Using the Cloze Technique with Math Algorithms.

math computation. Many math textbooks do not contain enough examples or provide enough practice and review for students. Even secondary teachers of students with learning disabilities indicate that commercial programs do not provide enough practice for mastery of specific skills (McLeod & Armstrong, 1982). Consequently, teachers at both elementary and secondary levels must use supplemental methods and materials to provide systematic, extended practice for students. When possible, the instructor should encourage the application of mathematical skills in other curricular areas, such as reading and science.

Copying

Some students have extreme difficulty copying math problems from a chalkboard or a math textbook. These students lose considerable instructional time in trying to reproduce problems accurately. Even some students at the secondary level find copying from the board as difficult as solving the problems on the worksheet (Masters & Mori, 1986). For students with this difficulty, an examiner should recommend that copying be eliminated and that all problems be prewritten on worksheets.

Estimation

Error monitoring in calculation requires the ability to estimate solutions. To improve this skill, students may record an estimated answer before solving the problem (Ashlock, 1982). Teachers may wish to develop worksheets that have two blanks recorded by a problem: one underneath for the solution and one to the side for the estimated answer. This procedure helps students develop the habit of asking whether or not an answer makes sense. When an examiner notes that many of a student's responses on the Calculation test are unreasonable, attention should be directed to developing concepts and skill in estimation.

Fact Charts

Simple charts that contain all of the basic facts may be developed for addition and subtraction, or multiplication and division. In creating the chart, the upper left square remains blank and then the numbers 1 through 9 are listed across the top of the paper and down the side of the paper. Solutions are entered into the appropriate square. Students may use these charts to perform computations when they have not memorized the math facts. Figures 6-10 and 6-11 provide fact charts for addition and multiplication.

Calculators

After observing and analyzing a student's performance in computational skill, an examiner may wish to recommend inclusion of a calculator in the student's program. The National Council for Teachers of Mathematics rec-

+	1	2	3	4	5	6	7	8	9
1	2	3	4	5	6	7	8	9	10
2	3	4	5	6	7	8	9	10	11
3	4	5	6	7	8	9	10	11	12
4	5	6	7	8	9	10	11	12	13
5	6	7	8	9	10	11	12	13	14
6	7	8	9	10	11	12	13	14	15
7	8	9	10	11	12	13	14	15	16
8	9	10	11	12	13	14	15	16	17
9	10	11	12	13	14	15	16	17	18

Figure 6–10. Addition Fact Chart.

x	1	2	3	4	5	6	7	8	9
1	1	2	3	4	5	6	7	8	9
2	2	4	6	8	10	12	14	16	18
3	3	6	9	12	15	18	21	24	27
4	4	8	12	16	20	24	28	32	36
5	5	10	15	20	25	30	35	40	45
6	6	12	18	24	30	36	42	48	54
7	7	14	21	28	35	42	49	56	63
8	8	16	24	32	40	48	56	64	72
9	9	18	27	36	45	54	63	72	81

Figure 6–11. Multiplication Fact Chart.

ommended the following nine uses for calculators in the classroom: (a) to encourage students to experiment with mathematical ideas, (b) to help students become wise consumers, (c) to reinforce learning of the basic number facts, (d) to increase students' understanding of algorithms through observation of repeated operations, (e) to verify the results of computation, (f) to promote independence in problem solving, (g) to solve lengthy problems that are impractical with pencil and paper, (h) to make generalizations from patterns of numbers, and (i) to reduce the time required to solve computations (Caravella, 1977).

Calculators may also be used in classrooms to check computation practice. If an examiner notes that a student makes a lot of careless mistakes, a calculator, which provides immediate feedback, may be the solution. The student may perform an error analysis, and, if he or she is unable to identify the mistake, a teacher or peer may provide assistance.

Meyer (1980) found that the calculator was a valuable teaching tool to supplement math instruction in a fourth-grade classroom. In addition to providing instant feedback on drill and practice activities, students learned how to reason logically through a problem to reach a solution. Students were also introduced to more advanced computational skills. Using calculators provided students with experiences such as adding and subtracting negative numbers, understanding place value up to eight place decimals, converting fractions to decimal equivalents, and adding and subtracting with decimals.

Meyer also noted that many students who disliked math changed their attitudes when provided with calculators. Students who have difficulty developing computational skill often lose interest in all of mathematics (Gawronski & Coblentz, 1976). Subsequently, for some students, the use of a calculator or microcomputer may be recommended as a motivational tool. This type of recommendation is particularly appropriate for secondary students who need to develop practical skill in mathematics but still have not memorized all of the basic facts. Without the use of a calculator, difficulty with facts may prohibit a student from progressing in math problem solving and higher-level thinking skills.

On some occasions, an examiner may encounter a student who has such extreme difficulty remembering math facts, that it is appropriate to recommend that a calculator be used whenever computational arithmetic is required. Before a calculator is introduced, however, the student should understand the basic operational concepts and be able to estimate approximate answers to problems. Once the student demonstrates understanding of the various operations, the examiner may recommend that the student use a calculator in the instructional setting. For example, Rich, a fifth-grade student, had extreme difficulty with all tasks requiring rote memorization. He had memorized only a few facts after studying his multiplication tables for 2 years. After talking with Rich, who agreed that this compensation was needed, the examiner recommended that Rich be permitted to use a calculator whenever necessary. This type of compensation for a student with a severe memory problem is similar to providing a typewriter to a student whose limited motor skill makes handwriting difficult.

Instructional Principles and Strategies for Basic Math Skills

Computational skill involves mastery of facts and procedures for the purpose of applying these different computations to real-life situations. The knowledge that is taught may be declarative (knowing number facts) or procedural (knowing how to perform the algorithm or steps in a problem) (Lloyd & Keller, 1989). Knowledge

of facts coupled with understanding the purpose and use of each operation provide a foundation for further development in mathematical concepts. Instruction must focus on both mastery of skills and conceptual development. Mastering the basic skills without developing conceptual understanding requires almost complete memorization. If any of the skills are forgotten, the learner is limited in how he or she can regenerate the forgotten facts or processes (Greenwood & Anderson, 1983). Instructional failure is often the result of inappropriate, incorrect, or inadequate instruction to develop the skill or concept being taught (Cawley, Fitzmaurice, Shaw, Kahn, & Bates, 1979a).

Programs that employ several principles of effective teaching have been shown to have positive effects on students' achievement in mathematics. In general, teachers are most effective when they view mathematics as a way of thinking, rather than as a collection of discrete computational skills (Fair, 1988). In summarizing the results of several research studies, Suydam and Dessart (1976) recommended that to help students retain mathematical skills and concepts, a teacher should: (a) teach skills and concepts in a meaningful way; (b) allow students to work at their own level; (c) provide intensive, specific, systematic review and practice; and (d) help students increase their motivation to learn.

In reviewing the research literature and analyzing teacher behavior patterns, Englert (1984) indicated that effective teachers: (a) maintain a brisk lesson pace; (b) provide success-oriented, systematic practice for students at accuracy levels of 80% or higher; and (c) provide immediate feedback, using reinforcement after correct responses and prompts or hints after incorrect responses. Prompting students to re-evaluate responses after errors were made was more effective than telling students the correct answers. Additionally, for reinforcement and feedback to be effective, students must understand what they are doing and know how to perform the problems (Lloyd & Keller, 1989).

In an extensive investigation, Good and Grouws (1979) observed mathematics teachers in natural settings and derived a set of factors that effective teachers employ in instruction. These factors, presented in Figure 6-12, were derived from both direct observations and research findings. Application of these instructional variables will improve student achievement. In a recent investigation, Kelly, Gersten, and Carnine (1990) found that use of these principles of curriculum design was significantly more effective than a basal approach for teaching students basic fraction concepts in high school remedial math classes. They concluded that the effectiveness of any mathematics curriculum can be increased by providing a wider range of examples, clearer step-by-step strategies, and discrimination practice in when to apply a particular strategy.

```
Daily Review (first 8 minutes except Mondays)
                (a) review the concepts and skills associated with the homework
                (b) collect and deal with homework assignments
                (c) ask several mental computation exercises
Development (about 20 minutes)
                (a) briefly focus on prerequisite skills and concepts
                (b) focus on meaning and promoting student understanding by using lively explanations,
                    demonstrations, process explanations, illustrations, etc.
                (c) assess student comprehension
                        (1) using process/product questions (active interaction)
                        (2) using controlled practice
                (d) repeat and elaborate on the meaning portion as necessary
Seatwork (about 15 minutes)
                (a) provide uninterrupted successful practice
                (b) momentum--keep the ball rolling--get everyone involved, then sustain involvement
                (c) alerting--let students know their work will be checked at end of period
                (d) accountability--check the students' work
Homework Assignment
                (a) assign on a regular basis at the end of each math class except Fridays
                (b) should involve about 15 minutes of work to be done at home
                (c) should include one or two review problems
Special Reviews
                (a) weekly review/maintenance
                        (1) conduct during the first 20 minutes each Monday
                        (2) focus on skills and concepts covered during the previous week
                (b) monthly review/maintenance
                        (1) conduct every fourth Monday
                        (2) focus on skills and concepts covered since the last monthly review
```

Figure 6–12. Summary of Key Instructional Behaviors. *Note.* From "The Missouri Mathematics Effectiveness Project: An Experimental Study in Fourth-Grade Classrooms" by T.L. Good and D.A. Grouws, 1979, *Journal of Educational Psychology, 71,* p. 357. Copyright 1979 by American Psychological Association. Reprinted by permission.

Prerequisite Skills

In addition to ineffective instruction, another major reason for instructional failure is that students often progress to more difficult tasks before mastering the prerequisites (Cawley, Fitzmaurice, Shaw, Kahn, & Bates, 1979a). For successful performance in all computations, students need to learn the underlying skills. Instruction should be sequential and build upon prior knowledge.

In some cases, an examiner may note that a student lacks the prerequisite skills for performing an operation. Even at the secondary level, students continue to have difficulty with math calculations. In a survey that examined the math difficulties of junior and senior high school students with learning disabilities, teachers reported that the six most common problems were: (a) division of whole numbers, (b) basic operations involving fractions, (c) use of decimals, (d) use of percents, (e) fraction terminology, and (f) multiplication of whole numbers (McLeod & Armstrong, 1982). Additionally, the survey results indicated that the majority of secondary students with learning disabilities had basic mathematical skills at the upper-third- to upper-fourth-grade level.

Consequently, remediation of basic math skills is often necessary with students at the secondary level.

Numeration

Number recognition, sequencing skills, and counting skills are necessary prerequisites for performing all math operations. A student who misses the first several items on the Quantitative Concepts and Calculation tests will likely need additional assistance in developing numeration ability before emphasis is placed on computational skill. Engelhardt, Ashlock, and Wiebe (1984) provided instructional ideas that correspond with 17 numeration readiness concepts.

With young students, many games will enhance numeration skill. For example, Sheridan (1973) described a class game for developing number recognition and sequencing skills. To begin, the teacher arranges large sturdy number cards along the blackboard in a sequence. One student leaves the room and another student picks the number to be removed. The first student then returns to the room to identify the missing number. If the answer is correct, the student replaces the card between the appropriate numbers. If the answer is incorrect, the teacher reviews counting and the concepts of *before* and *after*. Similar games may be designed with number lines and charts. The intent of mathematical games is to provide students with meaningful, problem-based experiences that will increase interest in mathematics and enhance conceptual development.

Use of Manipulatives

Concept development is aided by the use of manipulatives. Manipulatives help students form mental images of the processes that are associated with written notation (Dunlap & Brennan, 1979). Before students understand the use of symbols alone, they need experiences manipulating real objects, such as blocks, pennies, or beads. When using manipulatives in the classroom, a student should be actively involved; the actual moving of pieces helps students understand the process involved.

Once a child understands that he or she can count three blocks, three pennies, or three beads, pictures of objects may be introduced for counting. The child must develop the understanding that the number 3 represents any three objects. In assisting children to develop this concept, a teacher may progress from real objects, to pictures of objects, to representations of objects (lines or circles), to symbols. Many different types of examples should be provided.

Instructional sequence. Dunlap and Brennan (1979) suggested the following instructional sequence: (a) enactive or concrete level, where objects are used to represent symbols; (b) iconic or semi-concrete level, where pictures of sets are used to represent symbols; and (c) symbolic or abstract level, where numbers are used.

The use of symbols alone, without objects or pictures, is delayed until a student has developed a clear understanding of each symbol's meaning. When a student is able to manipulate objects to represent mathematical concepts and then is able, when given the symbolic form, to represent it with manipulatives, he or she is ready to move to the iconic level.

When introducing the iconic level, the student receives instruction in using math symbols to represent pictures. When a student is able to look at the math symbols and then draw a picture of the sets, he or she is ready to move to the symbolic level, or the use of symbols without aids.

Once a student has reached the symbolic level, drill activities may be introduced. Dunlap and Brennan cautioned that when drill activities are started too early, students become frustrated and have difficulty remembering or applying the skill at a later time.

Introducing new concepts. Manipulatives should also be used in upper grade levels whenever new mathematical concepts are introduced (Suydam & Dessart, 1976). For example, in introducing fractions, decimals, or percents, a teacher begins with a concrete, spatial representation, such as a paper folded into equal parts. Students then explore the new concept with manipulatives until they understand that the process illustrated by the manipulatives is the same as the pencil and paper task. Research results on fraction and decimal concepts indicate that the difficulty of many students in forming quantitative ideas results from inadequate presentation of concrete or spatial representations (Kelly, Gersten, & Carnine, 1990; Payne, 1980).

In some instances, an examiner may recommend that a student needs additional classroom work using manipulatives or pictorial representations. For example after analyzing errors on the Calculation test, an examiner observed that Wendy, a seventh-grade student, made errors on calculations involving fractions and decimals. Using informal assessment, the examiner asked Wendy to solve problems involving addition and subtraction of fractions using pictures. The examiner also asked Wendy to draw pictures to illustrate the fractions of 2/3, 3/4, and 7/8. Wendy did not understand how to represent fractions with drawings. In this instance, additional work with concrete or spatial representations is needed to help Wendy master and apply these skills.

Mastering Basic Facts

During an assessment, an examiner may observe whether a student has memorized several of the basic math facts. When watching Lewis, a fourth-grade student, complete problems on the Calculation test, the examiner noted that Lewis used finger counting for addition and subtraction problems and drew groups of sticks to solve multiplication problems. Although he demonstrated understanding of the underlying mathematical concepts, Lewis had not memorized number facts.

A student's basic knowledge about numbers is reflected in the strategies that are used for solving problems. Lewis, who counts on his fingers to solve an addition problem, is using a less efficient strategy than the student who retrieves the fact from memory. In summarizing the development of strategies for solving addition problems, Lloyd and Keller (1989) presented three generalizations regarding the acquisition of math skills: (a) strategies build on previously learned strategies; (b) as knowledge increases, learners become more flexible in using various strategies; and (c) as strategies are mastered, they increase in abstraction and efficiency. In planning an instructional program, emphasis should be placed on teaching concepts, while attempting to change inefficient procedural strategies.

A frequent goal of remedial programs is to help students respond automatically to the basic math facts. Initially, facts are taught at the procedural level and then brought to the automatic level through practice (Lloyd & Keller, 1989). The concept of automaticity refers to the belief that as the basic skills are practiced more, their execution requires less attention, and more cognitive processing capacity is left to execute higher level skills (Hasselbring, Goin, & Bransford, 1987). When students are accurate and fast in solving basic facts, more complex problems may be solved within a reasonable amount of time.

Basic guidelines. Many students with learning problems have trouble mastering or memorizing basic facts and, subsequently, have trouble developing computational skill. In developing a basic fact program for students with learning disabilities, Thornton and Toohey (1985) suggested that the following factors receive equal attention:

1. Review or reteach as necessary so that the prerequisites are mastered before a student is required to use them during fact learning.
2. Provide ongoing diagnosis and assessment.
3. Group facts by strategy for recall rather than by the size of the sum.
4. Teach strategies for working out unknown facts.
5. Match activities to the learning style of the student.
6. Control the pace of the program to ensure success.
7. Help students determine when a strategy applies and when it doesn't apply.
8. Provide verbal prompts to help children establish strategies.
9. Help students acquire self-monitoring skills.
10. Provide ample time for overlearning.

Improving retention. Some students have trouble retaining math facts because of poor short-term memory. Cawley (1984) suggested that the effects of memory deficits may be minimized by: (a) reducing the amount of material that the student is required to remember, (b) providing more repetition and review, and (c) emphasizing meaningfulness by developing experiences with the content and concepts.

Similarly, Hayes (1985) summarized several practices to facilitate the learning of math facts:

1. Select a small number of facts to work with one at a time. Do not introduce more facts until mastery is achieved.
2. Improve retention by providing oral repetition and written responses to flash cards.
3. Practice facts daily or two times a day for short periods of time.
4. Review all mastered combinations frequently. Include

one or two previously learned facts in the daily rehearsal.
5. Provide students with any unknown facts. Allow the use of charts or calculators until the facts have been mastered.

Hayes suggested following the same instructional guidelines for teaching math algorithms.

Direct Intervention

Often the most effective procedure for remediating difficulties in computation is to identify what a student knows and does not know, and then target appropriate remedial objectives. Careful error analysis often indicates the necessary remedial procedures. As early as 1926, Buswell noted that students' computation errors may be eliminated by basing remedial lessons on a diagnosis of errors. Once it has been determined that a strategy is inefficient (either too time-consuming or illogical), an efficient strategy is taught and practiced until the student understands and has mastered the process.

Direct instruction involves breaking down tasks into their component skills, teaching the components, and demonstrating how the components are combined (Silbert, Carnine, & Stein, 1981). Although many special commercial math programs exist, computational difficulties may often be resolved with task analysis, systematic teaching (including modeling and demonstrations), and corrective feedback and rewards. These types of procedures may be applied to the teaching of computations involving whole numbers, fractions, decimals, or percents.

Task analysis. Frank (1973) listed five steps in performing task analysis:

1. State the learning task or the objectives to be met by the student.
2. List all steps, operations, or prerequisite skills needed to meet the objective.
3. Place the steps and operations into a logical teaching sequence.
4. Determine through informal testing exactly what steps a student can and cannot perform.
5. Teach the steps in sequence.

This type of analysis allows an examiner to pinpoint specific problems and then design carefully sequenced learning activities. In selecting materials, the examiner or teacher should ensure that the material provides an appropriate instructional sequence.

Modeling, feedback, and reinforcement. Computational skill may be improved through the use of modeling, feedback, and reinforcement. Blankenship (1978) investigated the use of modeling plus feedback to reduce the number of systematic subtraction errors in nine elementary-age students with learning disabilities. In this procedure, the experimenter presented a student with a problem written on an index card and talked through the steps for its solution. Next, the student was asked to solve a problem. If the answer was correct, the student was presented with a set of problems and asked to complete them in the same way. If the answer was incorrect, the process was repeated using another pair of cards until the student was able to solve the sample problem correctly. When the assignment was completed, a "C" was placed by correct problems and a check mark by incorrect problems. Blankenship observed that modeling plus feedback enhanced rapid acquisition, promoted generalization, increased accuracy in subtraction, and fostered the maintenance of regrouping skills.

In several studies, significant improvements have been made in math rates by providing feedback and rewards as incentives (Johnson & McLaughlin, 1982; Luiselli & Downing, 1980; McLaughlin, 1981). Examples of effective reinforcement for completing a specified number of problems with accuracy include: contingent free time, praise, or points. In designing an instructional strategy, an examiner may wish to determine the type of reinforcement that would be most effective for improving a student's performance.

Multisensory Approaches

Just as with reading and spelling, a multisensory approach may help students memorize math facts. Some students will benefit most from saying the fact aloud, while looking at the fact. Others will prefer to look at the fact, say the fact, and then trace and write the fact.

Write-say procedures. Research results suggest that saying a problem before writing the solution improves arithmetic performance (Lovitt & Curtiss, 1968). Lombardo and Drabman (1985) examined two procedures similar to the Fernald approach in which six students wrote multiplication facts (Write procedure) or said them aloud while writing them (Write-Say procedure). Students were given study sheets with 72 multiplication problems. Answers were covered with tablets. After completing each problem, the student checked to see whether the answer was correct. If the answer was not correct, the problem was written five times. The students covered problems with their fingers to force writing from memory rather than simply copying. Although both procedures benefited five of the children, the Write-Say procedure seemed to accelerate learning more than the Write procedure. Similar to procedures used in spelling instruction, verbalizing

facts and then writing them from memory enhances the learning process.

Tracing. Thornton and Toohey (1985, 1986) described a procedure of writing a fact at the top of a piece of paper and having the student answer the fact, trace over the fact saying it aloud until it is remembered, and then folding the paper down, rewriting the fact, and opening the paper to check the answer. They recommended that this fold, write, and check procedure be performed until three consecutive correct answers are given.

They described a similar procedure called "ghosting," in which an unknown fact is written in large print on the chalkboard. The student traces over the fact, saying it aloud, until only the number "ghost" remains.

Tape recorders. A student may also tape-record facts he or she is practicing, leaving pauses before reading the answers. When the tape is played back, the student can try to say the answer faster than it is read on the tape (Thornton & Toohey, 1985). To increase the multisensory presentation of this procedure, a student may look at the problem while listening to the tape and then write the answer on a piece of paper.

Touch Math. Another multimodality approach to teaching the four basic computational skills is Touch Math (Bullock, 1986; Bullock & Walentas, 1989). This approach may be used with elementary students to supplement regular math instruction or to provide remedial instruction. The "touch" method adds the kinesthetic mode to the learning process. Students are taught to count by touching in sequence the points designated by large dark circles on each of the numbers from 1 through 9. Several steps progressing from simple to complex are involved in teaching the four basic operations: addition, subtraction, multiplication, and division.

For addition, the student touches the dots on the numbers and counts forwards. For subtraction, the student says the name of the larger number and then touches the dots while counting backwards. The entire program encourages verbal rehearsal strategies, visual cues, and other aids to help learners retain the necessary steps for each computational area. Students are encouraged to eliminate these steps when they are no longer necessary. Figure 6-13 illustrates samples from the Touch Math program.

Results of several research studies have supported the effectiveness of this approach with elementary students (Bullock & Walentas, 1989). Based on its multisensory nature, this approach may benefit elementary students who have trouble: (a) memorizing basic math facts, (b) understanding basic number concepts, or (c) completing problems with accuracy. For some students, simply teaching the use of touch points on numbers improves accuracy

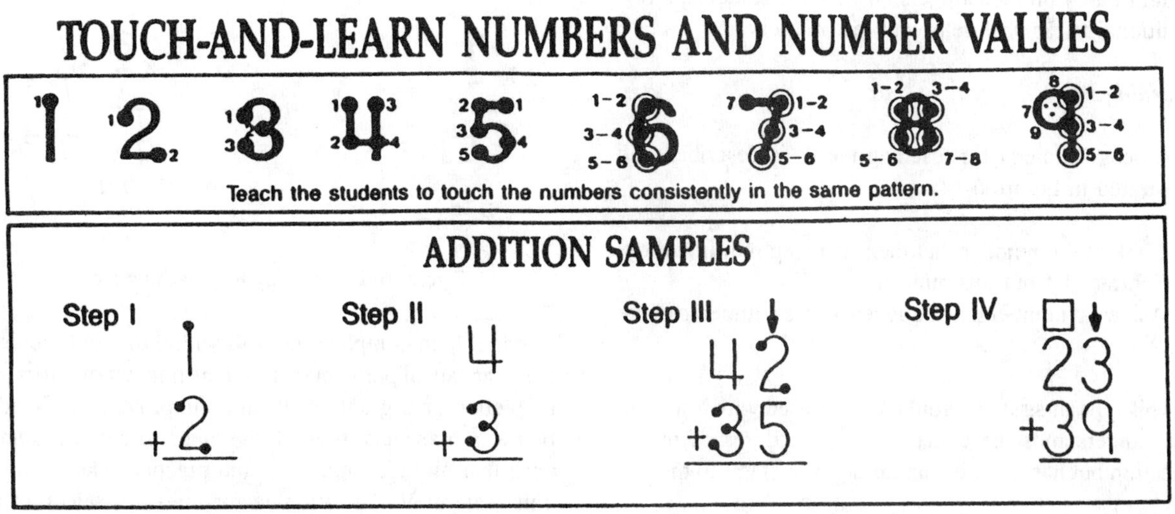

TOUCH-AND-LEARN NUMBERS AND NUMBER VALUES

Teach the students to touch the numbers consistently in the same pattern.

ADDITION SAMPLES

Step I   Step II   Step III   Step IV

Figure 6–13. Samples from the Touch Math Program. *Note.* From *Touch Math Instruction Manual* (p. 2) by J. Bullock and N. Walentas, 1989, Colorado Springs, CO: Innovative Learning Concepts. Copyright 1989 by Innovative Learning Concepts. Reprinted by permission.

in addition and subtraction. Touch points are eliminated as students become proficient in facts.

Supplementary Strategies for Addition Facts

Thornton and Toohey (1985) presented several strategies for helping students memorize basic addition facts. They cited research studies suggesting that modifying the instructional sequence and presentation of learning tasks improves fact learning among students with learning disabilities. The following strategies make it easier to memorize facts:

1. *Count-ons.* This strategy is used when numbers 1, 2, and 3 are added to a larger number. The student says the higher number and then counts on to the solution.
2. *Zero.* The student is taught that any number plus zero stays the same.
3. *Doubles.* Double facts are associated with pictures. When students see a double, they are instructed to think of the matching picture. The following facts are taught, two or three unknown facts at a time:

   2 + 2   car fact
   3 + 3   clover fact
   4 + 4   spider fact
   5 + 5   hand fact
   6 + 6   egg fact
   7 + 7   two week fact
   8 + 8   crayon or octopus fact
   9 + 9   tic tac toe or baseball team

4. *Near Doubles.* For problem solutions that are near to the doubles, such as 6 + 7, the student is instructed to think of the double fact and then just add one more. In introducing the unknown facts to a student, the teacher may progress from matching a picture of the near double to the double, a picture of the near double to a fact, and then the near double fact to the related double.
5. *9s.* Two strategies may be taught for the nine facts. The student may think of the 9 as a 10, and then subtract 1 from the answer. For example, for 9 + 5, the student would think 10 + 5, and then subtract 1. The other strategy is to think that the solution is always one less than the number being added. For example, with 9 + 5, the student records the 10 and then subtracts 1 from the 5 to obtain the answer.
6. *Near Tens.* The student learns the sums for 10, such as 6 + 4 and 7 + 3. When confronted with a problem, such as 7 + 5, the student is instructed to think of the 10 sum for help.

In addition, *turn-around* facts are used to demonstrate the cumulative property. Turn-around facts, such as 2 + 7 and 7 + 2, yield the same answer. Turn-arounds are learned for each group of facts as they are introduced.

Instruction using mnemonic cues and verbal prompts is effective for students with memory problems and attentional deficits. Similar procedures may be used to teach subtraction facts (Thornton & Toohey, 1986).

Supplementary Strategies for Multiplication Facts

Several of the multiplication facts are easily mastered: the 0s, the 1s, the 2s, the 10s. For the 5s, most students can count rapidly on their fingers. With some students, a few additional tricks will help with fact mastery.

Learning the 9s

An easy strategy for teaching the 9s is described and illustrated in Figure 6-14:

1. Look at the number that the 9 is being multiplied by.
2. Subtract 1 from this number.
3. Ask what number may be added to this number to make 9.

This type of strategy would only be used with a student who understands the concept and procedures of multiplication but has trouble committing basic facts to memory.

Another alternative is to teach students to think of the solution for 10 times the number and then subtract. For example, for $9 \times 4 = 36$, a student would think that $4 \times 10 = 40$, and then subtract 4 for the correct answer (Thornton & Toohey, 1985).

Rhymes

An additional strategy that may be used by children who have well-developed oral language skills, but trouble with rote recall, is rhyme or music. Flash cards are made for practicing any unknown facts. The problem and the first line of a poem are written on one side of the card, and the solution and the last line of the poem are written on the flip side. Cards are then appropriately illustrated. Students in a classroom may customize their cards by creating the rhymes and drawing the subsequent illustrations. Examples of a few rhymes created by a fourth-grade class for some more difficult facts follow:

(1) 8×7 can be done with sticks, (2) until you know that it's 56.
(1) 8×4 forgot what to do, (2) so she called up number 32.
(1) 7×7 was never on time, (2) until he ran into Mr. 49.

Students enjoy creating rhymes, drawing the illustrations, and practicing the facts. Gradually the rhyme cards are faded out and regular flash cards used. Song lyrics that include several facts may also be created for a familiar tune. These types of mnemonic strategies may help some students to memorize facts.

Timed Drills

Some students enjoy timed drills. A certain number of problems are identified and the student works as rapidly

Figure 6–14. Strategy for Teaching the 9s.

as possible to complete the drill within the set time limit. Both the rate of performance and the number of errors may be plotted on a graph to illustrate improvement. In addition to worksheets, several computer software programs exist that provide rapid drill and practice. The instructor must determine the rationale for the drill, select an appropriate presentation style, set a criterion level for performance, and then carefully document student progress. Investigations by Howell, Sidorenko, and Jurica (1987) have suggested that specific teacher intervention is necessary to maintain gains made with drill and practice software. In examining the effects of teaching multiplication facts to a student with learning disabilities, Howell et al. found that intervention was most effective when the teacher observed the student's methods and provided corrective techniques for inadequate strategies. These results suggest that when using a microcomputer, the combination of drill and practice software and specific teacher intervention produces the most lasting benefits.

Time-delay procedure. Mattingly and Bott (1990) described a constant time-delay procedure that was effective in teaching multiplication facts to four upper-elementary students identified as learning disabled, behavior disordered, or educable mentally handicapped. In this near-errorless learning procedure, 30 facts were identified as unknown and then randomly divided into six groups of 5 facts each. Facts were written on index cards. During the first session, the teacher presented the card, read the fact, and said the answer. The student then repeated the response. Each of the five facts was practiced five times. In the next sessions, the student read the fact and said the answer within 5 seconds. If unsure of the correct response, the student was told to wait 5 seconds and then the teacher repeated the fact and said the answer. The student was reinforced with a token both for correct responses and waiting 5 seconds because of uncertainty about the answer. This type of procedure resulted in mastery of multiplication facts with a low rate of student errors.

The intent of these types of instructional techniques is to teach automaticity with basic facts so that students can develop fluency in working mathematical problems. Efficiency with basic facts is directly related to successful performance in higher level arithmetic skills (Hasselbring, Goin, & Bransford, 1987). Although automaticity with math facts is important, care should be taken to insure that the central focus of mathematical instructional programs is problem solving and meaningful application of skills.

Flexible Problem Solving

In addition to mastering the facts, students also need to be encouraged to be flexible at problem solving with basic operations. Several activities may be used to promote conceptual development. The emphasis is not on speed but rather on understanding the relationships among the various processes.

One strategy is to present students with sets of completed problems with no arithmetical signs. The student then must determine which sign would produce the correct response for each problem (Thornton & Toohey, 1985). In addition to increasing understanding of the relationships among basic facts, this strategy may benefit students who tend to ignore mathematical signs.

Another method for increasing the learner's level of skill mastery is to present equations that are missing selected numbers. With some problems, students may be asked to provide several solutions. Figure 6-15 illustrates several sample problems using this technique. Because this activity requires students to engage actively in the arithmetic process, the relationships among numbers and operations become more apparent (Fearn, 1980). This strategy may work effectively with secondary students who need further work in computational skill.

Conclusion

Difficulty with basic concepts and computations may be attributed to a variety of factors, including inadequate instruction, lack of prerequisite skills, and memory problems. Analysis of performance on the WJ-R ACH Quantitative Concepts and Calculation tests will help an examiner to identify areas of need and determine whether a more in-depth analysis is necessary. These assessment results may then be used to plan effective instruction.

Basic math skill programs are designed to improve numeration skills, develop concepts and applications, and promote automaticity with facts and computations. Although extended practice is needed to memorize facts, computational skills are taught in meaningful contexts so they may be applied to problems in real-life situations. For increasing competencies in basic skills and independence in problem solving, students will benefit from a wide range of quantitative experiences, not just from computational practice. Instructional interventions, such as puzzles

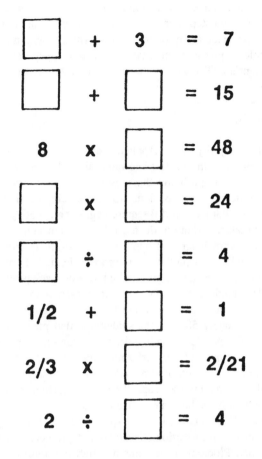

Figure 6–15. Cloze with Number Equations.

and problems that reveal the structure of mathematical operations, will encourage students to be mentally active and promote meaningful learning (Fair, 1988).

Mathematics Reasoning

The WJ-R ACH Applied Problems test measures mathematical reasoning or the ability to solve problems in practical situations. Even when students have mastered basic calculations, some have difficulty applying the operations to meaningful situations. Careful error analysis will help an examiner identify the reasons that a student is having difficulty.

Error Analysis of Applied Problems

The Applied Problems test contains a variety of problems. The items involve applications, such as: (a) counting, (b) solving simple one-step story problems, (c) reading digital and analog clocks, (d) identifying coins, (e) counting money, (f) solving problems with fractions, (g) making change, (h) determining miles on a map, (h) solving two-step story problems, (i) measuring figures, and (j) calculating interest rates. This wide range of problems provides the examiner with an overview of a student's ability to solve problems in a variety of situations.

Item Types

The majority of the Applied Problems items, with the exception of the easiest and most difficult items on the test, are word problems that require addition, subtraction, multiplication, or division. Approximately the first 10 items on Forms A and B require beginning counting skill with pictures. Many of the most difficult items on the test require knowledge and application of formulas. Figures 6-16 and 6-17 depict the word problem items in Forms A and B and the operations required to solve each problem.

The grade equivalent score after each item number indicates that the item would be answered correctly by approximately 50% of the students at that grade placement. For problems that require more than one step, each step is numbered. In performing an error analysis, an examiner may note that a student has difficulty solving problems that involve a specific operation, such as multiplication, or include more than one step.

An "E" is recorded by the specific items that include extraneous information. Several word problems on the Applied Problems tests contain extraneous information, either quantitative (an irrelevant number value) or qualitative (an irrelevant fact about a person, place, or thing). For example, Item 28 contains a quantitative distractor: "Sue walks 13 blocks to school, Mary walks 6 blocks, and Robert walks 8 blocks. How many more blocks does Sue walk than Robert?" To solve this problem, a student must be able to eliminate the quantitative distractor (Mary walks 6 blocks). A student who uses the number 6 in his or her computation is confused by the extraneous information.

Item 38 contains a qualitative distractor: "Ann lives 3 miles from school. She eats lunch at school. How many miles does she travel to and from school?" Although no extraneous numeric information is involved, a student may be confused by the qualitative distractor "She eats lunch at school" and, subsequently, have difficulty solving the problem. Through error analysis and observation of a student's performance on the Applied Problems test, an examiner may determine whether or not a student has difficulty identifying and eliminating extraneous information when solving word problems.

Students have difficulty solving story problems for several reasons. Cognitive, affective, and mathematical factors play an important part in successful problem solving (Bley & Thornton, 1981). In analyzing a student's

responses to the Applied Problems, an examiner should attempt to discover the reason that a student misses a problem. Possible reasons include: lack of prerequisite skills, errors in calculation, failure to comprehend the problem, or lack of knowledge regarding vocabulary or concepts.

Significant information may be obtained by recording and analyzing a student's responses. When evaluating a student's errors, an examiner should consider how the student arrived at a certain answer and whether or not the response is reasonable. After testing is completed, an examiner may obtain further information by analyzing a student's calculations on the Applied Problems Worksheet on the front cover of the Subject Response Booklet and by considering the student's performance in his or her instructional setting.

Analysis of the Applied Problems Worksheet

The Applied Problems Worksheet is provided to the student during testing. Figure 6-18 illustrates the Applied Problems Worksheet of Daniel, a fifth-grade student. Before beginning the error analysis, the examiner first determined which problem corresponded to each item and then drew boundaries to separate the problems.

On Item 30, Daniel recorded four 6s, then grouped them by twos and added them to make 12, and then added the two 12s to arrive at the correct solution. On Item 31, he added the two figures correctly. On Item 32, he started to multiply the 50 people by five chairs and then added the two 5s to arrive at the answer of 100. On Item 33, Daniel stated that the man would need two quarters, one dime, and five pennies to make a 65-cent phone call. On Item 34, he responded "two." He divided the four writing tablets in half.

On Item 35, Daniel began by listing the three notebooks and subtracting 2 dollars. He then added the four figures and produced the answer of $18.50. Daniel stated: "That can't be right." On his next trial, he listed three notebooks and added in the 2 dollars and came up with the same solution. On the third trial, he placed the 2 dollars on the top of the problem, and then stated that he could not determine how to solve the problem. On Item 36, he wrote down 5 days and 4 days and then multiplied them together. Analysis of Daniel's responses indicated that although he attempts to engage in logical problem solving, he lacks understanding of what steps to follow and how to select and apply the appropriate operations.

Figure 6-19 illustrates the Applied Problems Worksheet of Debbie, a seventh-grade student. On Item 35, Debbie added together the cost of the three notebooks, then subtracted from $2.00 to get the correct change. On Item 36, she made a chart listing the earnings of the three people: Two people making 5 dollars for three days, and

Applied Problems Form A: Analysis of Word Problems

Item Number	Median Grade	+	Operation -	x	÷	Extraneous Information
12.	<K.0		1			
14.	<K.0		1			
15.	K.1		1			
16.	K.2	1				
17.	K.4	1				
19.	K.8		1			
21.	1.2	1				
22.	1.2		1			
23.	1.2	1				
24.	1.6	1				
26.	2.0	1				
27.	2.6		1			E
28.	2.7		1			E
29.	2.7	1				
30.	3.6			1		
31.	3.7	1				E
32.	4.3				1	
33.	4.7	1				
34.	5.3				1	
35.	5.8	1	2			
36.	6.1	1		2		
37.	6.6			1		E
38.	6.8	1				E
39.	6.9		1			
40.	7.7	1			2	
41.	7.9	1		2		
42.	10.0			1		
43.	10.1				1	
44.	11.0				1	
45.	11.9		2	1		
47.	13.5			1		
48.	13.9			1		
49.	14.7	2		1	3	

Figure 6–16. Analysis of the Applied Problems Test, Form A.

one person making 4 dollars for three days. Then she added together the columns which resulted in an incorrect solution. On Item 37, Debbie added 22 miles four times to arrive at the correct solution. On Item 38, she added the denominators of the fractions together rather than the numerators. On Item 39, she wrote numbers to represent the hours from 4 o'clock to 1 o'clock and came up with the incorrect answer of 10. On Item 40, she attempted the first step of the problem by adding three of the costs. On Item 41, she began by listing the 37-mile trip to and from the job for 5 days. Although her initial reasoning was correct, she then wrote and completed the multiplication problem for 37×5. The examiner further noted that she placed the multiplication sign on the wrong side of the problem. On Item 43 she attempted to divide a yardstick into four equal parts by dividing 3 into 40 and then produced the answer of one foot and 33 inches. By performing this simple error analysis, the examiner noted that Debbie executes a plan for solving each problem but has difficulty with the application of multiplication, fractions, and measurement. These hypotheses may be verified with further information obtained from the WJ-R

Applied Problems Form B: Analysis of Word Problems

Item Number	Median Grade	+	−	x	÷	Extraneous Information
11.	<K.0		1			
14.	K.0		1			
15.	K.1	1				
16.	K.2		1			
17.	K.6	1				
19.	1.2	1				
21.	1.2		1			
22.	1.2	1				
24.	1.9	1				
26.	2.2			1		
27.	2.3	1				
28.	3.0			1		
30.	3.6	1				E
31.	3.6		1			E
32.	4.4				1	E
33.	4.4	1	2			
34.	5.7				1	
35.	5.1		1			
36.	5.9	1	2			
38.	7.4			1		E
40.	8.8	1	2			
41.	9.4				1	
42.	9.6			1		
43.	10.8	1	2			E
45.	10.8		2	1		
46.	10.2				1	
47.	13.7	2	3	1		
49.	14.5			1		
50.	13.7	2		1		

Figure 6–17. Analysis of the Applied Problems Test, Form B.

ACH Calculation and Quantitative Concepts tests and/or informal assessments.

Although the student is provided with paper and pencil, in some instances, a student will not perform any calculations on the Applied Problems Worksheet. Instead, the student attempts to solve the problems mentally. By analyzing a student's responses and errors, an examiner may note whether the student is accurate or inaccurate in performing mental computations.

Performance in the Instructional Setting

An examiner should attempt to determine whether or not a student's performance on Applied Problems is consistent with performance in the instructional setting.

Two major differences exist between the format of this test and the typical presentation format in instructional settings. First, the Applied Problems test is presented orally. This allows an examiner to observe how a student performs in math problem solving when no reading is required. Second, relatively simple calculations are required to control for the effects of low computational skill on problem solving. These two factors allow an examiner to obtain a more accurate assessment of mathematics reasoning by eliminating the effects of low performance in another area, such as reading.

A student may perform at an average or above-average level on the Applied Problems test but still have difficulty with problem-solving activities in the classroom. In an instructional setting, students have difficulty solving story

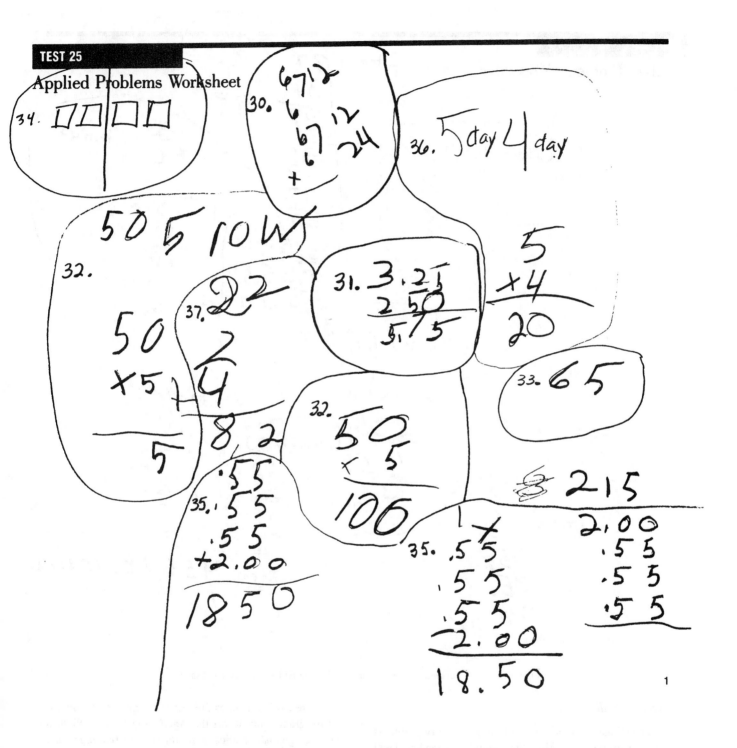

Figure 6–18. A Fifth-Grade Student on the Applied Problems Worksheet.

or word problems for several reasons. Difficulty with problems may be caused by the: (a) reading level, (b) computational requirements, (c) syntactical or linguistic complexity, or (d) conceptual complexity, including the use of extraneous information. By analyzing a student's performance on several clusters and tests of the WJ-R, an examiner may determine the major factors contributing to a student's difficulty.

TEST 25

Applied Problems Worksheet

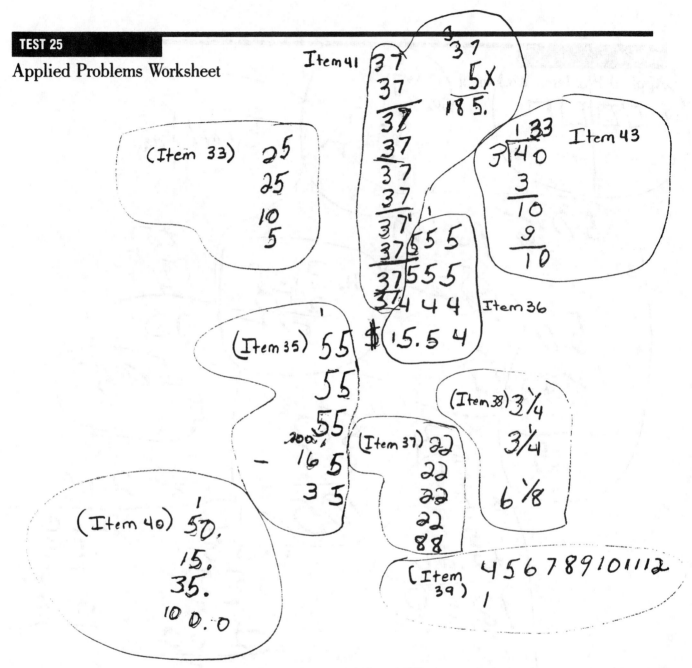

Figure 6–19. A Seventh-Grade Student on the Applied Problems Worksheet.

Reading Skills

To estimate a student's ability to solve story problems in an instructional setting, the individual's reading level must be considered. This may be done by comparing a student's performance on the Applied Problems test to performance on the WJ-R ACH reading tests. Some students are able to read at grade level but have difficulty solving even the simplest one-step story problems. Other students are able to solve complex story problems when the reading level is adjusted to their skill level.

Figure 6-20 illustrates the test performance of Phyliss, a fifth-grade student, on the Age/Grade Profile. Phyliss has average mathematics reasoning but low reading skills. In this situation, the examiner hypothesized that Phyliss' low reading performance was affecting her ability to solve problems in her math textbook.

Computational Ability

To estimate a student's ability to solve story problems in an instructional setting, the individual's level of com-

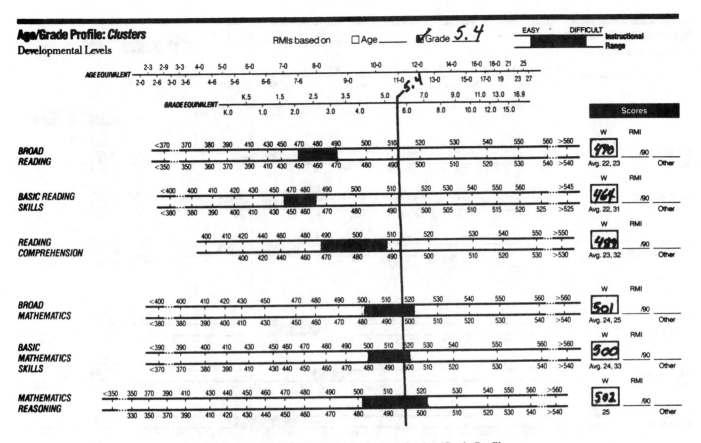

Age/Grade Profile: Clusters
Developmental Levels

Figure 6–20. A Fifth-Grade Student on the Age/Grade Profile.

putational skill must be considered. This may be done by comparing a student's performance on the Applied Problems test to performance on the Calculation test. Figure 6-21 illustrates the test performance on the Age/Grade Profile of Carlos, a ninth-grade student. Carlos has grade-level reading skills and problem-solving ability, but low basic math skills. Carlos' difficulty with problem solving is caused by computational errors and confusion regarding the application of more advanced calculations.

Linguistic and Conceptual Complexity

Some students have trouble understanding quantitative terminology or the math vocabulary words used in word problems. In addition, the complex/compound structure of sentences in word problems may confuse a student. Other students have trouble thinking through the various steps involved in problems. A student may be able to solve a one-step word problem, but have difficulty with two-step problems that require sequencing of steps. Additional information regarding linguistic and reasoning skill may be obtained by analyzing a student's performance on the Oral Language and Fluid Reasoning tests of the WJ-R COG.

Another major stumbling block to successful problem solving is the ability to select the appropriate operation (Zweng, 1979). When attempting to complete an item on the Applied Problems test, a student may ask the examiner: "Do I add, subtract, multiply, or divide?" Zweng noted that textbooks provide students with very little guidance on how to choose the correct operation. Subsequently, many teachers do not demonstrate or help children develop a language for problem solving. For example, when asked, "Why did you divide to solve that problem?" few students are able to explain that they needed to split the total number into equal parts.

Another factor that contributes to the conceptual and linguistic complexity of word problems is the use of extraneous information. The ability to eliminate extraneous information in word problems is a serious problem for many students (Cawley, 1985; Cawley, Miller, & School, 1987). In performing an error analysis, an examiner may note that a student has difficulty with the Applied Problems items that include extraneous information.

Additional Assessment of Problem-Solving Skills

An important aspect in assessing math problem solving is to determine the specific factors contributing to a

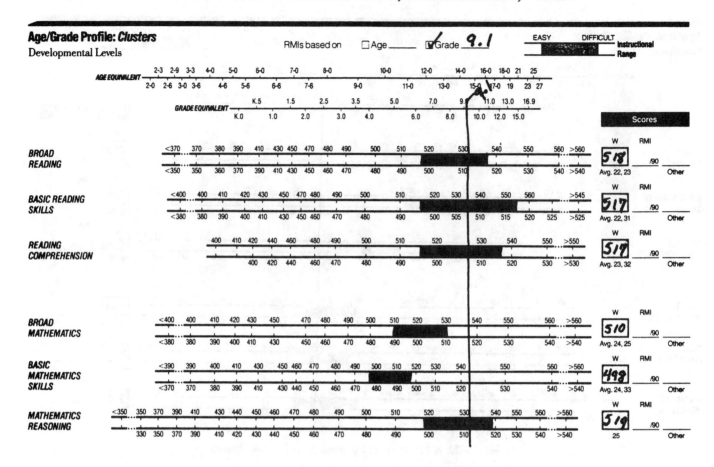

Figure 6–21. A Ninth-Grade Student on the Age/Grade Profile.

student's difficulty. In some cases, a more extensive evaluation may be needed. Based upon an initial analysis of an individual's performance on the Applied Problems test, an examiner will gain insight into the type of additional assessment that is needed.

Scope and Sequence Charts

Scope and sequence charts provide a hierarchical order for assessing and instructing basic math skills. Skills are identified for a particular area and then ordered by level of difficulty. District or school curriculum guides often include skills and competencies listed by grade level. Teacher's manuals in math textbooks also list skills for various grade levels.

When an examiner notes that a student has difficulty solving certain types of problems, a more in-depth informal assessment using an appropriate scope and sequence chart may be conducted. For example, the examiner noted that Miriam, a sixth-grade student, had difficulty on items that involve identifying coins and performing calculations with money. Subsequently, using

informal assessment, the examiner determined exactly what Miriam knows and what she needs to learn about money.

Diagnostic Approach

To analyze difficulty in problem solving in the classroom further, an examiner may wish to ask the student to solve several sample problems from the math textbook. If the student is unable to solve the problems, the examiner should attempt to determine the reason for the difficulty. To determine the level of problem-solving skill, an examiner may create simpler problems or select additional problems from a lower-grade textbook. The process continues until the examiner determines the level of student success.

Dimensions. An examiner may also present the student with a series of word problems that progress in difficulty on several dimensions. This analysis helps determine the type of problems that a student is able to solve independently. The dimensions may include: (a) number of steps, (b) reading level, (c) vocabulary level, (d) linguistic complexity, and (e) type of operation(s). The difficulty of possible problems ranges from simple one-step problems requiring addition and minimal reading to multistep problems that include extraneous information and require several different operations.

Steps. Enright (1987) described a thorough diagnostic approach for problem solving that includes five necessary procedural steps. The examiner attempts to determine whether the student: (a) reads and understands the problem, (b) organizes the information and facts, (c) determines the correct operation, (d) computes the answer, and (e) evaluates the answer. The goal is to identify the particular step(s) that are causing difficulty by establishing the point where the error began. Using a series of graded textbooks, the examiner prepares two items per skill in worksheet form. Instruction begins at the grade level of the first skill at which a student was unsuccessful. For example, if a student makes mistakes in the first step, understanding what is being asked for, remedial efforts are directed to reading and comprehension skills. If the student makes mistakes in the fourth step, computing the answer, then remedial efforts are directed toward computational skills.

Quantitative Vocabulary

As noted in the discussion of basic skills, some students may not have mastered necessary quantitative vocabulary. Limited vocabulary may also affect problem solving. For example, when presented with the word *earn* in a story problem, the student needs to know that the word implies an increase. An examiner may wish to list important vocabulary from a student's math textbook and then determine which words are known and which words need to be taught or reviewed.

Instructional Modifications

> If problem solving is truly the goal, obstacles to problem solving must be removed. A child who cannot solve problems because he or she cannot read the problems is not involved in problem solving, but is involved in reading.
>
> (Cawley & Miller, 1986, p. 47)

An examiner may wish to recommend several different types of modifications for a student who is having difficulty with math problem solving. The selected modifications should allow the student to engage successfully in problem-solving activities.

Reduce Number of Problems

One basic modification is to reduce the number of problems a student completes on a daily basis. A student may receive one or two word problems a day. This will allow an instructor and student to devote more time to discussing how solutions were obtained (Bley & Thornton, 1981).

Modify Level of Difficulty

As with any instructional material, the level of problem difficulty should match the instructional level of the learner. After analyzing a student's performance on the Applied Problems test and other tests of the WJ-R, an examiner may recommend that the word problems presented to the student in the classroom be controlled for: (a) reading level, (b) computational requirements, or (c) linguistic and conceptual demands. Often a lower level math textbook is not an appropriate solution as some aspects of the word problems are still too difficult, whereas other aspects are too easy. In selecting word problems for two different students, a teacher may present one student with problems that have a fourth-grade reading level, include extraneous information, but require simple computations. The other student may receive problems that are written at a second-grade level, without extraneous information, and require more advanced computations.

Even when the reading level and required computational skills are adjusted to a student's performance level, some students still have trouble solving story word problems. In addition to modifying reading level and computational skill, the complexity of the story problems or the clarity of the relationships should correspond to the student's general level of reasoning ability and language proficiency. If the goal of an activity is problem solving, then obstacles to problem solving must be removed (Cawley & Miller, 1986). Several strategies exist for modifying the difficulty level of word problems.

Rewrite Word Problems

One technique for controlling the difficulty level of word problems is to rewrite them. Word problems may be simplified by: (a) eliminating extraneous information, (b) controlling the vocabulary and sentence length, (c) drawing pictures and diagrams to illustrate the problems, (d) simplifying the required computations, or (e) reordering the numbers in the problem.

More skilled students may rewrite the problems in a math textbook for students with lower reading or computational skills. Cohen and Stover (1981) asked gifted students to rewrite story problems for less-skilled students. The gifted students altered the problems by simplifying the vocabulary, shortening sentence length, drawing diagrams, and eliminating extraneous information. Paraphrasing and rewriting word problems may also increase the skill of the writers. When students in regular sixth-grade classes were taught how to simplify story problems, they significantly outperformed the control group on a posttest of word problems.

Analyze and classify dimensions. As a teacher or students develop and create supplemental word problems, the problems may be analyzed and divided into sets. Problems may be classified along several different dimensions, such as: sentence structure and syntactical complexity, computational complexity, reading level, and the use of extraneous information (Cawley, Fitzmaurice, Shaw, Kahn, & Bates, 1979b; Fleischner & O'Loughlin, 1985). Problems may then be sorted and filed on index cards. Identifying the difficulty level across several dimensions allows a teacher to select from a variety of problems to meet individual needs.

Alter Instructional Sequence

For some students, the examiner will wish to recommend that the sequence of information presented in the math textbook be altered (Masters & Mori, 1986). For example, the examiner may determine that a student needs to review money concepts. Or, the instructor may wish to document a specific level of mastery before a student progresses to the next section in a text. Additionally, homework assignments may be selected that provide review by assigning a few problems from several different pages in previous chapters (Bley & Thornton, 1981).

Color-Coding

Story problems may also be modified and simplified through the use of color. Bley and Thornton (1981) recommended color-coding the sequence of steps in a problem. The first step is coded green and the last step is coded red. The color is phased out as the student begins to demonstrate proficiency. Although this type of modification may help a student sequence the steps, the main goals are to encourage the student to attend to the language of the problem and develop independence in problem solving. As skill develops, a student may be asked to color code the steps in a problem after reading the problem.

Color may also be used to draw attention to the necessary information. For example, a student may color the essential details green and mark out the extraneous information with red before completing a problem.

Calculators

Students with computational difficulty should use calculators for all problem-solving activities. In discussing the use of calculators in applied mathematics and verbal problem solving, Teitelbaum (1978) stated that a calculator relieves students of the tedious computational factor in the problem, allowing them to concentrate on how the problem is solved. When an examiner observes that a student has difficulty performing calculations, provision of a calculator for all problem-solving activities is an appropriate recommendation.

Instructional Strategies for Mathematics Reasoning

An examiner may recommend several different types of instructional strategies and procedures to assist a student who has difficulty in problem solving. For students with learning disabilities in mathematics, factors such as age, interests, level of ability, and present level of functioning serve to guide the selection of appropriate materials (Cawley, 1984).

General Guidelines

Several guidelines apply for developing appropriate student activities. In general, students should be provided with exercises that help them to see that mathematical patterns are logical and predictable. These activities should be meaningful and promote active student involvement.

In discussing the teaching and learning of mathematics, Greenwood and Anderson (1983) provided several principles for promoting growth in problem solving. These procedures focus on both the operational domain (basic skills and algorithms) and the conceptual domain (comprehension of the activity). Students need command of basic skills as well as ability to identify problem-solving strategies and relate them to a situation. Examples of teaching techniques that address proficiency in both skills and concepts include:

1. Provide an environment that encourages communication among students.
2. Require demonstration of conceptual understanding before requiring computational proficiency.
3. Recognize that computational proficiency includes both speed and accuracy and try to help learners attain a balance between these two features.
4. Emphasize students' ability to note patterns and relationships.
5. Value novel ways of approaching problems and provide opportunities for students to share their ideas.

Do:

1. Begin problem solving the day a child enters school.

2. Make problem solving the reason for computation.

3. Develop long-term programs of problem solving.

4. Conduct problem solving as a multimodal activity.

5. Partial out the effects of one variable on another. If the child cannot read the problem, rewrite it. If the computation is too complex, make it simpler.

6. Have children prepare or modify problems.

7. Differentiate between process and knowledge.

8. Prepare problems in such a way that children must act upon the information. Prepare a set of problems in which all problems have the same question.

9. Present problems dealing with familiar subject matter.

10. Constantly monitor progress and modify problems to fit the child's weaknesses and progress.

Don't:

1. Use cue words to signal an operation.

2. Teach children to use computational rules to solve problems. That is, do not tell children to add when they see three different numbers.

3. Use problem-solving activities as an occasional wrap-up to computation.

4. Mark a child wrong if he/she makes a computational error in problem solving if the operation is correct.

5. Train teachers to treat problem solving as secondary to computation.

6. Assume that because the child is able to perform an arithmetic operation that he/she can automatically solve problems that use that operation.

7. Conclude that an incorrect answer automatically indicates lack of facility in problem solving.

8. Fail to realize that problem solving is the most important aspect of mathematics for daily living.

9. Fail to seize the opportunities for training in problem solving in conjunction with other subject areas.

10. Present problem solving in a haphazard manner. Order and careful planning are essential.

Figure 6–22. Do's and Don'ts of Problem Solving. *Note.* From "A Brief Inquiry of Arithmetic Word-Problem-Solving Among Learning Disabled Secondary Students" by J.F. Cawley, J.H. Miller, and B.A. School, 1987, *Learning Disabilities Focus, 2,* pp. 91–92. Copyright 1987 by the Division of Learning Disabilities. Reprinted by permission.

6. Encourage students to assess the progress of their own learning. Promote self-diagnostic, self-evaluative, and self-awareness procedures for the purpose of identifying what skills have been mastered and which need to be strengthened and knowing what is understood and what is not.

Application of these principles and joint development of the operational and conceptual domains will help students become effective problem solvers.

Cawley, Miller, and School (1987) outlined several Do's and Don'ts for teaching problem solving to students with learning disabilities. These general principles are presented in Figure 6-22.

Teaching cue words. Cue or key words are words in a story problem that suggest the operation that should be performed. For example, the cue word *altogether*, suggests that the necessary operation is addition, whereas the cue word *remaining*, signals subtraction. Controversy exists regarding whether or not students should be directly taught to attend to cue words for problem solving. Thornton and Bley (1982) suggested that although the teacher

must be careful that a student does not become dependent on them, initially focusing on key words may help children with language deficits break through a learning barrier.

Others feel that because cue words are not useful in most practical situations and are only applicable to one-step problems, they should not be taught. Reliance on cue words does not help students think about the language of the problem or analyze the problem in any detail. The use of cue words encourages the student to remove the data without considering the context of the problem.

Unfortunately, the word problems in many school textbooks may be solved correctly by relying on cue words to select the appropriate operation. Some math programs even encourage children to color or underline any cue or key words before solving a problem. In discussing this type of procedure, Cawley and Miller (1986) stated:

> The extent to which this practice has dele-
> terious effects on the learning disabled has
> yet to be determined. However, if the meta-
> cognitive acts of planning, monitoring, and
> checking are integral to meaningful problem

solving, programs of this type appear det-
rimental because they teach the individual to
by-pass the information set, to ignore the
processes of analysis and interpretation, and
to circumvent the metacognitive sequence.
(p. 37)

Mathematics instruction should be based upon promoting
linguistic and conceptual understanding.

Story Problem Activities

The intent of practice activities in problem-solving
skills is not to teach students how to solve different types
of word problems commonly found in math textbooks but
rather to help students develop the language and thinking
skills needed for solving practical problems. A variety of
activities are appropriate, to assist students in solving story
problems. Examples include:

1. Help students develop mental images while they solve
story problems. This is accomplished by having students draw pictures to illustrate the message (Dunlap,
1982).
2. Alternate the order of problem-solving activities. Present solved problems and have students discuss the
steps. Present the steps in random order and have the
students arrange them in correct order (Thornton &
Bley, 1982). Younger students may be given pictures
to rearrange in the correct order or students may be
asked to devise word problems for given answers
(Bley & Thornton, 1981).
3. Create high-interest story problems. Capitalize on the
student's language and experiences.
4. Help students develop a language for problem solving.
In addition to teaching specific quantitative vocabulary, have children answer operation-related questions
(Zweng, 1979). Students need to be able to explain the
reason that they decided to add, subtract, multiply or
divide in specific story problems.
5. Do not limit problem-solving experience to paper-
pencil activities. Incorporate problem solving into
daily experiences.
6. Ensure that the reading level, the required computations, and/or the conceptual demands are not too
difficult for the student. Have the student restate
problems in their own words (Bley & Thornton, 1981).
7. Encourage instructor/student interaction.

Cawley (1984) described an interactive methodology,
designed to elicit oral responses from students, that contains four different combinations of interactions between
the instructor and learners: (a) manipulate-state, the teacher moves manipulatives and asks the students to explain
what has been done; (b) display-state, the students describe a visual display, such as a graph; (c) state-state, the
teacher gives a definition and asks the students to restate

it in their own words; and (d) write-state, the teacher writes
a symbol and asks the students to name it. By responding
orally to a variety of situations, the instructor provides
immediate feedback, and students are able to improve
their conceptual understanding.

Provision of many different types of problem-solving
activities will help students learn how to determine the
necessary information and the correct operation. Several
language-oriented techniques may be used to facilitate
verbal problem solving.

Story problems and language experience. A modified
language experience approach may be used to introduce or
help students understand story problems. Dunlap (1982)
suggested several activities progressing from concrete to
abstract that may be used with any process with students
at any grade level. These activities begin with parts of
story problems and have the student create a whole
problem. The following sequence may be used:

1. Concrete objects: Provide concrete objects and ask
students to manipulate them to illustrate a story problem.
2. Pictures: Provide two pictures and ask students to
create a story problem about the objects in the pictures.
3. Numbers: Provide two numbers and ask students to
write a story problem.
4. Number sentence: Write a number sentence on the
chalkboard and ask students to create story problems.

Dunlap suggested other activities that begin with story
problems and then have students interpret the parts.
Examples include:

1. Story to pictures: Read the story problem and demonstrate the message by drawing a picture.
2. Story to numbers: Identify the relevant numbers in a
problem or give problems without numbers and have
the students supply the numbers.
3. Story to question: Identify the central question in the
problem or give the story problem without a question
and have the students write the question.
4. Story to operation: Read the story and decide what
operation to perform.

Gradually, these steps may be integrated into solving
story problems by having the student: (a) read the problem, (b) paraphrase the problem, (c) draw a picture to
illustrate the message, (d) select the relevant numbers, (e)
identify the question, (f) select the operation, and (g) write
the number sentence (Dunlap, 1982).

Maze procedure. With the maze technique, the student
is provided with a choice of numbers or words and then
must select the correct answer. This technique may be
used to practice estimation skills (the student circles the
answer that looks the most reasonable) or to build math

```
Sally bought two apples.
                   bought
That afternoon she ate       three apples.
                   saw
Now she has five apples.


John has six tennis balls.
                              three
While playing in the park, he lost two     balls.
                              five
Now he just has one tennis ball.
```

Figure 6–23. Maze Procedure for Problem Solving.

```
Betsy bought six postcard stamps.
That afternoon she _____ two more.
Then she mailed eight postcards.

Marcos had twenty football cards.
He traded _____ of his cards for one of Sam's.
Marcos now has sixteen football cards.

Sid had fifteen balloons that he split among
_____ children.  Each child received
three balloons.
```

Figure 6–24. Cloze Procedure for Problem Solving.

vocabulary skills (the student selects the word with the most appropriate meaning). Figure 6-23 illustrates several different examples of using the maze technique for math problem solving.

Cloze procedure. With the cloze procedure the student must fill in a blank with either a word or a specific number. The cloze procedure may help direct a learner's attention to specified components of the information in a problem (Cawley, Fitzmaurice, Shaw, Kahn, & Bates, 1979a). Figure 6-24 illustrates several different examples of the cloze technique for math problem solving.

Problem solving with literature. As an alternative to math textbook problems, a teacher and students may create their own story problems. Cawley (1985) suggested using the knowledge base contained in the classroom reading program for building problem-solving experiences. Once students have read and discussed a story, the teacher builds sets of problem solving activities by adding numbers to the story content. This type of approach helps integrate reading and math activities. Students also see how numeric information is incorporated into meaningful contexts. Or, an instructor may use a workbook with interesting problems. For example, Kennedy and Thomas (1979) created a book of modern math story problems that illustrate the use of interesting tales.

After reviewing the literature on the history of story problems, McGinty and Van Beynen (1982) concluded that story problems should contain a real story and be much more interesting than those typically found in math textbooks. In discussing the need to revitalize the story problem, they cite a quotation from Weeks (1924):

> If problems could be restored to their pristine purity and beauty, it might still be possible to save Arithmetic, the Queen of Sciences. Problems should be so real as to fascinate a Boy. Every problem, without exception, should tell a story, and the story should often be of a sort to tempt the Boy to draw a picture or a map of it. To do so will prevent the Boy from falling asleep, and the contemplation of his drawings may keep the Teacher awake. Arithmetic might thus be transformed into the spring-board of the intelligence, allowing the happy Boy to develop fully the muscles of his imagination, for without imagination a Boy is nothing. Let the words *problem* and *story* come to mean as far as possible one and the same thing. (p. 310)

They suggested that teachers and students create story problems that are exciting and informative. This may be accomplished by having students develop a storybook set of their own word problems. To create high-interest problems, students may invent story problems as a creative writing assignment. If a student has difficulty including quantitative values in a story, the teacher first may have the student write the story and then help the student incorporate numeric information. The student, teacher, or peer may create several questions for the same story that require the reader to manipulate the presented data in several different ways.

Math journals. Burns (1988) suggested the use of math journals to help elementary students improve their understanding of verbal problems. Children work on the journals in small cooperative learning groups. The teacher presents a problem to solve, and the students study, discuss, and complete the problem. After the problem is completed, the students write a paragraph explaining how they obtained the solution. In addition to developing math skill, this approach integrates reading and writing activities into the math curriculum. The use of math journals may be particularly beneficial for students who have strengths in written expression but difficulty in math problem solving.

Story Problem Strategies

An examiner may recommend several different strategies that provide students with a step-by-step process or procedure for solving story problems. Bley and Thornton

(1981) summarized the following steps that are presented in many mathematics textbooks:

1. Read the problem.
2. Picture what is happening.
3. Think: What's the question?
4. What must you do to solve it (add, subtract . . .)?
5. Compute the answer.
6. Check. Is the answer reasonable?

In working with students with learning disabilities, Bley and Thornton recommended that after the students picture what is happening, they use objects or draw pictures to illustrate the problem. They continue through Step 4, and then the papers are checked. The computation is then completed, and the final answer is checked.

Fleischner, Nuzum, and Marzola (1987) reviewed the literature and determined that for successful problem solving students need information on how to identify the question, determine what information is needed to solve a problem, recognize unnecessary information, and know which mathematical operation is needed. They designed and evaluated the effects of an instructional program to teach fifth- and sixth-grade students with learning disabilities how to solve four kinds of story problems. The four problem types included: addition, subtraction, two-step problems, and problems with extraneous information. All students had adequate reading and computational skills, but lacked the procedural knowledge necessary to solve problems.

Students learned a sequence of steps to follow. For example, to help students discriminate between addition and subtraction problems, students circled the largest number in the problem and wrote it down. They then asked themselves, according to the action in the problem, what will happen to the largest number: Will it get larger or smaller? If the number becomes larger, I add. If the number becomes smaller, I subtract. Students were asked to highlight the question, and write down the label for the answer, such as inches, miles, etc.

Students were taught to master the procedures or strategies following the sequence outlined on prompt cards. The final prompt card included the following steps:

READ	What is the question?
REREAD	What is the necessary information?
THINK	Putting together? = Add
	Taking apart? = Subtract
SOLVE	Write the equation
CHECK	Recalculate
	Label
	Compare

In the final step, students used calculators to solve and check their problems.

Instruction was conducted for 30-minute segments twice a week for a 6-week period. Results from the study indicated that the experimental group, who received this direct instruction in problem solving, had more correct answers on story problems than the control group.

Similarly, Montague and Bos (1986) found that use of an eight-step cognitive strategy improved the verbal math problem-solving performance of secondary students with learning disabilities. The strategy combined the use of modeling, corrective feedback, verbal rehearsal, and self-questioning. The eight steps included:

1. Read the problem aloud and ask the teacher to explain any unknown words.
2. Paraphrase the problem aloud by stating the important information.
3. Visualize the information and draw a representation of the problem.
4. State the problem and underline the important information.
5. Hypothesize the number of steps and write the necessary operation signs.
6. Estimate an answer.
7. Show the calculation and circle the answer.
8. Check every step to ensure accuracy.

Montague and Bos noted that as testing progressed, students modified different strategy steps to meet their individual needs. In designing an individualized program, the examiner, teacher, or student may determine that certain steps of a strategy should be added, modified, or deleted.

Results from these two studies suggest that students who experience difficulty in solving story problems will benefit from explicit strategy instruction. As with methods in reading comprehension, the purpose of these approaches is to provide students with a structure that will increase success and independent learning. Students become successful when they are able to identify, organize, and sequence the necessary steps to solve meaningful problems.

Life-Skill Mathematics

For some low-functioning and severely learning disabled students at the secondary level, it is necessary to shift the emphasis from basic skill instruction to life-skill mathematics. This decision is made on an individual basis, based upon the student's abilities and progress in the math curriculum (McLeod & Armstrong, 1982). In making this recommendation, the examiner may also want to consider the individual's career goals.

Peterson (1973) identified several important skills for students to master if they are to develop functional use of mathematics. These functional skills include: (a) business and money-based vocabulary; (b) number symbols; (c) common measurement instruments, such as clocks, calendars, and thermometers; (d) liquid and dry measures for cooking; (e) map skills; and (f) financial concepts, such as credit cards and finance charges.

When administering the Applied Problems test to Katherine, a secondary student, the examiner observed that she had developed minimal skill in practical applications. For example, Katherine made mistakes adding together sets of coins that were under $1.00 in value. As a result of the assessment, the examiner recommended that Katherine participate in a program that would provide a functional mathematics curriculum and emphasize the application of mathematics to daily living.

Conclusion

Analysis of a student's performance on the WJ-R ACH Applied Problems test will help an examiner identify areas of need and determine whether or not additional assessments are necessary. Careful diagnosis that includes substantiation of both strengths and weaknesses will help an examiner design an appropriate individualized plan for enhancing problem-solving skill. The most important aspect of successful mathematics performance is the ability to apply mathematical processes to real-life, everyday problems. Fortunately, greater emphasis has been devoted to problem solving in the mathematics curriculum, and its presence will likely increase (Cawley & Miller, 1986). Problem solving is a way of teaching mathematics with the goals of helping students improve their conceptual understanding and quantitative thinking and become active, independent learners.

7

COGNITIVE ABILITIES: IMPLICATIONS FOR ACHIEVEMENT

Intellectual assessment within instructional settings has two main purposes: (a) to identify an individual's strengths and weaknesses within cognitive or intellectual areas and (b) to estimate the student's expected school achievement. Examining a student's performance on the WJ-R COG will assist an examiner with both identification of specific strengths and weaknesses and estimation of expected school achievement.

This chapter discusses the relationship between performance on the WJ-R COG and performance in an instructional setting by considering the potential impact that a deficiency in one or more of these cognitive factors may have upon academic performance. A brief description of the factors and examples of research related to each cognitive factor are included. Samples of educational recommendations that may be appropriate for individuals who have weaknesses in one or more areas, including oral language and attention, are presented. Additionally, the use of the WJ-R COG for predicting school achievement is discussed.

Considerable controversy exists in the field of learning disabilities and cognitive psychology regarding the relationship between cognitive factors or underlying mental processes and academic performance. In the past, direct perceptual or psycholinguistic training has failed to improve students' achievement. Consequently, this approach to identifying and directly remediating dysfunctions in psychological processes has been under attack and, in most instances, abandoned. The central problem of the process training approach was that the learning process was separated from the specific learning task and viewed as a discrete mental ability that could be trained in isolation. A more effective approach is to consider the interactive nature of cognitive processes, academic achievement, and affective and environmental variables. In general, cognitive abilities are seen as changeable and dynamic; that is, performance may alter through learning and experience.

Increasing evidence suggests that disruptions in certain psychological or cognitive processes may exert a causal influence on a student's learning ability. The extent of the influence will vary depending upon the learner's characteristics and the environmental setting, including the teacher, tasks, and instructional methods that are employed. Learning problems are addressed in the context of the interaction between the student and the environment.

The intent of discussing the cognitive factors and hypothesizing how they relate to achievement is not to encourage the remediation of underlying processes as discrete, isolated entities. Instead, identification of strengths and weaknesses in various cognitive abilities may help an examiner determine why a student is having difficulty and decide how to teach that student. Discussion of related research is presented to help clarify the potential impact a cognitive dysfunction may have upon academic performance.

The general recommendations provided for each cognitive factor are suggestions for an examiner to consider when a weakness is noted in a cognitive function and a problem is observed in an academic setting. These suggestions are based upon an integration of research results and clinical experience. Any recommendations made by an examiner should be tailored to an individual. In defining program modifications, an attempt should be made to explain why, when, and how a modification is made and who is responsible for implementation. The goal is to make appropriate program adjustments that will promote a student's educational achievement and success. In summary, although the relationship between cognitive abilities and achievement is at present a relatively uncharted region, the intent of this chapter is to explore how various strengths and weaknesses in cognitive abilities may influence an individual's ability to perform academic tasks.

Cognitive Factors

Can we reasonably suppose that all this utterly heterogeneous multitude of tendencies will by the most extraordinary chances sum up into anything that is in the slightest degree orderly?

(Spearman, 1927, p. 339)

The WJ-R COG Standard and Supplemental batteries contain tests that measure seven broad intellectual abilities: Long-Term Retrieval (Glr), Short-Term Memory (Gsm), Processing Speed (Gs), Auditory Processing (Ga), Visual Processing (Gv), Comprehension-Knowledge (Gc), and Fluid Reasoning (Gf). An eighth factor, Quantitative Ability (Gq), is measured by the Broad Mathematics cluster in the WJ-R ACH. These factors, defined in Chapter 2, are based upon the *Gf-Gc* theory of intellectual processing (Cattell, 1963; Horn, 1985, 1986; Horn & Cattell, 1966). This theory provides a data-based theoretical foundation for psychoeducational assessment.

Level of Processing

The *Gf-Gc* theory of intellectual processing provides a hierarchy of developmental functions. Figure 7-1 presents an adapted model of the eight WJ-R factors as they relate to the theory. In this model, the abilities at the bottom of the figure have low correlations with the abilities at the top of the figure (Horn, 1985).

Some students will have more difficulty with tests that involve lower level processing than on tests that involve higher level processing. Other students will have well-established lower level skills, but difficulty on the tests that involve higher level processing. Additionally, severe problems with the lower level perceptual skills may affect performance in the higher order cognitive processes.

Long-Term Retrieval

The Long-Term Retrieval factor is composed of Test 1: Memory for Names and Test 8: Visual Auditory Learning.

Supplemental information may be obtained by examining performance on Tests 15 and 16, the two Delayed Recall tests.

In some instances, an examiner may observe differences in a student's performance on these two tests. For a student with good oral language, the increased context in Visual-Auditory Learning may facilitate performance. For a student with a language impairment, the added context may hinder performance. Each of these tests requires a different response mode: In Memory for Names, the student hears and then points to the space creatures, an auditory-visual association task; in Visual-Auditory Learning, the student looks at and then orally identifies the symbols, a visual-auditory association task.

A student who performs poorly on the long-term retrieval tests may have difficulty with paired-associate tasks, such as learning the names of the letters of the alphabet or memorizing the times tables. Analysis of performance on the two Delayed Recall Tests may further substantiate this type of difficulty in recall. Figure 7-2 illustrates the Age/Grade Profile for Chuck, a fourth-grade student (4.9), on the four Long-Term Retrieval tests. Initially, Chuck's performance was significantly higher on the Visual-Auditory Learning test than on Memory for Names test. Upon retesting several days later, Chuck had extreme difficulty with both delayed recall tasks. In the classroom, Chuck was having difficulty with reading decoding, spelling, and memorization of math facts.

Related Research

The long-term retrieval tests, in contrast to the short-term memory tests require the student to store and retrieve symbol names over a period of time. The student must hold information in memory, while attending to new information. Some students with learning disabilities have difficulty with tasks similar to the Memory for Names and Visual-Auditory Learning tests that require the linking of verbal labels with visual information. Results from several studies have indicated that skilled readers retain verbally coded information better than learning disabled readers.

For example, Swanson (1986) attempted to determine if a failure to connect verbal and visual information was related to storage and/or retrieval operations. He compared the performance of skilled readers and learning disabled readers on different tasks involving viewing nonsense pictures with or without two types of names: names that emphasized the semantic aspect of the picture or names that were not associated with the picture. The results indicated that skilled readers were superior to disabled readers on tasks that involved pairing a picture with an associated name. Additionally, the name-associated labels increased memory for visual forms in the skilled readers but not in the disabled readers.

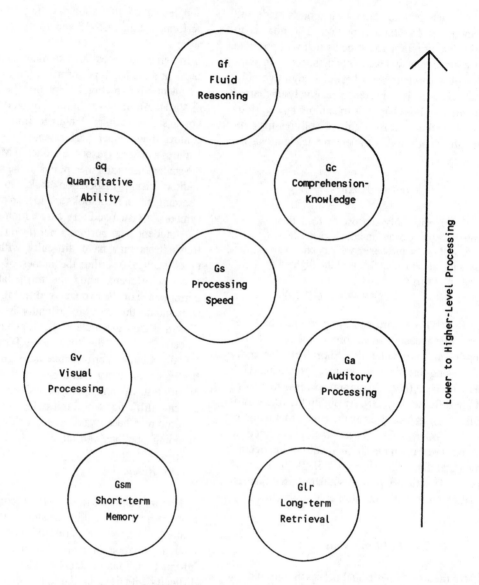

Figure 7–1. *Gf-Gc* Theory and the WJ-R Factors.

Swanson (1982) also found that naming of unfamiliar shapes enhanced recall for normal and deaf children but not for learning disabled students. These findings were interpreted as suggesting that some students with learning disabilities may have certain structural limitations in linguistic coding that may account for or contribute to their visual retrieval problems. Swanson (1983) hypothesized that because some learning disabled children have trouble relating visual stimuli with verbal codes, they tend to rely on nonverbal strategies for recall. He concluded that implicit linguistic coding (naming) differentiates normal from disabled readers on visual serial recall tasks.

Using meta-analysis, Kavale (1982) integrated the results from 161 studies that explored the relationship between visual perceptual skills and reading achievement. Results indicated that tasks involving visual-auditory

integration, the ability to match serially presented visual stimuli with auditory counterparts, were significantly correlated with reading achievement. Further research is needed to clarify the relationship between the WJ-R COG Long-Term Retrieval tests and academic performance.

Recommendations

To assist a student in tasks that require the formation and recall of associations, several recommendations based upon learning principles may be appropriate. Examples include:

1. Sequence materials from simple to more complex.
2. Provide intensive review, repetition, and overlearning at each step.

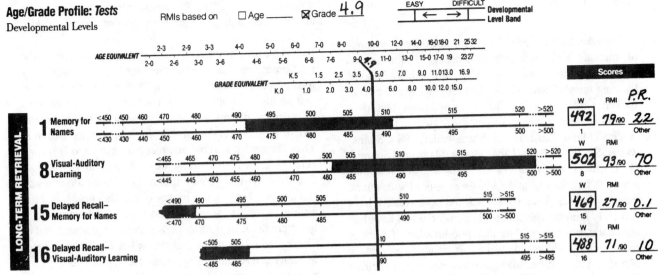

Age/Grade Profile: *Tests*
Developmental Levels

RMIs based on ☐ Age ____ ☒ Grade 4.9

Figure 7–2. Age/Grade Profile for a Fourth-Grade Student on the Long-Term Retrieval Tests.

3. Introduce only as many facts, words, etc., as the student is able to learn in a session.

4. Provide frequent opportunities for practice and review. Provide systematic review within a few hours of learning and review previous information in each lesson.

5. Integrate acquired knowledge with new knowledge whenever possible.

6. Provide the student with mnemonic aids or strategies for retention, such as the use of verbal mediation or rehearsal (saying the information to be remembered while looking at it).

7. Provide multisensory learning. Involve visual, kinesthetic, vocal, and auditory channels when appropriate. For example, have the student repeat step-by-step directions while he or she performs the task.

8. Provide immediate feedback of results. This may be accomplished with small group instruction, programmed learning materials, or a microcomputer.

9. Provide the student with a list of steps that will help organize behavior and, subsequently, facilitate recall.

10. Ensure conceptual understanding of any tasks that require operational efficiency, such as multiplication facts.

Short-Term Memory

Some students have weaknesses in short-term memory or the ability to recall and use information within a short period of time. The two primary measures of Short-Term Memory are Test 2: Memory for Sentences and Test 9: Memory for Words. Test 17: Numbers Reversed may be used as a supplemental measure of short-term memory.

The Memory for Sentences test measures short-term memory of sentences. For most students, short-term memory is enhanced in a meaningful, language-based context. In contrast, the Memory for Words test measures short-term memory for repeating unrelated words and has limited context. In some instances, an examiner may note performance differences on these two measures because of the types of tasks. For example, a student with average oral language skills, but low short-term memory, may have increased difficulty with the Memory for Words test. The examiner may also observe that the student has difficulty on the Numbers Reversed test. In contrast, a student with a language impairment may have more difficulty with the Memory for Sentences test than the Memory for Words test.

In addition to low performance on the short-term memory tests, a student with poor short-term memory may have trouble with other WJ-R COG tests that contain lengthy auditory instructions. Students with low short-term memory often experience difficulty in following oral directions. During testing, an examiner may note that the student asks for repetitions of information or has difficulty understanding the initial test directions. In an instructional setting, this type of student may become totally confused when the teacher states: "Open your books to page 52. Do problems 1 through 25. When you complete that assignment, turn in your worksheet and begin your Science unit."

The examiner may also observe that the student does not enjoy tests that require listening, such as Memory for Sentences, Incomplete Words, Memory for Words, Sound Blending, Numbers Reversed, and Listening Comprehension. For example, during an evaluation, Roger, a fifth-grade student, commented during the Memory for Sentences test: "I really hate to have to listen to things."

Related Research

Considerable research exists regarding the performance of students with and without learning disabilities on short-term memory tasks. Many students with reading and learning disabilities exhibit difficulty in the recall of spoken verbal materials. Research indicates that poor readers are less accurate in repeating sentences than good readers (Mann, Liberman, & Shankweiler, 1980; Shankweiler, Smith, & Mann, 1984). Brady, Mann, and Schmidt (1987) found that poor readers were less accurate than good readers on repeating four-item lists of consonant-vowel syllables. They concluded that poor readers have difficulty with the recall of spoken material and have less automatic, phonetic coding than good readers. This poor recall then contributes to reduced efficiency in processing phonetic information. Mann, Cowin, and Schoenheimer (1989) found that poor readers had difficulty holding spoken word strings in memory and, subsequently, experienced increased difficulty with sentence comprehension. They recommended that long sentences with complex clauses be avoided when giving instructions to poor readers.

Torgesen (1988) reviewed the results from several studies investigating short-term memory deficits. The research reviewed took place over a period of 4 years and involved studies of three different groups of learning disabled children with extreme memory span difficulties. This small subgroup of students with learning disabilities had general intellectual ability in the average range, but performed in the retarded range on tasks that required the immediate recall of sequences of items, such as digits, numbers, words, or letters. This type of student appeared to have difficulty in using phonological codes to store information in memory. In contrast, the students did not have difficulty on tasks that required them to retain visual figures that were difficult to label verbally. The WJ-R COG Picture Recognition Test would be an example of a task with visual figures that are difficult to mediate verbally.

Word identification. In regard to academic performance, the primary impact of a deficiency in short-term memory was upon acquisition of fluent word identification. The students with learning disabilities had difficulty in the rapid and accurate pronunciation of individual words. In contrast, the deficiency did not appear to affect comprehension of oral language or mathematics performance. Although their skills in mathematics were below grade level when compared to nondisabled students, the learning disabled students' math skills were not deficient when compared to other students with similar disabilities. Torgesen hypothesized that increased awareness of pho-

nological structure through intensive training in phonemic analysis may help these students develop decoding skill.

Early reading prediction. Research results support the relationship between verbal short-term memory and early reading performance. Mann and Liberman (1984) found that ability to retain a string of words and knowledge of the syllabic structure of spoken words were highly predictive of future reading problems for kindergarten children. They concluded that the adequacy of these two language skills is critical to reading development in first grade. Similarly, Badian (1988) found, in a longitudinal study that followed students from age 4 to eighth grade, that the ability to repeat increasingly complex sentences was a good predictor of reading performance at grades 3 and 8. These findings suggest that the WJ-R COG Short-Term Memory and Auditory Processing factors may be useful as part of a reading-readiness or kindergarten screening battery.

Spelling. Difficulty in short-term memory tasks may also influence spelling skill. Similar to younger spellers, students with learning disabilities have difficulty maintaining words in short-term memory long enough to encode the complete phonemic string (Gerber & Hall, 1987). Foster and Torgesen (1983) found that elementary learning disabled students with short-term memory deficits experienced severe and consistent problems in the acquisition of new spelling words. Even when words were studied using the same procedures as other children, the students' performance was still seriously impaired. In contrast, learning disabled students without short-term memory deficits profited from a directed study condition. These results suggest that learning disabled students with short-term memory deficits may require considerably more practice than their peers to acquire and retain spelling words.

Mathematics. Deficits in short-term memory may also influence development of computational skill. Webster (1979) examined the performance of mathematically proficient and mathematically disabled students on several types of memory-span tests, including digits and strings of nonrhyming consonants. The proficient students were at or above grade level on a math computation test. The disabled students were performing 2 or more years below grade level. Results indicated that the mathematically disabled students were significantly lower than proficient students on memory tests. These findings suggest that performance on memory-span tests is related to computational skill.

Prevalence. One important result of these studies is the estimate of prevalence of this subtype of disability: 15%

to 20% of school-identified learning disabled students in the fourth and fifth grades had this type of difficulty (Torgesen, 1988). Similarly, Speece (1987) found that 15% of 9- and 10-year-old children with reading disabilities had isolated difficulties on a digit span task. These findings suggest the existence of a subgroup of students with learning and reading disabilities who have poor performance on tasks that involve immediate verbatim recall of verbal information.

Hereditary component. A hereditary component may also exist. DeFries, Fulker, and LaBuda (1987) studied pairs of identical and fraternal twins in which at least one member of the pair was reading disabled. The heritability of reading, spelling, and related cognitive skills was tested. Results indicated that single-word reading, spelling, and verbal short-term memory, using a digit span test, were genetically influenced. In contrast, perceptual speed, motor speed, and reading comprehension were not. These findings indicate the importance of family history in identifying high-risk students for early intervention.

Adults. Deficits in short-term memory also persist in adults. In examining 80 young adults with learning disabilities, Blalock (1980) found that approximately one-third of the subjects had some kind of problem with auditory memory or memory span. The adults had trouble repeating series of digits and lists of unrelated words.

Recommendations

Several compensatory strategies may assist students with weaknesses in short-term memory. Recommendations may be provided to help students with: (a) following directions, (b) listening, and (c) reviewing materials.

Following directions. For students who have difficulty following oral directions, several modifications may be effective. Examples include:

1. Use short, simple sentences when speaking to the student. Be sure to keep verbal instructions at the student's vocabulary level.
2. Present one instruction at a time.
3. Stand near and look directly at the student when giving directions. If needed, place a hand on the student's arm or shoulder.
4. Ask the student to paraphrase instructions or to repeat the directions to the teacher before beginning an assignment.
5. Repeat directions as many times as necessary.
6. Write specific directions and assignments on the chalkboard for the student to copy.

7. Provide the student with assignments written on index cards.
8. Have a responsible peer record assignments for a student.
9. Have assignments on a tape recorder so the student can hit the pause button or replay the assignment as many times as needed.
10. Create an assignment notebook for the student to record all homework and test dates. In some cases, a parent or teacher will need to monitor the recording and completion of assignments.
11. Check frequently to ensure that the student understands the task.
12. Record key words on the board when giving assignments or group directions.

Listening. For students who have difficulty listening to orally presented material, several strategies may be recommended. Examples include:

1. Encourage the student to tape-record class lectures to be played back as soon as possible. The student should take notes while listening to the tape.
2. Provide practice for the student in retelling events or stories. For example, read the student a short story and ask the student to repeat the events in sequential order or to identify the major story components.
3. Use visual aids combined with verbal instruction whenever possible. For example, when giving directions or explaining terms, point to the area of the page or chalkboard that contains the relevant information. For many students, added visual, tactile, and contextual input enhances auditory recall ability. Write key terms on the board when giving oral directions.

Reviewing. Students with difficulty in short-term memory may need additional review of materials to aid retention. Examples of recommendations include:

1. Teach specific memory strategies and techniques that will improve immediate recall, such as the use of verbal rehearsal, grouping or chunking of information, making visual images, and mnemonics. The memory strategies should be taught within a context for which they may be used.
2. Teach specific learning or study strategies for each area of difficulty.
3. Ensure that the student continually reviews vocabulary words, math facts, or any information that requires extended practice for retention. Materials should be reviewed within hours of learning and then daily until mastery is insured.

4. Provide for overlearning by using intensive, systematic drill with index cards or with a microcomputer.

Processing Speed

The two primary measures of Processing Speed are Test 3: Visual Matching, which measures ability to identify matching numbers in a row of digits, and Test 10: Cross Out, which measures the ability to find five identical geometric drawings in a row. Additional information regarding Processing Speed may be obtained by administering Test 35: Writing Fluency in the WJ-R ACH.

Some students have trouble sustaining concentrated visual attention or working rapidly under timed conditions. This type of student may have difficulty with different types of tasks that require automatic processing. An examiner's observations may further substantiate a student's difficulty.

During testing, an examiner may note that a student attempts to cover up or block out other items while he or she is working. On the Visual Matching test, the student may become confused by the rows of numbers that contain reversible digits. Figure 7-3 illustrates the performance of Gary, a sixth-grade student, on the Visual Matching test. Gary missed several items that included reversible digits. When students have trouble with reversible digits, the difficulty may be more likely attributed to visual-processing or symbol-processing problems, rather than to problems in processing speed.

Related Research

Some evidence suggests that students with reading disabilities tend to score lower than controls on tasks that involve processing speed. Slow processing speed may also affect performance in mathematics.

Reading. Results from several research studies have demonstrated that some students with reading disabilities have symbolic processing deficits. As examples, Baker, Decker, and DeFries (1984) reported a difference in performance between reading disabled students and controls on symbol-processing speed measures. LaBuda and DeFries (1988) conducted a longitudinal study of children with and without reading disabilities who were administered a battery of tests three times over an average interval of 8.6 years. The tests measured three ability dimensions: reading, symbol-processing speed, and spatial reasoning. Although the students with reading disabilities showed deficits in all areas at each age, their rate of improvement in reading and spatial reasoning abilities was similar to the controls'. For symbol-processing speed, however, the difference between the two groups increased

with age. These results suggest that even though academic performance develops, some students may continue to have problems with the basic rapid processing of symbols into young adulthood. Decker and DeFries (1980) found that reading disabled children and their parents scored significantly lower than control families on tests of coding speed. The results demonstrate the persistence of symbol-processing deficits and also the familial nature of reading disability.

Arithmetic. Kirby and Becker (1988) found that students with learning problems in arithmetic were characterized by slow operation execution. Three groups of fifth-grade students were selected: a group with reading problems, a group with arithmetic problems, and a control group. The students with arithmetic problems had intelligence and reading scores within the average range. Operational efficiency was measured by performance on simple single-digit problems. Problems were presented on a microcomputer that recorded response time.

Although the student was required to perform simple computations, this type of task may be considered a measure of processing speed. Tasks of processing speed measure ability to perform relatively trivial tasks quickly. Prior to the study, the teachers concurred that all students in the samples would be able to solve all problems correctly. These results suggest that some students with learning problems in arithmetic are characterized by slow processing speed and/or lack of automaticity with facts. Although they may perform problems accurately, they do not perform simple computations quickly. Ackerman, Anhalt, and Dykman (1986) indicated that failure to automatize computational skills presages later arithmetical handicaps. Further research is needed to explore and clarify the relationship between Processing Speed on the WJ-R COG and math calculation ability, an aspect of Quantitative Ability.

Recommendations

Several recommendations may be appropriate for students who have low performance in Processing Speed. The intent of these compensatory strategies is to reduce distractions and enable students to work more rapidly and efficiently. Examples include:

1. Provide clearly duplicated worksheets that contain only a few problems and plenty of white space. Double-space all printed directions. If needed, type words in large letters with extra spaces in between. With some students, the use of large-print books may improve performance.
2. Seat the student in the front row near the chalkboard for all copying activities.

TEST 3

Visual Matching (cont.)

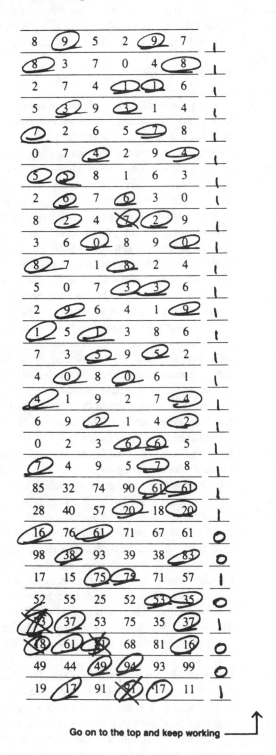

84	48	94	49	47	94
36	55	66	56	56	65
41	61	16	14	64	41
32	23	23	83	38	28
89	98	97	87	78	78
13	12	23	13	31	21
56	68	65	86	68	26
32	20	40	32	23	34
49	94	59	95	45	59
74	24	27	24	72	77
968	689	869	968	986	896
524	542	245	425	452	542
679	976	967	976	697	796
154	514	145	415	154	451
872	728	872	278	827	782
363	633	366	633	362	326
384	843	483	438	834	483
450	405	540	405	045	504
102	201	210	120	210	200
371	173	317	113	117	317
708	780	870	708	807	808
194	196	149	169	149	496
356	653	635	536	365	356
205	520	502	250	520	505
278	827	287	278	728	727
618	816	681	861	816	868
313	316	631	613	361	631
672	267	762	627	762	276
429	419	491	429	492	249
493	943	439	394	349	943

STOP

Go on to the top and keep working →

Figure 7–3. A Sixth-Grade Student on the Visual Matching Test.

3. Eliminate copying or limit the amount of material that a student is required to copy from the chalkboard or from a textbook. Do not require speed or accuracy in copying.

4. Provide practice with simple copying activities. Chart performance and reward the student for improved speed and accuracy.

5. Cut a window or box in a piece of cardboard so the student can frame and separate each problem as needed or have the student cover the part of the page that is not being worked on.

6. Point to all words and phrases while reading from the board.

7. To develop visual recall and perceptual speed, have the student reproduce words or phrases that are flashed on a tachistoscope or microcomputer. Gradually reduce the exposure time.

8. Allow the student to use an index card or finger for keeping his or her place in reading.

9. Encourage the use of graph paper in mathematics.

10. Extend the time for completing assignments.

11. Provide ample time for responding on written tasks.

12. Shorten assignments so that they may be accomplished in a reasonable time period.

13. Use visual clues to organize worksheets, such as instructing the student to place each answer in a box or folding the paper to make boxes.

14. Recommend visual tracking exercises or computer games that require rapid visual scanning.

15. Have the student copy letters, word sequences, or sentences using a typewriter or microcomputer.

16. Teach the use of verbal mediation when copying materials. The student should say each number, letter, or word as it is transferred from one place to another.

In some cases, an examiner may wish to recommend that the student obtain a full visual evaluation that emphasizes binocular coordination at near and far point, efficiency in changing visual fields, and other functional assessments of vision. This type of recommendation would be based upon observations of the student's classroom performance, as well as evaluation of assessment results.

Auditory Processing

The two primary measures of auditory processing are Test 4: Incomplete Words, which measures ability to analyze sounds, and Test 11: Sound Blending, which measures the ability to synthesize sounds. These tests require the student to use information about the phonology or sound structure of the English language. Additional information regarding auditory processing skills may be obtained by administering Test 18: Sound Patterns, a mixed measure of Auditory Processing and Fluid Reasoning, and Test 31: Word Attack in the WJ-R ACH.

Figure 7-4 illustrates the performance of Danny, an eighth-grade student, on the clusters of the Age/Grade Profile. Despite average performance in other cognitive skills, Danny was having extreme difficulty with decoding multisyllabic words, spelling, and learning Spanish.

Related Research

Clear associations exist between reading achievement and ability to analyze and interpret sounds in words. In reviewing a decade of research regarding phonological processing and reading disabilities, Wagner (1986) summarized the following conclusions: (a) phonological processing abilities may be measured; (b) they are related to the acquisition of reading skills; and (c) the relationship is at least partially causal for a subgroup of poor readers. Presumably, lack of phonological sensitivity makes it difficult to learn grapheme-to-phoneme correspondences (Stanovich, 1988). In examining the relationships between various reading and cognitive skills, Stanovich, Cunningham, and Feeman (1984) found that phonological awareness emerged as a separate predictor of reading skill that was independent of general verbal comprehension ability.

Students with learning disabilities often have more difficulty with tasks that involve reading phonically regular nonsense words, such as on the WJ-R ACH Word Attack test. For example, Kochnower, Richardson, and DiBenedetto (1983) found that when regular elementary children were matched with learning disabled children who were at the same reading level, the students with learning disabilities read fewer phonically regular real and nonsense words. They hypothesized that this deficiency interferes with development of reading vocabulary and is an important causal factor of reading disability.

In general, research on auditory closure, such as measured by the Incomplete Words test, is far less extensive than research on sound blending (Harber, 1980). In examining the performance of elementary students with learning disabilities, Harber found that tests of auditory closure and sound blending were most related to word analysis skills, rather than to oral or silent reading performance. Additionally, a significant relationship existed between auditory closure and word analysis skill.

Early reading and spelling. Considerable research literature supports the relationship between phonemic skills and learning to read and spell. In reviewing research on the cognitive processes that affect word decoding, Stanovich (1982a, 1982b) concluded that the low decoding skill of poor readers is primarily attributed to lack of phonological awareness that impairs their ability to segment, analyze, and synthesize speech sounds. Treiman (1985) and Wil-

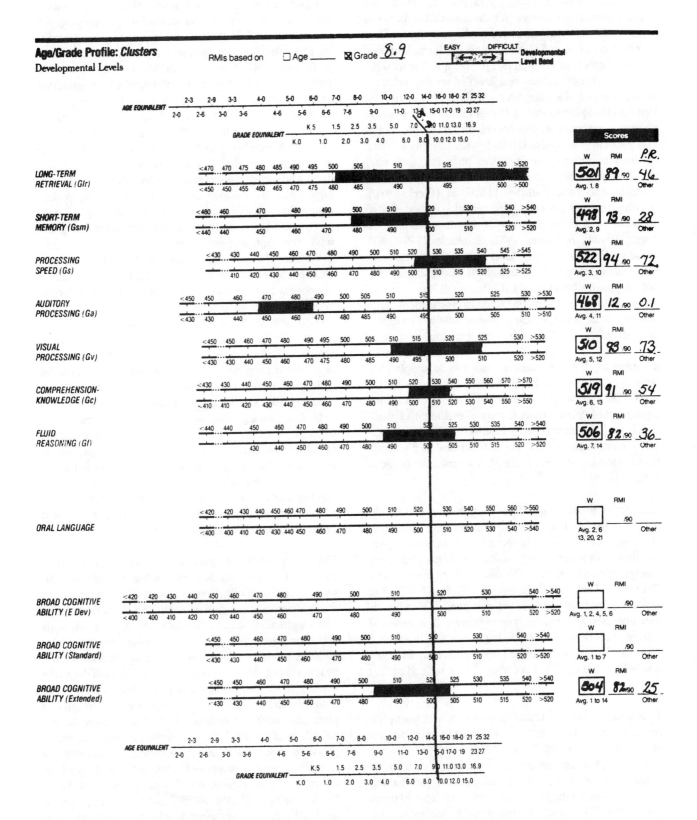

Figure 7–4. An Eighth-Grade Student on the Age/Grade Profile.

liams (1980, 1984) reviewed several research studies and found considerable support for the association between phonemic skill development and reading acquisition. In a longitudinal study of 543 children, Share, Jorm, Maclean, and Matthews (1984) found that phonological processing tasks were one of the best predictors of reading achievement at the end of kindergarten and first grade. Similarly, Perfetti (1985) found that in first-grade children, skills in phonemic analysis paralleled development in word decoding; phonemic analysis skill facilitated learning to read, but learning to read also facilitated phonemic analysis.

Auditory processing problems are often present in students who have spelling difficulties (Cicci, 1980). Spelling requires phonemic segmentation, the ability to attend to the detailed sequence of sounds in words (Gettinger, Bryant, & Fayne, 1982; Stanback, 1979-1980). Good spellers have a high level of auditory sequencing skill that enables generalization about letter patterns without necessarily being taught (Cotterell, 1974).

Two basic types of disabled students emerge: those with severe reading and spelling problems who are unable to take advantage of information from phonology because of serious difficulty with phonemic analysis and those who are generally better readers and can handle simple phonetic spelling (Stanback, 1979-1980). In discussing the results of a prior study, Rourke (1983) reported that students with phonetically accurate spelling had well-developed phonemic segmentation skill, whereas phonetically inaccurate spellers had deficiencies in phonemic segmentation, phonemic retrieval, phonemic synthesis, as well as visual memory.

Additional assessment. If an examiner notices weaknesses on the WJ-R COG auditory processing tests, he or she may wish to perform further informal analysis. Figure 7-5 illustrates a version of the Rosner Tests of Auditory Analysis Skills (Rosner, 1979) that has been expanded by Berninger, Thalberg, DeBruyn, and Smith (1987). The tasks proceed from syllables to single phonemes to blends and digraphs and require approximately 3 minutes of testing time. Berninger (1986) found that students with a score of 6 or below on this test at the end of kindergarten had below-average word decoding skill at the end of first grade.

Phonemic awareness training. Students with poor phonemic awareness are slow to develop word identification skill. Juel, Griffith, and Gough (1986) found that students with poor phonemic awareness could not read a single nonsense word at the end of first-grade despite having been exposed to large amounts of print and phonics instruction. They concluded that students will not acquire knowledge of spelling-sound correspondence until a prerequisite amount of phonemic awareness is attained.

Research results suggest that specific training in sound blending and phoneme segmentation (identifying the number of sounds within a word) improves general decoding ability in kindergarten and first-grade readers (Bradley & Bryant, 1985; Fox & Routh, 1984; Williams, 1980, 1984). Bradley and Bryant (1983) described a longitudinal study in which 400 children were tested on phonemic awareness prior to learning to read. They selected 65 students who were low in phonemic awareness and divided them into two groups, a control group and a group that received training in phonemic awareness. The students who received phonemic training scored significantly higher than the controls in reading and spelling performance. These findings support the need for oral phonological awareness training for students who enter first grade with poor phonemic awareness.

Specific training also appears to benefit elementary children. Vellutino and Scanlon (1982) found that training in phonemic segmentation improved the ability to decode nonsense words in both poor and good readers in the second and sixth grades. Overall, however, the poor readers did not perform as well as the good readers. Berninger, Thalberg, DeBruyn, and Smith (1987) indicated that examiners can make a valuable contribution by helping teachers to understand the relationship between phonemic skills and learning to read.

In categorizing various phonemic awareness tasks, Lewkowicz (1980) concluded that the tasks of sound blending and oral phonemic segmentation (separately articulating the sounds of a word in the correct sequence) are the most essential and closely associated with the reading process. Procedures that may be used to train sound blending and phonemic segmentation are presented in the section on Basic Reading Skills.

Secondary students and adults. Older students may continue to experience difficulty in tasks requiring auditory processing abilities, such as decoding, spelling, and foreign language learning. Russell (1982) conducted several longitudinal studies that followed dyslexic students and monitored their progress at regular intervals from childhood through adolescence or adulthood. Over several years many of the students attained a fairly high degree of reading proficiency. They continued, however, to have extreme difficulty on a test that required the reading of phonically regular nonsense words. Performance on this phonic reading test indicated continued impairment of phonetic processes even in adulthood. Additionally, a significant correlation existed between the severity of the disability and the score on the phonetic reading test. These findings suggest that the WJ-R Word Attack test, a test of phonically regular nonsense words, may have value in measuring enduring auditory processing impairments in older students and adults.

Modified (Expanded) Version of Rosner Test of
Auditory Analysis Skills* (Rosner, 1979)

I. Syllables — Kindergarten Level (5 initial, 5 final deletions)

Say	Now say it again, but don't say
baseball	base
cowboy	cow
*sunshine	sun
paper	pa
*cucumber	cu
*picnic	nic
morning	ing
seesaw	saw
bunny	ny
farmer	er

II. Single Phonemes — First Grade Level (5 initial, 5 final deletions)

Say	Now say it again, but don't say
*coat	/k/
*meat	/m/
pet	/p/
ball	/b/
*take	/t/
*game	/m/
make	/k/
*wrote	/t/
*please	/z/
coin	/n/

III. Blends/digraphs — Second Grade Level (8 initial, 2 final deletions)

Say	Now say it again, but don't say
*clap	/k/
*play	/p/
*stale	/t/
*smack	/m/
shoes	/sh/
chew	/ch/
teach	/ch/
string	/tr/
grow	/g/
trash	/sh/

Note: * indicates that item was on original Rosner Test of Auditory Analysis Skills (Rosner, 1979).

*The modification consisted of adding stimulus items so that there were 10 items each at the kindergarten, first grade, and second grade level.

Figure 7–5. Informal Assessment of Auditory Processing. *Note.* From "Preventing Reading Disabilities by Assessing and Remediating Phonemic Skills" by V.W. Berninger, S.P. Thalberg, I. DeBruyn, and R. Smith, 1987, *School Psychology Review, 16,* p. 565. Copyright 1987 by the National Association of School Psychologists. Reprinted by permission.

In addition to affecting the acquisition of reading decoding and spelling skill, severe auditory processing deficits may cause difficulty in interpreting lectures and understanding oral directions (Meyers, 1987). Another aspect of auditory processing is the ability to perceive speech under distracting conditions. Meyers described a secondary student with good reasoning skills and high knowledge in content areas who could not comprehend the orally presented lecture material in classes. As a result of his auditory processing disorder, his class notes, filled with gaps, were nearly useless.

Recommendations

Some students who perform poorly on the Short-Term Memory tests may also have trouble with the tests that measure auditory processing. In these cases, many of the recommendations for Short-Term Memory may be appropriate for the student. Other students will only have difficulty with the Auditory Processing tests. Depending upon the age of the student and the severity of the problem, several of the following recommendations may be appropriate:

1. Referral to the speech/language specialist for a more comprehensive language assessment.
2. Depending upon age, language, and reading achievement level, the student may benefit from specific training in phonemic segmentation and sound blending.
3. For young students, encourage the use of games that manipulate the phonological structure of words, such as rhyming games and nursery rhymes.
4. Develop skill in phonological awareness through counting activities that progress from counting the number of words in a simple sentence, to the number of syllables in a word, to the number of sounds within a word.
5. If the auditory processing deficits are not remediable, recommend a nonphonic reading approach.
6. In severe cases, the school will need to excuse the student from foreign language study in elementary school and waive the foreign language requirement at the secondary level.
7. Provide visual outlines and graphic organizers for tasks involving listening.
8. Give clear, direct instructions for all tasks, limited in length and complexity.
9. Do not penalize the student for difficulties in reading decoding or spelling.
10. Allow extra time for reading and writing activities.

Visual Processing

The two primary measures of Visual Processing are Test 5: Visual Closure and Test 12: Picture Recognition. Supplemental information may be obtained by administering Test 19: Spatial Relations. Students with low performance on these tests are likely to have difficulty with tasks that involve perceiving and thinking with visual patterns.

Related Research

The research on the relationship between visual processing and reading achievement is not as conclusive as the literature on auditory processing. After reviewing research that examined the relationships between visual-processing skills and reading achievement, Beech (1985) concluded that it is difficult to sort out the cause-and-effect relationship. Some research suggests that disabled readers perform as well as normal readers on nonverbal visual-spatial tasks (Swanson, 1983). Other studies have indicated modest relationships between visual processing skills and reading achievement.

In the most extensive work to date, Kavale (1982) conducted a meta-analysis of the results from 161 studies that examined the relationships among a variety of visual perceptual skills and reading achievement. The findings indicated that visual perceptual skills are an important correlate of reading achievement. The skills involved included: (a) visual closure, the ability to recognize a complete figure from fragmented stimuli; (b) visual spatial relationships, the ability to perceive the position of objects in space; (c) visual discrimination, the ability to perceive dominant features in different stimuli; (d) visual memory, the ability to recall the dominant feature of a stimulus or sequence of visually presented stimuli; (e) visual-motor integration, the ability to integrate vision with body movements; (f) visual association, the ability to relate visually presented stimuli conceptually; and (g) visual-auditory integration, the ability to match serially presented visual stimuli with auditory counterparts. All of these skills were significantly correlated with reading achievement.

In an analysis of the relationship among visual perceptual and reading achievement variables, three factors emerged. The first factor was a reading factor. The other two factors were a visual-cognitive factor, which included skills that require more cognitive involvement, and a visual differentiation factor, which included skills that are more automatic. This type of distinction also is apparent in the two WJ-R COG factors. The Processing Speed tests require rapid, automatic processing of visual symbols, whereas the Visual Processing tests are untimed and involve increased analysis and thinking. Further research is needed to clarify the relationship between the WJ-R COG Visual Processing tests and academic performance.

Recommendations

In general, recommendations for visual processing will include activities that increase awareness of spatial relationships and require visual thinking. Improvement in these skills is more related to artistic and manipulative skills than to academic abilities per se. Types of activities will vary based upon a student's age and interests.

Preschool and primary children. The following are samples of activities most relevant for preschool and primary children:

1. Provide activities such as puzzles, painting, drawing, bead stringing, pegs and pegboards, and building with blocks.
2. Provide activities with manipulative toys.
3. Have students arrange blocks or shapes on top of patterns.
4. Have children trace geometric shapes and other forms with their fingers or use plastic overlays with crayons.
5. Have students identify separate objects in pictures.
6. Have students sort shapes into categories.

7. Have students bend pipe cleaners to replicate designs and figures.
8. Provide experiences with a variety of geometric forms.

Upper-elementary and secondary students. The following are samples of activities that may be relevant for upper-elementary and secondary students.

1. Provide activities that require spatial organization and planning, such as paper folding, models, and three-dimensional puzzles.
2. Have students complete or develop mazes for younger children to solve.
3. Have students construct geometric patterns with blocks using design cards.
4. Provide practice with object assembly using materials such as nuts, bolts, and washers.
5. Provide opportunities for copying and drawing geometric patterns.
6. Use simple graphic patterns when illustrating key points.
7. Provide practice reading diagrams and charts.

Comprehension-Knowledge

The two primary measures of Comprehension-Knowledge are Test 6: Picture Vocabulary and Test 13: Oral Vocabulary. These two tests are also indicators of oral language proficiency. Supplemental measures of Comprehension-Knowledge may be obtained by administering Test 20: Listening Comprehension and the three WJ-R ACH Knowledge tests, Test 28: Science, Test 29: Social Studies, and Test 30: Humanities. Test 21: Verbal Analogies is a mixed measure of Comprehension-Knowledge and Fluid Reasoning.

Students who perform poorly on the Comprehension-Knowledge tests are likely to have reduced vocabularies and in some cases, limited background knowledge. Snider and Tarver (1987) discussed the effect of reading disabilities on knowledge acquisition. Because students with reading disabilities often devote so much time to decoding, their attention to comprehension is insufficient, and, consequently, they fail to acquire new knowledge. World knowledge is gained from a variety of reading experiences. If a student lacks reading fluency, he or she is unlikely to benefit from reading comprehension activities. As the student matures, reading comprehension depends more and more upon extensive background information in specialized content areas. Many students with reading or learning disabilities will not have acquired the fundamental vocabulary, concepts, and experiences that are necessary for understanding more complex text. Snider and Tarver suggested that because of a limited knowledge base, many learning disabled students with average intelligence are unable to demonstrate the higher level thinking skills that are required in reading comprehension.

By analyzing a student's performance on the Science and Social Studies tests, two supplemental measures of Comprehension-Knowledge, an examiner will have an estimate of knowledge in these two content areas. This estimate will help an examiner determine whether or not the student has an appropriate level of prerequisite background knowledge for comprehending textbooks in these two areas.

Related Research

Prior knowledge is important for both comprehension and problem solving. In terms of academic performance, the tests that measure Comprehension-Knowledge are most highly related to performance in reading comprehension. The relationship between vocabulary knowledge and reading comprehension has been documented in the literature through many factor-analytic and readability studies (Carnine, Kameenui, & Coyle, 1984).

Vocabulary and prior knowledge. Reading comprehension is not only influenced by linguistic cues and semantic content, but also by the knowledge that we bring to the passage (Lapp & Flood, 1983). Reading requires the ability to apply acquired knowledge to text. Prior knowledge also appears to facilitate vocabulary growth. Griswold, Gelzheiser, and Shepherd (1987) compared the performance of eighth-grade students with learning disabilities and normal-achieving students on a vocabulary learning task. They found that the learning disabled students retained fewer words than the normal-achieving students and that performance on the vocabulary tests was best explained by prior vocabulary knowledge and reading comprehension, rather than memorization strategies.

Both vocabulary and prior knowledge play critical roles in reading comprehension (Snider & Tarver, 1987). Several research studies have demonstrated the relationship among vocabulary knowledge, information tests, and reading comprehension. In a longitudinal study that followed a group of preschoolers from age 4 to eighth grade, Badian (1988) found that the best single predictor of reading comprehension performance was a test assessing factual knowledge. Stanovich (1988) found that one of the best predictors of reading comprehension in third- and fifth-grade children was a test of vocabulary. Evidence suggests that the importance of verbal comprehension ability increases as reading skill develops (Stanovich, Cunningham, & Feeman, 1984). Shanahan (1984) found that for beginning readers word production and recognition factors explained the largest amount of variance, whereas for advanced readers, vocabulary was more important.

One research study provides support for the relationship between the WJ-R COG Comprehension-Knowledge factor and reading comprehension. Santos (1989) administered 11 tests to 20 high school readers with learning disabilities and to 20 controls. The purpose of this experiment was to examine the relationship between reading comprehension performance and performance on tests of language skills and cognitive processes. As expected, the students with learning disabilities performed significantly lower on tests of language skills. Two of the six tests that had the highest correlation with reading comprehension were the WJ subtests of Picture Vocabulary and Antonyms/Synonyms (Woodcock & Johnson, 1977), the two tests that comprise the WJ-R COG Comprehension-Knowledge factor. Additionally, the Concept Formation test, a measure of Fluid Reasoning, was significantly related to reading comprehension.

In general, research supports the conclusion that instruction in vocabulary and prerequisite knowledge prior to reading improves comprehension. Snider (1989) investigated the effects of prior information and vocabulary on the reading comprehension performance of junior high students with learning disabilities. The results indicated that instruction designed to increase prior knowledge and vocabulary benefits reading comprehension performance.

Decline in scores. Several investigators have noted a decline in scores on acquired knowledge tests for students with severe reading impairments. Poor readers tend to display increasingly global cognitive deficits as they grow older (Stanovich, 1988). For example, Sinatra (1989) studied 14 males who were significantly disabled in word recognition skills. The first assessment was conducted when the students were on the average near the end of sixth grade. Students were then reevaluated after the age of 16. The findings indicated that scores on tests measuring acquired knowledge and vocabulary decreased, whereas scores on tests measuring visuo-spatial nonverbal processing remained constant. These results suggest that an examiner may note a decline across the years on the Comprehension-Knowledge tests for some students with a history of severe reading failure.

Listening comprehension. The Listening Comprehension test may be used to provide supplemental information about Comprehension-Knowledge. Considerable research has been conducted that addresses the relationship between listening comprehension and reading comprehension. For example, Wood, Buckhalt, and Tomlin (1988) tested 181 students on both listening and reading comprehension. The students ranged in age from 9 to 15 and

were selected from three different educational placements: learning disability, mild mental retardation, and regular education. As expected, the students with learning disabilities scored higher on the listening than on the reading comprehension tests and had a greater discrepancy between the areas than did the mildly mentally retarded or regular education students. Additionally, the students with learning disabilities scored higher on listening skills than the students with mild mental retardation, but lower than the students in regular education. Similarly, Spring and French (1990) found that the reading comprehension scores of 15 upper-elementary students with reading disabilities were significantly lower than their listening comprehension scores. In contrast, the reading comprehension scores of 15 nondisabled readers were not significantly different from their listening comprehension scores. These findings suggest that consideration of discrepancies between listening and reading comprehension may help examiners identify students with specific learning and reading disabilities.

Using the WJ-R, an examiner may gain insights into the effect of word recognition on reading comprehension performance by comparing a student's performance on the Listening Comprehension test that presents modified oral cloze tasks to his or her performance on the WJ-R ACH Passage Comprehension test that presents modified reading cloze tasks. Significantly higher performance on the Listening Comprehension test suggests that word recognition skill is interfering with reading comprehension performance. Significantly lower performance on the Listening Comprehension test suggests that word recognition skill improves comprehension. For example, students with a language impairment may score higher on the Passage Comprehension test than on the Listening Comprehension test because the printed words remain in front of them. The text facilitates processing and reduces the effects of low auditory memory on comprehension.

Although the Listening Comprehension test is not primarily a measure of short-term memory, some students may have difficulty retaining the information. Mann, Cowin, and Schoenheimer (1989) found that poor readers were less accurate than good readers in interpreting sentences because they were less able to hold phonological material temporarily in working memory. They found significant correlations between comprehension accuracy on sentences and the ability to hold spoken word strings in memory, such as measured by the Memory for Words and Memory for Sentences tests. Their findings suggested that sentence comprehension tests, when combined with tests that measure ability to hold linguistic material in short-term memory, may be a sensitive predictor of future reading ability.

The relationship between listening and reading comprehension increases through elementary school. Stanovich, Cunningham, and Feeman (1984) found that the correlations between reading comprehension and listening comprehension increased from first to third grade and from third to fifth grade. Both reading and listening comprehension involve several of the same abilities, such as reasoning, background knowledge, and vocabulary.

Recommendations

When students have difficulty on the Comprehension-Knowledge tests, several recommendations may be appropriate. Specific instructional strategies and methods for building background knowledge are presented in the section on Reading Comprehension and in Chapter 5. In addition to specific techniques, the following recommendations may be appropriate:

1. Encourage parents to read with their children and to help them acquire information through other means, such as discussions, educational television shows, and cultural events.
2. Develop study guides, vocabulary handouts, and presentation outlines for class lectures. Have the student follow along and add notes to the outline during each class presentation.
3. Provide direct cues to signify important information, such as informing the students during a lecture that certain points are important.
4. Begin all lectures with advance organizers. Inform the students of the important topics and what they will be expected to learn.
5. Use verbal organizational cues when lecturing, such as "first, second, and then the most important point . . . "
6. Use techniques that will help the student relate new knowledge to his or her existing knowledge.
7. Incorporate the student's interests and knowledge into instructional activities.
8. Preteach vocabulary and new concepts prior to asking students to discuss or read material.
9. When presenting directions and discussing concepts, use vocabulary that is understood by the student.
10. Provide activities designed to improve listening skill.
11. Provide specific instruction in vocabulary, such as teaching the student common prefixes and suffixes and how they alter word meaning.
12. Provide experiences in the community that will enhance a student's background knowledge.

Fluid Reasoning

The two primary measures of Fluid Reasoning are Test 7: Analysis-Synthesis and Test 14: Concept Formation.

Supplemental information may be obtained by administering Test 19: Spatial Relations and Test 21: Verbal Analogies. Students who perform poorly on these two tests are likely to have difficulty developing concepts and organizing and classifying ideas. This type of reasoning is required for both reading comprehension and math problem solving.

Bley and Thornton (1981) indicated that one of the most difficult areas for students with learning problems is that of abstract reasoning and mathematics. Furthermore, students who have difficulty with reasoning often are unable to: (a) verbalize what has been learned, (b) associate what is happening with symbolic representation, or (c) understand, auditorily or receptively, what is being explained. These difficulties with abstract reasoning make it hard for the student to sequence the steps in a problem logically (Thornton & Bley, 1982). Some students may understand initial concepts, but have trouble with tasks that require multiple associations. For example, a student may succeed on the initial items of the Analysis-Synthesis and Concept Formation tests, but become confused when the items involve two or more steps for a solution.

Related Research

Two recent studies have particular relevance to the WJ-R COG Fluid Reasoning factor. In examining the relationship between several cognitive tests and reading comprehension, Santos (1989) found that both the WJ Concept Formation and Analysis-Synthesis subtests (Woodcock & Johnson, 1977) were significantly related to reading comprehension performance in an adolescent population.

In a 10-year follow-up study that examined the ability of the WJ to predict future achievement, McGrew and Pehl (1988) found that Analysis-Synthesis was one of the top three subtests for predicting ninth-grade math performance (K. S. McGrew, personal communication, September 16, 1989). In the WJ-R COG, both the Analysis-Synthesis and Concept Formation tests, which were selected from the results of stepwise multiple regression studies, appear in the Math Aptitude cluster. As students mature, performance in mathematics becomes more strongly associated with reasoning skill. The findings from these two studies suggest that the Fluid Reasoning factor is related to mathematics achievement, and may be related to reading comprehension with older students.

Recommendations

In instructing students who have trouble formulating concepts, the most important recommendation is to make learning meaningful to the student. This may be accomplished by relating tasks to information that the student already knows. In order to comprehend concepts and rules, the student must organize the new information into his or her existing system of knowledge about the world. If a student is going to profit from instruction, the classroom tasks must be matched to the student's reasoning level. Further recommendations would include:

1. Encourage the use of manipulatives to develop concepts.
2. Attempt to teach concepts in a concrete manner. Use concrete cues in all directions, telling the student exactly what to do at each step.
3. Limit the amount of material presented at one time.
4. Select structured materials that are carefully sequenced.
5. Engage the student in demonstrations of the concept.
6. Have the student verbalize what he or she has learned.
7. Have the student teach a concept to younger students.
8. Provide ample opportunities for repetition and review.
9. Require a considerable amount of overlearning.
10. Teach the student strategies that may increase understanding and retention of a concept, such as verbalizing the steps of a task while it is being performed. Teach the student when and how to apply the strategy.
11. Provide the student with a list of procedures to follow when working with tasks that involve problem solving.
12. At the secondary level, select courses that do not require a high level of abstract reasoning.

Quantitative Ability

An examiner may also analyze Quantitative Ability as a cognitive factor. This factor, which measures calculation and problem-solving ability, is composed of two WJ-R ACH tests: Test 24: Calculation and Test 25: Applied Problems. If a student has low performance in Quantitative Ability, appropriate recommendations and instructional strategies may be found in Chapter 6.

Oral Language

The WJ-R COG Oral Language Cluster consists of five tests: Test 2: Memory for Sentences, Test 6: Picture Vocabulary, Test 13: Oral Vocabulary, Test 20: Listening Comprehension, and Test 21: Verbal Analogies. These tests measure several different aspects of expressive and receptive language. Figure 7-6 illustrates the various skills measured by the Oral Language tests.

Students with low oral language may have difficulty with both cognitive and achievement tests and may have trouble following directions or understanding compound and complex sentences. Some students with language impairments will request to have directions repeated. Others may not be self-monitoring well enough to recognize their lack of comprehension. On the WJ-R ACH, the student may have low written expression, poor basic reading skills and reading comprehension, or difficulty solving word problems in mathematics. In conversation, an examiner may note unusual patterns in the individual's use of language. The student may use vague pronoun referents, immature or nonspecific vocabulary, or have poor sentence structure.

In the classroom, the student may not contribute much to discussions and may respond in short, simple sentences. In some instances, a student will appear disorganized when relating a story or report events in an erroneous sequence. When asked a question, a student may demonstrate some knowledge of the topic, but not be referentially specific enough to communicate an appropriate response. Or, in other cases, a student may not be able to determine when enough has been said.

Language Processing

An examiner may perform a more in-depth assessment of language skill by analyzing a student's performance on several of the WJ-R COG and the WJ-R ACH tests. Figure 7-7 illustrates tests that measure various linguistic abilities. Verbal attention and memory include tests that require repeating or listening to auditory information; phonological awareness includes tests that involve analysis and synthesis of language sounds; semantics and morphology include tests that require knowledge of word meaning and language structure; verbal reasoning includes tests that require thinking and logical applications; and metalinguistic awareness includes tests that require awareness and knowledge of language uses in a variety of situations.

Auditory and Visual Tests

The WJ-R COG contains many auditory/oral language tests and several visual tests. Figure 7-8 illustrates the auditory and visual tests ordered from those that demand higher level mental processing (language and reasoning) and are more content-dependent to those that require primarily lower level mental processing (discrimination and perception) and are less content-dependent. Analysis of a student's performance across these tests may have implications regarding a preferred learning style.

Figure 7-9 illustrates the performance of Ike, an eighth-grade student, on the Age/Grade Profile for the WJ-R COG and WJ-R ACH clusters. In addition to low scores in oral language, Ike also had difficulty on the short-term memory and auditory processing tests. In contrast, he scored above grade level on the Processing Speed and

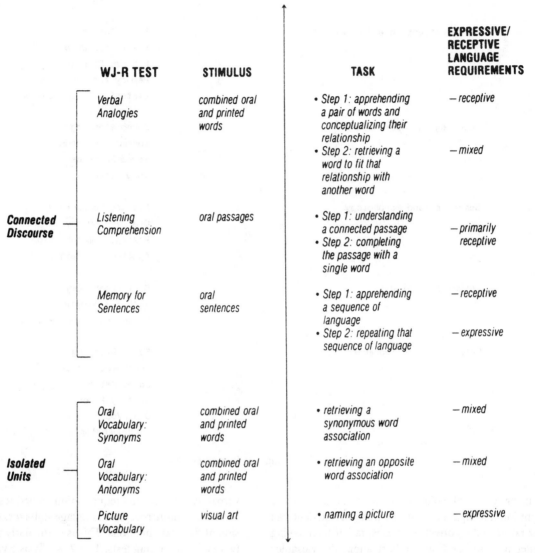

MORE COMPLEX

WJ-R TEST	STIMULUS	TASK	EXPRESSIVE/ RECEPTIVE LANGUAGE REQUIREMENTS
Verbal Analogies	*combined oral and printed words*	• *Step 1: apprehending a pair of words and conceptualizing their relationship* • *Step 2: retrieving a word to fit that relationship with another word*	*— receptive* *— mixed*
Listening Comprehension	*oral passages*	• *Step 1: understanding a connected passage* • *Step 2: completing the passage with a single word*	*— primarily receptive*
Memory for Sentences	*oral sentences*	• *Step 1: apprehending a sequence of language* • *Step 2: repeating that sequence of language*	*— receptive* *— expressive*
Oral Vocabulary: Synonyms	*combined oral and printed words*	• *retrieving a synonymous word association*	*— mixed*
Oral Vocabulary: Antonyms	*combined oral and printed words*	• *retrieving an opposite word association*	*— mixed*
Picture Vocabulary	*visual art*	• *naming a picture*	*— expressive*

Connected Discourse — (Verbal Analogies, Listening Comprehension, Memory for Sentences)

Isolated Units — (Oral Vocabulary: Synonyms, Oral Vocabulary: Antonyms, Picture Vocabulary)

LESS COMPLEX

Figure 7–6. Various Skills Measured by the WJ-R Oral Language Tests. *Note.* From *WJ-R Tests of Cognitive Ability—Standard and Supplemental Batteries: Examiner's Manual* (p. 28) by R.W. Woodcock and N. Mather, 1989, Allen, TX: DLM. Copyright 1989 by DLM. Reprinted by permission.

Visual Processing tests. In achievement, Ike was several years below grade level on both reading and written language tasks, but at grade level in mathematics. Presumably, Ike's generalized difficulty with auditory/language tasks has affected reading and writing performance more than mathematics performance.

Oral Response Requirements

In analyzing student performance, an examiner may also wish to consider the oral response requirements of the WJ-R COG tests. The majority of the tests require a single-word response; however, several tests do not require an oral response, whereas others require the student to produce a sentence. Figure 7-10 illustrates the oral response requirements for the cognitive tests.

For the tests that require minimal responses, the format could be altered, if necessary, so that no oral response is required. Although these types of modifications are rarely needed, they may be necessary for nonverbal students or students with severe expressive language impairments. On Analysis-Synthesis, the student could point to the solu-

Language Processing

	Tests
Verbal attention and memory	Sound Patterns
	Memory for Words
	Numbers Reversed
	Memory for Sentences
	Listening Comprehension
Phonological awareness	Sound Blending
	Incomplete Words
	Sound Patterns
	Word Attack
Semantics and morphology	Picture Vocabulary
	Oral Vocabulary
	Passage Comprehension
	Applied Problems
Verbal reasoning	Oral Vocabulary
	Verbal Analogies
	Listening Comprehension
Metalinguistic awareness	Sound Blending
	Incomplete Words
	Sound Patterns
	Writing Fluency
	Oral Vocabulary
	Verbal Analogies

Figure 7–7. Language Processing Tests.

tions using cards of colored squares. For the Picture Recognition and Spatial Relations tests, the student can simply point to the correct responses, rather than saying the letter names. For Concept Formation, the variables plus *and* and *or* could be presented on index cards and the student could select cards for each solution. For Sound Patterns, the two solutions, *Same* and *Different*, may be written on individual cards, or picture cards may be used such as a card with two faces with smiles (same) and a card with one face with a smile and one with a frown (different). After listening to the pair of sounds, the student then points to the appropriate card.

In assessing students with language impairments, an examiner may wish to consider the different response requirements in interpreting performance. Additionally, the examiner may wish to compare a student's performance on tests that are primarily verbal in nature to tests that are primarily nonverbal. Or, when assessing a student with limited English skills, the examiner may selectively decide to administer several tests that are primarily non-

verbal. A few tests that require minimal oral responses do, however, require receptive language skills for comprehension of the oral directions. This is particularly true for the two Fluid Reasoning tests, Test 7: Analysis-Synthesis and Test 14: Concept Formation, that provide the student with controlled learning instruction.

Informal Language Sample

In addition to analyzing performance on the WJ-R, an examiner should supplement an assessment with one or more taped language samples, if oral language performance is a major concern. An examiner may collect two samples: one of a spontaneous conversation and one of retelling a narrative. A conversation may center around a discussion of toys, objects, or events. A narrative may center around the retelling of a story, an experience, or a description of a favorite book or television show. Since the content may influence the quality of the student's speak-

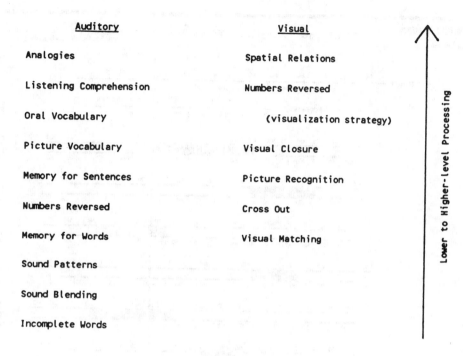

Figure 7–8. Auditory and Visual Tests on the WJ-R COG.

ing, an examiner may wish to select materials and topics that will generate a variety of concepts and ideas. The goal is to obtain a sample that is representative of what the student is competent of producing.

When listening to the samples at a later time, the examiner should ask questions that will facilitate the qualitative analysis. Examples of types of questions include:

Are the student's responses appropriate to the context?

Does the student use age-appropriate and varied vocabulary?

Does the student use simple, compound, and complex sentence patterns?

Does the student use correct grammar?

Is the sequence of ideas or events organized appropriately to the topic?

Does the student adequately introduce people and places in his or her narrative?

Does the student maintain the topic until completed?

Does the student answer questions appropriately?

Does the student use fillers excessively, such as "um" and "well," or phrases like "what'cha' ma' callits" to replace referents?

Does the student use a lot of empty words, such as "thing" and "stuff"?

Does the student have difficulty recalling certain words?

Does the student initiate conversation or merely respond?

Does the student introduce his or her topic to the listener?

Does the student provide adequate transitions to new topics?

Are the student's responses lengthy or minimal?

Recommendations

Students with severe oral language disabilities require extensive support services. Although recommendations are provided, in most instances, specific intervention programs will be designed by a speech/language specialist. Depending upon the age of the student and the severity of the problem, several of the following recommendations may be appropriate:

1. Referral to the speech/language specialist for a more comprehensive language assessment. If services are provided, the speech/language therapist should have ongoing communication with the student's classroom teachers.

2. Obtain recommendations from the speech/language therapist on methods and strategies for enhancing oral language in the instructional setting and for strategies that a teacher may use to facilitate oral comprehension.

3. Demonstrate or model what you want the student to do, talking through the task while performing it. Have the student talk through the task while doing it.

4. Encourage the student to use gestures if he or she

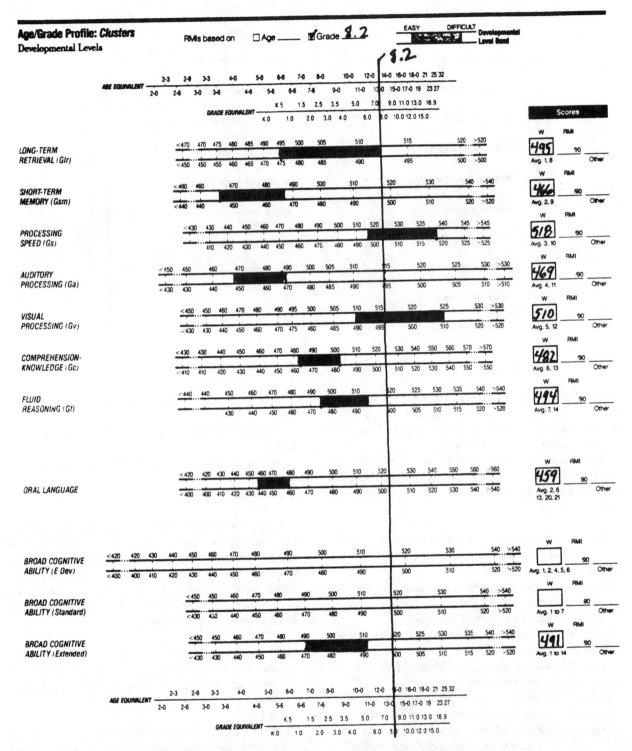

Figure 7–9. An Eighth-Grade Student on the Age/Grade Profiles.

cannot think of the necessary words for expression.

5. Provide plenty of opportunities for verbal responses.

6. Increase oral fluency by having the student say as many words in a category as he or she can think of within a minute time period.

7. Provide as much time as necessary for a student to respond to questions.

8. Have the student orally describe visual materials, such as a picture or poster.

9. Incorporate learning materials, enrichment activities, and games that will stimulate language development and encourage listening and speaking.

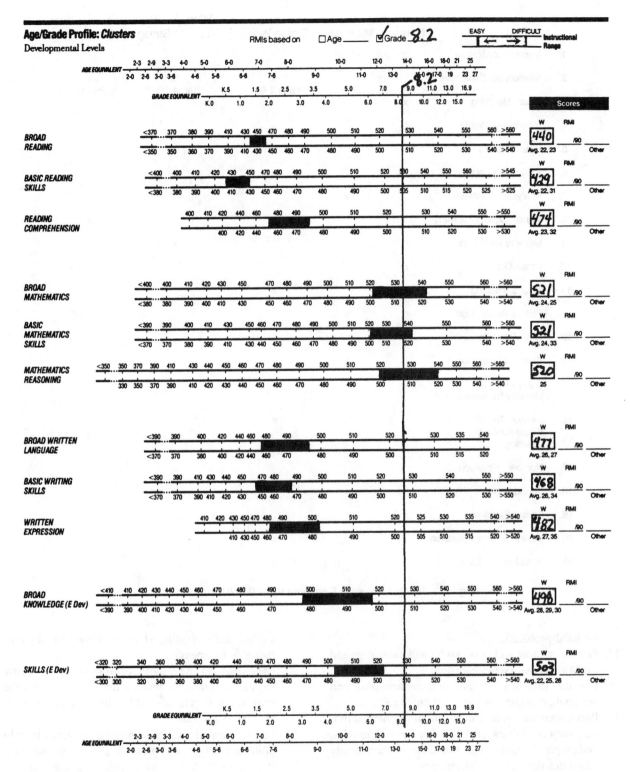

Figure 7–9 *(continued)*

10. Encourage both parents and teachers to read aloud to the student.
11. Explain and provide activities with important vocabulary words prior to assigning a chapter. Ensure that

new words are both pronounced and used correctly.
12. Teach content-related knowledge before requiring a student to perform a task, such as reading a story.
13. Avoid fill-in-the-blank tests for students with word

Test	None	Minimal	Single Word	Word/ Number String	Sentence
1. Memory for Names	x				
2. Memory for Sentences			x (Items 1-5)	x (Items 6-11)	x (Items 12-32)
3. Visual Matching	x				
4. Incomplete Words			x		
5. Visual Closure			x		
6. Picture Vocabulary			x		
7. Analysis-Synthesis		x			
8. Visual-Auditory Learning			x		x
9. Memory for Words				x	
10. Cross Out	x				
11. Sound Blending			x		
12. Picture Recognition		x			
13. Oral Vocabulary			x		
14. Concept Formation		x			
15. Delayed Recall - Memory for Names	x				
16. Delayed Recall - Visual-Auditory Learning			x		
17. Numbers Reversed				x	
18. Sound Patterns		x			
19. Spatial Relations		x			
20. Listening Comprehension			x		
21. Verbal Analogies			x		

Figure 7–10. Oral Response Requirements of the WJ-R COG Tests.

retrieval problems.

14. Pair the student with a peer who will encourage and facilitate verbal communication.

15. Use the student's interests and nonacademic and academic strengths as conversational topics.

16. Provide visual reinforcement for all listening activities, such as outlines, study guides, pictures, movies, and graphs. Ensure that the visual information clearly illustrates the auditory information.

17. Have the student sit close to the teacher or in the front of the classroom.

18. When teaching sight words and spelling words, ensure that the student understands the meaning of the words.

19. Help the student internalize a structure for telling stories, such as using story grammars to organize thoughts for speaking.

20. Use expansion and elaboration to show a student how to produce a more complex sentence. Paraphrase the student's sentence and add a little more detail or context to the idea.

21. Use reading and written language activities to help build oral language expression and comprehension.

22. Provide exemptions from foreign language classes.

23. Encourage and reinforce development of nonverbal and nonacademic strengths.

In planning instruction for students with language disabilities, an examiner should consider which language skills the student possesses and which language skills developmentally come next. After identifying the target skills, the new skills are presented in context using intensive practice and integrating the skills with past experiences (Bos & Vaughn, 1988).

Additional Considerations

While administering the WJ-R COG, an examiner will observe a student's ability to attend to a variety of tasks. Attention is crucial for academic success and a prerequisite to all learning. Some students with learning problems have trouble sustaining attention. Others have trouble attending to the relevant information.

Attention

Before making recommendations, an examiner will want to determine whether or not the problem is generalized (apparent when the student is engaged in most tasks) or task specific (apparent only when the student is engaged in specific tasks, such as math or reading assignments). For example, during testing an examiner noted that Steve was attentive for the majority of tests, but inattentive on any tests that involved listening. With another individual, an examiner may observe a difference in attention when the student is engaged in academic or cognitive tests. For example, the examiner noted that Betsy was inattentive on academic tests but attentive on novel cognitive tasks.

Differences in attention may also be observed in the classroom. For example, a student may be attentive during an art or physical education class but become highly distractible during reading lessons. Or, an examiner may note that a student is distractible during any academic task that requires independent seatwork. In observing Betsy in the classroom, the examiner noted that she was impulsive, called out answers without raising her hand, and had a heightened activity level. The classroom teacher also commented that Betsy is generally disorganized and has difficulty completing all assignments and homework.

To gain a more complete understanding of how attentional factors affect learning and behavior, an examiner should conduct several systematic observations of the student during both academic and nonacademic activities. Additionally, the examiner may need to conduct a parent conference to investigate the presence of these behaviors in other settings. Based upon observations, teacher reports, and parent reports, and in some cases student interviews, an examiner may determine that the possibility of attention-deficit-hyperactivity disorder (ADHD) should be investigated. In this situation, the examiner would refer the parents to a pediatrician with expertise in the diagnosis and treatment of ADHD. Ingersoll (1988) provides many suggestions for parents and teachers for helping a student with ADHD.

Recommendations

Although more intensive interventions such as behavioral therapy or management plans and/or medical therapies are often needed for students with attention deficits, several modifications may improve classroom success. Some possible recommendations include:

1. Begin with short, simple tasks that the student is able to complete and gradually increase the duration and complexity of the tasks.
2. Provide the student with a seat that is close to the teacher so the teacher can make frequent eye contact with the student.
3. Surround the student with peers who have good classroom behavior.
4. Provide an area where the student may work with limited distractions.
5. Develop procedures that will maximize the student's time on-task. Have the student record how much they have accomplished after a set period of time.
6. Make lists that will help the student organize and monitor daily tasks. Have the student check off tasks as they are completed.
7. Reinforce desirable behaviors. Praise the student for being on-task, completing assignments, behaving appropriately, doing good work, or sitting quietly. Try to keep comments positive.
8. Identify and provide appropriate reinforcements for the individual. Rewards can be tangible, such as food or stickers, or include special privileges, such as free time, computer time, library time, teacher helper, or no homework.
9. Increase attention span by rewarding on-task behavior at gradually decreasing intervals.
10. Give reduced assignments, such as only five problems on a page, so that the student is able to complete independent seatwork.
11. Provide immediate feedback on assignments. Incorporate programmed learning materials or computer programs, when possible.
12. Maintain a predictable classroom routine for the student to follow. Keep the daily schedule consistent as much as possible.
13. Help the student to make transitions from one activity to another. Remember that the most difficult transitions are from an unstructured activity, such as recess, to a structured activity, such as independent seatwork.
14. Prepare the student ahead of time for any changes in the schedule, such as an assembly or field trip.

15. Before addressing the student, speak the student's name and make eye contact. Keep oral directions short and uncomplicated. Ask the student to repeat the directions or, if the directions are lengthy, to write them down.

16. When directions are being given to a group, cue the student by placing a hand on the student's arm or shoulder to maintain attention.

17. In oral presentations, emphasize important information with advance organizers. For example, state: "This information is important to know."

18. Provide activities that require active participation, such as talking through problems or acting out the steps. Have students complete study guides or semantic maps while listening to presentations.

19. Use color on worksheets to draw attention to relevant details.

20. Permit movement in the classroom and provide frequent work breaks.

21. Use cooperative learning activities with small groups.

22. Teach social skills when necessary.

23. Provide the student opportunities to demonstrate his or her strengths in the classroom. Set up activities where the student may assist another student.

24. Insure that the student has all homework assignments recorded each day before leaving school. If necessary, set up a program where parents help the student organize his or her homework and then initial all completed assignments.

25. Coordinate a behavior management system between school and home. The goals of the program should be positive and attainable.

To assess whether or not a behavior management technique or intervention is effective, a teacher must keep careful data on a student's improvements in time on-task, time between activities, and classroom movement. One method is to monitor the student at regular intervals, such as every 10 minutes, and record the percentage of time that the student is on-task or engaging in appropriate behavior. This type of monitoring may also be done more intensively for shorter periods of time. For example, during an instructional period, a volunteer may record each 10 seconds whether or not a student is on or off task during a 20-minute period.

A student may also monitor and chart his or her own behavior with an attention tape (Glynn & Thomas, 1974; Ingersoll, 1988). An attention tape is completely quiet with the exception of a nonabrasive sound, such as a spoon tapping on a glass, at odd intervals. The recommended time intervals for a 30-minute tape are: 3, 4, 3, 5, 4, 2, 4, 3, 2.

To improve her ability to engage in independent seatwork, Betsy used an attention tape. Each time she heard the sound, she asked, "Am I on-task?" If so, she recorded a check and then resumed work. Betsy received points for increasing the number of checks she recorded within a time period. Within a month, Betsy increased her time on-task by 50%.

A timer may also be used. The student agrees to work a certain amount of time on a task and then sets the timer. Reinforcement is provided when the student works the agreed amount of time. A graph may used to chart the increased duration of attending behavior.

Predicting Achievement

In addition to revealing strengths and weaknesses within abilities, the other major purpose for administering an intelligence test is to estimate predicted achievement. For estimating expected achievement using the WJ-R COG, an examiner may use a full-scale score, Broad Cognitive Ability—Standard Scale (BCA), or the appropriate Scholastic Aptitude cluster. The Broad Cognitive Ability—Standard Scale provides an estimate of general intellectual functioning. The Scholastic Aptitude clusters allow an examiner to compare the most relevant set of cognitive skills to performance in a specific achievement area. The concurrent validity of both the BCA and the Scholastic Aptitude clusters in the WJ (Woodcock & Johnson, 1977) has been extensively documented (McGrew, 1986).

In addition to being a good predictor of present achievement levels, the WJ-R may also be useful for predicting future academic performance. McGrew and Pehl (1988) explored the predictive validity of the WJ. A group of 45 students were administered the WJ in third grade. Highly significant correlations were obtained between the third-grade intellectual and achievement scores and subsequent performance in reading and math 6 years later. These results provide support for usefulness of the WJ for predicting future achievement.

Aptitude Clusters

The main measures of potential on the WJ-R are the Aptitude clusters. These clusters provide a measure of predicted achievement based upon the specific set of cognitive skills that best estimate performance in that area. Using this procedure, a student's actual achievement is compared to the median average achievement of people with the same aptitude score (one-half would score above and one-half would score below). The discrepancy percentile rank indicates the percent of the population that has achievement as low or lower (below 50) or as high or higher (above 50). Figure 7-11 illustrates a completed Aptitude/Achievement Profile for Lynne, a fourth-grade student. When Lynne's reading achievement is compared

Aptitude/Achievement Discrepancies

CALCULATION OF EXPECTED STANDARD SCORES

Norms based on: ☐ Age ____ ☑ Grade 4.9

	APTITUDE SS		REF SS		DIFF (+ or −)	COLUMNS −DIFF −DIFF (F or G)	EXPECTED SS (D)
Oral Language	89 (PAGE 3)	−	100	=	−11	39 | 89	94
Reading	93 (PAGE 3)	−	100	=	−7	34 | 84 (+DIFF −DIFF)	95
Mathematics	89 (PAGE 3)	−	100	=	−11	36 | 86	93
Written Language	95 (PAGE 3)	−	100	=	−5	36 | 86	97
Knowledge	100 (PAGE 3)	−	100	=	0	37 | 87	100

CALCULATION OF DISCREPANCIES

	ACHIEVEMENT SS		EXPECTED SS		APTITUDE-ACHIEVEMENT SS DIFF (+ or −)	COLUMNS −DIFF −DIFF (F or G)	SIGNIFICANCE: PERCENTILE RANK* (H)	SIGNIFICANCE: SD DIFF** (H)
Oral Language	OR LANG SS: 99 (PAGE 3)	−	94	=	+5	22 | 72	67	0.45
Reading	READING SS: 72 (FROM WJ-R ACH)	−	95	=	−23	21 | 71	2	−2.15
Mathematics	MATH SS: 89 (FROM WJ-R ACH)	−	93	=	−4	21 | 71	35	−0.37
Written Language	WR LANG SS: 83 (FROM WJ-R ACH)	−	97	=	−14	22 | 72	11	−1.25
Knowledge	KNOWLEDGE SS: 98 (FROM WJ-R ACH)	−	100	=	−2	22 | 72	43	−0.18

*Percent of the population that has achievement as low, or lower, compared to expected achievement. (A PR over 50 indicates achievement is higher than expected achievement.)

**Difference between an achievement score and the expected achievement score in standard error of estimate units.

Figure 7–11. Aptitude/Achievement Profile for a Fourth-Grade Student.

to her predicted achievement, only 2% of the population with the same aptitude score has achievement as low or lower. In this situation, the examiner designed an instructional program for Lynne to enhance reading skill.

In another situation, Mary, a sixth-grade student, had low performance on the Reading Aptitude cluster and low performance on the Broad Reading cluster. Similarly, her performance on the Oral Language cluster and all other achievement areas fell within the low average range. The teacher also reported that Mary was slow to understand directions and acquire concepts. The examiner concluded that Mary did not have a discrepancy between predicted reading achievement and actual performance and recommended modifications in the level of instructional materials used in the regular classroom.

Conclusion

The relationships among some of the WJ-R COG factors and achievement are more clearly established than others. In many instances, further research is needed to clarify these associations. Presently, analysis of performance on the WJ-R COG tests may provide an examiner with helpful information regarding a student's strengths and weaknesses and predicted scholastic achievement.

Based upon performance, an examiner may recommend appropriate modifications or compensatory strategies that will help a student succeed. Students with severe language or perceptual impairments will also require an intensive instructional program for linguistic and academic development. In many instances, an examiner may suggest applicable recommendations and design an instructional or remedial program for a student. The previous chapters describe a variety of teaching techniques and methods that may be used for program design.

Through assessment, an examiner will be able to determine appropriate modifications and design instructional programs for students with varied types of scholastic learning difficulties.

Careful, individualized assessment leads to improved instructional planning. The diagnostic/prescriptive process is a repeating cycle in which problems are identified, programs are designed, and progress is monitored. When an examiner considers and integrates relevant data from assessment, error analysis, behavioral observations, and the environment into instructional planning, student learning and performance improve.

APPENDIX: SAMPLE PSYCHOEDUCATIONAL REPORTS

The intent of a psychoeducational report is to resolve the concerns of the referral source and to recommend appropriate treatment plans. When writing reports, the examiner must consider and integrate findings from behavioral observations, error analysis, and test scores. The communication of assessment results may be accomplished in several ways using a variety of report formats and styles. In some instances, an examiner may incorporate test scores into the report. In other instances, the examiner may attach the scores to the end of the report. The sections in a report will vary based upon the type and extent of the assessment performed. For example, for one evaluation, background information may be critical. In another case, the background section would be omitted. The amount of detail, the tests administered, and the number of recommendations provided will also vary based upon the purposes of the assessment.

An examiner may include scores in the body of the report or use a record form to summarize WJ-R test scores. Case # 1, Todd W., illustrates a summary of scores on a reporting form. Several other examples of reproducible reporting forms are included at the end of the Appendix. As an alternative, Compuscore printouts and WJ-R Profiles may be provided at the end of each report. As a sample, the Compuscore printout and WJ-R ACH Age/Grade Profile are included for Case #3, Andrew S.

As a guide for reporting WJ-R and other assessment results, the following report outline, adapted from Sattler (1988), may be used.

Sample Report Outline

1. Identifying Information
   (a) student's name and date of birth
   (b) student's age and grade
   (c) date of examination
   (d) examiner's name
   (e) teacher's name, parents' names, school (optional)
2. Reason for Referral
   (a) who referred the student
   (b) why the student was referred
   (c) specific concerns of the referral source
3. Background Information
   (a) relevant family history
   (b) current family situation
   (c) health/developmental history
   (d) relevant educational history
   (e) previous interventions and evaluations
4. Tests Administered
   (a) names of tests administered
   (b) other assessments used
   (c) results of previous assessments, if used in report
5. Behavioral Observations
   (a) reactions to assessment
   (b) general response style
   (c) activity and attentional level
   (d) language style
   (e) response to success and failure
6. Cognitive Abilities and/or Achievement

(a) report scores in text or attach scores
(b) interpret and integrate data
(c) consider findings from several sources
(d) separate paragraphs for results describing different areas, i.e., reading, mathematics
(e) use specific examples to document clinical interpretation

7. Recommendations
(a) base on strengths and weaknesses
(b) provide realistic and practical intervention goals and strategies
(c) suggest any further evaluation needed
(d) involve student, parents, and teachers

8. Summary and Conclusions
(a) review implications of results
(b) no new information
(c) optional

Sample Case Reports

When preparing psychoeducational reports, an examiner integrates information from all sources. The types of recommendations an examiner makes will depend upon the nature of the referral question, the prior instructional interventions, the present educational setting, and the service delivery system that is available. The content of reports and type of diagnosis made will also vary based upon the examiner's setting, i.e., public school, private school, vocational, clinical, or hospital, and the examiner's role within that environment. What is appropriate for one type of report is not appropriate for a report in another setting. For example, a private clinician may suggest a diagnosis of a learning disability, whereas an examiner in a public school would integrate information from the multidisciplinary team prior to categorizing the disability and determining whether the student qualified for special services. The selection of verbal labels will also depend upon the nature and purpose of the assessment. A psychologist in a vocational setting may classify a student's scores as falling in the Mentally Deficient range, whereas a school psychologist may describe the scores as falling in the Very Low range. The main goal of all psychoeducational reports is to translate clinical impressions gained from a variety of sources into meaningful recommendations that will increase a student's learning efficiency and behavioral adjustment. With the diagnostic/prescriptive model, assessments are conducted, recommendations are implemented, the progress of the student and the efficacy of the instructional techniques are monitored, and modifications and new plans are developed as needed.

The purpose of the following case studies is to illustrate the use of the WJ-R ACH for educational planning. These sample case studies depict several different types of students at a variety of age levels. Although information regarding cognitive abilities is presented, the emphasis of the reports is placed on interpreting and reporting information from the WJ-R ACH. With the exception of Case #1, Compuscore printouts were attached at the end of each report.

Name: Todd W.

Date of Birth: 3/29/81
Chronological Age: 8-9
Teacher: Mrs. Ashton

Dates of Testing: 1/9/90,
1/11/90
Grade: 2.4
Examiner:

Reason for Referral

Todd was referred by his second-grade teacher, Mrs. Ashton. Mrs. Ashton expressed concern regarding Todd's progress in school and his lack of self-confidence in his abilities. The purposes of the present evaluation were to provide information regarding the specific nature of Todd's learning difficulties and to make appropriate educational recommendations.

Background Information

Todd is currently enrolled in a second-grade program. Mrs. Ashton, his classroom teacher, reports that Todd has difficulty completing his work. In the classroom setting he spends much of his time looking at the paper, playing with objects, and staring into space. Even when he applies himself, he proceeds very slowly. Lack of speed is also noted in copying material from the blackboard. The classroom teacher also describes his handwriting as "extremely illegible all of the time."

Tests Administered

Todd was administered the Woodcock-Johnson Psycho-Educational Battery Tests of Cognitive Ability—Revised (Tests 1–14, 20, 21), the Woodcock-Johnson Tests of Achievement—Revised (Tests 22–31), and an informal reading inventory. Additionally, the examiner asked Todd to copy a series of shapes.

Behavioral Observations

Testing was conducted in two 2-hour sessions. Although Todd was cooperative throughout both testing sessions, he asked several times how much longer the testing would last. On several occasions, he started fiddling with some object on the table, such as a pencil or the knobs on the tape recorder. He also tended to become distracted by noises and inquire about extraneous environmental details, such as a fly resting on the window ledge. When prompted, he refocused on the task.

Comments throughout testing in all academic areas reflected his lack of confidence in his abilities. As ex-

amples, when asked by the examiner if he liked to read, Todd responded that he didn't know how to read. When asked to write some sentences, he stated that he didn't want to write because he wasn't any good at it. In solving math computations, when he came to a subtraction problem, he stated that he didn't know how to do subtraction problems and that he hated them.

Cognitive Abilities

When compared to grade-mates, Todd's overall cognitive performance fell in the Average range (Broad Cognitive Ability—Extended Scale SS = 107). Performance on all oral language tests fell within the Average to Superior range. Memory tasks that involved making and retrieving visual-auditory associations or required repeating words and sentences that he had heard also fell within the Average range. Both comprehension-knowledge tests, which include vocabulary development and cultural knowledge, and reasoning tests, which require problem solving in novel situations, fell within the Average range. In contrast, significant weaknesses were noted on tests that required rapid processing of visual symbols and informal tasks requiring copying of forms.

Achievement

With the exception of his Superior performance on the Social Studies test and his Average performance on the Science test, Todd scored below grade-mates in all academic areas. Based upon his aptitude scores, significant discrepancies exist between his predicted and actual achievement in reading, mathematics, and written language.

Reading

Presently, Todd has a beginning foundation in word identification. His instructional reading level ranges from beginning to mid-first grade level. Todd was able to identify common sight words when they were presented in a list but then misread these same words in connected text. As examples, when reading text, he misread "this" as "things," "he" as "I," "for" as "from," "fat" as "fast," "at" as "that," and "me" as "my." He tended to overlook details in words and confuse words with similar visual appearances. Additionally, on two occasions, he skipped entire lines of text. This visual confusion, coupled with below-average word attack skill, results in misidentification of words and a slow reading rate. Performance improves when he uses his thumb for tracking by placing it above the word he is reading.

When attempting to pronounce longer words in a list, he tended to ignore sounds within words. Although Todd does possess some word attack skill, he lacks confidence in his abilities and tends to give up if he does not immediately recognize a word.

Based upon assessment of his listening comprehension and oral vocabulary, Todd has average potential for reading comprehension. His present difficulties with reading comprehension tasks appear to be caused by low decoding skill and lack of confidence.

Written Language

Todd's most apparent difficulties with written language performance are in basic skills, primarily spelling and handwriting. Although Todd attempts to produce a phonetic representation of a word, he does not recall how common words look and does not listen carefully to the sounds that he is writing. For example, he spelled the word *bird* as *brid* and the word *new* as *now*. Reversals of the letters *b* and *d* were apparent in his spelling; he wrote the word *table* as *tadl* and the word *don't* as *bouwnt*. These types of errors provide further support for weaknesses in the processing of visual symbols.

Todd's handwriting is difficult to read and reflects his struggle with visual-motor tasks. He tends to run words together without spaces between them. His letters are inconsistent in size and poorly formed. When using lined paper, his letters tend to rise above the line. His handwriting deteriorates further when writing on unlined paper.

Todd also had difficulty writing complete sentences. On several items, he wrote lists of single nouns when asked to write a sentence.

Mathematics

Todd's instructional range in mathematics extends from mid-first-grade to second-grade level. No difference existed between calculation and problem-solving skills. Todd understood how to solve simple addition facts by counting on his fingers but had difficulty with subtraction. When asked to solve the problem $17 - 9$, Todd responded that he did not have enough fingers.

Knowledge

Todd's scores on the Knowledge cluster fell within the Average range which demonstrates his ability to acquire and retain information from his environment. His highest score was on the Social Studies test (GE = 4.3), whereas his lowest score was in Humanities (GE = 1.3), which measures knowledge of literature, art, and music. Todd commented that he was particularly interested in history but didn't care much about books. When asked to identify or complete several nursery rhymes, he stated that he had forgotten how they went.

Recommendations

To profit from instruction in a regular classroom setting, it will be necessary to modify educational materials to Todd's instructional levels. One major goal is to build independent working and study skills so that Todd will increase the time he spends on an assignment.

Classroom tasks that require efficient visual-perceptual and fine motor skills (hand-eye coordination) will be particularly difficult for Todd. Examples include handwriting, drawing, and copying material from the blackboard or a textbook. Todd will require additional time to complete these types of tasks.

Further Evaluation

1. Based upon Todd's classroom performance and test data, the multidisciplinary team may wish to consider referral to a vision specialist to examine visual efficiency.

2. If attentional difficulties continue to affect classroom performance, the team may wish to consider referral to a pediatrician for further investigation of attentional deficits.

Reading

1. In designing a reading program for Todd, high-interest books and stories should be used. The instructor may wish to begin using predictable books and the language experience approach.

2. Todd needs further assistance with word identification and word attack strategies. If skill does not develop naturally or cannot be integrated successfully into a language experience approach, he may benefit from a more structured approach, such as the Fernald method. The Fernald method will increase attention to visual details in words and may be used with the language experience approach: Todd writes original stories and then traces any unknown words that he needs for writing until he can write the word from memory.

Writing

1. Todd should be encouraged to engage in meaningful writing activities as often as possible. Attention should be directed to the communication of ideas; he should not be penalized for poor spelling. Todd would benefit from use of the writing process approach in the classroom where he engages in prewriting activities, drafting, revising, editing,

and publishing his stories.

2. Instruction should be provided to promote mastery of the spelling of high frequency words. Todd may benefit from a multisensory whole-word approach to spelling. An example would be an adaptation of the Fernald method for spelling. The following steps are used: (a) the teacher writes the word to be learned on a card and pronounces it; (b) the student repeats the word and then traces the word with a finger as many times as needed to write the word from memory; and (c) the word is removed and the student writes it from memory. The tracing used in this approach will also improve Todd's handwriting.

3. Todd should receive systematic instruction in handwriting. Cursive writing should be introduced as soon as possible. The rhythm and production of whole words in cursive are likely to make handwriting easier for Todd and help improve his legibility and spacing. Paper with structured visual guides illustrating a top line, dotted middle line, and a bottom line should be used for writing stories. When possible, handwriting practice should be integrated with meaningful writing activities, such as producing the final copy of a story for the bulletin board.

Mathematics

1. Todd needs to increase his knowledge of mathematical concepts associated with place value and regrouping. The teacher should provide concrete examples of when and how subtraction is used. Regrouping in subtraction should be introduced with manipulatives, and then Todd should learn to demonstrate the process with the objects. Once conceptual mastery is assured, emphasis can be switched to operational efficiency in computation.

2. Todd should not be required to copy math problems from the textbook for homework. Instead, problems should be presented on a clearly printed worksheet.

3. In the home, emphasis should be placed on developing practical skill in mathematics. For example, Todd needs to develop skill in identifying coins and counting up change to a dollar.

Attitude

A major concern is Todd's lack of confidence in his own abilities. His perception of himself as a learner is far lower than his actual performance level. After hearing Todd describe himself as a nonreader, the examiner was surprised to discover that Todd does possess beginning reading skills. Although Todd stated that he was "no good in writing," he was able to write several sentences that expressed appropriate content. A major goal should be to improve Todd's self-esteem and image of himself as a learner. This may be accomplished by providing him with realistic tasks and successful experiences. In addition to skill development, he needs constant reassurance that he is a capable individual. The following suggestions may help Todd improve his self-esteem:

1. Reinforce positive behaviors. Give five positive comments for each negative or correcting comment.
2. Provide positive reinforcement for appropriate social behavior (e.g., "We all appreciate it when you get ready quickly.")
3. Provide positive reinforcement for academic behavior (e.g., "Todd, you really worked hard on your math assignment today. You must feel good that your work is neat.")
4. Create opportunities for Todd to shine. When possible, take advantage of his good knowledge base and interest in social studies.

Educational Programming

Presently, an educational plan is needed to build academic skills, self-esteem, confidence, and ability to sustain attention to a task. School personnel should meet to determine whether Todd qualifies for special services within the school setting and to implement a treatment plan.

Summary

Todd's present school difficulties are caused by several factors. His primary cognitive weaknesses are in rapid processing of visual symbols, visual-motor skill, and ability to sustain attention. These weaknesses have affected acquisition of academic skills. Additionally, Todd's lack of confidence in his abilities and his low task persistence have contributed to academic difficulties.

Todd's instructional needs should be addressed immediately to reduce further damage to his self-esteem, ensure that he does not quit trying, and allow him to progress academically. With high-interest materials, a structured teaching situation, and successful academic experiences Todd should regain self-confidence in his learning abilities and his interest in learning.

Name _Todd W._   Grade _2.4_   Date of Test _1 - 11 - 90_

School _Sunset Elementary_   Date of Birth _3 - 29 - 81_

Teacher _Mrs. Ashton_   Chronological Age _8 - 9 -_

Examiner _N. Mather_   Norms based on: Age ___ Grade _X_

WOODCOCK-JOHNSON PSYCHO-EDUCATIONAL BATTERY - REVISED
TESTS OF COGNITIVE ABILITY

Test / CLUSTER	Factors	Age Equivalent	Grade Equivalent	Relative Mastery Index	Standard Scores SS	Standard Scores Range	Percentile Ranks PR	Percentile Ranks Range
STANDARD BATTERY								
1 Memory for Names	Glr	7-7	2.1	89 /90	98	94-102	45	34-55
2 Memory for Sentences	Gsm	8-10	3.5	95 /90	108	102-114	69	55-82
3 Visual Matching	Gs	6-5	1.1	61 /90	82	74-90	11	4-25
4 Incomplete Words	Ga	6-7	1.3	85 /90	94	87-101	35	19-53
5 Visual Closure	Gv	8-3	2.6	90 /90	100	92-108	50	30-70
6 Picture Vocabulary	Gc	11-0	5.6	99 /90	128	122-134	97	93-99
7 Analysis-Synthesis	Gf	7-10	2.5	90 /90	100	96-104	50	39-61
BROAD COGNITIVE ABILITY(E Dev)				/90				
BROAD COGNITIVE ABILITY(Std)				/90				
SUPPLEMENTAL BATTERY								
8 Visual-Auditory Learning	Glr	16-8	10.6	96 /90	120	115-125	91	84-95
9 Memory for Words	Gsm	9-2	3.8	96 /90	108	101-115	69	53-84
10 Cross Out	Gs	6-9	1.4	8 /90	87	79-95	19	9-37
11 Sound Blending	Ga	11-7	6.1	97 /90	117	112-122	86	79-93
12 Picture Recognition	Gv	8-4	2.9	92 /90	104	97-111	60	42-77
13 Oral Vocabulary	Gc	8-7	3.3	96 /90	112	106-118	80	66-88
14 Concept Formation	Gf	9-5	3.9	97 /90	113	110-116	81	75-86
COGNITIVE FACTOR CLUSTERS								
LONG-TERM RETRIEVAL	Glr	9-4	4.2	93 /90	109	105-113	72	63-81
SHORT-TERM MEMORY	Gsm	8-11	3.7	95 /90	109	104-114	72	61-82
PROCESSING SPEED	Gs	6-8	1.2	73 /90	90	74-86	10	4-18
AUDITORY PROCESSING	Ga	8-8	3.3	93 /90	107	102-112	68	55-79
VISUAL PROCESSING	Gv	8-2	2.7	91 /90	102	95-109	56	37-73
COMPREHEN.-KNOWLEDGE	Gc	9-6	4.2	97 /90	121	116-126	92	86-96
FLUID REASONING	Gf	8-8	3.3	95 /90	108	105-111	70	63-77
BROAD COGNITIVE ABILITY (Ext)		8-3	2.9	93 /90	107	104-110	67	61-75
APTITUDE CLUSTERS								
READING APTITUDE				93 /90	106	103-109	65	58-73
MATHEMATICS APTITUDE				91 /90	102	99-105	55	47-63
WRITTEN LANGUAGE APTITUDE				93 /90	108	105-111	71	63-77
KNOWLEDGE APTITUDE				95 /90	113	110-116	80	75-86
SUPPLEMENTAL TESTS 15 - 21								
15 Del. Rec.-Mem. for Names	Glr			/90				
16 Del. Rec.-Vis.-Aud. Lrng.	Glr			/90				
17 Numbers Reversed	Gsm,Gf			/90				
18 Sound Patterns	Ga, Gf			/90				
19 Spatial Relations	Gf, Gv			/90				
20 Listening Comprehension	Gc	8-7	3.1	93 /90	106	100-112	66	50-79
21 Verbal Analogies	Gf, Gc	7-11	2.5	90 /90	100	93-107	50	32-68
ORAL LANGUAGE								
ORAL LANGUAGE APTITUDE				/90				
ORAL LANGUAGE		8-11	3.5	96 /90	115	112-118	84	79-88

DM: 0003

Figure A–1. Test Report Form.

TESTS OF ACHIEVEMENT - STANDARD & SUPPLEMENTAL   Form __A__

Test / CLUSTER	Factors	Age Equivalent	Grade Equivalent	Relative Mastery Index	Standard Scores SS	Standard Scores Range	Percentile Ranks PR	Percentile Ranks Range
ACHIEVEMENT TESTS - STANDARD								
22 Letter-Word Identification		6-11	1.4	19 /90	77	73-81	6	4-10
23 Passage Comprehension		7-6	2.0	77 /90	94	90-98	35	25-45
24 Calculation	Gq	7-0	1.4	53 /90	82	77-87	11	6-19
25 Applied Problems	Gq	7-0	1.6	66 /90	87	82-92	19	12-30
26 Dictation		6-9	1.4	45 /90	76	71-81	5	3-10
27 Writing Samples		7-1	1.5	58 /90	87	84-90	20	14-25
28 Science	Gc	7-2	1.9	85 /90	97	90-104	41	25-61
29 Social Studies	Gc	9-8	4.3	98 /90	123	116-130	94	96-98
30 Humanities	Gc	6-8	1.3	79 /90	92	86-98	29	18-45
BROAD & EARLY DEVELOPMENT CLUSTERS								
BROAD READING		7-2	1.6	50 /90	86	83-89	17	13-23
BROAD MATHEMATICS*	Gq	7-0	1.5	58 /90	83	79-87	13	8-19
BROAD WRITTEN LANGUAGE		6-11	1.4	50 /90	84	81-87	14	10-19
BROAD KNOWLEDGE (E DEV)	Gc	7-10	2.4	91 /90	102	98-106	55	45-66
SKILLS (E DEV)		6-11	1.4	42 /90	78	75-81	7	5-10

*Also for use as a cognitive factor.

ACHIEVEMENT TESTS - SUPPLEMENTAL

Test / CLUSTER	Factors	Age Equivalent	Grade Equivalent	Relative Mastery Index	Standard Scores SS	Standard Scores Range	Percentile Ranks PR	Percentile Ranks Range
31 Word Attack	Ga	7-1	1.6	/90	91	87-95	27	19-37
32 Reading Vocabulary				/90				
33 Quantitative Concepts	Gq			/90				
34 Proofing				/90				
35 Writing Fluency	Gs			/90				
P Punctuation/Capitalization				/90				
S Spelling				/90				
U Usage				/90				
H Handwriting				/90				

BASIC SKILLS & APPLICATIONS CLUSTERS

Test / CLUSTER	Factors	Age Equivalent	Grade Equivalent	Relative Mastery Index	Standard Scores SS	Standard Scores Range	Percentile Ranks PR	Percentile Ranks Range
BASIC READING SKILLS		6-11	1.5	39 /90	87	84-90	19	14-25
READING COMPREHENSION				/90				
BASIC MATHEMATICS SKILLS	Gq			/90				
MATHEMATICS REASONING**	Gq			/90				
BASIC WRITING SKILLS				/90				
WRITTEN EXPRESSION				/90				

** Not an actual "cluster". The Applied Problems test measures Mathematics Reasoning.

INTRA-COGNITIVE DISCREPANCIES

COGNITIVE FACTOR CLUSTER	PR	SD DIFF
LONG-TERM RETRIEVAL		
SHORT-TERM MEMORY		
PROCESSING SPEED	1	-2.38
AUDITORY PROCESSING		
VISUAL PROCESSING		
COMPREHENSION-KNOWLEDGE		
FLUID REASONING		

INTRA-ACHIEVEMENT DISCREPANCIES

BROAD ACHIEVEMENT CLUSTER	PR	SD DIFF
BROAD READING (R)		
BROAD MATHEMATICS (M)		
BROAD WRITTEN LANGUAGE (W)		
BROAD KNOWLEDGE (K)	91	+1.34

APTITUDE/ACHIEVEMENT DISCREPANCIES

BASED ON: BCA _____   APTITUDE _____

ACHIEVEMENT CLUSTER	PR	SD DIFF
BROAD READING	3	-1.86
BROAD MATHEMATICS	5	-1.68
BROAD WRITTEN LANGUAGE	2	-1.96
BROAD KNOWLEDGE		
BASIC READING SKILLS		
BASIC MATHEMATICS SKILLS		
BASIC WRITING SKILLS		
READING COMPREHENSION		
MATHEMATICS REASONING		
WRITTEN EXPRESSION		

D Mc ACH/DISCREP 1

(continued)

Name: Sallie L.

Date of Birth: 9/11/81

Chronological Age: 8–2

School: Holy Cross

Dates of Testing: 10/25, 26, 11/6/89

Grade: 3.2

Examiner:

Reason for Referral

Sallie was referred for a psychoeducational assessment by both her mother and her third-grade teacher. Both parties were concerned about Sallie's difficulty with reading and writing, as well as her inability to stay on-task, both in school and at home. The purpose of the evaluation was to determine whether Sallie needed special services and to recommend strategies for improving performance.

Background Information

Sallie has a history of problems with short attention span, distractibility, and fidgeting in school. In first grade, she was diagnosed by her pediatrician as having Attention Deficit Hyperactivity Disorder (ADHD) and began taking Ritalin. Several months later, her mother decided that the medication was ineffective and discontinued its use. This year her mother reported that getting Sallie to concentrate on her homework at night is a constant battle. Mrs. L. noted that she had to sit with Sallie or Sallie would not work. She also indicated that Sallie was very frustrated at school and at home, often cried, and had nightmares about school assignments. Based upon the current behavioral profile and past diagnosis, Sallie was referred again to a pediatrician who reaffirmed the diagnosis of ADHD and placed Sallie back on Ritalin. Her mother has noted dramatic improvements in attention span, focus of concentration, neatness, and completion of work. Testing was postponed until after Sallie had been stabilized on Ritalin and had her reading glasses.

Tests Administered

Sallie was administered the Woodcock-Johnson Psycho-Educational Battery—Revised, a test of visual-motor integration, and an informal reading inventory. The examiner also collected a written language sample.

Behavioral Observations

Sallie was cooperative and cheerful during testing. She appeared to try her best on every item. She tended to be chatty and occasionally had to be reminded to attend to the task. Sallie was tested during the morning as her mother indicated that this was Sallie's best time of day.

Cognitive Abilities

Based on the results of the WJ-R COG, Sallie appears to be functioning within the Average range in global intelligence. No significant strengths and weaknesses were noted among the various cognitive skills assessed with the exception of Superior ability in visual processing speed.

Observations from a standardized test and informal analysis suggest that Sallie appears to demonstrate a relative weakness in visual-motor integration, or the ability to coordinate the fine motor movements of her hand to reproduce a visual image. Although her handwriting is legible, it is not neat. When Sallie was asked to write very carefully, she worked very slowly and was able to produce well-formed letters.

Achievement

Sallie is functioning in the Average to High Average range in all academic areas. In general, her problem-solving and comprehension abilities are slightly higher than her performance in basic skills.

Reading

Based on the results of the Broad Reading cluster score, Sallie's overall reading ability is in the High Average range when compared to grade-peers. Her Relative Mastery Index (RMI) of 97/90 indicates that she will have 97% success on reading tasks at grade level, while her average peers will be having 90% success. Throughout all reading activities, Sallie demonstrated behaviors consistent with good readers. She attempted to use structural analysis to identify unfamiliar words and was often successful in identifying prefixes, root words, and suffixes. She reread passages when items were difficult and consistently self-monitored for meaning. On the informal reading inventory, she was able to retell stories covering the main points and the supporting details.

Written Language

Based on the Broad Written Language cluster, Sallie is functioning in the Average range when compared to grade-peers. A difference existed, however, between performance on the Basic Skills cluster (RMI = 82/90) and the Written Expression cluster (RMI = 96/90). Sallie's abilities to articulate an idea in a structured writing task and to write quickly when the task is simple are significantly higher than her skills in punctuation, capitalization, and spelling. Although her handwriting was legible, her letters were somewhat poorly formed and of uneven and often incorrect height.

Mathematics

Sallie's performance on the Broad Math cluster was in the High Average range when compared to grade-peers. Her RMI of 95/90 indicates that she would be expected to demonstrate 95% mastery with similar tasks that average individuals in her grade would perform with 90% mastery. Sallie was able to add multidigit numbers with regrouping and subtract without regrouping. Her ability to apply mathematical knowledge in practical situations fell in the Superior range.

Knowledge

Sallie's performance on questions relating to three content areas placed her in the Average range compared to peers. These results suggest that despite an attentional problem, Sallie has picked up information from her environment, can retain this information over time, and can recall it when required.

Conclusions

Sallie appears to be a student of overall Average to High Average functioning in both cognitive and achievement areas. She appears to have a relative weakness in visual-motor integration. This weakness, in combination with ADHD, appear to have affected her ability to perform successfully in academic tasks in both the classroom and home.

Recommendations

Although special education services are presently not required, several recommendations will be of value in helping Sallie become more successful in the classroom and home.

Medication

1. Continue to observe Sallie closely to insure that the amount of medication she is taking is adequate to help her stay on-task and work carefully.

2. The classroom teacher must be responsible for reminding Sallie to take her medication, because the consequences for Sallie in poor-quality and incomplete

schoolwork have emotional as well as temporal ramifications (redoing the work as homework). One of the symptoms of ADHD is difficulty remembering responsibilities at specific times; therefore, it is unrealistic to expect Sallie to remember to take her medication.

Spelling

1. To improve spelling, teach Sallie a particular spelling study technique, such as Look-Say-Spell-Write. The following steps may be used:

a. Provide a list of spelling words, no more than five in a session, printed far enough apart so that each can be seen without seeing the others.

b. Have Sallie *Look* at the first word, *Say* the word, *Spell* the word as she looks at it until she is sure she can *Write* it from memory.

c. On a new piece of paper, Sallie should write the word without looking at the model. She then checks it against the model. If the word is correct, she repeats the writing-checking procedure three times. If the word is incorrect, she goes back and restudies the word.

d. After she has studied all of the words for the session, someone should test her on them. She should then be retested on the words the following day and restudy any words that were incorrect.

Handwriting

1. Teach Sallie cursive writing. Pay careful attention to the way she forms each letter (direction, proper sequence of strokes) as well as the appearance of the letter. Also help her notice height differences among letters (e.g., short letters live on the ground, tall letters go up in the sky, and some letters have their bottoms in the ocean.) Provide extensive practice in cursive as she learns it to give her a writing technique that is simultaneously fluent and neat. The formation of each letter must become absolutely automatic.

Punctuation and Capitalization

1. Reteach punctuation and capitalization rules that have already been presented in school. When she understands the rules, teach a proofreading strategy, such as COPS. For this strategy, Sallie will review her work for capitalization (C), overall appearance (O), punctuation (P), and spelling (S). Once this technique is learned, Sallie can use it independently.

Behavior

1. Work on behaviors that are interfering with Sallie's classroom functioning. Positive behaviors that would be

helpful to Sallie include: staying on-task, following directions promptly, and completing classroom assignments. Provide ample reinforcement for positive behaviors. If positive reinforcement is not sufficient, the teacher may develop a contract with Sallie.

a. Meet with Sallie privately. Tell her the behavior that you have noticed and why it is a problem (e.g., "When you hurry through your work, your writing is sloppy and it's hard for me to read your answers").

b. Suggest a contract in which she will earn one (or more) point each time she demonstrates a particular behavior. Agree on what her points will buy and when she will have a chance to spend them. At first she may need to be able to trade them in daily.

c. Write a contract that includes the student's name, the behavior to develop, a technique that may help the student (e.g., "Each time I notice the red dot on the index card on my desk, I will go back to work"), and the reward. Make

sure that the reward is positive, specific, and attainable.

d. Have the teacher and student sign the contract.

Homework

1. Before Sallie leaves school, check her assignment sheet to insure that all of the homework is recorded legibly.

2. When beginning nightly homework, Mrs. L. should help Sallie review all of the assignments, estimate the time each will take, and decide on their order of importance.

3. Mrs. L. can begin to decrease Sallie's dependence on her for constant supervision of homework by being nearby to provide help if asked, rather than sitting with Sallie. Periodically, Mrs. L. should look at Sallie's work, find something to praise, such as a neatly written sentence, the amount of time she has been working, or a detail in a story, and then move away again.

Name: Andrew S.

Date of Birth: 11/02/78
Chronological Age: 11–6
School: Sunshine School

Dates of Testing: 5/3, 5/5/90

Grade: 4.8
Examiner:

how he felt about school, Andrew commented that he liked school okay but he wasn't any good at it.

Reason for Referral

Andrew was referred for a psychoeducational evaluation by his clinical psychologist, Dr. Fenton. Dr. Fenton had noted perceptual problems that suggested some form of dyslexia and was concerned regarding Andrew's low levels of achievement despite average intelligence. Using the DSM-III-R criteria, Dr. Fenton indicated that Andrew would be classified as having a Developmental Reading Disorder. The purposes of the present evaluation were to provide information regarding the specific nature of Andrew's learning problems and to make appropriate educational recommendations.

Background Information

Andrew repeated third grade and is currently enrolled in a fourth-grade program in Sunnyside, Arizona. He receives special education services daily in the morning. This year his special education category placement was changed from Learning Disabled to Emotionally Handicapped. School records indicate that Andrew does not complete his work.

Tests Administered

Andrew was administered the Woodcock-Johnson Psycho-Educational Battery Tests of Cognitive Ability—Revised and the Woodcock-Johnson Tests of Achievement—Revised. The results from this assessment are attached. Additionally, the examiner listened to Andrew read a series of graded passages. After the instructional reading level was established, the examiner read several additional passages to Andrew and had him answer comprehension questions to estimate his level of listening comprehension.

Behavioral Observations

Testing was conducted in two 2-hour sessions. Andrew was cooperative throughout both testing sessions. On several occasions, he attempted to engage the examiner in conversations that were unrelated to the task. When asked

Cognitive Abilities

Andrew's overall cognitive performance fell in the Average range. Significant strengths were noted in both his auditory processing, or the ability to blend and synthesize sounds of the English language, and his comprehension-knowledge, which includes vocabulary development and cultural knowledge. In contrast, significant weaknesses were noted on all tasks involving short-term memory and retrieval of visual-auditory associations. Andrew had trouble repeating information he had just heard and reproducing information that he had just seen. On a delayed recall task administered 2 days later, Andrew was only able to recall two of the symbols that were learned in the previous session. He commented that he always "forgets stuff right after he learns it." These weaknesses in memory have made it difficult for Andrew to learn to decode, spell, and memorize math facts.

Achievement

With the exception of his performance on the Knowledge tests, Andrew is functioning several years below grade level in all academic areas. He has a significant discrepancy between his aptitude and achievement in both reading and written language performance. Based upon his cognitive abilities, one would predict a significantly higher level of academic performance.

Reading

Andrew's instructional reading level is approximately at beginning to mid-second-grade level. He did not recognize many simple sight words, such as "his," "went," and "must." When pronouncing words, he tended to ignore sounds within the words. He was unable to pronounce any words with more than one syllable out of context. His greatest weakness in reading was word attack, or his ability to pronounce phonically regular nonsense words. Presently, Andrew has not acquired a systematic strategy for word identification. He mispronounced simple consonant-vowel-consonant sound patterns and was unable to pronounce any multisyllabic nonsense words. When encouraged to make an attempt, his limited application of an efficient strategy is apparent.

In contrast to his low word identification skill, when passages were read to Andrew, he was able to retell and answer comprehension questions at the seventh-grade level. Based upon assessment of his listening comprehension and oral vocabulary, it appears that Andrew has average potential for reading comprehension. His present difficulties with reading comprehension tasks are caused by low decoding skill.

Written Language

Andrew's primary difficulty with written language performance is in basic skills. Although he has good ideas, his extreme difficulty with spelling decreases the amount of attention that he is able to devote to expressing his ideas. In several instances, it is impossible to decipher a word because of poor spelling. Although Andrew attempts to produce a phonetic representation of a word, he does not recall how common words look and does not listen carefully to the sounds that he is writing. For example, he spelled the word *with* as *whthe*. Andrew's handwriting is below average, but legible.

His difficulty with symbolic learning is evident in his frequent letter reversals in both reading and writing. For example, he pronounced the nonsense word "ib" as "id." When copying the word *big* from a list of three words, Andrew wrote *dig*. In writing sentences, he spelled the word *boy* as *doy*, and the word *bird* as *dird*.

Mathematics

Problem-solving skills are higher than computational skills. Andrew understood how to solve many problems but counted with his fingers for simple addition and subtraction facts and solved all multiplication problems by adding the numbers. For example on the problem 6 × 4, he added together two pairs of 6s, and then combined the two 12s to obtain the answer. He ignored the mathematical signs on simple subtraction problems and added the numbers. He was unable to solve subtraction problems that involved regrouping or to perform any simple division problems, such as 12 divided by 6.

Knowledge

Andrew's scores on the Knowledge cluster fell within the average range which demonstrates his ability to acquire and retain information through listening activities. His highest score was on the Science test. Andrew commented that this was his favorite subject in school.

Recommendations

To profit from instruction in a regular classroom setting, educational materials will need to be adapted to Andrew's instructional level. If modifications are not made, Andrew will not be able to read and profit from textbooks. Andrew may need to take exams orally and will need extra assistance with any reading or written assignments. Additionally, he is likely to have difficulty listening to oral presentations that do not have supplemental visual materials, such as an outline or a study guide to follow.

Classroom tasks that require visualization will be particularly difficult for Andrew. Examples include: memorizing sight words or math facts and copying material from the blackboard or a textbook.

Reading

1. Andrew needs further assistance with word identification and word attack strategies. Initially, he should be taught to decode using a structured phonics approach that is systematic and provides substantial repetition. His above-average performance on auditory processing tasks suggests that he will learn easily with this type of method. Examples of appropriate approaches would be the Slingerland or Orton-Gillingham approach, the Phonic Remedial Reading Lessons, or the Spalding method. Andrew should practice both pronouncing and blending sounds into words and then writing the words as he pronounces each letter sound in sequence. Initially, a linguistic reading program or a basal series with a controlled vocabulary should be used for reading. This type of instruction should be supplemented with high-interest reading materials so that Andrew does not lose interest in or lose sight of the purpose of reading.

2. As decoding skill improves, a fluency method should be used to increase reading rate. One possibility is the Neurological Impress Method, where the teacher or parent and the student read together while pointing to the words as they are read. This method may also be used to help Andrew read more difficult materials such as content area textbooks. Because of his good oral language and listening skills, Andrew would also benefit from following along with taped content area books.

Writing

1. Andrew should be encouraged to write as often as possible. Attention should be directed to the communication of ideas and he should not be penalized for poor spelling.

2. Instruction should be provided to promote phonetic spelling and mastery of the spelling of high-frequency words. Andrew is likely to benefit from a multisensory whole-word approach to spelling. An example would be an adaptation of the Fernald method for spelling. The following steps are used:(a) the teacher writes the word to be learned on a card and pronounces it; (b) the student repeats the word and then traces the word with a finger as many times as needed to write the word from memory; (c)

the word is removed and the student writes it from memory. As spelling skill improves, Andrew will benefit from word processing and the use of spelling checkers.

Mathematics

1. Andrew needs to learn the concepts that relate to place value and regrouping. The teacher should provide concrete examples of when and how subtraction, multiplication, and division are used. The teacher should also introduce fractions, decimals, and percentage.

2. Although memorization of math facts is important, Andrew may not be able to accomplish this. To continue his growth in math problem solving, he should learn how to use a calculator and be provided with one in the classroom. Emphasis should be placed on problem solving and development of practical skill in mathematics. For example, Andrew needs to increase his skill in counting coins and making change.

Educational Programming

Presently, intensive remediation is needed to build academic skills. Based upon the severity of his learning disability, one-to-one tutoring should be provided for Andrew during or after school. The tutoring should be three to four times weekly for an hour. The instructor should be a learning disability specialist with a strong background in special education methodology. For maximal growth, one-to-one therapy is critical.

Summary

The primary presenting problem is a severe weakness in memory that has affected acquisition of reading decoding skill, spelling, and memorization of math facts. These deficiencies in basic skill areas have subsequently affected performance in reading comprehension, math problem solving, and written expression. Andrew has significant discrepancies between his aptitude for scholastic success and his present achievement levels. He is clearly capable of making significant gains in academic areas with proper remediation.

Care should be taken to ensure that Andrew is not placed in an environment where he cannot succeed because of his level of academic skill. His instructional needs must be addressed immediately to reduce damage to his self-esteem and ensure that he does not quit trying. With a highly structured teaching situation, Andrew will make rapid progress and regain his self-confidence in his learning abilities. In the interim, he should receive constant support and reassurance that a lack of ability or low intelligence is not the reason for his learning difficulty.

COMPUSCORE FOR THE WJ-R

Norms Based on Grade

==
Name: Andrew S.   ID: Page: 1
==

Sex: M   School/Agency:
Examiner: Teacher/Dept:
Testing Date: 05/05/1990   City: State:
Birth Date: 11/02/1978   Adult Subjects
Age: 11 years 6 months   Education:
Grade Placement: 4.8   Occupation:
Years Retained: 1   Other Info:
Years Skipped: 0   Glasses: No   Used: No
Years of Schooling: 5.8   Hearing Aid: No   Used: No

Test Name	Raw Score	W	Age Equiv.	Grade Equiv.	RMI		SS	PR
1. Memory for Names	37-C	483	5-0	K.0[44]	61/90		76	6
						-1 SEM	72	3
						+1 SEM	80	9
2. Memory for Sentences	41	485	7-3	1.9	66/90		87	19
						-1 SEM	81	10
						+1 SEM	93	32
3. Visual Matching	34	488	9-0	3.6	73/90		88	21
						-1 SEM	81	10
						+1 SEM	95	37
4. Incomplete Words	31	508	23	15.4	96/90		117	88
						-1 SEM	109	73
						+1 SEM	125	95
5. Visual Closure	36	510	18-9	12.2	97/90		120	90
						-1 SEM	112	79
						+1 SEM	128	97
6. Picture Vocabulary	36	512	12-7	7.2	97/90		115	84
						-1 SEM	109	73
						+1 SEM	121	92
7. Analysis-Synthesis	20-F	494	8-8	3.4	82/90		94	35
						-1 SEM	89	23
						+1 SEM	99	47
BROAD COGNITIVE ABILITY (E Dev)	---	500	10-2	4.6	90/90		100	50
						-1 SEM	96	39
						+1 SEM	104	61
BROAD COGNITIVE ABILITY (Std)	---	497	9-5	4.2	87/90		94	34
						-1 SEM	90	25
						+1 SEM	98	45

Figure A–2. Compuscore for the WJ-R. Norms Based on Grade.

==
Name: Andrew S.   ID: Page: 2
==

Test Name	Raw Score	W	Age Equiv.	Grade Equiv.	RMI			SS	PR
8. Visual-Auditory Learning	36-K	485	6-7	1.1	68/90			74	4
						-1	SEM	69	2
						+1	SEM	79	8
9. Memory for Words	14	479	6-4	1.0	53/90			86	18
						-1	SEM	79	8
						+1	SEM	93	32
10. Cross Out	20	503	11-0	5.6	94/90			109	72
						-1	SEM	101	53
						+1	SEM	117	87
11. Sound Blending	25	508	13-10	9.4	96/90			111	77
						-1	SEM	105	63
						+1	SEM	117	87
12. Picture Recognition	16	500	10-3	4.8	90/90			100	50
						-1	SEM	93	32
						+1	SEM	107	68
13. Oral Vocabulary	22	505	11-4	5.9	95/90			108	71
						-1	SEM	102	55
						+1	SEM	114	82
14. Concept Formation	14-0	487	8-1	2.8	66/90			90	24
						-1	SEM	86	18
						+1	SEM	94	34
LONG-TERM RETRIEVAL (Glr)	---	484	5-9	K.4	66/90			74	4
						-1	SEM	70	2
						+1	SEM	78	7
SHORT-TERM MEMORY (Gsm)	---	482	6-9	1.4	61/90			86	18
						-1	SEM	81	10
						+1	SEM	91	27
PROCESSING SPEED (Gs)	---	496	9-9	4.4	88/90			97	42
						-1	SEM	91	27
						+1	SEM	103	58
AUDITORY PROCESSING (Ga)	---	508	16-4	10.7	96/90			115	84
						-1	SEM	110	75
						+1	SEM	120	91
VISUAL PROCESSING (Gv)	---	505	12-9	7.0	94/90			112	79
						-1	SEM	105	63
						+1	SEM	119	90

(continued)

```
================================================================================
Name: Andrew S.                        ID:                          Page: 3
================================================================================
```

Test Name	Raw Score	W	Age Equiv.	Grade Equiv.	RMI			SS	PR
COMPREHENSION- KNOWLEDGE (Gc)	---	508	11-8	6.4	96/90			112	80
						-1	SEM	107	68
						+1	SEM	117	87
FLUID REASONING (Gf)	---	490	8-4	3.0	75/90			91	26
						-1	SEM	87	19
						+1	SEM	95	37
BROAD COGNITIVE ABILITY (Ext)	---	496	9-4	4.0	87/90			94	35
						-1	SEM	91	27
						+1	SEM	97	42
READING APTITUDE	---	496	-----	-----	87/90			96	38
						-1	SEM	93	32
						+1	SEM	99	47
MATHEMATICS APTITUDE	---	494	-----	-----	82/90			92	29
						-1	SEM	89	23
						+1	SEM	95	37
WRITTEN LANGUAGE APTITUDE	---	496	-----	-----	87/90			95	37
						-1	SEM	92	30
						+1	SEM	98	45
KNOWLEDGE APTITUDE	---	498	-----	-----	88/90			97	42
						-1	SEM	94	34
						+1	SEM	100	50
15. Del. Recall- Mem. for Names	2-2	464	4-0[1]	K.0[1]	18/90			45	0.1
						-1	SEM	39	0.1
						+1	SEM	51	0.1
16. Del. Recall- V-A Learning	2-2	459	4-0[1]	K.0[1]	9/90			33	0.1
						-1	SEM	28	0.1
						+1	SEM	38	0.1
17. Numbers Reversed	5	453	5-5	K.1	5/90			58	0.3
						-1	SEM	52	0.1
						+1	SEM	64	1
18. Sound Patterns	23-S	503	10-7	5.1	91/90			102	55
						-1	SEM	97	42
						+1	SEM	107	68
19. Spatial Relations	18	499	10-4	4.7	90/90			100	50
						-1	SEM	93	32
						+1	SEM	107	68

Figure A–2. Compuscore for the WJ-R. Norms Based on Grade.

===
Name: Andrew S.   ID: Page: 4
===

Test Name	Raw Score	W	Age Equiv.	Grade Equiv.	RMI			SS	PR
20. Listening Comprehension	27	511	13-7	8.6	97/90			116	86
						-1	SEM	109	73
						+1	SEM	123	94
21. Verbal Analogies	15	504	11-0	5.6	93/90			105	64
						-1	SEM	99	47
						+1	SEM	111	77
ORAL LANGUAGE	---	503	10-8	5.4	93/90			105	63
						-1	SEM	102	55
						+1	SEM	108	70
ORAL LANGUAGE APTITUDE	---	486	-----	------	66/90			78	7
						-1	SEM	75	5
						+1	SEM	81	10

===
                Form A was used to obtain Achievement Scores
===

Test Name	Raw Score	W	Age Equiv.	Grade Equiv.	RMI			SS	PR
22. Letter-Word Identification	24	444	7-3	1.7	3/90			61	0.5
						-1	SEM	57	0.2
						+1	SEM	65	1
23. Passage Comprehension	13	466	7-8	2.2	23/90			73	4
						-1	SEM	67	1
						+1	SEM	79	8
24. Calculation	16	483	9-2	3.8	68/90			85	16
						-1	SEM	80	9
						+1	SEM	90	25
25. Applied Problems	29	485	8-10	3.3	68/90			88	21
						-1	SEM	83	13
						+1	SEM	93	32
26. Dictation	21	468	7-8	2.2	27/90			71	3
						-1	SEM	66	1
						+1	SEM	76	5
27. Writing Samples	15-V	475	7-3	1.7	39/90			71	3
						-1	SEM	66	1
						+1	SEM	76	5
28. Science	27	506	11-6	6.0	95/90			110	75
						-1	SEM	103	58
						+1	SEM	117	87

(continued)

===
Name: Andrew S.   ID: Page: 5
===

Test Name	Raw Score	W	Age Equiv.	Grade Equiv.	RMI		SS	PR
29. Social Studies	19	490	9-1	3.7	79/90		92	30
						-1 SEM	86	18
						+1 SEM	98	45
30. Humanities	26	500	10-2	4.8	90/90		100	50
						-1 SEM	95	37
						+1 SEM	105	63
BROAD READING	---	455	7-5	1.9	9/90		61	0.5
						-1 SEM	57	0.2
						+1 SEM	65	1
BROAD MATH (Gq)	---	484	9-0	3.6	68/90		84	15
						-1 SEM	80	9
						+1 SEM	88	21
BROAD WRITTEN LANGUAGE	---	472	7-5	1.8	34/90		67	1
						-1 SEM	63	1
						+1 SEM	71	3
BROAD KNOWLEDGE (E Dev)	---	499	10-0	4.7	90/90		100	50
						-1 SEM	96	39
						+1 SEM	104	61
SKILLS (E Dev)	---	466	7-9	2.1	23/90		69	2
						-1 SEM	66	1
						+1 SEM	72	3
31. Word Attack	5	469	7-3	1.8	25/90		74	4
						-1 SEM	69	2
						+1 SEM	79	8
32. Reading Vocabulary	16	480	8-5	2.7	58/90		81	11
						-1 SEM	77	6
						+1 SEM	85	16
33. Quantitative Concepts	26	481	8-10	3.4	61/90		84	14
						-1 SEM	78	7
						+1 SEM	90	25
34. Proofing	4	471	7-9	2.3	27/90		75	5
						-1 SEM	70	2
						+1 SEM	80	9
35. Writing Fluency	10	484	8-8	3.1	68/90		78	7
						-1 SEM	69	2
						+1 SEM	87	19

Figure A–2. Compuscore for the WJ-R. Norms Based on Grade.

```
================================================================================
Name: Andrew S.                         ID:                        Page: 6
================================================================================
```

Test Name	Raw Score	W	Age Equiv.	Grade Equiv.	RMI		SS	PR
P Punctuation & Capitalization	7	468	7-5	2.0	25/90		73	3
						−1 SEM	67	1
						+1 SEM	79	8
S Spelling	8	468	7-9	2.3	25/90		72	3
						−1 SEM	67	1
						+1 SEM	77	6
U Usage	4	472	7-8	2.2	34/90		79	8
						−1 SEM	73	4
						+1 SEM	85	16
H Handwriting	35	35	8-3	3.2	----		93	33
						−1 SEM	----	----
						+1 SEM	----	----
BASIC READING SKILLS	---	456	7-2	1.6	8/90		62	1
						−1 SEM	59	0.3
						+1 SEM	65	1
READING COMPREHENSION	---	473	7-10	2.4	39/90		76	5
						−1 SEM	72	3
						+1 SEM	80	9
BASIC MATH SKILLS	---	482	9-0	3.6	66/90		82	12
						−1 SEM	78	7
						+1 SEM	86	18
MATHEMATICS REASONING	Use scores from Test 25: Applied Problems							
BASIC WRITING SKILLS	---	470	7-8	2.0	29/90		73	4
						−1 SEM	69	2
						+1 SEM	77	6
WRITTEN EXPRESSION	---	480	7-10	2.3	55/90		75	5
						−1 SEM	71	3
						+1 SEM	79	8

(continued)

```
=========================================================================
Name: Andrew S.                        ID:                        Page: 7
=========================================================================
```

Intra-Cognitive Discrepancies

```
=========================================================================
```

	ACTUAL SS	OTHER SS	EXPECTED SS	SS DIFF	PR	SD DIFF
Long-Term Retrieval (Glr)	74	102	103	−29	1	−2.36
Short-Term Memory (Gsm)	86	100	100	−14	14	−1.08
Processing Speed (Gs)	97	98	98	−1	47	−0.07
Auditory Processing (Ga)	115	95	94	21	95	1.62
Visual Processing (Gv)	112	96	97	15	86	1.10
Comprehension-Knowledge (Gc)	112	96	94	18	95	1.61
Fluid Reasoning (Gf)	91	99	99	−8	25	−0.68

Aptitude/Achievement Discrepancies

```
=========================================================================
```

	ACTUAL ACH SS	APTITUDE SS	EXPECTED SS	SS DIFF	PR	SD DIFF
Oral Language	105	78	87	18	95	1.61
Broad Reading	61	96	97	−36	0.1	−3.36
Broad Mathematics	84	92	95	−11	15	−1.03
Broad Written Language	67	95	97	−30	0.4	−2.68
Broad Knowledge	100	97	98	2	57	0.18

Intra-Achievement Discrepancies

```
=========================================================================
```

	ACTUAL SS	OTHER SS	EXPECTED SS	SS DIFF	PR	SD DIFF
Broad Reading (R)	61	84	82	−21	1	−2.28
Broad Mathematics (M)	84	76	78	6	72	0.59
Broad Written Language (W)	67	82	82	−15	6	−1.55
Broad Knowledge (K)	100	71	74	26	99	2.55

Figure A–2. Compuscore for the WJ-R. Norms Based on Grade.

WOODCOCK-JOHNSON

Richard W. Woodcock
M. Bonner Johnson

F O R M   A

Tests of Achievement

WJ-R

S T A N D A R D   &   S U P P L E M E N T A L   B A T T E R I E S

T E S T   R E C O R D

Name __Andrew S.__ ID _____ Sex: ☑M ☐F Examiner _____

Grade Placement Ⓐ __4.8__ Years Retained Ⓑ __1__ Years Skipped Ⓒ _____ Years of Schooling Ⓐ + Ⓑ − Ⓒ = _____

	Year	Month	Day
Testing Date:	90	5	5
Birth Date: −	78	11	2
Difference:			
Age:	11	−	6

(Round to whole months)

School/Agency _____ Teacher/Department _____ City/State _____

Adult Subjects: Education _____ Occupation _____

Other Information _____

Does the subject have glasses? ☐Yes ☑No   Were they used during testing? ☐Yes ☐No
Does the subject have a hearing aid? ☐Yes ☑No   Was it used during testing? ☐Yes ☐No

Age/Grade Profile: Tests
Developmental Levels

RMIs based on ☐Age _____ ☑Grade __4.8__

EASY ← → DIFFICULT Instructional Range

Test	W	RMI	PR
22 Letter-Word Identification	444	5 /90	.5
23 Passage Comprehension	466	23 /90	4
31 Word Attack	469	25 /90	4
32 Reading Vocabulary	480	58 /90	11
24 Calculation	483	68 /90	16
25 Applied Problems	485	68 /90	21
33 Quantitative Concepts	481	61 /90	14

Do these test results provide a fair representation of the subject's present functioning? ☑Yes ☐No

If not, what is the reason for questioning the results? _____

DLM Teaching Resources
One DLM Park • Allen, Texas 75002

1

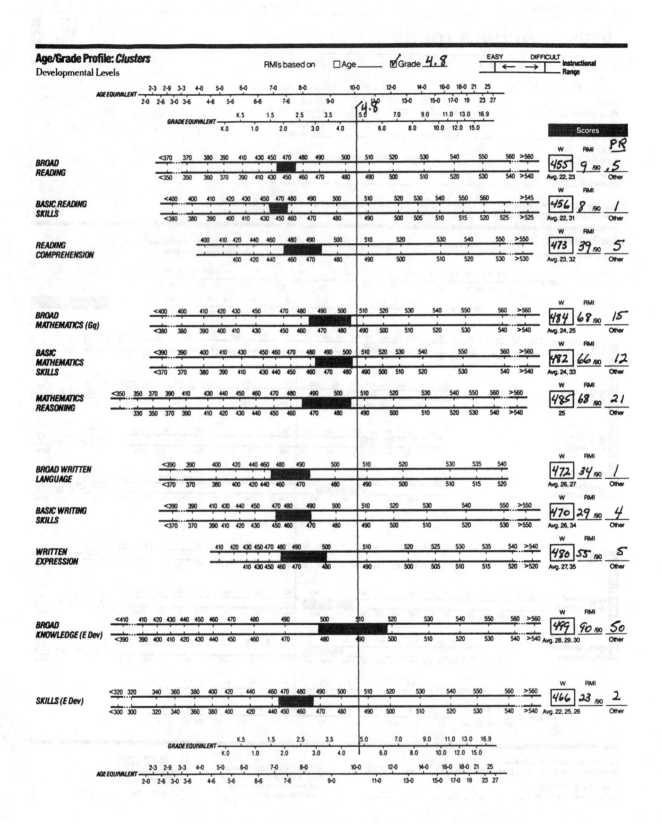

Figure A–3. Age/Grade Profile for the WJ-R. Norms Based on Grade.

Age/Grade Profile: Tests *(Continued)*
Developmental Levels

RMIs based on ☐ Age _____ ☑ Grade **4.8**

EASY — DIFFICULT · Instructional Range

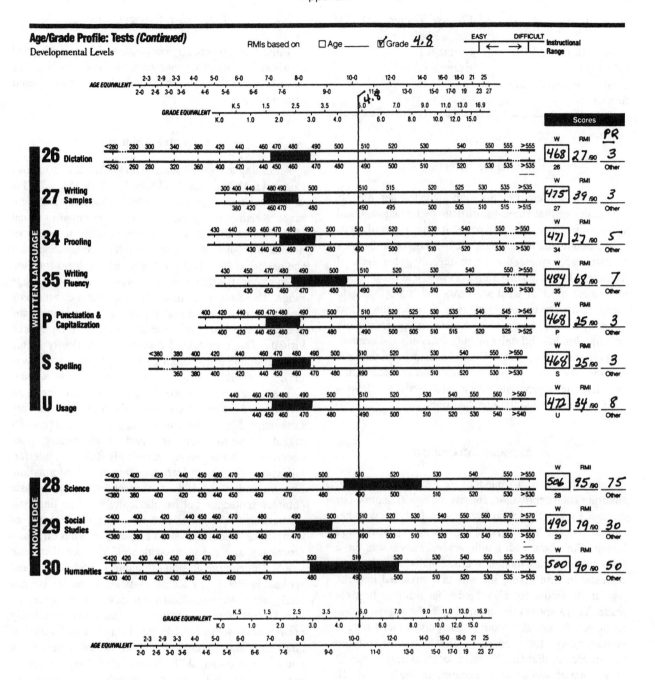

Name: Tanya F.

Date of Birth: 11/8/76
CA: 12–11
School: Hopper Middle
School

Dates of Testing:9/24, 25,
and 9/30/89
Grade: 6.1
Examiner:

Reason for Referral

Tanya was referred by her sixth-grade teacher, Mr. B., who indicated that Tanya has difficulty with language and a low vocabulary. Mr. B. wondered what types of strategies he could use to help Tanya in the classroom. Tanya's parents also expressed concern regarding her lack of learning. They noted that Tanya is aware that she does not understand most of what she hears and is beginning to verbalize her frustration. In contrast, they describe her as "visually astute." She is able to learn and perform daily activities but has difficulty making decisions and sequencing the steps of a process. Once she learns a routine, she performs it easily. The present evaluation was conducted to determine appropriate educational recommendations for Tanya in her sixth-grade classroom.

Background Information

Tanya has a background of severe abuse, neglect, environmental deprivation, and psychological trauma. For the past 3 years, Tanya has lived in a foster home with her two sisters. The home environment is stable, secure, and loving. For third and fourth grade, Tanya was in a self-contained classroom for Emotionally Handicapped students. In fifth grade, she was mainstreamed into the regular classroom for all subjects but reading. In sixth grade, Tanya spends the entire day in the regular classroom. Mr. B., her classroom teacher, noted that Tanya is missing many of the concepts with which other children her age are familiar and that she appears to be deficient in the amount of words that she understands and uses. Mr. B. also indicated that he spends a lot of extra time teaching Tanya vocabulary and concepts.

Tests Administered

Tanya was administered the Woodcock-Johnson Psycho-Educational Battery—Revised and an informal reading inventory. Additionally, the examiner collected an oral language and a written language sample.

Behavioral Observations

Tanya was exceedingly cooperative during testing and consistently worked hard and attempted to do her best. She stayed on-task 100% of the time during three 1-hour sessions.

Cognitive Abilities

According to her global score on the WJ-R COG Broad Cognitive Ability Cluster—Extended Scale (SS = 73; PR = 4), Tanya functions in the Borderline Mentally Deficient range. Relative strengths, however, were noted in visual skills. Tanya demonstrates average ability in speed of processing visual information as well as recognizing what she has seen. Her ability to learn and recall information when provided with visual clues was in the Low Average range. These results indicate that the visual channel is a strength for Tanya and that any new information that she is expected to learn and remember should be introduced visually. Tanya evidenced considerable difficulty on the fluid reasoning tasks, although a complicating factor was the lengthy verbal instructions that accompany these tasks.

Tanya's ability to process linguistic information at all levels, word through discourse, falls in the Low to Very Low range. She has difficulty with phonological processing at the word level. Her fund of vocabulary, from concrete to abstract levels, is severely deficient, interfering with her ability to learn new words and information. She can understand and use syntactic clues up to basic complex sentences, but has difficulty with the linguistic relationships inherent in understanding the meaning of complex sentences and relative clauses. She has difficulty processing and repeating sentences of more than nine words. Her comprehension of language, both written and spoken, is literal. Her ability to make inferences is most likely somewhat impeded by her lack of experience and world knowledge. Pragmatically, Tanya inappropriately presupposes listener knowledge of her topic and is unclear about pronoun referents. She does, however, have some good conversational skills. In discourse, Tanya is able to generate ideas, but needs cues to help her organize and separate critical from trivial information. Formal test results and listening comprehension measures indicate that Tanya has difficulty using verbal information for reasoning and problem-solving tasks.

Achievement

Tanya scored in the Low range on all achievement clusters with some relative strengths on certain tests.

Reading

Tanya's reading ability reflects her linguistic deficits in word attack, word recognition, vocabulary knowledge, syntax, linguistic relationships, recall of factual information, inference, and background knowledge. Her low vocabulary knowledge interferes with the meaning she is getting and affects her ability to guess at unfamiliar words. An interesting finding was that Tanya's performance on the WJ-R ACH Passage Comprehension test was significantly higher than her performance on the WJ-R COG Listening Comprehension test. This finding again demonstrates her learning advantage when she can use visual information. An important consideration is that when reading Tanya has control over how fast she takes in written information, but when listening, she must process information at the speaker's pace.

Written Language

Tanya's ability to express her ideas in writing, Low Average compared to age-peers, is significantly higher than her knowledge and use of writing mechanics. On the informal writing sample, her written composition was also somewhat better organized and more fluent than her spoken language. This is probably a result of the amount of time she has to organize her thoughts on paper as compared to when she is speaking.

Mathematics

Tanya's math achievement is significantly below that of age-peers. She can add and subtract with regrouping and solve simple one-digit multiplication problems. She is able to apply these skills to practical problems, such as money, but has difficulty with complex word problems and math vocabulary.

Knowledge

Tanya's score on the WJ-R ACH Broad Knowledge cluster is significantly below her other academic skills. This intra-achievement discrepancy may be understood in view of her deprived experiential background and her significant language and reasoning deficits. This lack of background knowledge in content areas inhibits her ability to learn from reading and spoken language.

Recommendations

Before specific recommendations are made for placement, further assessment is needed.

Further Evaluation

1. A test of adaptive behavior is needed to determine if the diagnosis of Borderline Mental Retardation is appropriate. Information about Tanya's ability to function independently in nonacademic areas such as personal living skills, community orientation, work-related skills, social-communication skills, and motor skills may be used to create goals and objectives that will help Tanya become prepared for independent living.

2. A more complete language evaluation should be conducted by the speech/language therapist.

School (General)

1. When providing instructions to Tanya, never assume prior knowledge or previous experience of words or information you are using to teach new concepts.

2. When teaching or speaking to Tanya, pause between phrases for processing time, limit sentence or clause length to approximately seven to eight words, use simple vocabulary, and give Tanya an opportunity to request repetition or clarification.

3. Teach everything that Tanya is expected to learn visually or with visual information that clearly illustrates the accompanying verbal information. Tanya is unlikely to benefit from activities that are purely auditory (including hearing someone else read from a text that is above her independent reading level).

4. When calling on Tanya in class, wait as long as necessary for her to organize her thoughts and formulate her response. Inform Tanya that she will have as much time as she needs and that she may say "I pass" if she does not know the answer.

5. Encourage Tanya to ask questions when she does not understand instructions, directions, or procedures.

Reading Comprehension

Tanya's instructional level ranges from primer to first-grade text. Materials will need to be at this level so that Tanya can master new concepts and vocabulary, understand the relationships among sentences, and associate the topics with personal experiences.

1. Directly teach Tanya how to interpret the relationships between phrases in complex sentences that appear in her reading (e.g., "since," "because," and "if/then" can denote cause/effect relationships).

2. Make sure that Tanya understands the meaning of vocabulary and concepts in her books prior to reading.

3. Teach Tanya to restate the main idea of a well-organized paragraph, and then to give related details.

4. Teach Tanya to read actively for meaning. Have her

attempt to associate the meaning with prior knowledge and experiences.

5. Teach Tanya specific strategies to use when she has not understood what she has read (e.g., reread, ask someone).

6. As she reads, teach Tanya to predict what will happen next and then to make judgments about the accuracy of her predictions.

Reading Basic Skills

1. Teach word attack and word recognition through word families or a linguistic approach. Capitalize on Tanya's visual memory by using well-established sight words to introduce phonic patterns and common word elements.

2. When teaching sight words, make sure that they are in her oral vocabulary.

Written Language

1. Use semantic mapping to help Tanya organize information prior to writing. Teach her to use this strategy as the basis for giving a short oral report.

2. Make sure that all words studied for spelling are part of Tanya's spoken and written vocabulary.

Mathematics

Practical math skills are a priority for Tanya. She should learn to apply computational skills to real-life problems, rather than to word problems in a book.

1. Emphasize the meaning of math by using visual aids and manipulatives to illustrate new ideas and extensions of previously learned concepts. Use real objects (e.g., money, liquid measures) as well as standard math teaching materials, such as Cuisenaire Rods and Unifix Cubes.

2. Provide considerable practice in application of any new arithmetic skill that Tanya is learning or has learned, both in story problems and in real-life applications (e.g., measuring for cooking, estimating how much groceries will cost).

3. Simplify the reading level and the linguistic complexity of word problems that Tanya is expected to solve.

Problem Solving

Teach Tanya problem-solving strategies. Overteach the strategy and provide extensive practice in a variety of situations. Emphasize the need to evaluate the effectiveness of the solution and change the strategy as needed. Most problem-solving strategies use the following steps: (a) identify the problem and determine what you want the outcome to be, (b) brainstorm possible solutions, (c) identify which solutions can be achieved, (d) select the solution that seems best, (e) try the solution, (f) ask if it is working, and (g) if it isn't working, modify it or select a different solution.

Summary

Tanya is a student with a severe language impairment who is significantly below average in reasoning and problem-solving abilities. In contrast, her visual processing abilities fall in the Average range and provide a critical channel for learning. Based upon her low performance in all achievement areas, extensive program modifications will be necessary. If adaptations cannot be made in the regular curriculum, placement in an Educable Mentally Retarded or Severe Oral Language Impaired program should be considered by the multidisciplinary team.

Name: Danny W.
Date of Birth: 10/16/1974
Chronological Age: 15–4
School: Redwood High School

Date of Testing:2/15/90
Grade: 9.9
Examiner:

Reason for Referral

Danny was referred by his mother because of concern regarding his continued difficulties in academic performance. The mother requested information regarding the nature of Danny's learning problems. In addition, she requested specific recommendations regarding an appropriate educational placement for Danny.

Background Information

Danny lives with his mother and younger sister. He plans to spend the majority of the summer with his father, who lives in California. Developmentally, speech was delayed and slow to develop. Danny was retained in kindergarten. He has received special education services and intermittent speech/language therapy from the second semester of first grade until the present date. Based upon the severity of his learning disability, his primary placements have been in self-contained Learning Disability classrooms. This year an attempt was made with limited success to return Danny to regular classes. He received failing grades in both his English and Spanish classes. He has presently completed his freshman year at Redrock High School and because of a family move will transfer to Douglas High School in the fall.

Tests Administered

Danny was administered the Woodcock-Johnson Tests of Cognitive Ability—Revised (Tests 1–14, 20) and the Woodcock-Johnson Tests of Achievement—Revised (Tests 22–30, 31, 32, 34, and 35). Test results are attached. Additionally, the examiner listened to Danny read a series of graded passages from an informal reading inventory.

Behavioral Observations

Danny was cooperative and maintained attention throughout the 3-hour testing session. He was generally quiet and tended to lack persistence when tasks became difficult. He had difficulty responding to test questions that required one-word responses or specific answers. Although he was unable to provide a specific answer on

several questions, he explained the function of the object or the general concept involved.

Cognitive Abilities

Danny's overall performance fell in the Low Average range. A significant strength was noted in his ability to process visual stimuli rapidly. In contrast, a significant weakness was noted in auditory processing, particularly his ability to analyze and blend sounds together to form words. When compared to his expected performance (based on his average performance on the other six cognitive factors), only 1 out of 1,000 students obtains a score that low in auditory processing. This inefficiency in the analysis of sounds has made it difficult for Danny to learn to decode and to spell. This type of disability may also have an impact on an individual's ability to listen to oral lectures and to learn a foreign language, such as Spanish. Danny also showed a relative weakness with short-term memory tasks, in both repeating information he had just heard and reproducing information that he had just seen. With the exception of mathematics aptitude (5% of the population would obtain a score that low or lower in mathematics), Danny does not exhibit discrepancies between his aptitude (predicted achievement) and his actual achievement in the areas of reading, written language, and knowledge.

Achievement

Danny is functioning several years below grade level in most academic areas.

Reading

Although Danny's instructional reading level ranges from approximately fourth to seventh grade, he has learned some good strategies for decoding words and for understanding what he is reading. His greatest weakness in reading is in word attack, or the ability to pronounce phonically regular nonsense words. He mispronounced several consonant-vowel-consonant sound patterns. His significant difficulty with sounds has made it hard for Danny to learn to decode and pronounce multisyllabic words. When Danny encounters an unfamiliar word in reading, he skips over it rather than attempting to figure it out. When encouraged to make an attempt, his limited application of an efficient strategy is apparent.

Written Language

Danny has difficulty both in written expression and in basic skills. Although he has good ideas, he has trouble expressing them clearly and in a logical sequence. In writing, he misspells many common words. For example, he spelled the word *bee*, *bea*, the word *table*, *tabale*, the word *both*, *bouth*, and the word *there*, as *ther*. Although Danny is attempting to produce a phonetic representation of a word, he does not recall how common words look. Although legible, Danny's handwriting is characterized by inconsistent slant and a mixture of lower- and upper-case letters.

Mathematics

Danny has difficulty with both computation and application of skills. Danny counted with his fingers for simple addition and subtraction facts. He left several problems blank, such as "17 – 9." When asked if he could solve the problem "17 – 9," Danny said that he did not know how. When asked to try, he arrived at the answer of "18." Danny was unable to perform any simple division problems, such as 8 divided by 2, and made mistakes on multiplication facts.

Recommendations

To profit from a mainstreamed or regular education course, materials will need to be at a lower readability level. Additionally Danny is likely to have difficulty listening to oral presentations or lectures that do not have supplemental visual materials, such as an outline or study guide to follow.

Reading

1. Danny needs further assistance with word identification strategies. Although he has developed some skill, he lacks confidence in his abilities. A method such as Glass-Analysis for Decoding could be used to build skill in structural analysis.

2. Instruction in specific comprehension strategies should also continue. Danny should be encouraged to stop and paraphrase material as he reads.

3. Danny should be provided with study guides to use when reading. These guides should list the important information that Danny is to locate as he is reading.

4. When possible, Danny should listen to taped books, as he follows along with the print.

Writing

1. When possible, Danny should use a word processor with a spelling checker. He should receive assistance in developing his ideas and revising his work and not be penalized for poor spelling.

2. To improve spelling, Danny should master the spelling of high-frequency words.

Mathematics

1. Danny needs to review the concepts associated with place value and regrouping. Although he is able to perform some operations successfully, he does not understand what he is doing. The teacher should provide concrete examples of when and how subtraction, multiplication, and division are used.

2. Danny should be introduced to fractions, decimals, and percentages.

3. Danny should learn how to use a calculator and, if necessary, be provided with one in the classroom.

4. In addition to intensive instruction, placement should be in a consumer or general math class.

Foreign Language

Based upon the nature and severity of Danny's auditory processing disability, any foreign language requirement in high school should be waived. A suitable substitute would be a computer course.

Conclusions

Danny is an individual with a severe learning disability. His weakness in auditory processing has interfered with and depressed his development in both cognitive and academic abilities. Because of continuing academic difficulties, his self-esteem is also low.

Presently, he is functioning significantly below the predicted level in mathematics. With direct instruction he is capable of making significant gains in mathematics. Additionally, attempts should be made to determine vocational interests and to provide Danny with appropriate experiences in the high school setting. Care should be taken that Danny is not placed into classes where he cannot succeed. The special education teacher from Redrock should meet with Danny's new teacher before school begins to insure a successful transition to the special program at Douglas.

Name: Monica H.

Date of Birth: 11/29/72
Chronological Age: 17–9
School: Cottonwood High

Dates of Testing: 8/10, 8/16/90
Grade: 11.9
Examiner:

Reason for Referral

Monica was referred by her parents due to their concerns regarding Monica's consistent difficulties in math, coupled with what appeared to be cycles of depression. Monica's grades vary from A to F, depending upon the course and level of interest. Monica's parents desired information regarding her learning skills to help guide them in continuing education and in making plans for college. Additionally, they wished to hire a tutor to assist Monica in mathematics.

Background Information

Monica is an attractive, 17-year-old girl, from a multilingual family. Her parents speak Spanish and French, as well as English. Although Spanish was her primary language, Monica speaks both Spanish and English fluently. Monica has never received special education services. At home, her mother describes her as generally disorganized: She loses personal and school items, forgets to turn in assignments, and keeps a disorganized notebook. Monica recognizes these characteristics and states that she has recently done a better job in keeping herself organized. Monica is presently preparing to begin her senior year at Cottonwood High School.

Tests Administered

Monica was administered several tests from the Woodcock-Johnson Psycho-Educational Battery—Revised. In addition, the examiner had Monica complete several informal assessments in mathematics.

Behavioral Observations

Monica presents herself as very poised and articulate. During the assessment, Monica tended to give up very easily when having difficulty. Rather than venturing a response to a test question, she would say that she did not know the answer. In general, Monica was personable, cooperative, and attentive throughout the sessions. At one point, she commented that she hated taking any kinds of tests.

Cognitive Abilities

Test results indicate that Monica has significant discrepancies between her strong linguistic abilities and her relatively weaker visual abilities. Monica's cognitive strengths lie in her ability to understand and use oral language and in memory for linguistically meaningful material. Monica performed in the High Average range on auditory processing tasks and in the Average range on visual processing tasks. Her ability to store and retrieve information that was not embedded in a strong linguistic context was significantly below her memory for meaningful language. Recall of less meaningful information after a delay of 4 days was in the Low Average range and suggests that Monica may have difficulty recalling information that was not fully meaningful to her at the time of learning.

Monica scored in the Low Average range in three cognitive areas that may interfere with ease of learning mathematics. Successful performance in mathematics requires reasoning, visual, and spatial abilities. Reasoning and problem-solving tasks that are composed of visual stimuli, rather than linguistic information, are a relative weakness for Monica. She is also relatively slow in processing visual information. This may indicate that she needs extra time to process, interpret, and manipulate the visual symbols involved in math. Thus Monica may have the capability to understand a particular math concept, but not have enough time to master it before the teacher moves on. Quantitative thinking may be considered a cognitive ability as well as an area of academic achievement. In this area, Monica has relative difficulties in comprehending quantitative concepts, understanding relationships, and in manipulating numerical symbols.

Monica's cognitive strengths in oral language, memory for meaningful information, and auditory processing provide a strong foundation for successful performance in reading and writing.

Achievement

Reading and Written Language

Results of the WJ-R ACH Broad Reading and Written Language clusters indicate that Monica's overall performance is in the Superior range when compared to grade-peers. A writing sample provided further support regarding writing skill. Monica's thoughts were well sequenced, had good transitions, and were clearly organized around the central theme. She made good use of examples, details, and description to add interest to her essay.

Mathematics

Although Monica scored in the Low Average range in broad math ability, her performance was significantly lower than predicted based on her other areas of academic achievement. Analysis of the three math tests indicated that Monica had difficulty with long division with a 3-digit divisor, reducing fractions, finding common denominators, multiplying with decimals, and converting fractions to percentages. She also made errors in basic quantitative concepts, such as the number of weeks in a year and the number of inches in a yard.

Monica's tendency to give up when she experiences difficulty in an area has likely had a reciprocal effect on her difficulty in mathematics. This style or coping strategy interferes with the acquisition and mastery of math concepts.

Knowledge

Monica's general knowledge of three content areas fell in the Average range with no significant differences among the tests of Science, Social Studies, and Humanities. This score is significantly below her performance within reading and written language, but within the predicted range based on her measured aptitude for Knowledge.

Recommendations

The high school counselor should be able to assist Monica in selecting appropriate course work for her senior year. Plans should also be made regarding an appropriate college setting. Monica may also benefit from counseling to help her overcome anxieties regarding scholastic performance and to help her establish realistic goals.

If Monica consents, her parents should enlist a tutor for the following purposes.

1. To provide Monica with support in her Algebra class, so that she learns the concepts and does not fail.

2. To teach Monica the more basic math skills that she is missing (e.g., balancing a checkbook, determining interest on a car loan, budgeting for family meals).

3. To review basic computational processes, involving fractions, decimals, and percentages.

4. To teach Monica a variety of efficient advanced reading and study strategies tailored to her learning style. Improving Monica's reading and study skills, even in her strong academic areas, will enable her to go into tests so well prepared that her anxiety will be greatly alleviated, allowing her the mental focus to demonstrate her knowledge. These techniques will also prepare Monica for college-level courses.

5. To teach Monica test-taking strategies other than pre-test studying.

6. To teach Monica to organize and prioritize her homework assignments so that she can handle academic requirements at college.

Name _____ Grade _____ Date of Test _____ - ____ - _____

School _____ Date of Birth _____ - ____ - _____

Teacher _____ Chronological Age _____ - ____ - _____

Examiner _____ Norms based on: Age_____ Grade_____

WOODCOCK-JOHNSON PSYCHO-EDUCATIONAL BATTERY - REVISED
TESTS OF COGNITIVE ABILITY

Test / CLUSTER	Factors	Age Equivalent	Grade Equivalent	Relative Mastery Index	Standard Scores		Percentile Ranks	
					SS	Range	PR	Range
STANDARD BATTERY								
1 Memory for Names	Glr			/90				
2 Memory for Sentences	Gsm			/90				
3 Visual Matching	Gs			/90				
4 Incomplete Words	Ga			/90				
5 Visual Closure	Gv			/90				
6 Picture Vocabulary	Gc			/90				
7 Analysis-Synthesis	Gf			/90				
BROAD COGNITIVE ABILITY(E Dev)				/90				
BROAD COGNITIVE ABILITY(Std)				/90				
SUPPLEMENTAL BATTERY								
8 Visual-Auditory Learning	Glr			/90				
9 Memory for Words	Gsm			/90				
10 Cross Out	Gs			/90				
11 Sound Blending	Ga			/90				
12 Picture Recognition	Gv			/90				
13 Oral Vocabulary	Gc			/90				
14 Concept Formation	Gf			/90				
COGNITIVE FACTOR CLUSTERS								
LONG-TERM RETRIEVAL	Glr			/90				
SHORT-TERM MEMORY	Gsm			/90				
PROCESSING SPEED	Gs			/90				
AUDITORY PROCESSING	Ga			/90				
VISUAL PROCESSING	Gv			/90				
COMPREHEN.-KNOWLEDGE	Gc			/90				
FLUID REASONING	Gf			/90				
BROAD COGNITIVE ABILITY (Ext)				/90				
APTITUDE CLUSTERS								
READING APTITUDE				/90				
MATHEMATICS APTITUDE				/90				
WRITTEN LANGUAGE APTITUDE				/90				
KNOWLEDGE APTITUDE				/90				
SUPPLEMENTAL TESTS 15 - 21								
15 Del. Rec.-Mem. for Names	Glr			/90				
16 Del. Rec.-Vis.-Aud. Lrng.	Glr			/90				
17 Numbers Reversed	Gsm,Gf			/90				
18 Sound Patterns	Ga, Gf			/90				
19 Spatial Relations	Gf, Gv			/90				
20 Listening Comprehension	Gc			/90				
21 Verbal Analogies	Gf, Gc			/90				
ORAL LANGUAGE								
ORAL LANGUAGE APTITUDE				/90				
ORAL LANGUAGE				/90				

DM: 0003

Prepared by David A. McPhail. Permission is granted to reproduce this form.

TESTS OF ACHIEVEMENT - STANDARD & SUPPLEMENTAL   Form____

Test / CLUSTER	Factors	Age Equivalent	Grade Equivalent	Relative Mastery Index	Standard Scores		Percentile Ranks	
					SS	Range	PR	Range
ACHIEVEMENT TESTS - STANDARD								
22 Letter-Word Identification				/90				
23 Passage Comprehension				/90				
24 Calculation	Gq			/90				
25 Applied Problems	Gq			/90				
26 Dictation				/90				
27 Writing Samples				/90				
28 Science	Gc			/90				
29 Social Studies	Gc			/90				
30 Humanities	Gc			/90				
BROAD & EARLY DEVELOPMENT CLUSTERS								
BROAD READING				/90				
*BROAD MATHEMATICS**	*Gq*			/90				
BROAD WRITTEN LANGUAGE				/90				
BROAD KNOWLEDGE (E DEV)	Gc			/90				
SKILLS (E DEV)				/90				

*Also for use as a cognitive factor.

ACHIEVEMENT TESTS - SUPPLEMENTAL

Test / CLUSTER	Factors	Age Equivalent	Grade Equivalent	Relative Mastery Index	SS	Range	PR	Range
31 Word Attack	Ga			/90				
32 Reading Vocabulary				/90				
33 Quantitative Concepts	Gq			/90				
34 Proofing				/90				
35 Writing Fluency	Gs			/90				
P Punctuation/Capitalization				/90				
S Spelling				/90				
U Usage				/90				
H Handwriting				/90				
BASIC SKILLS & APPLICATIONS CLUSTERS								
BASIC READING SKILLS				/90				
READING COMPREHENSION				/90				
BASIC MATHEMATICS SKILLS	Gq			/90				
*MATHEMATICS REASONING***	Gq			/90				
BASIC WRITING SKILLS				/90				
WRITTEN EXPRESSION				/90				

** Not an actual "cluster". The Applied Problems test measures Mathematics Reasoning.

INTRA-COGNITIVE DISCREPANCIES

COGNITIVE FACTOR CLUSTER	PR	SD DIFF
LONG-TERM RETRIEVAL		
SHORT-TERM MEMORY		
PROCESSING SPEED		
AUDITORY PROCESSING		
VISUAL PROCESSING		
COMPREHENSION-KNOWLEDGE		
FLUID REASONING		

INTRA-ACHIEVEMENT DISCREPANCIES

BROAD ACHIEVEMENT CLUSTER	PR	SD DIFF
BROAD READING (R)		
BROAD MATHEMATICS (M)		
BROAD WRITTEN LANGUAGE (W)		
BROAD KNOWLEDGE (K)		

APTITUDE/ACHIEVEMENT DISCREPANCIES

BASED ON: BCA _____   APTITUDE _____

ACHIEVEMENT CLUSTER	PR	SD DIFF
BROAD READING		
BASIC READING SKILLS		
READING COMPREHENSION		
BROAD MATHEMATICS		
BASIC MATHEMATICS SKILLS		
MATHEMATICS REASONING		
BROAD WRITTEN LANGUAGE		
BASIC WRITING SKILLS		
WRITTEN EXPRESSION		
BROAD KNOWLEDGE		

© Ms ACHDISCREP 18

Prepared by David A. McPhail. Permission is granted to reproduce this form.

Name_____ Grade_____ Date of Test _____ - __ - ____

School_____ Date of Birth _____ - __ - ____

Teacher_____ Chronological Age _____ - __ - ____

Examiner_____ Norms based on: Age_____ Grade_____

WOODCOCK-JOHNSON PSYCHO-EDUCATIONAL BATTERY - REVISED
TESTS OF COGNITIVE ABILITY - STANDARD & SUPPLEMENTAL

Test / CLUSTER	Factors	Age Equivalent	Grade Equivalent	Relative Mastery Index	Standard Scores		Percentile Ranks	
					SS	Range	PR	Range
LONG-TERM RETRIEVAL								
1 Memory for Names	Glr			/90				
8 Visual-Auditory Learning	Glr			/90				
LONG-TERM RETRIEVAL	*Glr*			/90				
15 Del. Rec.-Mem.for Names	Glr			/90				
16 Del. Rec.-Vis.-Aud. Lrng.	Glr			/90				
SHORT-TERM MEMORY								
2 Memory for Sentences	Gsm			/90				
9 Memory for Words	Gsm			/90				
SHORT-TERM MEMORY	*Gsm*			/90				
17 Numbers Reversed	Gsm,Gf			/90				
PROCESSING SPEED								
3 Visual Matching	Gs			/90				
10 Cross Out	Gs			/90				
PROCESSING SPEED	*Gs*			/90				
AUDITORY PROCESSING								
4 Incomplete Words	Ga			/90				
11 Sound Blending	Ga			/90				
AUDITORY PROCESSING	*Ga*			/90				
18 Sound Patterns	Ga, Gf			/90				
VISUAL PROCESSING								
5 Visual Closure	Gv			/90				
12 Picture Recognition	Gv			/90				
VISUAL PROCESSING	*Gv*			/90				
COMPREHENSION-KNOWLEDGE								
6 Picture Vocabulary	Gc			/90				
13 Oral Vocabulary	Gc			/90				
COMPREHEN.-KNOWLEDGE	*Gc*			/90				
20 Listening Comprehension	Gc			/90				
FLUID REASONING								
7 Analysis-Synthesis	Gf			/90				
14 Concept Formation	Gf			/90				
FLUID REASONING	*Gf*			/90				
19 Spatial Relations	Gf, Gv			/90				
21 Verbal Analogies	Gf, Gc			/90				
APTITUDE CLUSTERS								
READING APTITUDE				/90				
MATHEMATICS APTITUDE				/90				
WRITTEN LANGUAGE APTITUDE				/90				
KNOWLEDGE APTITUDE				/90				
ORAL LANGUAGE								
ORAL LANGUAGE APTITUDE				/90				
ORAL LANGUAGE				/90				
BROAD COGNITIVE ABILITY								
BROAD COGNITIVE ABILITY(E Dev)				/90				
BROAD COGNITIVE ABILITY(Std)				/90				
BROAD COGNITIVE ABILITY(Ext)				/90				

0 Mc 0001

Prepared by David A. McPhail. Permission is granted to reproduce this form.

TESTS OF ACHIEVEMENT - STANDARD & SUPPLEMENTAL   Form____

Test / CLUSTER	Factors	Age Equivalent	Grade Equivalent	Relative Mastery Index	Standard Scores		Percentile Ranks	
					SS	Range	PR	Range
READING								
22 Letter-Word Identification				/90				
23 Passage Comprehension				/90				
31 Word Attack	Ga			/90				
32 Reading Vocabulary				/90				
BROAD READING				/90				
BASIC READING SKILLS				/90				
READING COMPREHENSION				/90				
MATHEMATICS								
24 Calculation	Gq			/90				
25 Applied Problems	Gq			/90				
33 Quantitative Concepts	Gq			/90				
BROAD MATHEMATICS*	**Gq**			/90				
BASIC MATHEMATICS SKILLS	Gq			/90				
MATHEMATICS REASONING	Gq	Not an actual "cluster". The Applied Problems test measures Mathematics Reasoning.						

*Also for use as a cognitive factor.

Test / CLUSTER	Factors	Age Equivalent	Grade Equivalent	Relative Mastery Index	SS	Range	PR	Range
WRITTEN LANGUAGE								
26 Dictation				/90				
27 Writing Samples				/90				
34 Proofing				/90				
35 Writing Fluency	Gs			/90				
P Punctuation/Capitalization				/90				
S Spelling				/90				
U Usage				/90				
H Handwriting				/90				
BROAD WRITTEN LANGUAGE				/90				
BASIC WRITING SKILLS				/90				
WRITTEN EXPRESSION				/90				
KNOWLEDGE								
28 Science	Gc			/90				
29 Social Studies	Gc			/90				
30 Humanities	Gc			/90				
BROAD KNOWLEDGE	Gc			/90				

INTRA-COGNITIVE DISCREPANCIES

COGNITIVE FACTOR CLUSTER	PR	SD DIFF
LONG-TERM RETRIEVAL		
SHORT-TERM MEMORY		
PROCESSING SPEED		
AUDITORY PROCESSING		
VISUAL PROCESSING		
COMPREHENSION-KNOWLEDGE		
FLUID REASONING		

INTRA-ACHIEVEMENT DISCREPANCIES

BROAD ACHIEVEMENT CLUSTER	PR	SD DIFF
BROAD READING (R)		
BROAD MATHEMATICS (M)		
BROAD WRITTEN LANGUAGE (W)		
BROAD KNOWLEDGE (K)		

APTITUDE/ACHIEVEMENT DISCREPANCIES

BASED ON: BCA _____   APTITUDE _____

ACHIEVEMENT CLUSTER	PR	SD DIFF
BROAD READING		
BROAD MATHEMATICS		
BROAD WRITTEN LANGUAGE		
BROAD KNOWLEDGE		

	PR	SD DIFF
BASIC READING SKILLS		
BASIC MATHEMATICS SKILLS		
BASIC WRITING SKILLS		

	PR	SD DIFF
READING COMPREHENSION		
MATHEMATICS REASONING		
WRITTEN EXPRESSION		

D Mc ACHDISCREP 2

Prepared by David A. McPhail. Permission is granted to reproduce this form.

Name _____ Grade _____ Date of Test _____ - ___ - ___

School _____ Date of Birth _____ - ___ - ___

Teacher _____ Chronological Age _____ - ___ - ___

Examiner _____ Form _____ Norms based on: Age _____ Grade _____

WOODCOCK-JOHNSON PSYCHO-EDUCATIONAL BATTERY - REVISED
TESTS OF ACHIEVEMENT - STANDARD & SUPPLEMENTAL

Test / CLUSTER	Factors	Age Equivalent	Grade Equivalent	Relative Mastery Index	Standard Scores SS	Standard Scores Range	Percentile Ranks PR	Percentile Ranks Range
ACHIEVEMENT TESTS - STANDARD								
22 Letter-Word Identification				/90				
23 Passage Comprehension				/90				
24 Calculation	Gq			/90				
25 Applied Problems	Gq			/90				
26 Dictation				/90				
27 Writing Samples				/90				
28 Science	Gc			/90				
29 Social Studies	Gc			/90				
30 Humanities	Gc			/90				
BROAD & EARLY DEVELOPMENT CLUSTERS								
BROAD READING				/90				
*BROAD MATHEMATICS**	Gq			/90				
BROAD WRITTEN LANGUAGE				/90				
BROAD KNOWLEDGE (E DEV)	Gc			/90				
SKILLS (E DEV)				/90				

*Also for use as a cognitive factor.

ACHIEVEMENT TESTS - SUPPLEMENTAL

Test / CLUSTER	Factors	Age Equivalent	Grade Equivalent	Relative Mastery Index	SS	Range	PR	Range
31 Word Attack	Ga			/90				
32 Reading Vocabulary				/90				
33 Quantitative Concepts	Gq			/90				
34 Proofing				/90				
35 Writing Fluency	Gs			/90				
P Punctuation/Capitalization				/90				
S Spelling				/90				
U Usage				/90				
H Handwriting				/90				

BASIC SKILLS & APPLICATIONS CLUSTERS

Test / CLUSTER	Factors	Age Equivalent	Grade Equivalent	Relative Mastery Index	SS	Range	PR	Range
BASIC READING SKILLS				/90				
READING COMPREHENSION				/90				
BASIC MATHEMATICS SKILLS	Gq			/90				
*MATHEMATICS REASONING***	Gq			/90				
BASIC WRITING SKILLS				/90				
WRITTEN EXPRESSION				/90				

** Not an actual "cluster". The Applied Problems test measures Mathematics Reasoning.

INTRA-ACHIEVEMENT DISCREPANCIES

BROAD ACHIEVEMENT CLUSTER	PR	SD DIFF
BROAD READING (R)		
BROAD MATHEMATICS (M)		
BROAD WRITTEN LANGUAGE (W)		
BROAD KNOWLEDGE (K)		

Prepared by David A. McPhail. Permission is granted to reproduce this form.

Name _____ Grade _____ Date of Test _____ - _____ - _____

School _____ Date of Birth _____ - _____ - _____

Teacher _____ Chronological Age _____ - _____ - _____

Examiner _____ Form _____ Norms based on: Age _____ Grade _____

WOODCOCK-JOHNSON PSYCHO-EDUCATIONAL BATTERY - REVISED
TESTS OF ACHIEVEMENT - STANDARD & SUPPLEMENTAL

Test / CLUSTER	Factors	Age Equivalent	Grade Equivalent	Relative Mastery Index	Standard Scores SS	Standard Scores Range	Percentile Ranks PR	Percentile Ranks Range
READING								
22 Letter-Word Identification				/90				
23 Passage Comprehension				/90				
31 Word Attack	Ga			/90				
32 Reading Vocabulary				/90				
BROAD READING				/90				
BASIC READING SKILLS				/90				
READING COMPREHENSION				/90				
MATHEMATICS								
24 Calculation	Gq			/90				
25 Applied Problems	Gq			/90				
33 Quantitative Concepts	Gq			/90				
*BROAD MATHEMATICS**	*Gq*			/90				
BASIC MATHEMATICS SKILLS	Gq			/90				
MATHEMATICS REASONING	Gq	Not an actual "cluster". The Applied Problems test measures Mathematics Reasoning.						

*Also for use as a cognitive factor.

Test / CLUSTER	Factors	Age Equivalent	Grade Equivalent	Relative Mastery Index	Standard Scores SS	Standard Scores Range	Percentile Ranks PR	Percentile Ranks Range
WRITTEN LANGUAGE								
26 Dictation				/90				
27 Writing Samples				/90				
34 Proofing				/90				
35 Writing Fluency	Gs			/90				
P Punctuation/Capitalization				/90				
S Spelling				/90				
U Usage				/90				
H Handwriting				/90				
BROAD WRITTEN LANGUAGE				/90				
BASIC WRITING SKILLS				/90				
WRITTEN EXPRESSION				/90				
KNOWLEDGE								
28 Science	Gc			/90				
29 Social Studies	Gc			/90				
30 Humanities	Gc			/90				
BROAD KNOWLEDGE	Gc			/90				

INTRA-ACHIEVEMENT DISCREPANCIES

BROAD ACHIEVEMENT CLUSTER	PR	SD DIFF
BROAD READING (R)		
BROAD MATHEMATICS (M)		
BROAD WRITTEN LANGUAGE (W)		
BROAD KNOWLEDGE (K)		

Prepared by David A. McPhail. Permission is granted to reproduce this form.

REFERENCES

Abrahamsen, E. P., & Shelton, K. C. (1989). Reading comprehension in adolescents with learning disabilities: Semantic and syntactic effects. *Journal of Learning Disabilities, 22,* 569–572.

Ackerman, P. T., Anhalt, J. M., & Dykman, R. A. (1986). Arithmetic automatization failure in children with attention and reading disorders: Association and sequela. *Journal of Learning Disabilities, 19,* 222–232.

Adams, A., Carnine, D., & Gersten, R. (1982). Instructional strategies for studying content area texts in the intermediate grades. *Reading Research Quarterly, 18,* 27–55.

Allington, R. L. (1978). Word identification abilities of severely disabled readers: A comparison in isolation and context. *Journal of Reading Behavior, 10,* 409–416.

Alvarez, M. C. (1983). Sustained timed writing as an aid to fluency and creativity. *Teaching Exceptional Children, 15,* 160–162.

Anderson, R. G. (1938). A note on a case of spelling difficulty. *Journal of Applied Psychology, 22,* 211–214.

Ansara, A. (1982). The Orton-Gillingham approach to remediation in developmental dyslexia. In R. N. Malatesha & P. G. Aaron (Eds.)., *Reading disorders: Varieties and treatments*(pp. 409–433). New York: Academic Press.

Applebee, A. N. (1984). Writing and reasoning. *Review of Educational Research, 54,* 577–596.

Ashby-Davis, C. (1984). Levels of certitude for educated guessing in strict cloze passages. *Journal of Reading, 27,* 318–323.

Ashcraft, M. H. (1982). The development of mental arithmetic: A chronometric approach. *Developmental Review, 2,* 213–236.

Ashlock, R. B. (1982). *Error patterns in computation.* Columbus, OH: Charles E. Merrill.

Askov, E., Otto, W., & Askov, W. (1970). A decade of research in handwriting: Progress and prospect. *Journal of Educational Research, 64,* 100–111.

Aukerman, R. C. (1984). *Approaches to beginning reading* (2nd ed.). New York: John Wiley.

Badian, N. A. (1988). The prediction of good and poor reading before kindergarten entry: A nine-year follow up. *Journal of Learning Disabilities, 21,* 98–103, 123.

Baker, L. A., Decker, S. N., & DeFries, J. C. (1984). Cognitive abilities in reading-disabled children: A longitudinal study. *Journal of Child Psychology and Psychiatry, 25,* 111–117.

Bannatyne, A. D. (1971). *Language, reading and learning disabilities.* Springfield, IL: Charles C. Thomas.

Beach, J. D. (1983). Teaching students to write instructional reports. *Elementary School Journal, 84,* 213–220.

Beck, I. L., & McKeown, M. G. (1981). Developing questions that promote comprehension: The story map. *Language Arts, 58,* 913–918.

Beck, I. L., Omanson, R. C., & McKeown, M. G. (1982). An instructional redesign of reading lessons: Effects on comprehension. *Reading Research Quarterly, 17,* 462–481.

Beck, I. L., Perfetti, C. A., & McKeown, M. G. (1982). The effects of long-term vocabulary instruction on lexical access and reading comprehension. *Journal of Educational Psychology, 74,* 506–521.

Beech, J. R. (1985). *Learning to read: A cognitive approach to reading and poor reading.* San Diego: College-Hill Press.

Beech, M. C. (1983). Simplifying text for mainstreamed students. *Journal of Learning Disabilities, 16,* 400–402.

Begy, G., & Cahill, K. (1978). The ability of kindergarten children having completed a modified rebus readiness program to segment oral language into words. *Reading World, 18*(1), 27–32.

Bergerud, D., Lovitt, T. C., & Horton, S. (1988). The effectiveness of textbook adaptations in life science for high school students with learning disabilities. *Journal of Learning Disabilities, 21,* 70–76.

Berninger, V. (1986). Normal variation in reading acquisition. *Perceptual and Motor Skills, 62,* 691–716.

Berninger, V. W., Thalberg, S. P., DeBruyn, I., & Smith, R. (1987). Preventing reading disabilities by assessing and remediating phonemic skills. *School Psychology Review, 16,* 554–565.

Betts, E. A. (1946). *Foundations of reading instruction.* New York: American Book Company.

Betts, E. A. (1957). *Foundations of reading instruction* (2nd ed.). New York: American Book Company.

Billingsley, B. S., & Wildman, T. M. (1988). The effects of prereading activities on the comprehension monitoring of learning disabled adolescents. *Learning Disabilities Research, 4,* 36–44.

Blachowicz, C. (1977). Cloze activities for primary readers. *Reading Teacher, 31,* 300–302.

Blalock, J. W. (1980). Persistent auditory language deficits in adults with learning disabilities. *Journal of Learning Disabilities, 15,* 604–609.

Blankenship, C. S. (1978). Remediating systematic inversion errors in subtraction through the use of demonstration and feedback. *Learning Disability Quarterly, 1*(3), 12–22.

Blankenship, C. S. (1984). Curriculum and instruction: An examination of models in special and regular education. In J. F. Cawley (Ed.), *Developmental teaching of mathematics for the learning disabled* (pp. 29–53). Rockville, MD: Aspen Systems.

Bley, N. S., & Thornton, C. A. (1981). *Teaching mathematics to the learning disabled.* Rockville, MD: Aspen Systems.

Bookman, M. A. (1984). Spelling as a cognitive-developmental linguistic process. *Academic Therapy, 20,* 21–32.

Bormuth, J. R. (1968). The cloze readability procedure. *Elementary English, 45,* 429–436.

Bormuth, J. R. (1975). The cloze procedure. In W. D. Page (Ed.), *Help for the reading teacher: New directions in research* (pp. 60–90). Urbana, IL: National Conference on Research in English.

Bortnick, R., & Lopardo, G. S. (1973). An instructional application of the cloze procedure. *Journal of Reading, 16,* 296–300.

Bortnick, R., & Lopardo, G. S. (1976). The cloze procedure: A multi-purpose classroom tool. *Reading Improvement, 13,* 113–117.

Bos, C. S., & Anders, P. L. (in press). Interactive teaching and learning: Instructional practices for teaching content and strategic knowledge. In B. Y. L. Wong & T. E. Scruggs (Eds.), *Intervention research in learning disabilities* (pp. 166–185). New York, NY: Springer-Veralag.

Bos, C. S., Anders, P. L., Filip, D., & Jaffe, L. E. (1989). The effects of an interactive instructional strategy for enhancing reading comprehension and content area learning for students with learning disabilities. *Journal of Learning Disabilities, 22,* 384–390.

Bos, C. S., & Vaughn, S. (1988). *Strategies for teaching students with learning and behavior problems.* Boston: Allyn and Bacon.

Boyle, O. (1981). Mapping and composing. In M. H. Buckley

& O. Boyle, *Mapping the writing journey* (pp. 8–38). Berkeley: University of California Berkeley/Bay Area Writing Project, Curriculum Publication No. 15.

Bradley, L. (1981). The organization of motor patterns for spelling: An effective remedial strategy for backward spellers. *Developmental Medicine and Child Neurology, 23,* 83–91.

Bradley, L. (1983). The organization of visual, phonological, and motor strategies in learning to read and to spell. In U. Kirk (Ed.), *Neuropsychology of language, reading, and spelling* (pp. 235–254). New York: Academic Press.

Bradley, L., & Bryant, P. E. (1983). Categorizing sounds and learning to read: A causal connection. *Nature, 301,* 419–421.

Bradley, L., & Bryant, P. (1985). *Rhyme and reason in reading and spelling.* Ann Arbor: University of Michigan Press.

Brady, S., Mann, V., & Schmidt, R. (1987). Errors in short-term memory for good and poor readers. *Memory & Cognition, 15,* 444–453.

Bridge, C. A., Winograd, P. N., & Haley, D. (1983). Using predictable materials vs. preprimers to teach beginning sight words. *Reading Teacher, 36,* 884–891.

Briggs, E. (1970). Influence of handwriting on assessment. *Educational Research, 13,* 50–55.

Brigham, T. A., Graubard, P. S., & Stans, A. (1972). Analysis of the effects of sequential reinforcement contingencies on aspects of composition. *Journal of Applied Behavior Analysis, 5,* 421–429.

Bromley, K. D., & Jalongo, M. R. (1984). Song picture books and the language disabled child. *Teaching Exceptional Children, 16*(2), 114–119.

Brown, D. A. (1982). *Reading diagnosis and remediation.* Englewood Cliffs, NJ: Prentice-Hall.

Brown, R. (1981). National assessments of writing ability. In C. H. Fredericksen & J. F. Dominic (Eds.), *Writing: The nature, development, and teaching of written communication: Vol. 2. Process, development and communication* (pp. 31–38). Hillsdale, NJ: Lawrence Erlbaum.

Buckley, M. H. (1981). Mapping and thinking. In M. H. Buckley & O. Boyle, *Mapping the writing journey* (pp. 1–7). Berkeley: University of California Berkeley/Bay Area Writing Project, Curriculum Publication No. 15.

Bull, R., & Stevens, J. (1979). The effects of attractiveness of writer and penmanship on essay grades. *Journal of Occupational Psychology, 52,* 53–59.

Bullock, J. (Speaker). (1986). *Touch Math* (Video Cassette Recording). Colorado Springs, CO: Innovative Learning Concepts.

Bullock, J., & Walentas, N. (1989). *Touch math instruction manual.* Colorado Springs, CO: Innovative Learning Concepts.

Burns, M. (1988). Helping your students make sense out of math. *Learning, 16*(5), 31–35.

Buswell, G. T. (1926). Diagnostic studies in arithmetic. *Supplementary Educational Monographs, 23,* 185.

Caravella, J. R. (1977). *Minicalculators in the classroom.* Washington, DC: National Education Association.

Carbo, M. (1978). Teaching reading with talking books. *Reading Teacher, 32,* 267–273.

Carbo, M. (1987, February). Reading styles research: 'What works' isn't always phonics. *Phi Delta Kappan, 68,* 431–435.

Carnine, D., Kameenui, E. J., & Coyle, G. (1984). Utilization of contextual information in determining the meaning of unfamiliar words. *Reading Research Quarterly, 19,* 188–204.

Carnine, D., & Kinder, D. (1985). Teaching low-performing students to apply generative and schema strategies to narrative and expository material. *Remedial and Special Education, 6*(1), 20–29.

Carpenter, D. (1983). Spelling error profiles of able and disabled readers. *Journal of Learning Disabilities, 16,* 102–104.

Carpenter, D., & Miller, L. J. (1982). The spelling of reading disabled LD students and able readers. *Learning Disability Quarterly, 5,* 65–70.

Carver, R., & Hoffman, J. (1981). The effect of practice through repeated reading on gain in reading ability using a computer-based instructional system. *Reading Research Quarterly, 16,* 374–390.

Cattell, R. B. (1963). Theory for fluid and crystallized intelligence: A critical experiment. *Journal of Educational Psychology, 54,* 1–22.

Cawley, J. F. (1984). An integrative approach to needs of learning-disabled children: Expanded use of mathematics. In J. F. Cawley (Ed.), *Developmental teaching of mathematics for the learning disabled* (pp. 81–94). Rockville, MD: Aspen Systems.

Cawley, J. F. (1985, February). *Arithmetical word problems and the learning disabled.* Paper presented at the Association for Children with Learning Disabilities, International Conference, San Francisco, CA.

Cawley, J. F., Fitzmaurice, A. M., Shaw, R. A., Kahn, H., & Bates, H. (1979a). LD youth and mathematics: A review of characteristics. *Learning Disability Quarterly, 2*(1), 29–44.

Cawley, J. F., Fitzmaurice, A. M., Shaw, R. A., Kahn, H., & Bates, H. (1979b). Math word problems: Suggestions for LD students. *Learning Disability Quarterly, 2*(2), 25–41.

Cawley, J. F., & Miller, J. H. (1986). Selected views on metacognition, arithmetic problem solving, and learning disabilities. *Learning Disabilities Focus, 2*(1), 36–48.

Cawley, J. F., Miller, J. H., & School, B. A. (1987). A brief inquiry of arithmetic word-problem-solving among learning disabled secondary students. *Learning Disabilities Focus, 2*(2), 87–93.

Chall, J. (1983). *Stages of reading development.* New York: McGraw-Hill.

Childs, S. (1960, May). *Sound reading.* Paper presented at the International Reading Conference, New York.

Choate, J. S., & Rakes, T. A. (1987). Reading comprehension. In J. S. Choate, T. Z. Bennett, B. E. Enright, L. J. Miller, J. A. Poteet, & T. A. Rakes (Eds.), *Assessing and programming basic curriculum skills* (pp. 93–120). Boston: Allyn and Bacon.

Christine, R. O., & Hollingsworth, P. M. (1966). An experiment in spelling. *Education, 86,* 565–567.

Cicci, R. (1980). Written language disorders. *Bulletin of the Orton Society, 30,* 240–251.

Clark, F. L., Deshler, D. D., Schumaker, J. B., Alley, G. R., &

Warner, M. M. (1984). Visual imagery and self-questioning: Strategies to improve comprehension of written material. *Journal of Learning Disabilities, 17,*145–149.

Cohen, B. L. (1985). Writing: A new approach to the revision process. *Academic Therapy, 20,* 587–589.

Cohen, S. A., & Stover, G. (1981). Effects of teaching sixth-grade students to modify format variables of math word problems. *Reading Research Quarterly, 16,* 175–199.

Cohen, S. B., & Plaskon, S. P. (1980). *Language arts for the mildly handicapped.* Columbus, OH: Charles E. Merrill.

Cone, T. E., Wilson, L. R., Bradley, C. M., & Reese, J. H. (1985). Characteristics of LD students in Iowa: An empirical investigation. *Learning Disability Quarterly, 8,* 211–220.

Cook, J. E., Nolan, G. A., & Zanotti, R. J. (1980). Treating auditory perception problems: The NIM helps. *Academic Therapy, 15,* 473–481.

Cooper, C. (1973). An outline for writing sentence-combining problems. *English Journal, 62,* 96–102.

Cooper, C. (1975). Measuring growth in writing. *English Journal, 64,* 111–120.

Cotterell, G. (1974). A remedial approach to spelling disability. In B. Wade & K. Wedell (Eds.), *Spelling: Task and learner* (pp. 51–55). Birmingham, England: Educational Review.

Cox, L. S. (1975). Systematic errors in the four vertical algorithms in normal and handicapped populations. *Journal for Research in Mathematics Education, 6,* 202–220.

Cunningham, J. W. (1979). An automatic pilot for decoding. *Reading Teacher, 32,* 420–424.

Cunningham, P. M., & Cunningham, J. W. (1987). Content area reading-writing lessons. *Reading Teacher, 40,* 506–512.

Cunningham, P. M., Moore, S. A., Cunningham, J. W., & Moore, D. W. (1983). *Reading in elementary classrooms: Strategies and observations.* New York: Longman.

Curtis, M. E. (1980). Development of components of reading skill. *Journal of Educational Psychology, 72,* 656–669.

Curtis, M. E., & Glaser, R. (1983). Reading theory and the assessment of reading achievement. *Journal of Educational Measurement, 20,* 133–147.

Dagenais, D. J., & Beadle, K. R. (1984). Written language: When and where to begin. *Topics in Language Disorders, 4*(2), 59–85.

Dalke, C. (1988). Woodcock-Johnson Psycho-Educational Test Battery Profiles: A comparative study of college freshmen with and without learning disabilities. *Journal of Learning Disabilities, 21,* 567–570.

Darch, C., & Kameenui, E. J. (1987). Teaching LD students critical reading skills: A systematic replication. *Learning Disability Quarterly, 10,* 82–91.

Davis, D., & Miller, B. (1983). Why should I learn to write? *Academic Therapy, 18,* 431–435.

Decker, S. N., & DeFries, J. C. (1980). Cognitive abilities in families with reading disabled children. *Journal of Learning Disabilities, 13,* 517–522.

DeFries, J. C., Fulker, D. W., & LaBuda, M. C. (1987). Reading disability in twins: Evidence for a genetic etiology. *Nature, 329,* 537–539.

Delquadri, J. C., Greenwood, C. R., Stretton, K., & Hall, R. V. (1983). The peer tutoring spelling game: A classroom procedure for increasing opportunity to respond and spelling performance. *Education and Treatment of Children, 6,* 225–239.

Delquadri, J. C., Greenwood, C. R., Whorton, D., Carta, J. J., & Hall, R. V. (1986). Classwide peer tutoring. *Exceptional Children, 52,* 535–542.

Deno, S. L., Marston, D., & Mirkin, P. (1982). Valid measurement procedures for continuous evaluation of written expression. *Exceptional Children, 48,* 368–371.

Deno, S. L., Mirkin, P. K., & Wesson, C. (1984). How to write effective data-based IEPs. *Teaching Exceptional Children, 16,* 99–104.

Deshler, D. D., Ferrell, W. R., & Kass, C. E. (1978). Monitoring of schoolwork errors by LD adolescents. *Journal of Learning Disabilities, 11,* 10–23.

Dolch, E. W. (1941). *Teaching primary reading.* Champaign, IL: Garrard Press.

Douglass, B. (1984). Variation on a theme: Writing with the LD adolescent. *Academic Therapy, 19,* 361–363.

Dunlap, W. F. (sic) (1982). Readiness for solving story problems. *Academic Therapy, 17,* 581–587.

Dunlap, W. P., & Brennan, A. H. (1979). Developing mental images of mathematical processes. *Learning Disability Quarterly, 2*(2), 89–96.

Dwyer, E. (1980). Keeping a closed mind on reading. *Reading Improvement, 17,* 170–174.

D'Zamko, M. E., & Hedges, W. D. (1985). *Helping exceptional students succeed in the regular classroom.* New York: Parker.

Edgington, R. (1967). But he spelled them right this morning. *Academic Therapy, 3,* 58–61.

Eeds, M., & Cockrum, W. A. (1985). Teaching word meanings by expanding schemata vs. dictionary work vs. reading in context. *Journal of Reading, 28,* 492–497.

Ehri, L. C. (1980). The development of orthographic images. In U. Frith (Ed.), *Cognitive processes in spelling* (pp. 311–338). London: Academic Press.

Ehri, L. C. (1986). Sources of difficulty in learning to read and spell. In M. L. Wolraich & D. Routh (Eds.), *Advances in developmental and behavioral pediatrics* (pp. 121–195). Greenwich, CT: JAI Press.

Ehri, L. C. (1989). The development of spelling knowledge and its role in reading acquisition and reading disability. *Journal of Learning Disabilities, 22,* 356–365.

Enfield, M. L., & Greene, V. E. (1981). There *is* a skeleton in every closet. *Bulletin of the Orton Society, 31,* 189–198.

Engelhardt, J. M. (1982). Using computational errors in diagnostic teaching. *Arithmetic Teacher, 29,* 16–32.

Engelhardt, J. M., Ashlock, R. B., & Wiebe, J. H. (1984). *Helping children understand and use numerals.* Boston: Allyn and Bacon.

Englert, C. S. (1984). Effective direct instruction practices in special education settings. *Remedial and Special Education, 5*(2), 38–47.

Englert, C. S., Hiebert, E. H., & Stewart, S. R. (1985). Spelling unfamiliar words by an analogy strategy. *Journal of Special Education, 19,* 291–306.

Englert, C. S., & Lichter, A. (1982). Using statement-pie to teach reading and writing skills. *Teaching Exceptional Children,*

14, 164–170.

Englert, C. S., & Palincsar, A. S. (1988). The reading process. In D. K. Reid (Ed.), *Teaching the learning disabled: A cognitive developmental approach* (pp. 162-189). Boston: Allyn and Bacon.

Enright, B. E. (1987). Basic mathematics. In J. S. Choate, T. Z. Bennett, B. E. Enright, L. J. Miller, J. A. Poteet, & T. A. Rakes (Eds.), *Assessing and programming basic curriculum skills* (pp. 121–145). Boston: Allyn and Bacon.

Espin, C. A., & Sindelar, P. T. (1988). Auditory feedback and writing: Learning disabled and nondisabled students. *Exceptional Children, 55,* 45–51.

Fair, G. W. (1988). Mathematics instruction in the elementary grades. In D. K. Reid (Ed.), *Teaching the learning disabled: A cognitive developmental approach* (pp. 339–377). Boston: Allyn and Bacon.

Fearn, L. (1980). *Teaching for thinking.* San Diego: Kabyn Books.

Fernald, G. (1943). *Remedial techniques in basic school subjects.* New York: McGraw-Hill.

Fitzgerald, J. A. (1951). *A basic life spelling vocabulary.* Milwaukee: Bruce Publishing.

Fitzgerald, J., & Teasley, A. B. (1986). Effects of instruction in narrative structure on children's writing. *Journal of Educational Psychology, 78,* 424–432.

Fleischner, J., & Garnette, K. (1980). *Arithmetic learning disabilities: A literature review.* (Research Review Series 1979–1980). Research Institute for the Study of Learning Disabilities, Columbia University, NY. (ERIC Document Reproduction Service No. ED 210 843)

Fleischner, J. E., Nuzum, M. B., & Marzola, E. S. (1987). Devising an instructional program to teach arithmetic problem-solving skills to students with learning disabilities. *Journal of Learning Disabilities, 20,* 214–217.

Fleischner, J. E., & O'Loughlin, M. (1985). Solving story problems: Implications of research for teaching the learning disabled. In J. F. Cawley (Ed.), *Cognitive strategies and mathematics for the learning disabled* (pp. 163–181). Rockville, MD: Aspen Systems.

Flower, L., & Hayes, J. R. (1980). Writing as problem solving. *Visible Language, 14,* 388–399.

Foster, K., & Torgesen, J. K. (1983). The effects of directed study on the spelling performance of two subgroups of learning disabled students. *Learning Disability Quarterly, 6,* 252–257.

Fowler, G, L. (1982). Developing comprehension skills with primary and remedial readers through the use of story frames. *Reading Teacher, 36,* 176–179.

Fowler, G. L., & Davis, M. (1985). The story frame approach: A tool for improving reading comprehension of EMR children. *Teaching Exceptional Children, 17,* 296–298.

Fox, B., & Routh, D. K. (1984). Phonemic analysis and synthesis as word attack skills: Revisited. *Journal of Educational Psychology, 76,* 1059–1064.

Frank, A. R. (1973). Breaking down the learning tasks: A sequence approach. *Teaching Exceptional Children, 6,* 16–19.

Freeman, F. N. (1914). *The teaching of handwriting.* Boston: Houghton Mifflin.

Fry, E., Polk, J., & Fountoukidis, D. (1984). *The reading teacher's book of lists.* Englewood Cliffs, NJ: Prentice-Hall.

Gawronski, J. D., & Coblentz, D. (1976). Calculators and the mathematics curriculum. *Arithmetic Teacher, 23,* 510–512.

Gentry, J. R. (1978). Early spelling strategies. *Elementary School Journal, 79*(2), 88–92.

Gentry, J. R. (1982a). Developmental spelling: Assessment. *Diagnostique, 8,* 52–61.

Gentry, J. R. (1982b). An analysis of developmental spelling in GNYS AT WRK. *Reading Teacher, 36,* 192–200.

Gentry, J. R. (1984). Developmental aspects of learning to spell. *Academic Therapy, 20,* 11–19.

Gerber, M. M. (1984). Techniques to teach generalizable spelling skills. *Academic Therapy, 20,* 49–58.

Gerber, M. M., & Hall, R. J. (1987). Information processing approaches to studying spelling deficiencies. *Journal of Learning Disabilities, 20,* 34–42.

Gerber, M. M., & Lydiatt, S. (1984). Research and practice in teaching spelling. *Academic Therapy, 20,*5–10.

Gerhard, H. R. (1968). The failure strategies of third grade arithmetic pupils. *Arithmetic Teacher, 15,* 442–446.

Getman, G. N. (1985). Hand-eye coordinations. *Academic Therapy, 20,* 261–275.

Gettinger, M. (1984). Applying learning principles to remedial spelling instruction. *Academic Therapy, 20,* 41–47.

Gettinger, M., Bryant, N. D., & Fayne, H. R. (1982). Designing spelling instruction for learning disabled children: An emphasis on unit size, distributed practice, and training for transfer. *Journal of Special Education, 16,* 439–448.

Gibbs, V., & Proctor, S. (1982). "Read me a story": The presenting method works! *Academic Therapy, 17,* 619–622.

Gillingham, A., & Stillman, B. W. (1973). *Remedial training for children with specific disability in reading, spelling, and penmanship.* Cambridge, MA: Educators Publishing Service.

Giordano, G. (1982). CATS exercises: Teaching disabled writers to communicate. *Academic Therapy, 18,* 233–237.

Giordano, G. (1983a). Readiness skills for disabled writers. *Academic Therapy, 18,* 315–319.

Giordano, G. (1983b). Integrating remedial writing into reading programs. *Academic Therapy, 18,* 599–607.

Giordano, G. (1984). Analyzing and remediating writing disabilities. *Journal of Learning Disabilities, 17,* 78–83.

Glaser, R., Lesgold, A., & Lajoie, S. (1987). Toward a cognitive theory for the measurement of achievement. In R. R. Ronning, J. A. Glover, & J. C. Conoley (Eds.), *The influence of cognitive psychology on testing* (pp. 41–85). Hillsdale, NJ: Lawrence Erlbaum.

Glass, G. G. (1973). *Teaching decoding as separate from reading.* New York: Adelphi University.

Glass, G. G. (1976). *Glass-Analysis for decoding only teacher guide.* Garden City, NY: Easier to Learn.

Glynn, E. L., & Thomas, J. D. (1974). Effect of cueing on self-control of classroom behavior. *Journal of Applied Behavior Analysis, 7,* 299–306.

Gold, P. C. (1984). Cognitive mapping. *Academic Therapy, 19,* 277–284.

Gonzales, P. G., & Elijah, P. V. (1975). Rereading: Effect on error patterns and performance levels on the IRI. *Reading Teacher, 28,* 647–652.

Good, T. L., & Grouws, D. A. (1979). The Missouri mathematics effectiveness project: An experimental study in fourth-grade classrooms. *Journal of Educational Psychology, 71,* 355–362.

Goodman, L. (1987). LD students' writing: Analyzing errors. *Academic Therapy, 22,* 453–461.

Gordon, C., & Braun, C. (1983). Using story schema as an aid to reading and writing. *Reading Teacher, 37,* 116–121.

Graham, S. (1983). Effective spelling instruction. *Elementary School Journal, 83,* 560–567.

Graham, S. (1985). Evaluating spelling programs and materials. *Teaching Exceptional Children, 17,* 299–303.

Graham, S., & Freeman, S. (1985). Strategy training and teacher vs. student-controlled study conditions: Effects on LD students' spelling performance. *Learning Disability Quarterly, 8,* 267–274.

Graham, S., & Harris, K. (1986). *Improving learning disabled students' compositions via story grammar training: A component analysis of self-control strategy training.* Paper presented at the annual meeting of the American Educational Research Association, San Francisco, CA.

Graham, S., & Madan, A. J. (1981). Teaching letter formation. *Academic Therapy, 16,* 389–396.

Graham, S., & Miller, L. (1979). Spelling research and practice: A unified approach. *Focus on Exceptional Children, 12*(2), 1–16.

Graves, D. H. (1978). Handwriting is for writing. *Language Arts, 55,* 393–399.

Graves, D. H. (1983). *Writing: Teachers and children at work.* Exeter, NH: Heinemann Educational Books.

Graves, D. H. (1985). All children can write. *Learning Disabilities Focus, 1*(1), 36–43.

Graves, M. F., Cooke, C. L., & LaBerge, M. (1983). Effects of previewing difficult short stories on low ability junior high students' comprehension, recall, and attitudes. *Reading Research Quarterly, 18,* 262–276.

Gray, W. S. (1956). *The teaching of reading and writing.* (Monographs on Fundamental Education No. 10). Chicago: Scott, Foresman.

Gregg, N. (1983). College learning disabled writers: Error patterns and instructional alternatives. *Journal of Learning Disabilities, 16,* 334–338.

Gregory, J., & Morsink, C. (1984). Modifying the instructional program in mathematics. In C. V. Morsink (Ed.), *Teaching special needs students in regular classrooms* (pp. 211–237). Boston: Little, Brown.

Greenwood, J., & Anderson, R. (1983). Some thoughts on teaching and learning mathematics. *Arithmetic Teacher, 3,* 42–49.

Griffey, Q. L., Jr., Zigmond, N., & Leinhardt, G. (1988). The effects of self-questioning and story structure training on the reading comprehension of poor readers. *Learning Disabilities Research, 4,* 45–51.

Grinnell, P. C. (1988). Teaching handwriting and spelling. In D. K. Reid (Ed.), *Teaching the learning disabled: A cognitive developmental approach* (pp. 245–278). Boston: Allyn and

Bacon.

Griswold, P. C., Gelzheiser, L. M., & Shepherd, M. J. (1987). Does a production deficiency hypothesis account for vocabulary learning among adolescents with learning disabilities? *Journal of Learning Disabilities, 20,* 620–626.

Groff, P. (1969). New speeds in handwriting. In W. Otto & K. Koenke (Eds.), *Remedial teaching: Research and comment* (pp. 283–284). Boston: Houghton Mifflin.

Gurney, D., Gersten, R., Dimino, J., & Carnine, D. (1990). Story grammar: Effective literature instruction for high school students with learning disabilities. *Journal of Learning Disabilities, 23,* 335–342, 348.

Guthrie, J., Seifert, M., Burnham, N., & Caplan, R. (1974). The maze technique to assess, monitor reading comprehension. *Reading Teacher, 28,* 161–168.

Guyer, B. P., & Sabatino, D. (1989). The effectiveness of a multisensory alphabetic phonetic approach with college students who are learning disabled. *Journal of Learning Disabilities, 22,* 430–434.

Hagedorn, C. I., & McLaughlin, T. F. (1982). Assisted reading: A review and analysis of its effectiveness with remedial readers. *B.C. Journal of Special Education, 6,* 311–322.

Hagin, R. (1983). Write right—or left. *Journal of Learning Disabilities, 16,* 266–271.

Hall, J. K. (1981). *Evaluating and improving written expression: A practical guide for teachers.* Boston: Allyn and Bacon.

Hanover, S. (1983). Handwriting comes naturally? *Academic Therapy, 18,* 407–412.

Hansen, C., & Eaton, M. (1978). Reading. In N. G. Haring, T. C. Lovitt, M. D. Eaton, & C. L. Hansen (Eds.), *The fourth R: Research in the classroom* (pp. 41–92). Columbus, OH: Charles E. Merrill.

Harber, J. R. (1980). Auditory perception and reading: Another look. *Learning Disability Quarterly, 3*(3), 19–29.

Harp, B. (1988). When the principal asks: "Why are your kids giving each other spelling tests?" *Reading Teacher, 41,* 702–704.

Harris, A. J., & Sipay, E. R. (1985). *How to increase reading ability* (8th ed.). New York: Longman.

Harris, K. R., & Graham, S. (1985). Improving learning disabled student's composition skills: A self-control strategy training approach. *Learning Disability Quarterly, 8,* 27–36.

Harris, K. R., Graham, S., & Freeman, S. (1988). Effects of strategy training on metamemory among learning disabled students. *Exceptional Children, 54,* 332–338.

Hasselbring, T. S., Goin, L. I., & Bransford, J. D. (1987). Developing automaticity. *Teaching Exceptional Children, 19*(3), 30–33.

Hasson, E. (1983). The use of aural cloze as an instructional technique in kindergarten. *Reading Improvement, 20,* 197–199.

Hayes, A.M.F. (1985). Classroom implications. In J. F. Cawley (Ed.), *Cognitive strategies and mathematics for the learning disabled* (pp. 209–236). Rockville, MD: Aspen Systems.

Hayward, L. R., & LeBuffe, J. R. (1985). Self-correction: A positive method for improving writing skills. *Teaching Exceptional Children, 18*(1), 68–72.

Heckelman, R. G. (1965). The phonics bound child. *Academic*

Therapy Quarterly, 1, 12–13.

Heckelman, R. G. (1966). Using the neurological impress reading technique. *Academic Therapy, 1,* 235–239.

Heckelman, R. G. (1969). A neurological-impress method of remedial-reading instruction. *Academic Therapy, 4,* 277–282.

Heckelman, R. G. (1974). *Solutions to reading problems.* Novato, CA: Academic Therapy.

Heckelman, R. G. (1986). N.I.M. Revisited. *Academic Therapy, 21,* 411–420.

Henk, W. A. (1983). Adapting the NIM to improve comprehension. *Academic Therapy, 19,* 97–101.

Henk, W. A., Helfeldt, J. P., & Platt, J. M. (1986). Developing reading fluency in learning disabled students. *Teaching Exceptional Children, 18,* 202–206.

Henk, W. A., & Selders, M. L. (1984). A test of synonymic scoring of cloze passages. *Reading Teacher, 38,* 282–287.

Hennings, D. (1982). A writing approach to reading comprehension-schema theory in action. *Language Arts, 59*(1), 8–17.

Hessler, G. L. (in press). *Use and interpretation of the Woodcock-Johnson Psycho-Educational Battery—Revised.* Allen, TX: DLM.

Hildreth, G. (1955). *Teaching spelling.* New York: Henry Holt.

Hillocks, G., Jr. (1987). Synthesis of research on teaching writing. *Educational Leadership, 44*(8), 71–76, 78, 80–82.

Hofmeister, A. M. (1973). Let's get it write. Five common instructional errors in teaching writing. *Teaching Exceptional Children, 6,* 30–33.

Hoogeveen, F. R., & Smeets, P. M. (1988). Establishing phoneme blending in trainable mentally retarded children. *Remedial and Special Education, 9*(2), 46–53.

Horn, E. (1954). *Teaching spelling.* Washington, DC: American Educational Research Association.

Horn, J. L. (1985). Remodeling old models of intelligence. In B. B. Wolman (Ed.), *Handbook of intelligence* (pp. 267–300). New York: Wiley.

Horn, J. L. (1986). Some thoughts about intelligence. In R. J. Sternberg & D. K. Detterman (Eds.), *What is intelligence? Contemporary viewpoints on its nature and definition* (pp. 91–96). Norwood, NJ: Ablex.

Horn, J. L., & Cattell, R. B. (1966). Refinement and test of the theory of fluid and crystallized intelligence. *Journal of Educational Psychology, 57,* 253–270.

Horton, S. V., Lovitt, T. C., & Bergerud, D. (1990). The effectiveness of graphic organizers for three classifications of secondary students in content area classes. *Journal of Learning Disabilities, 23,* 12–22.

Hoskisson, K. (1975). The many facets of assisted reading. *Elementary English, 52,* 312–315.

Hoskisson, K. (1979). A response to "a critique of teaching reading as a whole-task venture." *Reading Teacher, 32,* 653–659.

Hoskisson, K., & Krohm, B. (1974). Reading by immersion: Assisted reading. *Elementary English, 51,* 832–836.

Houten, R. V., Morrison, E., Jarvis, R., & McDonald, M. (1974). The effects of explicit timing and feedback on compositional response rate in elementary school children. *Journal of Applied Behavior Analysis, 7,* 547–555.

Howell, R., Sidorenko, E., & Jurica, J. (1987). The effects of computer use on the acquisition of multiplication facts by a learning disabled student. *Journal of Learning Disabilities, 20,* 336–341.

Huey, E. B. (1968). *The psychology and pedagogy of reading.* Cambridge, MA: Massachusetts Institute of Technology Press.

Idol, L. (1987). Group story mapping: A comprehension strategy for both skilled and unskilled readers. *Journal of Learning Disabilities, 20,* 196–205.

Idol-Maestas, L. (1985). Getting ready to read: Guided probing for poor comprehenders. *Learning Disability Quarterly, 8,* 243–254.

Ingersoll, B. (1988). *Your hyperactive child: A parent's guide to coping with attention deficit disorder.* New York, NY: Doubleday.

Isaacson, S. L. (1985). *Assessing the potential syntax development of third and fourth grade writers.* Unpublished doctoral dissertation, Arizona State University, Tempe.

Isaacson, S. L. (1987). Effective instruction in written language. *Focus on Exceptional Children, 19*(6), 1–12.

Isaacson, S. L. (1988). Assessing the writing product: Qualitative and quantitative measures. *Exceptional Children, 54,* 528–534.

James, M. (1986). Self-selected spelling. *Academic Therapy, 2,* 557–563.

Janiak, R. (1983). Listening/reading: An effective learning combination. *Academic Therapy, 19,* 205–211.

Jenkins, J. R., Heliotis, J. D., Stein, M. L., & Haynes, M. C. (1987). Improving reading comprehension by using paragraph restatements. *Exceptional Children, 54,* 54–59.

Johns, J. L., & McNamara, L. P. (1980). The SQ3R study technique: A forgotten research target. *Journal of Reading, 23,* 705–708.

Johnson, D. D., & Pearson, P. D. (1984). Components of vocabulary instruction. In D. D. Johnson & P. D. Pearson (Eds.), *Teaching reading vocabulary* (pp. 9–16). New York: Holt, Rinehart, and Winston.

Johnson, R. J., & McLaughlin, T. F. (1982). The effects of free time on assignment completion and accuracy in arithmetic: A case study. *Education and Treatment of Children, 5,* 33–40.

Jones, K. M., Torgesen, J. K., & Sexton, M. A. (1987). Using computer guided practice to increase decoding fluency in learning disabled children: A study using the Hint and Hunt I program. *Journal of Learning Disabilities, 20,* 122–128.

Jones, M. B., & Pikulski, E. C. (1974). Cloze for the classroom. *Journal of Reading, 17,* 432–438.

Jongsma, E. A. (1980). *Cloze instruction research: A second look.* Newark, DE: International Reading Association.

Juel, C., Griffith, P. L., & Gough, P. B. (1986). Acquisition of literacy: A longitudinal study of children in first and second grade. *Journal of Educational Psychology, 78,* 243–255.

Juel, C., & Leavell, J. A. (1988). Retention and nonretention of at-risk readers in first grade and their subsequent reading achievement. *Journal of Learning Disabilities, 21,* 571–580.

Kann, R. (1983). The method of repeated readings: Expanding the neurological impress method for use with disabled readers. *Journal of Learning Disabilities, 16,* 90–92.

Kauffman, J., Hallahan, D., Haas, K., Brame, T., & Boren, R. (1978). Imitating children's errors to improve spelling performance. *Journal of Learning Disabilities, 11,* 33–38.

Kavale, K. (1982). Meta-analysis of the relationship between visual perceptual skills and reading achievement. *Journal of Learning Disabilities, 15,* 42–51.

Kelly, B., Gersten, R., & Carnine, D. (1990). Student error patterns as a function of curriculum design: Teaching fractions to remedial high school students and high school students with learning disabilities. *Journal of Learning Disabilities, 23,* 23–29.

Kennedy, D. (1974, November). The cloze procedure: Use it to develop comprehension skills. *Instructor,* pp. 82, 84, 86.

Kennedy, J., & Thomas, D. (1979). *A tangle of mathematical yarns.* Oxford, OH: Authors.

Kerrigan, W. J. (1979). *Writing to the point: Six basic steps* (2nd ed.). New York: Harcourt Brace Jovanovich.

Kirby, J. R., & Becker, L. D. (1988). Cognitive components of learning problems in arithmetic. *Remedial and Special Education, 9*(5), 7–16.

Kirk, S. A., & Chalfant, J. C. (1984). *Academic and developmental learning disabilities.* Denver: Love.

Kirk, S. A., & Elkins, J. (1975). Characteristics of children enrolled in the child service demonstration centers. *Journal of Learning Disabilities, 8,* 630–637.

Kirk, S. A., Kirk, W. D., & Minskoff, E. H. (1985). *Phonic remedial reading lessons.* Novato, CA: Academic Therapy.

Kochnower, J., Richardson, E., & DiBenedetto, B. (1983). A comparison of the phonic decoding ability of normal and learning disabled children. *Journal of Learning Disabilities, 16,* 348–351.

Kosiewicz, M. M., Hallahan, D. P., Lloyd, J., & Graves, A. W. (1982). Effects of self-instruction and self-correction procedures on handwriting performance. *Learning Disability Quarterly, 5*(1), 71–78.

LaBerge, D., & Samuels, S. J. (1974). Toward a theory of automatic information processing in reading. *Cognitive Psychology, 6,* 293–323.

LaBuda, M. C., & DeFries, J. C. (1988). Cognitive abilities in children with reading disabilities and controls: A follow-up study. *Journal of Learning Disabilities, 21,* 562–566.

Langer, J. A. (1981). From theory to practice: A prereading plan. *Journal of Reading, 25,* 152–156.

Langer, J. A. (1984). Examining background knowledge and text comprehension. *Reading Research Quarterly, 19,* 468–481.

Lapp, D., & Flood, J. (1983). *Teaching reading to every child* (2nd ed.). New York: Macmillan.

Larsen, S. C. (1987). *Assessing the writing abilities and instructional needs of students.* Austin, TX: PRO-ED.

Laughton, J., & Morris, N. T. (1989). Story grammar knowledge of learning disabled students. *Learning Disabilities Research, 4,* 87–95.

Lawlor, J. (1983). Sentence combining: A sequence for instruction. *Elementary School Journal, 84,* 53–62.

Leinhardt, G., Zigmond, N., & Cooley, W. W. (1980, April). *Reading instruction and its effects.* Paper presented at the annual meeting of the American Educational Research Associates, Boston, MA.

Lenz, B. K. (1983). Promoting active learning through effective instruction: Using advance organizers. *Pointer, 27*(2), 11–13.

Lenz, B. K., Alley, G. R., & Schumaker, J. B. (1987). Activating the inactive learner: Advance organizers in the secondary content classroom. *Learning Disability Quarterly, 10*(10), 53–67.

Lenz, B. K, & Hughes, C. A. (1990). A word identification strategy for adolescents with learning disabilities. *Journal of Learning Disabilities, 23*, 149–158, 163.

Lenz, B. K., Schumaker, J. B., Deshler, D. D., & Beals, V. L. (1984). *The word identification strategy.* Lawrence: University of Kansas.

Lesgold, A. M., Resnick, L. B., & Hammond, K. (1985). Learning to read: A longitudinal study of word skill development in two curricula. In T. G. Waller & G. E. MacKinnon (Eds.), *Reading research: Advances in theory and practice* (Vol. 4, pp. 107–138). Orlando, FL: Academic Press.

Leuenberger, J., & Morris, M. (1990). Analysis of spelling errors by learning disabled and normal college students. *Learning Disabilities Focus, 5*, 103–118.

Levine, M. D. (1987). *Developmental variation and learning disorders.* Cambridge: Educators Publishing Service.

Lewkowicz, N. K. (1980). Phonemic awareness training: What to teach and how to teach it. *Journal of Educational Psychology, 72*, 686–700.

Lickteig, M. J., Sr. (1981). Research-based recommendations for teachers of writing. *Language Arts, 58*, 44–50.

Litowitz, B. E. (1981). Developmental issues in written language. *Topics in Language Disorders, 1*(2), 73–89.

Lloyd, J. W., & Keller, C. E. (1989). Effective mathematics instruction: Development, instruction, and programs. *Focus on Exceptional Children, 21*(7), 1–10.

Lombardo, T. W., & Drabman, R. S. (1985). Teaching LD children multiplication tables. *Academic Therapy, 20*, 437–442.

Lopardo, G. (1975). LEA-cloze reading material for the disabled reader. *Reading Teacher, 29*, 42–44.

Lovitt, T. C. (1984). *Tactics for teaching.* Columbus, OH: Charles E. Merrill.

Lovitt, T. C., & Curtiss, K. A. (1968). Effects of manipulating an antecedent event on mathematics response rate. *Journal of Applied Behavior Analysis, 1*, 329-333.

Lovitt, T. C., & DeMier, D. M. (1984). An evaluation of the Slingerland method with LD youngsters. *Journal of Learning Disabilities, 17*, 267–272.

Lovitt, T. C., & Hansen, C. C. (1976). The use of contingent skipping and drilling to improve oral reading and reading comprehension. *Journal of Learning Disabilities, 9*, 481–487.

Lovitt, T., Rudsit, J., Jenkins, J., Pious, C., & Benedetti, D. (1985). Two methods of adapting science materials for learning disabled and regular seventh graders. *Learning Disability Quarterly, 8*, 275–285.

Lowenthal, B. (1987). Interviewing to diagnose math errors. *Academic Therapy, 23*, 213–217.

Luftig, R. L. (1987). *Teaching the mentally retarded student: Curriculum, methods, and strategies.* Boston: Allyn and Bacon.

Luiselli, J. K., & Downing, J. N. (1980). Improving a student's arithmetic performance using feedback and reinforcement procedures. *Education and Treatment of Children, 3*, 45–49.

Lutes, L. K. (1982). Clozing in on reading. *Academic Therapy, 17*, 523–528.

MacArthur, C. A., Graham, S., & Skarvoed, J. (1986). *Learning disabled students' composing with three methods: Handwriting, dictation, and word processing.* (Tech. Rep. No. 109). College Park, MD: Institute for the Study of Exceptional Children and Youth.

Maheady, L., & Harper, G. F. (1987). A class-wide peer tutoring program to improve the spelling test performance of low-income, third- and fourth-grade students. *Education and Treatment of Children, 10*, 120–133.

Maheady, L., Sacca, M. K., & Harper, G. F. (1988). Classwide peer tutoring with mildly handicapped high school students. *Exceptional Children, 55*, 52–59.

Mandoli, M., Mandoli, P., & McLaughlin, T. F. (1982). Effects of same-age peer tutoring on the spelling performance of a mainstreamed elementary learning disabled student. *Learning Disability Quarterly, 5*, 185–189.

Mann, V. A., Cowin, E., & Schoenheimer, J. (1989). Phonological processing, language comprehension, and reading ability. *Journal of Learning Disabilities, 22*, 76–89.

Mann, V. A., & Liberman, I. Y. (1984). Phonological awareness and verbal short-term memory. *Journal of Learning Disabilities, 17*, 592–598.

Mann, V. A., Liberman, I. Y., & Shankweiler, D. (1980). Children's memory for sentences and word strings in relation to reading ability. *Memory & Cognition, 8*, 329–335.

Maring, G. H., & Furman, G. (1985). Seven "whole class" strategies to help mainstreamed young people read and listen better in content area classes. *Journal of Reading, 28*, 694–700.

Markham, L. R. (1976). Influences of handwriting quality on teacher evaluation of written work. *American Educational Research Journal, 13*, 277–283.

Masters, L. F., & Mori, A. A. (1986). *Teaching secondary students with mild learning and behavior problems: Methods, materials, strategies.* Rockville, MD: Aspen Systems.

Mastropieri, M. A. (1988). Using the keyboard (sic) method. *Teaching Exceptional Children, 20*(2), 4–8.

Mastropieri, M. A. (1989, November). *Social studies can be multisensory: New ways to actively involve students in the learning experience.* Paper presented at "Building study skills and learning strategies for learning disabled students," Teachers College, Columbia, NY.

Mastropieri, M. A., & Scruggs, T. E. (1988). Increasing content area learning of learning disabled students: Research implementation. *Learning Disabilities Research, 4*, 17–25.

Mastropieri, M. A., & Scruggs, T. E. (1989). Mnemonic social studies instruction: Classroom applications. *Remedial and Special Education, 10*(3), 40-46.

Mastropieri, M. A., Scruggs, T. E., & Mushinski Fulk, B. J. (1990). Teaching abstract vocabulary with the keyword method: Effects on recall and comprehension. *Journal of*

Learning Disabilities, 23, 92–96, 107.

Mather, N. (1985). *The Fernald kinesthetic method revisited.* Unpublished manuscript, University of Arizona, Tucson.

Mather, N., & Healey, W. C. (1990). Deposing aptitude-achievement discrepancy as the imperial criterion for learning disabilities. *Learning Disabilities: A Multidisciplinary Journal, 1,* 40-48.

Mather, N., & Lachowicz, B. (in press). Shared writing: An instructional approach for reluctant writers. *Teaching Exceptional Children.*

Mattingly, J. C., & Bott, D. A. (1990). Teaching multiplication facts to students with learning problems. *Exceptional Children, 56,* 438-449.

Mayer, R. E. (1979). Twenty years of research on advance organizers: Assimilation theory is still the best predictor of results. *Instructional Science, 8,* 133–167.

McCabe, D. (1982). Developing study skills: The LD high school student. *Academic Therapy, 18,* 197–201.

McClure, A. A. (1985). Predictable books: Another way to teach reading to learning disabled children. *Teaching Exceptional Children, 17,* 267–273.

McCoy, K. M., & Prehm, H. J. (1987). *Teaching mainstreamed students: Methods and techniques.* Denver: Love.

McGinty, R., & Van Beynen, J. (1982). Story problems—Let's make them just that. *School Science and Mathematics, 82,* 307–310.

McGrew, K. (1986). *Clinical interpretation of the Woodcock-Johnson Tests of Cognitive Ability.* Orlando, FL: Grune & Stratton.

McGrew, K. S., & Pehl, J. (1988). Prediction of future achievement by the Woodcock-Johnson Psycho-Educational Battery and the WISC-R. *Journal of School Psychology, 26,* 275–281.

McGrew, K. S., Werder, J. K., & Woodcock, R. W. (1990). *Woodcock-Johnson—Revised Technical Manual.* Allen, TX: DLM.

McKeown, M. G., & Beck, I. L. (1988). Learning vocabulary: Different ways for different goals. *Remedial and Special Education, 9*(1), 42–52.

McLaughlin, T. F. (1981). The effects of a classroom token economy on math performance in an intermediate grade class. *Education and Treatment of Children, 4,* 139–147.

McLeod, T. M., & Armstrong, S. W. (1982). Learning disabilities in mathematics—skill deficits and remedial approaches at the intermediate and secondary level. *Learning Disabilities Quarterly, 5,* 305–311.

McLoone, B. B., Scruggs, T. E., Mastropieri, M. A., & Zucker, S. H. (1986). Mnemonic strategy instruction and training with learning disabled students. *Learning Disabilities Research, 2,* 45–53.

McLoughlin, J. A., & Lewis, R. B. (1990). *Assessing special students* (3rd ed.). Columbus, OH: Charles E. Merrill.

Mehlmann, M. A., & Waters, M. K. (1985). From write to right. *Academic Therapy, 20,* 583–586.

Memory, D. M. (1981). The impress method: A status report of a new remedial reading technique. *Journal of Research and Development, 14*(4), 102–104.

Mercer, C. D., & Mercer, A. R. (1985). *Teaching students with learning problems.* Columbus, OH: Charles E. Merrill.

Meyer, P. I. (1980). When you use a calculator you have to think! *Arithmetic Teacher, 27*(5), 18–21.

Meyer, V. (1981). Prime-O-Tec: Good news for adult disabled readers. *Academic Therapy, 17,* 215–220.

Meyers, M. J. (1987, November). LD students: Clarifications and recommendations. *Middle School Journal,* 27–30.

Miccinati, J. (1981). Teaching reading disabled students to perceive distinctive features in words. *Journal of Learning Disabilities, 14,* 140–142.

Mikkelsen, V. (1981). *The effects of a modified neurological impress method on developing decoding skills.* Paper presented at the East Carolina University Library Science Lecture Series. Greenville, NC. (ERIC Document Reproduction Service no. ED 209 638)

Miller, J. H., & Milam, C. P. (1987). Multiplication and division errors committed by learning disabled students. *Learning Disabilities Research, 2,* 119–122.

Miller, W. H. (1986). *Reading diagnosis kit* (3rd ed.). West Nyack, NY: Center for Applied Research in Education.

Monroe, M., & Backus, B. (1937). *Remedial reading,* Boston: Houghton Mifflin.

Montague, M., & Bos, C. S. (1986). The effect of cognitive strategy training on verbal math problem solving performance of learning disabled adolescents. *Journal of Learning Disabilities, 19,* 26–33.

Montague, M., Maddux, C. D., & Dereshiwsky, M. I. (1990). Story grammar and comprehension and production of narrative prose by students with learning disabilities. *Journal of Learning Disabilities, 23,* 190–197.

Moran, M. R. (1983). Learning disabled adolescents' responses to a paragraph-organization strategy. *Pointer, 27*(2), 28–31.

Moran, M. R., Schumaker, J. B., & Vetter, A. F. (1981). *Teaching a paragraph organization strategy to learning disabled adolescents* (Research Report No. 54). Lawrence: University of Kansas.

Moulton, J. R., & Bader, M. S. (1986). The writing process: A powerful approach for the language-disabled student. *Annals of Dyslexia, 35,* 161–173.

Moyer, S. B. (1982). Repeated reading. *Journal of Learning Disabilities, 15,* 619–623.

Neill, K. (1979). Turn kids on with repeated reading. *Teaching Exceptional Children, 12,* 63–64.

Neville, M. H., & Pugh, A. K. (1975). An empirical study of the reading while listening method. In D. Moyle (Ed.), *Reading: What of the future?* (pp. 95–106). London: Ward Lock Educational.

Newby, R. F., Caldwell, J., & Recht, D. R. (1989). Improving the reading comprehension of children with dysphonetic and dyseidetic dyslexia using story grammar. *Journal of Learning Disabilities, 22,* 373–380.

Newland, T. E. (1932). An analytical study of the development of illegibilities in handwriting from the lower grades to adulthood. *Journal of Educational Research, 26,* 249–258.

Nodine, B. F., Barenbaum, E., & Newcomer, P. (1985). Story composition by learning disabled, reading disabled, and normal children. *Learning Disability Quarterly, 8,* 167–179.

Nulman, J. H., & Gerber, M. M. (1984). Improving spelling performance by imitating a child's errors. *Journal of*

Learning Disabilities, 17, 328–333.

Nutter, N., & Safran, J. (1984). Improving writing with sentence combining. *Academic Therapy, 19,* 449–455.

Ogle, D. M. (1986). K-W-L: A teaching model that develops active reading of expository text. *Reading Teacher, 39,*564–570.

Oosterom, J. V., & Devereux, K. (1982). Rebus at Rees Thomas School. *Special Education: Forward Trends, 9*(1), 31–33.

O'Shea, L. J., & O'Shea, D. J. (1988). Using repeated readings. *Teaching Exceptional Children, 20*(2), 26–29.

O'Shea, L. J., Sindelar, P. T., & O'Shea, D. J. (1987). The effects of repeated readings and attentional cues on the reading fluency and comprehension of learning disabled readers. *Learning Disabilities Research, 2,* 103–109.

O'Sullivan, J. T., & Pressley, M. (1984). Completeness of instruction and strategy transfer. *Journal of Experimental Child Psychology, 38,* 275–288.

Otto, W., Peters, C., & Peters, N. (1977). *Reading problems: A multidisciplinary perspective.* Menlo Park, CA: Addison-Wesley.

Otto, W., & Smith, R. J. (1980). *Corrective and remedial teaching.* Boston: Houghton Mifflin.

Ownby, R. L., Wallbrown, F., D'Atri, A., & Armstrong, B. (1985). Patterns of referrals for school psychological services: Replication of the referral problems category system. *Special Services in the Schools, 1*(4), 53–66.

Pace, A. J. (1978). *The influence of world knowledge on children's comprehension of short narrative passages.* (Report No. CS 004 029). Toronto, Canada: Annual Meeting of the American Educational Research Association. (ERIC Document Reproduction Service No. Ed 153 188)

Palincsar, A. S. (1986a). The role of dialogue in scaffolded instruction. *Educational Psychologist, 21*(1,), 73–98.

Palincsar, A. S. (1986b). Reciprocal teaching: Can student discussion boost comprehension? *Instructor, 96*(5), 56–60.

Palincsar, A. S., & Brown, A. L. (1984). Reciprocal teaching of comprehension fostering and comprehension-monitoring activities. *Cognition and Instruction, 1,* 117–175.

Palincsar, A. S., & Brown, A. L. (1986). Interactive teaching to promote independent learning from text. *Reading Teacher, 39,* 771–777.

Palincsar, A. S., & Brown, A. L. (1988). Teaching and practicing thinking skills to promote comprehension in the context of group problem solving. *Remedial and Special Education, 9*(1), 53–59.

Palincsar, A. S., & Englert, C. S. (1988). Teaching learning disabled students to read. In D. K. Reid (Ed.), *Teaching the learning disabled: A cognitive developmental approach* (pp. 190–214). Boston: Allyn and Bacon.

Payne, J. N. (1980). Sense and nonsense about fractions and decimals. *Arithmetic Teacher, 27*(5), 5–7.

Pearson, P. D., & Johnson, D. D. (1978). *Teaching reading comprehension.* New York: Holt, Rinehart, & Winston.

Pearson, R. D., & Spiro, R. J. (1980). Toward a theory of reading comprehension. *Topics in Language Disorders, 1*(1), 71–88.

Perfetti, C. (1985). *Reading ability.* New York: Oxford University Press.

Personke, C., & Yee, A. H. (1971). *Comprehensive spelling instruction: Theory, research, and application.* Scranton, PA: Intext Educational Publishers.

Peters, M. L. (1974). Teacher variables in spelling. In B. Wade & K. Wedell (Eds.), *Spelling: Task and learner* (pp. 40–44). Birmingham, England: Educational Review.

Peters, M. L. (1979). *Diagnostic and remedial spelling manual.* (rev. ed.). London: Macmillan Education.

Peterson, D. L. (1973). *Functional mathematics for the mentally retarded.* Columbus, OH: Charles E. Merrill.

Petty, W. T., Petty, D. C., & Salzer, R. T. (1989). *Experiences in language: Tools and techniques for language arts methods* (5th ed.). Boston: Allyn and Bacon.

Phelps, J., & Stempel, L. (1987). Handwriting: Evolution and evaluation. *Annals of Dyslexia, 37,* 228–239.

Phelps-Teraski, D., & Phelps, T. (1980). *Teaching written expression: The Phelps sentence guide program.* Novato, CA: Academic Therapy.

Pieper, E. (1983). Technique for discovering LD adolescents' strategies for solving multiplication facts: Interviewing. *The Pointer, 27,* 40–41.

Polloway, E., Patton, J., & Cohen, S. (1981). Written language for mildly handicapped students. *Focus on Exceptional Children, 14*(3), 1–16.

Poplin, M. S. (1983). Assessing developmental writing abilities. *Topics in Learning and Learning Disabilities.3*(3), 63–75.

Poplin, M., Gray, R., Larsen, S., Banikowski, A., & Mehring, T. (1980). A comparison of components of written expression abilities in learning disabled and non-learning disabled students at three grade levels. *Learning Disability Quarterly, 3*(4), 88–98.

Poteet, J. A. (1987). Written expression. In J. S. Choate, T. Z. Bennett, B. E. Enright, L. J. Miller, J. A. Poteet, & T. A. Rakes (Eds.), *Assessing and programming basic curriculum skills* (pp. 147–176). Boston: Allyn and Bacon.

Pratt-Struthers, J., Struthers, B., & Williams, R. L. (1983). The effects of the Add-a-Word spelling program on spelling accuracy during creative writing. *Education and Treatment of Children, 6,* 277–283.

Pressley, M., Scruggs, T. E., & Mastropieri, M. A. (1989). Memory strategy research in learning disabilities: Present and future directions. *Learning Disabilities Research, 4,* 68–77.

Pumfrey, P. D. (1986). Paired reading: Promise and pitfalls. *Educational Research, 28*(2), 89–93.

Quillin, H. J., & Dwyer, E. J. (1978). Cloze modifications. *Journal of Reading, 22,* 200–201.

Rakes, T. A. (1987). Study and content area skills. In J. S. Choate, T. Z. Bennett, B. E. Enright, L. J. Miller, J. A. Poteet, & T. A. Rakes (Eds.), *Assessing and programming basic curriculum skills* (pp. 205–230). Boston: Allyn and Bacon.

Rakes, T. A., & McWilliams, L. (1981). Assessing reading skills in the content areas. In E. K. Dishner, T. W. Bean, & J. E. Readence (Eds.), *Reading in the content areas: Improving classroom instruction* (pp. 116–134). Dubuque, IA: Kendall/Hunt.

Rankin, E. F., & Overholser, B. M. (1969). Reaction of intermediate grade children to contextual clues. *Journal of Reading Behavior, 1,* 50–73.

Raphael, T. E., Englert, C. S., & Kirschner, B. W. (1986). *The impact of text structure instruction within a process writing orientation on fifth and sixth grade students' comprehension and production of expository text.* Paper presented at the American Educational Research Association, San Francisco, CA.

Readence, J. E., & Searfoss, L. W. (1980). Teaching strategies for vocabulary development. *English Journal, 69,* 43–46.

Reid, D. K. (1988). *Teaching the learning disabled: A cognitive developmental approach.* Boston: Allyn and Bacon.

Reid, D. K., & Hresko, W. P. (1981). *A cognitive approach to learning disabilities.* New York: McGraw-Hill.

Reisberg, L. E. (1982). Individual differences in learning disabled students' use of contextual cuing. *Learning Disability Quarterly, 5,* 91–99.

Reynolds, C. J., Hill, D. S., Swassing, R. H., & Ward, M. E. (1988). The effects of revision strategy instruction on the writing performance of students with learning disabilities. *Journal of Learning Disabilities, 21,* 540–545.

Reynolds, C. R., Gutkin, T., Elliott, S., & Witt, J. (1984). *School psychology: Essentials of theory and practice.* New York: Wiley.

Rhodes, L. K., & Dudley-Marling, C. (1988). *Readers and writers with a difference: A holistic approach to teaching learning disabled and remedial students.* Portsmouth, NH: Heinemann.

Rico, G. L. (1983). *Writing the natural way.* Boston: Houghton Mifflin.

Riegel, R. H., Mayle, J. A., & McCarthy-Henkel, J. (1988). *Beyond maladies and remedies.* Novi, MI: RHR Consultation Services.

Rieth, H., Axelrod, S., Anderson, R., Hathaway, F., Wood, K., & Fitzgerald, C. (1974). Influence of distributed practice and daily testing on weekly spelling tests. *Journal of Educational Research, 68,* 73–77.

Rieth, H. J., Polsgrove, L., & Eckert, R. (1984). A computer-based spelling program. *Academic Therapy, 20,*59–65.

Robinson, F. P. (1946). *Effective study.* New York: Harper & Row.

Rose, T. L. (1984). The effects of two prepractice procedures on oral reading. *Journal of Learning Disabilities, 17,* 544–548.

Rose, T. L., & Sherry, L. (1984). Relative effects of two previewing procedures on LD adolescents' oral reading performance. *Learning Disability Quarterly, 7*(1), 39–44.

Rosner, J. (1979). *Helping children overcome learning disabilities* (2nd ed.). New York: Walker.

Rourke, B. P. (1983). Reading and spelling disabilities: A developmental neuropsychological perspective. In U. Kirk (Ed.), *Neuropsychology of language, reading, and spelling* (pp. 209–254). New York: Academic Press.

Ruedy, L. R. (1983). Handwriting instruction: It can be part of the high school curriculum. *Academic Therapy, 18,*421–429.

Rumsey, I., & Ballard, K. D. (1985). Teaching self-management strategies for independent story writing to children with classroom behavior difficulties. *Educational Psychology, 5,* 147–157.

Russell, G. (1982). Impairment of phonetic reading in dyslexia and its persistence beyond childhood—Research note. *Journal of Child Psychology and Psychiatry, 23,* 459–475.

Russell, S. N., & Dunlap, W. P. (1977). *An interdisciplinary approach to reading and mathematics.* San Rafael, CA: Academic Therapy.

Rye, J. (1979). A closer look at cloze. *English in Education, 13*(3), 45–54.

Rye, J. (1982). *Cloze procedure and the teaching of reading.* London: Heinemann.

Sachs, A. (1983). The effects of three prereading activities on learning disabled students' reading comprehension. *Learning Disability Quarterly, 6,* 248–251.

Samuels, S. J. (1979). The method of repeated readings. *Reading Teacher, 32,* 403–408.

Samuels, S. J. (1986). Why children fail to learn and what to do about it. *Exceptional Children, 52,* 7–16.

Samuels, S. J. (1987). Information processing abilities and reading. *Journal of Learning Disabilities, 20,* 18–22.

Santos, O. B. (1989). Language skills and cognitive processes related to poor reading comprehension performance. *Journal of Learning Disabilities, 22,* 131–133.

Sassoon, R. (1983). *The practical guide to children's handwriting.* London: Thames & Hudson.

Sattler, J. M. (1988). *Assessment of children* (3rd ed.). San Diego: Author.

Schoenfeld, F. (1980). Instructional uses of the cloze procedure. *Reading Teacher, 34,* 147–151.

Schumaker, J. B., Denton, P. H., & Deshler, D. D. (1984). *The paraphrasing strategy (Learning Strategies Curriculum).* Lawrence: University of Kansas.

Schumaker, J. B., Deshler, D. D., Alley, G. R., Warner, M. M., Clark, F. L., & Nolan, S. (1982). Error monitoring: A learning strategy for improving adolescent performance. In W. M. Cruickshank & J. Lerner (Eds.), *Best of ACLD* (Vol. 3, pp. 170–182). Syracuse, NY: Syracuse University Press.

Schumaker, J. B., Deshler, D. D., Alley, G. R., Warner, M. M., & Denton, P. H. (1982). Multipass: A learning strategy for improving reading comprehension. *Learning Disability Quarterly, 5,* 295–304.

Schumaker, J. B., Deshler, D. D., Nolan, S., Clark, F. L., Alley, G. R., & Warner, M. M. (1981). *Error monitoring: A learning strategy for improving academic performance of LD adolescents* (Research Report No. 32). Lawrence, KS: University of Kansas Institute for Research in Learning Disabilities.

Scruggs, T. E., Mastropieri, M. A., Levin, J. R., McLoone, B., Gaffney, J. S., & Prater, M. A. (1985). Increasing content-area learning: A comparison of mnemonic and visual-spatial direct instruction. *Learning Disabilities Research, 1,* 18–31.

Seabaugh, G. O., & Schumaker, J. B. (1981). *The effects of self-regulation training on academic productivity of LD and NLD adolescents.* (Research Report No. 37). Lawrence: University of Kansas.

Shanahan, T. (1984). Nature of the reading-writing relation: An exploratory multivariate analysis. *Journal of Educational Psychology, 76,* 466–477.

Shankweiler, D., Smith, S. T., & Mann, V. A. (1984). Repetition and comprehension of spoken sentences by reading-disabled children. *Brain and Language, 23,*241–257.

Shapiro, E. S. (1989). *Academic skills problems: Direct assessment and intervention.* New York: Guilford Press.

Shapiro, E. S., & McCurdy, B. L. (1989). Effects of a taped-words treatment on reading proficiency. *Exceptional Children, 55,* 321–325.

Share, D. L., Jorm, A. F., Maclean, R., & Matthews, R. (1984). Sources of individual differences in reading acquisition. *Journal of Educational Psychology, 76,*1309–1324.

Sheridan, G. C. (1973). Number recognition and sequencing through games. *Teaching Exceptional Children, 5,*90–92.

Silbert, J., Carnine, D., & Stein, M. (1981). *Direct instruction mathematics.* Columbus, OH: Charles E. Merrill.

Silky, W, (1979). Cloze for instruction: A continuum. *Journal of Reading, 22,* 487.

Silverman, R., Zigmond, N., Zimmerman, J. M., & Vallecorsa, A. (1981). Improving written expression in learning disabled students. *Topics in Language Disorders, 2*(1), 91–99.

Simms, R. B. (1983). Feedback: A key to effective writing. *Academic Therapy, 19,* 31–36.

Simms, R. B. (1984). Techniques for improving student writing. *Academic Therapy, 19,* 579–584.

Sinatra, R. (1989). Verbal/visual processing for males disabled in print acquisition. *Journal of Learning Disabilities, 22,*69–71.

Sinatra, R. C., Berg, D., & Dunn, R. (1985). Semantic mapping improves reading comprehension of learning disabled students. *Teaching Exceptional Children, 17,*310–314.

Singer, H., & Donlan, D. (1982). Active comprehension: Problem-solving schema with question generation for comprehension of complex short stories. *Reading Research Quarterly, 17,* 166–186.

Sisneros, K., & Bullock, M. (1983). How do you spell Holiday? *Instructor, 93*(4), 60–61, 160.

Skrtic, T., Kvam, N., & Beals, V. (1983). Identifying and remediating the subtraction errors of learning disabled adolescents. *The Pointer, 27,* 32–38.

Slingerland, B. H. (1971). *A multisensory approach to language arts for specific language disability children: A guide for primary teachers.* Cambridge, MA: Educators Publishing Service.

Smith, G., & Smith, D. (1985). A mainstreaming program that really works. *Journal of Learning Disabilities, 18,* 369–372.

Smith, H. (1975). Teaching spelling. *British Journal of Educational Psychology, 45,* 68–72.

Snider, V. E. (1989). Reading comprehension performance of adolescents with learning disabilities. *Learning Disability Quarterly, 12,* 87–95.

Snider, V. E., & Tarver, S. G. (1987). The effect of early reading failure on acquisition of knowledge among students with learning disabilities. *Journal of Learning Disabilities, 20,*351–356, 373.

Solon, C. (1980). The pyramid diagram: A college study skills tool. *Journal of Reading, 23,* 594–597.

Spalding, R. B., & Spalding, W. T. (1986). *The writing road to reading* (3rd ed.). New York: William Morrow.

Sparks, J. E. (1982). *Write for power.* Los Angeles: Communication Associates.

Spearman, C. (1927). *The nature of intelligence and the principles of cognition.* London: Macmillan.

Speece, D. L. (1987). Information processing subtypes of learning disabled readers. *Learning Disabilities Research, 2,* 91–102.

Spring, C., & French, L. (1990). Identifying children with specific reading disabilities from listening and reading discrepancy scores. *Journal of Learning Disabilities, 23,* 53–58.

Stahl, S. (1983). Differential word knowledge and reading comprehension. *Journal of Reading Behavior, 15,* 33–50.

Stanback, M. (1979–80). *Teaching spelling to learning disabled children: Traditional and remedial approaches to spelling instruction.* (Report No. EC 140642). New York: Columbia University, Research Institute for the Study of Learning Disabilities. (ERIC Document Reproduction Service No. ED 210 842)

Stanovich, K. E. (1982a). Individual differences in the cognitive processes of reading: I. Word decoding. *Journal of Learning Disabilities, 15,* 485–493.

Stanovich, K. E. (1982b). Individual differences in the cognitive processes of reading: II. Text-level processes. *Journal of Learning Disabilities, 15,* 549–554.

Stanovich, K. E. (1988). Explaining the differences between the dyslexic and the garden-variety poor reader: The phonological-core-variable-difference model. *Journal of Learning Disabilities, 21,* 590–604, 612.

Stanovich, K. E., Cunningham, A. E., & Feeman, D. J. (1984). Intelligence, cognitive skills, and early reading progress. *Reading Research Quarterly, 19,* 278–303.

Stauffer, R. (1975). *Directing the reading-thinking process.* New York: Harper & Row.

Stein, M. (1983). Finger spelling: A kinesthetic aid to phonetic spelling. *Academic Therapy, 18,* 305–313.

Stewart, S. R. (1985). Development of written language proficiency: Methods for teaching text structure. In C. S. Simon (Ed.), *Communication skills and classroom success* (pp. 341–361). San Diego: College-Hill.

Stowitschek, C., & Stowitschek, J. (1979). Evaluating handwriting performance: The student helps the teacher. *Journal of Learning Disabilities, 12,* 203–206.

Suydam, M. N., & Dessart, D. J. (1976). *Classroom ideas from research on computational skills.* Reston, VA: National Council of Teachers of Mathematics.

Swanson, H. L. (1986). Learning disabled readers' verbal coding difficulties: A problem of storage or retrieval? *Learning Disabilities Research, 1,* 73–82.

Swanson, L. (1982). Verbal short-term memory encoding of learning disabled, deaf, and normal readers. *Learning Disability Quarterly, 5,* 21–28.

Swanson, L. (1983). A study of nonstrategic linguistic coding on visual recall of learning disabled readers. *Journal of Learning Disabilities, 16,* 209–216.

Tagatz, G. E., Otto, W., Klausmeier, H. J., Goodwin, W. L., & Cook, D. M. (1968). Effect of three methods of instruction upon the handwriting performance of third and fourth graders. *American Educational Research, 5,*81–90.

Teitelbaum, E. (1978). Calculators for classroom use? *Arithmetic Teacher, 26*(3), 18–20.

Thomas, C. C., Englert, C. S., & Morsink, C. (1984). Modifying the classroom program in language. In C. V. Morsink (Ed.), *Teaching special needs students in regular classrooms* (pp. 239–276). Boston: Little, Brown.

Thomas, K. (1978). Instructional applications of the cloze technique. *Reading World, 18*, 1–12.

Thomas, K. J. (1979a). Instructional applications of the cloze technique. *Reading World, 18*(1), 1–12.

Thomas, K. J. (1979b). Modified cloze: The intralocking guide. *Reading World, 19*(1), 19–27.

Thoreau, H. D. (1983). *A week on the Concord and Merrimack Rivers*. Princeton: Princeton University Press.

Thornton, C. A., & Bley, N. S. (1982). Problem solving: Help in the right direction for LD students. *Arithmetic Teacher, 29*(6), 26–27, 38–41.

Thornton, C. A., & Toohey, M. A. (1985). Basic math facts: Guidelines for teaching and learning. *Learning Disabilities Focus, 1*(1), 44–57.

Thornton, C. A., & Toohey, M. A. (1986). Subtraction facts: Hide-and-seek cards can help. *Teaching Exceptional Children, 19*(1), 10–14.

Thorpe, H., Nash, R., & Chiang, B. (1981). The effects of the kinesthetic-tactile component of the VAKT procedure on secondary LD students' reading performance. *Psychology in the Schools, 18*, 334–340.

Thurber, D. N. (1983). Write on! with continuous stroke point. *Academic Therapy, 18*, 389–395.

Thurber, D. N. (1984). *D'Nealian manuscript: A continuous stroke approach to handwriting*. Novato, CA: Academic Therapy.

Thurber, D. N. (1988). The D'Nealian pencil grip. *Communication Outlook, 9*(4), 11.

Tompkins, G. E., & Friend, M. (1985). On your mark, get set, write! *Teaching Exceptional Children, 18*, 82–89.

Topping, K. (1987a). Paired reading: A powerful technique for parent use. *Reading Teacher, 40*, 608–609.

Topping, K. (1987b). Peer tutored paired reading: Outcome data from ten projects. *Educational Psychology, 7*,133–145.

Torgesen, J. K. (1986). Using computers to help learning disabled children practice reading: A research-based perspective. *Learning Disabilities Focus, 1*, 72–81.

Torgesen, J. K. (1988). Studies of children with learning disabilities who perform poorly on memory span tasks. *Journal of Learning Disabilities, 21*, 605–612.

Torgesen, J. K., Dahlem, W. E., & Greenstein, J. (1987). Using verbatim text recordings to enhance reading comprehension in learning disabled adolescents. *Learning Disabilities Focus, 3*, 30–38.

Treiman, R. (1985). Phonemic analysis, spelling, and reading. In T. Carr (Ed.), *The development of reading skills* (pp. 5–18). San Francisco: Jossey-Bass.

Valencia, S. W., & Pearson, P. D. (1988). Principles for classroom comprehension assessment. *Remedial and Special Education, 9*(1), 26–35.

Vallecorsa, A. L., Zigmond, N., & Henderson, L. M. (1985). Spelling instruction in special education classrooms: A survey of practices. *Exceptional Children, 52*, 19–24.

Valmont, W. (1983a). Cloze and maze instructional techniques: Differences and definitions. *Reading Psychology, 4*, 163–167.

Valmont, W. (1983b). Cloze deletions patterns: How deletions are made makes a big difference. *Reading Teacher, 37*,172–174.

Valmont, W. (1983c). Instructional cloze procedures: Rationale, framework, and examples. *Reading Horizons, 23*, 156–162.

Van Allen, R. (1976). *Language experiences in communication*. Boston: Houghton Mifflin.

van der Leij, A. (1981). Remediation of reading-disabled children by presenting text simultaneously to eye and ear. *Bulletin of the Orton Society, 31*, 229–243.

Van De Weghe, R. (1978). *Research in written composition: Fifteen years of investigation* (Research report). Las Cruces: New Mexico State University (ERIC Document Reproduction Service No. ED 157 095)

Vellutino, F. R., & Scanlon, D. M. (1982). Verbal processing in poor and normal readers. In C. Brainerd & M. Pressley (Eds.), *Verbal processing in children: Progress in cognitive development research* (pp. 189–264). New York: Springer-Verlag.

Venezky, R. L. (1970). Linguistics and spelling. In A. H. Marckwardt (Ed.), *Linguistics in school programs: The sixty-ninth yearbook of the National Society for the Study of Education* (pp. 264–274). Chicago: University of Chicago Press.

Vogel, S. (1989). Some special considerations in the development of models for diagnosis of LD adults. In L. Silver (Ed.), *Crisis in education: Diagnosis of learning disabilities in public school* (pp. 111–134). Boston: College-Hill Press.

Vogel, S., & Moran, M. R. (1982). Written language disorders in learning disabled college students: A preliminary report. In W. Cruickshank & J. Lerner (Eds.), *The best of ACLD 1981: Vol 3. Coming of age* (pp. 211–225). Syracuse: Syracuse University Press.

Wade, S. E. (1983). A synthesis of the research for improving reading in the social studies. *Review of Educational Research, 53*, 461–497.

Wagner, R. F. (1981). Remediating common math errors. *Academic Therapy, 16*, 449–453.

Wagner, R. K. (1986). Phonological processing abilities and reading: Implications for disabled readers. *Journal of Learning Disabilities, 19*, 623–630.

Wallace, G. W., & Bott, D. A. (1989). Statement-pie: A strategy to improve the paragraph writing skills of adolescents with learning disabilities. *Journal of Learning Disabilities, 22*,541–543, 553.

Walmsly, S. A. (1984). Helping the learning disabled child overcome writing difficulties in the classroom. *Topics in Learning and Learning Disabilities, 3*, 81–90.

Webster, R. E. (1979). Visual and aural short-term memory capacity deficits in mathematics disabled students. *Journal of Educational Research, 72*, 277–283.

Weiss, H. G., & Weiss, M. S. (1982). Training kids to be winners in the handling of writing skills. *Academic Therapy, 18*,75–82.

West, P. V., & Freeman, F. N. (1950). Handwriting. *Encyclopedia of Educational Research*, 524–529.

Whaley, J. F. (1981). Story grammars and reading instruction. *Reading Teacher, 34*, 762–771.

Williams, J. P. (1980). Teaching decoding with an emphasis on phoneme analysis and phoneme blending. *Journal of Educational Psychology, 72,* 1–15.

Williams, J. P. (1984). Phonemic analysis and how it relates to reading. *Journal of Learning Disabilities, 17,*240–245.

Williams, J., & Wason, P. (1977). *Collaborative writing games.* (Report No. CS 203 907). London: University College. (ERIC Document Reproduction Service No. ED 150 594)

Wiseman, D. E., Hartwell, L. K., & Hannafin, M. J. (1980). Exploring the reading and listening skills of secondary mildly handicapped students. *Learning Disability Quarterly, 3*(3), 56–61.

Wiseman, D., & McKenna, M. C. (1978). Classroom uses of the maze procedure. *Selected Articles on the Teaching of Reading,* Set C, No. 41. New York: Barnell Loft.

Wong, B. (1979). Increasing retention of main ideas through questioning strategies. *Learning Disability Quarterly, 2*(2), 42–47.

Wong, B.Y.L. (1982). Understanding learning disabled students' reading problems: Contributions from cognitive psychology. *Topics in Learning and Learning Disabilities, 1*(4), 43–50.

Wong, B.Y.L. (1986). A cognitive approach to teaching spelling. *Exceptional Children, 53,* 169–173.

Wong, B., & Jones, W. (1982). Increasing metacomprehension in learning disabled and normally achieving students through self-questioning training. *Learning Disability Quarterly, 5,* 228–240.

Wood, T. A., Buckhalt, J. A., & Tomlin, J. G. (1988). A comparison of listening and reading performance with children in three educational placements. *Journal of Learning Disabilities, 21,* 493–496.

Woodcock, R. W. (1968). *Rebus as a medium of beginning reading instruction.* (Report No. IMRID-V4). Nashville, TN: Institute of Mental Retardation and Intellectual Development. (ERIC Document Reproduction Service No. 046 631)

Woodcock, R. W., Clark, C. R., & Davies, C. O. (1968). *The Peabody Rebus Reading Program.* Circle Pines, MN: American Guidance Service.

Woodcock, R. W., & Johnson, M. B. (1977). *Woodcock-Johnson Psycho-Educational Battery.* Allen, TX: DLM.

Woodcock, R. W., & Johnson, M. B. (1989). *Woodcock-Johnson Psycho-Educational Battery—Revised.* Allen, TX: DLM.

Woodcock, R. W., & Mather, N. (1989a). WJ-R Tests of Cognitive Ability—Standard and Supplemental Batteries: Examiner's Manual. In R. W. Woodcock & M. B. Johnson, *Woodcock-Johnson Psycho-Educational Battery—Revised.* Allen, TX: DLM.

Woodcock, R. W., & Mather, N. (1989b). WJ-R Tests of Achievement—Standard and Supplemental Batteries: Examiner's Manual. In R. W. Woodcock & M. B. Johnson, *Woodcock-Johnson Psycho-Educational Battery—Revised.* Allen, TX: DLM.

Zaner-Bloser Evaluation Scales. (1979). Columbus, OH: Zaner-Bloser.

Zweng, M. J. (1979). The problem of solving story problems. *Arithmetic Teacher, 27*(1), 2–3.

Index